The **Rough Guide** to

Panama

written and researched by

Sara Humphreys

with contributions by

Raffa Calv

D1466794

www.roughguides.com

Contents

The wildlife of **Panama** colour section following p.176

Arts and crafts colour section following p.240

Introduction to

Panama

Recalling the outstretched fingers of God and Adam on the Sistine Chapel ceiling, Panama's crooked form barely links the two continental masses of North and South America. The story of how the jungles covering this sliver of land were scythed open by the country's famous canal provides one of the most compelling tales of human sacrifice and triumph of recent centuries. But Panama is much more than a lucrative shortcut. Offering a surprisingly varied landscape, this slender, serpentine nation encompasses cloud-forested highlands, glorious palm-fringed islands, vibrant indigenous cultures and Central America's most ebullient capital city. And, remarkably, the vast tracts of rainforest that carpet the isthmus demonstrate an even greater density of biodiversity than Amazonia.

Yet, despite these attractions, Panama's charms have only just begun to be discovered by visitors. For many years even hardy backpackers "doing" Latin America skipped the country since the **Darién Gap** – the untamed mix of swamp and jungle that forms the hiatus in the Panamerican Highway – precluded any land route between Panama and South America. The country has also taken a long time to shrug off a serious image problem as a de facto 51st state of the US, founded to facilitate American ambitions through construction of the iconic waterway, with a dollarized economy and years of what was effectively US occupation in the former **Canal Zone**. Add to that Panama's not entirely undeserved reputation for money-laundering and the current trend of attracting North American retirees, and it's no wonder that tourists have initially been slow to appreciate the country's distinctive multifaceted identity and outstanding natural beauty.

Panama's compact size means the vast majority of its sights are easily accessible. From the comfort of your hotel in the capital, you can head out in the

morning to tramp in the footsteps of the conquistadors through spectacular, primate-packed rainforest, yet be swinging your hips to a salsa beat or dining on damask by candlelight in downtown Panama City the same evening. The ancient and modern, artificial and natural are irresistibly juxtaposed as vast computerized Panamax container ships transiting the canal slice through primeval rainforests teeming with monkeys, sloths, toucans, tapirs, fluorescent frogs and elusive wild cats only half an hour by dugout from where Emberá villagers practise subsistence agriculture. Visiting the country's fringes and little-visited interior, you can explore archipelagos and untracked jungle, basing yourself in small towns, friendly villages and remote eco-lodges, and from Volcán Barú – Panama's highest peak – you can witness the unique and breathtaking sight of the sun rising over both Atlantic and Pacific oceans.

The US is only one of many **cultural influences**, which derive from Spain and other parts of Europe, West Africa, the West Indies, China, India and

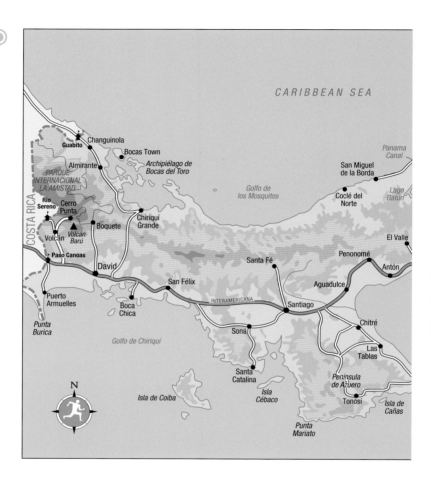

the Middle East – prompted by the need for migrant labour during the Panama Railroad, Canal and banana-boom eras – fused with the fascinating heritage of the eight indigenous peoples that survived the Spanish conquest.

Panama's complexities and contradictions confront you at every turn, which can intrigue and frustrate in equal measure. The Panamanian government has actively started to promote **tourism**, with plush new tourist offices mushrooming across the country, yet there's often very little information on offer, however well meaning the staff. The colourful traditional attire of Panama's indigenous populations is unashamedly used as photo fodder, but the people themselves are frequently ignored by their government, their lands under threat from development. Many inhabit the unique tropical rainforests of Panama's numerous national parks, which remain desperately underfunded

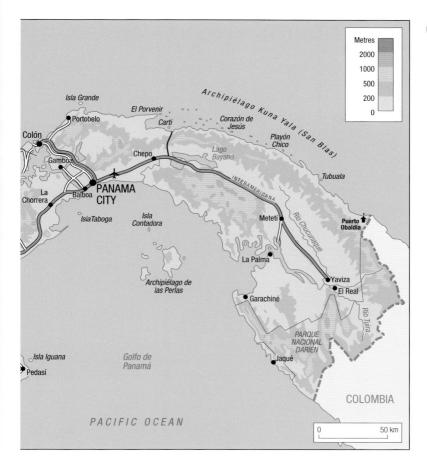

and are threatened by government-sanctioned projects, including hydro-electric dams and mining.

Indeed, it's hard to visit Panama and not be both amazed and perturbed by the pace of change in this small, young nation, as skyscrapers increasingly fill Panama City's skyline, motorways push deeper into the Darién and the country's heritage is at once bludgeoned and celebrated. Right now, the relatively undeveloped infrastructure and scarcity of tourists outside the main attractions means there are plenty of opportunities to get off the beaten track and interact with the population of a nation that – lest we forget – only took control of the world's grandest canal just over a decade ago. What the next ten years may hold for this invigorating, beautiful and contradictory country is anyone's guess, but it will emphatically not be dull.

Where to go

The vast majority of visitors fly in to cosmopolitan **Panama City**, where countless brash skyscrapers stare across the bay at the rocky peninsula of **Casco Viejo**, the city's rapidly transforming colonial centre, whose elegantly restored mansions, palaces and leafy plazas demand at least a day's leisurely exploration. If you're planning a short visit, it's easy to base yourself in the city and make daily forays to the Spanish **colonial forts** along the Caribbean coast near Portobelo, the monumental **Panama Canal** and the crumbling port city of **Colón**. Should the frenetic energy and interminable traffic din of the city's clogged arteries get too much, a quiet day lounging on a **Pacific beach**, birdwatching in the **Parque Nacional Soberanía** or fishing on **Lago Gatún** are all possible without foregoing the epicurean delights of the capital's sophisticated bars and restaurants in the evening.

After Panama City, the country's most popular tourist area is the Caribbean archipelago of **Bocas del Toro**, close to the Costa Rican border. Its deserted stretches of sand, powerful surf and colourful coral reefs are matched by an oft-forgotten mainland that offers opportunities for spectacular wilderness hiking as well as wildlife viewing in the Humedales de San San Pond Sak. Bocas's bohemian vibe and Afro-Caribbean culture contrasts with the vast stretch of **Kuna Yala**, an archipelago that extends for hundreds of kilometres and is home to Panama's most politically independent and culturally distinct indigenous people, the Kuna. Its densely populated islands provide a base from which to explore picture-postcard cays of white-sand beaches and coconut palms. With more time, you can explore the less accessible aquatic wonderlands of the Pacific coast, with world-class scuba-diving and sport fishing in

▼ Panama City, from Casco Viejo to Punta Paitilla

the mangrove-rich protected marine parks of the **Golfo de Chiriquí** and **Coiba**, the penal-colony turned wildlife-reserve, generally reached from the laid-back surfing hotspot of **Santa Catalina**.

From there it's short hop east to the rolling pastureland and quaint villages of the **Azuero Peninsula**, a region that revels in its colonial heritage. Once neglected by visitors, its festivals, including the country's most ardent Carnaval, overflow with enthusiastic accordion and violin playing, colourful costumes, masks, rodeos and lashings of seco – Panama's potent national tipple – and provide ample opportunities to interact with the outgoing local populace.

The dorsal mountain range dividing Panama's two coasts rises dramatically from the Pacific coastal plains that constitute the country's agricultural heartlands, with the most impressive peaks located in the spectacular **national parks** of Chiriquí's **Western Highlands**, surrounding the alpine towns of **Boquete** and the less touristed **Cerro Punta**. Here it's hard to resist the allure of verdant cloud forests filled with orchids, quetzals and hummingbirds, precision rows of shade-grown coffee plantations and fast-flowing rivers, perfect for whitewater rafting or kayaking. Further east, the **Cordillera Central** hosts other parks and rainforested peaks laced with waterfalls above the small communities of **El Copé**, **Santa Fé** and **El Valle**, all of which offer rewarding hiking, birdwatching and horse riding.

Few visitors venture east of Panama City to the **Darién** jungle, which has gained almost mythical status, as much for FARC guerrillas and drug-traffickers as for its spectacular scenery and wildlife. Requiring patience, money and more than a smattering of Spanish, the rewards are ample: sinuous river journeys by dugout, great canopies of cathedral-like rainforests sheltering some of Panama's most spectacular fauna, and remote indigenous communities, keen to share their skills and culture with visitors.

When to go

Squeezed between between seven and nine degrees north of the equator, Panama is located firmly within the **tropics**, with a climate to match: relentlessly hot and humid in the lowlands, cooling off fractionally to give balmy nights, whereas in the highlands, temperatures vary significantly with altitude, and can be chilly at night.

Most travellers visit during the shorter **dry season** (*verano*, "summer"), which runs from late December to the end of April, and with good reason. Azure skies predominate, at least on the drier Pacific plains, sheltered by Panama's mountainous spine. The firmer going underfoot makes it easier to travel on unpaved roads and explore the rainforests, and the reduced rainwater run-off ensures clearer waters to swim in. The dry season also includes the lively holiday periods of Christmas, New Year, Carnaval and Holy Week, when flights and hotels in popular tourist spots are at a premium.

You'll avoid the crowds and the mark-ups in the **rainy season** (*invierno*, "winter"), which stretches from May to December. Although the mountainous and rainforested regions in Panama are best avoided during the wettest months, since peaks are constantly swathed in cloud and tracks are boggy, if you stick to the lowland areas on the Pacific coast, the downpours, while frequent and intense, rarely last more than a few hours at a time, leaving plenty of sunny, dry periods to enjoy. In particular, the otherwise parched Azuero Peninsula offers much more picturesque scenery during its understated rainy season.

By contrast, the **Caribbean coast** receives almost twice as much rain as the Pacific, with virtually no recognizable dry season. Regional variations impact here too: the Trade Winds (at their strongest Dec to mid-Feb) make the water choppy and outer islands inaccessible in Bocas del Toro and Kuna Yala, while Bocas enjoys two relatively dry spells around March and October.

Average daily temperature and rainfall:

	Jan	Feb	Mar	Apr	May	Jun	Jul	Aug	Sep	Oct	Nov	Dec
Panama City												
Max/min (°C)	30/22	31/22	32/23	32/23	31/24	30/23	30/23	31/23	30/23	30/23	30/23	30/23
Max/min (°F)	86/71	87/71	89/73	89/73	87/75	86/73	86/73	87/73	86/73	86/73	86/73	86/73
Rainfall (mm)	33	18	13	74	201	203	178	198	198	262	254	137
Boquete												
Max/min (°C)	25/13	27/13	28/14	29/14	28/15	27/14	27/14	27/14	27/14	28/14	27/14	27/13
Max/min (°F)	77/55	80/56	82/58	84/59	82/59	80/58	81/58	81/58	80/57	83/57	81/56	82/56
Rainfall (mm)	2.5	38	81	231	472	432	467	660	546	925	376	121
Bocas del Toro												
Max/min (°C)	31/20	31/20	31/21	31/21	32/22	32/22	32/22	32/22	32/22	32/22	32/22	31/21
Max/min (°F)	88/68	88/68	88/70	88/70	90/72	90/72	90/72	90/72	90/72	90/72	90/72	88/70
Rainfall (mm)	204	235	188	323	273	287	387	346	254	219	390	485

16
things not to miss

It's not possible to see everything Panama has to offer in one trip – and we don't suggest you try. What follows is a selective taste of the country's highlights: remote islands, great coffee, colonial architecture and unique wildlife. They're arranged in five colour-coded categories, which you can browse through to find the very best things to see and experience. All highlights have a page reference to take you straight into the guide, where you can find out more.

01 Panama Canal Page **113** • The twentieth century's greatest engineering feat is best experienced first-hand with a transit through the locks.

02 **Archipiélago de las Perlas** Page 103 • Choose from a myriad of idyllic tropical islands ringed with white-sand beaches and turquoise waters.

03 **Chilling in Bocas** Page 250 • Glorious sunsets, party hostels, mellow lodges and Caribbean cuisine make Bocas a fine spot for anyone to let their hair down.

04 Diving and snorkelling
Page **43** • There's some great snorkelling to be done off the coral reefs of Bocas del Toro, while the aquatic paradise off Isla Coiba provides world-class diving.

05 Birdwatching Pages **42, 343**
& *Wildlife in Panama* colour section • Get close to the country's 972 bird species – including dazzling hummingbirds, the resplendent quetzal and crimson-backed tanager.

06 Santa Fé Page **176** • A delightfully fresh climate, abundant orchids and picturesque waterfalls make this mountainside village an appealing retreat.

07 Stay in an Emberá village Page **319** • Experience traditional village life with the Emberá in the Darién and learn the medicinal secrets of the rainforest.

13

08 Hiking Page **43** • Soak up the magnificent views in the rugged national parks of central and western Panama, with the stellar panorama from Volcan Barú, Panama's highest point, hard to beat.

10 Casco Viejo Page **68** • Seek out hidden gems in the colonial churches, leafy plazas and narrow streets of Panama City's colonial city centre.

09 Kuna culture Page **285** • Explore about the rich cultural traditions of the island-dwelling Kuna.

11 Coffee in Boquete Page **233** • Learn to detect floral, caramel, citrus and spice aromas in some of the world's finest gourmet coffee estates.

12 Adventure sports Pages **232 & 239** • From racing down the rapids of the Chiriquí Viejo to swinging on a canopy ride, the Western Highlands offer plenty to set your pulse racing.

13 Head into the Darién Page **314** • Glide upriver into one of the world's last wilderness areas, past vast buttress roots, tangled vines and the soaring forest canopy.

14 **Island life in Kuna Yala** Page **287** • Laze in a hammock strung between swaying coconut palms, dipping into the warm Caribbean waters to cool off, on one of many postage-stamp-sized islands in Kuna Yala.

16 **Festivals** Page **37** • Panama's diverse heritage has resulted in a fascinating array of festivals from Carnaval's wildest party in Las Tablas to the vibrant, rebellious celebration of Afro-colonial culture in the Caribbean's annual congos.

15 **Colonial architecture** Page **172** • From ruined Caribbean fortresses to Baroque Pacific churches, Panama possesses some fine conquest-era buildings, including the brilliant façade and intricate carved altars of the basilica at Natá.

Basics

Basics

Getting there

The vast majority of visitors to Panama arrive by air, landing at Tocumen International Airport in Panama City. Seats are generally more expensive and more heavily subscribed during the dry season (late Dec to April), especially the peak holiday periods of Christmas, Easter and Carnaval when many Panamanians living in the US return home. Though flights are easily booked through the internet it is still sometimes cheaper to make arrangements via a travel agent, bearing in mind the crucial distinction between Panama City in Central America (airport code PTY) and the one in Florida (airport code PFN). The $20 departure tax is now included in the ticket price.

Panama's reliable national carrier, Copa Airlines, often offers the best rates, has an efficient online booking service and still serves complimentary meals on flights. It flies to several US cities and to numerous destinations in Latin America and the Caribbean. All **ticket prices** given below include the relevant taxes.

Visitors travelling down from **Central America** may choose to make the longer but cheaper bus journey through Costa Rica, generally along the Pan-American Highway via the Pacific border crossing at Paso Canoas, though there are a couple of other border posts at Río Sereno in the Western Highlands and at Guabito on the Caribbean (or Atlantic) coast in Bocas del Toro.

Alternatives to flying from **South America** are a great deal more complicated, involving a number of boat and bus journeys on the Caribbean side, and are only for the adventurous. Cruise ship visitors will dock at the cruise ship terminals in either Colón, at the Caribbean end of the Panama Canal, or on the Amador Causeway in Panama City, on the Pacific side. Sailing boats carrying backpackers from Cartagena usually unload passengers in El Porvenir, in Kuna Yala, or in Puerto Lindo, further west along the coast in Colón Province. Other yacht arrivals will probably call in at the Balboa Yacht Club on the Amador Causeway or at the Shelter Bay Marina west of Colón.

Flights from the US and Canada

Given the historical links between the **US** and Panama it's no surprise that there are numerous direct flights; Continental, Delta and American Airlines, alongside Copa and TACA – actually a conglomerate of several Central American airlines – fly daily to Panama City from various US cities, including New York, Washington, Los Angeles, Orlando and Miami, with the latter the main portal, offering several daily connections.

Bargains are thin on the ground, though Copa often has special return **fares** for as little as $200 return for the three-hour trip from Miami. More typically, fares range from $300 (low season) to $500 (high season), costing more for the five-hour flight from New York or Washington ($350–550) and the six hours from Los Angeles ($450–750). It is often slightly cheaper to fly to San José, Costa Rica, and take one of the daily buses ($60 return) down to Panama (see p.20).

There are no direct flights from **Canada**; connections have to be made in the US, making it at least a nine-hour journey, with prices typically $600–1100. Slightly cheaper direct charter flights can sometimes be purchased in high season through Transat (Ⓦ www.transat.com) from Calgary, Montreal and Toronto or through Sunwing (Ⓦ www.sunwing.ca) from Montreal and Toronto.

Flights from the UK and Ireland

The dearth of direct flights from Europe in part explains the relatively low number of European visitors compared to the number of tourists from North America. There are currently no direct flights from the **UK** or **Ireland**, with KLM making the trip five times a week from Amsterdam (£500–800 from UK & Ireland) and Iberia operating frequent, but generally more expensive departures (£650–800) from several Spanish cities. The cheapest route from the UK or Ireland is often via the US with a US carrier (see p.19), which may save you over £100, though the extra hassle of clearing US immigration generally makes the KLM route via Amsterdam a more appealing option.

Flights from Australia, New Zealand and South Africa

From Australia, New Zealand and South Africa it is a long, expensive haul to Panama, with no direct flights. Most routes from **Australasia** (Aus$3500–4000) travel via the US, generally passing through Los Angeles, though flights via Santiago or Buenos Aires are also possible with the journey time (26hr-plus) much the same. From **South Africa** (30hr-plus), travel can be via London, South America or the US ($1500–2500). Given the huge cost, it is worth considering including Panama in part of a **round-the-world** ticket from these departure points – the price is comparable.

Flights from Central and South America

Various countries in **Latin America** have direct connections with Panama City either through their national carriers – Avianca flies from Colombia and Mexicana from Mexico – or through Copa, which connects with over forty destinations across Latin America and the Caribbean. In Costa Rica, award-winning Nature Air operates daily flights from San José to Bocas del Toro ($280 one-way, including carbon offsetting), while Panama's domestic carrier Air Panama makes three trips a week from San José ($250 return plus taxes) to David. TACA is due to restart flying this route too. From **Colombia**, AERES offers the cheapest fares though in small planes; you can usually get from Medellín or Cartagena to Panama City for under $220 one way, paying more from Bogotá.

By bus from Central America

It is possible to travel overland to Panama City (with drop-offs at David and Santiago en route) along the **Pan-American Highway** all the way from Tapachula, Mexico, with Ticabus (🌐 www.ticabus.com; $105 one way). Ticabus operates a series of comfortable long-distance air-conditioned buses with the obligatory diet of Hollywood movies that pick up (and drop off) passengers at the major cities in Central America en route, though you will have to spend a couple of nights in hotels on the way, which increases the cost. Transportes Galgos (🌐 www.transgalgosinter.com.gt) will also get you to Guatemala City from Tapachula ($25 one way), from where you can transfer to Ticabus. Agencia Tracopa (🌐 www.tracopacr.com; $15 one way) operates a daily service from San José to David.

Six steps to a better kind of travel

At Rough Guides we are passionately committed to travel. We feel strongly that only through travelling do we truly come to understand the world we live in and the people we share it with – plus tourism has brought a great deal of **benefit** to developing economies around the world over the last few decades. But the extraordinary growth in tourism has also damaged some places irreparably, and of course **climate change** is exacerbated by most forms of transport, especially flying. This means that now more than ever it's important to **travel thoughtfully** and **responsibly**, with respect for the cultures you're visiting – not only to derive the most benefit from your trip but also to preserve the best bits of the planet for everyone to enjoy. At Rough Guides we feel there are six main areas in which you can make a difference:

- Consider what you're contributing to the **local economy**, and how much the services you use do the same, whether it's through employing local workers and guides or sourcing locally grown produce and local services.

- Consider the **environment** on holiday as well as at home. Water is scarce in many developing destinations, and the biodiversity of local flora and fauna can be adversely affected by tourism. Try to patronize businesses that take account of this.

- Travel with a purpose, not just to tick off experiences. Consider **spending longer** in a place, and getting to know it and its people.

- Give thought to how often you **fly**. Try to avoid short hops by air and more harmful night flights.

- Consider **alternatives to flying**, travelling instead by bus, train, boat and even by bike or on foot where possible.

- Make your trips "**climate neutral**" via a reputable carbon offset scheme. All Rough Guide flights are offset, and every year we donate money to a variety of charities devoted to combating the effects of climate change.

By boat from Colombia

The only break in the 50,000-odd km of the Pan-American Highway is an 87km stretch of swamp and mountainous jungle between Carepa on the Colombian border and Yaviza in Panama in what is known as the Darién Gap (see p.313). Up until the early 1990s, thrashing your way through here **overland** was a famous challenge for adventurers. However, it is now forbidden as it is extremely dangerous due to the presence of drug-traffickers, Colombian paramilitaries and smugglers, with the threat of death or kidnapping adding to the usual jungle hazards. A (somewhat) safer alternative for those wanting to save money on air fares is to travel by **boat** along the Caribbean coast, though if you are out of luck with the weather, timings and bookings, the overall saving is likely to be negligible. Still, an adventure of sorts is guaranteed. This route requires a reasonable command of

Spanish or travelling with someone who has one. A multi-day sailing trip from Cartagena, in Colombia, to the western end of Kuna Yala or Colón Province is another possibility (see box, p.22).

To make the coastal journey from Colombia, it is first necessary to get to **Turbo**, a small city in Antioquia Department on the Pan-American Highway (accessible by regular buses from Medellín, which are safe during the day), and take the regular 9am launch across to Capurganá (2hr 30min; $25), a burgeoning low-key Caribbean resort unreachable by road but within striking distance by sea of Puerto Obaldía (1hr; around $15), a small military outpost across the border in Panama, at the eastern end of Kuna Yala. Since there is no regular crossing to Puerto Obaldía, departure times and charges depend on numbers, though **Capurganá** is a pleasant enough place to hang out for a few days

21

Getting there

while you're waiting for fellow travellers to roll up. Note also that both sea crossings can be exceedingly rough (especially between Nov and Feb) and are not for the faint-hearted; the boats are small and the waves loom large, though life jackets are provided. A large plastic bag to cover your luggage is a must as well as some waterproof protection for yourself.

Morning flights to and from **Puerto Obaldía** (1hr; $79) are operated by Air Panama (Tues, Thurs, Sun), though timings can vary. If you are feeling adventurous and prepared to hang around in Puerto Obaldía (see p.301), boat rides can be negotiated further up the coast, even as far as **El Porvenir**, often on Colombian trading vessels while a great way to explore some of the less touristy parts of Kuna Yala, it can end up as expensive as flying. Before leaving Colombia, get an exit stamp from **immigration** at Capurganá (daily 9am–5pm) and an entry stamp for Panama on arrival in Puerto Obaldía. Military police will meet the boat and escort you to the relevant authorities. Your belongings will be thoroughly searched for drugs and you are likely to be required to show proof of onward travel and possibly a yellow fever vaccination certificate (see p.33 & p.47) and sufficient funds (a credit card will do) to cover your stay. A serious grilling and further searches await you at customs and immigration at Albrook Airport in Panama City.

Airlines, agents and operators

Airlines

Aer Lingus ⓦ www.aerlingus.com.
Air Canada ⓦ www.aircanada.com.
Air France ⓦ www.airfrance.com.
Air New Zealand ⓦ www.airnz.co.nz.
Air Panama ⓦ www.flyairpanama.com.
AIRES ⓦ www.aires.aero.
American Airlines ⓦ www.aa.com.
Avianca ⓦ www.avianca.com.
British Airways ⓦ www.ba.com.
Continental Airlines ⓦ www.continental.com.
Copa Airlines ⓦ www.copaair.com.
Delta ⓦ www.delta.com.
Iberia ⓦ www.iberia.com.
KLM (Royal Dutch Airlines) ⓦ www.klm.com.
Mexicana ⓦ www.mexicana.com.
Nature Air ⓦ www.natureair.com.
Qantas Airways ⓦ www.qantas.com.
South African Airways ⓦ www.flysaa.com.
TACA ⓦ www.taca.com
United Airlines ⓦ www.united.com.

Online booking

ⓦ www.cheapflights.co.uk (UK & Ireland);
ⓦ www.cheapflights.com (US); ⓦ www .cheapflights.ca (Canada); ⓦ www .cheapflights.com.au (Australia & New Zealand);
ⓦ www.cheapflights.co.za (South Africa).
ⓦ www.ebookers.com (UK); ⓦ www .ebookers.ie (Ireland).
ⓦ www.expedia.co.uk (UK & Ireland);

Sailing to Panama

An increasingly popular passage from or to Colombia involves a four to five-day **sailing trip** from Cartagena or Sapzurro (close to the Colombia–Panama border), taking in some of the more remote tropical islands of Kuna Yala en route to El Porvenir, Cartí or Puerto Lindo (see also p.143). Typically backpacker rates are $375–400 per person including food and non-alcoholic beverages, though some require to you help around the ship, be it crewing or cooking. The more recent Sapzurro route has the advantage of usually being slightly cheaper, avoiding the roughest seas by hugging the coast, thereby affording more time to explore Kuna Yala. Be prepared to hang around at your departure point for a few days since preparations can take some time. Horror stories abound of drunken captains and poorly maintained boats, so do your homework; hostel recommendations of particular captains can be helpful but should be viewed critically since hostels usually receive commission for supplying passengers. You're best getting the lowdown from other travellers who have made the trip. Travelling between November and February can be dangerous with rough seas, so much so that some captains do not make the crossing during that period.

Ⓦ www.expedia.com (US); Ⓦ www.expedia.ca
(Canada); Ⓦ www.expedia.com.au (Australia);
Ⓦ www.expedia.co.nz (New Zealand).
Ⓦ www.flightcentre.co.nz (New Zealand).
Ⓦ www.justtheflight.co.uk (UK).
Ⓦ www.lastminute.com (UK & Ireland);
Ⓦ www.lastminute.com.au (Australia);
Ⓦ www.lastminute.co.nz (New Zealand).
Ⓦ www.travelocity.co.uk (UK); Ⓦ www
.travelocity.com (US); Ⓦ www.travelocity.ca
(Canada); Ⓦ www.travelocity.com.au (Australia);
Ⓦ www.travelocity.co.nz (New Zealand).
Ⓦ www.zuji.com.au (Australia); Ⓦ www.zuji
.co.nz (New Zealand).

Agents and operators

Aventouras US toll free ☏ 800 930 2846,
Ⓦ www.aventouras.com. Specialists in eco- and
community-based tourism in Latin America, with an
emphasis on cross-cultural interaction.
Exodus ☏ 020/8675 5550, Ⓦ www.exodus.co.uk.
Experienced UK-based adventure and activity holiday
operator, which offers cycling holidays in Panama as
well as water-based holidays in Bocas del Toro and
explorations of the canal area.
Journey Latin America UK ☏ 020/8622 8469,
Ⓦ www.journeylatinamerica.co.uk. Long-established

UK-based tour operator offering tailor-made itineraries
and tours, including a coast-to-coast jungle trek along
the conquistadors' Camino Real.
North South Travel UK ☏ 01245/608 291,
Ⓦ www.northsouthtravel.co.uk. Friendly,
competitive travel agency, offering discounted fares
worldwide. Profits are used to support projects in
the developing world, especially the promotion of
sustainable tourism.
STA Travel UK ☏ 0871/230 0040, US ☏ 1-800/
781-4040, Australia ☏ 134 782, New Zealand
☏ 0800/474 400, South Africa ☏ 0861/781 781;
Ⓦ www.statravel.com. Worldwide specialists in
independent travel; also student IDs, travel insurance,
car rental and more. Good discounts for students and
under-26s.
Trailfinders UK ☏ 0845/058 5858, Ireland
☏ 01/677 7888, Australia ☏ 1300/780 212;
Ⓦ www.trailfinders.com. One of the best-informed
and most efficient agents for independent travellers,
and includes a travel clinic.
Tucan Travel UK ☏ 020/8896 1600, Ⓦ www
.tucantravel.com. Award-winning small travel
operator offering Panama in combination with Costa
Rica and other Central American destinations on some
of their adventure overland tours.

Getting around

Panama has a fairly comprehensive and very efficient bus network, used by the majority of the population, which will get you around most of the mainland, though the level of comfort varies enormously. Along the western section of the Interamericana – the Panamanian section of the Pan-American Highway – luxury vehicles with reclinable seats, air conditioning, non-stop videos and onboard toilets speed along for several hours for a handful of dollars, while at the other end of the scale chivas – converted pick-up trucks packed like the proverbial sardine can – grind their way up twisting mountain roads to remote villages for not a lot less.

There are many good paved **roads** in central and western Panama, even to small villages up in the mountains, and dirt roads are also generally well graded though in the rainy season they can soon become a quagmire. East of Panama City there are few roads of any description.

For the longer trips from Panama City – over the Cordillera Central to Bocas, deep into Darién or to the more distant islands of Kuna Yala – an **internal flight** on one of Panama's two domestic airlines will save a lot of time. Indeed with only one road – sometimes impassable in the rainy season – into Kuna Yala, climbing aboard a plane is sometimes the only way into the archipelago. And to hop from island to island in Kuna Yala or ease upriver to visit Emberá villages in the Darién, the main mode of transport is a motorised **dugout** or *cayuco*.

While Panama City has a comprehensive **bus** system, it can be interminably slow on some routes, so taking a **taxi** is often easier and is inexpensive. In the other towns and cities, most places of interest are within easy walking distance though a taxi – rarely costing more than a couple of dollars – can save you from melting in the heat.

By bus

The vast brick building fronted by battalions of buses just down the road from Albrook Airport on the edge of Panama City is the Gran Terminal de Transportes de Panamá, the highly efficient hub of the **national bus system**. Most of the capital's local transport and all international and regional buses leave from here (see p.97).

The main centres, such as Santiago, Chitré and David, also have large efficient **bus terminals** on the outskirts of town complete with toilet, left-luggage and restaurant facilities; from there regional connections and local buses – usually a mixture of battered Toyota minivans with extra fold-down aisle seating and the more comfortable Coasters – head out into the countryside in centrifugal fashion. In the smaller settlements, minibuses or *chivas* hang out in the plaza or main street waiting

Finding your way

Panama is not without its frustrations: **streets** often have several names, rarely marked on a signpost; **telephone numbers** change frequently, especially for mobile phones and even for government offices; and **websites** are often not updated, or domain names left to lapse – all of which makes contacting people difficult. Moreover, the **pace of change** in Panama at the moment is phenomenal: new places to stay are mushrooming; bars, discos and restaurants, especially in Panama City and tourist areas, regularly open, close, move or change name, often lasting the summer partying and tourist season, but failing to last through winter. This guide will help you navigate this dynamic country, but it's always worth checking details on the ground.

for an adequate number of passengers. Generally, the more rural the location, the more laissez-faire the bus timetable and the more likely it is that passengers will be picked up anywhere along the route.

Along most regional bus routes from Panama City, transport runs from 5.30–6am until 9–10pm, whereas the first buses heading into the capital from the provinces may leave from 1–4am to ensure passengers arrive for the start of the commercial day. Local transport in the provinces usually peters out around 6.30–7pm, while in the capital the *diablos rojos* (see p.64) thunder along popular routes until around midnight. The bus timetables for many routes can now be consulted online at ⓦwww .thebusschedule.com/pa.

The Interamericana is punctuated with official and unofficial (generally at a major intersection) bus stops, where you can flag down transport, but on Friday and Sunday afternoons and at either end of a holiday period when buses are jam-packed you can be left stranded for hours.

Ticket prices range from 25c for any bus in the Panama City metropolitan area to around $4 for a two-hour ride in moderate comfort, or $15 for a relaxing seven-hour recline all the way to David. There are set prices for every route, often posted on the bus window, and tourists are rarely overcharged – if in doubt ask a local on the bus what the fare is in advance. **Luggage** generally goes for free, either on the roof or in the luggage compartment, although surfboards sometimes incur extra charges. Security is not usually an issue.

Booking ahead for busy holiday periods and international journeys is a must, though it is only possible for international and some long-haul domestic routes and entails going in person to the travel company ticket office, usually located in the bus terminal, in Panama City, David or Changuinola, to purchase the ticket in cash.

By air

Flying within Panama is a convenient and safe experience though you might have your heart in your mouth landing in the more flimsy twin-props at some of the more remote airstrips of Kuna Yala and Darién.

Panama has two **domestic airlines** – with little to choose between them – that serve the major urban areas, several locations along the largely inaccessible Comarca de Kuna Yala and a handful of destinations in the Darién, which are also hard to reach by road, especially in the rainy season. Both operate out of Marcos A. Gelabert Airport (☎238 2700), more commonly known as **Albrook Airport** after the former US air-force base it occupies, which lies 3km northwest of the city centre. All internal flights depart from or arrive here with the exception of the route across the Western Highlands from Enrique Malek Airport (☎721 1072) in **David** to Changuinola and Bocas Town in Bocas del Toro Province, which provides a welcome alternative mode of transport whenever the road route is blocked by landslides after heavy rains.

Propeller planes seating forty to fifty passengers generally ply the urban routes, while smaller twenty-seater puddle hoppers operate in the Darién and Kuna Yala to suit the shorter runways – sometimes only as long as the island they're on. **Aeroperlas** (☎378   6000,   ⓦwww.aeroperlas.com), the older, more established airline, serves fourteen destinations. **Air Panama** (☏316 9000, ⓦwww.flyairpanama.com) serves around twenty, including San José, Costa Rica, via a connecting flight from David. Prices for both airlines are the same and remain constant irrespective of the season, with the maximum domestic fare one-way currently around $110 (including taxes), but with many much cheaper. Both carriers accept online credit card bookings. Luggage allowances are 14kg for the David–Bocas route and 12kg on all other routes plus 2.3kg carry-on, but consult the airlines' websites for differing regulations about surfboards, which generally incur extra charges ($10–15).

Compared with the long-distance buses, plane **timetables** are fairly sketchily adhered to, especially in Kuna Yala and Darién. Flights to David, Bocas and the more touristed western end of Kuna Yala book up quickly in advance of a holiday weekend.

By car

Away from the traffic hell that is Panama City, **driving** in Panama is generally fairly straightforward, with very good, well-signposted roads connecting the main urban centres, though it can be a different story in some of the more remote or mountainous areas.

The **Interamericana** (also called the Carretera Panamericana), Panama's main thoroughfare – part of the Pan-American Highway that travels almost 48,000km from Alaska to Chile – runs 486km from the Costa Rican border at Paso Canoas in the west, skirting several major cities, crossing the canal and bludgeoning its way through the capital before continuing another 282km and grinding to an abrupt halt in Yaviza in the eastern Darién.

Traffic for the Azuero Peninsula peels off onto the **Carretera Nacional** at Divisa, 34km east of Santiago, and branches off north across the Cordillera Central at Chiriquí for the sinuous journey across the continental divide down to the islands of Bocas del Toro on western Panama's only transisthmian route. Though an excellent paved road, it is sometimes blocked by landslides during the wettest months of the rainy season.

The only other routes across the isthmus lie east of the canal. The frequently log-jammed **Transístmica** links the capital with the country's second city of Colón, and has recently been joined by the controversial **Autopista Panamá–Colón**, a toll road aimed at improving commercial traffic. An hour east of Panama City, beyond Chepo, a roller-coaster of a **dirt road** heads north from the Interamericana 30km over the mountains to Cartí, providing the only road link with Kuna Yala, but this is only accessible by 4WD in the dry season or in the drier moments of the wet season. The final stretch of the Interamericana, from Panama City to **Yaviza**, has finally been almost completely paved – only a short section of dirt just after Metetí, which becomes a quagmire in heavy rains, remains. Expect an increasing number of police checkpoints as you near the Costa Rican border, where you'll generally be waved on fairly nonchalantly, or along the road to Yaviza, where the bureaucratic rigmarole can take some time.

Despite Panama's decent road network, **driving at night** is best avoided because there's little illumination outside the urban centres, and drink driving, one of the main causes of accidents nationally, is common. Though there is a legal limit of 86 milligrams, it is rarely adhered to or enforced.

If you are involved in a car accident, Panamanian law requires that you should not move the vehicles but should wait near them until the traffic police (Transito) arrive; a statement from them is required to file any insurance claim. The **speed limits** are 40kph in urban areas, 60kph on secondary roads and 100kph on primary roads unless otherwise indicated but the speed limits are neither widely advertised nor followed. Two of the most dangerous roads are the Interamericana, which copious buses and heavy trucks thunder along, and the route across the Cordillera Central to Bocas del Toro, when bad weather can make the hairpin bends even more scary. Outside the hair-raising free-for-all of Panama City (see p.64), urban driving is not too threatening.

Hitching is possible, though with all the obvious attendant risks on the main thoroughfares, where it is unlikely anyone will stop. In the rural areas, where there is no or at best infrequent bus service, it is quite usual to thumb a lift on the back of a private pick-up, though you should offer to pay at least the equivalent of a bus fare.

Car rental

Renting a car enables you to cover more terrain in a shorter time, affords greater flexibility and makes it easier to explore some of the out-of-the way spots. Rental **costs** vary greatly among providers, so shop around and note that rates fluctuate according to season and demand. Virtually all rental vehicles have air conditioning. A manual economy car is the cheapest option (approximately $40/day, $250/week, including taxes and basic insurance cover). For a 4WD, which is probably only necessary if you want to get off the beaten track and into the national parks, bank on paying almost double that. **Fuel** is just over $3 a gallon and petrol stations (often 24hr) are liberally sprinkled along the main roads.

You'll find all the usual international **car rental firms** in Panama as well as local companies. The larger firms have their head offices at Tocumen International Airport, with many running a downtown office and sometimes branches at Albrook and David airports. Some operators have offices in other major cities and tourist towns.

Rates are sometimes cheaper if booked online in advance and fluctuate according to the season. The main reservations office number (generally in Panama City) has been given for each firm, though check the websites for other contacts. The minimum age for most car rental companies is 25 but 23 will suffice for some firms provided a credit card is produced as security. A driving licence – international or from your country of origin – as well as a passport will need to be shown.

Listings

Alamo ☎ 236 5777, ⓦ www.alamopanama.com.
Avis ☎ 278 9444, ⓦ www.avis.com.pa.
Barriga ☎ 269 0056, ⓦ www.barrigarentacar.net.
Budget ☎ 263 8777, ⓦ www.budgetpanama.com.
Dollar ☎ 270 0355, ⓦ www.dollarpanama.com.
Hertz ☎ 301 2611, ⓦ www.rentacarpanama.com.
Hilary (David) ☎ 775 5459, no website.
National ☎ 265 2222, ⓦ www.nationalpanama.com.
Thrifty ☎ 204 9555, ⓦ www.thriftycmla.com.

By taxi

A convenient and relatively cheap way to whizz round the capital – traffic permitting (see p.64), **taxis** are widely available in most of Panama's urban centres, ostensibly charging fixed rates according to zones or generally agreed prices for particular routes, which means that any trip within a town should not exceed a couple of dollars. A small surcharge is added for more than two passengers and prices are higher at night. While most Panamanian taxi drivers are very honest and adhere to standard rates, in Panama City and tourist areas like Boquete, the chances of a driver taking advantage of the uninformed increases so you should make local enquiries about likely charges and then agree on a price before getting into a cab.

Taxis, generally in the form of a 4WD twin cab, are also a practical way of reaching more rural locations which are poorly served by public transport. Official cabs should be yellow with their licence number on the door, though in the country you are more likely to come across unofficial drivers whose service is generally just as reliable. Taxi drivers can also be hired as **tourist guides** though most will only guide in Spanish – ask your accommodation for a recommended driver. There is no set hourly charge, but around $10 an hour is the going rate in Panama City, though petrol costs also need to be factored in.

By boat

Panama boasts over 1500 islands and it's almost inevitable you'll require water transport at some stage on your trip, be it smooth sightseeing in a canal transit or a bumpy water-taxi ride in Bocas. Fairly robust **ferries** equipped with life jackets and radio transmitters leave Panama City for Isla Taboga, and sometimes Isla Contadora, according to regular timetables, whereas in the remoter regions of eastern Kuna Yala you could be seated on a plank in a leaking motorized **dugout** bailing out with a yoghurt carton, having spent a couple of hours asking round for a ride. Frequent **water-taxis** serve Bocas from Almirante for fixed fares ($4), whereas any trip to the Pacific island of Coiba will probably mean getting a group of interested people together and negotiating a deal with a fisherman.

Travelling by motorized dugout or occasionally, if you're lucky, in a slightly more comfy **skiff** (*panga*), is the norm among the communities of Kuna Yala and Darién. If a boat is already heading the way you want to travel the fare will be fairly cheap. Otherwise, private boat hire (which needs to cover fuel and the boat operator's time and often their assistant) can be expensive; awareness of the going price for diesel will help your ability to haggle, as will knowledge of the amount of fuel necessary to cover the distance given the size of the engine. Note that the seaworthiness of vessels varies enormously and many are overloaded and lack life jackets even when heading for long trips on potentially hazardous waters. Every few months a boat somewhere sinks or capsizes and people

drown. Make sure you check out your transport before committing to a journey.

By bike

Away from the Interamericana and Panama City, **cycling** is pleasant – with wonderful views and quiet roads – and growing in popularity both as recreation and means of transport, though you won't find cycle lanes or cycle routes. Mountain bike **rental** is on the increase in tourist areas such as El Valle, Boquete, Bocas and Santa Fé, though the quality of the machine on offer is extremely variable, as are the rates ($3–5/hr, $10–15/day). In Panama City several rental places line the Amador Causeway, which actually possesses a cycle path, as does the recently inaugurated Cinta Costera. Exodus, the UK adventure holiday specialist (ⓦwww.exodus.co.uk), offers cycling holidays in Panama (see p.23).

Accommodation

From secluded mountain eco-lodges to thatched cane cabañas on a deserted island, from partying backpackers' hostels to smart boutique hotels, Panama offers a wide range of accommodation. Panama City inevitably has the greatest variety, though prices are generally a lot higher than in the rest of the country. In touristy areas such as Bocas and Boquete prices are creeping up and more lodgings now exist at the higher end of the market, though there is very little outside Panama City that could truly be described as luxury. Nevertheless, the number of comfortable lodges (often foreign-owned) and B&Bs is increasing. In Kuna Yala you could just as likely be sleeping in a hammock, while in the Darién you might be snoozing on the raised wooden floor of a traditional Emberá dwelling.

The names given to accommodation in Panama are equally varied. **Posada** and **lodge** usually indicate a fair degree of comfort in pleasant natural surroundings, whereas places prefaced with **hospedaje**, **pensión** or **residencial** are generally much simpler small family-owned lodgings. The word **cabaña** may conjure up an image of a simple thatched hut in an idyllic natural setting, but can just as easily mean a dark,

windowless cement cell in an unremarkable location. **Hostal** usually signifies a place with dorms for backpackers but occasionally is merely a synonym for a family-run hotel. **Hotel** too can cover a mixed bag from a plush international five-star high-rise to a dilapidated shack, and also includes the famous by-the-hour push-button motel, often referred to as **un push**, which rents out rooms short term for sexual liaisons. In

Accommodation price codes

The accommodation listed in the book has been assigned one of nine **price codes**, according to the cost of the cheapest double room (including taxes) in high season (generally Dec–April), not including the extra price hike some places indulge in for Carnaval, Christmas, New Year and other special holiday periods.

❶ $12 and under   ❹ $31–40   ❼ $91–120
❷ $13–20   ❺ $41–60   ❽ $121–200
❸ $21–30   ❻ $61–90   ❾ $201 and over

no way unique to Panama, they are scattered all over the country, most visibly along the Interamericana, with such enticing names as "*Sueño Lindo*" (Sweet Dreams) or "*Las Mil y Una Noches*" (Thousand and One Nights). As for the much abused prefix "eco", it may simply denote pleasant natural surroundings, and is no guarantee of sustainable environmental practices or social responsibility.

Neither name nor price is much of an indication of what you'll get for your money. **Hot water**, **air conditioning** and a **TV** (though not necessarily cable) is standard in hotels in all major cities and large towns and a private bathroom is often squeezed into fairly rudimentary and miniscule lodgings. In the lowlands, even the cheapest establishments usually have air conditioning, though not necessarily hot water; in the highlands air conditioning and fans are unnecessary and usually absent though hot water can be lacking at the budget end. As in most other Latin American countries, toilet paper should not be put down the **toilet**, but into the adjacent waste basket, because it can clog the system in all but the most modern top-end hotels; if in doubt, enquire at reception.

Hostels

Panama's **hostel** scene is expanding as the country attracts increasing numbers of backpackers. Currently there are still only around a dozen in the country – mainly in Panama City, Bocas and Boquete – which struggle to meet the growing demand, and advance booking is often necessary to be sure of a bed. A dorm bunk usually costs around $15, occasionally including coffee or a light breakfast, while some establishments also offer private rooms at $25–35. Most

have common areas, shared kitchens, free wi-fi or internet access and bags of useful information about the surrounding area.

Camping

There is virtually no organized **camping** in Panama, though a few lodgings allow tents if asked. In rural communities you can almost always find someone willing to allow you to camp on their land for a small fee. Alternatively, there are kilometres of empty beaches to pitch a tent on, although you should always seek local advice since they are not universally safe. Touristy areas such as Santa Clara and Isla Bastimentos have periodically reported theft and muggings while at night on a completely uninhabited island in Kuna Yala you run the risk of encountering the odd drug smuggler. The **national parks** (see p.39) seem more set up for camping since they have set fees (usually $5/person a night), but rarely offer facilities beyond those shared with the park wardens at the park entrance. Most of the parks and protected areas also offer dormitory accommodation (usually $15/person) and use of the kitchen.

Homestays

Homestays, a good budget accommodation option, often help the local economy more directly while providing an opportunity to engage in cross-cultural interaction. They may also be the only way of finding a room during major fiestas in a town that is short of formal lodgings. The tourist office, where one exists, is the best place to enquire. In Kuna Yala and Darién, a homestay is frequently the norm when overnighting in a village, which you will need to arrange with the chief or tourist co-ordinator on arrival.

Pricing and taxes

Most mid-range and high-end accommodation operates a dual **pricing system**: high season rates (mid-Dec to end of April) generally coincide with the dry season, whereas the rest of the year counts as low season, when it's possible to find significant discounts, especially for online bookings. On top of high season rates, some establishments in Panama City and the major holiday destinations hike their prices even higher for Carnaval, Easter (Semana Santa), Christmas and New Year. Some lodgings in places that are primarily weekend retreats, such as Isla Grande and El Valle, charge more Friday to Sunday, occasionally demanding a two- or three-night minimum stay.

All rooms are subject to ten percent **tourist tax**, which is not always included in the advertised rate but has been factored into our price codes (see box, p.29). Note too that in mid-range hotels a double room often means a room with two double beds and you might have to specify one double bed (*una cama doble*) – the assumption behind our price codes where this is an option – if you want to keep costs down. Room costs are usually based on two people sharing, but many rooms have an extra single bed, which a third person can have for an extra $10–15. Children under 12 are often admitted free.

Food and drink

Given Panama's clichéd status as the "melting pot of the Americas", it's no surprise Panamanian cuisine is infused with numerous culinary influences, notably Afro-Antillean, indigenous, Spanish, Chinese and American. Cosmopolitan Panama City offers the greatest variations in terms of gastronomy and price (see p.87), from a $2 plate of noodles and chicken in the public market to ornate fusion cuisine served on damask tablecloths. You can take your pick from Italian, Japanese, Lebanese, Brazilian, American – and thankfully not just McDonald's and KFC – Swiss or Indian fare. In the capital, Panamanian food rarely features on the menus of the mid- to high-end restaurants, outside a few tourist-orientated venues, but in markets, hole-in-the-wall restaurants and out in the interior, it's much easier to find local culinary specialities – often heavy on starch and frequently fried.

Outside the capital and the major tourist destinations of Boquete and Bocas, there is less variation and dining is often more informal and a lot cheaper; travellers on a tight budget can easily find simple well-cooked food in *fondas* (basic restaurants), which offer *comida corriente* (meal of the day) for very little. **Vegetarians** will be challenged since, as elsewhere in Central America, even the veggie staple of beans and rice can be cooked in pork fat. Your best bet is to head for a Chinese restaurant, present in most towns, or one of the proliferating pizzerias – incredibly there is even one now in Carti Sugdup, the first in Kuna Yala – or stock up with the fresh fruit and vegetables that abound in many local markets.

Breakfast

Panama's filling **desayuno típico** (traditional breakfast), aimed at sustaining workers for a hard day's labour in the fields, offers a chance to boost cholesterol levels. Panama's deep-fried favourites include *tortillas* (thick cornmeal cakes), *carimañolas* (mashed boiled yuca – cassava or manioc – stuffed with ground beef) and *hojaldres* (discs of sweetened leavened dough, which at best are delightfully crispy and tasty but at

Traditional dishes

Unless you are vegetarian, you should not leave Panama without sampling the country's **national dish**, *sancocho* – a tasty soup. Variations on the theme are served in many parts of Latin America and even within Panama the meal is prepared in numerous ways; essentially it's a hearty chicken-based soup with large chunks of yuca and other filling root vegetables, or maybe even plantain and sweetcorn, flavoured with cilantro – a herb similar to coriander but more pungent – exemplifying the Caribbean culinary influence. Other Panamanian variations of ubiquitous **Latin dishes** include the unappetizing-sounding *ropa vieja* ("old clothes" – spicy shredded beef over rice), *ceviche* (white fish, shrimp or octopus marinated in lime juice with chopped onion and garlic plus hot pepper and fresh coriander) and *mondongo* (a slow-cooked tripe and chorizo-based stew with plenty of root vegetables, laced with garlic and coriander or cilantro), the latter a traditional dish for celebration (*mondongada*) with family and labourers after the installation of the roof on a new house.

With so much coastline, it's no wonder seafood is a Panamanian staple in both the Pacific and Caribbean lowlands. In the latter, the Afro-Antillean influence is dominant – typical dishes include rice cooked in coconut milk and seafood prepared with spices and judicious amounts of lime. *Corvina* (sea bass) is the most widely eaten fish, but you can also find snapper, grouper, dorado, shrimp, langoustines, crab and lobster, though you should refuse the last four if offered them during the closed season (Dec 1 to April 15 in the Pearl Islands, March 1 to June 30 along the Caribbean coast) unless you know they have come from a freezer. Locally farmed trout is a speciality of the Chiriquí Highlands.

While starch and carbohydrates abound in most traditional foods, **greenery** is scarce. Don't be surprised if the salad accompaniment is merely a lettuce leaf supporting a slice of tomato and a couple of onion rings. Green vegetables are also conspicuous by their absence in many restaurants outside the capital, though they can often be found in local markets. Spices are generally used sparingly, but if you require more kick there's usually some *salsa picante* lurking on a table to take the roof of your mouth off.

worst are chewy and dripping in grease). Costa Rica's national dish, *gallo pinto* (literally "speckled rooster"), is another popular way to kick-start the day, a moist rice, beans and onions mix often accompanied with a dollop of *natilla* – a local sour cream that is also lavished on strawberries in the Chiriquí Highlands – and fried or scrambled eggs.

If such a heavy plateful is more than you can stomach first thing in the morning, head for a **panadería** (bakery) for a pastry and a shot of coffee, or pick up some fresh fruit at the local market. In the more expensive hotels in Panama City and in European or North American-owned establishments outside the capital, you can also expect combinations of cereals, fruit, yoghurt and toast.

Lunch and dinner

While it's possible to grab a light **lunch** – a flaky *empanada* (pasty) with a beef, pork or chicken-based filling or an *emparedado* (sandwich) – in urban areas, for most Panamanians lunch is the main meal of the day. In the *fondas* and cheaper restaurants ordering the *almuerzo del día* (lunch of the day) will get you a filling plate of chicken with rice, plus beans or lentils, or maybe fish and plantain down on the coast, for $2–3. Some places throw in a soup starter and dessert to give you a three-course set meal at very little extra cost. **Evening eating** is generally more low-key except when dining out for a special occasion.

Predominantly self-service *cafeterías* – the Panamanian equivalent of American diners – keep going from around 6 or 7am until 11pm or midnight in the urban centres. Out in the countryside, local restaurants and *fondas* may also open for all three meals but shut up shop shortly after nightfall, depending on demand. Lunch in formal dining establishments is usually served from noon until 3pm, dinner from 6 or 7pm until around 10pm, with the midday meal usually offering better value for money. Both may incur a ten percent **service charge**, which is not always included on the menu price list.

Street food and snacks

When tramping the big cities, you can sometimes find tasty morsels of **street food** to tide you over until mealtimes, from chunks of fresh pineapple or water melon to plantain crisps (*platanitos*) deep-fried on the spot. Small **roadside grills** often serve *carne en palito* (meat on a little stick) – fairly miniscule kebabs comprising slivers of (occasionally spicy) marinated beef, which take the edge of your appetite. During the day, you'll also see men pushing carts laden with fluorescent liquids and blocks of ice around the main squares, peddling **raspados** – paper cones filled with shavings of ice, drizzled over with a sickly flavoured liquid, made still sweeter by a slurp of condensed milk and much loved by kids.

Drink

Aside from Panama's tasty tap water, there's a wide range of beverages to sample, from lethal paint-stripper home-brews to delicious fruit concoctions served in a variety of manners, not to mention beer and rum, which are consumed in vast quantities during Panama's many festivals.

Beer is the most popular alcoholic drink; Panama's four main labels – Soberana, Panamá, Balboa and the ubiquitous Atlas – are all fairly inoffensive lagers, with Balboa slightly more full-bodied. Though none will set the pulse racing of beer aficionados, when ice-cold they definitely hit the spot, costing 60c swigged out of a bottle in a local cantina, and up to $4 served on a serviette in a frosted glass in a plush nightclub. Imported beers such as Heineken and Budweiser, and even Guinness, are widely available in Panama City and tourist towns but are more expensive.

The national tipple, the transparent, throat-singeing **seco** (a rough sugarcane spirit – see p.190), is significantly more potent (35 percent) and more commonly consumed by men in the interior, particularly during fiestas, as is rum. A lethal home-brew favoured by *campesinos* is *vino de palma*, made from fermented palm sap, as is *guarapo,* sugar cane juice distilled to knock-out strength. **Wine** – usually Chilean or Californian – is becoming increasingly available at reasonable rates in Panama City and in tourist areas such as Bocas and Boquete.

Away from the alcohol, there is a wide range of **fruit-based drinks**, which in most parts of the country (see opposite) you can enjoy with ice, safe in the knowledge that the water is drinkable. Mango, pineapple, soursop, passion fruit, tamarind and a host of other fruits can be savoured in a range of forms: as a *jugo natural* (pure fruit juice), a *licuado* (a fresh fruit, water and sugar shake), a *batido* (a milk shake) or a *chicha* (a sweet maize-based fruit concoction) – not to be confused with its alcoholic cousin, generally dubbed *chicha fuerte* – a potent fermented maize brew made in bulk for special celebrations, particularly among indigenous and *campesino* communities.

The similar-sounding *chicheme,* a surprisingly tasty Panamanian speciality of ground maize, milk, vanilla and cinnamon, most revered in La Chorrera, should be sampled at some stage. So should *pipa* – fresh juice sipped through a straw straight from the coconut – and Panamanian **coffee**. Outside the country, Panama's reputation as the world leader in producing gourmet coffee is a secret known only to connoisseurs; you can sample the most prized beans in Boquete and Panama City, though elsewhere you're more likely to be sipping the more mundane but perfectly satisfying Café Duran, which will be strong and is sometimes offered with condensed milk. While black **tea** is widely available in cities and tourist areas, tea lovers will usually have to content themselves with herbal varieties elsewhere – chamomile (*manzanilla*) or cinnamon (*canela*) are the most common offerings.

Iced **tapwater** is generally served on arrival in restaurants, except where water quality is poor – Bocas, the Darién and Kuna Yala – in which case you'll need to order mineral water.

Health

In the construction eras of the transisthmus railroad and canal, Panama was synonymous with disease, in particular yellow fever, malaria and cholera. Thankfully, times have changed, and most of Panama poses little threat to your health: yellow fever has been eradicated, malaria only persists in a few isolated areas, tap water is safe to drink in most of the country and sophisticated medical care is widely available in the main population centres. Your most likely medical ailment will be travellers' diarrhoea from a change of diet and climate, or sunburn from overdoing it on the beach.

That said, you should ensure that your basic **inoculations** are up to date and consult a travel medical centre professional to help you decide what other precautions to take. If you intend only to explore the canal area and chill on the beach, you'll probably need little more than sun block and insect repellent, but if you're bent on venturing into the Darién jungle, all kinds of insect- and water-borne hazards need to be considered. **Medical insurance** is essential – see p.48.

Inoculations

Most inoculations that involve multiple jabs need six to eight weeks to complete. There are no compulsory vaccinations to visit Panama but in addition to ensuring that your **routine injections** are current (tetanus, diphtheria and polio, MMR), hepatitis A and typhoid are generally recommended, though you can also have a combined hepatitis A and B jab, advisable for long-term travellers. **Yellow fever** is nearly always flagged up as a hazard on health websites in relation to Panama, although the last documented case was in 1974. Nevertheless, there is still deemed to be a very slight risk of the disease in the Darién and remoter parts of Kuna Yala. Moreover, since November 2008 the Panamanian government has required travellers entering the country from countries where yellow fever is listed as endemic, such as Colombia and Brazil, to carry proof of vaccination at least ten days prior to entry – ironic given that Panama is also on the list – though this requirement is rarely enforced.

Rabies is another potential hazard, more from vampire bats in cattle-ranching areas than from feral dogs, and one that should only really be considered by travellers expecting to spend time in the remoter rural areas.

General precautions

A major plus is that **tap water** in most of Panama is safe to drink, which means the usual travel worries about avoiding ice in drinks and salads washed in ordinary water can be dispensed with. The exceptions are in Kuna Yala, much of the Darién and the remoter parts of Bocas. On the main tourist islands of Kuna Yala and Bocas bottled water, though expensive, is widely available, but it is less easily obtained in the Darién. That said, since disposing of non-organic waste such as plastic bottles is a particularly acute environmental issue in these areas, try to use water purification tablets as much as possible. They are sometimes available in Panama City (see p.43) but it's a better bet to bring them with you. While vile-tasting chlorine or iodine tablets are still effective and widely available, some companies now produce tablets to neutralize the unpleasant aftertaste. Seek advice on the relative merits of chlorine versus iodine; the latter, for example, though considered more effective against giardia parasites, is generally not recommended for pregnant women. Campers with their own stove can of course boil water to sterilize it.

Since food safety is related to water safety and to food storage, exercise common sense when eating **salads** or **unpeeled fruit** in the few areas in Panama where the water is not potable. **Street food**, though frequently very tasty, is another potential minefield, particularly at fiestas when mounds of chicken and rice stand around in the hot sun for hours. Make sure the food is well cooked in front of you and, if the stall has been dishing up food all day, that any raw meat or fish has been stored in a cooler box with ice before cooking – and avoid anything swimming in mayonnaise.

Intestinal problems

Travellers' **diarrhoea** (TD) lasting a few days is the most common ailment encountered, as likely to be due to the change in diet and climate as to contaminated food or water carrying bacteria, viruses or parasites. If afflicted by the runs, the best cure is to rest and rehydrate, drinking plenty of clean water with rehydration salts. Sachets of Dioralyte or Electolade are worth keeping in your first-aid kit, though equivalents are easily purchased in pharmacies in the major urban centres. Diarrhoea remedies such as Imodium and Lomotil should only be used in emergencies, such as when embarking on a long-distance plane journey or a jungle trek, since stopping the flow is not actually healthy. If symptoms persist, especially if there is blood in the stool or vomiting occurs, consult a doctor, who will probably prescribe a course of antibiotics.

Sunburn and dehydration

Skin cancer is on the increase, largely because of overexposure to UV radiation – indeed it is the most prevalent form of cancer in the US. In the fierce tropical sun of Panama, a high factor sun cream (SPF 15 or higher with both UVA & UVB protection), a sun hat and sunglasses are an absolute must. Up to 40 percent of the sun's rays can be reflected back up from water or sand, even if you're sitting in the shade; nor is an overcast day free from damaging UV light. When travelling in a dugout – a likely scenario if exploring the Darién or Kuna Yala – you could be faced with hours without any protection. Serious sunburn, sun stroke and heat stroke are therefore all very real health hazards and far more likely than catching a tropical disease. Keeping up your fluid intake to avoid dehydration is just as essential.

Malaria

Though **malaria** was brought under control during the US canal construction era at the same time yellow fever was eradicated, it lingers on in isolated pockets. West of the canal, there is low risk of the disease in more remote areas of the Caribbean lowlands in Bocas and Veraguas, and a slightly higher risk east of the canal, in the Darién and in more isolated areas of Kuna Yala. Transmitted by a parasite in the saliva of an infected anopheles mosquito (active from dusk to dawn), its symptoms – fever, chills, headaches and muscle pains – are easily confused with flu.

It is most effectively combated through **prevention** – wearing long loose sleeves and trousers for protection, dousing yourself in repellent and sleeping under a mosquito net or in screened rooms. Most effective chemical insect repellents contain DEET, with the 25–35 percent varieties considered adequate for most needs. However, a few recent studies have started to raise questions about DEET's possible neurological side effects as well as damage to the environment. Whatever the medical opinions on the subject, you have to wonder about a solution that will melt your pen if it gets too close. Recently, more organic, non-chemical products, based on oils such as eucalyptus, citronella, cedar or verbena, are appearing on the market. They are generally more expensive but give less fierce protection, which wears off much more quickly. They can be effective enough when used with other preventive measures, although if you are in a malarial area you might want to stick to DEET. Mosquito coils are widely available across Panama, even in small villages; if seeking a natural alternative, candles can help deter the insects. In neither case should they be used in enclosed indoor environments.

A range of anti-malarial tablets are on the market, all of which should be purchased prior to arriving in Panama and started in advance of visiting the malarial area, though a public medical centre (*centro de salud*) in a malarial area should stock a supply for post-exposure treatment. West of the canal, chloroquine is the drug of choice, generally taken once a week a fortnight in advance of entering a malarial area and for four weeks afterwards.

East of the canal, where mosquitoes are chloroquine-resistant, mefloquine (also known as Larium) is often prescribed, though it can have particularly severe side effects. Malarone is a less controversial alternative but is currently the most expensive anti-malarial drug on the market. It is taken daily only two days before entering an infected area, to be continued for a week after leaving. Whatever you choose, it is important to finish the course of anti-malarials because of the time lag between bite and infection. If you become ill with flu-like symptoms after returning home, consult a doctor and inform them you've been to a malarial risk area.

Other bites and stings

Taking steps to avoid being bitten by **insects** is of paramount importance (see opposite). In addition to malaria, mosquitoes can transmit dengue fever, which induces flu-like symptoms similar to malaria but with more extreme aches. Sandflies (*chitras*) are a more likely pest for travellers, proliferating during the rainy season, and not only at the beach; almost invisible, you will become aware of them only when they bite. Sandfly bites itch more and for longer than mosquito bites – calamine lotion or antihistamine cream will usually reduce the aggravation. In forested rural areas in various parts of Panama bites from an infected sand fly can cause cutaneous leishmaniasis, whose symptoms can remain dormant for up to six months before sores and swellings break out on the skin. Though there is no vaccine, the disease is treatable through a series of jabs.

An overfamiliarity with Indiana Jones films can lead to the misconception that the greatest danger in the rainforest is a **snake bite**. While Panama has its share of venomous snakes – bushmaster, fer-de-lance and coral for starters – you are unlikely to see one, let alone get bitten. Nevertheless, donning long pants and closed shoes or (even better) boots reduces the risk, as does avoiding walking in the forest at night. Should a snake manage to get its fangs into you, immobilize the affected area, apply a light-pressure bandage (not tourniquet) above and below the bite and seek immediate medical attention. Even a local medical centre should have some anti-venom.

There's a whole host of **other beasts** on land that may bite or sting, but only when threatened: scorpions – more commonly seen at night – and some spiders, for example; while in the sea jelly fish, sting rays and fire coral can all be painful. If you are prone to allergic reactions to bites and stings, make sure you carry some antihistamine tablets, which can reduce swelling and itchiness, as well as antihistamine cream or calamine lotion to cool and ease the pain.

Medical resources for travellers

There are a number of useful **online resources**, though their information may not be sufficiently nuanced (see note on yellow fever, p.38) for your needs. The websites listed generally note travel medical centres, where you can get jabs, and give general advice on the most common ailments and diseases that you might encounter. Travel medical centre professionals generally have access to more detailed and specific health information; you are strongly advised to consult them as well as carrying out your own research.

US and Canada

Centers for Disease Control and Prevention (CDC) ☎ 800/232 4636 (24hr health helpline), ⓦ www.cdc.gov/travel. Official US government travel health site that's laden with info.
Public Health Agency of Canada ⓦ www .phac-aspc.gc.ca. Distributes free pamphlets on travel health and provides a comprehensive list of travel clinics in the country.
Travellers' Medical and Vaccination Centre ⓦ www.tmvc.com. List of travel health centres in Canada and vaccination costs plus brief travel health tips.

UK and Ireland

Fitfortravel ⓦ www.fitfortravel.nhs.uk. Excellent NHS (Scotland) public access site with country-specific advice, the latest health bulletins and information on immunizations.
Hospital for Tropical Diseases Travel Clinic ☎ 020/7388 9600 (Travel Clinic), ☎ 020/7950 7799 (24hr Travellers Healthline Advisory Service – see website for additional country-specific code at 50p/min), ⓦ www.thehtd.org.

MASTA (Medical Advisory Service for Travellers Abroad) ☎0870/606 2782, ⓦwww.masta.org. List of affiliated travel clinics, small health library and personalized country-specific health briefs (£4).
National Travel Health Network and Centre ⓦwww.nathnac.org. Excellent website for health professionals and the travelling public providing fact sheets on various travel health risks and a free database of country-specific health info.
Tropical Medical Bureau ☎1850/487 674, ⓦwww.tmb.ie. List of travel clinics in Ireland and country-specific info from US consular service.

Australia, New Zealand and South Africa

Travellers' Medical and Vaccination Centre ⓦwww.tmvc.com.au. User-friendly site listing travel clinics in Australia, New Zealand and South Africa plus accessible fact sheets on travel health and postings of health alerts worldwide.

Accessing medical care

Both state and private **medical care** is very good in Panama, particularly in Panama City; many doctors work in the public sector hospitals in the morning and run private clinics in the afternoon. The main problem the public sector faces is a lack of resources, particularly in the more remote rural villages, so most Panamanians who can afford private health care as well as almost all expats will head for a private clinic, where service is likely to be more immediate. The average cost of a consultation with a private doctor is $40–50, provided no x-rays or laboratory tests need doing, whereas a government-run doctor at the local clinic will see you for $3.

While **travel insurance** may cover costs, it will only do so after you file a claim on your return; you still need to be able to access sufficient funds to cover the bills at the time. Many doctors in the main cities have trained in the US at some stage and so speak good English. The US Embassy has a list of bilingual doctors in Panama City on their website (ⓦwww.panama.usembassy.gov /medical2010.html).

The media

Aside from one government TV channel and one radio station, the media in Panama is privately owned. The five national daily Spanish-language newspapers – and three Chinese-language papers – are widely available from street vendors in urban areas, and in supermarkets countrywide, while it's hard to escape TV in Panama – screens adorn most eating and drinking establishments, even upmarket restaurants, and are standard in most hotels.

Newspapers

The most respected **paper** is *La Prensa* (ⓦwww.prensa.com), which also produces informative supplements with in-depth writing and interesting features on tourism, history and culture. *La Estrella de Panamá* (ⓦwww.laestrella.com.pa) and *Panamá América* (ⓦwww.pa-digital.com.pa) also count as "quality press", with *El Siglo* (ⓦwww.elsiglo.com) and *La Crítica* (ⓦwww .critica.com.pa), the popular tabloid options, satisfying the masses with plenty of gore and scandal. While there is a strong tradition of investigative reporting and criticism of public officials, the relationship between the government and the press is uneasy, with periodic judicial and official harassment of journalists who take on the political elite.

Given the large US expat population, there is no shortage of **English-language news**. Aside from the imported *Miami Herald International Edition* and *USA Today*, there is the online *The Panama News* (ⓦwww .thepanamanews.com), which has the mantra "writing for thinking people not cattle". It pulls no punches and frequently contains features that border on the slanderous but, picking through them with healthy scepticism, you will gain some valuable insights into the dirty side of politics and business.

Liberally sprinkled round hotel lobbies and restaurants around the country, the free bilingual weekly *The Visitor/El Visitante* (ⓦ www.thevisitorpanama.com) offers a bland summary of Panamanian news, some features and a decent listings section of events in the main tourist zones of Panama City, Bocas and Boquete. The latter two expat enclaves also produce free monthly papers in English: *The Bocas Breeze* (ⓦ www.thebocasbreeze.com) and *The Bajareque Times* (ⓦ www.boquete -bajareque-times.com); primarily run by and for expats, they contain some useful listings.

TV and radio

On evenings in a bar or cafeteria you're likely to catch an unremittingly awful soap opera (*telenovela*) on one of Panama's six terrestrial **television** channels. Many middle-class Panamanians have access to cable TV with channels in Spanish and English, providing a heavy diet of Hollywood films, soaps, sitcoms and sport – baseball, football and boxing in particular – with periodic news bulletins.

Check out ⓦ www.coolpanama.com for a list of **radio stations**, frequencies and their musical preferences, ranging from traditional folk music, through western pop and rock, to reggaeton or salsa, plus live streaming. You can listen to a weekly roundup of Panamanian news in English on a Sunday (6–8pm) on Radio Metropolis (93.5FM), and Voice of America also broadcasts in Panama.

Festivals and public holidays

Panama is awash with festivals and public holidays. Alongside the numerous commemorations of historical events, there are copious Catholic celebrations – including each town's patron saint bash, agricultural fairs and cultural extravaganzas that reflect the country's ethnic diversity. Whatever the differences in the details, they all demand the ability to survive several days and nights of music, dancing and processions, fuelled on mountains of street food and gallons of booze. Head and shoulders above the rest stands Carnaval, a five-day marathon of hedonism (see box, p.197) at its most outlandish in the tiny Azuero town of Las Tablas. Check the tourist office website for festival and holiday dates (ⓦ www.atp.gob.pa), and see below and the relevant sections of the book for details of the major festivals.

Festivals

January

Feria de las Flores y del Café Mid-Jan. Ten-day celebration in Boquete to mark the coffee harvest with carpets of flowers, food and craft stalls, the daytime family entertainment followed by night-time discos.

February

Revolución Dule Feb 25. Celebrates the Kuna Revolution of 1925, their Independence Day, with colourful reenactments of battles against the Panamanian authorities held across the *comarca*.
Carnaval Four days of wild partying and processions running till dawn on Ash Wednesday. Celebrated countrywide, but especially in **Las Tablas** and **Panama City**, with an aquatic parade on the Saturday in Penonomé.

March

Semana Santa or **Holy Week** March–April. Celebrated everywhere, but most colourfully on the Azuero Peninsula.

37
■

Festival de los Diablos y Congos Vibrant biennial weekend event in Portobelo, showcasing Afro-colonial culture and resistance to the Spanish conquest in a mass of costumes, dances and devils (2011, 2013).

April

Feria de las Orquídeas Five days in early April in Boquete. Over a thousand orchids, craft stalls and a programme of cultural events.
Feria Internacional de Azuero Ten days in La Villa de Los Santos. Major agricultural fair with stalls, presentations and competitions reflecting the area's colonial and cattle-farming traditions.

June

Festival de Corpus Christi Late May/early June. Celebrated across the country but most spectacularly in La Villa de Los Santos with processions and dramatic devil dances.

July

Fiestas Patronales de la Virgen del Carmen July 16, Isla Taboga. The virgin gets to circumnavigate the island in a procession of decorated boats.
Fiestas Patronales de la Santa Librada July 20–22, Las Tablas. A mix of religious and folkloric parades incorporating the Festival de la Pollera, which showcases Panama's gorgeous national dress.

August

Festival del Manito Ocueño Thurs–Sun, dates vary. In Ocú, Azuero Peninsula. Lively folk festival featuring a mock duel and peasant wedding.

October

Feria de Isla Tigre Mid-Oct, Isla Tigre (Digir), Kuna Yala. Multi-day festivity of Kuna culture.
Festival de la Mejorana Five days in mid-Oct, Guararé, Azuero Peninsula. Panama's premier folk festival, involving music, dancing and parades.
Festival del Cristo Negro Oct 21, Portobelo. The most revered pilgrimage in the country, attracting thousands bedecked in purple robes.

November

Primer Grito de la Independencia Nov 10, La Villa de los Santos. The "First Cry of Independence", celebrated as part of "El Mes de la Patria". Patriotic

flag-waving parades and marching bands, attended by the president.

Public holidays

Panama has several national **public holidays** (see listings below), during which most government offices, businesses and shops close. When the public holidays fall on or near a weekend the government often grants a last-minute *puente* (bridge), usually a Monday or a Friday, making a long weekend and prompting a mass exodus from the city to the beach or the countryside, with a scramble for plane tickets and accommodation. ⓦwww.qppstudio .net/publicholidays.htm is a good source of up-to-date information. Note that services shut down in Panama City on August 15 to celebrate the foundation of Panamá La Vieja, while other towns and cities have their own multi-day festivities during which most services close down.

Over many public holidays, as well as during national elections, *ley seca* (literally **dry law**) is enacted, which means that, theoretically, alcohol can't be purchased or consumed during that period.

National public holidays

Jan 1 Año Nuevo. New Year's Day.
Jan 9 Día de los Mártires. Martyrs' Day, in remembrance of those killed by US troops in the 1964 flag riots.
Feb Carnaval. Four days up to and including Ash Wednesday.
March–April Viernes Santo (Good Friday)
May 1 Día del Trabajo. Labour Day.
Nov 3 Separación de Panamá de Colombia. Anniversary of the 1903 Separation from Colombia and primary Independence Day.
Nov 4 Día de la Bandera. Flag Day.
Nov 5 Día de Colón. Celebrating the city's Separation from Colombia.
Nov 10 Primer Grito de la Independencia. "First Cry of Independence", marking the unilateral declaration of independence from Spain in La Villa de Los Santos.
Nov 28 4 Independencia de Panamá de España. Independence from Spain – 1821.
Dec 8 Día de la Madre. Mother's Day.
Dec 25 Día de Navidad. Christmas Day.

National parks

Almost a quarter of Panama's land lies within the boundaries of its fourteen national parks – add in reserves, refuges and other protected areas, and the figure is over a third. Under siege on all sides from urban development, pollution and deforestation (see p.348), these nevertheless constitute one of Panama's major attractions: you can trek through pristine rainforest, explore Spanish colonial forts, haul yourself up volcanic peaks or swim with sharks and manta rays. Some, such as the legendary Darién, Central America's largest wilderness and Cerro Hoya, at the tip of the Azuero Peninsula, are particularly inaccessible and involve a lot of planning, perseverance and often money to reach; others, such as Camino de Cruces and Soberanía, are a stone's throw from Panama City, making an easy day-trip and providing a great opportunity to flush out some of Panama's dazzling birdlife.

Panama's ecosystems are astonishingly diverse – little surprise given that the country stands at the crossroads of two oceans and two continents, a vital link in the biological corridor between North and South America. Since the country is so slender, many of the parks offer a hugely varied **topography**: several straddle the continental divide, ranging from lofty moss-covered cloud forest pierced by rugged peaks to humid lowland rainforest; others protect dense swathes of mangrove, harbouring caimans, crocodiles and crustaceans while protecting vital mud flats for thousands of migratory birds. The

National park contact numbers

National Park	ANAM office	Telephone
Altos de Campana	Panama Oeste (Panama City)	☏254 2848
La Amistad	Bocas Regional Office (Changuinola)	☏758 6822
	Chiriquí Regional Office (David)	☏775 3163
Bastimentos	Bocas Regional Office (Changuinola)	☏758 6822
	Bocas Town, Isla Colón	☏757 9244
Camino de Cruces	Panama City – Metropolitan	☏6636 8606
Cerro Hoya	Los Santos Regional Office (Las Tablas)	☏994 7313
Chagres	Panama – Colón	☏320 7521
Coiba	Veraguas Regional Office (Santiago)	☏998 4271
Darién	Darién Regional Office (Metetí)	☏299 6965
General de División Omar Torrijos (El Copé)	Coclé Regional Office (Penonomé)	☏997 7538
Golfo de Chiriquí	Chiriquí Regional Office (David)	☏775 3163
Portobelo	Colón Regional Office	☏448 2165
Sarigua	Herrera Regional Office (Chitré)	☏996 7675
Soberanía	Panama City – Metropolitan	☏232 4192
Volcán Barú	Chiriquí Regional Office (David)	☏775 3163

three **marine parks** offer coral reefs, turquoise waters and islands encircled with sugar-sand beaches and coated in tropical forest that supports everything from fluorescent poison-dart frogs to primordial iguanas. Ruined colonial fortresses, a crumbling Devil's Island penitentiary and a rare tract of dry tropical forest also lie within national park boundaries.

Planning your trip

Which parks and reserves you decide to visit will depend on your interests and several practical concerns – transport, the time and money at your disposal, accommodation and the time of year. The map below gives a brief overview of the activities various parks offer. Further details are in the relevant chapters. Ⓦwww.anam .gob.pa/joomla has information in Spanish on flora and fauna, which is also available in a bilingual print version published by Ediciones Balboa (see p.354).

Eco-tourism is being championed as a viable way forward for local communities to make a living while protecting the environment, although concrete government support for projects is lacking. A handful of villages in the Chagres and Darién parks in particular have established links with local operators (listed in the relevant chapters – see p.44 for some Panama City-based companies) to receive tour groups and a few have even established their own

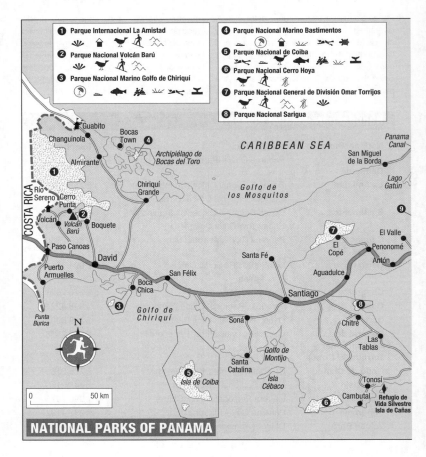

NATIONAL PARKS OF PANAMA

❶ Parque Internacional La Amistad

❷ Parque Nacional Volcán Barú

❸ Parque Nacional Marino Golfo de Chiriquí

❹ Parque Nacional Marino Bastimentos

❺ Parque Nacional de Coiba

❻ Parque Nacional Cerro Hoya

❼ Parque Nacional General de División Omar Torrijos

❽ Parque Nacional Sarigua

websites – though they're not always up to date – to encourage more independent travellers. While it is far less hassle to go with a tour operator, it is usually cheaper to organize your own visit, with the additional benefit of knowing that your money is going to the community rather than the agency.

Visiting the parks

The national parks are managed by the National Department for the Environment, the **Autoridad Nacional del Ambiente** (see ⓦwww.anam.gob.pa/joomla). Dealing with tourists is in theory the job of Panama's national tourist agency, the ATP, but ANAM staff in the regional and local offices, as well

as the *guardaparques* (park wardens) are often very helpful and likely to be of more direct use.

ANAM offices are generally open Monday to Friday from 8am to 4pm, though you can struggle to find anyone after midday before a long weekend or holiday period. If you need a permit, to book accommodation, or to hire a guide, it's best to drop by the regional or larger town offices to sort matters out in advance; if lucky with timings, you might even manage to get a lift to the park with a member of staff. If this is not possible, you can usually organize something on the spot – indeed, in theory, there should be a full-time resident warden at each national park entrance although in practice, in the

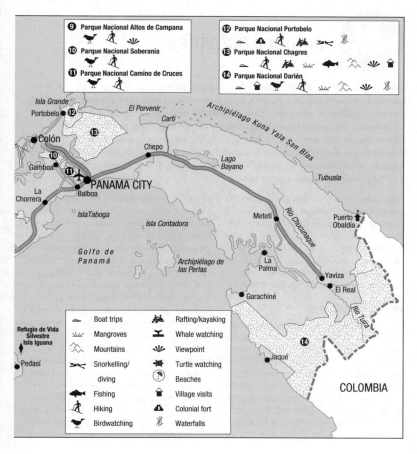

more remote and less well-funded outposts, it is not always the case.

If you decide to organize your visit by telephoning one of the ANAM offices, ask to talk to someone in *Aréas Protegidas*, and note that most ANAM employees only speak Spanish. With tourism very much a fledgling business in Panama, it may be some time before there is an integrated approach and anything like standardized **facilities** across the national parks. In most places, you will need to ask the park warden, and possibly hire them as a guide since maps and trail signs are conspicuously absent.

Given the general lack of infrastructure and information and the dilapidated state of some facilities, the park fees in some locations can seem excessive – though they are substantially less for nationals and residents. Most places charge $5–10 per person to visit, plus $5 per person to camp and around $15 for a bed for the night. Charges for the smaller reserves are generally around $3–5. However, these minor niggles are substantially outweighed by the outstanding beauty of the parks themselves, which you can often have all to yourself.

Outdoor activities

Both inside and outside the parks, Panama offers a host of outdoor activities, from swinging through the canopy on a zipline to tracking tapir prints in the mud of the Darién or lolling on a deserted beach. Some of these pursuits can be experienced as efficient packages from Panama City; others will need to be arranged more informally on the spot and a few require no organization whatsoever. Already renowned as a world-class birdwatching and sport fishing destination, Panama's reputation for outstanding diving, whitewater rafting and wilderness hiking is only just beginning to become established.

Several excellent **tour operators**, providing knowledgeable bilingual or multilingual naturalist guides work out of Panama City and offer tours around the country (see p.44) though for the more distant locations, such as Boquete or Coiba, you are better off looking for operators closer to the destination; they are listed in the relevant chapters.

Birdwatching

Panama offers first-class **birdwatching**, with Cana, deep in the heart of the Darién, recognized as one the world's top ten birding destinations. Boasting over 960 species of bird, including 55 varieties of hummingbirds and spectacular show birds such as the emerald and ruby resplendent quetzal (easy to see in the Chiriquí Highlands), the country also contains the world's largest concentration of harpy eagles (most likely to be

spotted in the Darién or in Amistad). Though Panama acts as a magnet for serious twitchers laden with tripods, checklists and hefty avian tomes (see p.354), it might persuade even those who have viewed birdwatching as a dull pastime, involving hours of trying to identify one indistinguishable brown bird from another, to think again. It's hard not to be impressed by the dazzling flashes of parrots and macaws in flight or the ludicrous painted bills of toucans swooping across the treetops.

Since many of these glamorous birds spend much of their time tantalizingly high up in the canopy, it is worth splashing out on at least a small pair of binoculars, which will significantly enhance your birdwatching experience. So too will engaging a **guide**. Alongside the big-name tour operators in the capital there are small-scale specialists, such as Birding

Panama (ⓦwww.birdingpanama.com) and Birding in Panama (ⓦwww.birdinginpanama.com), as well as numerous local residents scattered across the country, whose contact details are given in the relevant chapters. Daily rates for a professional bilingual naturalist guide contracted in the capital will be around $75–100 depending on how far you travel, but if you want something less expensive or just want someone to be able to point out some of the more obvious species, engaging someone locally from one of the villages for a few hours can cost as little as $15. A good way to start off is to attend one of the regular birdwatching-for-beginners walks ($5) in the Parque Natural Metropolitano in Panama City; organized by the Panama Audubon Society and advertised on their website (ⓦwww.panamaaudubon.org), they are open to all.

Hiking

Panama also affords a myriad of **hiking** opportunities. Vast wilderness areas such as La Amistad and the Darién are ideal for adventurous multi-day hikes across the isthmus, often involving bivouacking, staying in indigenous villages, fording rivers and wading through metres of mud. Aside from the Panama City operators, guides can be engaged locally in places such as Santa Fé, Boquete and Cerro Punta, at far less cost, though you'll need some Spanish. If you fancy a more modest outing, parks in the canal basin offer a range of trails from a gentle circular route to a reasonably strenuous rainforest tramp, following in the footsteps of the conquistadors. Note you'll need warm clothes for the chilly nights in the peaks of western Panama.

Basic hiking and camping gear can often be purchased at any of the Do It or Novey hardware shops in the main cities though the best selection (albeit still fairly limited) can be found at Acadia in Albrook Mall in Panama City (ⓦwww.acadiaoutdoors.com.pa). They also usually stock water filters and water purification tablets. Mirador Adventures in Boquete also rents out equipment.

Rafting and kayaking

The fast-flowing rivers that tumble down from the highlands of western and central Panama, carving their way through dramatic scenery, have put Panama on the map for **whitewater rafting** and **kayaking**. The top destination is the Río Chiriquí Viejo, replete with Class IV and V rapids, which runs parallel with the Costa Rican border – though it is in danger from a controversial hydro-electric project. The rivers are at their wildest during the heavy rains (May–Nov), but you'll manage to find enough water flowing somewhere to raft and kayak year-round. Boquete operators (see p.236) are best placed to organize Chiriquí destinations, while companies in the capital head for rivers in the Chagres basin or in neighbouring Coclé Province.

Sea kayaking is gradually growing in popularity, offering a great way to explore rocky coastlines and mangroves, and access remote beaches among the islands of Kuna Yala (see box, p.283), or round Coiba (see p.223) and Boca Chica (see p.236) in Chiriquí.

Diving

Diving in the **Pacific** can be truly spectacular, particularly in the Golfo de Chiriquí and the Archipiélago de las Perlas. Pick the right time of year (see p.347) and you're likely to spot manta rays, moray eels, sharks, schools of dolphins and migrating humpback and sperm whales – some scuba operators offer whale-watching tours. Large pelagic fish such as marlin, sailfish, amberjack, dorado and tuna also abound, which reel in sport fishing enthusiasts too (see p.44). The jewel in this marine crown is Isla Coiba; located on the edge of the second-largest reef on the Pacific side of the Americas, it offers world-class diving.

Among the coral reefs of Bocas and Portobelo on the **Caribbean** side, diving can also be enjoyable, if not as spectacular as at some other Caribbean destinations. Visibility can vary enormously, especially after heavy rain. However, the rainbow-coloured soft corals of Cayo Crawl off Isla Bastimentos make for breathtaking snorkelling and there are plenty of other fun spots to explore.

Reputable local **dive shops** operate out of Bocas, Portobelo, Santa Catalina, Isla Contadora and Pedasí, on the Azuero Peninsula, while Scuba Panama (ⓣ261 3841, ⓦwww.scubapanama.com), the country's oldest outfit, organizes expeditions from Panama City. Although the spooky Panama Canal dive has been shelved until the canal expansion programme has terminated, the gimmicky "two oceans in a day" trip allows you to plunge into the Caribbean waters off Portobelo before dashing back over the isthmus to dunk yourself in the Pacific.

Sport fishing

Panama means "abundance of fish" according to one reading of the indigenous language Cueva, and the country offers some phenomenal **fishing**. The Bahía de Piñas on the Pacific coast of the Darién, location of the exclusive Tropic Star Lodge (Ⓦ www.tropicstarlodge.com), is widely considered to be the world's top saltwater fishing destination, with the Golfo de Chiriquí, and Coiba in particular, a close second and the Pearl Islands not far behind.

Foreign-owned **fishing lodges** are mushrooming along the Pacific coast, most of which offer multi-day package deals that cover accommodation, meals and fishing excursions costing up to several thousand dollars. Recommended outfits include: Panama Big Game Fishing (Ⓦ www.panama -sportfishing.com), Coiba Adventure Sport- fishing (Ⓦ www.coibaadventure.com) and Pesca Panama (Ⓦ www.pescapanama.com).

Surfing

The Pacific coast offers some top-drawer **surfing**; in addition to the internationally renowned breaks round Santa Catalina, where the waves can reach 4m during February and March (though a good ride on 2m breakers is guaranteed year-round), there is some fine surfing to be had round Playa Venao and neighbouring beaches on the southern coastline of the Azuero Peninsula. Bocas offers varied breaks, plus welcoming bars and a decent après surf scene, while local surfers confined to Panama City tend to dash to the nearby Pacific beaches of Coclé for a weekend escape.

Other activities

Those who prefer an adrenaline rush in the air rather than on the water or up in the hills should head for the Boquete Tree Trek (see p.236), which can justifiably be considered the Tarzan of all **canopy adventures**, boasting a dozen zip lines, though more modest versions exist in El Valle (see p.160) and near Portobelo (see p.136). Similar adrenaline surges are guaranteed **skydiving** (Ⓦ www.panamaskydive.com) or **kitesurfing** at Punta Chame on the Pacific coast (see p.155).

If all that sounds too energetic there are plenty of ways to enjoy the outdoors without too much physical exertion; pass by any small fishing village and you can usually find a **boatman** willing to take you for a chug round the mangroves, drop you off for a laze on a deserted beach or even throw a line for a spot of fishing. Similarly relaxing is a plod along an empty beach or through the rainforest on **horseback**, which offers the chance to soak up the scenery without frightening away the wildlife – though don't expect a safety helmet, or a saddle that fails to remind you what you've been doing for the next week.

Mountain bikers in search of company might consider contacting Boa Panama (Ⓦ www.boapanama.com for English-speaking and Spanish-speaking contacts), an associa- tion of recreational off-road cycling enthusiasts, which organizes weekend outings.

Panama City tour operators

Advantage Tours ☎ 232 6944, Ⓦ www .advantagepanama.com. Specialies in birding tours, with a couple of great and affordable locations for multi-day excursions in the Darién. They also offer reasonably priced day-trips to an Emberá village and to Fuerte San Lorenzo, via Gatún Locks.

Ancon Expeditions ☎ 269 9415, Ⓦ www .anconexpeditions.com. Very professional and expensive outfit, offering top-notch bilingual naturalist guiding services for single-day excursions and multi-day adventures: birdwatching across Panama, trekking in the Darién or traversing the isthmus along the Camino Real. The unique experiences offered in the private reserves of Punta Patiño or Cana in the Darién are probably worth the extra outlay, but the inflated rates for a Panama Canal transit or Emberá village tour are harder to justify.

Aventuras Panama ☎ 260 0044, Ⓦ www .aventuraspanama.com. Adventure is the name of the game here, in particular kayaking and whitewater rafting down a variety of rivers within a couple of hours of Panama City in Panama and Coclé Provinces.

Ecocircuitos ☎ 314 0068, ⓦ www.ecocircuitous
.com. Actively involved in promoting sustainable
tourism and supporting several community-based
projects, this outfit offers a wide range of day and
multi-day excursions including sea-kayaking in Kuna
Yala. They also offer a honeymoon package to one of
the country's most luxurious hotels and stays at Isla
Contadora's *Punta Galeón* and the *Gamboa Rainforest
Resort*, neither of which is noted for its eco-credentials.

My Friend Mario ☎ 253 6500, ⓦ www
.myfriendmario.com. Popular local outfit from La
Chorrera offering inexpensive day-trips for budget
travellers – the Emberá village tour is particularly
good value.

Panama Exotic Adventures ☎ 314
3013, ⓦ www.panamaexoticadventures.com.
French-run organization (with Spanish and English
also spoken), specializing in multi-day adventure trips
to the Darién (and Kuna Yala).

Sendero Panama ☎ 390 5526, ⓦ www
.senderopanama.com. New professional outfit set
up by certified bilingual naturalist guides, at the more
expensive end of the market, offering a range of day-
trip and multi-day adventures.

Spectator sports

While football is popular in Panama, the
sport that arouses the greatest passions is
baseball. With a national team ranked ninth
in the world, and a number of successful
major league baseball stars to its credit,
including current New York Yankees closing
pitcher Mariano Rivera and the legendary
Rod Carew, after whom the national stadium
is named, baseball is Panama's national
sport. An inexpensive and captivating

evening's entertainment awaits if you attend
one of the fiercely contested national league
matches that take place in the dry season
– check ⓦ www.fedebeis.com for fixtures –
particularly in the more intimate stadiums in
the interior. Under the floodlights, a raucous
spirit prevails, with people partying in the
stands and screaming to the accompaniment of brass bands and drums, with plenty
of tasty street food on hand.

Close behind comes **boxing**, which has
produced more Panamanian world
champions than any other sport. Of these,
two stand out: "Panama Al Brown", a
bantamweight from Colón, who became the
first Latin American world champion in 1929,
and Roberto Durán, after whom the stadium
outside Panama City was named (see p.96
for more on going to a bout).

Less illustrious, though still given
passionate support when the occasion
demands, the national **football** team
won its first international trophy in 2009,
triumphing in the Central American champi-
onships. Generally, though, the team can
do with all the help it can muster so if you
fancy going to cheer them on check out
ⓦ www.panamafutbol.com, although the
professional league matches played out
in the low-key stadiums in the interior, at
Santiago or David, may provide greater
entertainment.

Another sport in which Panama enjoys a
rich heritage is **horse racing**, which is easily
accessible in Panama City (see p.96).

Travel essentials

Costs

Costs are higher than in Central American
countries such as Guatemala and Nicaragua,
and have risen to Costa Rican levels in some
areas. Staying in hostel dorms, eating in
inexpensive local restaurants and using
public transport you can easily survive on
$30–40 a day, less if camping, with anything

from $30–90 on top for a day's guided
excursion – snorkelling, surfing, fishing, horse
riding or kayaking, for instance.

Staying in more comfortable accommodation and eating in more touristy restaurants
can mean a daily food and lodgings budget
of $80 with excursions and maybe car hire
($40 per day) on top, though a lot depends

on whether you stay in Panama City and the canal area, where prices are significantly higher, or make for the interior.

High-end accommodation – only really available in Panama City and at a handful of resorts across the rest of the country – will set you back over $250 a night, with a three-course meal (without drinks) in one of the city's top restaurants averaging $35. For advice on tipping, see p.51.

Crime and personal safety

The presence of FARC guerrillas and cocaine smugglers in the Darién jungle has helped promote the popular misconception that Panama is a dangerous country to visit. In fact it is much safer than most other Central American states, with only a few areas to avoid or take special care.

The eastern strip of the **Darién** and **Kuna Yala** that borders Colombia tops the danger list as a no-go area; it contains the fabled Darién Gap, which has long held a fascination for travellers seeking adventure by hacking through jungle to the border. While this was difficult but feasible, it is now very dangerous and prohibited; since the 1990s several travellers attempting the overland route have been kidnapped or killed. There are still ways of visiting the Darién safely both in an organized group and as an independent traveller, and for crossing to Colombia on the Caribbean side by boat (see p.21), all of which can provide excitement without putting your life in acute danger.

The second major trouble spot is **Colón**, where extreme caution needs to be exercised even during daylight hours (see p.127). **Panama City** also has several areas to avoid, generally poor neighbourhoods with inadequate housing and high unemployment rates. As with many large cities in Latin America, **violent crime** is on the increase, but ninety percent of this is estimated to be drug-related, often among rival gangs; petty crime too is on the rise in some areas, especially where there are significant economic disparities between the general population and those who are making decent money from tourism, such as in Bocas. That said, by far the vast majority of visitors enjoy their time in Panama without incident, with the main issues being theft of money and/or passport and the odd traffic accident. The usual common-sense guidelines apply: don't wander around poorly lit or empty side streets at night; don't take money out of ATMs in poor neighbourhoods; don't walk about dripping in jewellery or flashing an expensive camera or watch; use maps discreetly; although a money-belt is often advised, it's another blatant signal that you're a tourist; don't give your address and room number to people you are unsure about; and if leaving a restaurant or nightclub really late, get the place to call a cab.

The police

If you are a **victim of crime**, report to the *Policía de Turismo* (Tourist Police) in Panama City (see p.97) – instantly recognizable in Casco Viejo since they're often on bikes sporting cycle shorts – or the main police station in other towns. Even though your possessions are unlikely to be recovered, a police report (*denuncia*) will be required to make an insurance claim. At the police station, you will probably need to present your ID, which by law you should always carry with you, though it is acceptable to carry a photocopy of your passport details provided it also includes a copy of the entry date stamp on the same page.

Culture and etiquette

No society is homogenous but Panama is particularly diverse, and customs vary widely. Overall, though, people are very courteous – driving in Panama City aside – and quite formal; **greetings** are customary before any exchange, such as asking for information, and the "usted" form of address is preferred to the "tu" form, which is reserved for close friends, although this is beginning to change among younger people or those who have spent significant periods of time out of the country. This formality is also reflected in **clothing**, particularly by the urban middle classes, who like to dress up to go out. Dress is also important on the beach; no nude sunbathing is permitted in Panama, except on one beach on Isla Contadora (see p.106), and beachwear should stay on the beach – cover your body in town.

Suitably modest attire (covered shoulders) is appreciated in churches. When visiting **indigenous communities**, cultural sensitivity is important as regards dress, alcohol and photography (see p.286).

Drugs

Drugs are widely available in Panama, **marijuana** and **cocaine** in particular, and you're quite likely to be offered something at some stage. However possession of either is illegal and makes those caught liable for a prison sentence. While the police might – and only might – turn a blind eye to a joint being smoked discreetly on a deserted beach, being caught with some weed trying to cross a border can have serious consequences. Possession of cocaine is punished very heavily, in part because Panama is a known transit point for drugs heading from Colombia to the US.

Electricity

The **voltage** in Panama is 110 volts and sockets take flat two- and occasionally three-pronged plugs. **Power cuts** and subsequent surges occur fairly frequently so if travelling with a laptop you may want to bring a surge protector. In many remote parts of the country, such as some islands of Kuna Yala, in national parks or in isolated villages, there is limited or no electricity at night so a torch is essential.

Entry requirements

Requirements for Panama can be confusing. They change frequently, but updates can take a while to filter through to all immigration officials, who may, for example, not agree on how long a tourist card is valid. Check for the latest regulations at a Panamanian consulate in advance of your trip and don't forget that if you are transiting via the US, you will need a transit visa, or a visa waiver application to be made online in advance of travel (see ⓦ www .usimmigrationsupport.org/visa_c1.html), as well as a machine-readable passport. The Panamanian immigration authorities' website is also worth checking (ⓦ www.migracion .gob.pa).

Depending on nationality, visitors are divided into three categories by the Panamanian

immigration authorities: those who need no visa, only a valid passport; those who need a tourist card; and those who need a tourist visa. This first category, requiring neither a visa nor a tourist card, currently includes citizens of **most European countries**, including the UK and Ireland, who will get a ninety-day stamp in their passport on arrival provided they can produce a passport valid for at least six months after departure, an onward (or return) bus or plane ticket and proof of funds (usually $500 or a credit card).

Citizens of **Australia**, **Canada**, **New Zealand** and the **US**, among others, do not need a visa, only a tourist card (*tarjeta de turismo*), which can be purchased on arrival in Panama for $5, or from your airline, and is valid for ninety days for US citizens, thirty days for the rest. It should be photocopied for security and then kept with your passport for presentation when necessary. Note that in the more remote border crossings of Río Sereno and Puerto Obaldía, immigration sometimes runs out of tourist cards so you may prefer to fork out for a stamped visa at the Panamanian embassy in Costa Rica or Colombia, respectively, in advance and save yourself some hassle at the border.

The third category of citizens – those requiring a visa – are subdivided into countries that need a stamped visa (*visa estampada*) and countries that need the more restrictive authorized visa (*visa autorizada*), which include **South Africa**, both of which are only available in advance from a Panamanian embassy or consulate. If you're arriving from one of the WHO-listed yellow fever countries you may be asked to produce your vaccination certificate (see p.33).

If you want to remain in Panama for longer, you can apply for an **extension** (*prórroga de turista* or *extensión de visa;* $15) for up to ninety days at any of the immigration offices listed in the relevant chapters.

Embassies and consulates abroad

Australia 1/234 Slade Road, Bexley North, NSW 2207 ☎ 02/9150 8409, ✉ panaconsul.sydney @bigpond.com.au.
Canada 130 Albert Street, Suite 300, K1P 5G4, Ottawa ☎ 613/236 7177, ⓦ www .embassyofpanama.ca.

New Zealand 300 Queen Street, Auckland Central
ⓣ09/379 8550, ⓔgthwaite@iprolink.co.nz.
South Africa 229 Olivier Street, Brooklyn, Pretoria
ⓣ012/460 6677, ⓔpanamaembassy@bodamail
.co.za.
UK Panama House, 40 Hertford Street, London W1J
7SH ⓣ020/7493 4646, ⓦwww.panamaconsul
.co.uk.
US 2862 McGill Terrace, NW Washington, DC 20008
ⓣ202/387 5601, ⓦwww.embassyofpanama.org.

Gay and lesbian travellers

Homosexuality was only decriminalized
in Panama in 2008, which is illustrative of
the country's prevailing social conserva-
tism but also of the fact that things are
beginning to change. The Asociación de
Hombres y Mujeres Nuevos de Panamá
(AHMN; ⓦwww.ahmnpanama.org) is
active in campaigning for LGBT rights and
low-key Gay Pride marches have been held
since 2005. The LGBT scene is discreet
in Panama; the clutch of nightclubs is not
widely advertised (see ⓦwww.farraurbana
.com and les-507.com) and on the
Panama pages of LGBT travel websites
(see for example ⓦwww.purpleroofs.com
/centralamerica/index-centralamerica.html,
www.gayjourney.com/hotels/panama.htm
and www.globalgayz.com) there are so far
only a handful of openly "gay-friendly" accommodation listings. In general hotels in Panama
City and North American and European-run
establishments are likely to be more tolerant.

Insurance

It would be unwise to head for Panama
without **insurance** that covers theft, loss,
illness, injury and flight cancellation. Before
you take out a new policy, make sure that
you aren't already covered: some all-risks
home insurance policies may cover your
possessions while abroad, and many private
medical schemes also apply when overseas.
In Canada, provincial health plans usually
provide some cover for medical treatment
when out of the country. Some student
insurance packages also include vacation
travel. When shopping around for a policy,
bear in mind that what are termed
dangerous sports, which usually include the
likes of scuba diving and whitewater rafting,
sometimes require an additional premium to
be paid. Should you have to seek medical
attention, keep all receipts, and if you lose
something valuable, get a police report
(*denuncia*). Whatever the situation you will
still need to access sufficient funds to cover
such emergencies (hence the usefulness of a
credit card) while on your trip, and apply for
reimbursement on your return home.

Internet

Cyber cafés come and go but there are
always a sufficient number to make internet
access easy, even in small towns, where the
local library usually has a couple of PCs.
Rates are generally $1–2 per hour and note
that the "@" sign is usually achieved by
pressing ALT, "6" and "4" keys simultaneously. Many hotels now offer wi-fi; it is
generally free in hostels and many budget-
end establishments but charges can verge
on the extortionate in the more expensive
hotels.

Language

Spanish is the official language of Panama
and the first language of over two million of

the population, though a recorded thirteen other first languages are spoken across the country. The latter are mainly indigenous but include Panamanian Creole English, preferred by around 100,000 Afro-Antillean Panamanians, primarily resident in Bocas, Colón and Panama City, and Cantonese or Hakka, spoken by around 60,000 Chinese-Panamanians. While many urban middle-class Panamanians speak **English**, some of whom are bilingual, the "everybody-speaks-English" myth is easily dispelled. Official estimates reckon around fourteen percent of the population can communicate in English but in small towns and rural areas you'll find many speak virtually no English and in a number of the remote indigenous communities some villagers, especially women, do not even speak Spanish. Your travel experience in the country will be greatly enhanced by learning at least the basics of Spanish before you arrive.

Learning Spanish in Panama

A good way of getting to grips with Spanish is to attend a **language school**. This also gives you an entrance into Panamanian life, especially if you take up the cultural immersion or homestay options and become involved in the volunteering projects on offer. Most schools run an extra-curricular programme, which almost inevitably includes salsa classes and excursions, while some courses specialize in language learning combined with activities such as scuba diving or surfing.

Group, small group (2–4) and one-to-one tuition is usually available; group classes, the cheapest option, generally comprise four hours of lessons per day at rates of around $160–260 per week, not including board and lodging. Make sure the institution is registered, that staff are qualified and that the teaching methodology is not just "chalk and talk" before committing any money. ⓦ www.languagestudy.goabroad.com /panama.cfm contains a list of recom-mended schools, but some of the more established ones are listed below.

Habla Ya Panama Plaza Los Establos, Boquete 20–22 ☏ 720 1294, ⓦ www.hablayapanama.com.
Spanish by the River Entrada a Palmira, Alto Boquete ☏ 720 3456, ⓦ www.spanishatlocations .com.

Spanish by the Sea Calle 4a, behind *Hotel Bahía*, Bocas del Toro, Isla Colón ☏ 757 9518, ⓦ www .spanishatlocations.com.
Spanish Panama Edif Americana No 1a, Vía Argentina, Panama City ☏ 213 3121, ⓦ www .spanishpanama.com, which has on-site hostel accommodation at *Anita's Inn*.

Laundry

Most mid-range and top-end hotels offer a **laundry** service, while aparthotels (see p.65) and some hostels have their own washing machines for guest use. Otherwise you have the choice of a *lavamático* (not as easy to locate in Panama City as in the provinces), an old-fashioned launderette, where you bundle your clothes into a machine, and then a dryer, paying no more than $3 for a load, including detergent and conditioner. It is only slightly more costly to go to one of the more ubiquitous *lavanderías*, which more closely resemble dry cleaners, where the same service will cost around $3–4, more if you want clothes ironed.

Living and working in Panama

If you're setting up your own business or are a foreign retiree who can fulfill the basic requirements, securing a **residential visa** is easy. Otherwise, residential and work permits are not easily come by unless you have specialist skills and – in theory at least – the recruiting company is unable to employ a Panamanian.

It's possible to arrange **voluntary work**, which can be carried out on a tourist visa, in advance. Try one of the various reputable international agencies, such as Volunteer Abroad (ⓦ www.volunteerabroad .com/Panama.cfm), or directly through the websites of Panamanian organizations; alternatively you may be able to show up on the spot. Key areas include conservation or social development projects, usually in poor, marginalized communities. Before you plunge into volunteering, do your homework to ensure that the programme is both bona fide and sustainable and that you are suffi-ciently skilled and experienced for the job. If training is provided, ensure that there is adequate time devoted to it – often a problem if organizations are hard-stretched.

Volunteering in projects, particularly with marginalized or vulnerable groups, is fraught with ethical dilemmas, which usually have no easy or "right" solution and can have unexpected negative side effects. While a couple of weeks on a turtle monitoring project may be fine, it's rarely a good idea to drop into a social development project for such a short time since a constant rotation of volunteers can be unsettling for individuals and communities, especially for vulnerable groups such as orphaned children.

That said, there are several well-established **programmes** in Panama. In Bocas del Toro, turtle conservation projects abound (see p.266) and various other long-standing social operations include: SOS Children's Villages (Asociación Aldeas Infantiles SOS de Panamá, Ⓦwww .sos-childrensvillages.org), which work with orphaned children; Fundación Pro Niños de Darién (Ⓦwww.darien.org.pa), an NGO operating in over a hundred communities in Darién, aiming to improve child nutrition through health education and the development of sustainable agricultural practices; and Nutrehogar (Ⓦwww.nutrehogar.org), which also focuses on child health. Various language schools (see p.49) also have volunteer programmes.

Mail

It is reliable, but if speed is of the essence the standard Panamanian **postal service** is probably not for you; a postcard from Panama can take five to ten days to reach North America (25c stamp) and a couple of weeks or longer to meander to Europe (40c stamp), Australasia or South Africa (50c stamp). Some of the high-end hotels sell stamps and may even post the letter for you; otherwise you need to locate a post office (*correos*), which are relatively elusive in Panama City (see listings, p.97) but more visible in the provinces – they are marked on our maps. Ensure that you're in the right line for stamps (*estampillas*). Opening hours (generally Mon–Sat 7am–5pm) vary, with more rural locations shutting earlier in the afternoon, especially on Saturdays. For a speedier delivery, send your letter or parcel EMS (Express Mail Services;

Ⓦwww.correos.gob.pa/ems.htm) from the post office, though this service is not valid for Europe. Alternatively, use one of the more expensive private mailing or courier services widely available such as Fedex (Ⓦwww.fedex.com/pa/) or Mail Boxes Etc. (Ⓦwww.mbe.com).

Post offices, recognisable by the COTEL, Correos y Telégrafos sign, also offer an *entrega general* (**poste restante**) service, keeping letters for up to a month. Passport ID needs to be shown when claiming post and you can't collect on behalf of another person. The sender should address items as follows: receiver's name, *Entrega General*, name of town, name of province, Republica de Panamá. If you are receiving post in Panama City then the postal zone also needs to be specified – enquire at the branch in question.

Maps

Both country and city **maps** of Panama are increasing in number and quality though there's still some way to go. There are also some rudimentary trail maps for the parks in the former Canal Zone, usually available from the park offices. International Travel Maps (1:300,000; available online at Ⓦwww.itmb.com and www.amazon.com; $13) and National Geographic (Ⓦwww .nationalgeographic.com) both produce good maps of Panama, and Rough Guides has a map covering Panama and Costa Rica. In **Panama** itself, large-scale maps are available at the Instituto Geográfico Nacional Tommy Guardia (Mon–Fri 8.30am–4pm) on Avenida Simón Bolívar, opposite the entrance to the university in Panama City, though some are several years out of date and would really only be of use if you were planning some wilderness hiking. Sufficient for most tourists' needs, Rutas de Aventuras (Ⓦwww.rutasdeaventura.com; $4–8) offers a series of glossy maps of the main tourist areas, enhanced with informative inserts (some in Spanish, some in English and Spanish) on the area's attractions and cultural events, available for purchase online or in tourist shops in Panama, though the quality across the series is uneven.

Money

Panama adopted **US dollars** (referred to as *dólares* or *balboas*) as its currency in 1904, shortly after separation from Colombia. Apart from a seven-day print flurry in 1941, producing what is known as the "seven-day-dollar" (now a collector's item), the country has always used US paper currency, though it mints its own coinage: 1, 5, 10, 25 and 50 centavo pieces, which are used alongside US coins. Both $100 and $50 bills are often difficult to spend, so try to have $10 or $20 as the largest denominations you carry.

Cards

With over nine hundred **ATMs** across the country, the most convenient way to access your money is by drawing some out on a credit card (you'll need your PIN number). Most home banks charge a fee for credit card withdrawal – check before departure – additionally since July 2009 all ATMs in Panama levy $3 per transaction. Visa and MasterCard are the most widely accepted **credit cards** across the country, both at ATMs (recognizable by the red *Sistema Clave* sign outside) and to pay for services such as plane tickets, tourist hotels, restaurants, goods in shops and car rental. American Express and Diner's Club tend to be more confined to Panama City. **Debit cards** such as Maestro and Cirrus are valid in many ATMs though they sometimes do not actually work in practice.

Most establishments in Bocas del Toro, Kuna Yala and the Darién only accept cash and denominations of $20 and below are preferred because of problems with counterfeit $50 and $100 bills. Note also that heading into a major holiday weekend, ATMs may run out of money, especially if there is only one machine in town.

You should inform your bank at home that you are travelling to Panama before your departure so that they don't block your credit card.

Banks, travellers' cheques and transfers

Most **banks** are open from 8am to 3pm Monday to Friday, and from 9am to noon on Saturday, though busier branches in the capital have extended hours; almost all branches have ATMs, as do many large supermarkets.

It is difficult to change foreign currency in Panama – change any cash into US dollars as soon as you can. In Panama City there are branches of the Banco Nacional de Panamá at the airport and on Vía España in the El Cangrejo district, or you could try Panacambios, a *casa de cambio* also on Vía España. Foreign banks will generally change their own currencies.

Travellers' cheques are best used as a back-up, if at all, since they are rarely accepted outside banks and even some branches of Panama's three major banks – Banco Nacional, HSBC and Banco General – refuse to handle them. American Express cheques in dollars are your best bet. Be sure to keep the purchase agreement and a record of the cheques' serial numbers safe and separate from the cheques themselves. In the event of loss, contact the issuing company immediately – they should be able to replace the cheques within 24 hours.

Money transfers can easily be carried out through Western Union (ⓦwww .westernunion.com), which has over one hundred offices sprinkled round the isthmus, with a concentration in Panama City.

Bargaining and tipping

Bargaining for goods is not the norm in Panama. If you're buying several items from a single stall in a craft market you can usually negotiate a slight discount (*descuento*), but it's rarely the lengthy social ritual it can be in some countries. Bear in mind too that while $40 for an intricate *mola* or $70 for a Panama hat may seem like a lot, they are likely to have taken several weeks to make.

Tipping is not universally expected and should be reserved for good service. While ten percent is customary in mid-range (or above) restaurants, it should not be automatic. In local *fondas* you might round up a $2.80 lunch to $3. Porters in hotels are usually tipped $0.50–1 per bag; the going rate at Tocumen airport is $1 per bag. In hotels you might consider leaving a tip of $1–2 per day for the person who has cleaned your room, but it's not *de rigueur*. It's not usual to tip taxi drivers or guides on organized tours. If, however, you hire the services of an ANAM park warden (*guardaparque*) to take you on a guided hike, you should ask what the going rate is; if there isn't one, $10–15 should be adequate for a full-day outing.

Overtipping is not helpful; it sets a precedent which other travellers may not be able to live up to, and can upset the micro-economy, particularly in small villages.

Opening hours

Opening hours vary from establishment to establishment, but generally businesses are open Monday to Saturday from 8–9am to 5–6pm. Government office hours are Monday to Friday 8am–4pm. Shops usually open their doors Monday to Saturday from 9am to 6pm, though places selling souvenirs and crafts to tourists may open on Sundays too and Chinese-Panamanian supermarkets often open early (6.30–7am) until late (10pm–midnight), with some of the larger ones operating 24 hours.

Museums – not a major attraction in Panama – are open from 8–9am to 4pm Monday or Tuesday to Saturday or Sunday with some of the provincial ones closing for lunch. **Churches**, which are all free to visit, are generally open from dawn until early evening, with the odd one closing for lunch.

Phones

Telephone boxes are found even in the smallest of villages, where the lone phone box – assuming it works – may be the community's only means of communication with the outside world. Easy to use, with instructions in English as well as Spanish, some phones accept both coins (5, 10 and 25 centavos) and cards; others only accept pre-paid phone cards (generally $3, $5, $10) purchasable at shops, Cable and Wireless offices and local pharmacies. Note that some cards can only be used for either interna-tional or local calls but not both. Seven-digit phone numbers denote **landlines** – the first three digits comprise the area code, whereas eight-digit numbers are for **mobile phones**.

Making a call

To make a call **to Panama** you need to dial the international prefix (generally 00),

followed by 507 – the country code for Panama – followed by the number. Phoning out **from Panama** you need to prefix the country code (UK – 44; Ireland – 353; US & Canada – 1; Australia – 61; New Zealand – 64; South Africa – 27) with 00. Local calls to landlines anywhere in Panama cost a pittance and are usually free from a hotel room. International calls are also relatively cheap provided you do not use a hotel phone. Some internet cafés (and Cable & Wireless offices) also have phone booths and offer decent rates for international calls as well as a degree of comfort, quiet and privacy. Off-peak time for international calls is between 6pm and 6am and weekends.

Mobile phones

Mobile phones have mushroomed in Panama, which now has as many different numbers – almost three and a half million – as it does people. Mobiles have trans-formed the lives of some indigenous communities that live far from the main population centres, and can be very useful for travellers too, especially in the more remote areas when wanting to confirm transport or a reservation from a dugout in the Darién. Crucially, though, **coverage** varies among the four service providers of Mas Móvil (from Cable & Wireless), Digicel, Movistar and Clarocom in particular regions, especially in the Darién and Kuna Yala, where your need is likely to be greatest. Enquire before you purchase. At the moment Mas Móvil & Movistar are currently the only two offering SIM cards though Digicel was set to do so in 2010. If you have an unlocked mobile phone on an 850 GSM (the setting for much of the Americas), you can easily purchase a SIM card on arrival from numerous corner shops in Panama City, or even online before you

Useful phone numbers

Police, including Transit Police 104
Ambulance: Red Cross 228 2187; Seguro Social 503 2532 – both are free
Directory enquiries 102
International operator 106

depart. Once the initial credit has expired, pre-paid airtime cards are available at shops around the country. Incoming calls are all free in Panama. Alternatively, you might consider renting a mobile or satellite phone; the executive business hotels can usually procure one for you.

Photography

The dazzling sunlight of any tropical country, especially in the dry season, can make it difficult to take decent **photographs**. The best times for the light are just after dawn and late afternoon to dusk, but since the sun rises and sets quickly it doesn't give you much time. If you need to purchase any photographic equipment, such as camera batteries or memory cards, Panafoto in Panama City (see Ⓦwww.panafoto.com) is really your only bet.

People are fascinating subjects, but be sensitive. If you want to photograph one or more people, rather than a market scene with people in it, you should ask their permission. In indigenous villages in particular, ask the village headman or the head of the tourist committee what the protocol is – some villages do not permit photography. Tour groups to a village may be encouraged to snap away but you should still ask for permission from the individuals concerned. In Kuna Yala, in particular, each island has its own regulations (see p.286).

Senior travellers

Given that Panama is one of the world's top **retirement** destinations, especially for North Americans, Panamanians are well used to meeting older foreign travellers. Though senior Panamanian and resident foreign retirees are eligible for incredible **discounts** on everything from flights to cinema tickets, visitors generally are not.

Time

Panama is four hours behind Greenwich Mean Time throughout the year, the same as Eastern Standard Time in the US, though note time changes for daylight-saving hours. Panama is one hour ahead of Costa Rica. If in doubt, consult Ⓦwww.timeanddate.com.

Toilets

Public toilets are thin on the ground in Panama. You will generally find them in bus terminals and airports, often requiring payment of a few cents to an attendant, who in return will hand you an inadequate few sheets of paper – always travel with an emergency toilet roll. Restaurants have facilities for customers – outsiders can usually sneak into fast-food joints and cafeterias, and petrol stations will usually hand you the key to an often less salubrious toilet if you're in need. Most places outside top-end or very modern hotels with their own septic system require you to throw used toilet paper into an adjacent basket – alas sometimes missing altogether from the most rudimentary establishments. In Kuna Yala and parts of Bocas, a toilet cistern is no guarantee of a water treatment system; everything may still flush straight out to sea.

Tourist information

The official **tourist agency** is the Autoridad de Turismo Panamá (ATP; Ⓦwww.atp.gob.pa), formerly the Instituto Panameño de Turismo (IPAT), whose acronym is still widely used. The recent tourist boom has caused a number of swanky new a/c tourist offices to be built in many of the major towns and resort areas though unfortunately most are not yet geared up to assisting passing tourists; nor is the website much help. You may be lucky enough to get a map and, if you have a specific question, the employee will probably do their best to help you, but do not expect lists of local accommodation or tourist attractions, nor assume the person will speak English. **Reception staff** at a good hostel or hotel are a far better bet for reliable information. Several tour operators based in Panama City (see p.44) can give you advice on the rest of the country, though they will naturally do so in the hope of selling you a tour.

The Visitor/El Visitante (Ⓦwww.thevisitorpanama.com), a free, weekly tourist promotion **magazine** in English and Spanish, omnipresent in hotels and touristy restaurants throughout the country, lists attractions and upcoming events. See p.37 and p.92 for other sources. Panama's **national parks** and other protected areas, which encompass many of Panama's natural wonders, are administered by the National Environment Agency, ANAM (Ⓦwww.anam.gob.pa; see p.39).

Travellers with disabilities

Organised tourism is in its infancy in Panama and awareness of the needs and rights of **people with disabilities** is a fairly recent phenomenon – they were only granted equal rights by law in 1999. As a result, Panama isn't really geared up to accommodate travellers with disabilities. That said, Tocumen International Airport has disabled access and many mid-range and luxury hotels in Panama City have facilities for people with disabilities, although as elsewhere in the world "disabled facilities" tends to be synonymous with "wheelchair access" rather than spanning the spectrum of special needs. The three resorts mentioned in "Travelling with children" (see below) also advertise "disabled access" and most cruise ships that take in Panama tend to be suitably equipped. Eco-Adventure International (Ⓦwww.eaiadventure.com) runs several tours to Panama for travellers with disabilities and senior travellers, though unlike Costa Rica the country does not yet feature as a destination on the dozens of other disability specialist travel websites (see Ⓦwww.disabledtravelers .com, www.wheeltheworld.com or www .flying-with-disability.com), which are nonetheless worth consulting for general travel advice and useful links on flying and travel agents.

Travelling with children

Latin cultures are very family-oriented and Panama is no exception. While there is no pre-packaged entertainment for **children** such as theme parks, there's plenty for kids to enjoy, including boat trips, snorkelling, horse riding, exploring the canal and walking in the rainforest. Many **hotels** have extra beds or pull-outs in rooms for children and under 12s are often free, with older kids admitted at discount rates. The large resort hotels – the *Decameron* at Farallón on the Pacific coast, the *Hotel Meliá* on Lago Gatún and the *Gamboa Rainforest Resort* – have special activities laid on and child-minding services. Small B&Bs and eco-lodges whose staff are concerned that kids may spoil the tranquillity sometimes do not permit children or have a minimum age of 12 or 14.

Habla Ya Language Centre (Ⓦwww .hablayapanama.com) in Boquete offers family and children's **Spanish courses**, while various tour operators in the UK and North America (check out Ⓦwww.wildland .com and www.familytrails.com in the US, and www.familytours.co.uk in the UK) now include **family-oriented itineraries** in Panama. Travelling to Kuna Yala and to the Darién, which can be challenging enough for adults, would be hard work with kids in tow unless you stay at the few high-end establishments. Sticking to Panama City and the canal area, the Pacific beach resorts, El Valle, Bocas and Boquete would be much easier and more enjoyable all round, especially if you're on a modest budget.

Women travellers

It is perfectly safe for women to travel alone in Panama. In **urban areas**, you might get the odd cat call or hiss and going alone to a bar in Panama City or a rural *cantina* the hassle is likely to be greater. In more **rural areas**, you may get some surprised looks and, depending on your age, questions about your presumed husband and children. In general you are likely to be treated with courtesy. As regards safety at night – in Panama City and Colón primarily but in other urban centres too – the same common-sense precautions apply as in cities in any country you're travelling in and whether female or male.

Guide

Guide

Panama City and the Golfo de Panamá

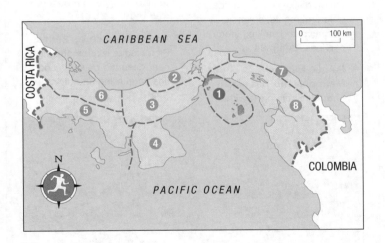

CHAPTER 1 **Highlights**

* **Casco Viejo** Perched on a rocky promontory, the evocative colonial centre has ancient churches, leafy plazas and grand buildings. See p.68

* **Cerro Ancón** Vantage point offering an unparalleled panorama of the city's towering skyscrapers and imposing canal. See p.82

* **Museo Antropológico** Vestiges of pre-Columbian life are on display here – intricate gold ornaments, splendid ceramics and striking stone carvings. See p.84

* **Parque Natural Metropolitano** This patch of tropical rainforest within the city limits provides the perfect spot to hone your birdwatching skills. See p.84

* **Panamá Viejo** The crumbling remains of the original Panama City, set in mud flats and mangroves on the outer limits of the metropolis. See p.85

* **Nightlife** Head for Calle Uruguay and kick-start the evening with a cocktail before hitting the dancefloor – choose from salsa to techno, reggae to reggaeton. See p.91

* **Archipiélago de las Perlas** Picturesque islands offering near-deserted beaches and fine snorkelling and diving. See p.103

▲ Casco Viejo from Cerro Ancón

Panama City and the Golfo de Panamá

P roudly positioned in the crook of land overlooking the Pacific, the soaring skyline of **PANAMA CITY** surveys the ocean before it, much as Vasco Nuñez de Balboa did when he chanced upon the body of water after a bloody journey south across the isthmus almost five hundred years ago. From its inception, the city has been situated on one of the world's great crossroads, and it has thrived on trade, attracting migrants from all over the world to a cosmopolitan melting pot bubbling with energy and ambition. Panama has long been considered a bridge between two continents and nowhere is this divided identity more apparent than in the capital, where glitzy skyscrapers, laser-lit nightclubs and chic restaurants more reminiscent of Miami than Latin America are juxtaposed with colonial churches, clamouring street vendors and chaotic traffic. Though it is the undisputed political, economic and social centre of Panama and home to almost a million – just under a third of the country's population – the city has very little in common with the rest of the country, which is often vaguely referred to as the "interior".

For the vast majority of visitors to Panama, the capital provides their first point of contact. Many spend their entire stay here, since it makes a good base from which to explore many of the country's attractions while enjoying the material comforts of sophisticated city living – the canal, a handful of national parks and the Caribbean coast as far as Portobelo can all be visited on day-trips. Other vistors, keen to leave behind the frenzied construction and thronging streets and escape into the country's outstanding wilderness areas, still linger a couple of days to savour the colonial architecture of Casco Viejo and the vitality of the modern city, including its many bars and restaurants.

While it is easy to tire of Panama City's irrepressible energy, oppressive heat and relentless traffic, it's just as simple to escape to nearby places of real tranquillity: the **Amador Causeway**, a breezy breakwater offering fabulous views of the canal and the city skyline; **Isla Taboga**, the sleepy "Island of Flowers" an hour's boat ride off the coast; or the **Parque Natural Metropolitano**, the only natural tropical rainforest within the limits of a Latin American capital. For those who really want to get away, join the capital's social elite and take a weekend break to the translucent waters and powdered beaches of the **Archipiélago de las Perlas**. Once the hideout of privateers and pirates, the islands now offer a more peaceful retreat.

Panama City

With a spectacular setting on the expansive Bahía de Panamá, flanked to the west by its great canal and to the north by lush, forested mountains, Panama City is an impressive metropolis. On the southwest end of the bay stands the old city centre of **Casco Viejo**, a jumble of immaculately restored colonial buildings, crumbling ruins and run-down housing on a rocky promontory while a few kilometres to the northeast rise the shimmering skyscrapers of **El Cangrejo** and **Marbella**, the modern banking and commercial district, and the penthouse apartments of **Punta Paitilla** and **Punta Pacífica**. Further east, amid sprawling suburbs whose tentacles extend 30km along the coast, stand the ruins of **Panamá Viejo**, the first European city to be founded on the Pacific coast of the Americas, while west of the city centre the former US Canal Zone town of **Balboa**, with its clipped lawns and restrained utilitarian architecture, retains a distinctly North American character despite having been turned over to full Panamanian control in 1999. In the background, the Panamanian flag proudly flies on the summit of **Cerro Ancón**, a surprising oasis of greenery on what was once a major US military base.

Some history

Founded by the conquistador Pedro Arias de Ávila, better known as **Pedrarias**, on August 15, 1519, Panama City quickly flourished as the base for further Spanish conquest along the Pacific coast, and later as the pivotal transit point for plundered treasure from South America and traded goods from the east bound for Spain. Brought ashore here, they were transported overland to Nombre de Dios and later, Portobelo, on the Atlantic coast, to be laden onto ships headed for Spain. By the mid-seventeenth century Panama City had a population of around five thousand, its customs house, cathedral and convents comprising some of the grandest constructions in the New World. The city's opulence invited numerous attacks by the **pirates** then ravaging the Spanish Main, and in 1671 the Welsh buccaneer **Henry Morgan** sacked the city (see p.331). The fire that then engulfed the city is commonly blamed on Morgan, although it is far more likely that flames spread from the detonation of the city's gunpowder supplies by the defeated Spanish governor. Known as **Panamá Viejo**, the ruins of Pedrarias's settlement still stand amid the sprawling suburbs of the modern city, and have been partially restored in recent years as a tourist attraction (see p.85).

Two years after Morgan's assault, the settlement was relocated on a rocky peninsula jutting out into the bay 8km to the southwest, a more defendable and salubrious site than its swampy predecessor. Named **Panamá Nuevo**, the new city developed in the area known today as **San Felipe**. No expense was spared in the fortifications, which were never breached again. As the community prospered, new churches, convents and municipal buildings were constructed, some using original stones from Panamá Viejo, though many were all but destroyed over the next century in a series of major fires – a common hazard of that period in urban areas crammed with wooden buildings.

Once the Spanish rerouted their treasure fleet around Cape Horn in 1746, Panama City's commercial importance slowly began to decline, only substantially picking up again in the mid-nineteenth century due to the isthmus's popularity as a transit point in the **California Gold Rush** and the completion of the **Panama Railroad** in 1855. The railroad, and subsequently the French and US canal construction efforts, brought immense prosperity and a wealth of new cultural influences that transformed the city and its inhabitants, who by 1920 totalled almost sixty thousand.

The **canal**, completed in 1914, confirmed Panama City's importance as a global trading centre yet immediately became a straightjacket for the capital, as the outbreak of World War I, two weeks prior to the waterway's official inauguration, opened the floodgates to large-scale **US military occupation** of the Panama Canal Zone, the 8km strip of land either side of the waterway under US juristiction. During World War II, defence installations proliferated and the predominantly US population topped one hundred thousand. Though other migrants continued to pour in, the lives of the city's population were regulated by the US military in the adjacent Canal Zone, who controlled everything from refuse collection and water supply to construction permits and whose affluence and spending power inevitably shaped commercial development. No surprise then that Panama City found itself at the forefront of increasing nationalist sentiment that periodically erupted into violence, most notably in the flag riots of 1964 (see p.337). Only after the handover of the canal had been assured, in the canal treaty of 1977, could the capital, and the country, start to plan its own path.

The introduction of banking secrecy laws in the 1970s led to the rapid expansion of the financial services sector, including an influx of **narco–dollars**. Despite the tightening of banking regulations, El Cangrejo remains a hive of intrigue and some of the luxury high-rise apartments there and in Punta Paitilla stand empty, the astronomical rents paid by their fictitious occupants providing a useful means of laundering money. With the handover of the last US bases to Panamanian control at the end of 1999, huge amounts of real estate were made available, enabling the city to expand further, though its spread inland is still checked by the backdrop of hills that form the protected Panama Canal Basin.

Arrival and information

Panama City is the country's transport hub for both international and national traffic, with an international and a domestic airport, a port, a cruise ship terminal and gigantic bus terminal. The main **tourist office** of the Autoridad de Turismo Panamá (ATP) in Panama City is behind the ATLAPA Convention Centre in San Francisco on Vía Israel, but it's not worth dragging yourself over there since you're unlikely to get more than the odd glossy brochure or map, if you're lucky. Much better sources of information are the hostels and some of the more upmarket hotels and tour operators.

By air

The entry point for most visitors to Panama is the **Aeropuerto Internacional de Tocumen** (☏238 2703), located about 24km northeast of Panama City. The recently renovated airport has a couple of helpful tourist information desks, a bank, ATM and a Cable and Wireless office upstairs providing internet and international phone call facilities. Eight **car rental** firms also have offices at the airport (see p.27). By far the easiest way to get into the city centre is by **taxi** though it is by no means cheap. There are two official taxi service providers, one of which maintains a desk in the entrance hall displaying the official rates, which you should consult if in doubt. At the time of writing rates were $28, including toll fees, for one or two people to central Panama City ($10/person for three or more passengers), and $33 for the Amador Causeway and Cerro Ancón.

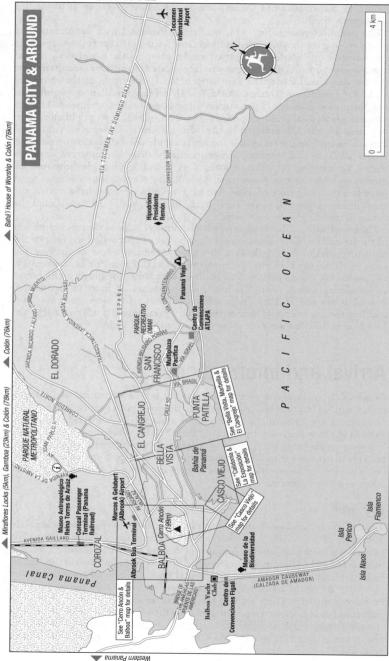

PANAMA CITY & AROUND

Eastern Panama ▲

Bahá'í House of Worship & Colón (76km) ▲

Colón (76km) ▲

Miraflores Locks (5km), Gamboa (23km) & Colón (78km) ▲

Western Panama ▲

4 km

N

PACIFIC OCEAN

Tocumen International Airport

VÍA TOCUMEN (AV. DOMINGO DÍAZ)

CORREDOR SUR

Hipódromo Presidente Remón

Panamá Viejo

VÍA CINCUENTENARIO

Centro de Convenciones ATLAPA

VÍA ESPAÑA

VÍA SIMÓN BOLÍVAR

TRANSÍSTMICA (AVENIDA SIMÓN BOLÍVAR)

AVENIDA RICARDO J. ALFARO (TUMBA MUERTO)

EL DORADO

PARQUE NATURAL METROPOLITANO

CORREDOR NORTE

AV. JUAN PABLO II

AVENIDA DE LA AMISTAD

AVENIDA BELISARIO PORRAS

PARQUE RECREATIVO OMAR

SAN FRANCISCO

Multiplaza Pacífica

VÍA ISRAEL

VÍA BRASIL

EL CANGREJO

CALLE 50

PUNTA PATILLA

BELLA VISTA

Bahía de Panamá

See "Bella Vista, Marbella & El Cangrejo" map for details

See "Calidonia & La Exposición" map for details

CASCO VIEJO

See "Casco Viejo" map for details

Museo Antropológico Reina Torres de Araúz

Corozal Passenger Terminal (Panama Railroad)

Marcos A Gelabert (Albrook) Airport

Albrook Bus Terminal

Cerro Ancón (199m)

See "Cerro Ancón & Balboa" map for details

BALBOA

COROZAL

AVENIDA GAILLARD

Panama Canal

Museo de la Biodiversidad

BRIDGE OF THE AMERICAS (PUENTE DE LAS AMÉRICAS)

Balboa Yacht Club

Centro de Convenciones Figali

AMADOR CAUSEWAY (CALZADA DE AMADOR)

Isla Perico

Isla Naos

Isla Flamenco

A far cheaper option is to get the **bus** from a bus stop at the other side of the road, about 200m from the terminal entrance. Buses with "Tocumen - Vía España" painted on the windscreen pass around every fifteen to twenty minutes and can take up to ninety minutes to make the journey in rush hour; the more infrequent ones (around 6.30am–6.30pm; every 30min; 75c with a/c) labelled "Corredor" take the toll road, which is much quicker and should reach the city centre in thirty to forty minutes. The slow-stopping buses to the city continue until around midnight, though hanging around the bus stop late at night can be risky. Both bus routes pass by the Plaza Cinco de Mayo, where you should alight if staying in Casco Viejo, before continuing to the main bus terminal.

Domestic flights from the country's two domestic carriers, Aeroperlas and Air Panama, touch down at low-key **Albrook Airport** (officially Marcos A. Gelabert Airport; ☎238 2700). This airport is only 3km northwest of the city centre, and taxis to most places in the city from here should not top $3, although the more luxurious cabs waiting immediately outside the terminal will charge you double the fare of a taxi flagged down on the road, which is easy to do during the day. Several **car rental** firms have offices here; there's also an ATM and a tourist desk.

By bus

All regional buses arriving in the capital deposit passengers on the upper level of the **Gran Terminal Nacional de Transportes**, known as "El Terminal", the national bus terminal 3km northwest of the city centre, close to Albrook Airport. A building of Stalinist proportions, 1km long, it has a similarly gargantuan shopping mall built opposite. To hop on a local bus into the city, go to the ground level, where a non-stop procession of buses drop off and pick up passengers in front of the terminal building – see below for the main routes. Taxis also stop there and should take you to your lodgings for no more than $3 for one or two passengers if you're heading for a central area such as Casco Viejo or El Cangrejo, though they may try to charge more if you arrive late at night or don't seem to know what you're doing.

City transport

Panama City's vast urban sprawl continues to expand outwards and upwards at an alarming rate, and navigating your way around can at first seem a daunting prospect. But as with most large cities, places of interest to tourists are concentrated in a few areas easily accessible by **bus** or **taxi**, or, in the case of Casco Viejo, on **foot**. Avoid travelling at rush hour (7.30–9am and 4.30–6.30pm), when traffic grinds to a halt in horn-honking mayhem.

Buses

Travelling by **bus** is the cheapest way to get about, costing a mere 25c, payable on exit, no matter where you travel within the metropolitan boundary. Known as **diablos rojos** ("red devils"; see box, p.64), these garishly painted buses constitute a tourist attraction in themselves and a ride on at least one is a must. Most circulate regularly – every few minutes on the busiest routes – from 5.30–6am until 11pm– midnight but less frequently on Sundays. Although there are official **bus stops**, some drivers will pick up and drop off at other places as the whim takes them. The final destination is painted on the windscreen with some of the major stopping places often indicated on a side window by the door. The city's main arteries and

Diablos Rojos

Whether as a cramped passenger or a terrified pedestrian, it's almost impossible to stay in Panama City without having life-threatening encounters with **diablos rojos** (red devils), the multicoloured converted old US school buses that clog up the city centre. Named for the devil-may-care attitude of many of the drivers, these anachronistic, fume-belching beasts are both safety hazards and cultural icons. The most exotic designs are air-brushed on and mix the religious and the profane: Jesus might jostle for position with pop singers in a psychedelic collage of fantasy landscapes, cartoon characters and Gothic monsters. Inside, feather boas, tassels and rosaries decorate the windscreen.

Arguably more is spent on the artwork than on maintenance, and many preventable **accidents** – some fatal – and breakdowns are caused by negligent owners or wild drivers, who enjoy racing *regatas* early in the morning or late at night when the roads are less congested. Add to that cramped seating, lack of ventilation and deafening music and it is easy to see why Panamanians have been pressing for the buses to be taken off the roads.

bus routes run vaguely southwest to northeast along Avenida Balboa and the Cinta Costera, Avenida Central (which becomes Avenida España) and Avenida Justo Arosemena (Av 3 Sur). No buses go into Panama City's historical centre, Casco Viejo; you'll need to get off at Parque Santa Ana or Plaza Cinco de Mayo and walk up the pedestrianized section of Avenida Central.

To reach the bus terminal from Casco Viejo, head for Cinco de Mayo and hop on any bus passing by the side of the Legislative Palace, where you can also hail the more sporadic, and often unmarked, minibuses heading for the Amador Causeway. Transport heading east can also be picked up at Parque Santa Ana. Most buses heading down Vía España towards Cinco de Mayo continue to the bus terminal at Albrook.

Taxis

Taxis are plentiful – around 28,000 in the city at the last count – and relatively cheap. They are supposed to follow an overcomplicated zonal pricing schedule (see Ⓦ www.transito.gob.pa) set by the transport authorities, but in practice the **price** is often down to supply and demand, your negotiating skills in Spanish and whether they want to take you. For most destinations in the city you shouldn't pay more than $2–3 during normal working hours, the exception being to Panamá Viejo or the Amador Causeway, where prices are often inflated (usually to a minimum of $5) because the driver is concerned about finding a passenger for the return trip. If you're unsure, ask around for the current rates beforehand and agree a price before getting into a cab.

Taxi drivers often serve as chauffeurs and unofficial city **tour guides**; $10–15 per hour is the going rate though you'll pay more for petrol if you want to travel some distance. Note that the more comfortable air-conditioned tourist taxis hovering outside the mid- to high-end hotels, recognizable by the **SET** licence plates, charge much higher rates.

Cars and bikes

Though **rental cars** are readily available from both airports and along Vía España near El Cangrejo (see p.27), it's not worthwhile until you're ready to leave the city since buses and taxis are cheap and plentiful. Besides, the lack of road signs and traffic signals, unmarked one-way streets and the free-for-all attitude of many drivers makes driving a stressful experience. You would need to have a death wish to **cycle** in most of Panama City. The exceptions are along the new Cinta Costera round the bay, and the Amador Causeway, where the existence of a cycleway and the general lack of traffic and fumes make for a pleasant ride. Three places on the causeway rent out bikes by the hour or for the day (see p.96).

Accommodation

There are **accommodation** options to suit all tastes and all budgets in Panama City, but beds are in short supply so it's a good idea to book ahead. If you're thinking of coming for Carnaval or any other busy holiday period, an advance reservation is an absolute must. Some mid-range hotels offer special business rates (open to all) or reductions for internet bookings.

Hot water is standard in hotels (though not necessarily in hostels) and most have air conditioning and cable TV, with many now offering wi-fi or other internet connections. If you're thinking of staying for a week or more, or are with a family, you might consider an **aparthotel**, which can be better value. These have kitchen/lounge/dining facilities but offer hotel services, such as cleaning, laundry and breakfast. Long-term rentals and corporate rates are often negotiable. Check out ⓦ www.panama.casa.com for smart modern apartment rentals ($700/week, $1700/month) in the banking district and its environs. Hotels located on a major bus route, such as Vía España or Avenida Perú, can get noisy from around 5.30–6.00am, when the grinding *diablos rojos* start up and the horn honking begins, until late at night, so ask for a room at the back on one of the higher floors.

There are three main areas to stay in Panama City. A growing number of budget travellers opt for a couple of friendly backpacker hostels in **Casco Viejo**, the old colonial centre, where there are also a couple of more comfortable options. The restoration of many of the area's historic buildings and absence of buses make it a pleasant retreat from the congestion and the pollution of the rest of the city. Various lively bars and restaurants have also made it a popular nightlife destination, though most places are relatively pricey.

Between Casco Viejo and the banking district of El Cangrejo lie the areas of **Calidonia** and **La Exposición**, which offer a wide selection of unexceptional but affordable modern hotels and *pensiónes*. Note that the streets off the main arteries are not very safe at night and some of the hotels offer rooms by the hour while places to eat are few and far between, though generally quite cheap. The safer and somewhat quieter districts of **Bella Vista**, **Marbella** and **El Cangrejo**, the hub of the city's nightlife and commercial activity, have the densest concentration of accommodation. Though prices are generally higher in these areas – apart from the hostels – you're within striking distance of most restaurants, bars, clubs, shops, casinos and cinemas and it's fairly safe to stroll around at night.

In addition to these neighbourhoods, there are an increasing number of lodgings scattered round the former **Canal Zone,** often offering greater tranquillity and, in some cases, superb views, though they are some distance from the main watering holes, which will mean spending more on taxi fares.

Casco Viejo

See map, p.69.

The Canal House C 5 at Av "A" ☏228 1907, ⓦ www.canalhousepanama.com. Elegantly restored colonial mansion just off the main square, comprising three stylish rooms (two of which are suites) with plasma TV, DVD player, wi-fi, etc. Breakfast is served in a spacious dining-lounge area, furnished in mahogany, which extends onto a large wraparound balcony. ❽

Los Cuatro Tulipanes Casa las Monjas, Av Central between C 3 & C 4 ☏233 1019,

Ⓦ www.loscuatrotulipanes.com. Experience Bohemian chic in Casco Viejo from a range of sumptuous apartments in beautifully restored colonial houses, offering traditional hotel services if required. Substantial discounts in low season. ❾

Hospedaje Casco Viejo C 8 nos. 8–31 ☏ 211 2127, Ⓦ www.hospedajecascoviejo .com. Clean, relaxed and surprisingly spacious hostel with numerous private rooms in a quiet street by the Iglesia de San José. The bathrooms have seen better days but you can't complain for the price. Small shared kitchen and interior patio plus free wi-fi. Dorms $10, doubles ❷

Luna's Castle C 9 Este between Av "B" & Av Alfaro ☏ 262 1540, Ⓦ www.lunascastlehostel.com. Great backpacker party venue set in a rambling property with balcony overlooking a square. Run by experienced owners, it offers free internet, shared kitchen, solar hot water, laundry, balconies, ping pong, a cine-centre, free pancake breakfasts and an on-site bar; just don't expect much sleep. Dorms $12, rooms ❸

Calidonia and La Exposición

See map, p.76.

Hostal Balboa Bay C 39 no. 21 ☏ 6538 3313, Ⓦ www.balboabaypanama.com. Small, quiet hostel tucked away off Av Balboa in a large converted house with a couple of small dorms (with and without a/c) and a few rooms. Free internet, TV room, washing machine and a couple of terraces to chill on, though it's hard to ignore the neighbour's a/c unit on one. Dorms $11. Rooms ❺

Hostel Mamallena Primera Calle Perejil off Vía España near the *Hotel Bella Vista* ☏ 6676 6163, Ⓦ www.mamallena.com. Popular backpacker place for chilling in a hammock on the communal balcony, or lounging in front of the TV. Dorms have a/c with quality mattresses while private rooms (also with a/c) have shared bathrooms. The friendly, helpful staff have bags of info and deals on trips and there are plenty of trimmings – free wi-fi and PCs with Skype, complimentary tea, coffee and all-day pancake breakfast, cheap airport transfer, washing machine. Only the location could be improved. Dorms $12. Rooms ❸

Hotel Acapulco C 30 between Av Cuba & Av Perú ☏ 225 3832, Ⓔ hotelacapulco@hotmail.com. A travellers' favourite for its solid value and friendly service. Some of the well-maintained, functional rooms have small balconies. ❹

Hotel Costa Inn Av Perú at C 39 ☏ 227 1522, Ⓦ www.hotelcostainn.com. Popular hotel with friendly staff, a small rooftop pool, secure parking and a restaurant. The recently refurbished rooms

have large beds, and a fridge. Apart from the *parillada* two blocks away, there's nowhere to eat nearby. ❻

Hotel Dos Mares Av Perú at C 30 ☏ 227 6149, Ⓔ dosmares@cwpanama.net. New and slightly more upmarket than many of its surrounding competitors, with bar-restaurant and fabulous rooftop pool and terrace – hosting Saturday-night barbecues – affording spectacular views of the bay. The comfortable modern rooms have spotless small bathrooms, and internet access in the foyer. Good value. ❺

Hotel Stanford Panama Plaza 5 de Mayo ☏ 262 4933, Ⓔ hotelstanford@cwpanama.net. Fantastic location overlooking the busy plaza offering slightly faded en-suite rooms with decent beds at afford-able rates. Go for a room with a view across the bay but away from the bar and casino and the rooftop terrace, which often throbs to the beat of weekend parties. ❹

Residencial Jamaica Av Cuba at C 38 Este ☏ 225 9870. Hidden behind a nicely trimmed hedge, Jamaica offers a good deal for the price – so is often full. Rooms are bright and clean. ❹

Bella Vista, Marbella and El Cangrejo

See map, p.78.

The Bristol Hotel Av Aquilino de la Guardia at C 50 ☏ 264 0000, Ⓦ www.thebristol.com. From the moment you glide across its gleaming marble foyer, this boutique hotel exudes exclusivity. The rooms are elegant and sumptuously furnished, while vast marble bathrooms, 24hr butler service and an award-winning restaurant mean the only thing lacking is a pool. ❾

Euro Hotel Vía España no. 33 by Colegio Javier ☏ 263 0802, ☏ 263 0927, Ⓦ www .eurohotelpanama.com. No-frills hotel with clean, compact rooms piped with ambient music, which thankfully can be switched off. Swimming pool, plus free wi-fi in the comfy lobby. ❺

The Executive Hotel C 52 at Aquilino de la Guardia ☏ 265 8011, Ⓦ www.executive hotel-panama.com. Long-established business hotel with a faithful Latin clientele. Rather faded rooms are offset by some terrific balcony views and excellent location. Rates include a substantial breakfast and some business centre facilities. Also with a 24hr coffee shop, a rooftop gym plus a bath-size pool and sundeck. ❽

Hotel California Vía España at C 43 Este ☏ 263 7736, Ⓦ www.hotelcaliforniapanama.net. Not the most convenient location but very popular hotel, offering good-value rooms, free wi-fi and a roof-top jacuzzi. ❺

Hotel Costa Azul C 44 Este at Av Justo Arosemena ☎225 4703, ✉hotelcostaazul @cwpanama.net. A small hotel with friendly service, internet, bar and parking. Rooms are bright, clean and spacious. ❺

🏃 **Hotel DeVille** C Beatriz M. Cabal at C 50 ☎206 3100, ⓦwww.devillehotel.com.pa. Plum in the heart of the financial district, this boutique hotel provides the best value for those seeking top-class accommodation with a more personalized service than the international luxury hotels can offer. Elegant, spacious rooms possess dark wooden furniture and opulent marble bathrooms. The strikingly designed on-site restaurant serves excellent French fusion cuisine. ❾

Hotel El Parador C Eusebio A. Morales opposite *Martin Fierro* ☎214 4586, ⓦwww.hotelparador panama.com. Another popular business hotel where you're lucky to get a booking. Rooms are bright with tiled floors and polished dark wooden furniture and some even have balconies. The rooftop pool is another draw. ❻

🏃 **Hotel Milan** C Eusebio A. Morales no. 31 ☎263 7723, ⓦwww.republicofpanama.net /Hotels/Hotel_Milan. Sought after hotel in a great location, so book well in advance. The place boasts sixty expansive spotless tiled rooms and suites (some with jacuzzi) with direct-dial phones. Good value if you take advantage of the 25 percent cash discount. Discounted! ❺

Jungla House Hostel C 49 Oeste off Vía Argentina, Edif. RINA no.11 ☎6920 4170. This well-located two-flat conversion tucked away round the back of El Cangrejo feels more like a house than a hostel. There's a shared kitchen and living room space and a nice balcony to sit out on. Has half-a-dozen bunks and a vastly overpriced private room (no bathroom). Dorms $15. Rooms ❺

Marriott Hotel C 52 & Ricardo Arias ☎210 9100, ⓦwwwmarriothotels.com. A Marriott that truly merits its 5-star rating, comprising excellent rooms and service with full business amenities, casino, pool and casino – located plum in the middle of the business district. ❾

Radisson Decapolis Hotel Av Balboa, Multicentro ☎215 5000, ⓦwww.radisson.com/panamacitypan. Brash or stylish (depending on your viewpoint) thirty-floor glass and steel edifice leading into the Multicentro Mall and Majestic Casino, offering big, tastefully designed rooms with all the frills – go for one on an upper floor with an ocean view. On-site restaurant (excellent breakfast buffet), sushi bar and pool. ❾

Residencial Los Arcos Av Justo Arosemena at C 44 ☎225 0569, ✉losarcos@cwpanama.net. Compact place on the edge of Bella Vista with

well-maintained rooms. The big plus is showers with proper showerheads – a rarity in this price bracket. ❹

🏃 **Sevilla Suites** C Eusebio A. Morales opposite *Rincón Suizo* ☎213 0016, ⓦwww.sevillasuites.com. Smart aparthotel aimed at the business market in a convenient location. Offers nicely furnished suites with kitchenettes, living/dining area, wi-fi. Enjoy the complimentary breakfast on the patio after a few lengths in the rooftop pool or a session in the mini-gym. ❽

🏃 **Torres de Alba** C Eusebio A. Morales at Vía Veneto ☎300 7130, ⓦwww.torresdealba .com.pa. Expansive well-furnished suites boasting lots of natural light, decent-sized kitchens (including washing machine) and all the usual mod cons. The gym and rather small pool are too close to street traffic to provide much relaxation. Great location but opt for a higher floor to escape the noise. ❽

Zuly's Backpackers C Ricardo Arias, at the end of a dead-end street by *Pizzeria Sorrento* ☎269 2665, ⓦwww.zulysbackpackers.com. Well-established hostel in new premises, which include balcony and small garden. Shared kitchen, living room, balcony, a rotating cast of international travellers and knowledgeable staff. Dorms $9. Rooms ❸

Former Canal Zone

Including the Amador Causeway, Balboa and Cerro Ancón, stretching to Albrook, Clayton and Miraflores Locks. See map, p.82, unless otherwise noted.

Albrook Inn C las Magnolias no. 14, Albrook ☎315 1789, ⓦwww.albrookinn.com. Convenient for early domestic flights from Albrook Airport and fine if you've your own transport, this otherwise out-of-the-way hotel is located in a tranquil residential suburb. Rates for comfortable motel-style rooms and suites include a buffet breakfast served in verdant surroundings. A small pool with jacuzzi provides another treat. ❻

Amador Ocean View Hotel & Suites Las Brisas, Isla Perico, Amador Causeway ☎314 3310, ⓦwww.amadoroceanview.com. Not mapped. Located above a restaurant walkway, expansive, well-equipped rooms peel off a single polished corridor. Get one facing Isla Taboga and the canal entrance else you're left contemplating the car park at the rear. Small pool and patio below. Breakfast included. ❽

The Balboa Inn Las Cruces, no. 2311a, Balboa ☎314 1520, ⓦwww.thebalboainn.com. Conveniently situated in the quiet residential area of Balboa, yet close to bus and taxi routes, this B&B

offers simple but nicely furnished rooms with excellent beds and plenty of natural light. The delightful garden breakfast terrace allows you to enjoy your granola while birdwatching. ❼

Country Inn & Suites Amador Causeway ☎211 4500, ⓦwww.panamacanalcountry.com. Not mapped. A standard motel in a stunning location, right by the canal entrance. Pay the extra $15 to watch the ships from your balcony – otherwise you get a view of the car park. The large, bright rooms are equipped with all conveniences. There's an onsite TGI Fridays and a couple of pools. Breakfast included. ❽

La Estancia B&B C Amelia Denis de Icaza, Quarry Heights, Ancón ☎314 1581, ⓦwww.bedandbreakfastpanama.com. The capital's best accommodation for nature lovers, halfway up Cerro Ancón, surrounded by trees, with agoutis and toucans nearby. The helpful owners oversee simple (not all en suite and none have TV), comfortable and light rooms and can arrange tours and transfers. You'll need a taxi to reach a restaurant but order a takeaway, grab some wine from the honesty bar and chill on the balcony. ❻

Holiday Inn Ciudad de Saber (City of Knowledge), Clayton ☎317 4000, ⓦwww.hinnpanama.com. Bang opposite the Miraflores Locks so you can watch the canal action night and day, though you'll need an upper floor room. The well-appointed, spacious rooms have giant plasma-screen TVs, crisp white sheets, sparkling bathrooms and the usual business amenities. But you are a long way from the city so taxi fares will hit the wallet hard. Breakfast included. ❾

Hostal Amador Familiar Av Amador, round the corner from Tamburelli's, Ancón ☎314 1251, ⓦwww.hostalamadorfamiliar.com. Bright yellow three-storey Canal Zone building with a laid-back atmosphere, attracting a mix of Panamanians and foreigners. Basic compact en-suite rooms, free wi-fi, laundry service and cheap airport transport, plus pleasant outdoor open-sided kitchen-cum-social area, where you prepare your complimentary DIY breakfast. Dorms with a/c $15, doubles from ❹

Other areas

Three other places worth considering lie in the El Carmen neighbourhood, just out from El Cangrejo along Vía España; in Betania, a quiet residential area 2km north of El Cangrejo; and close to Tocumen International Airport.

Casa Las Americas Rua Espíritu Santo, Betania ☎399 7783, ⓦwww.casalasamericas.com. See map, p.78. Intimate B&B, offering attractively furnished, comfortable rooms with a/c, wi-fi, shared or private bathroom, garden and a good-sized pool. Internet bookings are preferred – and much cheaper! ❻

Hostal La Casa de Carmen C 1 El Carmen no.32 ☎263 4366, ⓦwww.lacasadecarmen.net. See map, p.78. Strongly recommended by travellers of all ages and therefore usually full, so book ahead. A bit far out though just off the Vía España bus route but the attractions are numerous, including a pleasant patio and garden area with hammocks and barbecue – not to mention a pet parrot, plus the usual hostel amenities, and helpful staff. Dorm beds are good value, some of the rooms less so. Dorm $14.50, room ❹

Riande Aeropuerto Hotel & Resort Av Tocumen ☎291 9012, ⓦwww.hotelesriande.com /aeropuerto. Not a place to base a stay in Panama City, but this motel-like joint does the job if you've an early flight out of Tocumen (or a late arrival) as it's a couple of minutes away and offers a free airport transfer. ❼

Casco Viejo

Most of Panama City's historical monuments and tourist attractions are concentrated in the colonial city centre of **San Felipe** – more commonly called **Casco Viejo** (sometimes Casco Antiguo) these days – which makes it the best place to start your tour of the capital. For centuries the heart of Panama City's social and political life, and still home to the presidential palace, Casco Viejo, after decades of neglect, was declared a UNESCO World Heritage site in 1997 and is gradually being restored to its former glory. Now upmarket restaurants and cafés sit alongside chic offices and apartments in renovated colonial buildings, but the poor families talking on the doorsteps of crumbling, scarcely habitable houses are just as much part of the neighbourhood. Yet ongoing restoration projects are making it a much more pleasant place to visit and the increased police presence – including the highly visible tourist police, often on bicycles – ensures greater safety. Note that caution should still be exercised when walking around at night.

The best way to see Casco Viejo is on foot – you can reach it from the rest of the city by taxi or by taking any bus to Plaza Cinco de Mayo, then walking up Avenida Central, past Parque Santa Ana and the famous *Café Coca Cola* (both shown on the map below), as it narrows into a cobbled street, passing through the now invisible city walls into the historic centre. The rows of lottery ticket sellers – who number over ten thousand across the country – doing a brisk trade on the left-hand pavement provide an obvious clue to the function of the striking blue-and-white striped art deco building – one of two homes of the national lottery (the other lies on Av Perú, see p.77). A stone's throw further along on the left is the gleaming white and cream Neoclassical **Casa de la Municipalidad**, seat of the city's government. Next door stands the crumbling baroque façade of the city's oldest church, **Iglesia de la Merced**, which in 1680 was reconstructed on its present site using the original stones from Panamá Viejo. The façade is the best preserved section of the church, which gives way inside to some poorly conceived twentieth-century restoration work, though the gilded wooden altar retains some appeal.

Plaza de la Catedral

Further down Avenida Central the street opens out into the old quarter's most impressive square, **Plaza de la Catedral**, also known as Plaza Mayor and Plaza de la Independencia since the proclamations of independence from Spain and separation from Colombia were made here. Numerous busts of the nation's founding

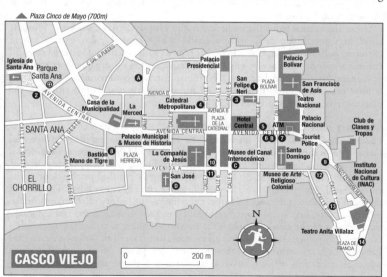

▲ Plaza Cinco de Mayo (700m)

CASCO VIEJO

0   200 m

ACCOMMODATION		RESTAURANTS & CAFÉS				BARS & CLUBS	
The Canal House	C	Las Bóvedas	14	Granclement	6	Café Havana	3
Los Cuatro Tulipanes	B	Buzios	13	Manolo Caracol	7	Casa Góngora	5
Hospedaje Casco Viejo	D	Café Coca-Cola	2	René Café	4	La Casona de	
Luna's Castle	A	Caffè Per Due	12	Supermercado		las Brujas	8
		Casablanca	1	Gourmet	10	Platea	9
		Diablo Rosso	11			Relic	A

fathers are scattered beneath the shady trees surrounding the striking central gazebo, with the Republic's first president, Manuel Amador Guerrero, taking pride of place. In the seventeenth and eighteenth centuries, the space was used for bullfights and theatrical presentations, becoming a park at the end of the nineteenth century, now frequented by elderly residents reading the paper and occasional street vendors. A small **fleamarket** (first non-bank-holiday Sun of the month 9am–5pm) is held in the square, with stalls selling arts, crafts and bric-a-brac.

Flanked by white towers sparkling with inlaid mother-of-pearl, the hybrid Neoclassical and baroque olive and cream sandstone facade of the **Catedral Metro-politana** dominates the square. It was built between 1688 and 1796 using some of the stone brought from the ruins of Panamá Viejo (see p.85). Three of its bells were also recovered from its ruined predecessor, and reputedly owe their distinctive tone to a gold ring thrown by Queen Isabella I of Spain into the molten metal from which they were cast. The cathedral's interior is tatty in places, though the large altarpiece carved from seven types of Italian marble is suitably imposing. To its right lies a trapdoor marking the entrance to tunnels – not open to visitors – designed as escape routes, connecting the cathedral to the churches of La Merced and San José.

The square is overlooked by several other historic buildings. Southeast of the cathedral is the **Palacio Municipal**, a splendid example of Neoclassical architecture. Originally constructed in 1910 on the site of the former city hall, its ground floor houses the **Museo de Historia de Panamá** (Mon–Fri 8am–4pm; $1), which offers a cursory introduction to Panamanian history, focusing on symbols of independence such as the national flag, the national anthem and the coat of arms, alongside an eclectic mixture of maps and artefacts, with explanations in Spanish. The languorous nude reclining in the entrance hall represents Panama bathing in the waters of the two oceans.

Across the square from the cathedral is the **Hotel Central**, once the plushest hotel in Central America, with a chandelier-lit central palm garden where glittering balls were held. It was here that crowds gathered in 1903 to celebrate full Panamanian independence by emptying a dozen bottles champagne over the head of General Huertas, the defecting Colombian garrison commander. The building is now being renovated to shine once more as a five-star hotel, although the original façade was demolished in 2009.

Museo del Canal Interoceánico

Plaza de la Catedral's most interesting site is arguably the excellent **Museo del Canal Interoceánico** (Tues–Sun 9am–5pm; $2; ☎ 211 1649, ⓦ www.museodelcanal .com, housed in a three-storey French colonial building, complete with mansard roof and shutters, next to the Palacio Municipal. The highly polished marble floor of the entrance hall bears witness to its former life as the city's grandest hotel. The bulk of the exhibition lies on the **second floor**, expounding the history of the transisthmian route, from the first Spanish attempt to find a passage to Asia to the contemporary management of the canal. Although the museum is rather text-heavy (in Spanish – the most conspicuous sign in English asks visitors to refrain from sitting on an original Panama Railroad waiting-room bench), there are plenty of photographs, video montages and maps offering striking comparisons between the different working conditions of the French and US canal eras which bring to life the enormity of the achievements.

With advance notice, the museum can arrange an English-speaking guide ($5/ hour for a minimum of three visitors). The **third floor** displays cover the apartheid living conditions of gold and silver roll employees (see p.336), more information and artefacts from the US canal drama and a barrage of press reports on the deteriorating Panamanian–US relations that eventually led to the handover of the canal. The museum has wheelchair access and a small **shop** selling modern and original canal memorabilia.

Palacio Presidencial

On the seafront, two blocks north of the square between Calles 6 and 5, stands the **Palacio Presidencial**. Originally built in 1673 for an unscrupulous colonial judge, who embezzled state funds to furnish his opulent mansion, it later served as a customs house, teacher training college and even a prison before being rebuilt in 1922 as the presidential residence in grandiose neo-Moorish style under the orders of President Belisario Porras. It is commonly known as the "Palacio de las Garzas" after the white egrets given to Porras by his poet friend Ricardo Miró, and they have lived freely around the patio fountain ever since. The pair of elegant blue cranes that also stalk the patio were donated by the South African government. The streets around the palace are closed to traffic and pedestrians but the presidential guards allow visitors access to view the exterior of the building during the day.

It is also possible to go on a free **guided tour** of the palace, which is well worth the hassle even though it only covers a few rooms and requires organizing several days in advance. A letter in Spanish suggesting possible dates needs to be e-mailed or hand-delivered to the Oficina de Guías (Mon–Fri 8am–4.30pm; ☎527 9740, ask for Sra Griselda Bernal, ⓔgbernal@presidencia.gob.pa), round the back of the yellow building on the waterfront by Calle 4. Visits (Tues, Thurs & Fri mornings) last about an hour – bring your passport. After admiring the marble floor and mother-of-pearl encrusted columns of the Moorish vestibule, the tour moves up to the first floor and the long *Salón Amarillo* (Yellow Hall), used for official ceremonies. From the presidential throne to the gilt mirrors and heavy drapes, the room is replete with shades of gold, amber and mustard, while striking murals by Roberto Lewis offer a selective romp through Panama's history. In the adjoining *Comedor del Palacio* (Dining Room), where state banquets are held, Lewis's distinctive murals are even more prominent, depicting idyllic country scenes. At the far end of the dining room a door leads off to the *Salón del Cabinete* (Cabinet Room), which contains portraits of all Panama's presidents. In addition to these main rooms, the tour allows you a peek at some of the splendidly tiled Moorish-themed ante-rooms.

Plaza Bolívar and around

Walking a block back from the waterfront and then east along Avenida B brings you out onto **Plaza Bolívar**, an elegant square dotted with manicured trees – the perfect spot for a glass of wine or meal at the two pavement café-restaurants, though it is periodically interrupted by the cries of primary-school children spilling out of class seeking out snow-cones (*raspados*) from the waiting vendors. Rebuilt after a fire in 1756, the plaza was dedicated in 1883 to Simón Bolívar, whose statue, crowned by a condor, stands at its centre.

The monument was erected in 1926 to commemorate one hundred years since the Amphyctionic Congress, the first Panamerican gathering, organized by Bolívar, aimed at unifying the newly independent Latin American countries in their relations with Spain. Although "El Libertador" (The Liberator) failed to attend the congress, and his dreams of unity ultimately foundered, it was considered a historic event. The meeting took place in the chapter house of the Franciscan monastery in the southeast corner of the square, now known as the **Salón Bolívar**. A small museum is enclosed within a glass casement, which includes a replica of the Liberator's gold ceremonial sword, encrusted with over a thousand diamonds, and the congress's original documents. Following restoration, it was due to reopen in 2010.

While the museum is likely only to attract serious history buffs, the surrounding **Palacio Bolívar** (Mon–Fri 8am–4pm; free), whose impressive peach and white facade extends along the eastern edge of the square, is well worth a peek inside. The building now houses the Ministry of Foreign Affairs, among other government offices, and has been beautifully restored, providing the courtyard – the **Plaza de los Libertadores** – with a magnificent translucent roof allowing in lots of natural light. From a raised platform at the far side a bronze bust of the visionary Liberator looks on.

Next door stands the **Iglesia y Convento de San Francisco de Asís**, which has been closed for restoration for some time. Built in the seventeenth century, the church was extensively modified following fires that all but destroyed it.

Teatro Nacional

Just off the square at the end of Avenida B stands the handsome **Teatro Nacional** (Mon–Fri 9.30am–5.30pm; $1; ☎262 3525). One of the first grand national buildings to be commissioned by the newly independent state, it was built on the site of a former convent and designed by Italian architect Genaro Ruggieri. The magnificent Italianate Neoclassical edifice opened its doors to the public in 1908 to initial success but the global depression of the 1930s brought a slump in the venue's fortunes, and it became a cinema for a while before falling into neglect. Extensively restored in the early 1970s, the theatre reopened in 1974 with a performance by Margot Fonteyn, the British ballerina and long-term Panama resident, whose bronze bust adorns the foyer, alongside that of Roberto Lewis, whose allegorical frescoes depicting the birth of the nation can be seen on the vaulted ceiling. The building was renovated again in the early 2000s, and it's well worth paying the $1 entry to poke around the splendid baroque interior, though finding the building open can be a challenge. One of the best ways to enjoy the theatre's splendour is obviously to attend one of the occasional productions, which are sometimes free (see p.92).

The ramparts

Outside, stroll across the car park at the end of Avenida B south along what once formed part of the the colonial city's ramparts; ahead, overlooking the sea to the left, is the shell of the **Club de Clases y Tropas**, the recreation centre for Noriega's national guard, which was largely destroyed during the US invasion, though the "N" for Noriega still lingers on the mosaic paving at its entrance.

A few metres beyond the Club de Clases y Tropas, take the steps up to the **Paseo Esteban Huertas**, a delightful, breezy bougainvillea-covered promenade that runs some 400m along the top of the defensive sea wall. The walkway along the ramparts is a favourite haunt of smooching couples – earning it the nickname Paseo de los Inamorados – and Kuna traders displaying their handicrafts to passing tourists. At the far end, before descending the steps into the Plaza de Francia, you get fine views across the bay. Peek over the wall here and you can glimpse the windows of the dungeons where prisoners were allegedly left at low tide to drown when the high tide flooded the cells.

Plaza de Francia

Descending the steps takes you to the **Plaza de Francia**, an irregularly shaped space bounded by the sea wall and the renovated arches of **Las Bóvedas** (vaults), Spanish dungeons that also functioned as storehouses, prison cells and barracks for the fort that occupied the plaza until the early twentieth century. They now contain a chic restaurant of the same name. The square was once the Plaza de Armas, the city's main square, but was remodelled in 1924 and now hosts a substantial monument dedicated to the thousands of workers who died during the disastrous French attempt to build the canal (see p.333). The centrepiece is an obelisk (with a secret door leading to a maintenance staircase behind one of the frieze panels) topped by a proud Gallic cockerel. It is ringed by busts of some of the key figures involved, including Ferdinand de Lesseps, the French diplomat who first conceived of the canal yet whose ignorance and vanity were central to the project's ultimate failure (see p.333). Behind the semi-circle of Neoclassical columns vast marble tablets chronologically outline the bare bones of the dream to build a transisthmian waterway.

The Neoclassical **French Embassy** overlooks the square from the north, fronted by a huge statue of former Panamanian president Pablo Arosemena. The large gleaming white building to the east was previously the city's main courthouse, badly damaged during the 1989 US invasion, and now home to the **Instituto Nacional de Cultura** (INAC, the National Institute of Culture), the body responsible for maintaining the country's museums. It was spruced up for the James Bond film *Quantum of Solace*, in which it featured as a Bolivian hotel. Adjacent is the intimate Teatro Anita Villalaz (see p.94).

Along Avenida A and up to Parque Santa Ana

Two blocks west along Avenida A from the corner with Calle 1 stands the ruined **Iglesia y Convento de Santo Domingo**, where restoration work is continuing apace. Completed in 1678, it is most famous for the **Arco Chato** (flat arch) over its main entrance. Only 10.6m high, but spanning some 15m with no keystone or external support, it was reputedly cited as evidence of Panama's seismic stability when the US Senate was debating where to build a interoceanic canal. Ironically, the arch inexplicably collapsed just after the centenary celebrations for Panama's independence in 2003, but has subsequently been restored to its former glory.

In the chapel next door, the absorbing **Museo de Arte Religioso Colonial** has a small collection of religious paintings, silverwork and sculpture from the colonial era, but has been closed to the public for some time as funding for renovation work has stalled. Take a quick detour down Calle 4 to the corner with Avenida Central, to take a look at **Casa Góngora** (Tues–Sun 10am–6pm; free), the city's oldest existing Spanish colonial home, which dates back to 1756. Built for a wealthy pearl merchant, the two-storey building retains many original features typical of the era and contains some period reproduction furniture. The house also provides a cultural space for art exhibitions and live music events (see p.93). Three blocks west along Avenida A stands the ruined shell of **La Compañía de Jesús**, a Jesuit church and the seat of the country's first university. Only the walls and ornate facade still stand but restoration is continuing, with plans mooted to create an orchid garden in the ruins.

Iglesia de San José

A block further west, set back on the corner with Calle 8, is the **Iglesia de San José**. Built in 1673, but since remodelled, the church is exceptional only as home to the legendary baroque **Altar de Oro** (Golden Altar), which illuminates the otherwise gloomy interior. A carved mahogany extravaganza gilded with 22-carat gold leaf, it was one of the few treasures to survive Henry Morgan's ransacking of Panamá Viejo in 1671 thanks, apparently, to having been painted or covered in mud to disguise its true value. One legend has it that on being asked by Morgan where the gold was, the priest pleaded poverty to explain its absence, even persuading the buccaneer to make a donation to the church.

Plaza Herrera

Continuing west another block, Avenida A emerges onto **Plaza Herrera**, a pleasant square lined with elegant nineteenth-century houses. This was originally

▲ Shoe-shining in Parque Santa Ana

the Plaza de Triunfo, where bullfights were held until the mid-nineteenth century, but was renamed in 1887 in honour of General Tomás Herrera, whose equestrian statue stands in its centre. Herrera – after whom the Azuero Peninsula province is named – was the military leader of Panama's first short-lived independence attempt in 1840. Just off Plaza Herrera to the west stands **Bastión Mano de Tigre** (Tiger Hand Bastion), a crumbling and indistinct pile of masonry that is the last remaining section of the city's original defensive walls on the landward side.

To the left is a striking wooden residential building, named La Boyacá after a nineteenth century gunboat, its front carved like the prow of a ship. Beyond, Avenida A heads into the poor barrio and no-go area of **El Chorrillo**, which was devastated during the US invasion, leaving hundreds dead and thousands homeless. It has since been rebuilt, but the coloured concrete tenements that replaced the old wooden slum housing are already run down. At night drug gangs run riot and the place is dangerous even during the day.

Parque Santa Ana

Head north out of the plaza and up Avenida Central, and you come out in **Parque Santa Ana**, the social and transport hub of the impoverished neighbourhood of Santa Ana. As the centre of activity outside the city walls in the early nineteenth century it hosted colourful markets and bullfights; now it offers some respite from the swirling traffic, and is often populated by many of the locality's older residents, discussing the latest news. The pedestrianized section of Avenida Central starts on the park's north-eastern side, where a row of shoe-shine booths provides another social focus.

Central Panama City

In contrast to the relative calm of the city's historical centre and ancient remains, the **modern city** streets of **central Panama City** reverberate with traffic noise and pavements are packed with people squeezing in and out of the patchwork of shops, banks, hotels and restaurants or threading their way through street vendors, hawkers and other shoppers. Wedge-shaped central Panama City arguably stretches 3km round the Bahía de Panama, from Avenida Central and Plaza Cinco de Mayo – home to the central government buildings – to Punta Paitilla, encompassing the older residencial and commercial districts of Calidonia and La Exposición, fanning out to include Bella Vista and the newer, plusher financial districts of Marbella and El Cangrejo.

Avenida Central

The pedestrianized stretch of **Avenida Central**, from Parque Santa Ana north as far as Plaza Cinco de Mayo, is one of the oldest and most colourful shopping districts. Blasts of air conditioning and loud music pour out from the huge predominantly Hindu-owned superstores that line the avenue selling cheap clothing, electronics and household goods, while on the street itself hawkers flog pirate DVDs and cheap sunglasses and vendors quench the thirst of shoppers with fruit or sugar cane juice. Nowhere is the enormous cultural diversity of the city more evident, a constant kaleidoscope of Hindus in saris, Kuna women in their traditional costumes, bearded Muslims in robes and skullcaps, *interioranos* in sombreros, Chinese, Afro-Antillanos and Latinos. In the evening, in the pedestrian area round Cinco de Mayo, extra food stalls pop up selling kebabs and sausages and as the night wears on, prostitutes tout for custom. Exercise caution when walking round the streets either side of Avenida Central and north of the Parque Santa Ana, and avoid wandering around the side streets at night.

Leaving Casco Viejo along Avenida B, at the junction with Avenida Balboa, the new **Mercado Publico** (Mon–Sat 6am–4pm, some stalls on Sun) contains a patchwork of stalls selling fresh produce, as well as clean public toilets, an ATM and a food hall, where you can join the breakfast or lunchtime crowds of locals selecting a heaped plateful of tasty fresh rice or noodles for under $3 from a selection of inviting *fondas*.

Plaza Cinco de Mayo and around

The pedestrian zone of Avenida Central spills out into the busiest square in the city, **Plaza Cinco de Mayo**, where the traffic mayhem takes over again. Several main roads converge here, resulting in *diablos rojos* roaring past in all directions as crowds congregate at street corners to flag them down. To the south the square is bordered by the neglected Neoclassical building that was originally the proud Panama Railroad Pacific terminal and more recently housed the national anthropological museum. Tucked away at its rear is a large, open-air **handicrafts market** (see p.95) which is worth a browse.

Over the road, by the pedestrian zone, stands a small fountain monument to the six volunteer firemen killed fighting an exploded gunpowder magazine in 1914. Diagonally opposite, on the northwestern side of the plaza, is the rather uninspiring **Palacio Legislativo** (Legislative Palace), home to the Asamblea Legislativa (Legislative Assembly), which stands in the raised park of the same name. Like many of the city's public spaces, it received a centennial facelift, and was renamed Parque José Antonio Remón Cantera, in honour of one of the country's former presidents, who was mysteriously gunned down at the hippodrome in 1955. Peer behind the towering black monolith at its centre and you are greeted by an enormous, rather unflattering head of the murdered president, protruding from the granite.

There are two places of potential interest up on the hill behind the Legislative Palace, though you need to cross the hazardous Avenida de los Mártires to reach them both. The first is the privately owned **Museo de Arte Contemporaneo** (Tues–Sun 9am–5pm; $5; ⓦ www.macpanama.org), across the road to your left, which has a permanent collection by Panamanian artists in a range of media and periodically hosts interesting exhibitions. The second building of note is the **Smithsonian Tropical Research Institute**'s Earl S. Tupper Research and Conference Centre (Ⓦwww.stri.org), which is set in leafy grounds on Avenida Roosevelt over to the right, where you'll need to show ID at the entrance. The centre has an impressive **bookshop** (Mon–Fri 10am–4.30pm), a research library and a very pleasant, modestly priced **cafeteria**. Visits to Isla Barro Colorado (see p.123) can be arranged at the bookshop.

Calidonia and La Exposición

Beyond Plaza Cinco de Mayo, Avenida Central continues to the northeast, the city's main thoroughfare and still a busy shopping street as it runs through **CALIDONIA** and **LA EXPOSICIÓN**. These twin barrios are sandwiched between Avenida Central, which soon metamorphoses into Vía España, and Avenida Balboa, which runs along the bay. Consisting of a dense grid of streets, where the sound of construction work is never far away, they are crammed with

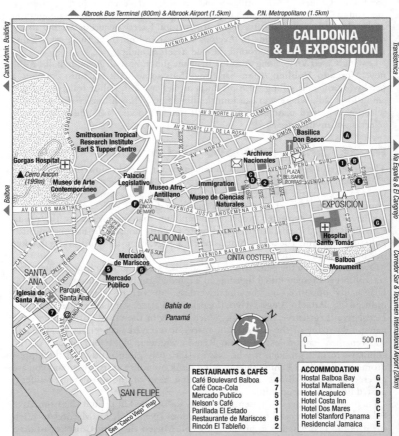

RESTAURANTS & CAFÉS	
Café Boulevard Balboa	4
Café Coca-Cola	7
Mercado Publico	5
Nelson's Café	3
Parillada El Estado	1
Restaurante de Mariscos	6
Rincón El Tableño	2

ACCOMMODATION	
Hostal Balboa Bay	G
Hostal Mamallena	A
Hotel Acapulco	D
Hotel Costa Inn	B
Hotel Dos Mares	C
Hotel Stanford Panama	F
Residencial Jamaica	E

cheap hotels though a sprinking of parks and museums provide welcome relief. This older section of the modern city dates back to the boom contruction eras of the Panama Railroad and Canal in the mid and late nineteenth century (see p.115 and p.335), when predominantly West Indian immigrants poured into the city, with a further influx forced out of the canal areas once the Zone was created.

Museo Afro-Antillano

A block down Avenida Justo Arosemena (also known as Av 3 Sur) on the corner with Calle 24, an unmarked wooden former church houses the **Museo Afro-Antillano** (Tues–Sun 9am–4pm; $1; ⓦ www.samaap.org), dedicated to preserving the history and culture of Panama's large West Indian population. The Church of the Christian Mission, as it was then, constituted the social centre of the barrio of El Marañon, a thriving Afro-Antillean community dating back to the construction of the railroad (see p.115). As property prices escalated in the 1970s and developers moved in with bulldozers, residents were forced out to the city suburbs. The community has maintained a precarious toehold in the centre of the city through this small but worthwhile museum, which highlights the pivotal role that Afro-Antilleans played in the construction of the railroad and the canal. The exhibits, featuring photographs, tools and period furniture, with texts in English, provide a sharp reminder of the harsh working and living conditions of black, "silver roll" canal workers, which contrasted acutely with the privileges of white American "gold roll" employees, in the days of the Canal Zone. The museum is also the focal point for the annual Afro-Antillean Fair that takes place over Carnaval.

Museo de Ciencias Naturales

Two blocks east of Avenida Central on Avenida Cuba, between Calle 29 and Calle 30, the **Museo de Ciencias Naturales** (Tues–Sat 9am–3.30pm; $1) offers a basic introduction to Panama's geology and ecology. For those who are not turned off by taxidermy and the musty smell of formaldehyde, the museum's modest collection may prove diverting, not least specimens of Panama's fauna that you are unlikely to see in the wild, such as the harpy eagle and jaguar. Up a block on Avenida Perú, the covered space that looks like a cattle market is actually the venue for the twice-weekly **national lottery** draw, which also features a folkloric show (every Wed, every Sun, last Fri of the month; 1pm). A little further along, a complete architectural contrast is provided by the splendid Corinthian capitols of the imposing Neoclassical home of the **Archivos Nacionales de Panamá**.

Plaza Belisario Porras

Moving another couple of blocks up Avenida Perú, on the right between Calle 33 and 34, lie the formal gardens of the **Plaza Belisario Porras**, honouring three-time president and founding father of the same name. In the vast monument to the former leader, Porras cuts a dashing figure, overlooked by splendidly restored government buildings and the balustraded Spanish Embassy. With your back to the monument, looking up Calle Ecuador to Avenida Central, you can spy the rose window of the neo-Romanesque **Basilica de Don Bosco** (daily 6am–6pm), built in the 1950s. As well as being pleasantly airy with some lovely stained glass, the place is a glittering blue mass of modern mosaics, crafted in Italy and then brought to Panama for the centennial celebrations.

Bella Vista, Marbella and El Cangrejo

The neighbouring areas of Bella Vista, Marbella and El Cangrejo form the financial and commercial core of Panama City – what is often nebulously referred

Avenida Central & Plaza Cinco de Mayo (1km)

Instituto Geografico Nacional 'Tommy Guardia'

TRANSÍSTMICA (AV. SIMÓN BOLIVAR)

Universidad de Panamá

Casco Viejo (2km)

VIA ARGENTINA

CALLE 53 OESTE

CALLE 43B OESTE

AV 3 B NORTE

AV 2 B NORTE

CALLE ARTURO MOTA OESTE

CALLE EUSEBIO A MORALES

EL CANGREJO

Supermercado Rey

CALLE GUATEMALA (AV 1B NORTE)

Iglesia del Carmen

VIA ESPAÑA

BELLA VISTA

LA EXPOSICIÓN

AVENIDA JUSTO AROSEMENA

Parque Urraca

AV CHILE (AV 5 SUR)

CINTA COSTERA

Cine Alhambra

Santuario Nacional

AVENIDA RICARDO ARANGO (AV 3A SUR)

MARBELLA

World Trade Centre

Plaza New York

AVENIDA BALBOA

Bahía de Panamá

Multicentro

VIA ISRAEL (AV 6 SUR)

CORREDOR SUR

PUNTA PAITILLA

0   500 m

BELLA VISTA, MARBELLA & EL CANGREJO

78

ACCOMMODATION		RESTAURANTS & CAFÉS				BARS & CLUBS	
The Bristol Hotel	O	3½	20	Niko's Café	23	BLG	2
Casa Las Americas	A	Antica	21	La Novena	3	La Bodeguita	37
Euro Hotel	G	Beirut	28	NY Bagel Café	4	The Gallery	41
The Executive Hotel	M	Café Suzette	11	Palacio Lung Fung	1	Guru	38
Hostal La Casa de Carmen	H	Caffè Pomodoro	9	Petit Paris	42	Lips Dance Club	7
Hotel California	I	Carlito's	29	Pita-Pan Kosher	43	The Londoner	
Hotel Costa Azul	K	Dolce	5	La Posta	31	Pub	34
Hotel DeVille	P	Eurasia	30	Del Prado	14	Moods	33
Hotel El Parador	E	Habibi's	34	Restaurante		Pangea	6
Hotel Milan	C	Limoncillo		Barandas	O	El Pavo Real	8
Jungla House Hostel	B	Pony Club	22	Restaurante		People	36
Marriot Hotel	N	Madam Chang	40	Jimmy	25	S6is	32
Radisson Decapolis Hotel	Q	Manolo's	17	Rincón Habanero	16	Sahara	35
Residencial Los Arcos	J	Martin Fierro	13	Siete Mares	19	Sparkles	39
Sevilla Suites	F	Masala	24	Las Tinajas	27	Hotel Veneto	
Torres de Alba	D	Matsuei	15	El Trapiche	12	Casino	18
Zuly's Backpackers	L	Napoli	26			The Wine Bar	10

to as the Área Bancaria. Just before Avenida Justo Arosemena joins up with Vía España, buses turn off right down Calle 50, entering the undulating leafy barrio of **BELLA VISTA**, once brimming with colonial mansions dating back to the 1930s. Despite the invasive tower blocks of the more recent construction boom, some delightful examples of colonial architecture still persist, their red-tiled rooftops peeking out from behind high stone walls and luscious gardens. A few now house some of the area's nicest restaurants. To the northeast on Vía España, over a kilometre beyond the Basilica Don Bosco, on the corner with Avenida Manuel E. Batista, stands the incongruous twentieth-century neo-Gothic wedding cake of the **Iglesia del Carmen**. Particularly impressive when illuminated at night, the stained-glass windows up the aisles depict tropical flowers, while those higher up in the nave relate tales from the Old and New Testament. The neo-Byzantine mosaic altarpiece also grabs your attention.

The church marks the beginning of **EL CANGREJO**, home to many of Panama City's classier hotels and restaurants, as well as upmarket stores and shopping centres selling designer fashions and state-of-the-art electronics. This, and the adjacent areas of Bella Vista and **MARBELLA**, is also where much of the city's nightlife is concentrated. These areas are all fairly safe at night.

Avenida Balboa and the Cinta Costera

The sweeping arc of Avenida Balboa that connected the city's historic heartland, Casco Viejo, to its symbols of industrial progress, the skyscapers of Punta Paitilla, has been irrevocably altered by the recent addition of the **Cinta Costera**. This multimillion-dollar undertaking aimed to ease the traffic congestion by constructing a parallel four-lane highway between the two areas on a vast tract of reclaimed land, alongside a promenade complete with trees, benches and leisure facilities for city residents enjoy. The jury is still out on the project, which appears to have provided more concrete than anything else.

At the southwestern end of the Cinta Costera stands the distinctive blue-roofed **Mercado de Mariscos** (Mon–Sat 6am–6pm, closed one Mon a month for

▲ *Diablos rojos* grind along Vía España

fumigation). A fabulous place to wander around, it sells all shapes and sizes of seafood, some waving their antennae at you from tanks. Tuck into an enormous *ceviche* for \$3, or choose a fish to fry yourself or take upstairs to *Restaurante de Mariscos* (see p.88), where for a few dollars they'll cook it for you. Nearby is the temporarily relocated **muelle fiscal**, from where occasional boats to the Darién, Colombia and the Archipiélago de las Perlas leave (see p.99).

The boulevard's main attraction, midway along, is the magnificent **Monumento a Vasco Núñez de Balboa**. Erected in 1913, it shows the sixteenth-century explorer atop a globe, sword in one hand and flag in the other; once looking out in perpetual triumph on the southern ocean he "discovered", he now seems a tad lost in the traffic. Set back across Avenida Balboa is the grand Neoclassical facade of **Hospital Santo Tomás**, the largest public medical facility in the country, while a further 800m along the embankment, the pleasant **Parque Urracá** is named after the indigenous chief who famously defeated the Spaniards and later escaped from captivity (see p.331).

Punta Paitilla, Punta Pacífica and San Francisco

Jutting out into the sea at the northeastern end of the bay, the artificial peninsula of **Punta Paitilla**, packed with over fifty shimmering skyscrapers, constitutes one of Panama City's most emblematic views. Built around 1970, the forty-storey high-rises containing luxury apartments, many of which lie empty due to absent or fictitious owners, became one of the most exclusive residential areas and – with a synagogue and various kosher food stores and restaurants in the vicinity – a major Jewish neighbourhood. There are no specific sights but the area merits a wander if only to experience the eerily deserted streets squeezed between precarious-looking tower blocks, where your only human encounter is likely to be with an aproned domestic servant out on an errand. Head along leafy Avenida Italia and you end up at a small secluded **park**, peeking out to sea.

Round the headland, the more recently built skyscrapers of **Punta Pacífica** – many still under construction – house yet more opulent ocean-view residences. Both exclusive enclaves form part of the broader district of **San Francisco**, which extends across the Corredor Sur, the bypass which cuts across the bay to Tocumen International Airport. A former upmarket residential suburb like Bella Vista, dotted with tiled colonial-style villas, San Francisco is also gradually falling prey to the city's skyscraper addiction. Its two main landmarks are the **Centro de Convenciones ATLAPA**, the city's main convention centre (see p.94), and Parque Recreativo Omar Torrijos, generally shortened to **Parque Omar**, the city's largest green space, after the Parque Metropolitano. Hundreds of city residents take their morning exercise here (see p.96) or laze about at weekends, and it's home to a lovely outdoor swimming pool.

Former Canal Zone

Established in 1903 to protect the canal, the **former Canal Zone** ran the length of the waterway extending approximately 8km either side of it, though excluding Panama City and Colón. Under US military control until 1977, it was jointly administered by the US and Panamanian authorities until the eventual handover in 1999 (see p.337). Though now gradually being swallowed up by Panama City's urban sprawl, **Balboa** – what was effectively the administrative capital of the "Zone" – still retains some of its pleasant leafy landscaping and original architecture, most notably the palatial **Canal Administration Building** and exclusive residential enclave of Quarry Heights. Above, **Cerro Ancón** affords splendid views of the city and canal, including south to the **Amador Causeway**, which marks the Pacific entrance to the canal, and north to the forested **Parque Natural Metropolitano**, which, together with the **anthropology museum**, makes a fascinating half-day excursion.

Amador Causeway (Calzada de Amador)

Away from the deafening traffic, accompanying pollution and stultifying heat of downtown Panama City, the refreshing breezes of the **AMADOR CAUSEWAY** (Calzada de Amador) – the canal's Pacific breakwater – have made it an attractive weekend recreational area for middle-class Panamanians as well as a draw for tourists. Reinvigorated as a trendy spot to dance the night away, the causeway is also a pleasant venue to wine and dine while enjoying close-ups of transiting ships or more distant views of the Paitilla skyline. More practically, it is the departure point for **ferries** to Taboga and the Archipiélago de las Perlas as well as for canal tours (see p.102, p.104 & p.114). Consisting of three interconnecting islands – Islas Naos, Perico and Flamenco – the 3km causeway first came into existence in 1913, to help prevent crosscurrents from silting up the entry to the canal. The causeway's strategic location, protruding out into the bay, also resulted in Isla Flamenco becoming the site for a US military base. The island now hosts the command centre for the Autoridad del Canal de Panamá (ACP), which controls all traffic transiting the canal.

The best way to explore the area is on foot or on a bike. **Getting there** in the first place by public transport can be tricky though. Occasional, poorly marked minibuses can be picked up at the side of the Legislative Palace (50c) at Plaza Cinco de Mayo. Primarily for transporting workers, they are generally more frequent early in the morning, at lunchtime, late afternoon and round 10 to 11pm, when bars and restaurants shut down. Taxis may charge anything from $5 depending on how far down the causeway you want to travel. At the entrance to the causeway, a couple of outfits rent out bikes (see p.96), which can provide a fun way to get around since a cycleway runs along most of its length.

The causeway

Leaving Balboa, the wedge-shaped area of Amador marks the unofficial entrance to the causeway, the monstrous Vegas-style **Centro de Convenciones Figali** on the right providing the most prominent landmark. Built in 2003 to stage the Miss Universe competition, it is the preferred venue for international rock concerts. En route, to the west of the road, you'll pass a 2003-built, rocket-shaped monument, **Plaza de Etnías y Culturas**, representing Panama's status as the bridge across two oceans and its ethnic diversity. Beyond, stretching out into the water, is the jetty for the Balboa Yacht Club, where you can purchase ferry tickets to Contadora or enquire about a job as a line-handler for a canal transit (see p.114).

At the tip of the Amador wedge, where the road funnels into the causeway proper, lies the most talked-about construction project of recent years, the **Museo de la Biodiversidad** (see ⓦwww.biomuseopanama.org). Already years behind schedule, the museum is due to be housed in an architectural space designed by Frank Gehry, famous for the Guggenheim Museum in Bilbao. It is hoped that the eventual rainbow-coloured, multi-faceted roof of the new museum will provide Panama City with a similarly iconic structure.

The islands

Moving down the causeway, along the palm-lined cycleway and jogging path dotted with benches, the first island you encounter is **Isla Naos**, location of a marine research centre for the Smithsonian Tropical Research Institute (STRI), which maintains a small reserve on the adjoining peninsula, Punta Culebra. The **Punta Culebra Nature Centre** (Jan–March daily 10am–6pm; April–Dec Tues–Fri 1–5pm, Sat & Sun 10am–6pm; $2) is worth popping into, especially if you are travelling with young children. Set in a rare patch of tropical dry forest, the reserve offers a small visitor's centre, a couple of pools containing marine life and a short trail through the forest, where you should keep an eye out for green iguanas and two-toed sloths. Next to the reserve entrance is the departure point for the ferry to Taboga.

Moving on to **Isla Perico**, the road curves round past Las Brisas, a strip mall of smart bars and restaurants that gaze out towards Isla Taboga. **Isla Flamenco** marks the end of the causeway, featuring a cruise terminal and a flash marina sheltering sleek yachts and motor boats, surrounded by various pricey bars and restaurants – a real tourist trap for unwary cruise ship visitors, though its wonderful views make the island a choice spot for a sundowner – see p.90.

Cerro Ancón and Balboa

Visible from most of the surrounding area, the huge Panamanian flag fluttering in the breeze on the summit of **Cerro Ancón** (199m) is one of the city's most distinctive landmarks. What's more, the hill is topped with a protected area of secondary forest harbouring white-tailed deer, agoutis, sloths, Geoffroy's tamarin and white-faced capuchin monkeys and offers unparalleled views of the city and the canal. Lower down the northwest slope, overlooking Albrook, the imposing sandy-coloured **Edificio de la Administración del Canal de Panamá** demands a visit for its striking **murals** celebrating the canal's completion, while from the building's rear there is a decent view of **Balboa**, the former Canal Zone administrative capital – an area that merits further exploration.

Exploring the hill

A stroll up **CERRO ANCÓN** is rewarded with sweeping **vistas** of both the city, from Punta Paitilla to Casco Viejo, and the canal, stretching from the Bridge of

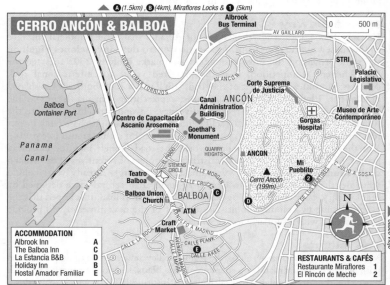

▲ **Ⓐ** (1.5km), **Ⓑ** (4km), Miraflores Locks & **❶** (5km)

CERRO ANCÓN & BALBOA

0   500 m

Albrook Bus Terminal

AV. GAILLARD

AVENIDA OMAR TORRIJOS

AV. ANCÓN

STRI

Palacio Legislativo

Balboa Container Port

Corte Suprema de Justicia

Canal Administration Building

ANCÓN

Centro de Capacitación Ascanio Arosemena

Goethal's Monument

Gorgas Hospital

Museo de Arte Contemporáneo

Panama Canal

QUARRY HEIGHTS

ANCON

AV. ROOSEVELT

EL PRADO

STEVENS CIRCLE

CALLE MORGAN

CALLE CRUCES

Cerro Ancón (199m)

Mi Pueblito **②**

JULIO A. SOSA

Teatro Balboa

BALBOA **Ⓒ**

Ⓓ

AV. DE LOS MÁRTIRES

Balboa Union Church

ATM

AVENIDA ARNULFO A. MADRID

N

Craft Market

CALLE LA BOCA

Ⓔ

CALLE PLANK

AVENIDA AMADOR

CALLE EMPIRE

CALLE AKEE

ACCOMMODATION	
Albrook Inn	**A**
The Balboa Inn	**C**
La Estancia B&B	**D**
Holiday Inn	**B**
Hostal Amador Familiar	**E**

RESTAURANTS & CAFÉS	
Restaurante Miraflores	**1**
El Rincón de Meche	**2**

▶ Casco Viejo

▼ Amador Causeway & Bridge of the Americas

the Americas as far as the Puente Centenario, which spans the entrance to the famous Gaillard Cut, 10km away. By the mirador overlooking the city, just below the flagpole, the seated serene bronze figure of poet **Amelia Denis de Icaza** is remembered for her poem "*Al Cerro Ancón*"; written in 1900, it served as a nationalist rallying cry.

Although you can get a **taxi** to the summit ($8–10 from any central area, including waiting time), it's well worth walking up in the early morning or late afternoon, when you're likely to encounter keel-billed toucans croaking from the treetops and a host of other wildlife. To reach there **on foot**, cross Avenida de los Mártires, behind the Palacio Legislativo on Plaza Cinco de Mayo, and cut through to the road that winds through the old Gorgas Hospital and Supreme Court (see map opposite). Skirting round the northern side of the hill, the road divides: to the right, it drops down to the Canal Administration Building, while ahead it climbs to **Quarry Heights**, the former US military command centre, which is now an exclusive leafy residential area (renamed Altos de Ancón) and is worth a short detour for its unique Zonian wooden architecture.

From the Quarry Heights security gate, it's a twenty- to thirty-minute hike to the summit; take first left, then immediate right. A few hundred metres later you'll pass a police checkpoint and gate, which is only open to traffic between 7am and 6pm, though you can slip through on foot at any hour. For an alternative and more direct route down the hill, take the unmarked steps here, which lead down to the theme-park-style **Mi Pueblito** (Tues–Sun 9am–9pm; $2), a set of four rather tacky replica villages, recreating various traditional architectural styles while flogging overpriced crafts. The main incentive is the **café-restaurant** *El Rincón de Meche* (daily 7am–early evening) on the pseudo-Spanish colonial square, whose fresh fruit juices aid recovery from any physical exertion on the hill. On Friday and Saturday evenings at 6pm there are free **folk-dancing** presentations.

The stately **Edificio de la Administración del Canal de Panamá** (Canal Administration Building), which dominates the hill's western slope, houses four arresting **murals** that celebrate the Herculean achievement of building the canal. (Tell the security guard that you want to see the "*murales*".). Decorating an elegant domed marble rotunda, just inside the main entrance, they were painted by New York artist William Van Ingen, known for his work in the Library of Congress in Washington DC, and they graphically convey the enormous scale and complexity of the labour. A series of evocative lithographs adorn the outer walls of the rotunda.

Balboa

The back terrace of L'Administración – push through the fire doors at the back of the rotunda – surveys the heart of **BALBOA**, namely **El Prado**, a palm-lined grassy rectangle measured to match the length and width of a lock chamber that cuts through the district, extending from the Goethals Monument at the foot of the administration steps to Stevens Circle at the far end. When George Goethals took over as chief engineer of the canal in 1907, he surveyed all that his predecessor, John Stevens, had achieved and prophetically wrote to his son, "Mr Stevens has done an amount of work for which he will never get any credit, or if he gets any, will not get enough." Nowhere is this more evident than in the monuments to their labours: while **Stevens Circle** consists of a small and rather neglected memorial down the far end of the Prado, the cream marble **Goethals Monument** monolith stands tall at the foot of the canal authority's seat of power with water cascading over three stepped marble platforms – symbolizing the three sets of locks – into a pool below.

Diagonally across from the monument stands the former Balboa High School, site of the dramatic "flag riots" (see p.337) of 1964 that culminated in the deaths of 21 Panamanians. At the back of the building on Avenida Roosevelt a breezeway leads to a steady burning flame, the centrepiece of a memorial to the 21 martyrs, whose names are inscribed on the surrounding pillars. The building is now the **Centro de Capacitación Ascanio Arosemena** (Mon–Fri 8am–5pm), which trains canal employees and contains an excellent collection of **photographs** of the canal construction and other **memorabilia**, including rusting tools, porcelain from the Tivoli Hotel – the grandest hotel of the Canal Zone era – and Goethals' hat rack. If your Spanish is not up to the canal museum in Casco Viejo then this exhibition, with bilingual labelling, will give you a good enough flavour. To reach the displays, enter the former school gates, taking the first right turn through a building, across a courtyard and into a second building.

A stroll down the Prado takes you to Avenida Arnulfo Arias Madrid, across which stands the faded Art Deco **Teatro Balboa**, worth peeking inside for its splendid mosaic floors. Built in the 1940s to entertain Zonians with a mixture of films and live shows, it is now home to Panama's national symphony orchestra (see p.94). Turning left along the main road, you hit the main intersection with Calle la Boca, where you cannot fail to notice the vainglorious bronze **monument** to former president Arnulfo Arias Madrid (see p.336), standing on the end of what looks like a giant seesaw with citizens imploring his help crawling towards him. Across from the monument, at the back of the former Army and Navy YMCA building, is one of the city's better **craft markets** (see p.95), which also has some stalls inside.

Parque Natural Metropolitano and Museo Antropológico Reina Torres de Araúz

After a few days in Panama City being deafened by the drilling of construction workers and roar of *diablos rojos*, you are likely to find yourself craving some peace and quiet. Though it's not quite far enough from the city centre to escape the hum of traffic, the **Parque Natural Metropolitano** (daily 6am–5pm; office hours Mon–Fri 8am–5pm, Sat 8am–1pm; $2; Ⓦ www.parquemetropolitano.org) nevertheless offers real tranquillity. An early morning stroll there combines well with a visit to the **Museo Antropológico Reina Torres de Araúz**, which houses most of the country's pre-Columbian treasures, a stone's throw from the park office at the junction of Avenida Ascanio Villalaz and Avenida Juan Pablo II.

Exploring the park

Three kilometres to the northeast of Albrook Airport, this hilly patch of semi-deciduous tropical forest offers some excellent **birdwatching** and glimpses of the city and canal area from three lookouts and five short but well-marked **trails**. Arriving early in the morning enhances your chances of seeing sloths entwined round branches, agoutis or koatis snuffling in the undergrowth and colourful and abundant birdlife, including golden-collared mannakins, slaty-tailed trogons and red-lored Amazon parrots. The most interesting meander is the 1.7km **Camino del Mono Tití**, named after the Geoffroy's tamarin monkeys that can occasionally be sighted when making the moderate climb to the viewpoint. From the main park entrance, you'll need to walk 1km along the **Sendero El Roble**, so called because of the pink-flowering oak trees along the path. To make a circular route, walk the Mono Titi trail one way, returning via the steeper but shorter **Sendero La Cienaguita** ("little marsh" – only visible in the rainy season).

Visiting the museum

The **Museo Antropológico Reina Torres de Araúz** (Mon–Fri 9am–3.45pm, closed Sat & Sun; $2; Ⓣ 501 4740) is Panama's finest anthropological collection, named after Panama's foremost anthropologist, Reina Torres de Araúz; the driving force behind the country's regional and national museums, and author of the first major published study of Panama's indigenous peoples, she was awarded the Orden de Vasco Nuñez de Balboa, Panama's greatest national honour. The museum itself contains an impressive array of **pre–Columbian gold**, some beautifully painted **ceramics** and a fascinating array of stone sculptures from the **Barriles culture** – believed to be the country's oldest civilization. Most of the gold items are *huacas* – precious objects recovered from the burial sites of prominent *caciques* (chiefs). These include weapons, tools and some very intricately carved jewellery, often in fantastical zoomorphic designs. The next section showcases some well-preserved ceramics, primarily for ceremonial use, comprising three distinctive regional designs. Spread out across the far end of the hall are stone objects recovered from Sitio Barriles, west of Volcán (see p.240), including ornate ceremonial *metates* (grinding stones) and curious large carved figures, some seemingly depicting chiefs or other prominent men being carried on the shoulders of slaves.

Practicalities

The main entrance, where the **park office** is located, lies 200m along Avenida Juan Pablo II after the junction with Avenida Ascanio Villalaz, where you can grab a free **map** or purchase a booklet (in English or Spanish) to guide yourself round Sendero La Cienaguita; if the place is closed, you can usually locate a warden in the vicinity but it's hard to get lost in the park since it's only about two square kilometres and the trails are well signed. With 24 hours notice, you can arrange for a **guided tour** in either English or Spanish (3hr; $15/group plus $3 entry/person). Birdwatching tours are also held periodically (see p.43).

Panamá Viejo and the eastern suburbs

You'll need some imagination to reconstruct the neglected ruins of Panamá La Vieja, or **PANAMÁ VIEJO**, as it's more often called, once the premier colonial city on the isthmus. Yet while there's no comparison with the magnificent Mayan sites elsewhere in Central America, the half-day excursion is made worthwhile by

> ## Panamá Viejo's treasure trail
>
> If you've buffed up on your history while touring Casco Viejo, you'll probably already be familiar with the tale of **Nuestra Señora de la Asunción de Panamá**, to give Panamá Viejo its full name. The original site of the Pacific settlement established in 1519 by the infamous Pedro Arias de Ávila, it was razed to the ground in 1671, following the Welsh pirate Henry Morgan's sacking of the city.
>
> Despite the surprisingly swampy location, Panama City prospered; by the early seventeeth century, it boasted an impressive cathedral, seven convents, numerous churches, a hospital, two hundred warehouses and around five thousand houses, driven by the city's commercial importance as the Pacific terminal of the Spanish Crown's **treasure trail**, sending silks and spices from the East and plundered silver and gold from Peru to Europe via the isthmus. This trade route necessitated the construction of a huge customs house, a treasury and a mint located in the most heavily fortified area of the Casas Reales (Royal Houses), the symbol of the Spanish Crown's might, originally separated from the rest of the city by a moat and wooden palisade. Little more than a pile of rubble now remains of these once impressive buildings, a result of some of the original stones being quarried for construction of the new city, coupled with modern governments' neglect, although the Iglesia del Convento de la Concepción and the cathedral bell tower have been restored.

the view from the bell tower alone, taking in Punta Pacífica to the southwest and, to the northeast, **Costa del Este**, the ambitious business and residential development built on the site of the former city dump.

More appealing vistas lie northwards across the eastern suburbs to the foothills of the Cordillera Central, where your eye is caught by the alien-looking hilltop dome that is the **Bahá'í House of Worship** (daily 9am–6pm; free). The faith developed in nineteenth-century Persia, and this is one of seven churches around the world, with the eighth being constructed in Chile. Interested visitors can attend the Sunday service (10am; 30min) or wander the flower-filled gardens. A taxi ride will cost a few dollars from Supermercado Rey at Milla Ocho – take any Transístimica bus going as far as San Isidro.

Museo del Sitio de Panamá la Vieja

Taking a combined ticket, which covers all the ruins and the museum, is the best option, visiting the **Museo del Sitio de Panamá la Vieja** (Tues–Sun 8am–5pm; $3 museum, $4 ruins, $6 combined ticket; ℡226 8915, ⓦwww.panamaviejo .org) first, as it will help orientate you. The two-storey block contains some interesting exhibits with information predominantly given in Spanish though with some summaries in English. The top floor displays items discovered during archaeological excavations, described in greater detail on the ground floor. There are some exquisitely preserved **pre-Columbian artefacts** – though labels are often frustratingly absent – together with pottery, coins and utensils from colonial times, and a useful interactive **scale model** of the city in 1671.

The ruins

Once outside the museum, backtrack 100m to peer over at the **Puente del Matadero** ("Bridge of the Slaughterhouse"), named after the neighbouring abattoir, which marked the western limit of the old city. Returning east along the shoreline, continue along the gravel path a few hundred metres past extensive mud flats being probed by hundreds of migrating waders. Passing the scarcely visible or recognizable Iglesia y Convento de la Merced, which survived Morgan's assault and was relocated to Casco Viejo, and the Iglesia y Convento de San Francisco, cross the road at the speed ramp, turning east down Calle de la Empedrada. To the left stands the well-preserved **Iglesia del Convento de la Concepción**, the city's only convent for women, built in 1597. Peer over the nearby wall and you'll find the impressive remains of the convent's seventeenth-century reservoir. The tour continues past the skeletal remnants of the Jesuit Iglesia y Convento de la Compañia de Jesús before reaching the Cincuentenario.

Once across the road, you are drawn to the vast open space of the **Plaza Mayor**, overlooked by the imposing cathedral **bell tower** (Tues–Sun 8.30am–6.30pm), one of Panama's most distinctive landmarks. It's here that you can best appreciate the city's former grandeur. The plaza constituted the social hub of the city, hosting events ranging from political rallies to bull fights, and it was surrounded by the most prestigious buildings, including to the east the *Cabildo* (City Hall) and the cathedral – **La Catedral de la Nuestra Señora de la Asunción**. The stone edifice that replaced the original wooden structure was completed between 1619 and 1629. The magnificently restored belfry now has a modern staircase, which is worth climbing for the views. Sporadic free guided tours are conducted in English and Spanish but depend on numbers, available staff and the weather. Enquire at the small information booth near the tower, or at the museum.

Leaving the cathedral by the vestibule, you can just make out the remains of the **Casa Alarcón**; formerly the domicile of the bishop, this nobleman's home dating back to the 1640s is the largest known and best preserved private house on the site. Beyond lies the crumbling Dominican Iglesia y Convento de Santo Domingo. A few hundred metres north along the Cincuentenario, little remains of the **Iglesia de San José**, which survived the fire of 1671 and contained the splendid golden altar that now sits in the church of the same name in Casco Viejo (see p.73). At the old northern city limit, a couple of hundred metres beyond, Panamá Viejo's famous **Puente del Rey** (King's Bridge) still spans the Río Gallinero, where it marked the gateway to the Camino Real, the conquistadors' mule trail across the isthmus. If you explore that far, exercise caution, since the surrounding Río Abajo neighbourhood is an impoverished barrio and tourist muggings are not unknown.

Practicalities

Getting to the ruins by **public transport** is easy. Direct buses from Albrook bus terminal with "Panamá Viejo" on the windscreen run about every thirty minutes, passing through Santa Ana and Cinco de Mayo before stopping some thirty minutes later outside the museum on the Cincuentenario. To catch the return bus from the ruins, wait on the corner of the road heading back into the city, near what is possibly Panama's only pedestrian crossing.

Restaurants and cafés

Panama City's cosmopolitan nature is reflected in its **restaurants**: anything from US fast food to Greek, Italian, Chinese, Japanese and French cuisine can easily be found in addition to traditional Panamanian dishes and excellent seafood. Bookings are advisable at weekends, if there's live music or a show, and during holiday periods. The most celebrated areas to eat out in are **Bella Vista** and **El Cangrejo** – along and around Vía España, Vía Argentina, Vía Veneto and Calle Uruguay – and **Casco Viejo**, with a handful of restaurants sprinkled along the **Amador Causeway**. Cheap hot and cold **takeaway** meals are available from the Rey supermarket (open 24hr) on Vía España, while the **food courts** in the city's numerous shopping malls are popular at weekends.

Casco Viejo

Casco Viejo is a destination for the city's smart set, jamming the streets in the evenings with their 4WDs as they head for the chic venues in converted colonial houses, though there are a few open-air restaurants, where you can soak up the historic surroundings, and the odd inexpensive hole-in-the wall joint, where you can get a meal for under three dollars. See map, p.69.

Las Bóvedas Plaza de Francia ☎ 228 8058. Soak up the history as well as the fine wine in the dimly lit caverns of former dungeons. The French-inspired cuisine is both mouthwatering and tastefully presented but plays second fiddle to the intimate ambience. Mains $16–25. Live jazz after 9pm on Fri and occasionally on Sat. Mon–Sat from 5.30pm.

Buzios C 1 Las Bóvedas ☎ 228 9045. One of the best places for alfresco dining in Panama City, on a paved terrace set amid lush tropical plants, offering an international menu with a Mediterranean seafood bias, accompanied by Brazilian music. Try the snapper fillet on ripe plantain and a bed of oriental vegetables, but leave room for the fresh fruit mousse. Most mains $12–17. Tues–Sun from noon.

Café Coca-Cola Plaza Santa Ana, C 12 at Av Central. The self-proclaimed "oldest café in Panama" and something of an institution among the city's older residents, who gather to drink coffee, read the paper and discuss the news. Filling Panamanian staples (ceviche, chicken with rice, soups) for about $3, and generously portioned breakfasts cooked to order. Good coffee. Daily 7am–11pm.

Caffè Per Due Av "A" at C 3. Italian-owned and operated, this little gem serves scrumptious oven-crisped pizzas ($5–9) and salads ($4–6) and is a popular spot for afternoon coffee and cake. Tues–Sun 8.30am–10pm.

Casablanca Plaza Bolívar at C 4 ☏ 212 0040. A delightful outdoor setting (with a/c inside if you prefer) plays host to well-prepared, wide-ranging dishes from burgers, kebabs and salads ($7–13) to more substantial seafood, meat or poultry mains. Kick-start dinner with a mojito before trying ribs in passion fruit sauce ($16.50). Daily noon until late.

Diablo Rosso Av "A" at C 7 ⓦ www.diablorosso .com. Eclectic mix of design boutique and funky art café, serving inventive salads, dips and delicious cakes. "*Cena cine*", involving food and a film, on Tues nights. Mon–Sat 8am–7pm.

🏃 **Granclement** Av Central at C 4. A fabulous indulgence after tramping the streets of Casco Viejo, this French-style artisanal ice-cream parlour offers flavours you wouldn't dream of – basil, lavender, Earl Grey tea – as well as chocolate every which way and an array of mouthwatering sorbets, though at a price. Mon–Thurs 11.30am–8pm, Fri & Sat 11.30am–11pm, Sun 12.30–8pm.

Manolo Caracol Av Central at C 3 ☏ 228 4640, ⓦ www.manolocaracol.net. Arguably Panama's most famous restaurant, offering an entertaining culinary bombardment of innovative tapas in a relaxed environment. You'll pay $12 for a five-dish lunch and $25 for a ten-dish dinner but with wine (over $30 a bottle) and tax on top you'll be hitting your wallet hard. Mon–Fri noon–3pm & 7–10pm, Sat 7pm–midnight.

🏃 **René Café** Plaza Catedral at C 7 ☏ 262 3487. Provided a 4WD isn't parked out front, the outdoor tables provide a splendid vantage point for admiring the cathedral while savouring a good-value five-piece tapas-style lunch ($9) washed down with a glass of wine. Dinner is a pricier $20 and better enjoyed in the intimate Provençal ambience inside. Mon–Sat 10am–3pm & 6–10pm.

🏃 **SuperMercado Gourmet** Av "A" at C 6. Upmarket café-shop serving delicious deli sandwiches and excellent light lunches for $4–7. Set yourself up for the day with a full breakfast ($4) and browse the selection of hard-to-find gourmet and imported goods. Mon–Sat 8am–7pm.

Calidonia and La Exposición

Reflecting their working-class populations, most dining options in these neighbourhoods are inexpensive and particularly busy at lunchtimes, serving up traditional Panamanian fare. See map, p.76.

Café Boulevard Balboa Av Balboa at C 31 Este. An a/c oasis of civilization in the dust, noise and endless construction work outside, livened up by a smart lunch-time business crowd. Specializing in toasted sandwiches ($3–4), the lengthy menu also includes more filling Panamanian dishes and a good-value three-course *menu del día* for $7.50. Mon–Sat 6.30am until late.

Mercado Publico Av "B" & Av Balboa. A dozen *fondas* serving heaps of tasty hot food for a couple of dollars (see p.75).

Nelson's Café Av Central at C 18 Este. Offers an appetizing plateful of *comida típica* for under $3, usually with a generous amount of vegetables. Daily early until late.

Parillada El Estado Av Perú at C 37 Este. Far from tourists and tourist prices, tuck into a delectable piece of grilled or fried fish or chicken with *patacones* and a smidgen of salad for $6. Mon–Sat 11am–10pm.

🏃 **Restaurante de Mariscos** Av Balboa, above the Mercado de Mariscos. Best for lunch so you can enjoy the hustle and bustle of the stalls below, where you can buy your seafood – the restaurant will cook it for a few dollars. Or opt for something from their own menu. Daily 11am–7pm.

Rincón El Tableño Av Cuba at C 31 Este. Popular cafeteria whose huge customer turnover ensures the *comida típica* is hot and fresh. Try the *tamales* or the house speciality, *chicheme chorrerano*, downed with a fresh juice. Panamanian breakfasts go for under $2 and lunch for under $3. Daily 6am–5.30pm.

Bella Vista, Marbella and El Cangrejo

From the converted colonial mansions of Bella Vista to the neon lights of **El Cangrejo**, this area offers by far the greatest variety of dining and drinking venues, mainly at the mid- to high-end of the price scale. See map, p.78.

3½ C Guatemala at C Eusebio A. Morales. Set back from the road, this self-effacing cafeteria offers superb value. $2 will get you a choice of three fresh vegetable dishes plus a bowl of soup. Mon–Sat 8am–7.30pm.

Antica Vía España at C Eusebio A. Morales. Funky, fluorescent Italian ice-cream parlour serving authentic *gelati* in a rainbow of flavours. If you need something to perk you up, try their cappuccino with croissant combo ($3). Free wi-fi. Mon–Sat 9am–11pm, Sun 2–10.30pm.

Beirut C 49A Este at Av Justo Arosemena, opposite the *Marriott*, ☎ 214 3815. A grotto-like ceiling, faux vines, murals and mosaics provide the setting for appetizers from $4 a dish and good-value, large combo platters, with mains from around $9. Hookah rental and occasional belly-dancing on weekends are additional attractions. Daily noon–late.

Café Suzette Vía Argentina opposite *Churrería Manolo's*. This delightful Venezuelan-run café-restaurant is a great lunch spot, serving delicious sweet and savoury crepes – try the smoked turkey and brie – for under $7. Mon–Sat noon–late, Sun from 1pm.

🏃 Caffè Pomodoro Vía Veneto at C Eusebio A. Morales in *ApartHotel Las Vegas* ☎ 269 5836. Extremely popular Italian place offering pasta and pizzas ($5–10). The tropical garden, decorated with fairy lights, is buzzing in the evening. Daily 7am–midnight.

Carlito's Parque Urracá at C 45 Este ☎ 225 0181. Very pleasant café-pizzeria with a leafy terrace, popular with families for filling empanadas and inexpensive, crispy pizzas (from $4.50 for a 10-inch one) with a vast range of toppings. Leave room for the tangy lemon pie. There's another outlet in Obarrio; both do takeaways. Mon–Sat 11am–10pm.

🏃 Dolce Vía Argentina between Av 3B Norte and Einstein's Head. Excellent funky little café and pastry shop, with a bar and book exchange – a great spot for a snack or light meal, including German specialities. Breakfast (oatmeal, waffles, eggs or fruit) is also a treat. Mon–Sat 8am–10pm, Sat & Sun 8am–6pm.

Eurasia C 48 between Av Federico Boyd & Parque Urracá ☎ 264 7859. Innovative fusion cuisine at its best, blending European and Oriental culinary traditions in this attractive high-end restaurant on the first floor of a Bella Vista colonial mansion. Mains average $20. Closed Sat lunch and all day Sun.

Habibi's C Uruguay at C 48 ☎ 264 3647. Buzzing corner terrace that's a well-established gathering spot for groups heading off to party. Prices alas have been shooting up with the place's popularity – $3 for a local beer or $12.50 for *corvina à la plancha*. Stick

to the tasty Middle Eastern dishes; mezes start at just under $20 for two. Daily noon–late.

Machu Picchu C Eusebio A. Morales ☎ 264 8501, next to *Martín Fierro*. The original Peruvian restaurant in Panama, decorated with pictures of its namesake and Andean weavings and specializing in seafood. The room is plain and the atmosphere low key but the moderately priced cuisine is decent and the pisco sours slip down a treat. Mon–Sat noon–3pm, 6–11pm, Sun noon–9pm.

Madam Chang C 48 between C Uruguay & C 49 ☎ 269 1313. The pre-eminent Chinese restaurant in Panama. Exquisitely prepared dishes from around the country (with a few Thai options thrown in) are given a contemporary twist and served in elegant surroundings. Daily noon–3pm, 6–11pm.

Manolo's Vía Veneto at C "D". A city institution with a popular corner terrace (or a/c dining), which is a great spot for a drink while people-watching. There's a good variety of light bites and more substantial mains on the menu but the food is no more than average and prices are creeping up. Daily 6am–2am.

Martin Fierro C Eusebio A. Morales at C Guatemala ☎ 264 1927. Forget the rest of the menu; meat takes centre stage here – reputedly the best steaks in the city ($15–25), to be accompanied by some fine red wine in elegant surroundings though standards can vary. Mon–Sat noon–3pm & 6–11pm; Sun noon–9.30pm.

Masala Av Justo Arosemena between C 44 Este & C 45 Este ☎ 225 0105. Cosy little restaurant with Indian trimmings and wooden tables or comfortable floor cushions for dining. Mains are around $14 and the *thali* platters, which could easily feed two, offer good value at $17. Mon–Sat 12–3pm & 6–10pm.

Matsuei C Eusebio A. Morales, no. 12A, opposite C "D" ☎ 264 9562. A Japanese restaurant with friendly service from waitresses in kimonos and a large menu that offers sushi, tempura, curries and teriyaki, involving a range of local and imported seafood. Prices range from $9 to $30 for a large sushi tray (which can be shared). Closed Sun lunch.

Napoli C 57 Este Obarrio, off Vía España ☎ 263 8800. Generally considered to dish up the best pizza in the city, this favourite of middle-class Panamanians is jammed with families at weekends. The thin-crust pizzas are excellent and the pasta dishes fine, but the atmosphere is bland. Tues–Sun 11am–midnight.

Niko's Café C 51 Este just off Vía España. The unpromising frontage masks another city institution. This no-frills 24hr cafeteria is the original of an expanding empire (also outlets in Albrook bus terminal, El Dorado Mall and C 50) You can take out or eat in various good-value hot dishes and sides for under $5.

🏃 **La Novena** Vía Argentina no. 71, opposite Happy Copy ☎ 264 3376. Named after Beethoven's Ninth Symphony, this vegetarian restaurant is a great lunchtime venue offering delicious prepared-to-order dishes (around $8) such as stuffed peppers, zucchini curry and range of wholesome soups, which you can follow with a wicked chocolate dessert. No alcohol, which makes it less popular in the evenings. Mon–Sat 10am–10pm.

🏃 **NY Bagel Café** Cabeza de Einstein, C Arturo Motta at Vía Argentina. A popular hangout for travellers, expats and local business folk, serving a wide variety of their namesake plus fruit smoothies, good coffee and more. Most items are under $5; free wi-fi. Mon–Fri 7am–8pm, Sat 8am–8pm, Sun 8am–3pm.

Petit Paris C 53 Este opposite *Felipe Motta*. A genuine French-run patisserie-boulangerie serving appetizing breakfasts and light lunches at Paris prices. Forget the delicious bread and quiches and indulge in the exquisitely crafted cakes and chocolates ($2–6), to be enjoyed with great coffee or a hot chocolate. Free wi-fi. Daily 7am–8pm.

🏃 **La Posta** C49 at C Uruguay ☎ 269 1076, ⊛ www.lapostapanama.com. The Fifties' Havana ambience of this beautifully restored mansion set in lush tropical gardens makes this a favourite of Panama's elite. The tiled floors, wooden ceiling fans and Cuban music all enhance your appreciation of the gourmet cuisine. Prices are not as exorbitant as they might be and you can get a bottle of wine for under $25. Mon–Sat noon–2.30pm & 7–10.30pm.

🏃 **Del Prado** Vía Argentina at C Guatemala. Long-standing, reliable 24hr diner with a pleasant outdoor terrace, indoor seating with a/c and an extensive, well-priced menu including chargrilled steaks, chicken or fish from $8. You can even get a bottle of wine for $12.

Restaurante Barandas *The Bristol Hotel*, Av Aquilino de la Guardia. Barandas, a byword for formal elegant dining, is renowned for exquisitely prepared, innovative Panamanian cuisine created by celebrity chef Cuquita Arias. Examples include green plantain wontons with mango sauce and sea bass in tamarind sauce. Prices are up in the stratosphere,

with the Sun brunch for just under $35 providing the best value.

🏃 **Restaurante Jimmy** C Manuel M. Icaza, just off Vía España. Extremely popular 24hr restaurant-cafeteria in the heart of El Cangrejo, with a wide choice of Panamanian and Greek food, plenty of light bites and fresh, strong coffee. A second larger open-air version serving succulent barbecued fare sits opposite the ATLAPA Convention Centre on Calle Cincuentenario (Daily 11.30am–11.30pm).

Rincón Habanero Vía Argentina, opposite *El Trapiche* ☎ 213 2560. Sample a slice of Cuba in this dark wood-panelled restaurant, from the rum to the cigars and even on the plasma screen. The handful of cosy tables are always packed with people enjoying reasonably priced food ($4–8) featuring copious black beans, accompanied by hot salsa tunes. Mon–Sat 11am–11pm.

Siete Mares C Guatemala at Vía Argentina ☎ 264 0144. Holding the reputation for the best seafood in Panama City, this place rarely disappoints. Mains from around $12 include corvina with crab in Pernod, and jumbo shrimps in passion fruit sauce, to be savoured in sleek surroundings, from the glass waterfall at the entrance to the piano bar accompaniment (Mon–Sat after 8pm). Daily 11.30am until late.

Las Tinajas C 51 at Av Federico Boyd ☎ 263 7890, ⊛ www.tinajaspanama.com. This delightful colonial mansion in Bella Vista is a favourite destination of tour groups, who flock here to experience authentic Panamanian food and a traditional dance show involving swishing *polleras* and devil dances. Grab a table early to ensure a decent view of the tiny stage. Shows are Tues–Sat at 9pm for $5 provided you spend at least $12 on food. Try the *surtido de mariscos*, a platter of seafood appetizers.

El Trapiche Vía Argentina between C Guatemala & Av 2B Norte ☎ 269 4353. Frequently billed as the place to go to try traditional food, such as *mondongo* (tripe) and *tamal de olla* (local tamale without the leaf wrapping), though it attracts Panamanians too. Prices are moderate (mains $8–13) and there is a lively atmosphere on the terrace, but the food quality is variable. Daily 7am–11pm.

Former Canal Zone

The **Amador Causeway** provides a cool, breezy setting with fabulous views across the bay. The downside is that a taxi there and back (there are few and infrequent buses) will add another $10–15 to your bill.

Café Barko Isla Flamenco, Amador Causeway ☎ 314 0000. Rather touristy spot aimed at luring visitors off their cruise ships, but the panoramic

views of Paitilla's silver skyline and Casco Viejo's church towers glistening in the afternoon sun are hard to beat. A great place for a sundowner, though you can also enjoy juicy seafood including sushi. Free traditional dance shows every Thurs. Daily 11am–late.

Kayuco Isla Flamenco, Amador Causeway. With outdoor tables overlooking the marina, it's by far the liveliest place in the area to enjoy a few sundowners with friends accompanied by some sizzling grilled seafood (from snacks at $2 to a mixed grill for two for $8.50) Daily 10am–late.

Mi Ranchito Amador Causeway, near the Punta Culebra Nature Centre. The restaurant's pleasant open-air tables are extremely popular with locals for enjoying cocktails, seafood and sunset city views. Mains $8–12. Daily noon–late.

Restaurante Miraflores Miraflores Visitor Centre, Miraflores Locks ☏ 232 3120. See map on p.112. A new chef has reinvigorated this restaurant, offering both buffet and à la carte formal dining, but you're still basically paying for the location so reserving a balcony table well in advance is a must. You'll see more canal action if you opt for the evening floodlit experience. It's not cheap, but it's a once-in-a-lifetime experience. Daily noon–11pm.

Al Tambor de la Alegría Las Brisas, Amador Causeway ☏ 314 3380. Another place offering a traditional food and dancing combo consisting of an hour-long romp through Panama's history using drama and dance, from Kuna Yala to the Azuero. The Sun breakfast buffet plus show (10am) is $12, whereas the evening performances (Wed–Sat 9.30pm) are pricier. Tues–Sun from 5pm & Sun buffet.

Other areas

There are several up-and-coming areas for wining and dining, including round the entrance to **Punta Paitilla** and the neighbourhood of **San Francisco**.

Limoncillo Pony Club C 69 Este, San Francisco, near Parque Recreativo Omar ☏ 270 0807. See map, p.78. Fine-dining favourite offering innovative modern American cuisine at reasonable rates, in stylish low-key surroundings. Closed Sat lunch & Sun.

Palacio Lung Fung Transístmica and C 62 Oeste ☏ 260 4011. See map, p.78. Some way from the action, in Los Angeles, but every taxi driver knows this vast oriental palace, whose thousand-seater upstairs ballroom with its glittering chandeliers is packed at weekends with Panamanians enjoying dim sum breakfast (until 11.30am). The food is average but the social experience makes it well worth the trip. Daily 7am–11pm.

Pita-Pan Kosher Bal Harbour, Punta Paitilla. See map, p.78. An illuminated 3D mural of Jerusalem welcomes you to this casual cafeteria popular with Jewish families, serving moderately priced appetizing dishes, with lots of veggie options – hummus, babaganush, falafel, alongside the ubiquitous pasta and pizza and even kosher sushi. Mon–Fri 7am–3pm (until 5pm Fri), Sun 9am–9pm.

Nightlife and entertainment

There's plenty to keep you entertained in Panama City – all night if you fancy. The vast array of **bars** and **restaurants** is complemented by all manner of entertainments: from a hip-swinging salsa session to an evening at the opera; from a flutter at the roulette table to an evening of jazz in Casco Viejo; from a booze cruise up the canal to a folk dancing performance. And of course there are several **cinemas** in the capital – mostly multiplexes in shopping malls showcasing the latest Hollywood offerings, generally in English with subtitles (*subtitulada*; see Ⓦ www.cinespanama.com), though less mainstream fare can be found – try La Casona de la Brujas in Casco Viejo (see p.93) and Cinepolis.

Panama City arguably has the best **clubbing** in Central America, although many places feel like imitations of Miami. Nightclubs are known as **discotecas** – ask for the former and you'll end up at a strip joint. Places open, close and reinvent themselves at an alarming rate: the current hotspots in terms of discotecas and bars are located in and around **Calle Uruguay** in Bella Vista, spreading out towards El Cangrejo and Marbella, blasting everything from techno to reggae and reggaeton to salsa. The new **Zona Viva** in the Amador Causeway offers an enclosed, mall-style "street" of bars, music joints and restaurants with secure parking, but is hard to reach via public transport and pricey in terms of taxis.

In contrast, an alternative scene is burgeoning in **Casco Viejo**, where, in the summer season, free open-air concerts are put on by the municipality in the main plazas. There are some fairly hip venues for live salsa and jazz in Casco Viejo though the January jazz festival (Ⓦwww.panamajazzfestival.com) – founded by Panama's internationally renowned jazz pianist, Danilo Pérez – will take you to venues across the city. You may also be lucky enough to catch Panama's most famous musical megastar on stage, Grammy-winning salsa artist, actor and sometime politician Rubén Blades.

Most **discotecas** are open Tuesday to Saturday, and get going around midnight. Entry will generally set you back $5–20 and may include an open bar up until a certain time and the usual "Ladies Night" enticements. Local beers cost around $3.50 with imports $4.50 and spirits and cocktails $5–6. If you're in a group, buying a bottle of spirits between you (which can sometimes get the entry charge waived) or a *cubetazo* (bucket of beer) will help keep costs down. In the smarter bars and clubs you'll need to dress up – no shorts or sandals. Try Ⓦwww.eyeonpanama .com for up-to-date reviews of bars and clubs. The **gay clubbing** scene, which is vibrant though fairly discreet, is currently concentrated in three main venues: Lips, BLG and Xscape Bar, and you can check out events at Ⓦwww.farraurbana .com and www.les-507.com.

Several large **casinos** are conveniently located near or in the high-end hotels. The larger ones, such as the Majestic (in Multicentro by the *Radisson Decapolis Hotel*) and the *Hotel Veneto Casino*, often have live music acts at weekends. There's also a great state-of-the-art **bowling** alley (Extreme Planet, Av Balboa) with vast sports screens, a bar and comfort food from Bennigans.

Though predominantly a party place, Panama City is enjoying a resurgence of **highbrow arts** with the reopening of the Teatro Nacional, where both the Ballet Nacional de Panamá and the Fundación Ópera Panamá (Ⓦwww .operapanama.com), aimed at nurturing local talent, periodically put on productions. For information and tickets, call Ⓣ262 3525, though tickets are often for sale at Blockbuster on Vía España in El Cangrejo. Those with decent Spanish who fancy a **play** should head for the Teatro En Círculo or the Teatro La Quadra; productions in English are put on by the Theatre Guild of Ancón.

To find out **what's on**, pick up a copy of *La Prensa* (or check online at Ⓦwww .prensa.com) or the free weekly *The Visitor/El Visitante,* which has a very accessible online version (Ⓦwww.thevisitorpanama.com). Equally useful are the listings websites at Ⓦwww.panamasocialcalendar.com (in English) and www .culturaplus.net (in Spanish); www.conciertospanama.org has up-to-date information on classical concerts; and www.panamarock.com keeps you abreast of the rock scene.

Las chivas parranderas

Increasing in popularity with locals and tourists, *chivas parranderas* – **party buses** – are generally remodelled *diablos rojos*, some of which flaunt the added danger of being open-sided, with only a few ropes to prevent rum-soaked revellers from flying out as the bus lurches round the corner on its city tour. Your $25–30 fee will cover a bilingual guide, a band or DJ and unlimited rum and seco. Tours (usually Fri & Sat 8pm–midnight) need a minimum number to run, so put your name down in advance. Around ten companies now operate variations on the theme – from a fire engine to a limo – though few are licensed. More established companies include Chiva Parrandera (Ⓣ225 8500), Chiva Parranguera (Ⓣ223 3977) and Chiva Fiestas (Ⓣ221 0399, Ⓦwwwchivafiesta.com).

Nightlife

Casco Viejo

Café Havana On the corner of C 5 & Av "B". A laid-back Cuban flavour permeates this intimate bar, from the atmospheric decor to the smooth mojitos. *Desayuno* and *menu del día* ($4–6) served. Daily 8am–late.

Casa Góngora C 4 at Av Central ☎506 5836. Free jazz on a Wed evening (8pm) at this restored colonial property, and occasional bolero performances on a Fri at the same time. Tables get snapped up quickly so arrive early. Bring your own drink and nibbles.

La Casona de las Brujas Plaza Herrera ☻ www.enlacasona.com. Affectionately known as "La Casona", this nomadic bohemian space, currently occupying the dilapidated Art Deco interior of the former City Bank, hosts a range of artistic events, from exhibitions to workshops, exhibitions, live theatre and music, ranging from indie to reggae or jazz. The vibe is mellow while drinks at the makeshift bar are inexpensive. Generally late Wed–Sat.

Habana Panamá C Eloy Alfaro at C 12, ☻www .habanapanama.com. Lavish evocation of the golden era of 1930s Havana, playing son, salsa and jazz. Live charanga orchestra plus food and bar. Thurs–Sat from 9pm.

Platea C 1 opposite Club de Clases y Tropas. Sophisticated, atmospheric bar in a restored colonial property, where staff in Panama hats mix cocktails for an older clientele. Great live music: Latin jazz on Thurs, salsa on Fri and classic rock on Sat. Mon–Sat 6pm–2am.

Relic *Luna's Castle*, C 9 Este between Av "B" & Av Alfaro ☻ www.relicbar.com. Funky plant-filled basement courtyard with subdued lighting and driftwood-hewn tables, accompanied by a mix of indie, hip-hop and rock. Inevitably populated with travellers from the adjoining hostel but the inexpensive drinks and vibrant scene attract some Panamanians too. Tues–Sat from 8pm; Wed live art event.

Bella Vista, Marbella and El Cangrejo

La Bodeguita C Uruguay between Av Balboa & C 47. Buzzing open-air venue with bamboo walls and thatched roof where Cuban salsa and cuba libres are de rigueur. Tues–Sat.

The Gallery C 50 Plaza New York, Marbella. ☻www.thegallerypanama.com Sophisticated party den for the capital's smart 20 somethings, with state-of-the-art lighting, themed evenings, thumping dance music and a long bar. Things get going late with dancing until daybreak at weekends. $10–20 entry. Tues–Sat.

Guru C 47 at C Uruguay ☻ www.gurupanama.com. The main mega-club for Panama City's gilded youth to party, with a large floor, dry ice and top-notch DJs pumping out reggaeton, hip-hop or salsa. You'll need to don your smart gear and shell out $10–20 to get in, but the drinks are not that pricey.

Hotel Veneto Casino Vía Veneto at C Eusebio A. Morales. Dull by day, but a festive atmosphere by night, especially at weekends, drawing a mixed crowd of casual and smart dressers who come to socialize, eat, listen to live music and watch sports on the myriad screens as much as to gamble. Daily 24hr.

Lips Dance Club Upstairs at Centro Comercial Splash, Av Manuel E. Batista, ☻www.lipspanama .net. Gay hotspot attracting a young crowd featuring colour-themed evenings, foam parties and glitzy drag acts. Entry $3–8. Open Fri–Sun from 10pm.

The Londoner Pub C Uruguay between C 47 & C 48. Leather-backed seats, walls plastered in rugby shirts and photos of London do a fair job of persuading you you're in Britain's capital. There's even English beer and cider on tap and some pricey fish 'n' chips on the menu. The pool tables are occupied by British expats and young Panamanian males. Mon–Sat from 5pm.

Moods C 48 at C Uruguay ☻ www.moodspty.com. Electronic music, including techno and reggaeton attracts Panamanians in their 20s and 30s. Wed–Sat with no cover on Wednesdays, which tends to increase the numbers.

Pangea C 53 Oeste near Vía Veneto ☻www .pangeapanama.com. Sumptuously furnished bar-restaurant with six themed rooms. Enjoy fine wines and spirits during happy hour (Mon–Fri 5pm), perched at the Raffles-style Singapore Bar, lounging on silken cushions in the Marrakesh tent, or ensconced in wicker chairs on the Bombay patio. Daily 11.30am–late.

El Pavo Real Vía Argentina at C Guatemala. In a new location with new owners but still the English-speaking expat haunt of choice, complete with pool tables, darts, pub grub, Guinness and soccer on TV. Often a live band plays at weekends. Mon–Sat noon–midnight.

People C Uruguay ☻www.peoplepanama.com. Lilac-lit 1970s decor with an upstairs lounge overlooking the dancefloor, where you'll dance to a crossover mix of electronica, hip-hop, salsa and reggaeton. Cover $10, with open bar some nights before 11pm.

S6is C Uruguay between C 48 & C 49. A mainstay of the party scene, popular with various age groups, this small cocktail lounge with DJ can get packed at weekends. It's pronounced "seis". Tues–Sat.

Sahara C Uruguay at C 48. A magnet for classic-rock-loving gringos, with videos to remind you of the glory days. Live bands (Wed–Sat), mainly perform covers, with reggae night on Wed. Pool tables and the pleasant patio are other draws. Happy hours 6–10pm. $5 entry at weekends.

Sparkles *Intercontinental Miramar Hotel*, Av Balboa near Parque Urracá. Sweeping vistas of the bay and city skyline fom this fifth-floor cocktail bar – ideal for a sophisticated sundowner. Happy hour Thurs & Fri 6–8pm; live music Fri from 8pm.

The Wine Bar C Eusebio A. Morales in *ApartHotel Las Vegas* ☎ 265 4701. The city's first wine bar provides a convivial setting amid faux vines, bottles galore and murals of rustic scenes, marred only by the over-vigorous a/c. Choose from over two hundred bottles, or just enjoy a glass while chilling to mellow live music (after 8pm). The food is secondary (and ordinary) but you can also order off the menu of the adjacent *Caffé Pomodoro* (see p.89). A new outlet is now in Las Brisas on the Causeway. Mon–Sat 5pm–late.

Other areas

BLG Transístmica, opposite the Ford Dealership. Laser light shows and plenty of drag and dance acts aimed at a gay and lesbian clientele. Cover charge from $5 but good drinks deals. Wed–Sat from 10.30pm.

Xscape Bar Av de la Amistad (by *Pizza Hut*), El Dorado. Gay and lesbian bar-lounge with pool table but also with DJs spinning the discs and live shows. Tues–Sat from 7pm, Sun T-dances from 5pm.

Zona Viva Amador Causeway, before Centro de Convenciones Figali. A constantly revolving strip mall of discos, bars and restaurants to suit every mood, from house to hip-hop, salsa to rock. Tues–Sat.

Cinemas

Alhambra Vía España, near Supermercado Rey ☎ 264 3217. Convenient location in El Cangrejo with seven screens.

Cinemark Albrook Mall ☎ 314 6001. Vast thirteen-screen complex.

Cinépolis Multiplaza Pacífica ☎ 302 6262, 🖰 www.cinepolis.com.pa. State-of-the art multiplex with 3D and VIP screens that also puts on occasional arthouse features advertised under *El Otro Enfoque*.

Extreme Planet Av Balboa ☎ 214 7022. Multiplex with several VIP screens complete with reclining chairs and the possibility of ordering food from *Bennigan's* next door.

Theatres and concert venues

Centro de Convenciones ATLAPA Vía Israel, San Francisco 🖰 www.atlapa.gob.pa. The centre has two auditoriums: Teatro Anayansi, seating almost three thousand, hosts pop, jazz, classical, ballet, circus acts and even ice-skating, with plays and beauty pageants in the smaller Teatro La Huaca.

Centro de Convenciones Figali Amador Causeway 🖰 wwwfigaliconventioncenter.com. The venue of choice for international rock artists.

Teatro Anita Villalaz Plaza de Francia, Casco Viejo ☎ 211 4017. Once part of the Supreme Court, this intimate 250-seater hosts a range of cultural activities, from poetry readings to reggae nights.

Teatro Balboa Av Arnulfo Arias Madrid, Balboa ☎ 228 0327. Spacious Art Deco theatre, staging all kinds of events, including concerts by the resident National Symphony Orchestra.

Teatro En Círculo Av 6C Norte 🖰 www.teatro encírculo.com. One of the premier venues for plays.

Teatro Nacional Av "B" between C 3 & C 4, Casco Viejo ☎ 262 3525. Savour a classical concert, ballet or opera in the sumptuous rococo interior of the capital's premier artistic venue.

Teatro La Quadra C "D", El Cangrejo 🖰 www .teatroquadra.com. Small theatre putting on experimental and avant-garde theatrical productions, with a strong social development focus.

Theatre Guild of Ancón At the foot of Cerro Ancón, by the police station 🖰 www.anconguild .com. Community theatre established to entertain Zonians that still puts on English-speaking amateur dramatics.

Shopping and markets

Despite the hype about duty-free shopping in Panama City, there's actually very little around and though the streets are bulging with malls and shops, you are unlikely to be overly impressed by either the selection or the prices – indigenous crafts and other souvenirs aside. The **Albrook Mall**, a two-storey kilometre of retail therapy with discount stores jostling for attention amidst more upmarket boutiques, is the number one shopping venue, due in part to its proximity to the bus terminal and the vast food court you can raid when you begin to flag. **Multicentro** (Av Balboa, Punta Paitilla) and **Multiplaza** (Vía Israel, Punta Pacífica) both have dozens of more upmarket boutiques. Vía España in El Cangrejo is another shopping area, containing an eclectic mix of bargain stores, would-be chic boutiques and tourist-oriented shops, while **Avenida Central**, a much older commercial area, is the place to browse if you're on a tighter budget and want a feel for the day-to-day transactions of the average city-dweller.

Arts and crafts

Of greater interest are the **arts**, **crafts** and other **souvenirs**. Some of the best quality *molas*, basketry and wood carvings are stocked in shops dotted round Casco Viejo, though the prices are higher. Vía Veneto is another area replete with souvenir shops and Gran Morrison, the department store round the corner on Vía España, has a reasonable selection. If a *mola* is on the shopping list, you'll probably get a better price from the Kuna craftspeople who spread out their wares on the pavements along Vía Veneto, or in the plazas of Casco Viejo, and who can often organize you a trip to Kuna Yala too. In the city's several **craft markets** the stalls are generally run by members of the community who made the crafts, with more money usually trickling down to the artisans.

Centro de Artesenías International Av Arnulfo Arias Madrid, behind the old YMCA, Balboa. Offers some of the better crafts available in the markets: hammocks, *molas* made into place mats, glasses cases and the like, basketry, earrings plus crafts from other Latin countries. Mon–Sat 9am–6pm, Sun 10am–5pm.

Flory Saltzman Molas Vía España at Vía Veneto (near entrance to *Hotel El Panamá*) Ⓦ www.florymola .com. Generally considered to have the best selection, with mounds of *molas* of varying designs and quality, but the real draw is the household and personal items – bedspreads, T-shirts, cushions, bags and wallets – where *molas* have been skilfully woven into the design. Mon–Sat 9am–6pm.

Galería de Arte Indígena C 1, Casco Viejo. The best selection of Wounaan and Emberá basketry in

the capital at suitably elevated prices, alongside high quality *tagua* and *cocobolo* carvings. Daily 9am–8pm.

Mercado de Buhonería y Artesanías Av 4 at Av "B" behind the old Pacific terminus for the transisthmian railway. Numerous stalls rarely frequented, including one selling a good range of hats and hammocks. Mon–Sat 9am–6pm.

Reprosa Av "A" at C 4, Casco Viejo & Av Samuel Lewis on the corner with C 54, Obarrio Ⓦ www .reprosa.com. Beautifully crafted gold and silver reproduction pre-Columbian and Spanish colonial jewellery. Daily 9am–6pm.

La Ronda C 1 Casco Viejo. Excellent selection of arts and crafts at Casco Viejo prices. Daily 9am–7pm.

Food

Turning to **food**, if you're self-catering or looking to stock up for a trip, you've several options. The large 24-hour Supermercado Rey on Vía España will satisfy most needs, while the El Machetazo stores on Avenida Central (near Parque Santa Ana and in Calidonia) are much cheaper, though choice is more limited. For a better selection of inexpensive fruit, vegetables and fish, visit the Mercado Publico (Av "B" at Av Balboa) and the Mercado de Mariscos (Av Balboa), respectively. Riba Smith (Ⓦ www.rimith.com), often dubbed the gringo supermarket, has several branches across town, stocking predominantly American imports, including a greater selection of veggie and organic products – though at a price. SuperKosher (C Sebastian, Punta Paitilla) in the car park beneath Multicentro is another more expensive supermarket but has a fabulous range of tasty bread, dried fruits and nuts and Indian foodstuffs. Felipe Motta (Ⓦ www.felipemotta.com) on Calle 53, Marbella, has the best selection of wines and a good deli counter.

Sports and leisure

There are not too many opportunities to watch or participate in sport in the capital but catching a **baseball** game ($5) at the Estadio Nacional Rod Carew (about 8km northeast from the city centre on Vía Ricardo J Alfaro, off the Corredor Norte) is a real treat worth the taxi fare (see Ⓦwww.estadionacional.com.pa and p.45). **Horse racing** has a rich tradition in Panama, and takes place 10km east of Panama City en route to the airport at the Hipódromo Presidente Remón (races Thurs 5.30pm, Sat & Sun 2pm; Ⓣ217 6060, Ⓦwww.hipodromo.com). Panama's recent resurgence as a global **boxing** powerhouse has encouraged an increased number of bouts in the capital city, above all in the slick new Arena Roberto Durán, named after Panama's former megastar. Watch the press for details and check out Ⓦwww .boxpanama.com.

For those who want to participate in sport rather than spectate, the leafy **Parque Recreativo Omar Torrijos** (on Av Porras, San Francisco) is a prime destination, with public facilities for tennis, basketball, baseball and football plus a jogging route as well as plenty of space to picnic. Best of all it has a lovely clean outdoor **swimming pool** (Tues–Sun; $2) though avoid the weekend crowds.

Of course most visitors to Panama come to go **hiking**, **birdwatching**, **surfing**, **fishing**, **diving** or **snorkelling**, some of which can be done as a day-trip from the capital, either independently or through a tour (see p.44).

Listings

Airlines Both domestic airlines have offices at Albrook Airport and in the city: Aeroperlas in the Hotel Sheraton C 53, Marbella Ⓣ270 1788 and in the TACA office (Ⓣ206 8210) in the Hotel Crowne Plaza, Av Manuel E. Batista, off Vía España by the Iglesia del Carmen.

Bicycle rental On the Amador Causeway, the safest place to cycle, Bicicletas Moses (Ⓣ211 3671), by the Museo de la Biodiversidad and Bikes & More (Ⓣ314 0103) by the Figali Centre. Both offer rental by the hour ($3–4/hr, $15–25/day), plus fun pedal buggies for two ($8/hr). Rates vary according to demand so check in advance. Both open 9am–9pm on summer weekends, with shorter hours midweek and in winter depending on the weather and business. Rali Carretero (Ⓣ263 4136, Ⓦwww.rali-carretero.com), on Vía España, with another branch at the Albrook bus terminal, repairs bikes and sells spares.

Bookstores Exedra Books (Mon–Sat 9.30am–9.30pm, Sun 11am–8.30am, Ⓦwww.exedrabooks .com) on Vía España is the largest, with selections in Spanish and English, though the quantity of books doesn't fill the space. Gran Morrison department store on Vía España has a reasonable selection in English on Panama. Librería Argosy (Mon–Sat 10am–6pm, Vía Argentina at Vía España) is a small, old-fashioned bookshop crammed with new and second-hand books, many by Panamanian authors. The Smithsonian bookshop (see p.76) stocks an excellent selection on wildlife, ecology and environmental issues in both Spanish and English.

Car rental See Basics, p.27.

Dentists Try Clínica Dental Fábregas (Ⓣ399 4251) in Hospital Punta Pacífica (see p.97) or the Eisenmann Dental Clinic (Ⓣ269 2750), C 53 at Av Samuel Lewis. Staff in both speak English.

Embassies and consulates Canada, C 53 Este, World Trade Centre, Marbella (Ⓣ264 9731, Ⓦwww.canadainternational.gc.ca/panama); Colombia, C 53 Este, World Trade Centre, Marbella (Ⓣ264 9266); Costa Rica, Av Samuel Lewis, Plaza Omega by the Santuario Nacional (Ⓣ264 2980, Ⓔembarica@cwp.net.pa); Ireland, C Elvira Méndez at Vía España (Ⓣ264 6633, Ⓔirishconspma@online.ie); South Africa, C 50 at C 69, Edif Plaza Guadalupe, Oficina 404, San Francisco (Ⓣ226 2559, Ⓔcralaw@cwpanama .net); UK, C 53, Torre MMG, Marbella (Ⓣ269 0866, Ⓦwww.britishembassy.gov.uk); US, Av Demetrio Basilio Lakas, Clayton (Ⓣ207 7000, Ⓦwww.panama.usembassy.gov). There is no consular representative for Australia or New Zealand though Australia has an agreement with the Canadian embassy.

Hospitals Excellent medical care is available in the city in both the public and private sector with many US-trained and English-speaking staff. Recommended public hospitals include Hospital Santo Tomás, C 34 Este at Av Balboa (☏227 4122, emergencies 507 5600), and Hospital Santa Fé, Vía Simon Bolívar at Av Frangipani (☏227 4733, ⓦwww.hsantafe.com). Recommended private medical care is available at Clínica Hospital San Fernando, Vía España, Las Sabanas, next to *McDonald's* (☏305 6300, ⓦwww .hospitalsanfernando.com); and Centro Medico Paitilla, Av Balboa at C 53 (☏265 8800, ⓦwww .centromedicopaitilla.com. The Centro de Medicina Natural on C 42 Este at Av Mejico, Edif Guadalupe (☏225 0867) offers natural and traditional methods of treatment.

Immigration (*Migracíon*) Av Cuba at C 29 (Mon–Fri 8am–4pm; ☏507 1800).

Laundry See p.49.

Maps Free city maps of variable quality abound, generally with the advertising hotels, restaurants and tourist services marked; the Rutas de Aventura (ⓦwww.rutasdeaventura.com and see Basics, p.50) city map ($8) is available at Gran Morrison stores, various hotels and souvenir shops.

Money exchange If you need to change currency, head for Panacambios (Mon–Sat 9am–6pm) on the ground floor of the Edif Plaza Regency on Vía España.

Pharmacies Pharmacies are plentiful. Farmacias Arrocha is the largest chain, often open 24hr with a huge branch on Vía España, in front of the *Hotel El Panamá.*

Police Policía de Turismo, Vía España opposite the Riande Hotel Continental (☏269 8011) and Av Central at C 3, Casco Viejo (☏511 9261).

Post office The main office is opposite the Basílica Don Bosco, on Av Central, between C Ecuador & C34 Este. Other convenient branches are on in the Plaza Concordia (below the *Hotel El Panamá*), El Cangrejo, Calidonia and in Balboa at the end of the Prado on Av Arnulfo Arias Madrid. See Basics p.50 for hours and details on receiving post.

Telephones The main Cable & Wireless office (Mon–Fri 8am–6pm & Sat 8am–4pm) is on Vía España, next to the National Bank and Plaza Concordia, and has comfortable facilities to make international phone calls, as do some internet cafés. For phone boxes see p.52.

Moving on from Panama City

Most people use the country's efficient and extensive **bus system** to travel around though **internal flights** are plentiful, reasonably priced and simple to arrange. They're particularly useful for reaching Kuna Yala, Bocas del Toro and remote areas of the Darién. **Car rental** is also easy though fairly pricey (see p.27) but worth it if you're heading off the beaten track. The Archipiélago de las Perlas and the Darién are the only likely destinations for visitors moving on by **boat.**

By bus

All regional buses leave from the **national bus terminal** at Albrook, where you need to purchase a ticket from the appropriate ticket office inside the building, before passing through a turnstile (a 5c coin is needed) to a numbered departure bay at the back. For several major destinations, there is more than one company operating transport, some offering both express and cheaper stopping buses, though companies charge the same price for the same service.

On buses for Tocumen International Airport, which drop you a few hundred metres from the **airport** entrance, you buy a ticket on board, after passing through turnstiles at a separate inconspicuous entrance labelled "Corredor", midway along the ticket hall. However, note that the first airport bus from Albrook leaves 9.30–10am; if you need an earlier bus, catch one from the large bus stop (and shelter) on Avenida Justo Arosemena, close to Plaza Cinco de Mayo. To get to the bus terminal from the city centre, hop on a bus on Vía España or at the side of the Legislative Palace off Plaza Cinco de Mayo.

The box on p.98 gives information on the most common regional bus destinations. For details of the return journey, consult the relevant chapters.

Major domestic bus routes

Destination	Frequency	Duration	Cost
Aguadulce	Every 25min, daily 4.15am–9pm	3hr	$6
Antón	Every 20min, daily 5.20am–8pm	2hr	$3.50
Bayano (Vía Chepo)	Every 40min, daily 5.30am–5.45pm	2hr 30min	$1.25
Chame	Every 15min, daily 5.30am–9pm	1hr 20min	$2.15
Changuinola (via Almirante)	Daily 8am & 8pm	10hr	$24
Chitré	Approx every hr, daily 6am–11pm	3hr 30min	$7.50
Colón	Every 30min, Express bus 4.40am–10pm Every 20–30min, regular bus 3.40am–1am	1hr 15min–2hr	$2.50 $1.50
El Copé	Hourly, Mon–Fri 6am–7pm, Sat & Sun 6am–6pm	3hr	$5.50
David	Two companies run hourly buses, daily 5.30am–8.30pm. Both have express services at 10.45pm & midnight	7hr	$12.60 $15 express
Gamboa	Daily 5am, 5.45am, 6.30am (6am on weekends), 8am, 10am, noon, 2pm, 4.30pm, 6.30pm, 9pm; Mon–Fri also 1 & 3pm	45min	$0.65
Penonomé	Every 20min, daily 4.45am–11pm	2hr	$4.35
San Carlos	Every 20min, daily 6am–8.30pm	1hr 30min	$2.70
Santiago	Two companies run 37 buses between them, daily 1am, 3am & 6am–midnight	4hr	$7.50
Soná	Every 2hr, daily 8.20am–5.45pm	5hr	$8
Las Tablas	Hourly, daily 6am–7pm	4hr	$8
El Valle (de Antón)	Every 25min, daily 6.30am–7pm	2hr	$3.50
Villa de Los Santos	Hourly, daily 6am–11pm	3hr 30min	$7.50
Yaviza and Metetí	Daily 3.15–7.30am, then hourly departures as far as Metetí until 4.30pm. From Metetí, take a local bus to Yaviza (6am–9pm; 1hr; $5)	6–7hr to Yaviza; 5–6hr to Metetí	$14 ($9)

Travelling to Costa Rica

Ticabus (☎ 314 6385, ⓦ www.ticabus.com), with an office at the terminal, runs overnight and daytime buses (11am & 11pm; 15–16hr; $40 & $30) to **San José**, Costa Rica. Advance booking is advisable. Alternatively, take a Padafront bus to the border at Paso Canoas (see p.218) (9 buses daily; $14, $17 for the overnight express), via David, and transfer to Costa Rican transport.

By air

The country's two domestic airlines (see p.25) conveniently fly out of Albrook Airport, just north of Cerro Ancón, where each has its own check-in lounge-cum-waiting-room. **Aeroperlas** (☎ 378 6000, ⓦ www.aeroperlas.com) serves thirteen destinations while **Air Panama** (☎ 316 9000, ⓦ www.flyairpanama .com) serves nineteen, including San José, Costa Rica, via a connecting flight from David. Prices for both airlines are the same and both accept online credit-card bookings.

By boat

The main reason for wanting to leave Panama City by **boat** (other than to visit the Archipiélago de las Perlas and Isla Taboga, see p.102 & p.104), is to go to the Darién. Check in with *Transportes Multimar*, down by the temporarily relocated main wharf (*muelle fiscal*) by the Mercado de Mariscos (see p.79). They make a couple of weekly deliveries to La Palma and Jaqué and sometimes take passengers, though there's no comfort in the lengthy ride. You can put your name down for passage to La Palma ($15) or Jaqué ($20), though for the former it is quicker and cheaper via bus and water-taxi on the Metetí–Puerto Quimba–La Palma route (see p.307).

Golfo de Panamá

Covering 2400 square kilometres, the **GOLFO DE PANAMÁ** is dotted with over a thousand islands, many uninhabited, including tiny sandy cays little more than the size of a football pitch. A popular day-trip destination, **Isla Taboga**'s mellow pace offers relief from the frenetic energy of Panama City. Further afield, the two-hundred-plus islands, pristine beaches and azure waters of the **Archipiélago de las Perlas**, also accessed from the capital, form the area's most compelling destination, and are a major magnet for diving and sport fishing.

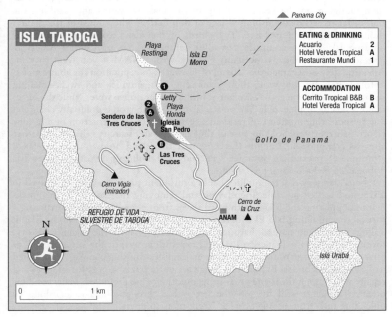

▲ San Pedro, Isla Taboga

Isla Taboga

Twenty kilometres off the coast and about an hour away by boat, the lush hills of **Isla Taboga** (ⓦ www.taboga.panamanow.com) have provided one of the most popular weekend escapes for Panama City residents since the capital's sixteenth-century foundation. These days most visitors are day-trippers, who spend their time lounging on the beach, bathing in the shallow waters and strolling the traffic-free streets of the fishing village of **San Pedro**, where most of the island's thousand-odd inhabitants live. Two-thirds of the island, together with neigh-bouring Isla Urabá, comprise a wildlife refuge for one of Central America's largest colonies of brown **pelicans** – check with ANAM if you want to visit. Affectionately nicknamed the "Island of Flowers", its reputation for abundance is unfortunately on the wane; though hibiscus, bougainvillea and sweet-smelling jasmine are in evidence, they are not as prolific as they once were, while the once-famous succulent pineapples are now a rarity. The vibe too is gradually changing due to increasing numbers of resident expats, with the construction of a luxury resort – currently on hold because of the island's water scarcity – likely to further alter its complexion. But for the most part the island holds on to its relaxed atmosphere: packed on summer weekends and holidays, at other times Isla Taboga can feel gloriously deserted.

Taboga's present-day tranquillity belies a turbulent past. The Spanish arrived in 1515, and wasted no time in enslaving and removing the native Cueva Indians before populating the island with freed slaves from elsewhere and constructing a fort on the adjoining **Isla El Morro** – its cannons are sprinkled round the island. Taboga's excellent natural harbour has crucially shaped the island's history, forming the base for Francisco Pizarro's expeditions against the Incas, as well as pirates such as Morgan and Drake. After an English steamship company established its headquarters on Isla El Morro, Taboga became a buzzing port for supplies and repairs and, though the island's maritime importance has dwindled, many contemporary Taboganos still live off the sea, either through small-scale fishing or unloading tuna from fishing boats to larger trans-shippers.

The Island

A day-trip still gives you plenty of time to explore San Pedro's meandering narrow streets, hike to the island's highest point, Cerro Vigía, and enjoy a beer on the beach.

San Pedro

Approaching the floating pier, you are greeted by the whitewashed buildings and red rooftops of San Pedro, strung out to the left behind **Playa Honda**, a shingly strip dotted with small fishing boats. Turning right after leaving the pier takes you to Taboga's better beach, **Playa Restinga**, a golden crescent, half of which forms a sand bar reaching to Isla El Morro, which is submerged at high tide. Its appeal is somewhat diminished by the piles of overgrown rubble from the demolished *Hotel Taboga* at the back. Crowds of Panamanians happily swim off both beaches, but it is worth considering that much of the island's sewage flows into the bay, while after heavy rains rubbish can wash up on the shore.

The rest of the island

Heading back towards the village, along the jasmine-scented Calle Abajo, a steep path to the right leads up to the **plaza**, the social hub of the island – where villagers of all ages gather to watch or play football or volleyball, dance or simply hang out. At one end, steps lead up to the gleaming white stucco walls of the **Iglesia San Pedro**, built in 1550 and reputedly the second oldest church in the western hemisphere. Leaving the square via Calle Arriba at the opposite end, and turning left you come across a shrine to the Virgen del Carmen and the house where Pizarro apparently lived, while a brightly tiled plaque nearby commemorates the painter Paul Gaugin, who had a short stint working on the canal before heading off for the South Seas.

It's definitely worth summoning up the energy to do one of the island's two walks. The shorter hike to **Cerro de la Cruz** takes an easy thirty minutes. Leaving town along Calle Abajo, you pass the delightful **casa de la concha**, on the right, decorated by former owner and one-time pearl fisher with scallop and pearl shells, and the site of old French canal-era **sanitorium**, which the Americans later converted into a rest and recuperation centre for "gold roll" canal employees before upgrading it to a hotel. After the weed-strewn **cemetery**, take the dirt road down to the left, then a path up an embankment to the right 100m later, after which it's an easy walk to the gigantic sixteenth-century cross, where you can soak up the sweeping sea view.

The panorama is even more spectacular from the mirador at the top of **Cerro Vigía** (370m). After the turn to Cerro de la Cruz, the main path continues to a junction. Straight ahead lie the ANAM offices, the island's desalination plant and the refuse dump; to the right, the widening dirt road meanders slowly up the hill. The more direct route to the summit, up the **Sendero de las Tres Cruces**, presents a more challenging climb through lush forest, not least because of poor signposting. After heavy rain, the path becomes a mudslide, but the rewards are almost-guaranteed sightings of green and black poison-dart frogs and tarantulas. The route is indicated from the plaza, by the phone box; after the housing ends, turn sharp right and then ten minutes into the forest bear left at a fork, traversing a stream, which the path crisscrosses several times before arriving, forty-five minutes later, at three well-tended crosses – the burial sites of a trio of buccaneers who foolishly tangled with some Taboganos. Bearing left again, the trail soon emerges from the undergrowth onto the dirt road to the summit.

Other popular diversions include a **boat trip** round the island, which allows close-ups of pelicans thrusting fish down the gullets of squawking chicks in the nesting months of January to June. There is also reasonable **snorkelling** on the far side of Taboga and Isla El Morro and round a wreck off Isla Urabá, though currents can be strong. A couple of hours in a *panga* should cost around $60.

Practicalities

The fifty-minute **boat trip** across to the island on the Calypso Queen (☎314 1730) is one of the highlights of a visit, giving passengers close-ups of the ships waiting to transit the canal and a chance to glimpse dolphins and even migrating whales (July–Oct). There are daily departures from La Playita on the Amador Causeway, near the entrance to the Punta Culebra Nature Centre (Mon, Wed & Fri 8.30am & 3pm, returning from Taboga at 9.30am & 4.30pm, Tues & Thurs 8.30am, returning 4.30pm, Sat, Sun & public holidays 8am, 10.30am & 4pm, returning 9am, 3pm & 5pm; $11 return). On weekends and public holidays in particular you'll need to get there an hour in advance to be sure of a seat. On busier weekends the new Calypso King also zips across in thirty minutes. Make sure you take sufficient cash with you as there is **no ATM** on Taboga.

The nicest of the limited and overpriced accommodation options is the Spanish colonial hacienda-style *Hotel Vereda Tropical* (☎250 2154, Ⓦwww .veredatropicalhotel.com; ◎), its rooms tastefully decorated with rustic tiling, although only some have ocean views and the service can be desultory. The friendlier *Cerrito Tropical B & B* (☎6489 0074, Ⓦwww.cerritotropicalpanama .com), further up the hill, offers both plain rooms equipped with air conditioning, fan, private bathroom with shared balcony (◎) and one- to three-bedroom apartments with kitchenettes and private balconies ($140–300). Budget travellers should note that some locals rent out rooms informally in their houses for $20–40, often meeting the morning ferry to seek out guests; otherwise enquire at *Restaurante Mundi* by the jetty.

Eating options on the island are similarly restricted and service is slow, so if you join the summer weekend crowds it's probably worth bringing a picnic. The terrace of the *Hotel Vereda Tropical* provides lovely views to accompany excellent food – try the house *corvina* in coconut and passion-fruit sauce ($14) – but prices are high and service is hit and miss. For delicious home cooking at modest prices, head for the delightful *Acuario* (daily 8am–8pm), a few hundred metres along from the jetty on Calle Abajo – the house lemonade is a must. Next to the jetty, the informal *Restaurante Mundi* (daily 8am–5pm) serves simple plates of seafood and rice ($6–9), even delivering to the beach if required.

Slaves, pirates and pearls

Little is known about the **indigenous population** of the archipelago, which was wiped out in the sixteenth century after news of the abundance of **pearls** reached the conquistadors' greedy ears. Needing labour to harvest them, the Spanish brought over African slaves, the ancestors of most of the current population. Over the next few centuries, the maze of islands provided hideouts for pirates plundering Spanish galleons en route from Peru, often with the help of local bands of *cimarrones* (escaped slaves).

The end of Spanish rule did not spell the end of the pearl trade, which thrived until the oyster beds became diseased in the 1930s. Though they have recovered to an extent – pearl fishers still operate from Isla Cayeta – there's little chance of a new pearl rivalling the archipelago's most famous find, the pear-shaped Peregrina ("pilgrim"). Plucked in the sixteenth century, it belonged to Spanish and English royalty before ending up with Hollywood legend **Elizabeth Taylor**.

Tourism in the islands took off in the 1970s when businessman and diplomat Gabriel Lewis Galindo bought the island for a bargain $30,000. By constructing roads and selling off plots to other wealthy Panamanians, he established Panama's first resort island.

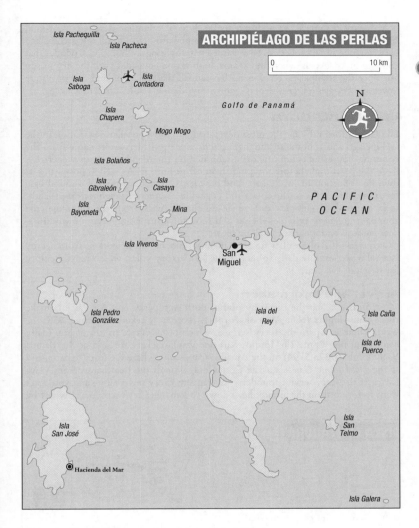

Archipiélago de las Perlas

Set in coral-rich crystalline waters in the Golfo de Panamá only a twenty-minute flight southeast of Panama City, the 220 islands and islets that comprise the **Archipiélago de las Perlas** (Pearl Islands) were named by Vasco Nuñez de Balboa in 1513 after their once prolific black-lipped pearl oysters. Sprinkled over an area of around 1700 square kilometres, only a handful of islands are actually inhabited and many remain under-explored, though various controversial multimillion-dollar luxury development projects are threatening to change that. Currently, the attractive **Isla Contadora** is the only island with a developed tourist infrastructure though **Isla Saboga**, **Isla del Rey** and **Isla San José** (the latter's wonderful coral and beaches only accessible via the exclusive *Hacienda del Mar* – see Ⓦ www.haciendadelmar.net)

hold plenty of appeal. In addition to the lure of countless deserted sugar-sand **beaches** and **reefs** teeming with multicoloured fish, a visit to the archipelago between June and October can be rewarded with sightings of humpback **whales** that come to breed. As elsewhere in Panama, high season coincides with the dry season but since the archipelago receives far less rainfall than the mainland and prices are lower and beaches less crowded, it's worth considering a visit at other times.

Isla Contadora

Isla Contadora is by far the most developed and most popular destination in the archipelago and is home to the main public airstrip. It derives its name from the counting house the conquistadors established on the island to tot up their riches from the pearl trade before shipping them off to Europe. As well as possessing its own fine selection of lovely soft-sand beaches, Contadora provides a sound base for snorkelling trips to the corals and crystalline waters of neighbouring islands, visits to sea-bird colonies and whale-watching. Away from the shoreline, the abundant greenery provides shelter and food for a surprising array of wildlife – deer, agoutis and iguanas can all be spotted.

Only a handful of families are permanently resident, while workers from nearby Isla Saboga commute daily to service the 180 luxury villas, which remain empty for much of the year.

Arrival and information

Most tourists reach the island by **plane**. Both Aeroperlas and Air Panama make twice-daily flights from Albrook Airport, more at weekends (20min; $58 one way). There is a periodic **ferry** service, which often falters in low season (daily 8am, returning 2pm; 1hr 15min; $30 one way). Tickets are sold at the Balboa Yacht Club (☎228 5794) on the Amador Causeway, where the ferry departs, and at the *Hotel Punta Galeón* on Isla Contadora, though the boat leaves from Playa Larga. If the ferry service founders – as happens every few years – and you don't want to fork out on the airfare, head down to Panama City's temporary wharf by

ACCOMMODATION				EATING & DRINKING			
Cabañas de Contadora	**F**	Hotel Perla Real	**D**	Gerald's	**2**	Restaurante Romantica	**E**
Casa del Sol	**C**	Sagitario	**A**	El Manguito	**4**	Rincón Romantico	**3**
Contadora Inn B&B	**B**	Villa Romantica	**E**	Restaurante Punta Galeón	**1**	Sagitario	**B**

the Mercado de Mariscos (see p.79) and negotiate a boat ride for around $30, less if a *colectivo* is leaving.

All accommodation on Contadora offers airport or ferry transfer, though at 1.3 kilometres square, nowhere is far to walk. The **main square** on the island is a two-minute stroll west of the airstrip, containing a police booth, small medical centre (Mon–Fri 8am–3pm) a couple of restaurants and some public phones. Given the high cost of living on Contadora, it's unfortunate that there's **no bank** or ATM here or anywhere else in the archipelago. Thankfully most accommodation and restaurants and some tours take credit cards. It's worth bringing some supplies as well as cash, since the three mini-supermarkets, clustered around the square, offer limited variety and very little fresh produce, although the Pacific Island Shoppette stocks a rack of Moët & Chandon.

If getting around on foot doesn't appeal, you might consider renting a golf cart or ATV – the more expensive hotels and the diving operator Coral Dreams do a thriving trade. Prices vary from $25–35 per hour or $50–70 for 24 hours, so shop around. The one taxi driver, César, (T 6583 1231), charges an astronomical $5 per trip. Mountain bikes can be hired from *Casa del Sol* ($3/hr, $14/day). The *Contadora Inn* runs a welcome centre by the airport for its guests, which also serves as a part-time **internet** café.

Accommodation

There's no such thing as budget **accommodation** on Contadora, with nothing below $40, and most lodgings are overpriced for what they offer but have a/c unless otherwise indicated. Outside Christmas, Carnaval and Easter, rates drop considerably and are often negotiable. *The Contadora Inn, Casa del Sol* and *Perla Real* are clustered together in a quiet residential area inland on the western part of the island, a few minutes walk from the beach, while *Villa Romantica* has a coastal location. **Camping** is frowned upon, though you can easily arrange transport to camp on one of the nearby uninhabited islands.

Cabañas de Contadora T 393 0307, W www.cabanasdecontadora.tripod.com. Four light studio *cabañas* overlooking the airstrip (but still with a sea view) offer the island's best value. Each has a comfy double bed, fan and mosquito screens, plus a kitchenette with fridge, minibar and dining table and a small balcony complete with hammock. In the house two slightly pricier rooms with a/c include use of the kitchen-living area and shared bathroom. Breakfast is included and other meals can be ordered. **⑤**

Casa del Sol T 250 4212, W www.panama-isla -contadora.com. Neat, cosily decorated room with fridge, breakfast bar and private patio or a slightly larger studio flat with living area and kitchenette, including breakfast. Cash only. Single room **⑥**, studio flat **⑦**

Contadora Inn B&B T 6699 4614, W www .contadoraislandinn.com. Gorgeous two-house B&B offering excellent service with nine beautifully appointed en-suite rooms. In each of the two houses, guests share a spacious kitchen and lounge area with TV/DVD player, books and games opening out onto a large balcony backed by luscious forest, with a cooler hammock-strewn *rancho* below. **⑦**

Hotel Perla Real T 6513 9064, W www.perlareal .com. Delightful Spanish colonial-style hotel set around a central patio and fountain (only running in the rainy season!). The four fairly compact rooms with private bathrooms containing hand-painted tiling and basin are well appointed with terracotta floor tiles, tasteful artwork and French windows. Two suites are available with kitchenette. **⑦**

Sagitario T 250 4091. The four cheapest rooms on the island, tucked away behind the restaurant of the same name, are overpriced for what they offer. Though clean they range from a dark, hot cell with fan but no window to a slightly larger room with fan, TV and window. Contact Sra Mathilde, usually found in the shop adjoining the restaurant. Cash only. **④**

Villa Romantica Playa Cacique T 250 4067, W www.villa-romantica.com. Superbly located on the bluff overlooking the beach, though the quirky decorations – seemingly straight out of Vegas – may not be to everyone's taste; walls display extravagant murals of castles or Neoclassical bas-reliefs while bathrooms range from ostentatious marble and antique mirrors to shell-encrusted showers. Beds are large and comfy and rooms have cable TV but you'll want to have a sea view to justify the price. **⑦**

The Island

The **beaches** and island **views** constitute Contadora's main attractions and you can easily complete an initial reconnaissance of them all in a couple of hours, selecting your favourites for a more leisurely lounge later. **Playa Larga** provides the longest stretch of sand and the most sheltered swimming in the warmest water, on the island's eastern side, with two abandoned ferries the only eyesore. Moving south round the headland, **Playa de las Suecas** ("Swedish Women's Beach"), Panama's only public nudist beach, is suitably secluded and also offers the island's best snorkelling round the headland towards Playa Larga, where sharks, stingrays and turtles can often be seen. Another few minutes' stroll, skirting the end of the runway, past the dark sand of the unfairly labelled **Playa Fea** ("Ugly Beach"), brings you to the island's loveliest swathe of soft, sugary sand, **Playa Cacique**. Backed by lush vegetation interspersed with a few select residences and the *Villa Romantica*, it looks out through anchored yachts across turquoise waters to nearby Isla Chapera. Round a rocky promontory at the west end of the beach is the smaller **Playa Camarón**, while further along, the west end of the island possesses a few unremarkable and fairly inaccessible beaches, which can be reached with a little entertaining rock scrambling at low tide. Giving the island's dump on the southwestern tip a wide berth, follow the road down the slope to the north to Contadora's fledgling yacht club, which looks out towards Isla Saboga.

The centre of the island is occupied by a football pitch, which comes alive in late afternoon. South of the pitch there's a small whitewashed church, while the road up the eastern side of the pitch passes one of island's two **lakes**, on the left, which are magnets for thirsty wildlife such as magnificent frigatebirds that skim the surface scooping up water. Further along, the road sweeps down to the charming sheltered cove of **Playa Ejecutiva**, backed by manicured grass dotted with shady trees and overlooked by the house that hosted the exiled Shah of Iran in 1979. Returning to the northern end of the airstrip, the *Hotel Punta Galeón* surveys the beach of the same name.

Activities

Most organized **activities** on Contadora involve getting on or in water, which your hotel can usually arrange for you. Alternatively, stroll down to Playa Galeón, where boats are likely to be bobbing around off the beach, and negotiate a price for what you want, finding out the going rates – around $35 per hour at the last enquiry – in advance and agreeing on an itinerary. If you're travelling on your own, it will probably be cheaper to join an organized tour.

There's reasonable **snorkelling** to be enjoyed off some of Contadora's beaches, but there is more to see a little further afield. The PADI-certified Coral Dreams (℡6536 1776, ⓦwww.coral-dreams.com), down by the airport, offers half-day snorkelling ($35 including equipment and soft drinks) and **diving** for both beginners and certified divers ($65 for a one-tank dive including equipment). Tourists can be packed rather sardine-like in the boat in the busy summer months, so check on numbers in advance. The snorkelling excursion usually takes in the islands of **Chapera**, **Mogo-Mogo** and the sandy cay of **Boyarena**, which lie in a cluster south of Contadora and were locations for several series of the US reality TV show *Survivor*. Though Chapera is a private island, you are unlikely to be hassled by the owner for strolling along its beaches, since he was arrested in 2007 for money laundering (though is still awaiting trial) and his assets, including the island, were seized by the government.

While you'll see more fish off Chapera, bathing in the translucent water of Mogo-Mogo's crescent-shaped bay is blissful. Alternatively, arrange to be dropped at one of the nearby islands, with a tent (or sheet sleeping bag and mosquito net) and some supplies, and arrange to be picked up a day or two later. On a clear night the stars are truly scintillating.

For those who want to enjoy the sea life without getting wet, *Villa Romantica* offers a similar itinerary in a **glass-bottomed boat** for the same price. The rugged coastline of Contadora is good to explore in a **kayak**, which can be hired at Punta Galeón for around $5 per hour. Even more leisurely is a day-long cruise on a **catamaran** (contact Amanda or Xavier on ☎ 6413 7128, ⓦ www.lasperlassailing .es.tl) or **sailboat** (contact Guido or Patrizia on ☎ 6723 1147); at $80 a person both the catamaran and sail-boat excursions offer excellent value, as they include food, drinks and a couple of snorkelling stops.

Birding enthusiasts will want to hire a boat to observe the nearby **sea-bird colonies**, though it isn't possible to land on the islands. Pacheca, about 3km northwest of Contadora, is home to thousands of tropical cormorants, magnificent frigate birds and brown pelicans, who nest atop the guano-covered cliffs, while the smaller Pachequilla is packed with brown and blue-footed boobies.

Eating and drinking

As with accommodation, **eating** options are limited and supply problems from the capital can mean some dishes are not always available. Avoid lobster between December and mid-April, as it's closed season across the archipelago.

Gerald's By the airstrip ☎ 250 4159. Tiled *rancho* with comfortable wooden furniture providing a congenial ambiance to enjoy the best cuisine on the island. Specialities are seafood and meat dishes (mains from $8), accompanied by moderately priced wine served in elegant lead crystal glasses. Daily noon–3pm, 6–10pm.

El Manguito Just off the square. What passes for nightlife on the island – a dim pool hall selling beer all week and pumping out the sounds on a weekend.

Restaurante Punta Galeón Playa Galeón ☎ 250 4220. This open-air bar-restaurant is the top spot on the island to sip a cocktail at sundown, though the food is variable. The extensive menu offers international cuisine plus a range of kosher and vegetarian dishes. Most mains $14–20. Daily 7am–11pm.

Restaurante Romantica Playa Cacique ☎ 250 4067. The food's usually decent enough, but the

delightful breezy cliff-top setting is the real draw. Everything is grilled, with seafood, including lobster and crayfish, the house speciality ($10–40). Hearty buffet breakfast ($8.50) also available. Daily 7am–3pm, 6–10pm.

Rincón Romantico Main square ☎ 675 05640. Owned by Charley of *Villa Romantica*, this fairly new addition to the island's culinary scene offers pleasant dining on a covered patio. The menu centres on (pricey) pizza ($12) plus straightforward pasta and salad dishes. Daily 11am–3pm, 7–10pm.

Sagitario Main square. The better of the two cheap local *fondas*, offering a shady terrace overlooking the square and a good place to chat to locals. The *menu del día*, usually involving chicken or fish with rice and lentils, is tasty and good value at $3.50; other mains $6–9. Daily 6am–9pm.

Isla Saboga

Just across from Contadora lies the slightly larger **Isla Saboga**, whose four hundred inhabitants populate the main village, **Puerto Nuevo**, perched on the hilltop above the main pink-shell beach. Many commute to Contadora to work; others fish and ferry tourists in their boats or carry out subsistence agriculture. This may soon change as Saboga is set to be transformed by an international development consortium aiming to pump $1.5 billion into constructing a vast complex of luxury hotels and condominiums (see ⓦ www.islasaboga.org), laughably termed a "community development" project. So get there quickly to take advantage of the unhurried pace of life and gloriously deserted beaches.

The island can be reached by a ten-minute **boat** ride from Isla Contadora's Playa Galeón ($3 for a regular passage), making it an easy day-trip destination.

A great place to take a picnic, there is also a community-run bar-restaurant on the main fishing beach plus a couple of *fondas* up in the village. The eighteenth-century hilltop church – one of the few traces of Spanish occupation left in the archipelago – is worth a quick peek inside before you head across to the delightful Playa Encanto. At low tide, it's an exciting two-hour scramble south over rocks and across coves, passing scores of cormorants and pelicans sunning themselves, to the soft salt-and-pepper expanse of the island's premier beach, Playa Larga, from where you can hike down a dirt road back to the village in under half an hour.

Isla del Rey and around

The greatest land mass in the archipelago is Isla del Rey (sometimes referred to as Isla San Miguel); at almost 240 square kilometres, it is Panama's second largest island after Coiba. **San Miguel**, its main population centre, is a fishing village of some eight hundred people situated on a kilometre-long stretch of beach on its north coast. There are no tourist facilities, so accommodation is very basic and it will only appeal to hardy travellers who speak reasonable Spanish and aren't put off by being offered iguana for lunch or witnessing a violent bout of cockfighting, the main evening entertainment. It's easy to engage a local guide to take you to explore some of the nearby rivers and waterfalls, or go horse riding. The only **accommodation**, *Hotel San Miguel* (T 6661 7198), lies just up from the beach, offering rudimentary rooms with fan and shared cold-water bathroom ($10), while a couple of streets away, a local restaurant will serve you a plateful of simple food for under $3. The most practical way to reach the island is to fly with Air Panama (Tues, Thurs & Sat 10.30am; 20min; $58 one way).

Isla Viveros, just off the northwest coast of Isla del Rey, is home to another multimillion-dollar development enterprise pushed through despite concerns over its environmental impact. Its new marina, international airport and hotel were due to open in 2010 (W www.islaviveros.com). **San Telmo**, a small nature reserve to the southeast of Isla del Rey, is noted both for its primary rainforest and for the extraordinary curiosity of a Jules Verne style **submarine** visible at low tide. One of the world's first, this rusting beached whale has been resting on the shore since 1869 when its pearl-fishing crew surfaced too quickly and so died from decompression sickness. At over 40km round-trip this would be a costly full-day undertaking, hiring the services of a boatman in San Miguel.

The Canal, Colón and the central Caribbean coast

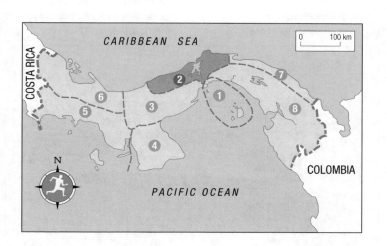

CHAPTER 2 # Highlights

* **Canal transit** Experience the great, iconic waterway on a boat and marvel at the tropical scenery. See p.113

* **Miraflores Locks** Get a close look at the precision manoeuvring of gargantuan container vessels as they squeeze through the lock chambers. See p.115

* **Birdwatching in Soberanía** Over 525 bird species have been recorded here: grab your binoculars and scan the canopy at dawn. See p.117

* **Hiking** Follow in the footsteps of the conquistadors along the old booty trails of the Camino de Cruces or Camino Real through tangled, lush rainforest. See p.116, p.118 & p.125

* **Stay in an Emberá village** Overnight in traditional thatched homes, sharing Emberá culture and learning about the surrounding rainforest. See p.124

* **Spanish colonial forts** Step back in time at the desolate, evocative ruins of Fuerte San Lorenzo, or the well-preserved forts of Portobelo. See p.133 & p.137

▲ A cruise ship transits the canal, Lago Gatún

The Canal, Colón and the central Caribbean coast

Running 80km across the isthmus between the Pacific and Atlantic oceans, straddling the provinces of Panama and Colón, the **Panama Canal** remains a colossus among engineering achievements, a truly awe-inspiring sight and justifiably the country's prime tourist attraction. What's more, it can easily be explored on an excursion from Panama City, with the **Centro de Visitantes de Miraflores** offering the best location from which to view the action. Though the corridor that flanks this vital thoroughfare is home to almost two-thirds of Panama's population, for much of its length the waterway cleaves through pristine rainforest, large tracts of which are protected within several national parks. **Parque Nacional Soberanía** is one of the most accessible tropical rainforest preserves in Latin America, while **Isla Barro Colorado** is home to the world-renowned Smithsonian Institute. Both support an exceptional degree of biodiversity and offer easy day-trips from the capital. The quiet town of **Gamboa** is the embarkation point for excursions to the island and for most tours offering partial transits of the canal; it is also the starting point for rainforest hikes and birdwatching outings along the famous **Pipeline Road**. Three of the area's national parks – Soberanía, the smaller adjacent Parque Nacional Camino de Cruces and the larger, somewhat less accessible Parque Nacional Chagres – also offer the opportunity to walk along the remnants of the historic, partially cobbled **Camino de Cruces** and the **Camino Real**, which mule trains carved across the forested spine of the isthmus in colonial times to transport Spain's plundered treasures from Panama City to the Caribbean coast.

The canal reaches the Atlantic at **Colón**, Panama's second city, synonymous with poverty and crime in the minds of many Panamanians, yet compelling and rich in history, with a strong Afro-Antillean and Afro-Colonial heritage. Either side of Colón stretch kilometres of Caribbean coastline peppered with small communities, more or less untainted by tourist development, as well as the country's most impressive colonial ruins. To the west, along the **Costa Abajo**, the formidable remains of the colonial **Fuerte San Lorenzo** still guard the mouth of the Río

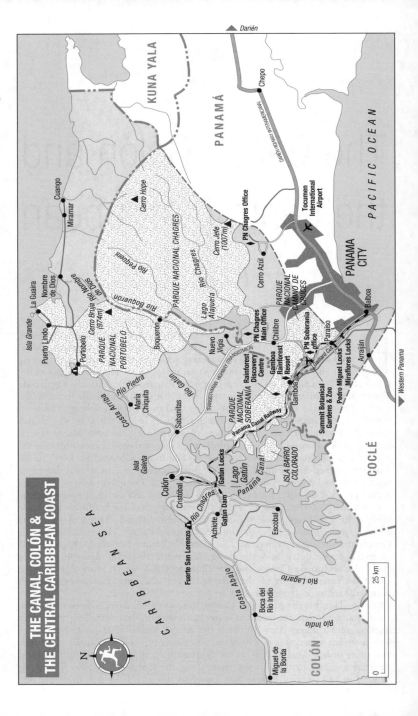

THE CANAL, COLÓN & THE CENTRAL CARIBBEAN COAST

N

CARIBBEAN SEA

PACIFIC OCEAN

Darién

KUNA YALA

PANAMÁ

Chepo

Tocumen International Airport

PANAMA CITY

Balboa

Arraiján

PN Chagres Office

Cerro Hope

Cerro Jefe (1007m)

Cerro Azúl

PARQUE NACIONAL CHAGRES

Río Pequení

Río Chagres

Lago Alajuela

Río Boquerón

PARQUE NACIONAL CAMINO DE CRUCES

PN Chagres Main Office

Chilibre

PN Soberania office

Paraíso

Gaillard Cut

Pedro Miguel Locks

Miraflores Locks

Cuango

Miramar

La Guaira

Nombre de Dios

Isla Grande

Puerto Lindo

Portobelo

Cerro Brúja (974m)

PARQUE NACIONAL PORTOBELO

Boquerón

Costa Arriba

Río Piedra

María Chiquita

Sabanitas

Nuevo Vigía

Río Gatún

TRANSÍSTMICA HIGHWAY (TRANSÍSTMICA)

Gamboa Rainforest Resort

Gamboa

Rainforest Discovery Centre

PARQUE NACIONAL SOBERANÍA

Panama Canal Railway

Summit Botanical Gardens & Zoo

Isla Caleta

Colón

Cristóbal

Gatún Locks

Gatún Dam

Achiote

Fuerte San Lorenzo

Río Chagres

Lago Gatún

Panama Canal

ISLA BARRO COLORADO

Escobal

Costa Abajo

Río Lagarto

Boca del Río Indio

Río Indio

Miguel de la Borda

COLÓN

COCLÉ

Western Panama

0   25 km

◀ Western Panama

Chagres amid untouched tropical rainforest; to the northeast lies the **Costa Arriba**, an isolated region of rich coral reefs and laid-back fishing villages, much of which is nominally protected by the **Parque Nacional Portobelo**, set around the ruins and beautiful natural harbour of the old Spanish port of **Portobelo**.

The Panama Canal

Panama's canal is the country's most recognizable landmark, crucial to its economy and inextricably entwined with its historical and cultural development. Arguably, the world's most important waterway, it sees around fourteen thousand vessels and three hundred million tons of cargo pass through its locks every year – a figure that may double once the canal's ambitious expansion plan has been realized. A gargantuan feat of engineering, the construction of the **PANAMA CANAL**, completed in 1914, set the standards for twentieth-century engineering. At \$352 million it was the most expensive project ever undertaken, with the world's largest earthen dam creating the world's largest artificial lake. The most enormous locks ever built contained the greatest amount of concrete ever used – just over three million cubic metres, the equivalent of sixty Empire State Buildings – and possessed the largest ever swing doors. Yet it is the combination of the scale and ingenuity of the achievement with its ruggedly beautiful tropical setting that makes the canal so special.

There are several ways to appreciate what the canal has to offer, all of them within easy striking distance of the capital. Most people take a trip to **Miraflores Locks** – a convenient fifteen-minute bus ride out of Panama City – which has a well-situated visitor centre with a museum and viewing platform, offering a fine view of ships as they pass through. Facilities at the canal's other viewing platform, across the isthmus at the equally impressive three-chamber **Gatún Locks**, are not as developed and take longer to reach, though you can get even closer to the action (see p.132). Different perspectives again are offered by fishing or boating trips on **Lago Gatún**, and by speeding across the isthmus and alongside the canal by **train**. But by far the best way to get your head around the technical brilliance, natural beauty and sheer magnitude of the feat is to travel along the canal – known as a transit – on a **boat**.

Transiting the canal

To fully appreciate the canal, you need to see it up close. Things may not be quite as you'd expect – the gargantuan Panamax vessels (the largest on the canal) are manoeuvred with surprising delicacy, while the banks of this vast commercial enterprise are lined with jungle and spotted with unspoilt islands. In a **partial transit** from Gamboa to the tip of the Amador Causeway (or vice versa) you get to experience the excitement of passing under the impressive Bridge of the Americas, through the narrow Gaillard Cut and being raised and lowered in the lock chambers of both Miraflores and Pedro Miguel Locks. The **full transit** takes in the most breathtaking scenery, crossing Lago Gatún and weaving among tiny forested islands. You'll glide past a silent stream of giant ships before passing through the enormous Gatún Locks and terminating in Colón, from where it can be up to a two-hour bus journey back to Panama City.

Although completing a full transit might hold a certain cachet, the advertised 8–9 hours can often be a lot longer if you get caught up in one of the frequent log jams in Gatún Locks. A partial transit provides enough excitement and interest for most people and if you take a northbound trip, docking around 1pm in Gamboa, you can skip the bus transfer to enjoy a coffee or a cocktail at the *Gamboa Rainforest*

The Big Ditch

Erroneously nicknamed **The Big Ditch**, the 77km canal eschews straight lines as it weaves its way from the Pacific to the Caribbean or Atlantic entrance, which is actually 42km to the west, on account of Panama's eel-like shape. British politician and historian James Bryce dubbed the waterway "the greatest liberty Man has ever taken with nature", though ironically it has resulted in a symbiotic relationship between the two: the canal's constant thirst for water to feed the locks is highly dependent on the preservation of the adjacent national parks to protect the water catchment area.

The vast **lock chambers** measure 304.8m by 33.53m, affording colossal Panamax vessels a mere 0.6m of leeway either side, yet they function in much the same way as they did when they were first used. Once the gates are closed, these vast vessels are kept aligned by cables attached to pairs of electric locomotives known as mules (*mulas*). The huge tunnel-like culverts then kick in with phenomenal efficiency, taking only eight minutes to fill the giant chamber with the equivalent of 43 Olympic swimming pools.

Tolls for ships are calculated depending on type of vessel, size and type of cargo. The average toll for the largest vessels is $126,000 for the 8–10 hour transit but the costs don't stop there, since up to three tug boats are also required for the more difficult stages of the operation at a cost of $3000 per hour per boat, not to mention the obligatory canal pilot. It is no wonder that in 2008 annual revenues topped $2 billion. Yet for all the sums, the canal still represents a major saving in time and money for ships that would otherwise have to travel 15,000km round the treacherous seas of Cape Horn.

Resort before getting the public bus back to the city, with the added bonus of avoiding the inflated taxi fare from the causeway at the other end.

The two companies listed below offer similar **trips**, charging $165 for the full transit and $115 for the partial, which includes a transfer between the relevant marina on the Amador Causeway and the boat, bilingual guided commentary, soft drinks, meals and snacks. In the tourist season (Dec–April) there are frequent transits; out of season they tend to be restricted to Saturdays, with a full crossing only once a month. Various **tour operators** also offer canal transits though they all use the boats listed below – you're essentially just paying to be picked up from your accommodation.

The cheapest way to see the canal is to try and get a job as a **line-handler** – a person who helps keep the boat positioned in the locks; it a requirement for all transiting cruising vessels to have four line-handlers. If interested, ask around at the Balboa Yacht club on the Pacific side and in Shelter Bay Marina on the Atlantic side.

Canal and Bay Tours ☎ 209 2009, ⊛ www .canalandbaytours.com. Two larger craft are used for full transits, while the partial transit often employs the smaller *Isla Morada*, a 1912 wooden vessel said to have been previously owned by Al Capone. All tours leave from La Playita, Isla Naos, at 8am.

Panama Canal Tours ☎ 226 8917, ⊛ www .pmatours.net. The company caters predominantly to foreign tourists. Southbound partial transits leave from Flamenco Marina at 10am; northbound partial transits and full transits leave at 7.30am.

The Panama Canal Railway Company

Leaving the city along Avenida Omar Torrijos, with the towering cranes and vast stacks of shipping containers of the Port of Balboa away to your left, the Corozal Passenger Terminal of the **Panama Canal Railway Company** (☎ 317 6070, ⊛ www.panarail.com) is the first place of interest, and departure point for the scenic transisthmian train journey. The original Panama Railroad, built in the 1850s during the California Gold Rush (see box below), transported over $700 million in gold before the completion of the Union Pacific Railroad across the US in 1869 made it obsolete, forcing it into bankruptcy. A short revival transporting workers and equipment during the canal's construction, the railway fell into disrepair until 1998 when the government agreed to privatize it. Though the railway company predominantly ferries freight to and from the Atlantic and Pacific container ports, it offers a commuter passenger service to Colón that is very popular with tourists. A supremely comfortable way to enjoy the canal, it serves up old-world elegance in wood-panelled, carpeted carriages with large windows. In fine weather, make sure you also get out onto the open viewing deck. Departures from the Corozal Passenger Terminal (Mon–Fri; 1hr; $22 one way) are at 7.15am, with the return trip leaving Colón at 5.15pm. Reservations are not necessary though it's worth getting there early (6.30am) to secure your vantage point. Taxis charge around $5 from the city centre.

Miraflores Locks

A mere fifteen minutes from downtown Panama City along the Avenida Omar Torrijos are the **Miraflores Locks**, where the **Centro de Visitantes de Miraflores** (Miraflores Visitor Centre; daily 9am–5pm, including holidays; $8 museum and viewing decks, $5 lower viewing deck only; ⑦ 276 8617, ⓦ www.pancanal.com) provides a prime location for observing the canal in action. Marking the Pacific entrance to the waterway, the locks raise or lower vessels 16.5m between sea level and the artificial Lago Miraflores in two stages, a process best appreciated from the upper observation deck of the visitor centre only metres away from the water. Optimum viewing times for vessels transiting are before 11am, when ships are usually entering the canal from the Pacific, and after 3pm, when they are exiting.

The four-storey visitor centre – a rather unappealing monolith – also contains an impressive museum, which serves to promote the Autoridad del Canal de Panamá (ACP) as much as to inform you about the canal. Both the French and US

Building the Panama Railroad

So often overshadowed by the building of the Panama Canal, the **Panama Railroad** was the world's first transcontinental railway and a phenomenal engineering feat in its own right. Anticipating the gold rush, wealthy American businessman William Aspinwall constructed a 76km track linking the Atlantic and Pacific Oceans to facilitate trade between New York and the East Coast and rapidly developing California. At an incredible total cost of almost $8 million (six times the original estimate), it became the most expensive track per mile in the world, though the hefty first-class transit fee, $25 in gold, also made it one of the most profitable.

The **human costs** were brutal. During the five years of construction an estimated 6000–10,000 workers died, though appallingly records were only kept of the white employees, who constituted a fraction of the work force. The high death toll enabled the railroad to sustain a grisly sideline in pickling bodies in barrels to sell to hospitals worldwide. Although most of the labourers came from the Caribbean, others migrated from as far as India, Malaysia and Ireland. Despite the constant influx, work occasionally stalled since at any one time only a third of the men, who spent long days up to their waists in swamp, attacked by mosquitoes and disease, were fit enough to wield a shovel.

Little sign of the appalling human cost remained when the inaugural transit was made in 1855 amid much pomp and champagne. As one of the passengers wrote, "It affords the observant traveller an opportunity of an easy enjoyment and acquaintance with intertropical nature unsurpassed in any part of the world". The same is still true today.

construction efforts are squeezed into the ground floor exhibition – for more in-depth coverage go to the canal museum in Casco Viejo (see p.70). Against a vast montage of historical photos and a soundtrack of blasting dynamite, the bare bones of the enterprise are covered through impressive scale models and bilingual texts. Sound effects continue on the first floor as the focus shifts to the biodiversity of the canal's catchment area, while on the floor above, the spotlight turns to engineering; highlights include a virtual high-speed transit of the canal, complete with illuminated 3-D topographic map, and experiencing life inside a lock culvert (thankfully without the water). The centre also houses a couple of thinly stocked **cafés**, a **restaurant** and a gift shop.

It's a fifteen-minute ride on any Gamboa or Paraíso **bus** from the Albrook terminal to the Miraflores stop.

The road to Gamboa

Leaving behind the Miraflores and Pedro Miguel Locks, the road to Gamboa (Carretera Gaillard) skirts the emerald rainforest of the contiguous **Parque Nacional Camino de Cruces** and **Parque Nacional Soberanía**, both of which have trails to suit hikers, bird lovers and anyone interested in the Spanish conquest. It then ascends to the continental divide at the **Summit Botanical Gardens and Zoo**, before swooping down to the bridge across the Río Chagres, which marks the entrance to the somnolent canal-era town of Gamboa. Unfortunately buses to Gamboa, though regular, are infrequent, so that visiting several sites in one day is tricky unless you have your own transport.

Parque Nacional Camino de Cruces

Despite bearing the name of the conquistadors' famous trade route across the isthmus (named after the now-submerged settlement of Cruces), the **Parque Nacional Camino de Cruces** is often overlooked as a tourist destination, with the adjoining Parque Nacional Soberanía attracting far more visitors. Yet, while it is hard to escape the dull sounds of traffic thundering along the motorway that cuts across a corner of the park, the reserve is a prime location for spotting sloths and provides important traces of colonial times.

There are four **trails** on offer: the **Sendero Capricornio** is the shortest and most popular, an easy 1km circular stroll from the administration building through

Paja canalera

Travelling alongside the canal on the Pacific side, you can't fail to notice what appear to be streaks of shimmering silk against the verdant backdrop of rainforest – actually a rampant cream-tipped mass of swaying **elephant grass** (*saccharum spontaneum*). Introduced to the Canal Zone from Asia by the Americans in the 1950s and 1960s, earning it the nicknames of *paja canalera* (canal grass) and *paja gringa* (gringo grass), it is unclear whether it was planted on the canal banks to help prevent erosion or arrived accidentally in a shipment of equipment from Vietnam. Either way, the result has been devastating. An invasive species, the grass now covers at least twenty square kilometres between the Soberanía, Camino de Cruces and Metropolitano parks, and is creeping into parts of the Darién, Coclé and Veraguas, rendering soil unfit for any other purpose. Since the grass needs bright sunlight to thrive, ANAM has started a reforestation programme of native trees that will produce a lot of shade to stem its spread.

some of the park's mainly dry semi-deciduous forest. But it's worth expending slightly more energy on the **Sendero Mirador** (3.2km total), which offers a moderate hike up to a breezy wooden watchtower, affording an impressive panoramic view of the canal and distant city skyscrapers. The remaining two trails, the **Ruinas de Cardenas** and **Camino de Cruces**, are both still in need of clearance work, though you don't need to venture far along the latter before you'll come across some of the original cobblestones.

Any of the **buses** going from Albrook bus terminal to Paraíso and Gamboa will drop you off at the bottom of the Carretera Chivo Chivo, a couple of bends after the Miraflores Locks and before the road crosses the Miraflores Ponds, where you can often spot ducks and jacanas, and occasionally caimans. From there it's a 2km hike up a dirt road requiring a high clearance vehicle, or 4WD in the rainy season, to the **park office** ($5 entry, $5 camping), where **camping** is permitted, though there are no facilities beyond a bathroom and running water.

Pedro Miguel Locks and the Gaillard Cut

A short drive or bus ride further up the road takes you to the smaller **Pedro Miguel Locks**, which though closed to the public can be viewed from a parking spot just beyond them. The canal then narrows into the infamous **Gaillard Cut**, where around seventy percent of all canal excavation occurred. Its 13km stretch posed the most persistent technical headache for engineers, and severe landslides continued long after the eventual opening of the canal. On the left, a little beyond Paraíso, the canal's former dredging headquarters, rows of small white crosses mark the **French Cemetery**, which sits on the continental divide, a poignant reminder of the doomed French attempt to build a canal in the 1880s. The road then climbs a couple of kilometres, with a turn-off to the elegant, cable-stayed **Centennial Bridge**, opened in 2004 to celebrate Panama's hundred years of independence, and providing a second link between the east and west of the country and easing congestion on the Bridge of the Americas, the only other exit west from Panama City. After 3km of dense rainforest the road forks: to the right it cuts through the Parque Nacional Soberanía to the Transístmica and the new motorway, which both link Panama City with Colón, while to the left it continues to Gamboa.

Parque Nacional Soberanía

Providing the most accessible substantial body of tropical rainforest from Panama City, a mere thirty-minute drive away, the **PARQUE NACIONAL SOBERANÍA** is one of the country's most visited national parks and well worth exploring. A long, thick, broadly rectangular strip that stretches north and west from the **park office**, which lies 15km northwest of Panama City, it hugs the canal and encircles Gamboa, covering over 190 square kilometres. The park encompasses a stretch of the majestic Río Chagres, the canal's lifeblood, which you can explore by boat, and several well-maintained trails either side of the town, including a stretch of the historic Camino de Cruces and a world-renowned birding hotspot, the Camino del Oleoducto (Pipeline Road).

Harbouring 525 recorded bird species, 105 mammals, 79 reptiles and 55 amphibians, the chances of spotting **wildlife** in the park are high. White-tailed deer, agoutis, coatis, pacas, howler monkeys and Geoffroy's tamarins are fairly commonplace, but you'll need a good guide to locate the rarer, more elusive nocturnal kinkajous or silky anteaters. Following an extensive breeding programme, several harpy eagles have been released into the park in recent years so there is a slim chance of catching sight of these endangered birds (see box, p.320). Other birds to

▲ Admiring the Río Chagres in Parque Nacional Soberanía

look out for include crested eagles, red-lored Amazons, great jacamars and trogon – the park's symbol.

The trails

There are three substantial trails and one small circuit within the park, although they're not particularly close to each other or the park office, arguably making the area best enjoyed with a car, parking at the various trailheads, or on a tour (see p.44).

By far the most tramped trail is the unpromising-sounding **Camino del Oleoducto** (Pipeline Road), so named because it was originally built to service an oil pipeline constructed across the isthmus by the US in World War II in case transportation via the canal became impossible. The pipeline was never used but the 17.5km dirt-road service track, which lies a kilometre beyond Gamboa, draws birding enthusiasts from around the world. Though visually unremarkable since it is no wilderness trail, the likely wildlife sightings more than compensate. As elsewhere, the forest is at its most active at daybreak, though you're likely to find something to catch your eye whatever time you go. Even if you can't tell a white-whiskered puffbird from a band-tailed barbthroat, you cannot fail to be impressed by the array of brightly coloured birds and you'll see a great deal more if you go with a good guide (see p.42 & p.44).

A 10km section of the isthmus-crossing **Camino de Cruces** traverses the park's dense vegetation from the borders of the Parque Nacional Camino de Cruces (see p.116) – to access the trailhead, head 6km up the road that forks right at the park office, which connects with the Transístmica and the new Panama City–Colón motorway. The trail ends up at the shores of the Río Chagres, site of the barely distinguishable remains of the Ruinas de Venta de Cruces, which served as a resting post for weary, booty-laden mules and conquistadors. However, you don't have to venture that far to get a flavour of the history – a ten-minute hike along the path will bring you to a restored section of the original sixteenth-century paving stones.

If you decide to walk the whole trail, there are two options to avoid returning along the same route (the round-trip is an exhausting eight-hour trek). One is to hop across the Chagres to the *Gamboa Rainforest Resort* (see p.120) and revive yourself with a drink, before catching one of the regular buses back. You would need to organize a boat to meet you in advance, which the park wardens can arrange for a couple of dollars, or you can seek out a boatman at the town jetty in Gamboa. Alternatively, hike half of the Camino de Cruces, breaking off down the 5km **Sendero de la Plantación**, the gravelly remnants of a paved thoroughfare that once led to the largest private agricultural venture in the old Canal Zone, harvesting rubber, coffee and cocoa, which you can still occasionally spot growing wild amid the rainforest. It eventually disgorges you onto the road to Gamboa, where you can flag down one of the regular Gamboa–Panama City buses – you can also park at this end of the track.

A few hundred metres along the main road from the Plantation Trail lies the entrance to **Sendero El Charco**, a short circular route.

Practicalities

Buses from Panama City's Albrook terminal drop off at the park office, several kilometres away from the main trails and at the entrance to the Sendero de la Plantación (also the turn-off for the *Canopy Tower Ecolodge* – see p.120). For the Pipeline Road, alight at the park in Gamboa, walk 1km along the road parallel to the railway and canal, then follow the signs up a dirt road to the right to the (infrequently staffed) entrance barrier. Anyone travelling by car can park at any of the trailheads.

You can pick up a **map** and pay your fee ($5) at the **park office** (☎232 4192) or at the entry barrier to the Pipeline Road. Although most of Soberanía's trails are easy and safe enough to do on your own, you're strongly advised to hike the **Camino de Cruces** with a guide as the trail is overgrown and difficult to follow in places. Several Panama City tour operators do the trip, as well as offering excursions to the Pipeline Road (see p.44), which would solve the transport difficulties, or you can hire a park ranger from the park office as a guide – a much cheaper option, though you're unlikely to get an expert naturalist. The fit and adventurous might consider a two-day hike along the whole of the Pipeline Road and beyond, down to Frijoles, a further 7km and across Lago Gatún by boat, though you would need a guide as the trail becomes indistinct after Río Agua Salud. Most visit the park as a day-trip from Panama City, although there is accommodation in Gamboa (see p.120) if you're keen to make an early start in the forest. You can also arrange to **camp** ($5) along the Plantation or Pipeline Roads (no facilities but near running water) or lodge at the basic **ANAM refuge** at the trail end, but you will need to carry your own food.

Summit Botanical Gardens and Zoo

The formerly down-at-heel **Summit Botanical Gardens and Zoo** (daily: Jan–March 9am–5pm; April–Dec 9am–4pm; $1; ☎232 4854, ⓦwww .summitpanama.org) is undergoing an ambitious overhaul. Though some of the animal cages are still depressingly small, Summit merits a visit in order to see fauna that you are unlikely to spot in the wild and it is a pleasant place to stroll and birdwatch. In the early rainy season you may see colonies of oropendolas and caciques, while hummingbirds and toucans are more common year-round. The gardens' star attractions are some of Panama's most endangered and elusive residents – a jaguar, tapir, a forlorn harpy eagle, and some golden frogs in a new amphibian rescue unit that was due to open in late 2010.

The gardens are a popular picnic spot so during weekends and school holidays your ears are more likely to be greeted by reggaeton than birdsong. To get here, take any Gamboa **bus**, getting off at the stop right outside the park gates.

Gamboa and around

Surrounded by the luxuriant vegetation of the Parque Nacional Soberanía and bordered by the impressive Río Chagres and Lago Gatún, into which the river spills, you would expect **Gamboa** to be a thriving tourist destination. Yet despite being the portal to a variety of attractions on and off the water, the sleepy former Canal Zone town has yet to be revitalized by the tourist traffic, partly since most visitors tend to make day-trips out from Panama City. For nature lovers and birding enthusiasts in particular, Gamboa provides access to the legendary Pipeline Road and the adjacent Rainforest Discovery Centre. It is also the departure point for excursions to the scientific research station on **Isla Barro Colorado**, for boats offering Pacific-bound partial canal transits, fishing trips or wildlife viewing on **Lago Gatún**, and for cultural excursions to indigenous **Emberá communities** upriver. The town is easily accessed by bus and though some activities need organizing in advance, others require no planning or can be arranged on the spot.

Gamboa

Situated at the entrance to Lago Gatún – the loveliest section of the Panama Canal – at the junction with the powerful Río Chagres and surrounded by exuberant rainforest, **GAMBOA** is an attractive, quiet town, the most noticeable activity taking place weekdays on the lake shore, where the canal dredging division is located, and at the town's eastern perimeter, where the gargantuan luxury *Gamboa Rainforest Resort* perches high above the banks of the Chagres. Commanding imperious views of the surrounding scenery, it offers a bewildering array of activities to both residents and day visitors.

Arrival and information

Gamboa is a thirty-minute drive or fifty-minute **bus** ride from Panama City. Buses (☎314 6013) make regular daily departures (5am, 5.45am, 6.30am - 6am on weekends, 8am, 10am, noon, 2pm, 4.30pm, 6.30pm, 9pm; Mon–Fri also 1 & 3pm; 55c) from the very far end of the Albrook terminal (by *Niko's Café*). After crossing the bridge into Gamboa, the bus circles the tree-filled park, where you alight for the Pipeline Road or Rainforest Discovery Centre, before it heads up towards the *Gamboa Rainforest Resort*, where it turns, taking the same route back. Catch it back to Panama City outside the entrance to the dredging division, at the park corner. A taxi will set you back $25.

The town has two **ATM** machines, at the resort and at the entrance to the dredging division, opposite which there is a **post office.**

Accommodation

The *Gamboa Rainforest Resort* dominates, but there are a few other options.

Canopy Tower Ecolodge Semaphore Hill, Parque Nacional Soberanía ☎264 5720, ⓦwww .canopytower.com. US radar tower converted into a four-storey, twelve-room eco-lodge with a genuine commitment to conservation. Simple, functional, single rooms with shared bathroom are offered alongside more comfortable en-suite doubles and suites; all have screens, fans and hot water. Guests get a free guided walk each day, with excursions catering primarily for birders. Rates (multi-day packages offer good deals) include full

board, with decent meals served from the wonderfully panoramic dining lounge. ⑨
Gamboa Rainforest Resort ☎314 5000, ⓦwww .gamboaresort.com. Sprawling luxury mega-resort in a stunning location overlooking the river, predominantly attracting US couples and families who want nature activities laid on. There are spacious rooms and suites in the main building, with all mod cons plus good-sized balcony and great views, or cheaper "villa apartments" in renovated canal-era houses. Facilities are endless:

two vast pools, tennis courts, mountain bikes, gym, spa, plus a marina complete with kayaks and boats. Activities (some included) range from bingo to a visit to an Emberá village. Service at the resort and in the three restaurants, two bars and disco is variable, as is the quality of the cuisine. ⑨

🐾 **Ivan's Bed & Breakfast** Central Gamboa ☎ 314 9436, ⓦ www.gamboaecotours .com. Tucked away in a delightful old wooden canal house, this friendly establishment run by Gladys and Ivan Ortíz is aimed primarily at birdwatchers, comprising four simply furnished

but comfortable en-suite rooms with fans and hot water. Continental breakfast is included with other meals provided on request. Ivan leads local birding tours and can help organize other excursions. ⑥

Soberanía Research Station and Lodge Central Gamboa ☎ 6676 2466, ⓦ www.advantagepanama .com/soberania. The best budget option, run by Advantage Tours, often hosting Smithsonian scientists and visiting student groups. Offers a handful of simply furnished doubles with a/c, private bathroom and hot water, and shared kitchen. ⑤

The Town

Isolated **Gamboa** – its only road access via an old single-track bridge shared with the Panama Railroad – has never been a major scene of activity. Built in 1911 as a settlement for around seven hundred "silver roll" employees and families (see p.336), its population did not increase significantly until the canal's dredging division relocated there from Paraíso in 1936. As the white US canal workers and military personnel who could not be accommodated on bases moved in, the earlier inhabitants were squeezed to the town's margins. By 1942, Gamboa's residents exceeded 3800, much more than the current population, and the community could boast a cinema and golf course. Once the Panama Canal Authority started to transfer operations to Panama City following the 1977 treaties, services began to close and the town dwindled, although the **golf course** has recently been upgraded (ⓦ www.summitgolfpanama.com). There's little to do in the town except soak up the tranquil yesteryear feel, taking in the attractive (and often empty) canal-era architecture, indulging in a little birdwatching around the wooded fringes, or strolling along the Chagres, looking out for iguanas and turtles sunning themselves along the riverbanks, and marvelling at the constant procession of container ships.

The Gamboa Rainforest Resort

Announcing its pre-eminence with a large sign directing you right as you enter Gamboa, the imposing **Gamboa Rainforest Resort** is the centre of attention in town. Much more than just a place to stay (see opposite), the resort offers a wealth of activities for residents and non-residents both in its extensive grounds and by way of excursions organized by Gamboa Tours, based in the hotel (ⓦ www .gamboatours.com). However, unless you like pre-packaged nature tourism, you're unlikely to want to do more than stop for a bite to eat or a drink. Activities include the popular but expensive **aerial tram ride** (Tue–Sun 8.45am, 10.30am, 1.30pm, 3pm; $53), an hour-long guided tropical chairlift excursion. Other low-key **diversions** include a butterfly house, orchid nursery, serpentarium and miniature aquarium containing caimans and crocodiles, though it's more rewarding to spot them in their preferred habitat, the shallows of the Chagres, on a night boat tour ($42) or from the vantage point of the riverside restaurant, *Los Largatos*.

Eating and drinking

The best bet for a bite to eat is the *Gamboa Rainforest Resort*, though you'll be paying elevated tourist prices and the quality of food and service is variable. A lunchtime buffet is available at the main *Corotú* restaurant (daily 6.30am–10.30pm), while snacks and cocktails are served at the Monkey Bar terrace, a splendid breezy spot with fabulous views across the Chagres, and the riverside *Los Lagartos* (Tue–Sun 11.30am–5pm) offers superlative opportunities for wildlife viewing. During the week, inexpensive meals are available from the makeshift **fondas** opposite the entrance to the canal's dredging division, which close after feeding lunch to the workers. Otherwise there is a hard-to-locate – so ask - small **shop** at the back of some houses on the way to the Pipeline Road, or bring a picnic.

The Rainforest Discovery Centre

A couple of kilometres along the Pipeline Road from Gamboa, the **Rainforest Discovery Centre** (daily 6am; ☏ 264 6266 in Panama City, ☏ 314 9386, ⓦ www .pipelineroad.org) boasts an impressive canopy observation tower with multi-level viewing platforms, a series of short trails and an interpretive centre, whose main draw is the observation deck, where bird feeders attract scores of hummingbirds. The drawback is the hefty entrance fee ($20) if you arrive during prime birding time (6–10am; $15 thereafter), though it's definitely worth the outlay if you're keen on birds or you make a day of it, taking a picnic. Profits go towards environmental education, research and conservation projects.

Canopy Tower Ecolodge and Nature Observatory

For serious nature lovers who can't afford the overnight rates, it's still worth considering a day-trip ($85–95) to the **Canopy Tower Ecolodge** (☏ 264 5720, ⓦ www.canopytower.com). These are actually partial day-trips, which have to be organized in advance, and include one meal, the park fee and a guided walk, where you're likely to spot manakins, antbirds, tinamous, sloths, coatis and agoutis, as well as an abundance of butterflies and insects. You also get time on the truly special canopy-level observation deck, which is equipped with a telescope and even sun loungers, allowing you to indulge in some spectacular armchair birdwatching. To get there take a taxi ($20) or the Gamboa **bus**, which will drop you off at the drive entrance, from where it's a steep 1km to the lodge.

Lago Gatún

Following the damming of the Río Chagres in 1910, the waters took three years to rise, culminating in the formation of **LAGO GATÚN**, the largest artificial lake in the world at the time, covering 425 square kilometres – roughly the size of Barbados. The lake now provides 33km of the waterway's total 77km length, with the ships following the original course of the Río Chagres, where the lake is at its deepest, and collects and releases the 43 million gallons of water necessary for each vessel to transit the canal.

The undulating topography ensured that this impressive body of water developed into a place of great beauty, with dozens of peninsulas and tree-topped islands, and a myriad of inlets easing their tentacles into the lush rainforest, all of which are best explored by boat. Favourite destinations are **Isla Barro Colorado** (see opposite) and the archipelago of **Islas Tigre** and **Islas Brujas**, formerly the collective home of a primate sanctuary, where for over twenty years abandoned "pet" or confiscated trafficked monkeys were rehabilitated to the wild. Though the sanctuary is now closed the monkeys remain happily marooned there. You can't land on the seventeen or so islands, but with a good pair of binoculars you can usually observe some of the islands' inhabitants cavorting in the trees from your boat. Several tour operators include the islands on their wildlife viewing trips (see p.44) though some, unfortunately, can't resist the urge to feed the monkeys.

Other wildlife to look out for includes crocodiles and caimans slithering in the muddy shallows, as well as sloths and snakes entwined round branches, which can easily be spotted while on a fishing trip. The lake is famous for its prolific peacock bass, and fishermen hanging out at the public dock, before the bridge, will happily take you out for a few hours angling for around $60 for the boat.

Isla Barro Colorado

Home to the most studied patch of tropical forest in the New World is **Isla Barro Colorado** (BCI), whose name derives from the dominant reddish clay (*barro colorado*). Designated a biological reserve in 1923, it is administered by the Smithsonian Tropical Research Institute (STRI), drawing scientists from all over the world to pore over the sixteen square kilometres of flora and fauna. Once only accessible to scientists, the island can now be visited either through the STRI (☎212 8951, ⊛www.stri.org; or in person at the STRI's Earl S. Tupper Building – see p.76), or with a select few tour operators, and it makes for a diverting outing.

Tours last all day (Tues, Wed & Fri 7.15am–4.10pm, Sat & Sun 8am–3.30pm; $70) and depart from the STRI jetty, 1km beyond Gamboa. Rates include the boat transfer and lunch, though you have to get yourself to Gamboa first. After a short **talk**, you set out on a **guided walk**, during which you'll learn about some of the island's 1300 plus plant species and 110 odd species of mammal, over half of which are bats. A favourite route leads to the "Big Tree", an enormous 500-year-old kapok with a 25m diameter, laden with epiphytes. Although the small island is home to both ocelots and pumas, you're unlikely to see more than their prints in the mud. Much more visible are the vast colonies of leafcutter ants, estimated to chew fifteen percent of all leaves produced in the forest to feed the fungus they eat in their subterranean nests. After **lunch** in the cafeteria, you are left to your own devices to watch for wildlife around the immediate vicinity of the research station. You're likely to see howler monkeys at the very least. Unfortunately, it's not permitted to return to the forest on your own – you might be able to coax your guide back for a second outing before the boat leaves, but it depends on the individual and on the weather.

Parque Nacional Chagres

North of Panama City, encompassing large tracts of the Provinces of Colón and Panama, the vast, sprawling rainforested wilderness of **Parque Nacional Chagres** stretches from the northern rain-soaked mountains overlooking the Caribbean to the park's highest peak, Cerro Jefe (1007m), in the south. The tropical vegetation harbours large but elusive populations of tapirs, endemic salamanders and an abundance of birdlife, including harpy eagles and the rare Tacarcuna bush tanager, and is laced with waterfalls and rivers rich in fish as well as otters, caimans and crocodiles. Hikers are also drawn to the area, particularly by the prospect of following in the steps of the conquistadors along the Camino Real, which slices across the western edge of the reserve.

At the heart of the park, the powerful Río Chagres and its tributaries – home to several Emberá and Wounaan villages that welcome visitors – carve their way through rugged terrain spilling into the scenic elongated **Lago Alajuela** at the park's southwest corner. A reservoir, Lago Alajuela was built to help regulate the water level in Lago Gatún further downriver.

Supplying forty percent of the water necessary for the canal to function and providing all the water for domestic and industrial consumption – as well as electricity through **hydro-electric power** – in Panama City and Colón, the Río Chagres is of vital importance to the country. In order to protect the river and its catchment area, the national park was formed in 1985, its 1296 square kilometres making it one of the country's largest protected areas.

Accessing the park

Despite three park offices within easy reach of main roads from Panama City, the reserve's vastness and the lack of tourist development make access difficult, especially if you're reliant on public transport. So most tourists visit with a tour operator (see p.44), generally bound for the western end, round **Lago Alajuela**, which lies around 35km north of the capital by road. There, several jetties serve as departure points for kayaking, fishing or rafting excursions, or for visiting an Emberá village or hiking along the Camino Real. Other than die-hard birdwatchers, few tourists head for the other main entry point into the park, in the hillside community of Cerro Azul, which lies 40km northeast of Panama City by road. From there you can hike to **Cerro Jefe**, an important location for endemic mosses, orchids, ferns and bromeliads but besides an impressive mirador and a couple of short **birding** trails, there's no infrastructure for venturing into the park's wilderness areas.

Visiting an Emberá community

At only a couple of hours travel away from Panama City and Colón, the **Emberá village tour** is now an established favourite with cruise ships and tour operators (see p.44). Publicity brochures glibly talk about the Emberá "living much as their ancestors did centuries ago" and although the communities ensure that you get a varied and traditional cultural experience during the visit, you don't need to look further than the use of outboard motors, mobile phones and Spanish – not to mention the jeans and T-shirts often donned once the tourists have evaporated – to see that the Emberá are undergoing radical change. Staying **overnight**, or preferably for several nights, affords a better opportunity to interact with villagers and venture deeper into the forest. That said, the day-tours can still offer visitors a fascinating partial snapshot of Emberá life, and there are obvious benefits to communities: income that will afford them greater self-determination, renewed cultural pride and a revival of ancestral skills and traditions. Yet for some of the younger generation, donning a loincloth and dancing is merely a means to a financial end, lacking any deeper cultural signifi-cance, and it's hard to gauge the impact on communities and the surrounding forest of increasing hordes of visitors in peak cruise-ship season (Oct–April), which causes village life to stand still.

Although the villages inevitably vary in setting and character, the excursions follow much the same **itinerary**. Do your homework, though: prices ($75–150, not neces-sarily including the $5 park entry fee) and tour group sizes vary, though even travelling in a small party is no guarantee you won't be cheek by jowl with other tourists once in the village. Morning pick-up (8am–8.30am) is followed by an hour's bus journey to Lago Alajuela, where life-jacketed tourists fan out towards different villages in motorised dugouts, piloted by men strikingly clad in loincloths (*antia* or *wuayuco*) and beaded necklaces. The boat trip (30–60min depending on the village location and river water levels) is itself a highlight, gliding through vine-laden forest with raptors wheeling overhead and metallic kingfishers flashing past. At the villages, traditional wood and thatch buildings sit on stilts, and you'll be greeted by enthusiastic kids and women, who form a dazzling collage of fluorescent sarong-like skirts (*uhua*) and multicoloured bead and silver coin necklaces, their hair often adorned with hibiscus flowers.

Activities generally include a village tour, a talk about the traditional Emberá way of life (see p.306) and a demonstration of basketry or wood carving as well as a short walk into the rainforest with one of the village elders to learn about medicinal plants, dealing

Río Chagres and around

Most tourist activities rely on the area's main artery, the Río Chagres, be it **whitewater rafting** the cascading torrents of the upper river or more leisurely **kayaking** along the slower, lower stretches, both of which are generally organized as day-trips from Panama City (see p.44). One of the best ways to explore the park is by visiting one of the numerous **Emberá** communities, sprinkled along the banks of the Chagres and its tributaries (see box below). The Emberá, together with the closely related Wounaan, have been relocating from the Darién since the late 1960s. Since their traditional means of livelihood – semi-nomadic subsistence agriculture and hunting – are now largely denied to them thanks to the restrictions of living within a national park, they are being encouraged to make a living from tourism, often aided by NGOs and Peace Corps workers.

As with the neighbouring parks of Camino de Cruces and Soberanía, Parque Nacional Chagres also includes important traces of the country's colonial past, containing a lengthy portion of the **Camino Real**, one of the conquistador mule routes across the isthmus, which skirts the eastern shores of Lago Alajuela. There is currently no clearly marked route but several tour companies offer day or multi-day guided hikes along this historic trail (see p.44).

with everything from extracting snake venom to enhancing your love life. A simple lunch – usually fried fish and plantain, plus fruit – precedes traditional dances accompanied by drums, bamboo flutes and maracas, after which tourists are left to get their bodies painted with jagua dye, frolic with the kids in the river and peruse the numerous finely made crafts on display, sold at fixed prices. Unlike the Kuna, the Emberá are fairly comfortable being photographed and general shots of the village (though not inside homes) and dances are allowed, though permission should be sought from individuals. Most tours pile back into the dugouts 2.30–3pm for the return trip.

It is possible and cheaper to visit **independently** – several of the communities have their own website with mobile phone contact numbers (listed below). They generally charge around $70 per person (1–2 people, less for more) for the day ($30 per night), which is approximately what they receive per tourist from the tour operators. But you'll still need to ring in advance to ensure a boat ride, and reaching Puerto de Corotú, the departure point for most villages on Lago Alajuela, is time-consuming on public transport (2hr 30min) and will probably also require some travel by taxi. To reach Corotú, take any *diablo rojo* signed "Transístmica" from the front of Albrook bus terminal. Change at San Miguelito onto a bus bound for La Chibima. After the bus stop, turn into the first road on your right, where you can find a taxi to take you to the port ($8–10). If you want to increase your chances of a less touristy scene, visit an Emberá community in the Darién (see p.319), where with far fewer and smaller tour groups – the odd exception aside – it's easier to learn about village life without disrupting it.

Community contacts

Comunidad Drua ⊛ www.trail2.com/embera.

Comunidad Parará Puru ⊛ www.emberavillagetours.com.

Comunidad Tusipono Emberá ⊛ www.emberatusipono09.blogspot.com.

Just outside the park boundaries

Emberá Errebachi Tulio ☏ 275 3076, ✉ tuliotours@gmail.com. On the Río Piedra, Colón (see p.137).

Comunidad San Antonio ⊛ www.authenticpanama.com/wounan/htm.

Comunidad Emberá Quera ⊛ www.emberapanama.com. On Río Gatún.

Cerro Azul and Cerro Jefe

Though designating both a mountain peak and a nearby village, **Cerro Azul** generally refers to the mountainous area around both, on the southern edge of the national park, 40km from Panama City. It is very popular with more affluent Panamanians – and increasingly with foreign retirees – many of whom have second homes peppered along the fringes of the park boundary, attracted by the accessible fresh mountain air and great views (when the mists clear). It's not as wild as the Darién or Amistad, but for birdwatchers and nature lovers with limited time, Cerro Azul makes for a convenient break from Panama City, with a number of comfortable accommodation options within reach of the forest. You can easily get within striking distance of the park with an ordinary vehicle or by bus, since the roads are asphalt as far as the gated residential area of Altos de Cerro Azul.

The main draw is the park's highest point, **Cerro Jefe**, though two short birdwatching trails are located near the summit. To reach there from the park office the route is less interesting, between open fields for about 3km before plunging into elfin forest, where the road forks. From there it's another 1.5km through cloud forest up to the antenna-covered Cerro Jefe, beyond which a **mirador** offers a splendid panorama along the Pacific coast and across the unending canopy of Chagres, even as far as the Caribbean on a clear day.

A little further along, two paths head off down the steep hill, eventually petering out, forcing you to return the same way: along the narrow and frequently boggy **Sendero Vistamares** and the **Sendero Xenoris**, 1.5km further along on the left. Both offer the chance to see speckled antshrikes, crested guans, yellow-eared toucanets and crimson-bellied woodpeckers. If you really want to explore, **Sendero Guayaral** is a tough but rewarding tramp from the park office at Cerro Azul to a refuge at Cerro Brewster (9km each way), which can be made easier by hiring horses to take your gear; arrange a guide in advance with the office in charge of the park at the ANAM Headquarters in Albrook in Panama City.

Practicalities

The western end of the park, around Lago Alajuela, is about a forty-minute drive from Panama City. The park headquarters (℡320 7521; $5) are at **Campo Chagres**, a small headland jutting into Lago Alajuela. To get there, take a Colón **bus**, getting off at Mini Super Mario along the Transístmica, and walk the remaining 3km. An ordinary car will also manage the journey. Though this is primarily a destination for day-trippers from the capital, you can **camp** here. The jetties at Madden Dam, Nuevo Vigia and Victoriano Lorenzo, further round the lake, are the embarkation points for visits upriver to Emberá communities (see box, p.124).

To reach **Cerro Azul** by **car**, head east along the Corredor Sur from Panama City; 6km past the airport turn-off, you enter the nondescript town of 24 de Diciembre, where Cerro Azul is signposted off to the left, just before Supermercado Xtra. By **bus**, take any transport bound for 24 de Diciembre or Chepo from Albrook terminal, getting off at La Doña Super 99 (just before Xtra); cross the road to the bus terminal at the back of the shopping centre, where minibuses wind up to Cerro Azul (every 30–45min, 6am–6pm; $1). On the right just after the entrance to Altos de Cerro Azul, *Fonda Bruni* serves filling *comida típica*. The buses turn just by the park office (no phone, contact the Campo Chagres office; $5 park fee).

ANAM camping Campo Chagres and Cerro Azul offer camping space with cold-water showers and shared kitchen facilities with the wardens but you'll need to bring all your food. Both prefer advance notice. $5

Cabañas 4x4 Cerro Azul, 5km beyond the park office ℡6680 3076, ⊛www.cabanas4x4.com. Four rustic but rather dark self-catering log cabins (for 2–8 people) and a couple of indigenous *bohíos* with thatched upstairs sleeping areas, set in delightful wooded surroundings with a natural swimming pool. Various spa services are also available. 4WD access necessary or arrange transport at the park office for a fee. Cabin $45/person, *bohío* $15/person.

Ginger House Altos de Cerro Azul ☎297 7037, ⓦwww.gingerhouse-panama.com. Well-appointed guesthouse providing home comforts set in lovely gardens offering three spacious, spotless rooms (private or shared bathroom) plus communal lounge, patio and hammock areas, affording wonderful views. ⑥

Posada de Ferisse Cerro Azul ☎297 0197, ⓔlaposadaferhisse@hotmail.com. Six double en-suite rooms (TV, a/c and private patio space). The on-site open-sided restaurant offers a mix of Panamanian and Cuban–Caribbean dishes and there's also a swimming pool. Though the views are great, it's some way from the forest. Breakfast included. ③

Colón and the Costa Abajo

Situated at the Atlantic entrance to the Panama Canal, with a population of around 42,000, **Colón** makes it into few holiday brochures; for most Panamanians its name is a byword for poverty, violence and urban decay. Yet vestiges of its former grandeur remain, worth exploring for an afternoon before heading out to several tourist destinations of note which lie within striking distance. Southwest of Colón a road runs through to the enormous **Gatún Locks**, where you can get up close to gigantic container ships being raised and lowered between sea level and Lago Gatún. Once across the canal, the road divides: to the right it meanders 22km through dense forest to the evocative ruins of the colonial **Fuerte San Lorenzo**, standing guard at the mouth of the Río Chagres; to the left, it rises above the shoreline of Lago Gatún, offering splendid views across the water and its sprinkling of tree-topped islands before undulating through agricultural land to the rarely visited coastal communities of the **Costa Abajo**.

Colón

While it's true that much of the city is run-down, following decades of neglect and decline, and the threat of violent crime is ever-present, **COLÓN** retains the decadent charm of a steamy Caribbean port, its former glory still evident in a few surviving monuments. Moreover, the people of Colón, mostly descendants of West Indians who came here to build the canal, are as warm and friendly as anywhere in the country and just as fond of partying. Sadly, most visitors come here solely to shop at the **Colón Free Zone**, a walled enclave on the edge of the city, where goods from all over the world can be bought at very low prices.

Safety in Colón

Although sometimes exaggerated, Colón's reputation throughout the rest of the country for **violent crime** is not undeserved, and if you come here you should exercise extreme caution – mugging, even on the main streets in broad daylight, does happen, with the preferred method a knife discreetly pointed at some point of your anatomy until you hand over the goods, which you should do without fuss. Don't carry anything you can't afford to lose, try and stay in sight of the police on the main streets, and consider renting a taxi (recommended by your hotel) to take you around, both as a guide and for protection. They charge about $15 an hour.

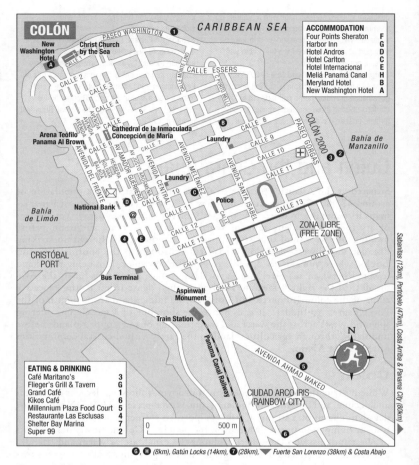

COLÓN

CARIBBEAN SEA

PASEO WASHINGTON ①

New Washington Hotel **A**

Christ Church by the Sea

CALLE 1

CALLE ESSERS

CALLE MONTE LIMO

C. PORTO BELLO

CALLE 2

CALLE 3

CALLE 4

5

AVENIDA CALLE

AVENIDA

AVENIDA

Arena Teófilo Panama Al Brown

Cathedral de la Inmaculada Concepción de María

AV. AMADOR GUERRERO

AV. JUSTO AROSEMENA

CALLE 5

CALLE 6

CALLE 7

AVENIDA MELÉNDEZ

AVENIDA CENTRAL

AVENIDA SANTA ISABEL

PASEO GORGAS

COLÓN 2000

Bahía de Manzanillo

CALLE 8

Laundry **B**

CALLE 9

CALLE 10

✚

② ③

AV. AMADOR GUERRERO

AV. HERRERA

AV. BOLÍVAR

CALLE 10

CALLE 11

Laundry

National Bank

Bahía de Limón

@ **D**

Police **C**

CALLE 11

CALLE 12

CALLE 13

CALLE 13

ZONA LIBRE (FREE ZONE)

④ **E**

CALLE 14

CALLE 15

CALLE 16

CRISTÓBAL PORT

Bus Terminal

Aspinwall Monument

CALLE 16

Train Station

Panama Canal Railway

N

AVENIDA AHMAD WAKED

F
⑤

CIUDAD ARCO IRIS (RAINBOW CITY)

⑥

| 0 | | 500 m |

Sabanitas (12km), Portobelo (47km), Costa Arriba & Panama City (80km) ▶

ACCOMMODATION
Four Points Sheraton	**F**
Harbor Inn	**G**
Hotel Andros	**D**
Hotel Carlton	**C**
Hotel Internacional	**E**
Meliá Panamá Canal	**H**
Meryland Hotel	**B**
New Washington Hotel	**A**

EATING & DRINKING
Café Maritano's	**3**
Flieger's Grill & Tavern	**G**
Grand Café	**1**
Kikos Café	**6**
Millennium Plaza Food Court	**5**
Restaurante Las Esclusas	**4**
Shelter Bay Marina	**7**
Super 99	**2**

Ⓖ, Ⓗ *(8km), Gatún Locks (14km),* ❼ *(28km),* ▼ *Fuerte San Lorenzo (38km) & Costa Abajo*

Some history

As work began on the construction of the Panama Railroad in 1850, the settlement now known as Colón began to mushroom on a low-lying lump of coral known as **Isla Manzanillo**. Surrounded by mosquito and sandfly-infested mangrove swamps and lacking a source of freshwater, the location was so unfavourable that the workers initially lived on a brig anchored in the bay rather than on the island itself. American historian H.H. Bancroft, on his arrival in 1851, summed up the general view: "The very ground on which one trod was pregnant with disease, and death was distilled in every breath of air". Yet the Americans in charge of the railway bewilderingly insisted on establishing the **Atlantic terminal** here, and in 1852 unilaterally named the place Aspinwall after one of the railway's owners. This upset the New Grenadan (present-day Colombia and Panama) authorities, who insisted that it be called Colón, after Cristobál Colón (aka Christopher Columbus), leading to a long-running dispute that the Colombians finally won by ingeniously instructing the postal services not to deliver letters from the US if addressed to Aspinwall.

The railway brought many immigrants and a degree of prosperity to the town despite the constant threat of yellow fever, malaria and cholera. Since then, wealth – via canal construction, a spell as a fashionable cruise-ship destination in the 1950s and the success of the Free Zone, founded in 1949 – has come and gone, and Panama's main port predominantly remains a slum city. In the face of extreme poverty and soaring unemployment levels, it is little surprise that many have turned to crime, particularly drug and arms trafficking, as a way to survive.

Arrival, information and transport

By far the most comfortable way to reach Colón is to splash out on the fabulous Panama Canal Railway **train** ($22 one way, $44 return; see p.115) to the Atlantic terminus, from where it's a short taxi ride ($1–2) or ten-minute walk to the bus terminal. If you walk, make sure you stay on the left-hand side of the road, hugging the fence, otherwise you are likely to get mugged. Most people travel to Colón by **bus**, arriving at the bus terminal (on the corner of Av del Frente and C 13), surprisingly one of the safer areas of town during the day. Buses arrive from and leave for Panama City every twenty minutes between 4am and 10pm though it's worth paying a little extra for the half-hourly express coaches (90min; $2.50). Try to arrive in daylight. If you arrive by **boat** from Kuna Yala, you'll come in at Coco Solo port, a $3 taxi ride from the city centre (but see p.279 for much safer transport options to and from the archipelago).

Though the city centre is compact, you are strongly advised not to wander around but to use licensed yellow **taxis** or the fancier, pricier tourist taxis (white with a yellow band) wherever possible. Consult your hotel about hiring a reliable driver to do your sightseeing; hourly rates (approximately $15) depend on where you go and the number of passengers. Though there are several banks and **ATMs** the safest places to withdraw money are in the Zona Libre and in Super 99 in Colón 2000. The **tourist office** on C 1 (Mon–Fri 8am–4pm; ☎441 9644) does not have much information and will be very surprised to see you.

Accommodation

Colón's budget options are in areas best avoided but there are sufficient **business hotel** options, some quite affordable. It's worth splashing out on a place that has armed security and a restaurant, so you won't have to go out at night. For those who prefer to give Colón a wide berth, there are a couple of places in the former Canal Zone by Lago Gatún, 10km or a $5 taxi-ride away, and conveniently situated for the locks and San Lorenzo, and one up in the hills east of Colón.

Four Points Sheraton Millennium Plaza, Av Ahmad Waked, Corredor Zona Libre ☎447 1000, ⓦwww.fourpoints.com. Colón's top hotel offers fifteen storeys of stylishly furnished rooms with all the usual luxuries and bright, floor-to-ceiling windows that afford splendid panoramas of the city. ❽

Hotel Andros Av Herrera, between C 9 & C 10 ☎441 0477, ⓦwww.hotelandros.com. Six floors of clean, tidy en-suite rooms (cable TV and decent furniture) arranged round an impressive central stairwell with wrought-iron balconies. Also with internet and an inexpensive restaurant (closed Sun). ❺

Hotel Carlton C 10 at Av Meléndez ☎447 0111, ⓦwww.elhotelcarlton.com. Slightly faded but full of character, with photographs of the canal, a display of flags and an impressive central staircase in the lobby. The rooms (en suite with a/c & cable TV) though a reasonable size, are nothing special but the hotel has a good selection of in-house services including a restaurant (mains $6–8; closed Sun), laundry, pharmacy and internet access. The first-floor patio terrace is also a plus. ❹

Hotel Internacional Av Bolívar at C 12 ☎445 2930, ⓦwww.hotelinternacional.es. A good deal located on one of the safest streets in the city (all things being relative), within a stone's throw of the bus terminal. Rooms are basic but comfortable providing cable TV and clean bathrooms. There's wi-fi throughout, a couple of

PCs, a (sporadically open) rooftop bar and a reasonable restaurant (closed Sun). **④**

Meryland Hotel C 7 opposite Parque Sucre ☎441 7055, ⓦwww.hotelmeryland.com. Behind the fancy pseudo-colonial facade lies a somewhat overpriced business hotel. The area is quiet and leafy, and the beds are really comfy, but the en-suite rooms (cable TV and a/c) are tired and functional. Facilities include an on-site restaurant (closed Sat 3pm to Sun 3pm), internet access and laundry service. **⑥**

New Washington Hotel C 1, Paseo Washington ☎441 7133. Superbly situated right on the water-front, the hotel's ornate facade and impressive marble entrance hall hark back to its long history. One step inside an overpriced tatty room, however, brings you back to the hotel's less illustrious present. Service is poor, though there are tennis courts, a pool, and great views from some rooms. **⑥**

Outside the city

Harbor Inn Residencial Espinar, Lago Gatún ☎470 0640, ⓦwww.harborinnpanama.com. Safe and tranquil B&B in the old Canal Zone offering simply furnished en-suite rooms (with a/c & wi-fi) at moderate rates. If the limited grill fare at the restaurant (closed Sun) doesn't grab you, it's a short hop round to more exciting cuisine at the *Meliá*. **④**

Meliá Panamá Canal Residencial Espinar, Lago Gatún ☎470 1100, ⓦwww.meliapanamacanal .com. The former home of the controversial School of the Americas – a US training academy for the Latin American military elite – sits on a peninsula jutting out into Lago Gatún, and has now been transformed into an elegant luxury resort. It boasts two restaurants, a couple of bars and a disco as well as an endless list of sporting and outdoor activities, including kayaking and boat trips on the lake. **⑧**

Sierra Llorona Lodge Santa Rita Arriba, 25km from Colón on the western tip of Chagres National Park ☎6574 0083, ⓦwww.sierra llorona.com. This private lodge with landscaped grounds is set in lush forest. Popular with birdwatchers and a treat for all nature-lovers, the lodge itself offers superb panoramic views, and consists of eight simple, comfortable and breezy en-suite rooms (no TV, phone or a/c). Meals can be provided on request, and knowledgeable guides can be hired for hikes or birdwatching ($15–20/person). Accessible by 4WD, bus plus 4.5km uphill hike, or pre-arranged pick-up. Breakfast included. **⑦**

The City

At the entrance to Colón, opposite the train station, is the **Aspinwall monument**, a rather dull column honouring the American founders of the city and owners of the Panama Railroad. Keeping left, the road leads to the bus terminal, where a further left turn takes you north up dilapidated **Avenida del Frente**, once the city's main commercial road, which runs along the waterfront of Bahía Limón. Most of the shops are closed now and the elegant two- and three-storey buildings with pillared overhanging balconies are crumbling, their pastel paintwork peeling and covered in graffiti. Opposite the corner with Calle 8 is the abandoned **train station**, built in 1909 for the original Panama Railroad. Just off Avenida del Frente on Calle 6 is the **Arena Teófilo Panama Al Brown**, Colón's boxing stadium; its namesake was the first Latin American world champion in the 1930s and one of the greatest boxers of all time. Four blocks down Calle 8 stands the **Catedral de la Inmaculada Concepción de María,** built between 1929 and 1934 with high, neo-Gothic arches and some attractive stained-glass windows.

Back on Avenida del Frente, it's six blocks north to the still-spectacular **New Washington Hotel**. Initially constructed in wood around 1870 to house railway engineers, it was rebuilt several times, most notably on the orders of US President Taft, who commissioned the splendid stone edifice that you see today to accommodate government officials and the increasing numbers of American tourists flocking to see the canal construction. Inside a large palm-filled walled enclosure, lapped by the Caribbean waters, the hotel's neo-colonial elegance, complete with chandeliers and ornate double marble staircase, is a reminder of Colón's former splendour.

To the left of the hotel as you look towards the city is the unassuming dark stone Episcopalian **Christ Church by the Sea**, the first Protestant church in Central America, built in the mid-1860s for the railway workers. Although in poor repair, the church contains some delightful intricate stained-glass windows, some of which were damaged in the 1989 US invasion (see p.338). Four blocks east along the seafront, a statue of Christ the Redeemer, arms outstretched, faces down **Avenida Central**, which is lined with **monuments**: a grandiose statue of Columbus with a cowed indigenous girl; Quibián, the indigenous leader who led the resistance against Columbus; and a bust of Aminta Meléndez, a young heroine of Panama's separation from Colombia. Behind the bus terminal is the port enclave of **Cristóbal**, formerly part of the Canal Zone and still one of Latin America's busiest ports, handling more than two million tons of cargo a year.

Zona Libre de Colón and Colón 2000

The southeast corner of Colón is occupied by the **Zona Libre** (Ⓦwww .colonfreezone.com), a citadel covering more than a square kilometre. This is the second largest duty-free zone in the world, after Hong Kong. With an annual turnover of more than $16 billion and a contribution to the economy of around $1.3 billion, the Zona provides eight percent of Panama's GDP and is experiencing substantial growth. All manner of consumer goods are imported here and then re-exported across Latin America and the Caribbean, and it is visited by thousands of businesspeople every day. The Zona Libre is basically a forbidden city for Colón residents unless they work there – indeed many workers are bussed over from Panama City, which is a source of much friction locally. Tourists are allowed in on presentation of a passport at the gate but to purchase anything proof of passage out of the country will need to be shown.

Inside the Zona, the contrast with the rest of Colón could not be greater – immaculate superstores line clean, well-paved streets and the only smell is of money and expensive perfume. Most of the trade is in bulk orders; it's debatable how much of a saving you make if you're just shopping for the odd item. A more recent initiative to help revitalize the city's economy is an enclave near the Zona Libre known as **Colón 2000**, which attempts to lure some of the two hundred thousand cruise ship passengers that pass through Colón annually but has little to offer besides the odd souvenir and coffee shop.

Eating and drinking

Though Colón's **restaurants** are known for their Caribbean influence and heavy reliance on seafood, spices and coconut milk, the most authentic places are too riskily situated to visit safely. Thus, you are often best off eating in or near your hotel, especially in the evening. If you do decide to go out – which you may have to do since some hotel restaurants are closed at the weekend – take a taxi for all but the shortest journeys. The *Radisson* and *Four Points Sheraton* both offer bountiful buffet breakfasts open to non-residents.

Café Maritano's Colón 2000. The best bet for cruise ship passengers to grab a frappé or a latte with a slice of cake before heading back to their ships. Daily 7am–10pm.
Flieger's Grill & Tavern Ⓦwww.harborinn panama.com/fliegers.html. Moderately priced American-style grill and big-screen sports bar serving up ribs, wings and burgers with fries. Attached to the *Harbor Inn*, it's also open to non-residents. Mon–Fri 12–3pm, 6–10pm, Sat 2–10pm. Closed Sun.
Grand Café Northeast end of town near Washington Drive. Lebanese cuisine features

heavily here – *mutabal*, *kafta* and falafel, as well as the regular meat, chicken and seafood options, plus several veggie dishes. At $12–15, prices are on the high side, though you can get a small pizza from around $4. Smoke a hookah and enjoy the view of the boats bobbing off shore. Daily 8am–11pm

🏃 **Kikos Café** ☎441 9643. A $2 taxi ride to the relatively calm Arco Iris neighbourhood (aka Rainbow City). A cosy lunchtime venue, the owner keeps a watchful eye so that you can relax and enjoy stuffed fish ($6), *bacalao* ($6) or smoked pork chops ($6) with coconut rice or *patacones* on the shady terrace. Mon–Sat 11am–10pm.

Millennium Plaza Food Court Av Ahmad Waked, Corredor Zona Libre. Crammed with fast-food joints serving pizzas, burgers, burritos and teppanyaki, it's hardly a gourmet's Mecca but it is one of the few places open on a Sunday (though choice is limited then), and it's safe. Daily 10am–10pm.

🏃 **Restaurante Las Esclusas** C 11 & Av Balboa ☎ 445 0904. Security guard and CCTV make this first-floor venue a reliable evening dining option outside your hotel. Despite an atmosphere on a par with a motorway service station, service is professional and food decent; alongside appetizing seafood mains ($8–10) there's a variety

of salads, sandwiches, chicken and pork dishes. Daily 9am–10pm.

Shelter Bay Marina Fort Sherman ☎ 433 0471, ⓦ www.shelterbaymarina.com. Lovely bayside setting for sipping a cocktail or enjoying a leisurely lunch on your way back from San Lorenzo. The food's nothing fancy – soups and salads (around $5), gourmet sandwiches and burgers ($7–9) and a few flame-grilled options ($11–14) – but the location provides adequate compensation. Daily 7.30am–9.30pm.

Super 99 Colón 2000. About the only place besides the top-class hotels to get a bite to eat on a Sunday morning before 10am. It's basic fare but at rock-bottom rates and you can grab a local paper there to peruse at the same time. Open 24hr.

Listings

Banks There is a branch of Banco Nacional on Av Bolívar near C 10 (Mon–Fri 8am–3pm) and in the Free Zone on C 14, but the safest bet for getting cash is the ATM in *Super 99* in Colón 2000.

Car rental Budget (☎ 441 7161) and Hertz (☎ 441 3272) both have offices in Colón 2000.

Hospital Hospital Amador Guerrero, C 10 at Paseo Gorgas ☎ 475 2211.

Internet Infotech (daily 8am–8pm; $1/hr) is on Av Herrera near C 10.

Laundry On the corner of Av Santa Isabel and C 9, in a relatively safe part of town.

Pharmacies In the Super 99 supermarkets on Av Bolívar and in Colón 2000.

Police station Av Meléndez between C 11 & C 12, ☎ 441 5255.

Post office On C 9 near Av Balboa (Mon–Fri 7am–6pm, Sat 7am–5pm).

Telephones There are public phone boxes in Colón 2000.

Isla Galeta

About 12km northeast of Colón lies **Isla Galeta**, which is actually a headland and home to the Smithsonian's marine research and education centre (Tues–Sun 9am–3pm; ☎ 212 8191, ⓦ www.stri.org; $2). A far lesser known attraction than Isla Barro Colorado, the centre is more on the scale of Punta Culebra (see p.82), its main attraction a modest boardwalk through the **mangroves**, where crabs and tree snakes can be spotted. There's also an **interpretive centre** and a handful of exhibits, including touch pools and the 15m skeleton of a Bride's whale. With no public transport, and at 12km from Colón, a taxi including wait time will set you back around $20, it's only worthwhile if you have your own transport – it's easily accessible in a normal car; see the website for directions.

Gatún Locks and Gatún Dam

Eight kilometres southwest of Colón, accessible by bus or taxi, are the truly impressive **Gatún Locks**. Comprising three sets of double lock chambers, they stretch for 3km, if you include the approach walls, which made them the greatest concrete structure in the world until the Hoover Dam's completion in 1930. The dam is to your left a couple of kilometres further along the road after crossing the bridge below the locks – an experience which affords a rare close-up of the tremendous studded steel plate breastplates of the lock's mitre gates. Despite being the longest in the world when it was built, at 2.3km, and a brilliant technical achievement, the earthen **Gatún Dam** is not as visually impressive as it should be, though the curved concrete **spillway** at its centre can be. Following heavy periods of rain its fourteen gates open, offering a terrifying spectacle – visible from the road – as a torrent of frothing water gushes forth from Lago Gatún. The energy is harnessed through an adjacent hydro-electric generating station, which provides power for various canal operations.

The poorly signposted **Gatún Visitors Pavilion** (daily 8am–4pm; $5; ☎443 8878) receives far fewer visitors here than at Miraflores, in part because the viewing platform, though close – allowing you to marvel at the magnitude of the operation – does not look down on the action, and the place lacks a full-scale visitor's centre. You can get to the locks and the dam by catching any Costa Abajo **bus** (see p.136). For the locks, get off just before the traffic lights at the swing-bridge across the canal and walk a few hundred metres up the road on the left. For the dam, take the first left after the locks. A **taxi** from Colón would take you to the locks and back for around $15–20 including wait time.

Fuerte San Lorenzo and the Área Protegida San Lorenzo

The **Área Protegida San Lorenzo** stretches over 120 square kilometres along the Caribbean coast and the shores of Lago Gatún, encompassing the grand colonial defences of **Fuerte San Lorenzo** and a swathe of secondary forest and swampland, which provide excellent **birdwatching**. Though the only developed trail lies close to the village of Achiote (see p.135), a wander down any of the tracks off the road to the fort with your binoculars is likely to be productive. Some areas are still out of bounds on account of unexploded mines that the US military left behind after deciding it was too expensive to clear – there are warning signs about the dangers but they are not everywhere, so stick to the paths.

The Fort

Perched high on a rocky promontory, standing guard over the mouth of the Río Chagres, the well-preserved ruins of **Fuerte San Lorenzo** bear witness to its importance during Spanish colonial times. Its spectacular location, commanding views of both the brooding river and the glistening Caribbean, coupled with its isolation at the end of a 12km dirt road, which slices through thick forest, make it a far more evocative place than the more accessible and more visited Portobelo. Construction of the original sea-level earth-and-wood fort began in 1595 to protect loot-laden Spanish boats sailing down the Chagres to Portobelo from attack by foreign vessels. Though Francis Drake failed to take the place in 1596, it fell to one of **Henry Morgan**'s privateers in 1670, enabling Morgan and his band to pass unhindered up the river and destroy Panama City. The fort was rebuilt in coral stone in the 1680s in its present cliff-top location, where it was eventually ruined in 1740 by the British, apparently in revenge for the Spanish coastguards' wounding of a British merchant captain, Robert Jenkins, in what became known rather farcically as the War of Jenkins' Ear. Although San Lorenzo was rebuilt and further strengthened – the impressive remains visible today – the fortifications were never really tested again, though they were used as part of the US military defences in World War II – note the still visible anti-aircraft platform next to the tower.

Along with the forts at Portobelo, the place was declared a World Heritage Site in 1980 and is now a popular destination on the cruise-ship circuit, but if you get there early (or visit during the rainy season) you can often have the place to yourself. As you cross over the **drawbridge** (not the original one) and through the smart squat stone-and-brick **guard house**, the main entrance to the fort, you come out onto the **esplanade**, which offers the best view of the fort and served to collect rainwater that was channelled off into a **water tank** over the parapet in front of you. The vast grassy area below is the **parade ground**, containing the ruined troops' and officers' quarters. Taking the ramp down, follow the wall along to the ruins of the **powder magazine** and the **tower** built into the side of the hill, now scarcely more than a deep hole filled with litter. Though the adjacent wall parapets and cannons have now gone, the view is as it always was, and it's easy to picture watchmen anxiously gazing out towards the horizon for enemy ships. Before climbing back up towards the guard house, peer inside some of the many remarkably preserved **vaults** underneath the esplanade, used to store equipment and food and, much later, prisoners. Crossing the drawbridge once more you'll find yourself on the **exterior platform**, with the one surviving sentry box to the left. Here the parapet is still intact, as are the nine **cannons** pointing out towards the putative enemy.

Practicalities

With no public transport to San Lorenzo, your best bet is to go on a **tour** – several operators (see p.44) run day-trips from Panama City combining San Lorenzo with a visit to Gatún Locks. Alternatively, **rent a car** for the day since a **taxi** (including waiting time at the fort) will set you back around $30, whereas car rental would not cost much more and would allow you to stop off at Gatún Locks on the way or explore more of the protected area before grabbing a bite to eat at the *Shelter Bay Marina* (see p.132) on the way back. Once over the canal, take the well-signposted road straight ahead towards Fort Sherman, the former US military base. After crossing the remains of excavations made for the French canal, the road continues for 12km, reaching a checkpoint at the entry to the former fort, where you'll need to show ID. The road to San Lorenzo bends off to the left, continuing for another 10km along a good-quality dirt track to the fort. You'll come across the **park office** after a couple of kilometres, where if you're lucky there'll be someone to relieve you of your park fee ($3).

The Costa Abajo

A left turn after crossing the canal takes you towards the **Costa Abajo**, as yet an undeveloped stretch of rugged, windswept Caribbean coastline, reached via a picturesque undulating road that skirts the shores of Lago Gatún before cutting through a mix of forest and pastureland to the sea. A hinterland in tourist terms – though several projects are said to be in the pipeline – the area will really only appeal to avid birdwatchers and those who want to get off the beaten track.

Two villages here earn a trickle of visitors. **Escobal**, attractively situated on Lago Gatún, is a pleasant spot to engage in a little kayaking, fishing or horse riding while **Achiote**, further inland, is a prime location for birdwatching. The other settlements strung out along the wild, windswept coastline rarely see tourists, though the recent tarring of the road as far as Miguel de la Borda may soon change this.

Escobal

The road to Escobal and Cuipo periodically offers glimpses of sparkling Lago Gatún and its many wooded islands through the trees and prolific elephant grass. After about 10km the road divides: to the right it heads back up towards the coast via Achiote; ahead it continues to the sprawling lakeside fishing village of **Escobal**, which enjoys an ethnically diverse population, primarily populated by descendants of canal labourers and communities displaced by the damming of the Río Chagres. It's an attractive spot to relax and engage a boatman to explore some of the tiny islands and secret inlets on the vast reservoir, or go horse riding or hiking in the forest. At restaurant *Doña Nelly* (T 434 6029), right by one of the bus stops, Aida González or Saturnino Díaz can help sort out homestay **accommodation** and arrange activities. Alternatively, if you have a tent, head for Sra de

Tuñon's (☎ 6638 4912) – take the last road on the left when leaving the village – which offers a lovely camping spot down by the lakeside, where you can enquire about a boatman to take you out on the lake.

Daily buses marked "Costa Abajo Cuipo" pass through Escobal (6.30am, 8am, then every 40min until noon & hourly until 7–8pm; 45min–1hr; $1.50).

Achiote

Located in a flat-bottomed valley just outside the Área Protegida San Lorenzo, the hamlet of **Achiote** provides a good base for exploring the area. Strung along the main road backing onto a flower-filled and forested hillside and surrounded by bucolic countryside, its five hundred inhabitants primarily survive on livestock rearing and subsistence agriculture, with coffee the main crop. It is also home to a community-based eco-tourism project, which focuses on birdwatching and hiking as well as offering a tour of a local coffee farm.

The 435 recorded bird species are spread across the Área Protegida San Lorenzo, which encompasses tracts of mangrove, cativo and palm swamps and vast swathes of other secondary forest types, including some deciduous growth. The main birdwatching trail is the **Sendero El Trogón** ($5 combined entry to the path and the park), which lies 4km before Achiote, within the park boundary, and was so named on account of the three types of trogon that frequent the area. Although a pleasant trail, the birding is often easier (and free) along the more open areas of the main road. If you're willing to dodge the occasional speeding bus or truck, you'll get a chance to see brilliant chestnut-mandibled and keel-billed toucans, blue-headed parrots and beautiful blue cotingas. To venture further into the reserve, you need to arrange a **guide** for hiking or birdwatching (approximately $25 for 2hrs) with the local ecotourism group, *Los Rapaces* (☎ 6664 2339, although they can also be hard to reach), which can also organize homestays and a visit to the local coffee farm in the harvesting season (Dec–Jan). Alternatively, drop by *Centro El Tucán* (Mon–Fri 8am–4pm and on weekends on request; ☎ 6567 5634; dorm $8/person), which has two basic dormitories (fans, mosquito screens and cold-water showers). There's an on-site kitchen, though if you don't fancy catering, note that the inexpensive community restaurant *La Cascá* (☎ 6637 8522; open until early evening), 1km down the road, serves up tasty, filling fare, though it'll often be a case of eating what's in the pot that day. A day's notice is preferred but it's hard to get anyone on the phone.

Along the coast to Miguel de la Borda

Beyond Achiote the road rises, twists and turns the next 12km, offering views of the pleasantly undulating pastures before reaching the coast at the village of **Piña**. Here bracing winds and waves batter the rugged coastline while treacherous currents throw up driftwood and fishing debris on the black-streaked beaches. It's well off the tourist trail and therefore makes for an interesting drive or bus trip, the coastal road meandering 40km from Piña through a string of settlements of cement block houses and the odd wooden *costeño* lodging, each with its painted church.

The road ends at the village and river of **Miguel de la Borda**, where the truly adventurous can negotiate passage by boat (around $10/person) to the small community of Coclé del Norte, in the remote western part of Colón Province, which maintains links with the rest of the country via motorized dugout up the river of the same name to Coclecito, followed by a *colectivo* to Penonomé (see p.164). The boats leave infrequently and hardly at all when the seas are rough (Nov–Feb). There are currently no places to stay along this stretch of coast though you can probably find a very basic bunk or hammock for the night, or pay to pitch a tent, with a little Spanish and perseverance.

Public transport along the Costa Abajo is fairly frequent, though early morning or late afternoon the bus may have to wait up to forty minutes to cross the canal, which makes timetables unpredictable. To reach Achiote take the bus bound for Miguel de la Borda (approx every hour, daily 6.30am–6pm; 45min–1hr to Achiote, $2.50; 2hr 30min to Miguel de la Borda; $4) or, more commonly, Río Indio, also confusingly marked "Costa Abajo". Note that the last bus back to Colón from Achiote leaves around 4pm. Make sure you have sufficient cash with you since there are **no banking facilities** outside Colón.

Portobelo and the Costa Arriba

For lovers of the outdoors or enthusiasts of Spanish colonial history, there are several attractions along or around the **Costa Arriba**, the crinkly coastline east of Colón. The area's main draw is the scenically situated town of **Portobelo** – in colonial times the most important settlement on the isthmus after Panama City since all the plunder from South America passed through here en route for Spain. The ruined **fortresses**, remnants of the conquistadors' attempts to safeguard the treasure from the envious grasp of pirates and privateers, constitute the town's primary tourist sites, while two of Panama's most vibrant **festivals** define the town for many visitors. Outside of the town, there is good **diving** and some attractive nearby **beaches** and in the lush interior a little further afield at the scenic Río Piedra there's an impressive **canopy adventure** and opportunities for camping, horse riding or hiking in magnificent rainforest.

East of Portobelo, the road forks left towards the picturesque sheltered bay of **Puerto Lindo**, a lovely spot to hang out for a couple of days and a common departure point for travel to Colombia by sail boat. Beyond, the gravel road continues to the fishing village of La Guaira, providing access to the weekend party island of **Isla Grande**. Most of these attractions lie within the little-respected boundaries of the **Parque Nacional Portobelo**. Bearing right at the fork, the road tracks east through a string of coastal villages, the most appealing of which is the one-time colonial port of **Nombre de Dios**.

The road to Portobelo

The unmissable El Rey supermarket in the unremarkable settlement of **Sabanitas**, 12km east of Colón on the Transístmica, bound for Panama City, marks the turn-off to Portobelo and the Costa Arriba, and the starting point for an increasingly pleasant drive as the traffic and houses are left behind and the road heads towards the coast. After about 12km, you come to **Playa María Chiquita** and, 4km later, **Playa La Angosta**, two dark golden-sandy beaches flecked with black (accessible by any Portobelo-bound bus from Colón via Sabanitas). Packed with families fleeing the city at weekends, they are deserted midweek and have a certain windswept charm. La Angosta offers the better and more developed beach with a few cement cabins, a restaurant and picnic tables though María Chiquita has a minor surf break.

Between the two beaches, a signed turn-off leads to the province's most recent adventure attraction, **Panama Outdoor Adventures Canopy Tour**, ☎6030 9515, ⓦ wwww.panamaoutdooradventures.com), just under 4km up a dirt track along the picturesque Río Piedra valley. Though not on the scale of the Boquete Tree Trek (p.236), it is still quite impressive, with some of its nine cables over 30m from the ground, allowing you to soar across the valley and among the tree-tops.

Close by the river, where you can swim, and surrounded by rainforest, it's a delightful place to **camp** ($10/person, $15 with tent hire) though you'll need to bring your own food. Activities include **river tubing**, **horse riding**, which can include a visit to an **Emberá village** just across the river ($55) or a whole day in the saddle ($95), and wildlife spotting along the well-tended **trails**. You can hike in from the road or arrange a pick-up.

There's more **accommodation** slightly further up the valley, along the river bank, where the *Finca Los Tucanes* (☎6683 5318, ✉miguelyan2000@yahoo .com.ar) offers three basic rustic wooden cabins accommodating up to four ($40 per cabin plus an extra $10 to use the *finca*'s kitchen, or $30 per person for bed and full board). The *finca* is owned by a Basque-Argentinian artist couple, and as well as the customary hiking, birdwatching and fishing excursions, they offer activities such as tagua carving and painting.

Portobelo

A soldier's eye view across the turquoise bay from the rusting Spanish cannons of a **PORTOBELO** fort is one of the most popular postcard views in Panama, conveying the impression of a remote military outpost surrounded by dense vegetation. It therefore comes as a shock to most visitors to find the forts smack in the middle of an economically deprived modern town, with dilapidated houses propped up against the historical ruins and kids playing football in what was once a parade ground. The town itself is mostly squeezed along a thin strip of land between the main road and the bay, which spills into the Caribbean. A half day provides ample time to explore the colonial relics, leaving you the afternoon to enjoy a nearby beach or arrange a rainforest hike.

Portobelo gets busy for two famous **festivals** (see box, p.138): the Festival del Nazareño in October and the hugely enjoyable Afro-colonial Festival de Congos y Diablos, which takes place every two years in March, with smaller celebrations taking place along the coast in the weeks leading up to Carnaval.

Some history

Christopher Columbus, so the story goes, believing himself to be on the verge of death after days on a storm-tossed sea, spotted a beautiful sheltered bay surrounded

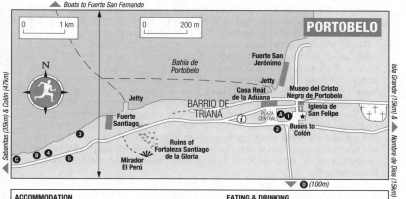

ACCOMMODATION				EATING & DRINKING			
Coco-Plum Eco-Lodge Resort		Hostel Portobelo	D	Las Anclas	4	Restaurante Yaci	1
Hospedaje La Aduana	A	Scuba Portobelo	C	El Castillo	3	La Torre	5
	B			Restaurante Arith	2		

by forested hills and gratefully exclaimed, "Che porto bello". While the name stuck, the strategic importance of the natural harbour was not truly appreciated until 1585, when it became clear that Nombre de Dios – then the principal Spanish port on the Panama's Caribbean coast – was too exposed and should be relocated to Portobelo. As if to reinforce the point, Sir Francis Drake promptly destroyed Nombre de Dios in 1595 and was on the verge of attacking Portobelo when he died of dysentery – his coffin supposedly lies at the bottom of the ocean at the entrance to the bay, near an islet which bears his name.

In 1597 San Felipe de Portobelo was officially founded, prompting further fortification and providing a new target for spoil-hungry pirates and privateers, including notorious buccaneer Henry Morgan, who pounced at night in 1668, and squeezed one hundred thousand pesos from the Spanish authorities in exchange for not levelling the place. British naval commander Sir Edward Vernon, attacking seventy years later, made no such concession and destroyed the two fortresses. Though new forts were built in the mid-eighteenth century – those still visible today – they were smaller since Portobelo's commercial importance was already waning as the Spanish had rerouted their ships round Cape Horn. When the Spanish garrison finally abandoned the town in 1821, its 150 years of strategic significance came to an end.

Arrival, information and orientation

It is possible to visit Portobelo as a day-trip from Panama City, though you'd be looking at over two hours on public transport each way. Take any Colón-bound

---

The festivals of Portobelo

Two very different **festivals** bring this otherwise lethargic town to life, causing traffic to grind to a halt well before the first fort, and streets to heave with people, as you find yourself knee-deep in discarded polystyrene containers, beer cans and chicken bones.

El Festival del Nazareno

In mid-October, Portobelo explodes into a frenzy of religious fervour and wild partying at the *Festival del Nazareno* – more commonly dubbed the **Festival del Cristo Negro** (Black Christ Festival) after Panama's most revered religious icon, a striking, dark-skinned Christ with a penetrating gaze and bearing the cross, which resides in the Iglesia de San Felipe. Legends differ regarding how the effigy ended up in the town, though all agree that its iconic status was cemented when, in 1821, it spared the townsfolk from an epidemic that was sweeping the isthmus.

Though the main **procession** occurs on October 21, the build-up begins days before as up to forty thousand pilgrims, including general party-goers and a small number of criminals wanting to atone for their crimes, march on town. Thousands walk the 35km from Sabanitas and a handful hoof it from further afield, some crawling the last stretch on their hands and knees, a few in ankle-length purple robes, urged on by faithful companions wafting incense, rocking miniature shrines in front of their eyes, or even pouring hot wax on their backs. To compound the suffering, they're frequently overdosing on carbon monoxide from the festival traffic, which weaves in and out of the pilgrims struggling along the scorching asphalt. Shelters, food stalls and medical posts are set up along the route while the town itself is jam-packed with makeshift casinos, stalls selling religious paraphernalia and food outlets dishing out chicken and rice.

At 8pm an ever-changing cohort of robed men begin to parade the icon, bedecked in a claret robe, round the packed town in a rhythmical swaying, to the accompaniment of brass and drum, followed by the penitents. Once the candlelit litter has been

express bus, getting off at the El Rey supermarket at the Sabanitas junction, where you can hop on a Portobelo bus (every 30min, 6am–8pm, 6pm on Sun; 1hr 30min; $1.30) heading out from Colón bus terminal. They take about twenty minutes to cover the 12km to Sabanitas and a further hour for the remaining 35km to Portobelo. At busy festival or holiday times, it's worth going into Colón itself to make sure of a seat. All buses from Colón labelled "Costa Arriba" also stop in Portobelo. Return buses to Colón leave from the square in front of the Iglesia de San Felipe, the last leaving Portobelo at 6pm.

Taxis are scarce but the town is small and distances are easily walkable. The **tourist office** (Mon–Fri 8.30am–4.30pm; ☎ 448 2200) is in a beautifully restored old merchant's house at the corner where the road forks coming into town. There is no **ATM**; the nearest is inside the supermarket at Sabanitas. On the square, there's a **payphone** and an **internet** café (Mon–Fri 9am–5pm).

Accommodation

Portobelo's better **accommodation** lies slightly out of town on the road to Colón, offering lovely views across the bay, with cheaper alternatives in town. There's nowhere safe to camp around the town itself but you could pitch a tent on one of the beaches if you get a boat out there, though there are no facilities. If you're hitting town for a festival, you will need to make a **reservation** well in advance. The tourist office can assist you in finding an inexpensive **homestay**.

returned to the church around midnight, the pilgrims discard their robes at the entrance as an explosion of fireworks marks the start of a hedonistic feast of drinking, gambling and dancing that continues through the night. "El Naza", as the statue is affectionately known by some devotees, gets another celebratory town outing on the Wednesday of Holy Week, this time clothed in purple, though the festivities are not quite as grand.

Congos and devils

At weekends leading up to Carnaval, **congo** societies along the Costa Arriba erupt in colourful explosions of traditional song, dance and satirical play-acting that originated in the sixteenth century among outlawed communities of escaped slaves, known as *cimarrones*. Congregating in mock palaces – a parody of the Spanish court – each with its king (*Juan de Dios*) and queen (*Mecé*) togged out in extravagant costumes and ludicrously large crowns, they communicate in their own dialect. The men sport painted faces, conical hats and outlandish tattered clothes, worn inside-out and decorated with everything from empty beer cans to teddy bears; the women wear multicoloured *polleras*, their hair garlanded with flowers, and dance to beating drums and choral chants. In the many comic rituals, "prisoners", including the odd unsuspecting tourist, are taken and released for ransom – a few coins or an offer of a beer will usually do. The celebrations reach their climax on Ash Wednesday with the Festival de los Diablos. The ferocious scarlet-and-black devils (representing the evil spirits of the Spanish colonials), who have been previously running amok in frightening masks, brandishing whips, are captured by a posse of angels, who drag them off to be baptised.

In an attempt to preserve this waning culture, and aware of its potential to generate tourist income, the Portobelo authorities support a biennial *Festival de los Diablos y Congos* (see ⓦ www.diablosycongos.org) in March, which is well worth getting to see.

Coco-Plum Eco-Lodge Resort Main road, 2.5km before town ☎ 448 2102, ⓦ www .cocoplum-panama.com. The nicest place to stay but overpriced: cheerful with a dozen funkily furnished though dark en-suite rooms decorated with conch shells and marine-themed murals (a/c & TV) set in a plant-filled garden. There's a hammock-strewn jetty, a thatched balcony bar with pool table and a scuba outfit on site (see opposite). ⑤

Hospedaje La Aduana Plaza Central ☎ 448 2925. Four good-value basic rooms (one with a/c, three with fans, two with private bathroom), plus a great shared balcony, with rocking chair and hammocks, overlooking the action of the main square. The bar-disco underneath means limited sleep at weekends. ②

Hostel Portobelo Casa 3c la Guinea 2min uphill from town ☎ 696 1554, ⓦ www .hostelportobelo.com. The best value in town offering two dorms, one private room with shared kitchen, TV room and lovely terrace with BBQ overlooking the town. Dorm $10, room $25.

Scuba Portobelo Main road, 2.5km before town ☎ 261 3841, ⓦ www.scubapanama.com. Although catering for divers, anyone can stay. Five light, en-suite a/c rooms and shared balcony with hammocks affording superlative sea views. Spread around pleasant grounds, six slightly older bungalows with similar amenities accommodate up to four, plus there's a ten-bed dormitory with a/c. A low-key restaurant serves a few filling staples but there are good restaurants within walking distance. Dorm bed $15. ⑤

The town and forts

Fuerte Santiago is the first fort you encounter before entering the town proper from the west, built in the mid-eighteenth century following the destruction of the original fortifications by the British. The main entrance takes you through a vestibule protected by gun ports to the now grassy **parade grounds**, where the ruined walls of the officers' quarters, barracks, kitchen and artillery emplacement are visible to your left. More impressive are the lower and upper **batteries**, their moss-covered cannons pointing out across the bay. If you've time, it's worth crossing over the road for the steep five-minute climb to the **Mirador El Perú**, on the site of a watchtower of the former **Fortaleza Santiago de la Gloria**, whose scarcely visible overgrown ruins are now bisected by the main road below. Across the bay you can make out the remains of **Fuerte San Fernando** peeking through dense foliage. To reach the fort, take a water-taxi ($2) from the jetty by Fuerte Santiago. Though smaller than its sister fort, the scenic spot gives a different perspective on the town.

▲ Fuerte Santiago, Portobelo

Moving further into the town, you pass through the former **Barrio de Triana**, an area marked out in the sixteenth century for slaves, to the small **Plaza Central**, dominated by the two-storey coral stone and brick **Casa Real de la Aduana**, built in 1638 to replace an earlier wooden structure. A third of the world's gold, alongside copious other treasures, passed through here for over a century, and the customs house was required to have only one entrance and one exit to reduce fraud and theft and ensure the Crown got its full royal cut of the spoils. Destroyed in an earthquake in 1882, it underwent a $1 million restoration in 1997 and now houses a small, diverting two-room **museum** (daily 8am–4pm; $1) containing models of the original forts, costumes and other exhibits including the obligatory pile of cannon balls.

Beyond the customs house, down by the waterside and hemmed in by housing, lies **Fuerte San Jerónimo**, the town's largest and most impressive ruins. The former **parade ground** stretches along the eighteen gun emplacements of the lower battery, with nearly all the original rusting cannons intact. It's worth walking along to the high battery, where you can still see the rainwater reservoir, storage rooms for gunpowder and the latrines, and get a soldier's eye view of the entrance of the bay.

The town's other major landmark, and focus of the annual Festival del Nazareño (see box, p.138), is the **Iglesia de San Felipe**, which overlooks another square. Although its construction started in 1606, it was only completed in 1814, making it the conquistadors' last religious building in Panama, with the bell tower added in 1945. Inside you'll find white walls and a large carved gilt mahogany altarpiece, though the focus of attention inevitably is on the object of so much devotion, the so-called Black Christ, a dark-skinned, lifelike statue of Jesus bearing the cross that peers out from behind a glass casement.

Behind the church lies the newly restored Iglesia de San Juan de Dios, containing the new **Museo del Cristo Negro de Portobelo** (daily 8am–4pm; $1; check at the Aduana if it's shut), which is well worth a peek since it displays many of the luxurious velvet robes which wealthy devotees have donated for the Christ to wear. The amount of intricate gold and silver thread work involved is astounding, with pride of place going to robes given by boxing legend Roberto Durán (on the former altar) and Puerto Rican salsa star Ismael Rivera (the crimson robe on the right-hand wall). Rivera attributed his recovery from drug addiction and the subsequent rejuvenation of his career to the Nazareño, and a gaudy bronze and lilac statue to the singer now stands on the right-hand side of the main road as you enter town.

Activities

Given the numerous reefs and scuttled ships in the waters round Portobelo, it is no surprise that it's one of the country's top **diving** and **snorkelling** destinations – though you won't get the diversity and quantity of fish that you can find in the Pacific. Popular dive spots include a B-45 plane wreck by Drake's Island, where some still hold out hope of uncovering the privateer's sunken lead coffin amid the encrusted coral; the varied marine flora and fauna of the Three Sister Islands; and the labyrinth of canyons off Isla Grande. The town's two main scuba companies are located on the main road on the left shortly before Portobelo; both are PADI-certified with good reputations. Panama Dive Adventures (T 279 1467, W www .panamadiveadventures.com) is based in Panama City but operates out of *Coco-Plum Eco-Lodge*, whereas Scuba Portobelo (T 448 2147, or 261 4064 in Panama City, W www.scubapanama.com), a little further out, has its own lodgings.

To explore on land, contact Selvaventuras (T 442 1042, E selvaventuras @hotmail.com; or ask at *Coco-Plum*), a popular local outfit that offers various excursions, such as **hikes** through rainforest to refreshing pools and waterfalls ($20) and horse riding. Alternatively, for a leisurely **boat trip** engage Moisés Zapata of Taxi Acuático (T 448 2105), 50m before the tourist office on the left on the main road. Likely as not he'll be trimming someone's beard as he's also a barber. Two popular excursions include a two-hour cruise round the bay and up into the mangroves of the Río More ($25 for two) or a drop-off and pick-up at **Playa Blanca**, Portobelo's prettiest beach, reachable only by boat ($30). You can also contract boatmen hanging round the main **jetty** by Fuerte Santiago.

Eating and drinking

In the town itself, there are several inexpensive **restaurants** and *fondas* round the two plazas, with the pricier, more touristy places by the waterfront on the main road into town offering more varied menus.

Las Anclas *Coco-Plum Eco-Lodge*. Don't let the fun fishy decor distract you from the tasty squid, lobster, crab and the like (mains from $8) plus daily specials prepared by the Colombian chef. Daily 8am–8pm.

El Castillo Main road, 500m before Portobelo. A cheesy pirate statue guards the entrance to this mock galleon bar-restaurant (with the emphasis on bar), splendidly situated over the water. Daily 11am–9pm; closed Wed off-season.

Restaurante Arith Main road, before the church. A busy, thatched open-sided place with wooden beams draped with fishing nets, which serves breakfasts and lunches of inexpensive solid staples, including fantastic *patacones*. Daily 7am–5pm.

Restaurante Yaci Church square. A plate of fried fish or chicken heaped with coconut rice for a couple of dollars. Daily 7am–6pm.

La Torre Main road 2km before Portobelo T 448 2039. A breezy upstairs open-sided restaurant preparing good, reasonably priced seafood – try the *cambombia en salsa de coco* ($8.50) or *almejitas al jingebre* ($7). Daily 8am–6pm.

Parque Nacional de Portobelo

Bordering the Parque Nacional Chagres, the **Parque Nacional de Portobelo** covers 360 square kilometres of varied landscape around Portobelo. From Cerro Bruja (979m), the carpet of rainforest sweeps down to a 70km wriggle of coastline, taking in coral reefs, mangroves – home to crab-eating raccoons – and golden beaches, where four species of turtle come to lay their eggs. There are also significant populations of green iguana. Deforestation was already a major concern before the area was declared a park in 1976, but continued surreptitious tree-felling is putting even greater strain on the park's scarcely protected and highly fragmented natural resources.

Leaving Portobelo, the paved road tracks east through flattish pastureland, where it's hard to credit that you're still within the national park boundaries. A few kilometres out of town, in the unremarkable village of Nuevo Tonosí, you can find the **park office**. As yet, no trails or accommodation have been developed, though ANAM can supply a guide to hike in the local area for a modest fee. While in the village, stop by the large roadside **restaurant** *Don Quijote* (T 448 2170; Fri–Sun & hols 8am–9pm), which serves up delicious moderately priced French–Italian cuisine, including home-made pasta, tasty thin-crust pizzas and an assortment of *parilladas* and Panamanian favourites.

A few kilometres further on, at a junction known as "La Cruce", the road divides: the right-hand fork continues to Nombre De Dios, where it rejoins the coast, whereas the left-hand road keeps you within the park, taking you into the small, partially forested peninsula between the Bahía de Portobelo and Bahía San Cristóbal. Most only pass through it en route to the weekend holiday retreat of Isla Grande, but it constitutes a scenic diversion in itself and the quiet bayside hamlet of **Puerto Lindo** makes a tranquil base for exploring the area.

Puerto Lindo

The nicest place to hang out on the peninsula is **Puerto Lindo**, a small fishing village en route to Isla Grande, its clutch of simple dwellings strung out along a sheltered, palm-fringed bay, where fishing vessels and yachts bob nonchalantly in the natural harbour. It's become a popular transit point for travellers heading to or from Cartagena, Colombia, by sailboat (see box, p.22). The consequent increase in backpacker traffic has meant that – as well as a shop selling basic supplies and a reasonable **restaurant** and bar – there's some decent **accommodation**, offering meals, tours and a fine spot for simply relaxing.

Bambu Guest House ☏448 2247, ⓦwww .panamaguesthouse.com. Dutch-run establishment nestled in a luscious garden overlooking the bay with three stylishly furnished en-suite rooms and an upstairs communal dining balcony, affording great ocean views. Yacht tours (see ⓦwww .oceantrips.com) or rainforest walks with a local guide can be arranged. Breakfast included. ⑥

🏃 **Caballo Loco** 2–3km before Puerto Lindo, on the right ☏448 2291, ⓦwww .flordecafe.com. Although the two rustic wooden A-frame cabins with fans and mosquito nets are nothing special ($60 for six people, $50 for four), the open-sided garden restaurant of this French-run establishment is a delight, as is the exquisitely prepared fusion of French and Panamanian cuisine (mains $9). Get in touch before you roll up since although the place is open Fri–Sun for lunch and dinner (and for all meals when the cabins are occupied), it closes early if business is slack.

🏃 **Casa X** In the village by the waterside ☏6689 6923, ⓔcasaxparavacacionar @hotmail.com. Small, bland one and two-bedroom suites overlook the water, but the star is a great restaurant, where you can enjoy delicious, inexpensive freshly prepared meals ($6) in a delightful waterside setting. ⑥

🏃 **Hostal Wunderbar** On the left just after the turn-off to Cacique ☏448 2426, ⓦwww .hostelwunderbar.com. Mellow lodgings offering dorm beds, hammocks and two doubles with shared bathroom, some in a large Kuna-style open-sided bamboo house that also contains a distinctly un-Kuna pool table. Wake up to howlers in the morning and chill out in the evening to the sound of crickets and frogs. Boat trips to Isla Grande and other nearby islands or mangroves, plus sailboats to Colombia via Kuna Yala can be arranged (see p.22). *Cayucos* and bikes are also available for rent and horse riding, hiking or fishing in the national park are possible with local guides. Dorm $12. ⑥

Isla Grande

Isla Grande's popularity as a weekend getaway for Panamanian urbanites has often led to hyperbolic descriptions of its beaches and overall beauty. In truth, it doesn't measure up to the stunning islands of Kuna Yala or Bocas del Toro, but if you're in the area, or have been cooped up in Panama City and want a quick shot of Caribbean vibe, a dose of fresh air and a splash in the sea before tucking into some Creole cuisine, then Isla Grande will do very nicely, though you'll be lucky to get anyone to serve you a meal midweek during the rainy season.

Arrival and information

Access to the island is generally from the fishing village of **La Guaira**, where a 200m water-taxi ($2) across the water takes you to the main jetty by *Cabañas Jackson*, which is the unofficial information point – for a little extra you can be taken directly to lodgings further afield. The *Bananas Village Resort* has its own secure parking and boat transfer in the nearby village of **Juan Gallegos**. Alternatively, *Hostal Wunderbar* in **Puerto Lindo** can organize boat transport locally ($3.50 return).

Those driving can leave the car by La Guaira dock for free, or in the more secure partially fenced area nearby ($2 a day). Either way, don't leave valuables in the car. Infrequent **buses** make the two-hour journey to La Guaira from Colón (every 2hr, 9.30am–5.30pm; $2.85) via Sabanitas and Portobelo. The last bus back to Colón is usually at 1pm (4pm on Sun), though check with the bus driver that these times still hold. With **no ATM** on the island you'll need to bring cash, although most of the accommodation options take credit cards.

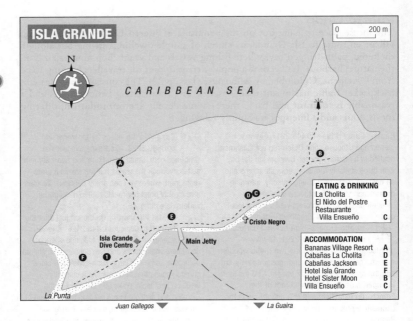

ISLA GRANDE

N

0   200 m

CARIBBEAN SEA

A

B

D C

E

† Cristo Negro

Isla Grande
Dive Centre   Main Jetty

F   1

La Punta

Juan Gallegos ▼   ▼ *La Guaira*

EATING & DRINKING

La Cholita	D
El Nido del Postre Restaurante	1
Villa Ensueño	C

ACCOMMODATION

Bananas Village Resort	A
Cabañas La Cholita	D
Cabañas Jackson	E
Hotel Isla Grande	F
Hotel Sister Moon	B
Villa Ensueño	C

Accommodation

There's a reasonable range of basic **accommodation** on the island, none of it particularly cheap, though low season midweek you can bargain for better rates. *Bananas* and *Sister Moon* are located on the north side and towards the northeastern tip of the island, respectively; most other places are concentrated in the centre of the village along the coastal path.

Bananas Village Resort ☎ 448 2252, ⊛ www .bananasresort.com. The priciest and most comfortable place to bed down. Set in a secluded bay with a negligible beach, its eight spacious two-storey A-frame cabins (a/c, cable TV, erratic hot water) come with patio/balcony overlooking the sea. $45 more gets you a more luxurious seafront suite. Costs include breakfast, pool, kayaks, snorkelling gear, pool table and fishing tackle, with boat trips extra. The overpriced restaurant is the only evening dining option so bills can mount up. ❽

Cabañas La Cholita ☎ 448 2962. Twelve simple rooms with cheerful mosaic tiling set around a pleasant garden. All are a/c (6pm–10am), with private bathrooms but cold water. The quieter, pricier rooms towards the back have pleasant patios furnished with table, chairs and hammock. ❺

Cabañas Jackson By the main jetty ☎ 448 2311. The cheapest, most basic cinder-block rooms (fan or a/c, cold water and private bathrooms)

accommodate 2–8 people, with adjacent shop selling basic provisions plus the beachside *Restaurante Parillada Olympia*. ❸

Hotel Sister Moon ☎ 236 8489, ⊛ www.hotelsistermoon.com. Scattered over the breezy hillside overlooking the island's only surf break, thatched cabins (fans and mosquito screens) on stilts comprise the island's nicest accommodation – make sure you get a full sea view. Next to the cosy restaurant is a small pool and sun deck providing an excellent view of the waves. Breakfast is included. Dorm beds $25. ❺

Villa Ensueño ☎ 448 2964, ⓔ villaen@cwpanama .net. Very popular, comprising sixteen clean brightly painted en-suite rooms (firm beds, a/c 6pm–9am, mosquito screens) and shared porches looking onto a garden. This gets noisy and lacks privacy at weekends since picnic tables in the grounds are rented out ($15, including use of showers) to day-trippers. Boat trips can be arranged at the hotel. ❺

The Island

At just 3km long and under a kilometre wide, with only a couple of paths and no roads, it's easy to orient yourself on Isla Grande. Most of the island's four hundred residents of predominantly Afro-Antillean descent live off fishing and tourism and reside in the **main village**, which is strung out along a coastal footpath running the length of the island. The village jetty, by *Cabañas Jackson*, constitutes the hub of "downtown" Isla Grande, where most accommodation options, bars and restaurants are located and the reggae vibe is at its most pronounced. At weekends in the dry season and peak holiday times, when the island bulges with up to a thousand fun-loving Panamanians, the place is throbbing, often with music blaring from portable stereos (despite the island's attempts to ban them) and the one decent beach at La Punta, on the southwestern tip, is inevitably packed.

The more accessible strips of beach with shallow water good for swimming are in the village, overlooking the mainland, while there's decent snorkelling off the northern coast, by *Bananas*. Isla Grande Dive Centre (☎232 6994), an experienced dive outfit lying west of *Cabañas Jackson*, can take you out to sample some of the underwater sites a short boat ride away, or further afield in Kuna Yala. A popular boat excursion leads you through a mangrove "tunnel of love" to the best local white-sand beach and snorkelling destination, **Isla Mamey**. A half-day trip (approx \$40) can be arranged through your hotel or directly with one of the guys hanging out at the main jetty. Surfers should head for Playa Grande on the mainland towards Nombre de Dios.

Behind the village, a steep flight of concrete steps pushes through the dense foliage across the island to *Bananas*. If you don't fancy the climb, hop in a water-taxi. A less well-trodden route to the resort, involving some shoreline scrambling, heads uphill from just before *Sister Moon*, turning left in front of a large house, crossing the saddle and descending into the bay. On the island's highest point stands the 85m **lighthouse** built by the French in 1894, which is worth ascending for its superb panoramic views.

Eating, drinking and nightlife

Restaurants generally belong to the hotels and predominantly serve fresh seafood almost straight from the boats, often accompanied by coconut rice or plantain. *Restaurante Villa Ensueño*, built out over the water next to the island's own Cristo Negro, is one of the best places to dine, offering inexpensive delights including *fufú* (fish soup in coconut milk, \$4) and lobster, while in neighbouring *La Cholita* try island-style conch (\$9). Follow the loudest music along the front at weekends and you've found the island's **nightlife**.

Along the Costa Arriba to Cuango

Keeping right at the fork after Nuevo Tonosí, the undulating road hits the sea once again at **Nombre de Dios**, before hugging the windswept coastline through a string of sparsely populated villages – Viento Frío, Palenque and Miramar, before terminating at Cuango. With a 4WD vehicle it's possible to cross the Río Cuango and adventure a little further but for most, including the five daily buses from Cólon, **Cuango** is the end of the road, with an appropriate end-of-the road feel. There's actually little reason to travel beyond Nombre de Dios unless you're seeking an isolated surf spot at Playa Palenque or Playa Cuango, or hoping to get a boat ride to Kuna Yala from Miramar, which is also the only place to get petrol.

Nombre de Dios

The most compelling of the coastal settlements, **Nombre de Dios** is famed as the Atlantic terminus for the Camino Real, where in colonial times treasure was transferred from exhausted mules to ships bound for Spain. The village derived its name from the apocryphal words of its founder, Diego de Nicuesa, who, desperate to land his starving crew, espied the spot and cried out, "Paremos aquí en el nombre de Dios!" Sadly no trace remains of the town's famous historical past, largely thanks to Sir Francis Drake, who razed the place to the ground in 1595, thus persuading the Spanish to move their operation to Portobelo.

Nevertheless Nombre de Dios is a scenic place to stroll through, situated on the palm-fringed Río Fato, and with a pleasant five-minute meander up to a **mirador** established by a local environmental group offering a view of the village and the turquoise sea beyond. **Playa Damas** is the best local beach, a short hop by boat (try down by the bridge). If you want **accommodation**, ask around for the community-owned *Hospedaje a Nombre de Dios* (no phone, ❶) on the square, which has ten very basic rooms, though *Casita Rio Indio* (ⓦwww.panama-casitarioindio .chez-alice.fr, Ⓔcasitarioindio@yahoo.fr; ❷) is a more appealing option. Five minutes along the Nombre de Dios road from Portobelo after the fork to La Guaira, set well back from the road in verdant surroundings overlooking a forested stream, it consists of a simple wooden *cabaña* with two very rustic rooms at bargain rates. The friendly French owners can provide inexpensive breakfast and dinner but you'll need to venture out to the kiosk down the road, or bring supplies, for lunch. Activities such as horse riding ($20) or night outings to look for caimans can be organized. Ask the Nombre de Dios bus to drop you off, or catch a taxi ($8) from Portobelo.

Cuango and around

There's little reason to stop off in windswept **Viento Frío** and **Palenque** though you can enjoy a simple seafood lunch at the *Restaurante el Puerto* (☎6573 4469) in the latter, which sits plum on the beach. At the forlorn port of **Miramar**, the next village along, you can negotiate passage to El Porvenir in Kuna Yala ($20/person for a minimum of nine people; 90min), but you'd be well advised to find out in advance about possible departures since they are irregular and rare in the storm season (Dec–Feb). Try contacting Sr or Sra Magan, who have three simple rooms by the port (☎6693 5186; ❷), though if you need to overnight in the village, *Bohío Miramar* (☎6452 0446; ❹), right on the beach, offers much nicer accommodation, with a/c and an adjoining restaurant. It goes without saying that there are no ATMs or banking facilities in any of these places; you'll need to bring sufficient cash from Sabanitas or Colón. At the end of the tarred road lies **Cuango**, where the only sound is of waves breaking over the rocks and grey-sand beach, and the settlement's desolation is tangible. Beyond the river, a rough dirt road penetrates dense jungle.

At the far eastern tip of the province, near the community of Santa Isabel close to the border with Kuna Yala, lies the province's one luxury eco-resort, *Coral Lodge* (ⓦwww.corallodge.com), which can be accessed by boat from Miramar. Buses to Cuango from Colón (9am, 11am, 1pm, 3pm, 4.30pm; 2hr 30min; $4.70) are marked "Costa Arriba–Cuango" and the last return bus departs at 2–3pm.

Central Panama

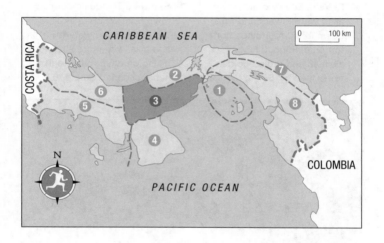

CHAPTER 3 # Highlights

* **Parque Nacional y Reserva Biológica Altos de Campana** Spectacular views greet hikers in this rugged landscape, only an hour from Panama City. See p.152

* **Santa Clara** A couple of vibey bars and casual restaurants make this the mellowest stretch of beach in the area. See p.155

* **El Valle** Lovely crater town filled with flowers and fruit trees, its surroundings home to horse riding, hiking, ziplines and fabled golden frogs. See p.156

* **Parque Nacional Omar Torrijos** Hire a local guide to scale the rainforested peaks of this little-explored park or get the binoculars out for some birdwatching. See p.168

* **Natá** One of the oldest churches in the Americas, with a dazzling white exterior and intricate wooden carvings adorning the interior. See p.172

* **Santa Fé** Tranquil mountain town from which to explore the surrounding waterfalls and hills, with more strenuous hiking on offer in the nearby national park. See p.176

▲ The famous golden frogs of El Valle

3

Central Panama

t was on the Caribbean coast of **central Panama**, at the foot of the steep rainforested slopes that straddle the provinces of Colón and Veraguas, that Christopher Columbus tried – and failed – to settle in 1502 (see p.329), though not before his reports of gold had reached the ears of the Spanish Crown. The isolated black communities sprinkled along the coastline today are descended from the African slaves who were brought over to work in the gold mines that the conquistadors eventually established. Across the continental divide, the Pacific coastal plains of Coclé and Veraguas were some of the first areas to be settled by the colonizing Spanish, who drove the indigenous population up into the forested mountainous spine of the Cordillera Central, where, several hundred years later, their descendants, the Ngöbe and Buglé, still live and fight – this time against the Panamanian government and international hydro-electric and mining companies.

Lower down, the gentler, denuded Pacific slopes are predominantly populated by peasant farmers, claiming varying mixtures of indigenous, African and Hispanic ancestry, and the land is taken up with arable and cattle farming. For this reason, central Panama is often ignored by tourists as they speed along the Interamericana, heading for the loftier peaks of Chiriquí or the golden beaches of Bocas. Yet there are good reasons to linger along the way. Accessible **beaches** are strung out along the Pacific coast, only an hour's drive from the capital, luring surf- and beach-loving urbanites in equal measure, but it is the mountains that hold most appeal, offering a splendid array of hiking and birdwatching opportunities. The volcanic tors of **Parque Nacional Altos de Campana** afford sweeping vistas of the coastline, while the scenic crater town of **El Valle** boasts outdoor activities and a lively craft market. **Parque Nacional Omar Torrijos** offers peaks shrouded in mist and a chance to explore the little-visited rainforested Caribbean slopes, and, further west, the delightful mountain town of **Santa Fé** is surrounded by cascading waterfalls and orchids that can be enjoyed on foot or horseback. Back down in the plains, the cities of **Aguadulce**, **Penomené** and **Santiago** have their own, low-key appeal, and provide access to some of the country's most important historical sites, such as the old colonial churches at **Natá** and **San Francisco**, which both contain wonderful wooden carvings, and the pre-Columbian remains of **El Caño**, an important ancient ceremonial and burial site.

CENTRAL PANAMA

CARIBBEAN SEA

COLÓN

PARQUE NACIONAL
GENERAL DE DIVISIÓN
OMAR TORRIJOS (EL COPÉ) ▲ Cerro Marta
(1046m)

Cerro Peña Blanca
(1314m)

El Copé

VERAGUAS

Río Grande

Cerro Cenizo
(1626m)

COCLÉ

Santa Fé

Cerro Alto
del Cigueral
(1510m)

Laguna de la
Yeguada

El Caño

Nata

Calobre

San Francisco

Aguadulce

INTERAMERICANA

David (170km)

INTERAMERICANA

Divisa

Santiago

HERRERA

The road to El Valle

All buses heading west out of Panama City cross the **Bridge of the Americas**, suspended 1600m above the mouth of the canal, where the **Interamericana** starts its journey to the Costa Rican border almost 500km away. After grinding through the urban sprawl of **La Chorerra**, 40km to the southwest, the road crests at Loma Capana, where you've scarcely time to gasp at the views across the sparkling Golfo de Panamá and the brooding peaks of the Cordillera Central – assuming you dare risk taking your eye off the hair-raising traffic – before

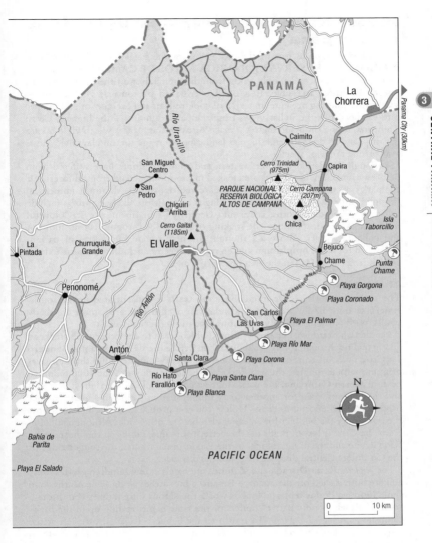

it swoops down like a rollercoaster onto a narrow alluvial plain hemmed in between the mountains and the Pacific.

Just before the descent, a road off to the right winds up to the country's oldest **national park**, which provides some enjoyable hiking and birdwatching. Once down on the flatland, a string of entrances to various **beaches** peel off the Interamericana, providing the nearest decent stretches of sand to Panama City, with spots to appeal to all kinds of beach-lovers, most reachable by bus. Shortly after crossing over the border from the Province of Panama into Coclé, a road heads north into the mountains and the delightful weekend resort of **El Valle**.

Parque Nacional y Reserva Biológica Altos de Campana

Established in 1966 as part of the protection for the canal basin, the **PARQUE NACIONAL Y RESERVA BIOLÓGICA ALTOS DE CAMPANA** is Panama's oldest national park and at only 55km from the capital, just off the Interamericana, one of the most accessible. It is often overlooked by tourists, visited only at weekends by fleeing urbanites in search of cool fresh air and exercise, or enthusiastic birdwatchers. But the stellar views from the park's summits – the highest, Cerro Campana, tops a thousand metres – make Altos de Campana a worthwhile hiking day-trip, and its dramatic and singular landscape of craggy tors and lava fields hosts a surprising range of species.

Although the denuded lower western and southern slopes have suffered from deforestation, elsewhere peaks are cloaked in pre-montane and tropical forest. Of the park's 39 **mammal** species, the black-eared opossum is the most numerous, though it'll be tucked up in its den during the day. More likely sightings include two- and three-toed sloths, coatis and Geoffroy's tamarin monkeys. Colourful **birds** also abound, including the striking orange-bellied trogon, rufous motmot and collared aracari. Above all, though, the fifty square kilometres of park is renowned for its 62 **amphibian** and 86 **reptile** species, including the near-extinct golden frog (see p.160) in the area's western fringes.

The trails

The park's network of five interconnecting **trails** is concentrated in the south-eastern section. Easily accessible and relatively well demarcated, most are shady strolls, with one a moderately strenuous hike through scenic forest.

The flattish **Sendero Panamá** (1.5km), which leads to the other trails, makes a gentle incline through forest for about 800m before the well-maintained **Sendero La Cruz** peels off to the right. After a steep twenty-minute climb through trees dripping with epiphytes, the path forks: to the left it climbs to the 1000m domed peak of **Cerro Campana**, the park's highest point, while to the right it descends and then climbs again for another forty minutes, culminating in a giant boulder topped with an enormous cross. Unless you're a proficient rock-climber, follow the trail under the boulder for an easier clamber the other side. Although at 860m Cerro La Cruz is lower, it affords the better panorama, taking in the meandering Río Chame and the distant blocks of the Pacific beach resorts, the rugged ridge of the Cordillera Central disappearing into the distance.

The *senderos* **Rana Dorada** and **Zamora** are barely a few hundred metres long, and are both signed off the Sendero Panamá a bit further along. The nearby loop trail, **Sendero Podacarpus** (600m), is worth the detour since it takes you through some of Panama's only native conifers of the same name, ending up in the park's campsite at *Refugio Los Pinos*. To return to the Sendero Panamá, turn left at the T-junction below the campsite, then left again once you reach the main path to return the way you came, or right at the second junction to descend what becomes a disintegrating asphalt road down to the main road.

If you've time, a visit to the village of **Chicá**, a few kilometres along the road at the end of the bus route, makes a pleasant postscript, with bougainvillea-filled gardens and several *fondas* serving traditional **food**. Although most joints only open up at weekends, *Johany's Café Comedor* serves up tasty dishes all day on the refreshingly breezy terrace for under $3.

Practicalities

Grab any San Carlos, Capira or Chame **bus** from the Albrook terminal to the town of Capira ($1.50), about 50km west of Panama City. Ask to be dropped off on the

Interamericana a few hundred metres after the Shell garage at *Restaurante Lily's*, where minibuses bound for the mountain village of Chicá, via the park, depart (hourly, 7am–8pm, returning on the hour; 40min). If you've time, stock up with supplies at the nearby Quesos Chela, one of Panama's gastronomic gems, producing fresh yoghurts and empanadas as well as its renowned cheeses.

The **park office** ($5 entry, $6 extra to camp), where you may get a map, is perched on the left-hand side of the road, after around a twenty-minute winding ascent. Unfortunately, it's over 3km further up the mountainside to the park itself and the trailhead, though you may be able to persuade the bus to wait while you sort out the formalities. The park entrance lies on the right after a sign declaring "No Estoy". If you've come by car – a straightforward drive since the park is signposted off the Interamericana 5km beyond Capira – park here. Follow the path up beside the large house, where a sign marks the trailhead.

Although you can **camp** at the back of the park office, it's much nicer in the park at *Refugio Los Pinos*, a pleasant spot surrounded by pine trees about a thirty-minute hike from the trailhead. There's a latrine and space to make a fire but no water or electricity.

The Pacific beaches

Once the Interamericana hits the coastal plain at the western edge of Panama Province, roads start to branch off the main artery like blood vessels, feeding the various **beaches** along the Pacific coast, with locations to suit surfers, swimmers and sunbathers and sand ranging from charcoal grey through tan to pale cream. The eastern stretch is dominated by **surfing** waves, from Gorgona to Río Mar, while the most attractive beaches, accompanied by the best selection of accommodation and eating options and a fair bit of development, lie a further 20km west, at **Farallón** (Playa Blanca) and **Santa Clara**. The closest decent stretches of sand to the capital, reachable in a couple of hours, they are packed at weekends and holidays with Panamanian families escaping the city heat, but midweek they can be deserted. Many tourists give the area a miss, preferring the white picture-postcard sand of the Pacific or Caribbean islands. But if you're a windsurfer or kitesurfer, or a surfer without the time to get down to Santa Catalina (see p.221), or you want a quick dip in the sea or a trot along the sands on horseback, then at least one stretch of the coastline should appeal.

Arrival and information

Life is a whole lot easier with your own transport, especially since **buses** generally only drop off passengers at the "*entrada*" on the Interamericana, from where a ten-minute stroll or a sweaty 8km hike – depending on the destination – will get you to the beach, though sometimes **taxis** are available. Banks and ATMs are scarce, so check in advance which places accept credit cards and make sure you have enough cash for your trip.

Those heading for **Punta Chame** should hop on a Chame-bound bus (from Albrook every 15 mins) as far as Bejuco (70min; $2.15) and transfer to the hourly(ish) pick-up trucks ($1.25) or taxis ($15–20) for the remainder of the journey. Machete Kiteboarding (see p.155) can organize transport for their clients from Panama City for $50. The turn-off to **Gorgona** is 8km further west of the Punta Chame junction, with the beach in walking distance, whereas minibuses (50c) and taxis ($3–4) at the Coronado exit, a little further along the Interamericana, shuttle folk to the sand. The highly visible El Rey **supermarket**, which contains an **ATM** and is next to a **petrol station**, marks the turn-off.

Keen surfers heading for **Playa El Palmar** and **Playa Río Mar** should jump on a bus bound for Antón and will probably need to hike down the road from the

Interamericana stop to the beach. Beach-goers aiming for **Santa Clara** are likely to find taxis hanging round the turn-off from the highway, or can arrange a pick-up in advance (℡ 6606 9084). If you're bound for **Farallón** (Playa Blanca) you'll also need to get off a bus heading for Antón on the Interamericana though guests at the *Decameron* and *Playa Blanca* resorts can arrange a transfer from or to Panama City for around $35. There is an **ATM** in the *Decameron* resort.

Accommodation

The **accommodation** is as varied as the sand along this stretch of coastline; you can take your pick from a thousand-room all-inclusive resort to a tent on the beach. Our list below runs from the surf-happy eastern stretch, where Playa Coronado offers the best options, westwards towards Santa Clara, which boasts a mega-resort and plenty of popular hammock and tent spots.

The eastern beaches

Coronado Golf & Beach Resort Av Punta Preita, Playa Coronado ℡ 264 3164, ⓦ www.coronado resort.com. Sprawling hacienda-style place 1km off the beach in extensive, landscaped grounds. The 18-hole golf course, Olympic pool, tennis court, stables and chocolate massage at the spa help entertain guests before they've even thought about the sea. Very busy at weekends. ❾

El Littoral Punta Prieta, Coronado, ℡ 240 1474, ⓦ www.litoralpanama.com. Classy if pricey B&B with swimming pool and covered dining terrace. Five tasteful, well-appointed rooms offer a/c, cable tv, wi-fi and private or shared bathrooms. ❼

Punta Chame Motel Punta Chame ℡ 240 5498. Packed with windsurfers during the season (Dec–April), this eleven-room hotel offers simple but well-equipped rooms and a reasonably priced *rancho*-restaurant on the beach. Breakfasts around $4, fish and seafood mains around $8. ❺

Río Mar Surf Camp Near Río Mar, San Carlos ℡ 240 9128, ⓦ www.riomarsurf.com. Overpriced, dark two-bunk rooms with fan ($10 more for a/c) set on a grassy mound just off the sand but it's the only place on the beach for surfers to bed down. Board and cooler rental. Extra $5 for use of the kitchen. ❹

Playa Santa Clara and Farallón

Cabañas las Veraneras Playa Santa Clara ℡ 993 3313, ⓔ lasveraneras@cwpanama.net. Offers laid-back vibes and nice thatched *cabañas* (with fan or a/c) on the beach, with split-level versions on the ridge above, though the booming beats from the nearby bar-restaurant make early

nights tricky. Larger, quieter cement rooms with kitchen lie further back. ❻

Restaurante y Balneario Playa Santa Clara Playa Santa Clara, near *Las Sirenas* ℡ 993 2123. A rare opportunity for organized camping – $5/person – on the beach, including security and showers. For $10 you can bag a simple *rancho* during the day, complete with hammocks for lolling in, and use of showers and bathrooms. There's a simple on-site seafood restaurant, and day-trippers can use the showers for $3.

Royal Decameron Golf Beach Resort & Villas Farallón (Playa Blanca) ℡ 993 2255. You'll either love or hate this four-star all-inclusive behemoth hogging 2km of fantastic beach. With over 1000 rooms, 10 restaurants, 11 bars, a spa and 18-hole golf course plus a mind-boggling array of organized daytime and evening activities, there'll scarcely be time to sleep. Advance internet bookings can be good value. ❽

Las Sirenas Playa Santa Clara ℡ 223 0132 (Spanish speakers) or 993 3235 (English speakers), ⓦ www.lasirenas.com. Tranquil, fully equipped one- or two-bedroom cottages (accommodating 4 or 6) located either over the hilltop in bougainvillea or plum on the beach. Add to each a large patio, hammock and BBQ, and you have the nicest lodgings in the area. $143 for the cottage.

Villa Botero Panamá B & B Playa Santa Clara, C Aviación at C Arroyo ℡ 993 2708, ⓦ www.villaboterobb.com. A short hop from the beach, this charming B&B offers a couple of exquisitely furnished rooms in a colonial-style tiled-roof cottage with all mod cons – wi-fi, flat-screen cable TV, fridge – overlooking a pool and surrounding garden with use of a shared kitchen. ❻

The beaches

Travelling west along the Interamericana, the first exit travels the length of a 12km sandy spit to the low-key fishing village of **Punta Chame**, where the vast flat beach, strong winds and choppy waters have transformed this otherwise deserted swathe of sand into Panama's centre of **kitesurfing**; two schools operate during the season (Nov–May; ⓦwww.kitesurfingpanama.com, www.machetekites.com. Beware the stingrays at low tide. At the mouth of the more sheltered Bay of Chame sits Isla Taborcillo, dubbed Isla de John Wayne, which was purchased by the iconic actor after shooting *Río Bravo* in Panama and has now been converted into a family resort complete with swinging saloon doors, sheriff's office and swaggering gun-slinging tough guys.

Next up are Playas **Gorgona** and **Coronado**, once the most fashionable weekend destinations for middle-class residents of Panama City, with beach-front properties overlooking the marbled charcoal sand. There are two surfing magnets in the neighbourhood – at Playa Malibu in Gorgona and at Punta Teta (predictably dubbed "Tits" by surfing gringos), 3km down a dirt road not long after the Coronado exit. The only substantial settlement in the area, 12km on from El Rey, just off the Interamericana, is **San Carlos**, worth noting mainly as a place to buy provisions and catch a bus. Transport from Panama City terminates here at twenty-minute intervals ($2.70) while minibuses also leave every thirty minutes for the popular resort of El Valle ($1.50). The other surfing hotspots in the area lie down two asphalt roads a few kilometres west of San Carlos at **Playa El Palmar** and **Playa Río Mar**. Non-surfers should continue a further 20km to hit the best beaches on this stretch of coast.

Playa Santa Clara, 30km east of Penonomé, is probably the loveliest beach, a seemingly endless belt of pale sand lapped by calm waters with pleasantly informal bars and restaurants – though large concrete developments are beginning to encroach here, and quad bikes and jet skis roar about the place at weekends. A few kilometres further along the coast, at the equally impressive beige swathe of **Farallón** (slowly being rebranded as Playa Blanca), things are even busier, and the local fishing village is becoming increasingly hemmed in among greedy resorts, condominium complexes and gated retirement communities. Since all beaches are public in Panama, you can still occupy the sand, though splashing out on a *Decameron* day pass ($45) is good value for some hedonistic pleasure – all you can eat and drink and full use of resort facilities, including some of the water toys. Most accommodation can fix up some gentle **horse riding** along the beach or a **boat trip** with one of the local fishermen.

Eating, drinking and nightlife

The large resorts take care of the catering and evening entertainment for their guests. Otherwise there is a sprinkling of local **bars** and **fondas** amid a handful of **restaurants** aimed exclusively at tourists and expats.

The eastern beaches

🏃 **Los Camisones** La Ermita, km 104 off the Interamericana to the right between San Carlos and Santa Clara ☎993 3622, ⓦwww.loscamisones.com. Its reputation for serving the best seafood in the country (including paella) has pushed the prices up in recent years, though this Spanish-Panamanian restaurant rarely disappoints. A changing menu dependent on available fresh produce is enjoyed in a relaxed large *rancho* set in a pleasant garden. Most mains $10–20. Daily 9.30am–9pm, Fri–Sun until 11pm.

Restaurante El Parque Centre of San Carlos. Reliable, inexpensive local place (with a/c) selling platefuls of Panamanian and Chinese regulars

for under $4, and the *menu del día* for even less. Daily 8am–10pm.

Rincón del Chef On the road into Coronado ☎240 1941, ⓦwww.elrincondelchefpanama.com. Delightful colonial-style establishment, a favourite among gringo expats, serving a wide-ranging menu of local and imported products. Meat and fish mains around $10. Daily 8am–9pm, Fri & Sat until 10pm.

Playa Santa Clara and Farállon

Fonda Adela Playa Santa Clara. Inexpensive seafood options ($4–7) bang on the beach near *Cabañas las Veraneras*. Only open at weekends.

Restaurante y Balneario Playa Santa Clara. Beach *rancho* with wooden picnic tables selling moderately priced fish and seafood (most under $9) and cheap chilled beer. Great for soaking up the sunsets.

Pipa's Beach Bar Farallón (Playa Blanca) Ⓦ www.pipasbeach.com. At the end of the sandy road, past the *Decameron*, this informal bar-restaurant is smack on the sand. The excellent lobster and trimmings will set you back a hefty $25 but most other fresh seafood dishes are $6–9. Tues–Sun from 10am.

Restaurante Las Veraneras Playa Santa Clara. Vibey bar-restaurant on the beach, which serves decent fish and seafood, with the party atmosphere picking up on weekends. Daily 10am–9pm.

El Valle and around

About a 100km southwest of Panama City, just beyond San Carlos, a windy road ascends 600m into the cordillera – Panama's mountainous spine – to **EL VALLE** (Ⓦ www.el-valle-panama.com), a small town of around seven thousand inhabitants nestled in the crater of a now-extinct volcano. Undulating hills rise to the south and west, ascending to more dramatic, forested peaks to the north, often shrouded in mist. The picturesque location, cool climate and relative proximity to the capital (90min by car) have made El Valle the holiday-home location of choice for Panama City's elite and is increasingly attracting foreign retirees. Quiet during the week, the place comes alive at weekends and on public holidays as a stream of 4WDs arrives from the city and the otherwise still roads resound with the sound of clopping hooves or revving quad bikes.

The huge explosion that blew the top off the volcano three million years ago left a vast caldera that over time filled with rain water. When the crater-lake drained, it left behind a flat layer of rich volcanic soil. Perfect for agricultural production, the fertile earth also nourishes the vast expanses of trimmed lawn, abundant fruit and flower-laden trees, and attendant hummingbirds tucked away down El Valle's side streets, which are central to the place's charm.

The town's surroundings are instantly impressive. Spectacular stream-filled cloud forests envelope the elevated mountain reserve of **Monumento Natural Cerro Gaital**, which provides first-rate birdwatching opportunities, and visitors can also explore the puzzling petroglyphs of **La Piedra Pintada** and the spectacular falls of **Chorro El Macho**. If you enjoy fresh mountain air, meanwhile, there are enough decent hiking, horse riding and cycling opportunities to keep you in El Valle for several days.

Arrival and information

Buses pull in across from the covered **market** on nondescript Avenida Central (also known as Avenida or Calle Principal), which acts as the town's unofficial bus terminal and forms the social and administrative centre of the village, with the **post office** tucked in behind. Most other amenities are spread out along the road, which forks at its western end, leading off to some of the area's major natural attractions: La Piedra Pintada, Chorro El Macho and La India Dormida. Buses from Panama City arrive here (every 30min 7.30am–6.30pm; 2hr; $3.50), as do regular minibuses from San Carlos, twenty minutes down the road.

Once in El Valle most places can be reached **on foot** and there are even pavements along some parts of the main road. Cycling is also convenient and **bicycles** can be hired at *Hotel Don Pepe* ($2/hr, $10/day) or at several lodgings in the town. **Taxi** rides should not cost more than a couple of dollars to most places though finding one available is about as easy as locating one of El Valle's fabled golden frogs. During the day, occasional blue buses circulate round the village ($0.25) and will drop you off wherever you want, while half-hourly yellow school buses shuttle back and forth from Capirita, at the eastern end of the village, to La Pintada to the west. **Minibuses** also head up the mountain to **La Mesa** (every 30min 7am–4pm), the access point for Cerro Gaital.

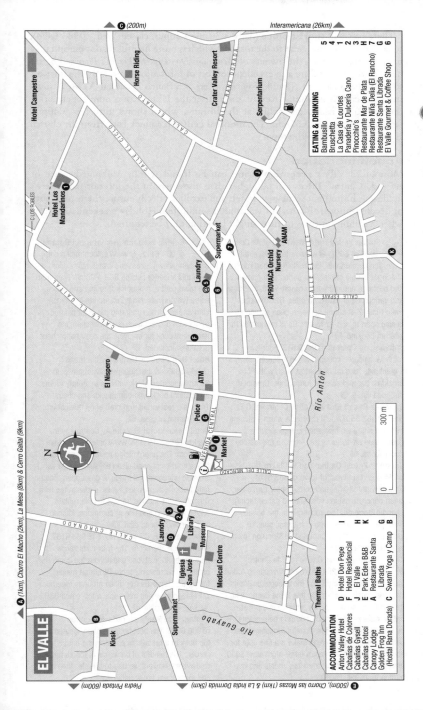

EL VALLE

▲ A (1km), Chorro El Macho (2km), La Mesa (8km) & Cerro Gaital (9km)

C (200m) ▲   Interamericana (26km) ▲

Hotel Campestre

Horse Riding

Crater Valley Resort

Serpentarium

Hotel Los Mandarinos ❶

CLUB ROBLES

CALLE EL CICLO

CALLE EL HATO

CALLE RANA DORADA

CALLE EL GAITAL

J

7

Laundry
@ 5
6

Supermarket

APROVACA Orchid
Nursery

ANAM

CALLE EL VALLE

CALLE ESPAVE

K

El Níspero

F

ATM

Police
G

AVENIDA CENTRAL

CALLE DEL MERCADO

LOS MANDARINOS

Río Antón

Río Anton

N

300 m

0

El Valle Gourmet & Coffee Shop

H I
Market

B

i

3
2 4

Laundry

Library

Museum

D

Iglesia
San José

Medical Centre

CALLE CORONADO

Supermarket

Kiosk

B

Thermal Baths

Río Guayabo

E (500m), Chorro las Mozas (1km) & La India Dormida (5km) ▼

Piedra Pintada (600m) ▼

EATING & DRINKING
Bambusilio	5
Bruschetta	4
La Casa de Lourdes	1
Panadería y Dulcería Cano	2
Pinocchio's	3
Restaurante Mar de Plata	H
Restaurante Niña Delia (El Rancho)	7
Restaurante Santa Librada	G
El Valle Gourmet & Coffee Shop	6

ACCOMMODATION
Anton Valley Hotel	I
Cabañas de Colores	H
Cabañas Gysell	K
Cabañas Potosí	G
Canopy Lodge	B
Golden Frog Inn (Hostal Rana Dorada)	C
Hotel Don Pepe	D
Hotel Residencial El Valle	F
Park Eden B&B	J
Restaurante Santa Librada	E
Swami Yoga y Camp	A

3

CENTRAL PANAMA

157

There's a small **tourist office** (daily 8.30am–4.30pm, closed Wed; ☎ 983 6474), squeezed into a kiosk next to the market, which is more helpful than some and may have a map, although the owners of *Artesanías Don Pepe* or *David's Place* sell better maps of the area and are also excellent sources of local information. By the turn-off to El Nispero Zoo on Avenida Central, there is a Banco Nacional **ATM**. A small **internet café** is in a small row of shops after the Hong Kong mini-supermarket though you can also get online at the **library**, which shows films (Fri 6.30pm, family screening Sat 3.30pm). The **medical centre** is a block back from the church at the western end of the town.

Accommodation

Most of El Valle's **accommodation** can be found within walking distance of Avenida Central. Prices can be higher than elsewhere in the interior (and there's no decent hostel) but some new hotels and excellent B&Bs ensure there are plenty of decent options, all with hot water unless indicated. Holiday weekends are busy, when a minimum two- or three-night booking may be required.

Anton Valley Hotel West end of Av Central ☎ 9836 6097, ⊛ www.antonvalleyhotel .com. Ten comfortable, tastefully furnished rooms sharing a couple of pleasant patios with games and books to entertain. Bike rental, wi-fi, massage and various other extras on offer. The breakfast room (daily 7–9.30am) serves a good spread and is also open to non-residents. Good reductions for internet booking. ➏

Cabañas de Colores ☎ 9836 613. Four twee rainbow-coloured cottages set in a garden down a quiet side road off Av Central, each with TV, breakfast bar and eclectic furnishings. Cramped, but good value. ➍

Cabañas Gysell East end of Av Central at C El Hato ☎ 983 6507 You'll receive a warm welcome at these small whitewashed cottages, with good-value en-suite rooms – ignore the kitschy decorations. ➍

Cabañas Potosí On the road to Chorro las Mozas, 1km west of town ☎ 983 6181, ⓔ dnnswnthld3@hotmail.com. Simply furnished, clean concrete cabins with shared patios facing La India Dormida. The cockerels in the flower-filled grounds, where you can camp, should ensure an early start. Camping $15/person (own tent $10/person) ➎

Canopy Lodge On the road to Chorro El Macho ☎ 264 5720, ⊛ www.canopylodge .com. Though not actually in the canopy (unlike its Gamboa cousin, see p.120), this lodge overlooking the Río Guayabo is superbly situated in a private nature reserve. It's aimed at birding enthusiasts, but the fine surroundings, tasteful furnishings and comfortable common areas make it a fine spot for anyone to unwind. Minimum three-night stay: $900 in total including airport transfers, meals and two birding tours per day. ➒

Golden Frog Inn (Hostal Rana Dorada) ☎ 983 6117, ⊛ www.goldenfroginn.com. Satisfying views across the crater valley floor from this superior hillside B&B a 20min walk from the town centre. A handful of rooms and suites, some with private verandas, are set in a nicely landscaped garden (ignoring the giant painted frogs) with a small pool, shared kitchen and hammock deck for enjoying the daily happy hour. Breakfast included. ➏

Hotel Don Pepe Av Central by the market ☎ 983 6835, ⓔ hoteldonpepe@hotmail.com. Centrally located block with clean, comfy rooms, an upstairs deck with hammocks and chairs. There's a restaurant and craft shop downstairs and internet access. ➎

Hotel Residencial El Valle Av Central, by the market ☎ 983 6536, ⊛ www.hotelresidencialel valle.com. The unpromising motel-like exterior belies light comfy and clean en-suite rooms with sizeable windows and fridge. A great open-sided hammock deck provides views across to the hills. Other benefits include free wi-fi, bike rental ($2/hr, $10/day) and use of communal kitchen and laundry. A good deal. ➎

Park Eden B&B C Espavé No. 7 ☎ 983 6167, ⊛ www.parkeden.com. The frilly furnishings may not be to everyone's taste, but the comforts provided (microwave, cable TV, coffee maker, fridge) and fabulous tree-filled grounds together with friendly service make this a top-notch B&B. Packages available. ➐

Restaurante Santa Librada Av Central ☎ 986 6376. The best budget option, located at the back of a restaurant and opening onto a small garden. The handful of basic, clean rooms have cold-water showers; some are brighter than others and mattresses are variable. ➋

Swami Yoga y Camp ☎ 983 6540, ⓔ swami camping@yahoo.com. Informal campsite and yoga centre with shared kitchen in a delightful orchard on the road to Chorro El Macho. The bargain rates include a veggie meal and you can borrow a tent if necessary. A dorm is planned. $5/person.

The Town

Town life revolves round the daily **market**, which draws the largest crowds at weekends, especially on Sundays, when farmers and artisans pour in to sell fruit, vegetables, flowers and handicrafts. It's Panama's best-known craft market outside the capital and you'll find a decent range of ceramic figurines, painted wooden trays (*bateas*) and soapstone carvings (mostly by Ngöbe or Buglé artists) alongside Kuna *molas* and Emberá or Wounaan basketry as well as straw hats (see *Art and Crafts* colour section). Also of interest is Bambusillo (Wed–Sun 9.30am–6pm), an excellent **art gallery** located next to the pharmacy further east on the main road.

Arts and crafts aside, El Valle's low-key sights are nearly all signposted off Avenida Central. The **serpentarium** (daily 8.30am–5.30pm; $1), on the right as you head into town, could display its charges more appealingly – specimens are crammed into home-made boxes – but if your Spanish is up to it, you can still be treated to an informative tour and handle the friendly boa. The **APROVACA Orchid Nursery** (daily 9am–4pm; $2) is on the left a few blocks later, by the ANAM office. It nurtures around five hundred of Panama's twelve hundred orchid species, including the country's rare endemic national flower, the delicate *flor del espíritu santo* – named for the centre of each bloom, which resembles a white dove.

For many, El Valle is synonymous with golden frogs (see box, p.160) and your best chance of glimpsing the diminutive amphibians is at the local zoo, **El Níspero**, (daily 7am–5pm; $3), where they form the proud centrepiece of the impressive new Centro de Conservación de Anfibios de El Valle (EVACC for short), which should definitely feature on your itinerary. Sixteen other threatened native species of frog, toad and salamander have also been collected for study and breeding in captivity, with a view to releasing them back into the wild once the fungus is no longer a threat. The rest of the zoo – which started life as a plant nursery and still

▲ The market in El Valle

La Rana Dorada – Panama's threatened Golden Frog

Decorating everything from pre-Columbian talismans to tacky T-shirts and lottery tickets, Panama's **golden frog** (*rana dorada*) is one of the country's most enduring cultural icons, associated above all with El Valle since the surrounding cloud forest provides its only known habitat. In ancient times the Guaymí (or Ngöbe) revered the frog, carving ceramic and golden likenesses for jewellery and *huacas* – precious objects buried with chiefs and other prominent citizens – of this symbol of fertility and prosperity. Indeed legend had it that possessing one of these "true toads" in life would ensure good fortune in the afterlife as it would transform into a golden *huaca*. Even today it is believed that a glimpse of this tiny dazzling amphibian in the wild will bring good luck, though a sighting is highly improbable thanks to the deadly chytrid fungus, which decimated amphibian populations worldwide and wrought devastation in the area in 2006. The water-borne fungus, which attacks the skin and suffocates the animal, was thought to have wiped out the wild population – you can see captive frogs at El Nispero (see p.159). Promisingly, though, there have been recent isolated sightings in the forest of these emblematic amphibians, which together with some successful breeding in captivity give hope for their eventual recovery in the wild.

functions as such – crams 55 species of bird, alongside ocelot, margay, capybara, several types of monkey and even Manuel Noriega's tapirs, adopted after the US invasion, into inadequate cages. To get there, take a right turn just before the police station, and follow the rocky unmade road for about 1km.

Continuing up Avenida Central, past the market on the left, takes you to the whitewashed twin towers of the small **Iglesia de San José**, behind which is a modest one-room **museum** (Sun 10am–2pm, but ask around for access on other days; 50c). Much of the displays – lumps of volcanic rock, household objects and contemporary crafts – are forgettable, but there are some striking polychromatic pre-Columbian ceramics and interesting carved faces.

Beyond the church, a side road leads down to the low-key **thermal baths** (*pozos termales*; daily 8am–5pm; $1) by Río Anton, which allegedly have medicinal powers. The weekends are hectic, but the warm cement pool can be a pleasant experience midweek – take your swimming costume. There are also a couple of pots of exfoliating, mineral-rich mud on hand. Leaving the hot springs, hang a right down the aptly named Calle de los Millonarios (Millionaires' Road), and take a peek at some of the immaculately maintained gardens and luxury weekend homes of Panama's wealthy elite.

Walks and activities

Though not as lofty as the peaks of Chiriquí, the mountains encircling El Valle still provide picturesque scenery ideal for a range of outdoor activities: whizzing along a zipline, horse riding or abseiling, and – a little further afield – kayaking or whitewater rafting. In particular the area offers a wealth of **hiking** opportunities, ranging from the most popular route, a moderate two-hour excursion up and along the pastured contours of La India Dormida to a strenuous two-day trek to Altos de Campana. Not that you have to head for the mountains to spot birds, since hummingbirds, motmots, euphonias and the like can easily be seen flitting round the fringes of the village as you stroll to the town's nearby waterfalls and petroglyphs.

Chorro El Macho and the Canopy Adventure

Across the bridge over the Río Guayabo at the east end of Avenida Central, the road forks three ways. A thirty-minute walk up the right fork takes you up to

Chorro El Macho (daily 6am–5pm; $3.50), a picturesque 35m **waterfall** set in a private ecological reserve. A short circular path leads to a viewing platform at the base of the falls, where lizards bask on the rocks and hummingbirds dart through the foliage. Though you can't take the plunge here, near the entrance there is delightful natural swimming pool in the river, or you might prefer a guided nature walk ($35) with a bilingual guide.

The **Canopy Adventure** (daily 6am–4pm; ℡983 6547; $52.50), accessed via the park entrance, adds adrenaline to the delightful flora and fauna and its five cables – one taking you across the face of the falls – forms one of El Valle's major attractions. $12.50 will get you a one-line traverse over the river, which seems scarcely worth it. If you're heading for Chiriquí you might want to save your cash to do the more impressive Boquete Tree Trek (see p.236). But here the adventure has the potential to combine thrills with wildlife viewing, especially if you arrive close to 6am, when there is a greater chance of seeing wildlife.

Chorro Las Mozas and La Piedra Pintada

The left fork from the bridge over Río Guayabo leads to the smaller and far less dramatic **Chorro Las Mozas** falls; fifteen minutes walk from town, it's a popular place for the local youth to splash around, especially at weekends.

In contrast, a fifteen-minute walk along the central prong of the fork leads to a massive petroglyph known as **La Piedra Pintada**. An enterprising group of locals have recently started charging 25c entry, supposedly to keep the trail clean, and there's no shortage of kids offering to guide you to the giant rock face and attempt to explain the mysterious pre-Columbian carved spirals and anthropomorphic and zoomorphic figures. You can continue up the path that follows the stream, which becomes more of a scramble as it forges through the forest, passing three pretty waterfalls. Ten minutes after the third one, to the right, stands the smaller petroglyph of **Piedra El Sapo**, named after the toad-like shape of one of its hieroglyphs, before the path continues up to the mythical ridge of La India Dormida (see box below).

Longer hikes

For most hikes you'll need a **guide**, since trails are not well marked and if the mist descends it's easy to lose your way, though on a clear day you can manage **La India Dormida** without being accompanied. There are several routes up the legendary hill, the most direct being to follow the path up past the Piedra Pintada, hugging the stream until you reach the top. A better circular route heads out past the baseball stadium, bearing left at the next fork. When the road ends, a path

---

La India Dormida

The undulating hilltop at the western end of El Valle, known as **La India Dormida**, is believed to be the slumbering silhouette of Flor del Aire, beautiful daughter of Urracá, the indigenous chief famed for his fierce resistance to Spanish colonization. The story goes that while battles were raging, Flor fell in love with one of the conquistadors, unaware that she was admired by Yaraví, the tribe's most courageous warrior. Failing to get Flor's attention, Yaraví took the drastic measure of hurling himself off a mountain in front of the whole village. Understandably distraught, Flor renounced her love for the Spaniard and wandered off into the forested hills, where she eventually died of grief. Her body, it is said, is immortalized in the shape of a mountain. With a great deal of imagination and a little prompting from a local resident, you can usually make out her recumbent form, denuded of trees except for the distinct forested section to the right-hand side, which more clearly resembles the tresses of her hair.

off to the right brings you out on the lower part of what is presumed to be Flor's body (see box, p.161). Walking north along the deforested ridge, you can enjoy the splendid views across the crater before taking the path down from the "head" that eventually passes the refreshing waterfalls and natural swimming pools near La Piedra Pintada, where you can cool off.

A more challenging hike scales the area's highest peak, the forbidding forest-clad **Cerro Gaital** (1185m), for which you'll need a permit from ANAM ($5) either from the office in town, by the orchid nursery, or the one at the northern entrance to the reserve near La Mesa, which is often unstaffed. The most direct route involves a steep climb from a path behind *Hotel Los Mandarinos*, for which you'd need a guide. Alternatively, you can labour 7–8km up the road to La Mesa (or take the bus), bearing right at the fork after the village and arriving, a few hundred metres later, at the entrance of the **Monumento Natural Cerro Gaital**. The orchid-rich reserve is as a haven for **birdwatchers** as well as hikers, harbouring a rainbow of hummingbirds, honeycreepers, toucanets, tanagers and trogons, as well as the elusive black guan. A 2.5km loop trail, Sendero El Convento, winds through cloud forest, circling the summit, with a turn-off to a mirador which on a clear day affords stellar views down to the coast.

Other activities

The *Crater Valley Resort* at the eastern end of town hosts the Panama Explorers Club (☏983 6942, ⓦwww.pexclub.com), which organizes a range of other outdoor activities in the area, including **abseiling** (rappelling), **whitewater rafting** (rapids Grades I to III), **kayaking** and **mountain biking** (around $90 for the day; six needed so sign up in advance).

For **horse riding** (☏6646 5813; $8/hr), visit the long-established stables on Calle El Hato, opposite the shrine, just before *Hotel Campestre*. It's worth paying a little extra for a guide (Spanish-speaking) to accompany you. A popular route, lasting around four hours, takes you round Cerro Gaital.

Eating, drinking and nightlife

Though El Valle is never exactly humming in the evening, aside from the local Friday-night *cantina* parties, **restaurants** can be quite full at weekends and during holiday periods.

Finding a guide

Guides of all ages and experiences are available in El Valle; a necessity if you intend to do some serious **hiking**, they can also ensure you see a lot more when **birdwatching**. For a few dollars – which can be a vital source of family income – kids will interpret the squiggles on La Piedra Pintada and entertain you with tales (in Spanish) to accompany you up La India Dormida. For expert knowledge and bilingual guiding you'll need to pay a lot more; the most obvious choices (though likely to be booked up) are **Mario Bernal** (☏231 3811 or 693 8213, Ⓔmariobernalg@hotmail.com – an internationally renowned naturalist from El Valle) and **Mario Urriola** (☏6569 2676, Ⓔinfo@panamabirdguide.com – a professional biologist and enthusiastic ornithologist, who also runs the serpentarium). For Spanish speakers seeking less specialized expertise, **Rodolfo Mendez**, better known as "El Chacal" (contact *Hotel Don Pepe*, or ☏660 75174), has a good general knowledge of the area while AGUITEVA, a recently formed local eco-tourism group, offers English-speaking guiding ($5/person/hr, though less if 3–4 people; Ⓔaguiteva @hotmail.com, or enquire at the tourist kiosk). Many of the hotels also have their own local guides whom they regularly call on.

Bambusillo Av Central. Relaxed café attached to the art gallery serving a changing menu of inexpensive veggie dishes using seasonal local produce (Wed–Sun high season, Sat & Sun low season).

Bruschetta Av Central ☎6518 4416. The lively but cosy atmosphere here – where Panamanian dishes and pseudo-Italian bruschettas ($3.50–5.50) are on the menu – together with the moderate prices (salads $4–6; seafood dishes from $7) make this a popular place. Since there's only a sprinkling of the sought-after patio tables, it's worth booking ahead at weekends. 11.30am until late, closed Tues.

La Casa de Lourdes C El Ciclo, tucked behind *Hotel Los Mandarinos* ☎983 6450, ⊛www.lacasa delourdes.com. Lovers of fine dining should make the pilgrimage to the spectacular Tuscan-style villa-restaurant of celebrity chef Lourdes Fábrega de Ward, where inventive gourmet Panamanian cuisine (mains around $25) is served on the elegant poolside terrace. Reservations a must at weekends. Daily lunch noon–3pm, dinner from 7pm.

Panadería y Dulcería Cano Av Central. Just the place to stock up with some sticky buns, cakes and bread to keep you going on a hike. Daily 7.30am–8pm.

Pinocchio's Good-value thin crust pizzas ($5–7) and a few pasta regulars are on offer in this no-frills venue. Cocktails are also available, though the ambiance doesn't really fit. Daily noon–9pm.

Restaurante Mar de Plata Av Central below *Hotel Don Pepe* Great, cheerful café-restaurant which is a favourite lunchtime stop for Panamanian families. Tasty traditional mains from $6, including top-quality *patacones* with a few Peruvian additions – try the fried *ceviche* – to wash down with delicious home-made juices and *batidos*. Daily 7am–11pmish.

Restaurante Niña Delia (El Rancho) Av Central. A simple restaurant under a thatched roof serving good *comida típica*. Full breakfasts available for under $3 with mains from $5. At weekends it's packed with families profiting from the $7 bargain buffet lunch (noon–5pm), which includes a drink and dessert.

Restaurante Santa Librada Av Central. The best and most popular inexpensive option serving Panamanian favourites for under $9 plus the more unusual *corvina al curry* and several chargrilled dishes.

El Valle Gourmet & Coffee Shop Av Central. Deli-cum-café with pleasant outdoor seating overlooking a stream, where you can enjoy a large mug of your favourite brew while tucking into a fancy sandwich (around $3) or cake. Thurs–Sun 8–9am to 6pm or so; daily in high season.

Moving on from El Valle

Getting to Panama City is easy enough as **buses** (Mon–Sat dawn–4pm, Sun dawn–6pm; 2hr; $3.50) leave approximately every 25 minutes from the petrol station (*la bomba*) opposite the market. Going west is trickier; take a San Carlos minibus (every 30min until 6pm), completing a circuit of the town before heading for the highway. Get off at the "*entrada*" on the Interamericana at Las Uvas ($1.20), where you have to flag down a westbound bus. The large ones to Santiago or David are almost always full and so rarely stop; your best bet is to get a smaller bus to Penonomé and change, though on Friday afternoons or at the start of a public holiday you could be in for a long wait no matter which vehicle you try to ambush.

Penonomé and central Coclé

The capital of the province of Coclé, **Penonomé**, was founded by Spanish colonisers in 1581 and briefly served as capital of the isthmus after the destruction of Panamá Viejo. Standing at the geographical centre of Panama (a plaque marks the fact), this bustling market town remains important both as a transit point and for the fertile land that surrounds it, which is used for fruit, vegetables, rice and maize as well as for pig, poultry and cattle farming. The seventeen thousand inhabitants are predominantly mestizo, while some have Arab and Chinese origins. Fittingly for a town that served as a *reducción de Indios* – a place where conquered indigenous groups were forcibly resettled – Penonomé was named after Nomé, a local chieftain cruelly betrayed and executed.

The town makes a decent base for visiting other places of interest nearby, notably the tranquil village of **La Pintada**, famed for its finely woven **sombreros** and the scenic mountains to the north, including **Chiguirí Arriba**, with its hiking trails and spectacular views and the vibrant Cucua community of San Miguel Centro. Topping the mist-swathed peaks to the northwest, **Parque Nacional Omar Torrijos** is a treat for birdwatchers and hikers.

Penonomé

Aside from a small museum and the cathedral's lovely new stained-glass windows, **PENONOMÉ**'s charms are fairly low-key, although its aquatic celebrations for *Carnaval* are a real crowd-puller (see p.37).

Arrival and information

Public transport in Penonomé is not as straightforward as it might be. **Buses** pour in from Panama City (every 20min; 2hr; $4.35) from early in the morning until after midnight, dropping passengers off at the turn-off (*entrada*) into town along its busy commercial main street, called both Vía Central and Avenida J.D. Arosemena, heading for what can loosely be termed the "bus terminal", comprising a couple of streets by the market, just southeast of the main square. Transport leaves for Panama City from the south side of the Interamericana opposite the *Hotel Dos Continentes* at similar intervals.

For those heading west, the large buses to Santiago, Chitré and Las Tablas pull in for a pit stop at the *Restaurante Universal*, just east of the *Hotel y Suites Guacamaya*; David buses rarely stop since they're usually full. Other westbound transport picks up passengers at the Esso station at the Interamericana junction with Avenida J.D. Arosemena. Regular minibuses for the beachside resort of Santa Clara leave from 200m down J.D. Arosemena at the junction of Calle Victoriano Lorenzo, whereas all other minibuses can be located in the mêlée round the market place, which resembles the dodgems at times. Destinations of interest include

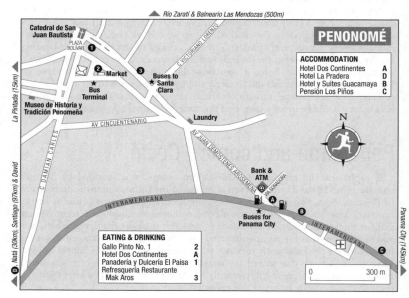

Río Zaratí & Balneario Las Mendozas (500m)

PENONOMÉ

ACCOMMODATION
Hotel Dos Continentes	A
Hotel La Pradera	D
Hotel y Suites Guacamaya	B
Pensión Los Piños	C

Catedral de San Juan Bautista
PLAZA BOLÍVAR
Market
Bus Terminal
Museo de Historia y Tradición Penomeña
Buses to Santa Clara
C VICTORIANO LORENZO
AV CINCUENTENARIO
Laundry
AV JUAN DEMOSTENES AROSEMENA
C DAMIAN CARLES
Bank & ATM
VIA SUMADORA
INTERAMERICANA
Buses for Panama City
N

La Pintada (15km)

D. Natá (30km), Santiago (97km) & David

Panama City (145km)

EATING & DRINKING
Gallo Pinto No. 1	2
Hotel Dos Continentes	A
Panadería y Dulcería El Paisa	1
Refresquería Restaurante Mak Aros	3

0   300 m

Festival del Toro Guapo

The small agricultural town of **Antón**, just off the Interamericana almost midway between Farallón and the provincial capital, Penonomé, really only registers on the tourist radar once a year, during the festival of **Toro Guapo** ("Fierce Bull") in mid-October, when the pleasant colonial square and whitewashed church are transformed by hordes of visitors.

The fun-filled five-day extravaganza takes its name and much of its action from the cattle farming that has defined the area for centuries and is well worth sampling. Alongside the usual array of folkloric dancing, colourful street parades, beauty pageants and progressively more drunken revelry are **toros** – men who cavort around the streets, charging at all and sundry. They dress in fantastical costumes draped over wooden or bamboo frames, topped with a bull's head adorned with ribbons and mirrors.

Many of the surrounding villages produce such a beast, with the creativity of the costume and acrobatic skills of the wearer a source of local pride, to be displayed during the parade on the final morning. After being blessed in the church, the bulls are led round the town as they playfully harass the *pollera*-swishing dancers, accompanied by bands of drummers. Listen out among the beats for the distinctive chime of the *almirez* – a bell-shaped bronze mortar of Afro-colonial origin that pharmacists once used to grind their medicinal herbs and is now a musical instrument unique to Antón.

Other festival highlights include **water fights** (*mojaderas*), competitions testing traditional **rural skills**, such as carrying firewood, peeling coconuts and milking a cow, and dancing by extravagantly dressed **diablos limpios** ("clean devils" – see p.193). Strangest of all is the **cutarras**, when a poor cow is wrestled to the ground by several farmers, often the worse for wear, who then struggle to fix sandals (*cutarras*) over the hooves, recalling an old trick of cattle rustlers attempting to hide the tell-tale hoof prints.

Reaching Antón by **bus** is easy from Panama City (every 20min, 5.20am–8pm; 2hr; $3.50), especially as additional buses are laid on during the festival. The two main **accommodation** options are both on the Interamericana: *Pensión Panamá* (☎987 3042; ❶) offers rudimentary, clean rooms with fan and cold-water showers (extra for TV), while the slightly more upmarket *Hotel Rivera* (☎987 2245; ❸) across the road has air-conditioned rooms with TV.

Aguadulce (hourly 5am–7/8pm; 1hr; $1.50); Chiguirí Arriba (6am, 9am then every 60–90min until 6.30pm; 1hr 15min; $1.75); El Copé (every 20min; 1hr; $1.50); La Pintada (every 10min 6am–8pm; 20min; 85c); and San Miguel Centro (infrequently; 1hr 30min; $3.50).

Avenida J.D. Arosemena contains most other amenities – a couple of **banks**, **ATMs**, **pharmacies** and an **internet café**, plus several places to eat.

Accommodation

All the **accommodation** listings given here lie on the northern side of the Interamericana and are suitably motel-like, with midweek reductions. Cheaper, very basic lodgings can be found round the plaza in town.

Hotel Dos Continentes At the junction with Av J.D. Arosemena ☎997 9325, ⓦwww.hotel doscontinentes.net. Long-standing labyrinth of rather faded rooms with decent beds and noisy a/c units, offering reasonable value nevertheless. ❸
Hotel la Pradera Several hundred metres west of town ☎991 0106, ⓔhotelpradera@cwpanama .net. The top spot to bed down with decent modern amenities plus an on-site bar-restaurant and small pool. ❺

Hotel y Suites Guacamaya Close to the junction with Av J.D. Arosemena ☎991 0117, ⓔhguacamaya@cwpanama.net. The glitzy exterior fronts forty modern rooms, (with cable TV & a/c), a good restaurant (mains $5–8) and a cramped bar and casino that have pretensions. ❹
Pensión los Piños A few hundred metres east of town ☎997 9518. Easily missable squat building offering eleven cheap basic rooms with bathroom and fan (extra for a/c & TV). ❶

▲ *Campesinos* enjoying lunch in Penonomé

The Town

Though a provincial capital and major agricultural centre, Penonomé is a surprisingly small town, with a very rural feel, containing a couple of modest sights and a pretty river all within walking distance. The main drag, Avenida J.D. Arosemena, runs a few hundred metres from the Interamericana to the pleasant **Plaza Bolívar** (also known as Plaza 8 de Diciembre). Featuring a statue of Simón Bolívar, the square is flanked by government buildings and the **Catedral de San Juan Bautista**, where the early morning or evening light projects dancing rainbows of colours through the new stained-glass windows. To the east of the cathedral, a small *plazuela* features monuments to Penonomé's glitterati including a bust of **Victoriano Lorenzo**, a local nationalist hero who was eventually tricked into capture and executed by firing squad (see p.334).

Southeast of the plaza, the streets around the lively **market** and the ad-hoc **bus terminal** are busy with *campesinos* from local villages loading and unloading their produce and minibuses scooting off in all directions. In contrast, a block further along Calle Damián Carles, then two blocks right, takes you to quiet San Antonio, the oldest part of town, where the **Museo de Historia y Tradición Penonomeña** (Tues–Sat 9am–4pm, Sun 9am–noon; $1) is located. A tiled blue-and-white *quincha* (wattle and daub) building contains a modest collection of pre-Columbian ceramics, colonial religious art and period furniture.

If the heat gets too much, a five-minute walk out of town in the other direction will take you to the **Balneario Las Mendozas**, a popular swimming area in the Río Zaratí, location of the aquatic parade at Carnaval when the floats are literally floated down the river. Though a party place at weekends and during holidays, you can enjoy a quieter dip here at other times, or upstream at **Las Tres Peñas**, a more attractive pool.

Eating and drinking

More varied menus are available in the hotel **restaurants**, with inexpensive places serving traditional food along the main street and around the market.

Gallo Pinto Ubiquitous chain with *comida típica* for under $2.50 in all its outlets, though you can't beat *Gallo Pinto #1*, on the corner overlooking the market, for people-watching. Daily 6am–8pm.

Hotel Dos Continentes The glass-fronted restaurant is justifiably popular, serving a good range of international dishes and Panamanian staples. Breakfasts are excellent.

Panadería y Dulcería El Paisa Av J.D. Arosemena. Bakery with a couple of stand-up tables inside and some outdoor seating. Good for a cup of coffee or a fruit juice and a sticky bun. Daily 6am–9.30pm.

Refresquería Restaurante Mak Aros Av J.D. Arosemena. A local open-sided cafetería popular for breakfast, offering similar food and prices to *Gallo Pinto*. Daily 6am–8pm.

La Pintada

Aficionados of Panama's hats – as opposed to Panama hats, which are made in Ecuador – should consider making a detour out to the village of **La Pintada**, 15km northwest of Penonomé in the foothills of the cordillera, which is famed for its high-quality palm-woven *sombrero pintado* or "*pintao*" (see box below). It is a major and expanding business in the village and surrounding area, involving several thousand individuals. The **Mercado de Artesanías La Pintada** (daily 9am–4pm), which displays the crafts of around a hundred local families, sells a wide range of hats in addition to decorated gourds, soapstone carvings, pots and various knick-knacks, though finding the place open can be tricky, especially in the rainy season. Not so with master hat-maker Señor Quirós, next door, who lives at the back of his shop, **Artesanías Reinaldo Quirós** (daily 8.30am–7.30pm), and also has a good collection. Both locations are on the left-hand side of the football pitch and are easy to spot.

Another place of potential interest is the local **cigar factory**, *Cigarros Joyas de Panamá* (Mon–Sat 7am–5pm; ☎692 2582), now garnering an international reputation for its hand-rolled organic Cuban-seed tobacco cigars. Just drop by and witness the dexterity with which some workers roll up to six hundred cigars a day. Single or boxed cigars can be bought on the spot.

Panama's hat – the sombrero pintado

Though not as famous or sought after as its Ecuadorian cousins, Panama's own straw hats are growing in reputation. Ubiquitous in rural Panama, worn by men and women, both as everyday work attire and a luxury accessory, they vary in style according to province and function. But while the hats have their origins in indigenous societies, Coclé's **sombrero pintado** or *pintao* ("painted hat"), which takes its name from the black and white design, has become the most popular and emblematic.

Quality (and therefore price) is principally determined by the number of **rings** (*vueltas*), but takes into consideration the consistency and fineness of the weave. A coarse seven-ring weave takes a week to make and costs around $10 whereas a twenty-ring *fino* usually requires a month and can set you back $100, more if bought in Panama City. The cost may seem high, but immense and skilled labour is involved. Once cut, the fibres are stripped from the leaves and cooked to be made pliable before being dried and bleached in the sun. For a high-quality *sombrero pintado*, the finest fibres are culled from bellota alongside coarser junco fibres, naturally dyed by being boiled with chisná leaves and buried in earth for several days, to form the distinctive black rings, while fine threads of sisal (pita) are used to stitch everything together.

Practicalities

Visiting La Pintada is an easy half-day excursion, with **minibuses** (every 10min, 6am–8pm; 20min; 85c) from behind the market in Penonomé rolling to a halt between the village plaza and the football pitch. Return buses run to a similar timetable. However, if you'd rather be up in the hills for the night, *Nature's Inn* (☎983 0005 for Spanish, ☎6539 6118 for English, ⓦwww.naturesinnpanama .com; dorm $15, ❹) is a new, tastefully designed B&B a few kilometres beyond the village and reachable by bus. Perched on a hill, with a pleasant woodland walk down to a river, where you can bathe, it also offers hiking and horse riding ($10). Full board is available; otherwise, you can share the kitchen, treating yourself to the occasional excursion to La Pintada, where a few inexpensive local restaurants are dotted round the village, and a posh new steakhouse, *Restaurante La Casa Vieja* (☎983 0597; Tues–Sun 11am–9.30pm), has opened up in the plaza.

Chiguirí Arriba and El Valle de San Miguel

From the market area in Penonomé, *chivas* head off through the surrounding cultivated fields to villages scattered in the folds of the cool, forested mountains that rise to the north. **Chiguirí Arriba**, 30km to the northeast, makes an easy day-trip (buses 6am, 9am then every 60–90min until 6.30pm; 75min; $1.75) with plenty of good hiking trails, spectacular views across forested limestone hummocks and a 30m waterfall, Cascada Tavida, nearby – local children will happily guide you there for a small tip. The best **accommodation** in the area is *La Posada del Cerro La Vieja* (☎983 8905, ⓦwww.posadalavieja.com; ❼), a lovely eco-resort and spa at the foot of the brooding mountain of the same name. It offers spacious terracotta-tiled cabins with private balconies set amid beautiful gardens on reforested pastureland. Rates include breakfast, with other meals ($12) and guided excursions ($10–15/person) extra. More adventurous trips across the mountains to El Valle, or over to the Caribbean rainforests can be organized though there's no reason – with a little Spanish, a local guide and the right supplies and equipment – why you can't do this independently.

If you're in the area in late January, it is worth hopping off the bus en route in the village of **Churruquita Grande** for the citrus-filled **Festival de la Naranja** to marvel at the elaborate and inventively crafted wood and thatch displays overflowing with local produce, vying for the prize of best stall. A different kind of experience awaits in **San Miguel Centro**, 35km northeast of Penonomé, home to the **Cucua** community, which offers a community-based eco-tourism project (contact Angel Brennan ☎983 0254, ✉dbrennan07@yahoo .com). They are famed for their devil dance conducted in elaborate cream-coloured pyjama-like costumes made from *cucua* bark, painted with geometric shapes using natural dyes and topped with a fanciful deer mask complete with real antlers. Simple **homestay** lodging is offered for a modest fee; extra is charged for a performance by the dance troupe. *Chivas* for San Miguel Centro (1hr 30min; $3.50) leave infrequently from Penonomé bus terminal.

Parque Nacional Omar Torrijos

A difficult place to get to, this little-visited 250-square-kilometre protected carpet of lush forest astride the continental divide is well worth the effort. The national park's mouthful of a full name, **Parque Nacional General de División Omar Torrijos Herrera**, was given on its formation in 1986 in remembrance of Panama's flamboyant populist leader, whose plane mysteriously crashed into one of the area's highest peaks, Cerro Martha, in 1981. These days it is more usually referred to as "Parque Omar Torrijos" or "El Copé" after the nearby village. Averaging twenty degrees Celsius in the cloud-forested peaks of the Cordillera

Central, the canopy cascades down to the more moist vegetation of the Caribbean side, where temperatures average 25°C and the area receives an incredible 4m of rainfall. There's some fine **wildlife**: tapirs, peccaries and all five of Panama's species of large cat roam the undergrowth, while red-fronted parrotlets, orange-bellied trogons and the extraordinary bare-necked umbrella bird draw birdlovers. You're more likely to hear than see the three-wattled bellbird, which has one of the loudest bird calls in the world – a bizarre metallic "dong" that carries almost a kilometre.

A few hundred metres beyond the park entrance, an informative **visitors centre**, with a rear balcony offering splendid views, marks the start of a couple of fairly short, well-kept circular routes (2km and 4km) and an interpretive loop, aimed at enhancing visitors' appreciation of the abundant and diverse flora. **Hikers** should consider aiming for **Cerro Peña Blanca** (1314m), which occasionally peeks out from the mist to the west of the park entrance. The moderately strenuous four-hour trail ascends west from Barrigón and on a rare clear day you are rewarded at the summit with spectacular views of both oceans. The other popular route heads over the continental divide from the park entrance down to the community of **La Rica**, a good four-hour hike away. A guide is essential for both these excursions. Set in verdant surroundings laced with waterfalls and natural swimming pools and within reach of giant guayacán, cuipo and cedar trees, La Rica is the perfect spot to appreciate the park's natural beauty, though getting there can be a very muddy affair for much of the year.

Practicalities

One of the reasons this wonderful park is often overlooked is that getting here is no easy task. First you need to reach the mountain village of **El Copé**. Direct **buses** head from Panama City (on the hour from 6am; 3hr; $5.50), while minibuses from Penonomé are even more frequent (every 20min; 1hr; $1.50). Once in El Copé, climb aboard the occasional connecting minibus (7am–5pm) that struggles 3km up the gravel road to the even smaller village of **Barrigón**, after which only a 4WD can crawl the remaining steep 4km to the **park entrance** ($5 entry); on foot the hike will take well over an hour. To arrange 4WD transport in advance, contact Faustino Ortega (☎983 9265) or Joel Santana (☎983 9110). Neither El Copé nor Barrigón has a **bank** so you will need sufficient cash. If self-catering, stock up on supplies in Panama City or Penonomé.

There are now several options in terms of **accommodation** and **guiding** thanks to several emergent community-based eco-tourism initiatives.

AGLAC Ecotours El Copé, behind the police station ☎6652 1922, ⓦwww.aglacecotours.com. A local outfit that can arrange simple accommodation at Las Yayas, a waterfall in Barrigón, and offers various day-hikes or more strenuous overnight expeditions in the park, for which you'll need your own tent and kit.

Albergue Navas Barrigón ☎983 9130. Anna and Santos Navas are warm, long-standing hosts providing three simple cinder-block rooms with shared outside toilet and shower; meals, made with fresh produce from their *finca*, are served in the family kitchen. Santos and his sons are wonderfully knowledgeable guides, whose services can also be hired by non-guests,

though you'll need some Spanish. The family also owns a rustic cabin within the park. Meals and guide included. ❸

ANAM Park entrance. Contact Hellington Ríos Barrera at ☎997 9805 in the ANAM regional office, Penonomé, though you can usually organize something on the spot. A spacious solar-powered cabin near the entrance affords sweeping vistas, though conditions are often misty, and comprises a large lounge, a dormitory with four bunks and a kitchen equipped with a stove, fridge and basic utensils. Bring a sleeping bag as it's chilly at night. The park wardens are usually willing to be hired as guides. Camping is possible but there is no electricity and it is likely to be very wet. Bunk $15/person, camping $5/person.

La Mica Just outside El Copé ☎6746 3942, Ⓦwww.lamica.org. A new biological station offering basic cabin, dormitory or camping facilities and guided nature hikes of the area. They can also help arrange homestays in the scenically located community of Santa Marta (or contact Adalberto Lorenzo ☎6774 5061) on the park border. Dormitory or cabin $12/person; camping $5/tent.

Aguadulce and western Coclé

Travelling west along the Interamericana, across the flatlands of Coclé, the terrain becomes duller and drier as you pass endless fields of sugar cane and cattle and enter the crescent known as the Arco Seco (Dry Arc), which sweeps round the Bahía de Parita west of the Pacific beaches to the eastern section of the Azuero Peninsula. Plum in the middle of what transforms into an unpleasant dust bowl in the dry season stands the important agro-industrial town of **Aguadulce**, synonymous with sugar, salt and – more recently – shrimps. Though the town itself is unremarkable, at the right time of year you can observe its agricultural processes first-hand, while avid birdwatchers head for the saltpans of **Playa El Salado** to the southeast. East of Aguadulce lie two of Panama's major historical attractions, the intriguing pre-Columbian site of the **Parque Arqueológico El Caño** and the splendid colonial church of **Natá**.

Aguadulce

Salt had been harvested in the area by the indigenous population long before a boat load of colonizers landed in the mid-nineteenth century, naming the place **AGUADULCE** ("freshwater") – apparently amazed at the purity of the water they'd drawn from a local well given its proximity to the sea. The town's coastal location allowed it to develop into a major port during the twentieth century but with the access channel constantly silting up and competition from road transport along the Interamericana, the port scarcely functions these days.

Arrival and information

Buses from Panama City (every 25min, 4.15am–9pm; 3hr; $6) halt at two **bus stops** on the Interamericana for Aguadulce; the western one by the *Hotel Inter-americana* is the main one; return buses to Panama City (similar timetable) leave from the nearby junction with Avenida Rafael Estévez, which leads into the town centre. If you don't fancy hoofing it to downtown Aguadulce, regular **minibuses** costing a few centavos run along the road while **taxis** only charge $1. Three hundred metres nearer town, buses leave for Santiago (every 20min, 5.30am–6.30pm; 1hr; $2.50), though they tour the plaza first. Other popular destinations include Chitré (every 20min, 4am–6pm; 1hr; $2.50), Penonomé (hourly, 5am–7pm; 1hr; $1.50) and El Copé (every 45min, 6am–6pm; 1hr; $1.50). Buses leave from the plaza. The large buses to David stop, if they have a spare seat, across the road from the *Hotel Interamericana*.

Most amenities lie on or around the central plaza: several **banks** and **ATMs** line Avenida Rodolfo Chiari, and there's a decent **supermarket** with **ATM** in the shopping mall round the corner from the *Hotel Interamericana*.

Accommodation

There are only three **accommodation** options to choose from, none too pricey.

Hotel Carisabel Calle Vía El Puerto ☎997 3800, Ⓦwww.hotelcarisabel.com. Pleasant, compact rooms with more furniture and better paintwork than the *Interamericana* with the same amenities including a fishpond-size pool and a bar-restaurant offering decent food. ❹

Hotel Interamericana Intermaricana ☎997 4363. Bland but functional en-suite rooms (hot water, cable

TV, a/c & fan), though the main attraction is the excellent large swimming pool, which transforms into a local party place at weekends, so select your room carefully. The on-site restaurant has a vast menu to suit most palates (mains $4–9) and lunchtime family meal deals. ❹

The Town

As usual, life centres on the main square, **Plaza 19 de Octubre**, where the **Iglesia de San Juan Bautista** exhibits a mishmash of styles, the original altar frescoes having disappeared beneath an expensive pile of red brick – the current altarpiece. Look out for the incongruous German grandfather clock inside.

Across the park, the charming two-storey nineteenth-century building, which was once the post office, now houses the Museo Regional Stella Sierra (named after a local poet, whose work is on display), much better known by its previous title, **El Museo de la Sal y el Azúcar** (Mon–Sat 8am–4pm; $1). Since the roof collapsed, the exhibition rooms have been squeezed onto the ground floor, displaying an assortment of pre-Columbian relics, photos and instruments from the early days of the salt and sugar industries plus some weaponry and uniforms from the civil war, during which two major battles were fought in the town.

Eating and drinking

Aside from the hotel restaurants, there are plenty of decent inexpensive places to **eat** in town, with the bright and airy cafeteria-style *Panadería y Restaurante la Espiga* (daily 6.30am–10.30pm) a good starting place, serving decent food from sandwiches, through burgers and salads to traditional Panamanian mains ($4–7); it is particularly popular at weekends when locals come to socialize over breakfast (including great fresh juices) and enjoy the paper. *Fonda la Fula* (Thurs–Sun 6am–late) on Avenida Rodolfo Chiari, heading out of town towards the Interamericana, has the best reputation for traditional food; a basic affair with long aluminium tables under a corrugated iron roof, it is famous for its *sancocho*.

Around Aguadulce

As well as its own modest sights, Aguadulce provides a decent base for trips to **El Caño**, one of Panama's most important archeological sites, and **Natá**, one of its grandest churches. Other intriguing excursions can be made to the **Ingenio de Azúcar de Santa Rosa** (Santa Rosa Sugar Refinery) during the harvest (Jan–March; tours Mon–Fri 7am–4pm, Sat 7am–11am; ☎ 987 8101; free), an easy 15km west of Aguadulce, and to a stretch of nearby coastline rich in birdlife.

Parque Arqueológico El Caño

Some 18km north of Aguadulce (25km west of Penonomé), just off the Interamericana, the **Parque Arqueológico El Caño** (Tues–Sat 8am–4pm, Sun 9am–1pm; $1; ☎ 228 6231) is one of Panama's most significant pre-Columbian archeological sites. Sadly, a combination of plunder, vandalism and neglect means there is relatively little for the lay visitor to appreciate, while the park's floodplain location makes it a mosquito-infested quagmire in the rainy season.

An important ceremonial site from 500 to about 1200 AD, El Caño later became a cemetery, and was still in use as such after the conquest. One of the most fascinating finds was over a hundred basalt statues that formed what was described as the "Temple of the Thousand Idols", which were illegally decapitated by an

American Indiana Jones-style adventurer in the early twentieth century, and the best of their zoomorphic and anthropomorphic heads are now scattered in museums in the US, with a few in Panama City's anthropological museum. The site narrowly escaped bulldozing in the 1970s, and now consists of several **funeral mounds**, a **cacique's hut** and lines of headless **standing stones**. A small **museum** displays ceramics and lesser stone statues but otherwise there's nothing to delay you for more than half-an-hour.

There's no direct public transport to El Caño, but you can get dropped off on the Interamericana at the entrance to the village, from where it's a further 3km down a dirt road to the site – a taxi from Natá ($5) might be easier (see below).

Natá

It's hard to picture **NATÁ**, a quiet backwater 7km south of the El Caño turn-off (11km north of Aguadulce), as the major Spanish settlement it once was, until you arrive at the plaza to be confronted with the expansive dazzling white baroque façade of the **Basílica Menor Santiago Apostól**. Possibly the oldest church in the Americas still in use, and recently fully restored to its former glory, it bears testament to the town's historical importance and merits a detour. Founded in 1522 by Gaspar de Espinosa (whose bust surveys the church from the square) and named after the local indigenous chief, the town supposedly gained its subsequent full name, **Santiago de Natá de los Caballeros**, from a hundred knights (*caballeros*) – hand-picked by King Charles V of Spain – who were sent to subjugate the local population and spread the Catholic word. The surrounding fertile plains made Natá a perfect base for confronting the main indigenous resistance forces under Cacique Urracá, who relentlessly attacked the site (see p.331), and for providing supplies to the now long-abandoned gold mines on the Caribbean coast. Apart from the splendid bell tower, the main attractions are the ornately **carved wooden altars** framed by exquisite columns laden with vines, flowers and angels, which adorn an otherwise simple wooden interior. Though the least elaborate, the main altar importantly contains images of the patron saint, Santiago el Menor (James the Lesser), and the co-patron, San Juan de Díos, who are removed from their niches and paraded round the town on their saint days of July 25 and March 8, respectively.

Regional **buses** westbound to Aguadulce or eastbound to Penonomé will drop you at the entrance to Natá or El Caño on the Interamericana, and local shuttles between Aguadulce and Penonomé may even enter for a quick sweep of the plaza at Natá. Otherwise, from the highway it's a ten-minute walk into the village, passing *Restaurante Vega*, which serves inexpensive Panamanian and Chinese dishes.

Playa El Salado

Driving southeast out of Aguadulce, a newly tarred road showcases the town's other two major industries as it navigates 8km between mud and salt flats and shrimp farms to the mangrove-lined coast at **Playa El Salado**. In the dry season, salt is heaped like snow by the evaporation pools while September and October are the best months to catch flocks of migrating waders; among the numerous sandpipers and plovers, look out for striking black-necked stilts probing the mud for crustaceans and lovely roseate spoonbills filtering the tidal pools.

At weekends, many Aguadulceños head this way to escape the heat of the town and lounge on the pleasant beach, or loll about in **Las Piscinas**, shallow stone baths built on the flats, offering views of the bay, that catch the salt water as the tide moves out to provide a warm pool, though a sharp exit is necessary once the tide turns. El Salado is famous for its jumbo shrimps, which you can sample at one of the **restaurants** dotted along the road. They generally open around noon, daily during the dry season, and at weekends the rest of the year. Most famous is *Johnny Tapia* (Thurs–Sun out of season; ℡6556 6655), an unpromising concrete block with a tin roof, overlooking mangroves, just after the village mirador. The owner is lively and the food great, especially the shrimps (around $8) and *pescado*. Alternatively, try the more scenic, furnished thatched terrace of *Restaurante Reina del Mar* (℡997 2960 weekends and holidays out of season) towards the end of the village on the right.

Getting to Playa El Salado by car is straightforward; by public transport it's trickier as only half a dozen **minibuses** ($1) leave the main square each day and times are irregular. **Taxis** charge $5.

Santiago and the central highlands

At Divisa, on the border between the provinces of Coclé, Herrera and Veraguas, 23km beyond Aguadulce, the road forks: the Carretera Nacional turns south into the Azuero Peninsula, while the Interamericana continues a further 37km west to busy **Santiago**, the provincial capital of Veraguas. Situated almost halfway between Panama City and David, Santiago is a major transit point as well as a marketing centre for the livestock, rice, maize and sugar from the surrounding farmlands. Of greater interest to the tourist is the city's status as the entry point to the undulating Pensinsula de Soná, at the tip of which lies Santa Catalina, the

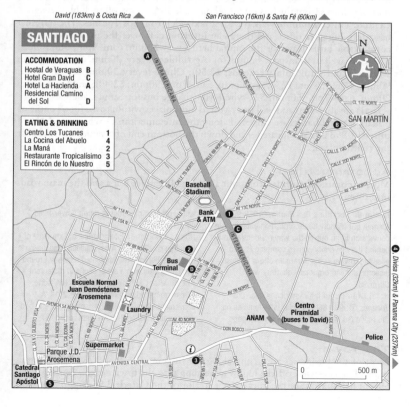

SANTIAGO

ACCOMMODATION
Hostal de Veraguas B
Hotel Gran David C
Hotel La Hacienda A
Residencial Camino del Sol D

EATING & DRINKING
Centro Los Tucanes 1
La Cocina del Abuelo 4
La Maná 2
Restaurante Tropicalísimo 3
El Rincón de lo Nuestro 5

David (183km) & Costa Rica ▲   San Francisco (16km) & Santa Fé (60km) ▲

SAN MARTÍN

Baseball Stadium

Bank & ATM

Bus Terminal

Escuela Normal Juan Demóstenes Arosemena

Laundry

Supermarket

Parque J.D. Arosemena

Catedral Santiago Apóstol

ANAM

Centro Piramidal (buses to David)

Police

Divisa (32km) & Panama City (237km)

0   500 m

173

country's surfing capital (see p.221), and as gateway to the cooler mountain slopes of the Cordillera Central, which are sprinkled with tranquil farming villages and the charming hilltop town of Santa Fé.

Santiago

The administrative, economic and cultural capital of the province, **SANTIAGO** is a bustling centre of around forty thousand inhabitants. Founded in its present location in 1637, and previously of great agricultural importance, it is now a thriving commercial hub – evidenced by the proliferation of banks and a new state-of-the-art baseball stadium. If travelling round Panama by public transport, it's highly likely that at some stage you will, at the very least, spend time in the bus terminal or stranded on the Interamericana, though there's little incentive to venture further into town unless you happen to coincide with the *patronales* around July 25, which draw in the crowds for some serious partying.

Arrival and information

The large express buses running between Panama City and David make their pit stops at one of two service areas, Centro Los Tucanes or Centro Piramidal, at Santiago's eastern and western exits to the Interamericana respectively. If they have space, they will pick up extra passengers but at peak times – Friday afternoons and holidays – you can be waiting hours for a vacant seat and may have to resort to short hops on local transport, which can be a lengthy process. All other transport leaves from the **bus terminal** on Calle 10A Norte, often dubbed Avenida Central, a fifteen-minute walk (or $1–2 taxi ride) from Los Tucanes. The terminal has a **left-luggage** office and there's an **internet café** over the road. Smaller, less comfortable buses leave for the capital here (every 30min, 6am–9pm; 3hr 30min; $7.50) as well as transport bound for Aguadulce (every 20min, 5am–10.45pm weekdays and until 7pm weekends; $2.50); Chitré (every 30min, 5.30am–9pm; 90min; $2.50); Santa Fé (every 30min, 5am–7pm; 90min; $2.40); and Soná (every 20min, 6am–7pm; 50min; $2), where you change bus for Santa Catalina.

    Taxis are abundant and will ferry you to most places within town for a couple of dollars. Several **banks** are clustered along the Interamericana – where the **ANAM office** (T 998 0615) is located – and down the bottom end of Avenida Central near the central plaza.

Accommodation

Most **accommodation** is strung out along the Interamericana and the main roads into town.

Hostal de Veraguas San Martín, T 958 9021. A small but friendly hostel-cum-homestay house conversion in an out-of-the way residential area behind the university, where camping is also possible. Owner Lydia Jaramillo offers Spanish lessons and can organize voluntary work. Dorm $8.

Hotel Gran David Interamericana near *Los Tucanes* T 998 1866. Popular with families on the move (so is often full) and provides good

value, offering nice rooms round flower-filled gardens. ❸

Hotel La Hacienda Interamericana, 3km west of Santiago T 958 8580. A psychedelic Mexican-style ranch, its vibrant, well-appointed rooms set round two courtyards with a small pool and restaurant. ❺

Residencial Camino del Sol Calle 10A Norte, across from the bus terminal T 998 2114. A convenient, cheap though uninspiring place to bed down, with functional, clean, dark rooms. ❷

The Town

Most of the businesses are strung along the Interamericana and Avenida Central, which branches west off the highway heading into the town centre, coming to an abrupt halt in front of the impressive exterior of the **Catedral Santiago Apóstol**, now stunningly illuminated at night. Across the square, the provincial museum, housed in the former prison, where three-time president Belisario Porras was incarcerated during the civil war, has been closed for restoration for some years. In the centre of the busy plaza, the unassuming **Parque Juan Demóstenes Arosemena** takes its name from the former president, who is revered here for choosing the town as the site for Panama's first teacher-training institution. The college, **La Escuela Normal Juan Demóstenes Arosemena**, lies several blocks northeast of the square on Calle 8A Norte and is the architectural jewel of Santiago, with a majestic baroque frontispiece worth checking out if you're in town.

Around town

A few kilometres outside Santiago are a couple of delightful village **churches** worth a detour, and both accessible by **bus** (Atalaya every 15min, 5am–10pm; 30min; 50c; San Francisco every 30min, 7am–6pm; 20min; 75c). **La Iglesia San Francisco de la Montaña** is on the road heading to the mountains of Santa Fé, 16km north of Santiago, in a village of the same name. Hop off the bus at the fork by the police post and bear right a few hundred metres. The simplicity of the small stone church, believed to have been built around 1727, belies the wonderfully elaborate wooden interior, with nine intricately carved baroque altarpieces betraying both Spanish and indigenous influences.

In the opposite direction, 8km southeast of Santiago, the **Iglesia Atalaya** resembles an inauspicious two-tier wedding cake from the outside, its lofty vaulted ceilings covered in splendid frescoes and lovely stained-glass windows more than compensate. Tucked away in a side altar, the Cristo de Atalaya, said to date back from before 1730, is one of Panama's most venerated icons, a magnet for thousands of pilgrims every first Sunday in Lent.

Eating and drinking

As befits a provincial capital there is a range of places to **eat**, from inexpensive local dishes to pricier international cuisine.

▲ Detail from La Iglesia San Francisco de la Montaña

Centro Los Tucanes Interamericana. Hordes of bus passengers pile into Panama's equivalent of a motorway service station, where a range of hot dishes, including daily specials, salads and sandwiches, are available at reasonable rates. Daily 11am–10.30pm.

La Cocina del Abuelo Interamericana, Plaza Hotel Gran David (not to be confused with *Hotel Gran David*) ☎958 9168. The city's main gourmet restaurant, though rather touristy, offering excellent international cuisine (main $7–14) with live music at weekends and an adjacent bar. Daily 11am–10pm.

La Maná Av 10B Norte, opposite the bus terminal. Cosy cafeteria offering filling inexpensive dishes. Daily 6am–8pm.

Restaurante Tropicalísimo Av Central at C 17. A range of mid-priced Cuban and Panamanian dishes (most mains under $8) can be enjoyed, such as *lechón habanero,* the house speciality, in pleasant terrace or indoor surroundings. Mon–Sat 9am–11pm.

El Rincón de lo Nuestro La Placita, near the main square. A busy daytime watering hole, serving up Panamanian breakfast fry-ups and the *almuerzo del día* for under $2, plus local specialities such as *gaucho de mariscos* (seafood stew and rice). Daily 6am–3pm.

Santa Fé

A small hilltop town about 60km north of Santiago, **SANTA FÉ**, is a jewel of a mountain retreat that has been a well-kept secret for years. Surrounded by a stunning necklace of verdant mountains sprinkled with sparkling cascades and serene stretches of river, with easy access to a forested swathe of national park, it is a hiker's and birdwatcher's dream. Thanks to its 500m altitude, Santa Fé enjoys a pleasant, fresh climate, and while the arrival of a real estate office may herald further development, for the moment its absence of traffic and low population density, with houses strung across the tree-dotted hillside, gives it a peaceful village feel. Santa Fé is famous for its floral abundance, boasting over three hundred species of **orchids**, which are celebrated in an annual three-day August festival, when most are in bloom, attracting aficionados from around the country (contact the tourist office in Santiago for dates on ☎998 3929).

Arrival and information

An undulating rollercoaster of a road leads up to Santa Fé, which is served by **minibuses** from the main terminal in Santiago (every 30min, 5am–7pm; 90min; $2.40). For the return trip they leave from outside the "bus terminal" by the restaurant. The **taxi** fare to or from Santiago is $30 but the one taxi driver in the town, Tomás, is a busy man and needs to be booked in advance (☎6818 1191).

Santa Fé has **no bank**, though there is a **post office**, a couple of supermarkets, several grocery stores and a market to stock up on provisions for hikes up in the hills. The Fundación Héctor Gallego (Mon–Fri 8am–8pm, Sat & Sun 8am–6pm; ☎954 0737), along from the hostel, now offers **internet** services.

Accommodation

Santa Fé's dearth of upscale **lodgings** and fancy **restaurants** has helped preserve its relative anonymity. Currently, there are three places to stay in town, though the local cooperative is planning to build an eco-lodge up by the park.

Centro Turístico Alto de Piedra No phone. 5km above Santa Fé, on the park doorstep, a small-scale enterprise has started up, which currently consists of two cement rooms with shared outside toilet and a restaurant or space to camp. Guided hikes and horse riding can be arranged. Reachable by 4WD and the village taxi ($6 one way) only, there is also a very infrequent *chiva* that runs there

from Santa Fé, but it is a remote spot, more so when the weather is bad. ❷

Hostal La Qhia Near the bus terminal ☎954 0903, ⓦwww.panamamountain house.com. A relaxed yet efficient chalet-style hostel with a bohemian feel set in a lush garden and run by an Argentine–Belgian couple. Comprising only a small dorm and two private

The wildlife of Panama

This field guide provides a quick reference to help you identify some of Panama's more common or interesting birds, mammals, reptiles, amphibians and insects. Photos show easily identified markings and features, while notes give clear pointers about the kinds of habitat in which you are most likely to see each species, its behaviour and general tips about sighting. For further details on the country's wildlife, see p.342.

 HABITAT 🦃 BEHAVIOUR ✓ VIEWING TIPS

Magnificent frigatebird

Fregata magnificens (Fragata magnífica)

- Common around both coasts and islands, and in the canal area. Nests year-round on Isla Iguana.

- Feeds by snatching food from the sea or other birds, rather than diving. Males inflate enormous scarlet pouches (gular sacs) to attract females.

✓ Easily recognizable by its forked tail and 2m wingspan, circling high in the air.

Blue-crowned motmot

Momotus momota (Barranquero)

- One of Panama's four species of motmot, with a distinctive "racket tail", found in open lowland woodland or the fringes of rainforest, mainly on the Pacific side.

- Nests in long burrows in earthbanks. Often seen in pairs.

✓ Sits motionless for a long time on the underbranch of a tree before darting out for prey.

Keel-billed toucan

Ramphastos sulfuratus (Tucán pico iris)

- One of Panama's seven species, found in moist lowland forest across the Caribbean slope, in the canal area and on the Pacific side in eastern Panama, including the Darién.

- Travels in small flocks, with a swooping flight, and roosts and nests in the hollows of trees.

✓ Easily distinguished from other toucans by its mainly lime-green bill. Has a very distinctive monotonous croaking call and is best spotted very early morning or late afternoon in the canopy seeking fruit.

White-necked Jacobin

Florisuga mellivora (Colibrí nuquiblanco)

- One of 55 species of hummingbird in Panama; found in lowland forests (up to 1300m) and forest edges.

- Feeds on nectar in tall trees and epiphytes, but also takes insects on the wing.

✓ Distinctive white underbelly and neck stripe, with metallic dark blue head and straight bill.

HABITAT   BEHAVIOUR   ✓ VIEWING TIPS

Northern jacana

Jacana spinosa (Jacana Centroamericana)

 Freshwater marshes, lakes and slow rivers across western Panama and in the canal area.

 Giant spindly feet allow it to walk on floating vegetation in search of insects and seeds. Females mate with several males, who incubate the separate clutches of eggs.

 Easily distinguished from the wattled jacana, by its lack of red facial wattles. Displays lemon yellow flight feathers.

White ibis

Eudocimus albus (Ibis blanco)

 One of six species of ibis in the country, inhabiting the coastal mud flats and mangroves of the Pacific, including Coiba and the Archipiélago de las Perlas.

 Gregarious, nesting and roosting in large colonies.

 Look for them at low tide probing the mud for small fish and crustaceans, or returning to roost in mangroves at dusk.

Chestnut-headed oropendola

Psarocolius wagleri (Oropéndola cabecicastaña)

 The most common of the four species in Panama, widespread in Caribbean and Pacific lowlands, in the forest canopy and edges, and on old plantations.

 Weaves hanging nests in colonies of forty to fifty, returning to the same tree each year to nest between January and May.

 Travelling in small noisy flocks, they make a range of gurgling, squawking and bell-like sounds, displaying their golden tail feathers in flight.

Crimson-crested woodpecker

Campephilus melanoleucus (Carpintero crestirrojo)

 Secondary forests and open woodland on both Pacific and Caribbean slopes.

Lays two eggs in a hole in a dead tree, incubated by both parents.

Look and listen for it hammering its way up a tree trunk searching out insects. Distinguishable from the similar but smaller lineated woodpecker, whose white shoulder markings do not meet on the back.

 HABITAT   BEHAVIOUR   VIEWING TIPS

Red-legged honeycreeper

Cyanerpes cyaneus (Mielero patirrojo)

 Lowland tropical forest, open or residential areas below 1000m.

 Eats insects on the wing, fruit seeds and nectar.

 The most common and widespread honeycreeper, often seen in small groups or pairs (the female is olive green).

Spectacled owl

Pulsatrix perspicillata (Búho de anteojos)

 Mature forest on both Pacific and Caribbean slopes.

 Noctural, resting in dense foliage during the day though it may be active on overcast days.

 Large owl (48cm), instantly recognizable by its white "spectacles", though juveniles are equally striking with white head and black eye rings.

Resplendent quetzal

Pharomachrus mocinno (Quetzal mesoamericano)

 Prevalent in the cloudforest canopy and sub-canopy of western Chiriquí.

 Solitary fruit- and insect-eaters except during breeding season. Males grow long streamer-like tail feathers and perform acrobatic aerial courtship displays.

 Look out for them very early in the morning, or before dusk during the breeding season (late Dec–April) when pairs can sometimes be seen on the ground. They have a distinctive whistle, and the female is a duller brownish-green.

Scarlet macaw

Ara macao (Guacamaya rojo)

 Now confined to a sizeable colony in the lowland rainforest of Coiba.

 Seen in pairs or small flocks in the treetops wrestling seeds, fruit and nuts from branches in the canopy.

 Likely to be heard before being seen, uttering a range of screams and squawks.

 HABITAT   BEHAVIOUR   ✓ VIEWING TIPS

Blue-headed parrot

Pinuus menstruus (Loro cabeciazul)

 Common in lowland forest and semi-open areas up to 1200m on both slopes, but in greater numbers on the Caribbean.

 Particularly noisy parrots, they feed on fruit, seed and grain.

 Look out for them at dawn and dusk leaving or arriving at their communal roosting areas in palms and other tall trees.

Slaty-tailed trogon

Trogon massena (Trogón coliplomizo)

 Found in damp lowland forests.

 Often sits motionless on a branch for a long time, waiting for insects to prey on.

 Note that the female has a grey head.

White-faced capuchin Monkey

Cebus capucinus (Mono cariblanco)

 Arboreal, frequenting low and high-level forests up to 2000m.

 Noted for their dexterity and use of tools, both as weapons, or to get food – they are omnivorous.

Possessing unmistakable humanoid pink faces, they generally live in troops of about fifteen.

Mantled howler monkey

Aloutta palliata (Mono aullador)

 Widespread in tropical forest up to 2500m.

 Live in troops of ten to twenty with an Alpha male, feeding off fruit, leaves and flowers.

 To locate a troop, follow the distinctive bellowing sound made by males at dawn and dusk, and also when disturbed, which is a warning to other males.

 HABITAT   BEHAVIOUR   ✓ VIEWING TIPS

Paca

Cuniculus paca (Conejo pintado)

 Found in forests near small rivers.

 Solitary nocturnal animal that often jumps into water to escape danger.

✓ Distinguishable from its smaller, more common diurnal relative, the agouti (*ñeque*), by its white spots. Can be identified on a night hike by its brilliant yellow or orange eyes when spotlit.

Brown-throated three-toed sloth

Bradypus variegates (Perezoso de tres dedos)

 Inhabits various forest-types.

 The more commonly seen of Panama's two sloths, being more numerous and both diurnal and nocturnal, though it spends much of the time asleep to conserve energy. It descends to the ground to defecate once a week.

✓ When entwined round a branch asleep, with fur camouflaged by greenish algae, it resembles a large insects' nest.

Baird's tapir

Tapirus bairdii (Macho de monte)

 Panama's largest land mammal (250–400kg) prefers dense swampy rainforest, sticking close to water.

 Primarily nocturnal, it often spends hours resting in a waterhole during the hottest part of the day.

 Being very shy with acute hearing, tapirs are very difficult to see, though they have occasionally been spotted in the Darién.

Jaguar

Panthera onca (Jaguar or tigre)

 The largest of Panama's five cat species, it prefers large territories of dense low- to mid-elevation forest such as in Amistad and the Darién.

 Solitary nocturnal predator that stalks and ambushes its prey – ranging from mice to tapirs – often by biting straight through the skull.

 Virtually no chance of seeing one in the wild but look in the morning mud for four rounded toe prints, about 10cm wide.

 HABITAT 🦇 BEHAVIOUR ✓ VIEWING TIPS

Northern tamandua

Tamandua Mexicana (Hormiguero bandera)

 Commonly found in forests and more open habitats on both Pacific and Atlantic coasts.

 A solitary diurnal and nocturnal animal that uses its long tongue (40cm) to lick up 9000 ants or termites a day.

 Look out for it feeding along the branches of trees and on the ground.

Bushmaster

Lachesis muta (Verrugosa)

 Huge venomous snake (2–3m) that frequents remote, rocky forests such as the Darién and Amistad.

 Unlike most pit vipers, it lays eggs (10–16) in a burrow; after hatching, the young continue to live underground until they are fully adult.

 Nocturnal, so rarely seen, but recognizable as a pit viper by its triangular head; much heavier than the fer-de-lance.

Green iguana

Iguana iguana (Iguana verde)

 Across the country in lowland forest near water but also on semi-arid islands such as Isla Iguana.

 Arboreal, diurnal and herbivorous, it spends much of the time basking on a branch or rock. The male's dewflap is used in territorial displays and courtship during the breeding season, when eggs are buried in the ground.

 Look along branches overhanging water or on rocks. Colours vary from lime green to orangey-brown.

Strawberry "blue jeans" poison-dart frog

Oophaga pumilio (Rana venenosa roja y azul)

 Humid lowlands in Bocas del Toro.

Males are very territorial and "wrestle" each other over territory. Both parents care for the eggs; once hatched, the female carries them piggy-back style, one at a time, to a safer location, such as a bromeliad.

 Look in the leaf litter round the base of trees for them feeding on ants.

 HABITAT BEHAVIOUR ✓ VIEWING TIPS

West Indian manatee

Trichechus manatus (Manatí del Caribe)

🌸 Moves easily between marine and freshwater wetlands along the Caribbean coast, but with some in Lago Gatún.

🌱 Munching on floating vegetation most of the time, they otherwise float in the water like large logs.

✓ Main sightings are early morning in the Humedales de San San Pond Sak in Bocas del Toro.

Hercules beetle

Dynastes Hercules (Escarabajo Hercules)

🌸 Found across the country in moist rainforest.

🌱 Primarily nocturnal, it feeds on rotting fruit and tree sap but can be active during the day when looking for a mate, typically during the rainy season.

✓ The male is instantly recognizable by its long horn, used to tussle with other males over females.

Blue morpho

Morpho menelaus (Morpho azul)

🌸 Inhabits the rainforest canopy countrywide but occasionally found lower down in clearings.

🌱 Drinks the juice of rotting fruit through its proboscis and has an erratic zigzagged flight.

✓ Unmistakable iridescent blue in flight (up to 15cm wingspan), but displays its camouflaged underside when resting on a leaf.

Green sea turtle

Chelonia mydas (Tortuga verde or Tortuga blanco)

🌸 Though it nests in greater numbers on the Pacific side, including the Archipiélago de las Perlas and Golfo de Chiriquí, it can be seen feeding in the coastal shallows off both coasts.

🌱 Mostly herbivorous, it predominantly eats seagrass.

✓ Easiest to see when nesting during peak season (June–Oct) in Bocas del Toro.

🌸 HABITAT 🌱 BEHAVIOUR ✓ VIEWING TIPS

Héctor Gallego and the Santa Fé Cooperative

In the middle of the night of June 9, 1971, **Padre Héctor Gallego**, the 33-year-old priest of Santa Fé, was abducted by two uniformed men of Omar Torrijos's National Guard and was never seen again. In 2002, the Truth Commission set up by President Moscoso to examine crimes committed during Panama's two dictatorships found what they believed to be the tortured remains of the revered priest. It is generally presumed that Manuel Noriega, then head of the secret service, gave the orders, though it seems likely that Torrijos, even if unaware of events at the time, was complicit in the cover-up.

Gallego had arrived in Santa Fé from Colombia in 1967 as the town's first parish priest, and was appalled at the exploitation of the local farmers by the wealthy merchant elite, whose clout within the town and access to outside markets allowed them to buy the farmers' goods for a pittance and sell them on for a fat profit. Gallego set about educating and organizing the peasant population into becoming self-reliant, helping them to establish a cooperative so their products could be sold directly to the market, bypassing the merchants. It is not known exactly what threat this posed to the authorities: perhaps they feared a radicalization of the movement, though the priest never encouraged violent rebellion. Some suggest it was a more personal grudge since the local *cacique* was a cousin of Torrijos. Whatever the reason, a campaign of intimidation began, starting with insults and threats, escalating into arson and culminating in the priest's final "disappearance". "If I disappear," Gallego announced before his death, "don't look for me. Continue the struggle." His prophetic words now figure on the monument to him in the town.

rooms with hot-water bathrooms, you'll need to book. A lovely hammock-strewn balcony and *rancho* complete the tranquil scene though the morning cockerels will ensure an early start. Tasty breakfasts and international and vegetarian dinners are served, and maps and guides can be arranged for excursions. Dorm $10. ❸

Hotel El Sol de Santa Fé (Formerly *Hotel Santa Fé*). Main road ☎954 0941, ⓦwww.hotelsolsantafe .com. Perched on the hillside 500m before town,

this institution has for years attracted fleeing urbanites at weekends seeking fresh mountain air and relaxation. Under new management, it has been repainted but rooms (for 2–5 people) remain dark with no frills. Onsite bar-restaurant. ❷

Jardín Santafereño ☎6436 2454. Four recently renovated basic dark cement *cabañas* set on a wooded hilltop, overlooking the town, though the restoration of the nearby *cantina* and restaurant for weekend parties might alter the ambiance. ❹

The Town

Daily activity centres on the small covered **market** area, where fresh local produce is on display alongside a smattering of predominantly Ngöbe craft stalls. Across the road stands a monument to the town's most famous resident, **Padre Héctor Gallego** (see box above), whose kidnap and murder has left the town emotionally scarred. A non-profit foundation that bears his name continues his community development work, offering support and skills training to local farmers and artisans. More visibly, the priest's legacy resides in the continued success of the cooperative he helped found; it includes a couple of supermarkets, several grocery stores, a restaurant, bus and taxi services, and the jewel in the crown, the local organic coffee mill, **Café El Tute** (☎954 0801). Tours (in Spanish) of the processing plant, where you can buy some of the delicious product, and to a nearby organic coffee farm, can be organized through the tourism cooperative (☎954 0737), which has a smart *rancho* near the centre of town.

Activities

The area's natural beauty makes it perfect for **hiking**, **birdwatching** and **bathing** in clear streams and rivers – provided the weather holds – though the mountainous topography means there'll be steep inclines wherever you wander. *Hostal La Qhia* has home-made maps to guide guests to local waterfalls and natural swimming pools; otherwise a good start is to head down to the river, before the entrance to the village, below the *Hotel El Sol de Santa Fé*, or follow the road up towards Alto de Piedra

If you intend to tackle the area's loftiest peaks, Cerro Tute (930m) and Cerro Mariposa (1200m), cloaked in montane forest, or want to penetrate the wilderness areas of the park, then hiring a **guide** (around $15–25/person/day depending on numbers) is a must. Ask your accommodation, the tourist cooperative or try Artesanías Santa Fé, which, though short on the advertised crafts, offers some interesting hikes including a night excursion. Edgar Toribio (℡6713 2074, ℮edgar_toribio@yahoo.es) comes recommended for hiking and wildlife. Popular destinations include the impressive Salto Alto de Piedra and Salto El Bermejo, as well as the 30m cascade of El Salto, slightly further afield. It's even possible to organise a multi-day trek over the Cordillera to the Caribbean coast, involving hiking and river transport by dugout.

Two of the most pleasurable activities, given the magnificent scenery, are **horse riding** (contact César Miranda ℡6792 0571, ℮aventurascesamo@hotmail.com; $40 for two) and **tubing**, floating down the nearby river for over an hour, gliding past kingfishers, herons and egrets. Ask for directions to the house of William Abrega (℡6583 5944; $5/person, life jacket provided), whom it's well worth employing to show the best line into the occasional rapids. Panama Dreamfinders, the real estate office near the town entrance now rents **bicycles**, but you'll need to be fit to deal with the very steep roads.

Eating and drinking

The handful of local **restaurants** (daily, usually 6am–7pm) all serve much the same filling traditional Panamanian fare at rock-bottom prices, usually involving chicken, beans, rice and soup, with a greater choice at lunchtime when hungry farm workers flock in. Both the agricultural and tourism cooperatives run restaurants, as does the bus terminal.

The Azuero Peninsula

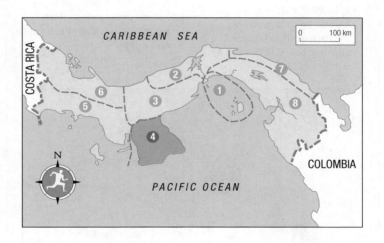

CHAPTER 4 # Highlights

✳ **Azueran artesanía** Catch the artisans at work in village workshops, where they craft exquisite ceramics, devil masks and straw hats, as well as embroidered *polleras* and *montunos*. See p.187

✳ **Festivals** Get caught up with the peninsula's major fiestas: the Rio-style glitz of Carnaval at Las Tablas; devil dances for Corpus Christi celebrations in La Villa; and the nation's biggest folkloric jamboree, the Festival de la Mejorana, in Guararé. See p.197, p.193 & p.194

✳ **Isla Iguana** A wildlife retreat of black and green iguanas, chest-puffing frigatebirds and shoals of rainbow-coloured fish. See p.201

✳ **Playa Venao** A lovely swathe of beach best appreciated by surfing the waves or horse riding along the sands. See p.203

✳ **Isla de Cañas** Camp out among the turtles that arrive in their thousands to nest along glorious sand each year. See p.204

▲ Magnificent frigatebirds at Isla Iguana

The Azuero Peninsula

4

THE AZUERO PENINSULA

M ention the **AZUERO PENINSULA**, the box-shaped land mass that protrudes into the Pacific, and clichéd images abound of smiling women dancing around in *polleras*, cowboys lassoing cattle and quaint village squares with whitewashed colonial churches. Yet the peninsula often delivers on such images: peasant farmers stride off to the fields at the crack of dawn, *sombrero* on their head, and machete slung across the shoulder; some hamlets still contain adobe houses adorned with bougainvillea, topped with terracotta tiles; and small villages celebrate their saint day with bands of accordionists and fiddlers playing foot-tapping folk melodies. That said, the pace of development is increasing: trucks rattle along tarred rather than dirt roads; towns often now include hideous cement-block mini-supers with zinc roofs; and vast tracts of land are being gobbled up by mushrooming real estate agents and mining companies, looking to force rapid and irrevocable social change on communities. For the moment, though, cattle farming and agriculture still prevail in the interior while coastal communities continue to derive their livelihood from fishing.

The peninsula, which covers a substantial 7616 square kilometres, is sometimes referred to as Eastern and Western Azuero, with no connecting road across the dividing mountainous spine that runs down the western flank. The former comprises the vast bulk of the terrain and the small provinces of Herrera and Los Santos, clustered around their respective provincial capitals of **Chitré** and **Las Tablas**, which make good bases for exploring the region. The Western Azuero, on the other hand, is an oft-forgotten sliver of Veraguas Province that trickles down the western seaboard, dotted with small ranching and fishing communities and ending in one of Panama's least explored wilderness areas, the **Parque Nacional Cerro Hoya**, which nourishes sparkling waterfalls and is home to several endemic species of animals and plants. That and the little-visited **Reserva Forestal El Montuoso** contrast acutely with the rest of the peninsula, which more than anywhere else in the country has been stripped of forest due to excessive logging and slash-and-burn agriculture. The desert-like **Parque Nacional de Sarigua**, at the heart of the **Arco Seco** (Dry Arc) – Panama's driest, hottest region that curves around the eastern shore of the Azuero – is a compelling reminder of the consequences of such practices. For a visitor, this means choosing your time to visit carefully; when fed by the rains, the verdant rolling pastures punctuated by villages ablaze with flowers and fruit trees make up a picturesque landscape, but when the clouds dry up, they lose much of their natural beauty, becoming parched and dusty as temperatures soar. Panama's Spanish colonial heritage is also at its most visible and vibrant in the Azuero, from cattle ranching and bullfighting through baroque churches to elaborate costumes – the best examples of which are crafted on the peninsula – and distinctive music that enliven the numerous

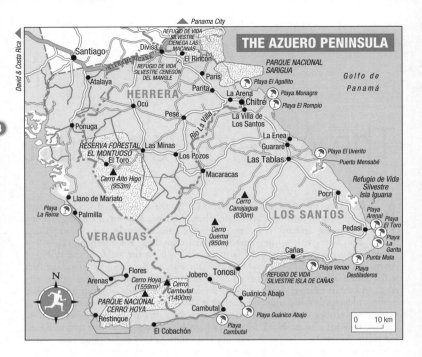

THE AZUERO PENINSULA

Panama City

David & Costa Rica

Santiago — Divisa — El Rincón — REFUGIO DE VIDA SILVESTRE CIENEGA LAS MACANAS

INTERAMERICANA

Atalaya — REFUGIO DE VIDA SILVESTRE CENEGÓN DEL MANGLE — Paris — Parita — La Arena — Chitré

HERRERA — Ocú — Pese — La Villa de Los Santos

PARQUE NACIONAL SARIGUA

Golfo de Panamá

Playa El Agallito — Playa Monagre — Playa El Rompio

Ponuga — RESERVA FORESTAL EL MONTUOSO — Las Minas — Los Pozos — La Enea — Guararé — Las Tablas

El Toro — Cerro Alto Higo (953m) — Macaracas

Playa El Uverito — Puerto Mensabé

Llano de Mariato — Cerro Canajagua (830m) — LOS SANTOS — Pocrí

Refugio de Vida Silvestre Isla Iguana

Playa La Reina — Palmilla — VERAGUAS — Cerro Quema (950m)

Playa Arenal — Playa El Toro — Pedasí — Playa La Garita — Punta Mala

N

Cañas

Flores — Jobero — Tonosí — Arenas — Cerro Hoya (1559m) — Cerro Cambutal (1400m) — PARQUE NACIONAL CERRO HOYA — Guánico Abajo — Cambutal — Restingue — El Cobachón

REFUGIO DE VIDA SILVESTRE ISLA DE CAÑAS — Playa Venao — Playa Destiladeros

Playa Guánico Abajo — Playa Cambutal

0   10 km

religious festivals. This has led to the region being fondly dubbed the *cuña* (cradle) of national culture and traditions by many Panamanians – a statement which takes little account of the cultural affinities or contributions of the country's non-mestizo populations and conveniently ignores the existence of much earlier cultures. Vestiges of pre-Columbian communities, the most ancient of which was an eleven thousand-year-old fishing village at Sarigua – currently the oldest known settlement on the isthmus – provide evidence both of an earlier history and of the conquistadors' brutal efficacy in wiping it out, still notable today when you notice the absence of indigenous communities in the region.

The Azuero's greatest appeal lies in its **festivals**, which reel in thousands of Panamanians from all over the country, particularly for the major parties of **Carnaval** in Las Tablas and Chitré, **Corpus Christi** in La Villa de Los Santos and the **Festival de la Mejorana** in Guararé, though only recently have foreign tourists started to take an interest. Despite being championed as fine examples of the country's Spanish heritage, the festivities actually illustrate its hybridity: solemn religious ceremonies combine with pagan rituals and hedonistic excess; traditional folk groups are followed by DJs blasting out reggaeton, rap and salsa; and stylized Andalusian-inspired dances such as the *tamborito* (Panama's national dance) and *punto* are imbued with African and pre-Columbian rhythms using drums, gourds and seed pods. Over five hundred festivals are held annually in the region, so you could spend a whole year here in a permanent alcoholic haze drifting from one celebration to the next, soaking up (literally and metaphorically) the legendary Azueran hospitality.

But there's more to the peninsula than partying: for the nature lover, **Isla Iguana** and **Isla de Cañas** offer very different but fascinating wildlife experiences, the former a major nesting site for the chest-puffing frigatebirds, boasting coral beaches and rich snorkelling, while the latter affords a rare opportunity to witness the mass breeding of olive ridley **turtles**. The peninsula's eastern seaboard hosts various important **wetlands** teeming with birdlife. Deserted **beaches** fringe the coastline – broad tan, chocolate and black stretches of sand welcome top-notch **surfing** waves while world-class **sport fishing** takes place off the legendary "Tuna Coast", with many enthusiasts using understated **Pedasí** as a base.

Chitré and around

CHITRÉ is the main urban centre in the Azuero Peninsula, and it makes an ideal base for exploring the surrounding area and for attending the region's numerous festivals. To the north, the contrasting wetland reserves of **Ciénaga Las Macanas**, the **Reserva de Vida Silvestre Canegón del Mangle** and the desertified **Parque Nacional de Sarigua** are within easy reach. So too is the picturesque colonial village of **Parita**, just off the main road, and the nearby settlement of **La Arena**, famous for its ceramics. Further inland you can access a string of small traditional towns and villages and feel as if you're stepping back in time.

Chitré

A laid-back commercial town with an attractive colonial centre, **CHITRÉ** was founded in 1848, though indications are that conquistadors had been there since the mid-1500s. For the provincial capital of Herrera Province, life centres on the bustling streets around Calle Manuel María Correa, where you'll also find the interesting regional **museum**, and the well-manicured **Parque Unión**, flanked by the splendid **cathedral**, notable for its impressive yet restrained wooden interior.

Arrival and information

Chitré's large **bus terminal** (☎ 996 6426) is 1km south of the town centre on the bypass, Vía Circunvalación, with frequent **minibus shuttles** to the main plaza (25c), where you can catch the return bus; or you can jump in a **taxi** ($2), paying the same fare to most places in town. Getting to Chitré from Panama City involves taking one of the regular large **buses** (hourly, 6am–11pm; 3hr30min; $7.50), which return to the capital at similar intervals (1.30am, 2.45am, then hourly, 4am–6pm). Other routes served include Aguadulce (every 20min, 4am–6pm; 1hr; $2.50), Las Minas (every 30min, 6am–6pm; 1hr; $2.20), Ocú (every 30min, 6.30am–7pm; 1hr; $2.20), Macaracas (hourly, 6am–6pm; 1hr; $2.20), Pesé (every 15–20min, 6.30am–6.30pm; 30min; $1), Santiago (every 30min, 5am–6.30pm; 1hr10min; $2.40), Las Tablas (every 10–15min, 6am–9pm; 40min; $1) – where you'll need to change for Pedasí and Tonosí. To get to David, take one of the many frequent Divisa shuttles ($1.25) to the junction with the Interamericana, where Panama–David buses will stop if they have space, so avoid peak travel times; alternatively, catch a bus to Santiago and change there. For the short hop to La Villa de Los Santos, a mere 4km south down the main road, buses depart around every ten minutes (6am–9pm; 15min; 35c).

Approaching the town by road from the north, the dual carriageway of Paseo Enrique Geenzer squeezes into the bottleneck of Calle Manuel María Correa, one of the principal commercial roads, whose pavements are packed with shoppers and business folk. After crossing Avenida Pérez, the town's other main artery, traffic is often close to a standstill. Most of the **banks**, **ATMs** and **shops**, including several **pharmacies**, are located along here and around the main square while the **post office** (Mon–Sat 7am–5pm) is a block up on Avenida Pérez, on the corner with

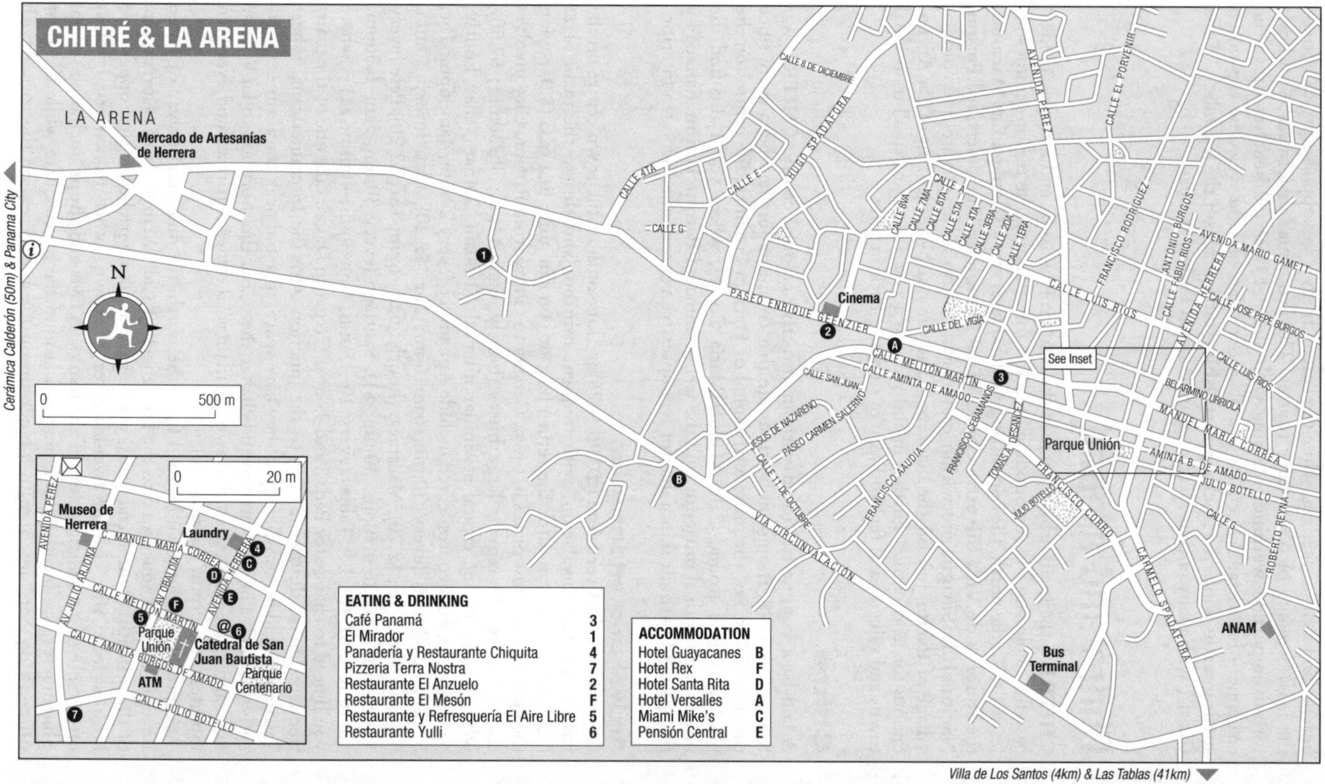

CHITRÉ & LA ARENA
LA ARENA
Mercado de Artesanías de Herrera
Cerámica Calderón (50m) & Panama City
N
0 500 m
Villa de Los Santos (4km) & Las Tablas (41km)
Cinema
See Inset
Parque Unión
Bus Terminal
ANAM
PASEO ENRIQUE GEENZIER
CALLE MELITÓN MARTÍN
CALLE AMINTA DE AMADO
CALLE LUIS RIOS
AVENIDA PÉREZ
AVENIDA HERRERA
AVENIDA MARIO GAMETT
CALLE JOSE PEPE BURGOS
CALLE FABIO RIOS
ANTONIO BURGOS
FRANCISCO RODRIGUEZ
CALLE EL PORVENIR
BELARMINO URRIOLA
MANUEL MARÍA CORREA
AMINTA B. DE AMADO
JULIO BOTELLO
CALLE G
ROBERTO REYNA
CARMELO SPADAFORA
FRANCISCO CORRO
TOMAS A. DESANCEZ
FRANCISCO CEBAMANOS
FRANCISCO AAUDIA
VÍA CIRCUNVALACIÓN
CALLE 11 DE OCTUBRE
JESUS DE NAZARENO
PASEO CARMEN SALERNO
CALLE SAN JUAN
CALLE DEL VIGIA
HUGO SPADAFORA
CALLE 8 DE DICIEMBRE
CALLE E
CALLE 4TA
CALLE G
CALLE A
CALLE 8VA
CALLE 7MA
CALLE 6TA
CALLE 5TA
CALLE 4TA
CALLE 3ERA
CALLE 2DA
CALLE 1ERA
0 20 m
Museo de Herrera
Laundry
Parque Unión
Catedral de San Juan Bautista
Parque Centenario
ATM
AVENIDA PÉREZ
C. MANUEL MARÍA CORREA
AV. JULIO ARJONA
AV. OBALDÍA
AVENIDA HERRERA
CALLE MELITÓN MARTÍN
CALLE AMINTA BURGOS DE AMADO
CALLE JULIO BOTELLO
EATING & DRINKING
Café Panamá 3
El Mirador 1
Panadería y Restaurante Chiquita 4
Pizzeria Terra Nostra 7
Restaurante El Anzuelo 2
Restaurante El Mesón F
Restaurante y Refresquería El Aire Libre 5
Restaurante Yulli 6
ACCOMMODATION
Hotel Guayacanes B
Hotel Rex F
Hotel Santa Rita D
Hotel Versalles A
Miami Mike's C
Pensión Central E

Calle Belarmino Urriola. The **hospital** (℡ 996 4444) is south of town on Avenida Carmelo Spadafora. **ANAM** (℡ 996 7619) is also rather out in the sticks but you will need to contact them for permission to visit La Reserva Forestal El Montuoso (see p.191) or the Parque Nacional de Sarigua (see p.188). It might be worth **renting a car** (4WD in the rainy season) for a couple of days, especially to get to the less accessible protected areas or to explore further inland. Budget (℡ 996 0027) and Hertz (℡ 996 2256) have offices on Vía Circunvalación whereas Thrifty (℡ 996 9565) lies on Paseo Enrique Geenzier, not far from *Hotel Versalles*. You can get free **wi-fi** in *Café Rex*, and there are several **internet cafés** near Parque Unión, where **public phone boxes** are also conveniently located.

Accommodation

As the peninsula's main urban centre, Chitré possesses a range of **accommodation** though nothing at the very top end of the scale.

Hotel Guayacanes Vía Circunvalación ℡ 996 9758, ⓦ www.losguayacanes.com. Rather far out and pricey but offering decent rooms with all mod cons plus a bar-restaurant, swimming pool and casino. Breakfast included. **❼**

Hotel Rex Parque Unión, C Melitón Martín ℡ 996 4310, ⓔ hotelrex@cwpanama.net. You're paying more for its prime location on the plaza so it's worth splashing out for the French windows and a view over the park. Slightly faded furnishings but pleasant wooden panelling and comfy beds make it a reasonable option for the unfussy traveller. Takes credit cards. **❺**

Hotel Santa Rita C Manuel María Correa at Av Herrera ℡ 996 4610. Good value in a prime location, this aging but well-maintained hotel has dark, simple en-suite rooms (a/c, cable TV, good bed and hot water) off long corridors at modest prices. **❸**

Hotel Versalles Paseo Enrique Geenzier ℡ 996 4422, ⓦ www.hotelversalles.com. Don't delude yourself with visions of Parisian splendour, though rooms in this functional motel-like business hotel on the main approach road are well equipped (a/c, phone, wi-fi, cable TV and hot water), if lacking in character. Small pool and bar-restaurant. **❺**

Miami Mike's Av Herrera at C Manuel María Correa ℡ 6603 9711. Shambolic small-scale hostel offering little more than a bunk, kitchen and a fantastic rooftop view but run by an affable American, at rock-bottom rates. Dorm $9.

Pensión Central Av Herrera at C Melitón Martín ℡ 996 0059. Somewhat run-down but clean and basic, with a/c, cable TV and cold water. Breakfast included. **❷**

The Town

The compact colonial quarter of Chitré can easily be explored in a couple of hours. The most obvious place to start is the imposing **Catedral de San Juan Bautista**. Constructed between 1896 and 1910, it underwent a major restoration in the late 1980s, which took the unusual step of exposing some of the exterior stone walls, to provide a striking contrast with the snow-white facade and bell towers. The restrained polished wooden interior also makes a refreshing change from the ornate decor in many Catholic churches, especially the gilded mahogany altar, which is complemented by bright stained-glass windows. To the side of the cathedral are the immaculate formal gardens of the **Parque Unión**. The neatly clipped flowerbeds and swaying palm trees around a stately bandstand provide the backdrop for the mixing of modernity and tradition: young suited executives hold forth on their mobile phones while elderly *campesinos* in *montunos* and *sombreros de junco* – the traditional embroidered shirts and workday straw hats – discuss the local news.

Stroll two blocks east to **Parque Centenario**, a more low-key affair, surrounded by squat red-tiled houses with wrought-iron grillwork. Head north a block down the side of a colourful corner fruit and vegetable **market**, then west for three blocks, along bustling Calle Manuel María Correa, which is the heart of the town's commercial life, and you come to **Parque Bandera**, adorned with large coconut

▲ Museo de Herrera, Chitré

palms. Here you'll find the **Museo de Herrera** (Tues–Sat 8am–4pm; $1), housed in an elegant converted colonial mansion and former post office. Probably the best museum outside Panama City, it is nevertheless quite modest (explanations only in Spanish). Downstairs focuses on the pre-Columbian era: a couple of fine ceremonial **metates** stand out, as well as the impressive collection of **ceramics**. A reproduction **burial chamber** shows a life-size model *cacique* decked out in his gold arm and leg bands while copies of gold **huacas** from the anthropological museum in Panama City line the walls. Upstairs, fast forward several hundred years to the colonial and post-colonial periods, with displays of **traditional musical instruments** and **costumes**, which inevitably include elaborate *polleras* and devil outfits, and various **tools** from rural life, some of which are still used today. Don't miss the pouch made from a bull's scrotum used to carry staples for mending fences. The museum also offers **cultural tours** of the area, but only in Spanish.

Eating, drinking and entertainment

Outside festival times, town **nightlife** isn't exactly swinging. **Cines Modernos** (☎996 6121, ⓦwww.cinespanama.com; $3.15) – set back from Paseo Enrique Geenzier, heading out past the *Hotel Versalles* on the right – produces a predominantly Hollywood diet, mainly dubbed. The *Break Bar and Lounge* at the *Hotel Guayacanes* is the hottest spot to dance the night away while the adjoining *Fiesta* is the most diverse of several **casinos**. Chitré is noted for its **fresh fish**, which you can sample at one of the town's numerous inexpensive restaurants.

Café Panamá Paseo Enrique Geenzier, next to Global Bank. Popular roadside café serving tasty dishes accompanied by beans, rice, plantain and salad for a few dollars. Daily 6am–8pm.

El Mirador Well signposted up the hill off the Carretera Nacional between Chitré and La Arena. Atmospheric open-air hilltop spot to enjoy a beer while admiring the sunset or the twinkling night lights of Chitré. Daily 4pm until late.

Panadería y Restaurante Chiquita Av Herrera at C Manuel María Correa. Large open-sided cafeteria serving pastries, snacks and inexpensive mains for under $5. Daily 5am–10pm.

Pizzeria Terra Nostra C Aminta Burgos de Amado near Parque Unión. Reputedly the town's best pizzas, with a wide selection of toppings. Greek specialities, tacos, burritos and other comfort food available. Mon–Sat 10am–10pm, Sun 4–10pm.

Restaurante El Anzuelo Paseo Enrique Geenzier. Pleasant breezy rancho bar-restaurant next to the new *Gran Hotel Azuero*, serving mid-priced sizzling grilled meats and seafood (under $8), with delicious fresh fruit juices. The jumbo mixed platter ($22.50) should feed several mouths. Tues–Sun noon–11pm.

Restaurante El Mesón Downstairs at the *Hotel Rex*. Eschew the a/c dining room for the much nicer open-air café overlooking the park. Breakfasts under $3, while lunch and dinner mains start at around $6.50, and include well-prepared snacks (toasted sandwiches, burritos), the usual Panamanian and international regulars and Spanish specialities like paella, chorizo and tongue. Free wi-fi. Daily 6am–11pm.

Restaurante y Refresquería El Aire Libre Parque Unión, Av Obaldía. Pleasant open-sided restaurant overlooking the park; packed at lunch, offering a cheap *menú del día* – the customary plateful of rice, beans and chicken or fish. Daily 6am–10pm.

Restaurante Yulli C Melitón Martín near Parque Centenario. Nice cafeteria food lacking the usual grease. Wash it down with chilled fruit *chicha*. Mon–Sat 6am–4pm, Sun 6am–2pm.

La Arena

The only reason travellers stop off at **La Arena**, a suburb-like village 5km west of Chitré, is to peruse the **ceramics**, for which it is famous. Get off the bus (from the bus terminal or the centre of town) or abandon your taxi ($2.50) along the Carretera Nacional once you see roadside displays of pottery, which include anything from vast urns (*tinajas*), plant pots and household ornaments to oversize frogs – Panama's answer to the garden gnome. In addition to the renowned traditional ceramics with pre-Columbian motifs, you'll find gaudier glazes and a fair amount of tack. Other potential souvenirs include traditional folkloric instruments, such as the five-string guitars (*mejoraneras*), drums (*tambores*) and gourd rattles (*churucas*), as well as beaded jewellery, hammocks and devil masks. The two best-known places to shop are the **Mercado de Artesanías de Herrera** (daily 8.30am–4.30pm), which is on the right coming from Chitré, where the road forks; and **Cerámica Calderón** (☏974 4946; daily 7am–4pm), a little further along the main road, where you can witness the pots being moulded and fired in giant kilns on the premises. There are plenty of other places in the vicinity to shop; you just need to ask or wander around.

Parita

Founded in 1556, **Parita** is one of the oldest, best preserved and most picturesque villages on the peninsula. Arrive shortly after sunrise or just before dusk to catch the best light for photographs. At only 1km northwest of Chitré, a few hundred metres off the Carretera Nacional, the village is easily reachable by public transport (take any Divisa bus; 50c). Take in the sparkling white eighteenth-century **Iglesia Santo Domingo de Guzmán**, with its attractive clay-tiled roof. Peek inside and you'll see some ornately carved wooden altarpieces and a similarly elaborate pulpit. Surrounding

---

Mask-makers

Ghoulish devil masks, which form the centrepiece of Corpus Christi celebrations (see p.193) across the country and feature in other festivals throughout the year, make great souvenirs. Though you'd be hard put to squeeze a full-size headpiece into your hand luggage, increasingly smaller versions are being made for the tourist trade. Available in various craft centres and agricultural fairs, you can also visit some of the mask-makers in their workshops. Expect to pay $8–10 for a small mask and from $45 for a large one. Two renowned artisans are:

José González (☏996 2314) His workshop in the outskirts of Chitré is tough to find but ring and he'll pick you up, or enquire at the Museo de Hererra (see p.186).

Dário López (☏974 2933) Hard-to-miss workshop on the Carretera Nacional, just north of Parita beyond the petrol station, that specializes in *diablos sucios*.

the plaza, terraces of pastel-coloured traditional adobe (*quincha*) cottages with tiled roofs take you back in time, though a line of telegraph poles remind you that the village was not totally bypassed by the twentieth century. Party time in Parita occurs in the days leading up to August 8, the celebration of the village's foundation.

Wildlife reserves along the coast north of Chitré

The **mangroves** and **mud flats** along the coast north of Chitré attract prolific birdlife, particularly migratory waders, though without your own transport, some of these locations are not easily accessible, especially in the rainy season.

Playa Agallito

Despite the continued clearing of mangroves to make way for shrimp farms, the silty mud and salt flats of **Playa Agallito** still provide sustenance for thousands of shore birds and waders, many migratory, who return to the same spot to feed each year. This avian feast is the main reason to come here, as it's one of the country's top spots for catching sight of the splendid roseate spoonbill as well as American oystercatchers and wood storks, amid a potpourri of terns, egrets, herons and sandpipers. The best time to visit – bring the binoculars – is at high tide when birds feed close to shore. Buses run every half hour between Chitré and Playa Agallito, via Avenida Herrera, from around 6am to 6pm.

Parque Nacional de Sarigua

The contrast could not be greater a little further up the coast at **PARQUE NACIONAL DE SARIGUA** (8am–4pm; $5), which comprises a desert-like wasteland, covered with a layer of surreal bronze-coloured dust. Birdlife is restricted to a coastal sliver of threatened mangrove. This eighty-square-kilometre protected reserve stretches out into the Bahía de Parita and is squeezed between Río Santa María and Río Parita on land. Behind the mangroves, vast salt flats and tracts of dry forest lie bleak saline-streaked gullies dotted with cactus, acacia and snowy blobs of wild cotton. Less a tourist attraction, as it is often heralded, than a cautionary tale, Sarigua is testament to the devastating consequences of a century of slash-and-burn agriculture and overgrazing that resulted in poor acid soils being exposed to erosion. It is by far the hottest and driest area in the country, averaging just over a metre of rainfall annually, with temperatures soaring to mid-30°C during the day, and even above 40°C at the back end of the dry season, when dust storms rage and wind speeds can reach 70kph at night.

The silver lining to this sad tale of environmental degradation is that the erosion has helped uncover important archeological remains, including evidence of an eleven-thousand-year-old fishing village, the oldest known settlement on the isthmus, and more recent traces (between fifteen hundred and five thousand years ago) of an ancient farming community. When walking around the park it's easy to stumble on shards of ancient ceramics or discarded shells, just as the sparse vegetation makes it easier to spot boas curled around parched branches, armadillos digging in the undergrowth or lizards and iguanas sunning themselves.

The landscape is best appreciated from the top of the rickety **mirador** by the **ranger station**, from where you can also make out distant shrimp farms. Drinking water and toilets are located at the park office, where rangers offer guided walks for a tip. The place is rather undeveloped, with only one very short trail so far, and though **camping** is permitted, it's hard to see the attraction. Theoretically there should always be a warden on site though it's best to contact the ANAM office in Chitré (p.185) beforehand, especially if you intend to camp ($5/person) or would like a guide.

To reach Sarigua either take a bus to Parita (50c) and a taxi ($3) from there, or fork out the whole taxi fare ($10) from Chitré. By car (4WD necessary in the rainy season) the turn-off is well signposted off the Carretera Nacional just north of Parita.

Refugio de Vida Silvestre Cenegón del Mangle

At the mouth of the Río Santa María, with around eight square kilometres of mangrove rich in wildlife, the **Refugio de Vida Silvestre Cenegón del Mangle** (8am–4pm; $3) has previously been an important stop on any serious nature lover's itinerary of the peninsula. Heronries packed with grey and tri-coloured herons and great white and cattle egrets earned it the nickname *ponedero de garzas* (heron's nest), prompting construction of a 500-metre boardwalk through the mangroves to better view the birds, especially during the nesting season (Jun–Sept). Sadly, though, heron numbers have decreased while the boardwalk had been allowed to rot, so check with ANAM in Chitré (✆996 8216) on its current state. In the dry season, there's little reason to visit.

With no bus service from Chitré, transport options are taxis (from Chitré $20, or Parita $10) or private vehicle. By car, it's a 45-minute ride from Chitré: 7km north of Parita, turn right at a bus shelter and petrol station to París – a far cry from its namesake in Europe, and actually named after a local indigenous chief. At the fork by the village church, bear right and then right again at an unmarked crossroads a few hundred metres later. The tarred road soon peters into dirt, which continues another 4km before signs to the reserve re-emerge, which you follow to the park office.

La Ciénaga de las Macanas

Another 10km north (just over 7km south from the junction at Divisa) of the Cenegón del Mangle junction is the turn-off to the region's largest freshwater wetland area, **La Ciénaga de las Macanas** (entry $3). A shallow lake with swampy surroundings and patches of dry forest set on Río Santa María's floodplains, it attracts an abundance of resident and migratory birdlife. The reserve's best vantage point is the **observation tower** near the water's edge, where it's easy to pick out the iridescent glossy ibis or wattled jacana picking their way across carpets of lilies and water hyacinth; less so to identify the fluffy rear end of a diving fulvous or black-bellied whistling duck. Brahman cattle chomping through the greenery might come as more of a surprise, but they help regulate the invasive water hyacinth and since the marsh-cum-lake is a multi-use site, limited farming and fishing is allowed, though conservationists are keen to reduce the number of grazing livestock.

Amenities are better here than at nearby Cenegón del Mangle: beside the tower are toilets, picnic tables, a short interpretive path and a jetty protruding over the water, with a couple of boats tethered. If you fancy boating on the water to get closer to wildlife or throw a fishing line, contact one of the eco-tourism groups in the nearby village of **El Rincón** (de Santa María). GEMA (contact Hector Escudero, ✆6021 4919) offers guiding services (in Spanish) and boat trips, and can arrange transport for you. El Rincón is reachable by **bus** from Chitré. From there it is around 4km to the marsh (right at the church, then right at the fork.)

The central peninsula

The best way to get a feel for rural life in the Azuero, which in some places has remained much the same for over a century, is to head west of the Carretera Nacional into the **agricultural heartland** of the peninsula. Here you pass rolling hills of pastureland sprinkled with giant hardwoods, fields of sugar cane and flower-filled towns and villages, where the unhurried pace of life is infectious.

There is precious little accommodation in these places, but the main population centres are well connected by public transport on decent roads and two or three can easily be combined into a day-trip. To experience life in the more remote villages, pack a sleeping bag or tent and clamber aboard one of the infrequent *chivas* from the plaza of one of the larger centres and improvise once you reach the end of the road – literally. The hospitality of most people on the peninsula is such that you're bound to find somewhere to spend the night for a few dollars, with a bar and a hole-in-the-wall *fonda* nearby to sustain you.

Pesé

One of the prettiest towns within reach of Chitré, lying 24km southeast and surrounded by a carpet of sugar cane, **PESÉ** is known for its Good Friday re-enactment of the Passion of Christ, and its liquor; the ironic juxtaposition of faith and booze is evident the moment you set eyes on the church, which looks disapprovingly across the road at the *Varela Hermanos* **distillery**, producer of Panama's national knock-out (35 percent) tipple, seco. What Spanish émigré and founder José Varela started up as a sugar mill and refinery in 1908, became a distillery in 1936 and the business has never looked back, now supplying ninety percent of Panama's spirits, with outlets across Latin America. As you can find out for yourself on a tour of the place (Jan–April), the factory produces a million cases of spirit a year, much of which ends up down the throats of revellers at the Azuero's many festivals, such as the annual **Festival de la Caña de Azúcar** held in Pesé to celebrate the end of the harvest. Opposite the distillery, the smartly painted grey-and-white **church** stands beside a small park, which faces a neat line of traditional terracotta-tiled houses fronted by flowering shrubs. If passing at lunchtime, note that *Restaurante Marithel*, a shady patio draped with foliage and hibiscus flowers, serves a decent plate of *comida típica* for around $2. Over the road is an **ATM**. **Buses** leave Chitré and meander along to Pesé (6.30am–6.30pm; 30min; $1) every twenty minutes.

Ocú

Twenty kilometres west of Pesé, the larger village of **OCÚ** makes up for the lack of quaint charm by attracting visitors for its **festivals** and hat-making. The **Festival del Manito** (Aug 16–20) is the premier event to attend. Apart from the usual parades of *polleras* and *montunos*, accompanied by music, dancing and drinking, there are two stand-out elements: the **tamarind duel** (*duelo del tamarindo*) and the **peasant wedding** (*matrimonio campesino*). The latter is self-explanatory but a wonderful sight: following a mock church wedding, the bride, decked out in an all-white *pollera*, is paraded on horseback through the streets while the groom holds an umbrella above her head to protect her from the sun (or rain). In contrast, testosterone-fuelled duels from bygone days, when men fought to the death over women, family honour, or simply from overdoing the liquor, are re-enacted every year with swords and sabres on a platform in the centre of the plaza. The town's other five-day extravaganza, la **Feria de San Sebastián** (Jan 16–20), is an agricultural fair honouring the patron saint.

Ocú is also renowned for **hat-making**, though its star has faded of late as more accessible Penonomé (see p.167) has garnered a greater share of the market. Nevertheless, the distinctive white sombrero Ocueño, with a thin black trim, is still produced in the town's home-based workshops. Try **Artesanías Ocueña**, a women's cooperative on the way into town, which also produces fine *polleras, montunos* and other embroidery items. **Buses** to Ocú from Chitré (every 30min, 6.30am–7pm; $2.20) can take around an hour, as can transport from Santiago (every 20–30min, 6am–6.30pm; $2).

Las Minas, Los Pozos and Macaracas

Though Pesé and Ocú are the more common day-trip destinations in the central peninsula, it is a pleasant drive, by bus or car, to cover the further 30km through **Las Minas** and **Los Pozos**, before either returning to Chitré or continuing southeast to **Macaracas**. The picturesque lush rolling hills (which metamorphose into increasingly parched and dusty mounds in the dry season) become more pronounced between Las Minas and Macaracas, as the road skirts the fringes of the western massif. From Macaracas, which sits just over the border in Los Santos Province, the road divides: turning northeast it heads back to the Carretera Nacional, joining it 15km south of La Villa de Los Santos; continuing south, the less travelled route slowly twists its way 50km down to Tonosí. There's nothing particular to see or do in any of these places, except chill out and watch rural life unfold. The party most likely to attract outsiders occurs in Macaracas. The **Fiesta de los Reyes Magos** (Three Wise Men) features a two-hour dramatization of the Adoration of the Magi, which has taken place in the church plaza every January 6 for almost two hundred years.

Reserva Forestal El Montuoso

Up the valley from Las Minas, the seriously denuded peaks of the optimistically named **RESERVA FORESTAL EL MONTUOSO** pale in comparison with the richly forested mountain ranges in Chiriquí, Bocas or the Darién, so if you're heading for one of those locations, El Montuoso can easily be skipped. But if you're lingering in the Azuero and aching to get into the hills, this is the best place to come, until the rugged wilderness of Parque Nacional Cerro Hoya (see p.205) becomes more accessible.

The 120-square-kilometre reserve, dubbed the *"pulmón"* ("lung") of Herrera, was created in 1977 to safeguard the five rivers that rise in the mountainous region – some of the Azuero's major water sources – and to protect the rapidly vanishing tracts of forest being eaten away by illegal farming and timber extraction. In response, several reforestation projects have been initiated. Though only twenty percent of the reserve is now forested, what remains is concentrated around the reserve's highest point, Cerro Alto Higo (953m). Steep-sided mountains cleaved by river-eroded ravines harbour plenty of wildlife to interest the visitor, such as red brocket and white-tailed deer, howler monkeys, white-faced capuchins and collared peccaries. This is also one of the easiest places to spot the endemic brown-backed dove while other specialities include violet sabrewings and blue-throated goldentails – both hummingbirds – and the ever-acrobatic orange-collared manakin. The **park office**, located in Tres Puntas, 4km before the straggling hilltop village of Chepo, is a great place to **camp**, set in a lovely orchard, where a short, pretty trail crisscrosses the nascent Río La Villa up to a cascading pool. The main trail, **Sendero Alto Higo**, leads up the mountain of the same name, heading off to the left after Chepo, at a place known as the Caras Pintadas (Painted Faces), an imaginative reference to the petroglyph near the start of the path, where rare sundews are in evidence in winter. A moderately strenuous hike of just over an hour brings you out at a peak by a radio mast, which offers a tantalizing restricted view – thanks to some unfortunately located trees – towards the Golfo de Montijo.

Practicalities

Reaching the hillside village of Las Minas is straightforward enough by **car** or by **bus** (every 30min, 6am–6pm; 1hr; $2.20) from Chitré though the remaining 11km to the reserve requires a 4WD in the rainy season, or a ride in the sporadic *chiva* bound for Chepo. Visitors to the reserve stay at the **park office** ($5 entry,

$15 dorm or $6 camping), a five-minute walk from the road at Tres Puntas, which has two comfortable dormitories and use of a shared kitchen and a camping area. You'll need to stock up with food before you reach the limited shopping options of Las Minas and note that alcohol is prohibited at this particular park.

The road to Las Tablas

Just south of Chitré, the Carretera Nacional crosses Río La Villa, the peninsula's longest river, which marks the provincial boundary between Herrera and Los Santos, and continues southeast, running parallel to the coast, a few kilometres inland. After skirting the diminutive yet historically important town of **La Villa de Los Santos**, whose small museum and impressive church interior merit a detour, the road bypasses tiny **Guararé**, host to the country's largest folkloric festival, before arriving in the provincial capital, **Las Tablas**, about halfway down the peninsula.

La Villa de Los Santos

LA VILLA DE LOS SANTOS is famous for the vibrant costume-clad celebrations of Corpus Christi, an historic rebellion against Spanish colonial rule, and the **Feria Internacional de Azuero** (Ⓦwww.feriainternacionaldeazuero.com), the peninsula's annual five-day agricultural jamboree. If you arrive outside party time, though, it's easy to be disappointed. "La Villa" or "Los Santos", as the town is usually called, is much smaller and quieter than neighbouring Chitré, and not as spruced up or as vibrant as La Tablas. You'll need little more than an hour to check out its two main attractions – the church and museum, both on the central plaza.

Arrival and information

Buses shuttling between Chitré and Las Tablas (every 10–15min, 6am–9pm; 35c) can drop you off on the Carretera Nacional by the **bus terminal**, which has a **taxi rank** nearby, or further south by the fairground. From Panama City transport pours down the peninsula, with direct buses heading for La Villa hourly from 6am to 11pm (3hr 30min; $7.50) and buses leaving as frequently for Las Tablas, which can drop you here, or for Chitré, from where it's a short hop by minibus. For the return to Panama City, or other major destinations, board a Chitré-bound minibus on the main road, opposite the bus terminal.

The Town

The Carretera Nacional slides around the town centre, separating the colonial core from newer suburban developments, including the town's two hotels and the fairgrounds, which lie 1km further south. The **main plaza** is aptly named after the great Latin American liberator **Simón Bolívar** since it was to him that the town's influential citizens addressed a letter on November 10, 1821, asking to join his revolutionary movement against Spain, in what was called the *Primer Grito de la Independencia* (First Cry for Independence). This unilateral declaration started the domino effect that led to national independence from Spain eighteen days later and is celebrated annually with the customary flag-waving parades of marching bands, traditional folk costumes, speeches and fireworks. The room in which the letter was penned, complete with original furniture, forms part of the beautifully restored **Museo de la Nacionalidad** (Tues–Sat 8am–4pm, closed for lunch; $1), which sits on the north side of the square. Making the most of the town's historical status, much of the museum – which was formerly a school and a prison (though not at the same time) – overflows with details (in Spanish) of various leading characters in

El Festival de Corpus Christi

By far the most fascinating and famous of La Villa's celebrations is the **Festival de Corpus Christi**, a heady mix of **Christian** and **pagan** imagery in an exciting narrative of dance, drama and dialogue. It features a cast of larger-than-life characters and dancers decked out in extravagant costumes, interwoven with a series of religious ceremonies. Corpus Christi became an important tool in Spanish colonization across Latin America, as the invaders attempted to woo the indigenous population to the Christian faith by incorporating elements of their traditions and rituals into the ecclesiastical ceremonies. Though there is plenty of local variation, the basic good-versus-evil plot is the same.

The action starts on the Saturday before Corpus Christi when church bells at noon bring hordes of *diablos sucios* (dirty devils) rampaging onto the streets. Clad in crimson-and-black-striped jumpsuits, wearing ferocious devil masks with flame-coloured headdresses and letting off firecrackers at will, they terrify all and sundry to the beat of drums and whistles. Fast forward to Wednesday, several masses later, when at 11.30am on the Eve of Corpus Christi, the Diabla or Diablesa (though as with all roles, performed by a male) also races around the town announcing the arrival of her husband, the Diablo Mayor, who convenes with three other devils in the central plaza. Joking and knocking back the booze, they carve up the globe in a bid for world domination. Before dawn on Corpus Christi, Santeños roam around town, on foot and on horseback, in search of the Torito Santeño – a man in a bull's costume – who is causing havoc, but is eventually rounded up in the **Danza del Torito** as the party proceeds through the streets to a large communal breakfast. The centrepiece of the drama unfolds mid-morning before the church, on a magnificent carpet of petals, as the Archangel Michael and the *diablos limpios* (clean devils), distinguishable from the bad guys by their white sleeves and a rainbow of handkerchiefs attached to the waist, vanquish the villains in the Danza del Gran Diablo o Diablitos Limpios before allowing them in to the service. All the dance troupes – including an assortment of dwarves, roosters, vultures, Mexican conquistadors and escaped African slaves – attend the mass, which then relocates outside as Holy Communion is offered to the townsfolk before the serious partying begins.

Further merrymaking takes place a week later culminating in Saturday's **Día del Turismo**, which provides a highlights show on stage in the plaza, and Sunday's Día de la Mujer, offering Santeñas, whom tradition has prohibited from participating thus far, the chance to dust off their *polleras* and join in the fun.

the independence movement. These include **Rufina Alfaro**, a local 20-something lass, whose actual existence is in doubt but who has nevertheless passed into national mythology as the heroine of the resistance. Exploiting the local Spanish commander's affections, and securing crucial intelligence for the independence movement about when to attack the army barracks, she then headed the march there that cemented the bloodless coup. Check out **Parque Rufina Alfaro**, which lies three blocks southeast of the plaza on Avenida 10 de Noviembre, where a monument to the plucky Santeña – which has her seemingly emerging from a swamp – upset folk from her presumed birthplace on account of her wide girth and substantial bosom when from all accounts she was a diminutive maid.

On the northeastern side of the plaza, which has remained much as it was in 1821, the **Iglesia San Atanasio** has been undergoing a painfully slow restoration. Though the first stones were laid some time between 1556 and 1559, the edifice was not completed until two hundred years later in 1782. The dilapidated exterior gives little indication of the architectural gems inside, which include a series of magnificent carved altars – a profusion of spiralling columns adorned with vine leaves, winged cherubs and flowers, all dripping with gold. Most splendid of all is the main altar, framed by an even more opulent archway that predates the completion of the church. Note also the painted wooden tracery above the nave and the life-size entombed Christ figure in the glass sepulchre, which is paraded around the streets on Good Friday in a candlelit procession. The church is also the focal point for the town's famous **Festival de Corpus Christi** (see box, p.193). Although it is celebrated throughout Panama, the festivities in La Villa stand head and shoulders above the rest.

Practicalities

There are only two **hotels** in the town. The better one is *Hotel La Villa* (T 966 8201; ❸) a few hundred metres off the Carretera Nacional; though you'll either love or hate the folkloric-themed decor, this is a pleasant low-key place with good-value rooms (a/c, hot water, cable TV and firm beds) in a garden setting with a pool and moderately priced restaurant. Just south of the bus terminal, *Hotel Restaurante Kevin* (T 966 8276, E hotelranchokevin@yahoo.com; ❹) comprises compact, clean functional rooms with the standard amenities set round a grassy area. Filling *comida criolla* is served at the restaurant. In town, *Refresquería Yonell* on the main plaza serves simple dishes for under $2, with a view across the park thrown in, while close to the fairgrounds on the main road, *Zapatos los Cuates* (Tues–Sun 3pm–midnight), a gringo-run Mexican joint, has opened up under a breezy rancho, selling tacos, burritos and the like for under $5. On the corner of Avenida 10 de Diciembre there is a **bank** with an **ATM**.

Guararé

The somnolent town of **GUARARÉ**, 6km north of La Tablas, springs to life once a year, as enthusiastic crowds arrive in droves to enjoy the nation's largest and best folk festival, named the **Festival de la Mejorana** (W www.festivalnacionaldela mejorana.com) after Panama's five-stringed guitar, the *mejoranera*. The five-day jamboree, which coincides with the *patronales* for the Virgen de la Mercedes on September 24, is for lovers of Hispanic traditions; there's not a techno-beat in earshot, and although the booze flows as at most Panamanian festivals, it's a less hedonistic affair than many. The plaza resounds with folk music day and night, and dancers and musicians from around the country converge on the otherwise empty main square to entertain and compete. Adults and children vie for medals in violin, accordion, or *mejoranera* playing, and drumming, singing or dancing. Even traditional work clothes are judged, during which competitors pretend to

---

La Reina del Festival de la Mejorana

It's hard to grasp the appeal of being the **Festival de la Mejorana queen** – spending hours on stage, weighed down by a heavy crown and smiling through interminable drum and accordion solos – until you recognize the social prestige of the position, a national honour that lasts beyond the queen's year-long reign. What's more, families are prepared to shell out $15,000 for the privilege, and that's just for starters. Should there be more than one candidate at the October deadline, a run-off is held over three rounds (*escrutinios*) lasting several months, during which the candidates' families have to outdo each other in fundraising – a prospect that has the organizing committee rubbing its hands in glee since it means more cash for the festival coffers. The belle with the most financial backing at the end gets to wear the crown; her rivals have to settle with being princesses. The highest sum paid so far to secure festival glory is $70,000, some of which the queen gets to spend on her regalia – no cheap matter given that the elaborately embroidered *polleras de gala* cost several thousand dollars – and on other necessities such as dancing lessons and float decoration.

carry out everyday tasks: grinding corn, carrying water or attending mass. Bullfights are also on the agenda, usually dominated by seco-sodden guys staggering around a muddy field waving a filthy rag at a tired bull, cheered on by supporters – a far cry from the celebrity matadors of Spain. The festival highlight on Sunday morning is the **Gran Desfile de Carretas**, when superbly decorated ox-carts parade through the town, accompanied by *tunas* (African-inspired bands of call-and-response singers and drummers). Inevitably all eyes are on the float carrying the **Reina del Festival de la Mejorana**, decked out in her *pollera de gala* finery, topped by a gold crown (see box opposite).

The festival, first held in 1949, was the brainchild of a local chemistry teacher, Manuel Zárate, whose nostalgia for Panama while studying abroad made him realize the need to promote and preserve the country's cultural traditions. The **Casa Museo Manuel Fernando Zárate** (Tues–Sat 8am–4pm; $1), located in his former home five blocks downhill from the church, chronicles Zárate's life and the festival's history. Walls are plastered with photos, including portraits of previous *reinas*, some antique *polleras* and menacing devil costumes.

Aside from the festival, Guararé's other claim to fame is as the birthplace of Panama's greatest sporting legend and one of the all-time greats of world boxing, **Roberto Durán**, better known as Manos de Piedra ("Hands of Stone").

Any of the numerous Chitré–Las Tablas **buses** can drop you off on the Carretera Nacional at Guararé, whose northern entrance is conveniently marked with a large billboard of a *mejoranera*. There are two places to stay, both on the main road – the very basic *Hospedaje Eida* (℡6447 0601; $18.50) and the much better equipped *Hotel La Mejorana* (℡994 5794; $22), though it's near impossible to get a room here during the festival.

Las Tablas and around

Famed for hosting Panama's wildest Bacchanal during *Carnaval*, at any other time of year **LAS TABLAS** moves at a much more sedate pace. In comparison with neighbouring Chitré, the provincial capital of Las Tablas is a modest town, though it possesses a sprinkling of the necessary amenities to satisfy a passing tourist, as well as an attractive **church** and a small **museum**, dedicated to Belisario Porras, three-time president and Las Tablas's most famous citizen. Spanish nobles apparently founded the town in 1671; having fled Panamá Viejo after its sacking by pirate Henry Morgan, they were swept by fierce winds onto the shores of the Azuero. Here – so the story goes – among a pile of stones and bathed in light, an image of the **Virgen de Santa Librada** appeared before them as a statue, which they interpreted as a sign that their new settlement should be established on that very spot. Santa Librada, unsurprisingly, was adopted as the patron saint. The name Las Tablas is thought to have derived from the planks (*tablas*) salvaged from the ships and used to construct the initial houses.

Arrival and information

Transport from Panama City (hourly, 6am–7pm; 4hr; $8) pulls in at the **main bus terminal**, from where it's an easy walk four blocks down Avenida 8 de Noviembre to the main square. The departure and arrival point for regular buses to and from Chitré (every 10–15min, 6am–9pm; 45min; $1.25) and Pedasí (every 15 min, 6.30am–7.30pm; 40min; $1) and sporadic transport to and from Tonosí ($3.50) and Cañas ($3.50) is located outside Supercentro Praga on Avenida Belisario Porras, a few blocks from the plaza. **Banks**, **pharmacies**, an **internet café** and **public phones** are clustered round the square while the **post office** lies four blocks north on Calle Francisco González.

La Villa de Los Santos (37km) & Chitré (41km)

LAS TABLAS

0   500 m

ACCOMMODATION
Hospedaje Martha	**B**
Hotel Don Jesús	**A**
Hotel Piamonte	**C & D**
Hotel Sol del Pacifico	**E**

EATING & DRINKING
Billar Cincuentenario	**3**
Jair Sports Bar	**2**
Panadería y Refresquería Pan Caliente	**6**
Restaurante El Caserón	**4**
Restaurante Los Portales	**5**
TripWay Disco	**1**

VIA CIRCUNVALACIÓN

Bus Terminal

Police

CALLE SANTA LIBRADA

CALLE EMILIO CASTRO

VÍA CIRCUNVALACIÓN

AV CARLOS LÓPEZ

CALLE FRANCISCO GONZÁLEZ

AVENIDA 8 DE NOVIEMBRE

CALLE LOS SANTOS

CALLE 12 DE OCTUBRE

CALLE DEL ESTUDIANTE

CALLE RAMÓN MORA

AVENIDA ROGELIO GAEZ

Estadio Olmedo Solé

Stadium

Cemetery

Iglesia Santa Librada

Laundry

Escuela Presidente Porras

CALLE MOISÉS ESPINO

Museo Belisario Porras

AVENIDA BOLÍVAR

Buses to Chitré & Pedasí

CALLE AGUSTÍN BATISTA

CALLE 3 DE NOVIEMBRE

N

ANAM (400m), Pedasí (40km) & Playa Venao (70km)

Accommodation

For a provincial capital, Las Tablas has a small spread of **accommodation**, but during Carnaval, residents rent out rooms to cover any shortfall.

Hospedaje Martha C Moisés Espino ☎ 994 1012. Ideal for budget travellers, offering small, clean a/c en-suite doubles plus cheaper options with fan and shared bathroom. ②

Hotel Don Jesús C Ramón Mora, four blocks north of plaza ☎ 994 6593, ✉ hoteldonjesus @gmail.com. The town's nicest lodgings in a converted family home with well-appointed rooms and good service. Guests share a comfortably furnished lounge-balcony area for breakfast and chilling out. A pond-size pool and wi-fi are welcome extras and there's a restaurant. ④

Hotel Piamonte Av Belisario Porras ☎ 994 6372. This hotel has taken over the *Residencial Mariela* and *Hotel Manolo* across the road, offering cheaper accommodation on one side and slightly pricier rooms with frillier bedspreads across the road, though the rooms overlooking the street on the cheaper side are the nicest. ④

Hotel Sol del Pacifico C Agustín Cano Castillero ☎ 994 1280. This fairly central three-storey modern block offers the best value for money in town, with clean, comfortable rooms – though it's worth checking out several – and decent hot-water showers. ④

The Town

Most business in Las Tablas is conducted along the two main streets, Avenida 8 de Noviembre (also Av Carlos López) and Avenida Belisario Porras, which converge in the leafy **main plaza** – the vortex of the maelstrom that is Carnaval but at any other time a tranquil shady spot to enjoy a snow-cone or ice cream. The **Iglesia de Santa Librada**, whose roof has suffered serious damage from errant fireworks during the festivities, overlooks Parque Belisario Porras with a figurine of the patron saint set at the facade's apex. The magnificent golden altar, which suffers from an overdose of pale-faced cherubs, illuminates the otherwise pedestrian interior though look out for the reliquary said to contain a segment of the saint's leg. Although originally built in 1789, a lot of the church structure visible today dates from the late 1950s, having suffered an earthquake in 1802 and a major fire in 1958. Diagonally across the square the neat red-tiled **Museo Belisario Porras** (Mon–Sat 8am–4pm; 50c) celebrates the life of Panama's most illustrious president in the house of his birth. Ironically its most striking exhibit is the Napoleonic-size tomb intended to house Porras' remains, which lies empty as family members wrangle over whether the bones should be moved from the prestigious Cementerio Amador in Panama City, where they are currently interred. Walls in the single display room are plastered with faded photos, certificates and memorabilia. These only partly succeed in conveying (in Spanish) the extent of his many achievements (see p.336). On one famous occasion the statesman's bust, which stands outside the museum, was stolen and discarded in a latrine. On hearing the news, Porras wryly remarked: "*Mis enemigos, no pudiendo llegar hasta mí, mi han hecho descender hasta ellos*" ("Since my enemies cannot reach me, they have dragged me down to their level"). **El Pausílipo**

Carnaval and the Festival de Santa Librada

For many people Las Tablas is synonymous with **Carnaval**, the nation's wildest party, which sees an estimated eighty thousand people squeeze into the narrow streets and central plaza for the five-day Bacchanal. Though scaffolding is erected and people cram every window and balcony ledge, it is still a crush, so it's not for the claustrophobic or faint-hearted. The festivities revolve around a five-day Montagues-versus-Capulets-style feud renewed every year that divides the town down the middle in their loyal support for either **Calle Arriba** (Ⓦwww.carnavalescallearriba.com) or **Calle Abajo** (Ⓦwww.calle abajolastablas.com), during which swords are substituted for water pistols and the Calles shell out $500,000 each year to compete for the best music, supporters, fireworks, costumes, floats and queen. The proceedings start on the Friday night in a blaze of fireworks with the coronation of the new queens, followed by dancing until dawn in a swirl of seco and sweat. Mornings kick-start around 10am with *culecos* or *mojaderos*, which essentially entail being doused by hosepipes from large water tankers as you dance in the street. The queens parade around the square enthroned on gigantic themed floats followed by percussion and brass *murga* bands, who work themselves up into a frenzy to inspire the *tunas* – the all-singing all-dancing support groups – to pump up the volume and outdo the opponents with insulting lyrics. The glam factor is ratcheted up a few notches at night, both on the streets and on the even more extravagant and glitzy floats, and general hedonism takes off until people flake out, often in cars or in the park, before starting all over again the next day. The good times are formally ended when a sardine is symbolically buried in the sand at dawn on Ash Wednesday to mark the start of Lent.

Commemorated annually from July 19 to 22 is the **Festival de Santa Librada**. Though there is no shortage of boozing and carousing, the event is less frenetic and a shade less hedonistic than Carnaval, though with all the usual attractions of traditional costumes, dancing and music, street food, bullfighting, fireworks and, of course, the religious devotions. They start on July 19 as the pilgrims file into town, bearing an effigy of the saint, who is dripping in gold jewellery given by devotees, but for tourists July 22 is the day to aim for since it incorporates the **Festival de la Pollera**, offering a chance to see streams of women decked out in Panama's glorious national dress sashaying through the streets.

(Tues–Sat 8am–5pm; $1), Porras' simple country house, which lies a few kilometres out of town, has also been turned into a museum, though there is little to see.

The only other building of note in town, and possibly the most enduring product of the Porras presidency in Las Tablas, is the **Escuela Presidente Porras**, with a smart maroon-and-cream exterior, and a distinctive clock tower and majestic portal. Built in 1924, this immaculately kept state school possesses high ceilings, large windows and beautiful louvered shutters.

Eating and drinking

It's perhaps in response to all the festival boozing for which Las Tablas is famous that the town's two best-known **restaurants** do not sell alcohol, though there are plenty of places that do. Evenings midweek are quiet unless there's a baseball match on at the Estadio Olmedo Solé (Jan–May; ⓦ www.fedebeis.com) – a highly entertaining party atmosphere to be savoured even if you don't know a home plate from a dinner plate.

Billar Cincuentenario Av 8 de Diciembre on Plaza Belisario Porras. With great views over the plaza from its first-floor balcony, this unpromising-sounding joint is a relaxing place to enjoy a chilled beer, with a video jukebox as well as pool tables for entertainment. Daily 10am until late.

Jair Sports Bar C Emilio Castro, along from the baseball stadium. A popular weekend hang-out with disco, serving up American-style snacks – buffalo wings, nuggets, burgers – to help soak up the seco. Thurs–Sat.

Panadería y Refresquería Pan Caliente Av Belisario Porras on Plaza Belisario Porras. Just the place to nip in for a pastry and a shot of coffee. Daily 6am–10pm.

Restaurante El Caserón C Moisés Espino and C Agustín Batista. Top billing goes to this congenial open-sided joint with outdoor terrace. It serves up plenty of moderately priced seafood and *parrilladas* (mains $5–9) and you can bring a beer to have with the meal. Daily 7am–11pm.

Restaurante Los Portales Av Belisario Porras at C Los Santos. Offering inexpensive dishes – a range of rice combinations with chicken, pork or beef, as well as seafood regulars (most $5–8) washed down with fresh fruit juices (no alcohol) – this charming crumbling colonial house overlooks the action on the main street. It also serves a mean Panamanian fry-up breakfast. Mon–Sat 7am–9pm, Sun 7am–3pm.

TripWay Disco C Ramón Mora near Av 8 de Diciembre. The town's only nightclub blasts out a mix of reggae, salsa and reggaeton. Fri & Sat, and occasionally Thurs; $1–3.

Playa El Uverito and Puerto Mensabé

Playa El Uverito, 10km from Las Tablas, is a favourite beach of Tableños for weekend partying and picnicking, though if you come midweek, you can have a scenic stretch of chocolate sand (ignoring the piles of rubbish on the way down to the beach) all to yourself. Two lovely guesthouses, just back from the beach, are ideal getaways for a couple of nights' quiet self-indulgence with the possibility of water-based activities if you want. *B&B Posada del Mar* (ⓣ 394 2049, ⓦ www.posadamar .com; $66) has five well-appointed en-suite rooms (a/c, fan, TV and wi-fi) and a spacious patio balcony overlooking the beach. Even nicer, a few hundred metres further south along the dirt road facing the sea, lies the artistically designed *Hotel La Luna* (ⓣ 6525 9410, ⓦ www.hotel-laluna.com; $67), complete with lovely pool, vast tiled rooms, minimalist decor, floor-to-ceiling glass windows and sofas on the balcony to sink into and watch the waves (make sure you get an upstairs room). *El Rincón del Faro* (ⓣ 994 8264; Tues–Sun noon–10pm), right above the beach, offers good views and excellent seafood (mains from $8). A day pass ($24) includes two meals and snacks, use of the small pool and beach showers. *Restaurante Vista del Mar* (from noon; closed Wed), a stone's throw from the *Posada del Mar*, serves simpler seafood, as well as *comida corriente* (under $2). A bus service is on the cards but in the meantime grab a **taxi** from Las Tablas ($6). Another kilometre further south, at the river mouth, **Puerto Mensabé** also has a pleasant **beach** and excellent casual **restaurant**; the fish could hardly be fresher since it's right next to where the fishermen land and fillet their catch.

The southern coast

At the flat southeastern tip of the peninsula, the tiny, quaint colonial town **Pedasí**, 40km down from Las Tablas, is becoming the centre of an unlikely development boom, attracting tourists and luxury real estate developers in equal measure though as yet, its character remains relatively intact. The nearby wildlife refuges of **Isla Iguana** and **Isla de Cañas** draw wildlife enthusiasts while the waves that batter the headland and southern coastline act as magnets for surfers. As the main road turns southwest, beyond Pedasí, skirting the golden arc of Playa Venao and mangrove-lined bay encircling Isla de Cañas, the farmland becomes hillier and more rugged, eventually arriving in **Tonosí**, the Peninsula's last main town, nestled in a valley. Heading south from there, the road deteriorates before petering out at the remote coastal community of **Cambutal**, halfway along the coast. To the west, the Azuero's western massif looms, containing its highest peaks, which top 1500m and crown the little explored **Parque Nacional Cerro Hoya**. With a dearth of public transport connections and poor roads, this corner of the peninsula sees few visitors.

Pedasí and around

Near the southeastern corner of the peninsula lies the small fishing town of **PEDASÍ**. It was catapulted into the national consciousness a few years ago when it became known as the birthplace of Panama's first female president, Mireya Moscoso (see p.339), a fact that immediately hits you on arrival: a vast billboard shows a photo of the woman herself, complete with presidential sash, with a bronze bust in the main square a further reminder, if you needed one. There's nothing to really see or do in Pedasí, once you've glanced around the plaza, but it is a tranquil place to hang out, and it has an amazingly wide range of lodgings and restaurants given its size, which make it an excellent base for trips to Isla Iguana and Isla de Cañas, as well as being within easy reach of a string of great surfing beaches. Pedasí is clearly heading to be a major centre for tourist

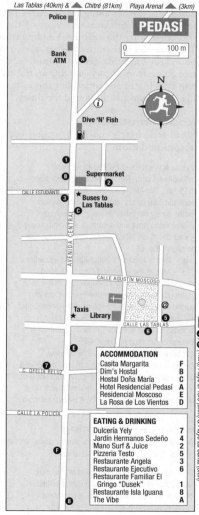

Las Tablas (40km) & ▲ Chitré (81km) Playa Arenal ▲ (3km)

PEDASÍ

Police

Bank
ATM Ⓐ

0   100 m

N

ⓘ

Dive 'N' Fish

❶
Ⓑ   Supermarket
           ❷
CALLE ESTUDIANTE
❸ ★ Buses to
Ⓒ   Las Tablas

AVENIDA CENTRAL

CALLE AGUSTÍN MOSCOSO

Taxis   @
★ Library   ❺
           CALLE LAS TABLAS
Ⓔ   ❻

❼
C. OFELIA RELUZ

CALLE LA POLICÍA

Ⓕ

❽

▶ ④ Ⓓ (1km), Playa El Toro (3km) & Playa La Garita (3km)

ACCOMMODATION
Casita Margarita	F
Dim's Hostal	B
Hostal Doña María	C
Hotel Residencial Pedasí	A
Residencial Moscoso	E
La Rosa de Los Vientos	D

EATING & DRINKING
Dulcería Yely	7
Jardín Hermanos Sedeño	4
Mano Surf & Juice	2
Pizzeria Testo	5
Restaurante Angela	3
Restaurante Ejecutivo	6
Restaurante Familiar El Gringo "Dusek"	1
Restaurante Isla Iguana	8
The Vibe	A

development on the Azuero, due in no small part to the impetus given by the village's most famous daughter.

Arrival and information

Almost any service you need – money, food, accommodation, transport, tours – is available along the 800m of Avenida Central (effectively the Carretera Nacional), where the frequent buses from Las Tablas deposit passengers. Note that the bank's **ATM** is the last on the peninsula so if you're heading towards Playa Venao or Cambutal you'll need to get enough cash here. The recent Azuero tourism boom has also earned Pedasí two **flights** a week from Panama City, in a small twelve-seater plane operated by Aeroperlas (Mon & Fri 12.30pm, returning at 1.40pm; 55min; $80 one way). It has also prompted a new **tourist office**, which lies further along by the Accel petrol station, but don't hold your breath for any useful information. Most of the restaurants and all of the lodgings are sprinkled along the next few hundred metres as well as a couple of supermarkets. The **internet** café sits on the plaza, two blocks east of the main drag. Minibuses bound for Las Tablas (every 15 min, 6.30am–7.30pm; 40min; $1) wait under the tree across from *Restaurante Angela*; the elusive buses bound for Cañas and Tonosí also stop by the restaurant but there are only a couple a day and timetables shift like quicksand so ask around for times.

Accommodation

Small-scale hotels and B&Bs strung out along the high street comprise Pedasí's **accommodation**.

Casita Margarita ☏ 995 2898, Ⓦ www .pedasihotel.com. The nicest but priciest place in Pedasí, this American-owned five-room boutique B&B offers spotless well-appointed rooms nicely furnished in wood, with elegant shared living area and hammock-strung balcony. A vast buffet breakfast is included and trips can be organized. ❼

Dim's Hostal ☏ 995 2303. The attraction here is the wonderful hammock-filled *rancho* beneath two vast mango trees at the back of the glorified eight-room tree-house. Cosy and quirky, the rustic en-suite rooms nevertheless offer a/c, cable TV, hot water and wi-fi. Breakfast is included and the welcoming owner can arrange excursions for modest sums. ❺

Hostal Doña María ☏ 995 2916, Ⓦ www .hostaldonamaria.com. Superior though overpriced B&B in a delightful two-storey house containing six bright, nicely furnished en-suite rooms with large windows, fans and a/c, plus TV. A pleasant shared terrace overlooks a garden with hammocks and a BBQ area. Midweek reductions. ❻

Hotel Residencial Pedasi ☏ 995 2490, Ⓦ www .residencialpedasi.com/espanol.mht. The twenty rooms are nondescript but are clean and tidy with a/c, good beds and decent hot showers, which together with the garden setting and free wi-fi make it good value. ❸

Residencial Moscoso ☏ 995 2203. Ironically, given that it shares the name of the ex-president, it's the cheapest budget option in town, with very small rooms with reasonable beds and a choice of fan, a/c, TV and shared or private bathroom. ❶–❸

La Rosa de los Vientos On the road to Playa El Toro ☏ 677 80627, Ⓦ www .bedandbreakfastpedasi.com. Delightful, colonial-style architecture set in tropical grounds 1km outside Pedasí and within walking distance of the beach. Three crisp, bright rooms open out onto a shared porch. ❺

Eating and drinking

A clutch of **restaurants** and **cafés** are sprinkled along the main drag and in the plaza, most of which close early.

Dulcería Yely C Ofelia Reluz, just off the main road. Dalila Vera's bakery is a national institution that has served delicious home-made cakes to locals, Hollywood film stars and presidents. Specialities include *queques* (coconut cakes made with local sugarcane honey and a touch of aniseed) and *flan casero*, to take out or enjoy there with a cup of *chicha* or *chicheme*. Daily 7am–9pm.

Jardín Hermanos Sedeño C Las Tablas, four blocks down from the plaza. Occasionally active *cantina* at weekends or during fiestas.

Mano Surf & Juice C Estudiante ⓦwww .manosurf.com. A surf shop with a pleasant outdoor café serving fresh juices and healthy snacks. Daily 9am–6pm.

Pizzeria Testo The plaza. No-nonsense place serving filling sandwiches, tacos and pizzas (and some less enticing sweet goodies) to eat in or take out. Daily 8am–10pm.

🏃 Restaurante Angela Av Central. Popular spot with locals, serving a well-prepared traditional breakfast or lunchtime *menu del día* ($2) on nicely maintained patio tables. Mains all under $5. Daily 7am–8.30pm.

Restaurante Ejecutivo C Las Tablas on the plaza. Solid Panamanian dining option with non-stop TV, inexpensive heaped platefuls of rice and noodles in various guises, plus seafood and meat options ($4.50–9). A good variety of traditional fried breakfasts are on the menu for $2.50. Daily 8am–11pm.

🏃 Restaurante Familiar El Gringo "Dusek" Av Central. This restaurant with a pleasant outside terrace (TV aside) offers *comida criolla*, mariscos and a variety of salads. Additional attractions include fresh vegetable accompaniments, wine by the glass and great desserts. Thurs–Tues noon–10pm.

Restaurante Isla Iguana Av Central. The place to go for a special meal (though it's not overly gourmet) with a reputation for savoury seafood. Thurs–Tues 11am–10pm.

The Vibe At the back of *Hotel Residencial Pedasí*. Mellow, comfy place to have a drink. Tues–Sat 5–10pm.

Activities

There's plenty to do around Pedasí, depending on the time of year. Dive 'N' Fish (ⓣ 995 2894, ⓦ www.divenfishpanama.com; Mon–Fri 7am–5pm), the town's sole tour operator and only PADI-qualified outfit on the Azuero, organizes **scuba diving** either around Islas Frailes ($100) or Isla Iguana ($85), where **snorkelling** ($45) is also an option, along with **horse riding** ($65), **kayaking** ($65) and **sport fishing** ($450/day, maximum of 6 people). **Turtle watching** on Isla de Cañas ($65) is a night trip, leaving at 10pm. Located by the petrol station, the company also operates out of *Pedasí Sports Club*, located at the entrance to the town, where it offers discounts. Most activities need a minimum of two people. *Casita Margarita*, *Dim's Hostal* and *Hostal Doña María* also offer outings to their guests at varying rates – the most common excursion being to Isla Iguana (see below) – while most lodgings will provide you with the name of a reliable guide, boatman or taxi driver if you prefer to arrange something yourself. Recommended (Spanish-speaking) local independent naturalist guides include Edison Cedeño (ⓣ 6660 9709), Mario Espino (ⓣ 6681 7046) and Victor Vera (ⓣ 6505 4357, ⓔ victorvera56@gmail.com). Pedasí also provides a sound base for a day's **surfing** at the beach; the town's new surf shop, Mano Surf & Juice (ⓦ www.manosurf .com), organizes **excursions**, and does **board** and **bike rental**.

Refugio de Vida Silvestre Isla Iguana

Undoubtedly the best day-trip to make from Pedasí is to **Isla Iguana**, a tiny lump of basalt 4km offshore, which forms the centrepiece of the **REFUGIO DE VIDA SILVESTRE ISLA IGUANA** (ⓦ www.islaiguana.com). The reserve was created in 1981 to protect one of the largest and oldest coral reefs in the Golfo de Panamá, home to over two hundred species of colourful fish though the coral is not in great condition, thanks in part to the US military; in the 1990s a large chunk of the reef was blown off when two large bombs – relics of US training during World War II – had to be detonated. Though covered mainly in dry scrub and grass, a grove of tall coconut palms and a sprinkling of other fruit trees hark back to the 1960s when Isla Iguana was last inhabited. The rugged coastline of guano and cactus-covered basalt is interrupted by two coral-sand beaches: the larger **Playa El Cirial**, where all boats pull up, accommodates the **park office** and a modest visitor's centre; and a 200m **path** across the island through iguana-favoured scrub takes you to **Playita del Faro**, a small patch of sand squeezed between rocks and named after the nearby lighthouse. Strong offshore currents mean swimming and snorkelling are sometimes prohibited here, but at low tide rock pools offer plenty to explore. The basalt outcrop to the left as you reach the beach provides a vantage point for one of the island's main attractions: Panama's largest colony of **magnificent frigatebirds**, estimated to be around five thousand. January to April offer the best chance of seeing males puffing out their extraordinary inflatable scarlet pouches, yet nesting goes on all year. Other birdlife to look out for includes the resident osprey, oyster catchers and the island's distinctive variant yellow warbler. Rustling in the scrub, green and black versions of Isla Iguana's namesake can be glimpsed while seven species of crab, of all colours and shapes, take over the rocks and sand when visitors are scarce. Playa El Cirial's small crescent of silky sand backs a sheltered cove of translucent water barely covering coral formations inhabited by a rainbow of reef fish, making it a superb spot for **swimming** and **snorkelling**; further out you may encounter turtles (though they don't nest on the island) and reef sharks. In the migratory season (June–Dec, but especially Sept and Oct) **humpback whales** are visible, sometimes in the company of **dolphins**. The area's rich marine life makes it popular with **scuba divers** (see p.201).

Practicalities

Avoid travelling to Isla Iguana during major holiday periods if you want any chance of enjoying the natural beauty and tranquillity the place has to offer. Despite repeated attempts by ANAM to control the number of visitors, fishermen desperate for extra income continue to bring boatloads of tourists, which can total six hundred in a day at peak times, inevitably putting huge pressures on the island's natural resources. Dive 'N' Fish arranges **snorkelling** ($45) and **diving** trips ($85 for two tanks) to the island and most hotels can, at the very least, provide contact details of a fisherman with a boat at **Playa Arenal** and a **taxi** driver to get there ($2 one way) since there are no buses. Arrange a pick-up time with the taxi since the public phone on the beach is often broken. An average price is $60 for a small boat for a half-day trip; the crossing can take upwards of forty minutes depending on conditions. Despite greater visitor numbers in the dry summer months, Isla Iguana is a far better destination between May and December as the calmer conditions make for a smoother crossing and more rewarding snorkelling; the sea can be so rough between January and March that it's sometimes too dangerous to set out. Park **fees** ($10 admission and $10 to camp) are payable on the island. There is no bunkhouse but rudimentary **camping** facilities exist in the form of a latrine and a rancho to pitch the tent under. Electricity is lacking, and you'll need to bring water as well as food and a camping stove with you.

The surfing beaches

The southeastern tip of the Azuero Peninsula offers desolate beauty: kilometres of smooth dark sands punctuated by rocky outcrops and pounded by surf, with a few (foreign-owned) intimate lodgings spaced along the coast, ranging from an informal surf camp to one of the top boutique hotels in the country. Although not as renowned as Santa Catalina, the beaches around the southeastern tip of the Azuero Peninsula, all within striking distance of Pedasí, offer excellent surfing, with some waves reaching four metres. Though the most consistent waves are encountered between March and November, the coastline is surfable all year round.

Around Pedasí

Playa El Toro and **Playa La Garita** are a walkable 3km or two-dollar taxi ride away from Pedasí; follow the road out of the main square until the fork, heading left to El Toro and right to La Garita. Three kilometres south of Pedasí at the village of El Limón, a road leads off 7km ($5 from Pedasí by taxi) to the band of chocolate sand and rocks at **Playa de los Destiladeros** (bear right at the fork), which offers good surfing as well as fabulous views across the ocean. Two lovely French-owned hotels are located here. The exclusive, rather formal *Villa Camilla* (☎232 0171, Ⓦwww.villacamillahotel.com; ⑨), perched on the hilltop, its terracotta exterior visible from the road, also houses a pricey gourmet restaurant open to non-guests for dinner. From *Villa Camilla*, it's a ten-minute walk to the beach, where the secluded *Posada de los Destiladeros* (☎995 2771, Ⓦwww.panamabambu.net; ⑥ cash only, including breakfast) offers better value for money with its nine rustic bungalows set in tropical grounds. Sundecks overlooking the beach, a pool and comfortable communal areas ensure total relaxation. Both places can arrange horse riding, snorkelling, fishing trips and island excursions.

Playa Venao and around

Moving around the peninsula, 35km from Pedasí, the road crosses the Río Oria and heads towards the coast. At the small fishing village of El Ciruelo, a few kilometres before Playa Venao, are a couple of small B&Bs where you can laze in a hammock doing very little, canter along the sands or head out on a fishing trip. A little further along the road lies **Laboratorio Achiotines**, an international research station for the threatened yellowfin tuna. It overlooks the protected **Bahía de Achiotines**, whose mainland coral reef – one of the very few on the Pacific coast of Central America – attracts 150 odd species of fish, making it a pleasant spot to don mask and snorkel. A couple of kilometres further west, a dirt road heads down to the quirky *La Playita* resort (Ⓦwww.playitaresort.com). Ignore the tacky skeletal *objets d'art* which would not look out of place in a natural history museum, and head for the secluded soft-sand **beach** that provides the most **sheltered swimming** in the area. Midweek and off season, you'll have the place to yourself; at other times it's teeming. Most visitors come for the day ($5); snorkel hire is extra ($6) and you can paddle around in a **rowing boat** ($5/hr) before tucking in to some tasty seafood at the rancho **restaurant**.

Rounding the headland, you come to the imposing 3km swathe of charcoal-coloured sand that is **Playa Venao** (or Venado). The region's best known surfing spot provides waves suitable for beginners and more experienced practitioners alike. A glorious arc, its beauty is now threatened by a massive, controversial residential and hotel development project set to alter the landscape dramatically. A few kilometres out from the bay, the guano-flecked rocky stacks of **Islas Frailes** are at times covered in thousands of nesting sooty terns and other passing sea birds though you'll need a good pair of binoculars to get a decent view from the boat since landing is impossible.

Accommodation

A handful of pleasing **lodgings** exist in the vicinity of Playa Venao, where you can arrange horse riding and boats for fishing or visiting Isla de Cañas, Isla Iguana or Islas Frailes.

Casa de Estrella El Ciruelo ☎6471 3090, Ⓦwww .casadeestrella.com. Laidback and modestly furnished, with a great shared balcony overlooking the sea, TV/DVD, dining room and kitchen. There's also a gas barbecue grill to cook up your catch. ⑤

Eco Venao Playa Venao ☎ 832 0530, Ⓦwww.ecovenao.com. Superb hilltop overlooking the bay, 1km beyond the main beach. The lovingly restored wooden farmhouse offers

eight bunks and a couple of simple private rooms with shared kitchen and bathrooms. Also, moderately priced cane-and-thatch *cabañas* and two stone bungalows are spread across the grounds. Campers ($5.50) share the lodge facilities, including the numerous hammocks and a volleyball court. Boat trips can be arranged, or you can explore the bay on horseback or in a kayak. Dorm $11, double ③.

Sereia do Mar El Ciruelo ☎ 6523 8758, ⓦ www.sereiadomar.net. Smart, tranquil retreat (rooms with a/c, TV, DVD and fridge) with a lovely long balcony overlooking the sea and a hammock-strewn rancho. The $5 kitchen charge, though, is a cheek. Surf lessons are also on offer. ⑥

Villa Marina Playa Venao ☎ 263 6555, ⓦ www.villamarinapanama.com. Tucked away at the east end of the beach, this spacious hacienda-style boutique hotel is set in lush grounds surrounded by tropical forest with a stone infinity pool overlooking the beach. Tastefully designed with all mod cons (a/c, cable TV and wi-fi). ⑧

Tonosí, Cambutal and Guánico Abajo

For most people Playa Venao is remote enough, though die-hard surfers may want to try the even more out-of-the-way spots around **Cambutal**, a small fishing village another 60km through undulating cattle country – spectacularly lush in the rainy season, desperately barren once the moisture has been sucked out of it – down a deteriorating road. Here the picturesque, charcoal Playa Cambutal and some of the surfing beaches further west get serious three-metre waves while non-surfers can explore the caves, blowholes and crevices of this impressively rugged coastline. The new colonial-style *Hotel Playa Cambutal* (☎ 832 0948, ⓦ www.hotelplayacambutal.com; ⑧ including breakfast), on the beach, offers spacious ocean-view rooms. Fishing charters, kayaking, horse riding and hiking excursions can all be arranged. At the other end of the price range, the breezy hilltop hostel of Kambutaleko (☎ 6627 2389, ⓦ www.hotelkambutaleko.blogspot.com; ④), above the village, offers half a dozen simple fan-ventilated doubles with private bathroom – more for a suite with fridge – and shared ocean-view terrace. An open rancho kitchen is on the cards and there are a couple of cheap local restaurants in the village.

Fifteen kilometres east, around Punto Morro, is the less publicized **Guánico Abajo**. There are some basic *cabañas*, good surf, mangroves to explore and the nearby **Playa Marinera**, cream-coloured sands hemmed in by cliffs, where over thirty thousand olive ridley turtles lay their eggs each year.

In the dry season a high clearance saloon car can just make it down to Cambutal and Guánico Abajo, but once the rains start a 4WD is a must, and even then, locals often find themselves towing city surfers out of the mud. To reach both places you first have to pass through Tonosí, a glorified regional crossroads surrounded by hilly cattle ranches but which has all the basic amenities around the main square: a **bank** (though no ATM), a couple of **pharmacies**, a **post office**, **hospital** and a **supermarket**. If you're heading for Isla de Cañas or Parque Nacional Cerro Hoya, you'll need to drop in at the **ANAM** office (☎ 995 8180) though for the former you can contact the island directly (see below).

All transport leaves from the plaza: a sprinkling of **buses** run via Macaracas to Las Tablas (1hr 30min; $3.50) while a handful of *chivas* serve Cambutal, Guánico Abajo and surrounding villages. If you miss your beach-bound transport, don't worry as Tonosí possesses a couple of reasonable places to crash for the night: *Residencial Mar y Selva* (☎ 995 8003; $20), approaching town along the Pedasí–Las Tablas road, has ten clean, modern en-suite rooms (a/c and hot water) and a restaurant, which serves plates of *comida típica* for under $4. The owner, Bolívar Domínguez, is a good source of information on the national park and a potential guide. Heading south out of town, *Pensión Boamy* (☎ 995 8142; $20) offers similar accommodation and also has a restaurant, though the best place to eat, beneath a rancho 1km further out, is *El Charcón*, which specializes in succulent grilled meat.

Refugio de Vida Silvestre Isla de Cañas

In the next bay beyond Playa Venao, nestled among the mangroves and a stone's throw from the swampy shoreline, lies the long sliver of land that is **ISLA DE CAÑAS**, a place synonymous with **turtles**, which arrive annually in their thousands, availing themselves of a glorious 14km band of sand to lay their eggs. Five species of turtle nest on the island, the most numerous being the world's tiniest sea turtle, the olive ridley. Their extraordinary mass nesting, or *arribada* (arrival), when thousands storm the beach over several nights, is a sight to behold. Pacific green turtles also nest in large quantities alongside significantly smaller numbers of loggerhead, leatherback and hawksbill. Nesting primarily takes place between May and November, with September to November considered the peak months, though timing your visit to coincide with an *arribada* – generally several days either side of a full moon – is tricky. The island was designated a protected area in 1994 and many of the eight hundred-strong population are involved in a cooperative protecting the turtles – for which they are permitted to harvest a percentage of the eggs for consumption and sale. Villagers also act as turtle-watching guides ($10), an offer worth taking up if only to increase the likelihood of more eggs hatching rather than being sold on the black market. Since female turtles are easily spooked by bright lights, it's better not to bring cameras, or torches, unless infra-red; rely on the guide and let your eyes adjust to the light (see p.266).

Turtles are not the only attraction since the reserve extends into a swampy tangle of mangroves both on the island's shore-side and along the mainland, providing roosting and nesting sites for water birds, which can be seen close-up on a round-the-island **boat tour** ($200 for up to 7, bring own food), or even on the shorter excursion ($40 for up to 6), which also takes in a pre-Columbian archaeological site (with little to see) and a strangely formed cave dubbed the "*casa de piedra*". A couple of hours gentle **fishing** will set you back $20 (for up to four) as will a ride in a horse and cart (for up to 6) around the island's beaches and cultivations – rice, maize, banana and cocoa are all grown alongside vast quantities of juicy water-melons, which should be sampled while you are there.

Practicalities

It can be difficult to reach Isla de Cañas by public transport since there are only two buses a day from Las Tablas via Pedasí (8am, 4pm; 45min; $2.25). Jump off at the eminently missable turn-off to the dock, 6km west of Cañas village, from where it's a 4km hike down a dirt road (4WD necessary in the rainy season) unless a few extra dollars can persuade the bus driver to go down to the dock. Alternatively take a taxi from Pedasí ($20), or bus it to Cañas village and take a **taxi** to the jetty ($2), where there may be a boat waiting. If not, bang the makeshift "gong" hanging nearby to alert someone on the island (it's very close), who will send some transport over ($1). If the tide is out, expect to get very muddy (dress accordingly) as you will have to wade through the sludge to meet the boat. Though the turtle action happens after dark, boats only cross to the island during the day (unless you come with an organized tour), which means staying the night. The village cooperative, which jointly manages the turtle project with ANAM, will sort out a guide and accommodation: the cooperative has very rudimentary **cabins** ($10), for which you'll need a mosquito net, or you can pitch a tent ($5). There is also a small inexpensive **restaurant**. Although there is a small **ANAM** outpost on the island, the admission charge ($10) needs to be paid in Las Tablas. For more information or advance booking ring the public phone (T 995 8002) and ask for Pablo Pérez.

Parque Nacional Cerro Hoya

While the Darién is often considered Panama's "final frontier", the country's most inaccessible park is possibly **PARQUE NACIONAL CERRO HOYA**, 325 square kilometres of the Isthmus' most ancient volcanic rocks tucked away in the southwest corner of the Azuero Peninsula. Reaching the area requires an adventurous spirit since formal trails and accommodation are both lacking and transport is tricky. But the rewards are plenty: giant mahogany, cedar, cuipo and ceiba trees soar above carpets of moist forest, containing over thirty species of endemic plants, which rise up from the sea to lofty Cerros Hoya (1559m), Moya (1478m) and Soya (1326m). A few scarlet and great green macaws maintain a fragile foothold in the forests, as does the endemic Azuero parakeet; other critically endangered species include the Azuero spider and howler monkeys while substantial populations of white-tailed deer pick their way through the forest floor, shared with agoutis, collared peccaries and coatis. As the park's name suggests (*hoya* means river bed), the massif nourishes over ten major rivers, home to caimans and otters, and hundreds of streams that tumble down to the coast, leaving natural swimming pools and waterfalls in their wake. The protected area extends out into the sea, including precious mangroves and secluded coves enclosed by sheer cliffs, providing sheltered sands for hawksbill, olive ridley and even some leatherback turtles to lay their eggs.

Created in 1985, in a desperate attempt to stop the Azuero's haemorrhaging of forest though destructive agricultural practices, the national park and its protecting agencies are helping the population of about two thousand – scattered around 25 communities – to make a livelihood from sustainable agroforestry, eco-tourism, animal husbandry and fishing projects. The best time to visit is in dry season when the views are more spectacular, the mud less overwhelming and the hiking more pleasurable, though waterfalls and rivers – two of the major attractions – are inevitably less impressive.

Practicalities

Reaching the park is easier from the west, where a tarred road leaves the Interamericana just east of Santiago, skirting the coast over 100km down to the villages of **Arenas** and **Flores**. Both are served by a handful of buses a day from Santiago bus terminal. Arenas is home to a small ANAM office (no phone) and two knowledgeable guides: Ricuarte Moreno, a former ANAM warden, and Isidro Castro, who knows the area well; both are contactable via the public phone box (T 999 8143). Though there are some trails in the area, to reach the park proper necessitates travelling along a dirt road, and crossing two major rivers for the remaining 18km to Restingue, a coastal hamlet at the park boundary. This is only possible in the dry season; once the rains start, the Río Varadero becomes impassable. If all that sounds like too much hassle, consider exploring the park with Tanager Tourism (T 6715 7471, W www .tanagertourism.com; $25), which organizes ecology-focused activities, particularly birdwatching, in the western Azuero. Based in the village of **Palmilla** (take the Mariato bus from Santiago, hourly, 6am–5pm; 90min; $3), midway down the peninsula's western coast, it offers camping under a raised rancho, with tent and mattresses provided. Rates include breakfast and are less if you have your own tent.

To access Cerro Hoya from the east, take the poor dirt road west from Cambutal, which hugs the coastline for 22km to the clutch of houses comprising the community of **El Cobachón**. Here, Marcelino Rodríguez usually accepts campers at his place while Daniel Saénz comes highly recommended as a guide, and can also arrange horses. Whether on horseback, in a 4WD or on foot (which entails some shortcuts along the beach at low tide, so a tide timetable is a necessity), the road from Cambutal is still only accessible in the dry season since several rivers need to be forded. Alternatively, take a boat from Cambutal or Los Buzos, which will be costly ($80), unless you can cadge a lift with ANAM or catch a *colectivo* heading that way. Whichever side you choose to tackle Cerro Hoya, you will need to see consult with **ANAM**: in Las Tablas (T 994 7313) or Tonosí (T 995 8180) approaching from Los Santos; or in Santiago (T 998 4271) and Arenas (no phone) from the Veraguas side. For any expedition to Cerro Hoya, you will need to be self-sufficient – tent, sleeping bag, food, stove, water bottle (and purification tablets), mosquito net, repellent, sun cream, first-aid kit and torch are all essentials.

5

The Western Highlands and the Golfo de Chiriquí

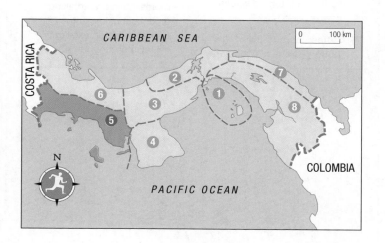

CHAPTER 5 # Highlights

* **Parque Nacional Marino Golfo de Chiriquí** Head out in a boat to explore swathes of mangrove, abundant marine life and idyllic tropical islands. See p.218

* **Santa Catalina** The country's capital of surf boasts first-class waves and a laid-back ambiance. See p.221

* **Parque Nacional de Coiba** Outstanding diving, whale-watching and pristine rainforests are among the attractions of this penitentiary turned wildlife reserve. See p.224

* **Coffee** Learn to tell a "buttery" from a "chocolatey" aroma on some of the world's finest gourmet coffee estates in Boquete. See p.233

* **Birdwatching** Seek out the resplendent quetzal and rare hummingbirds in the eerie cloud forests of the Chiriquí Highlands. See p.234

* **Volcán Barú** On a clear day, sunrise on Panama's highest peak affords a unique, spectacular panorama taking in both oceans. See p.235

* **Whitewater rafting** Dramatic rapids set in breathtaking mountainous make the Río Chiriquí Viejo an exhilarating whitewater run. See p.235

▲ Surfing at Santa Catalina

5

The Western Highlands and the Golfo de Chiriquí

From the raging torrents of the Río Chiriquí Viejo and the verdant peaks of the Cordillera Central to the marine-rich coral, swampy mangroves and empty sands of the Golfo de Chiriquí, **western Panama**'s diverse scenery offers some of Panama's top natural attractions. Magnificent in their own right, they also provide the setting for a range of exhilarating outdoor adventure activities, including whitewater rafting, kayaking, hiking and zip-lining.

Most of western Panama lies within the provincial boundaries of **Chiriquí**, which, Chiricanos will proudly remind you, is the *granero* (granary) or *canasta de pan* (breadbasket) of Panama. This is no idle boast: the region produces the bulk of the country's agricultural produce, as varied as the land on which it is cultivated, from the paddy fields round Alanje to the strawberries of lofty Cerro Punta. To the south lie the **Tierras Bajas** (Lowlands), home to the otherwise tranquil provincial capital of **David**, which comes alive every March when it hosts a major international agricultural fair; the region's other main festival, celebrating flowers and coffee, takes place in Boquete every January.

South of David lies the **Golfo de Chiriquí**, a vast body of water with beautiful coastal fringes and deserted islands that stretches from the Azuero Peninsula in the east to the Costa Rican border. Surrounded by nutrient-rich waters that attract dazzling aquatic life, including humpback whales, the gulf contains the mangroves and coral of the **Parque Nacional Marino Golfo de Chiriquí** and the former penitentiary of **Isla Coiba**, which is renowned for its scuba diving and pristine rainforest. It is most easily accessed from **Santa Catalina**, a mellow fishing village tucked away in the southwestern corner of Province Veraguas, and the country's top surfing venue.

Yet it is the **Tierras Altas** (Highlands) to the north that attract the most attention and tourists, with the cool, sunny climate and spectacular scenery of **Boquete** a magnet for North American and European retirees. The town provides a great base for exploring the surrounding cloud forests or ascending Panama's highest peak,

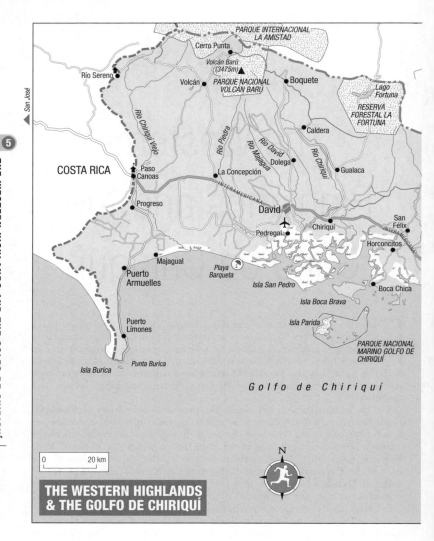

THE WESTERN HIGHLANDS
& THE GOLFO DE CHIRIQUÍ

Volcán Barú, which can also be approached from the less touristy settlements of **Volcán** and **Cerro Punta** on its western flanks. The latter provides a convenient springboard for the rugged, little-explored peaks of **Parque Internacional La Amistad**. A large area of the forested slopes of eastern Chiriquí form part of the **Comarca Ngöbe-Buglé**, which extends over the continental divide into Bocas del Toro and Veraguas (see p.250).

Some history

The **Ngöbe** and closely related **Buglé** – both recognizable by the women's brightly coloured cotton dresses – were collectively referred to as Guaymí in colonial

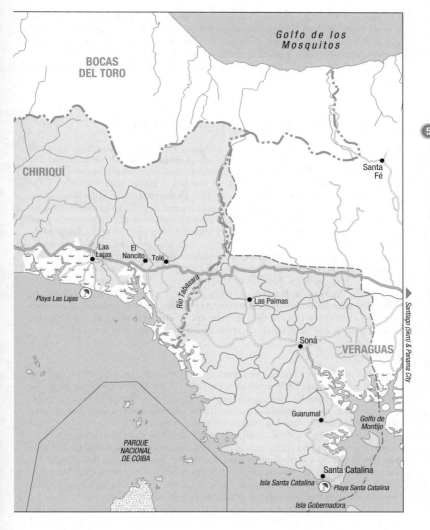

accounts, featuring prominently as fierce warriors. Their various tribes, alongside many others that never survived the colonial struggle, were pushed up into the mountains by the **Spanish**, who moved into the region in the late sixteenth century. Founding major centres in Remedios (1589) and Alanje (1591), the colonizers also established numerous mission towns such as San Félix, San Lorenzo and Tolé, located just off the Interamericana. Though some Guaymí succumbed to their evangelizing efforts, others formed alliances among themselves and with passing pirates, and the towns were regularly raided and sometimes destroyed.

Following separation from Colombia, the province of Chiriquí, which had been established in 1849, gained its own railway – though it folded around 1980 – in recognition of its agricultural importance, which further increased once the United Fruit Company began banana production round Puerto Armuelles in 1927 and coffee plantations started to thrive. It is on such plantations that the Ngöbe and Buglé now work, travelling great distances throughout the provinces of Chiriquí and Bocas del Toro – migrant wage labourers on rich lands that once belonged to their ancestors.

David and the Chiriquí Lowlands

In contrast to the fresh highlands – the destination for the vast majority of visitors to the province – the oppressive heat of the **Lowlands** does little to attract the punters. Nor do endless fields of maize, rice, bananas, sugar cane and cattle. Still it's hard to avoid **David**, or at least the city's vast bus terminal, since virtually all the province's transport passes through here – though the road under construction that skirts the southern slopes of Volcán Barú may change that. What's more, Chiriquí's capital is gradually growing in appeal as a place to chill out for a couple of days and enjoy a few city comforts – increasingly varied dining options and a fairly lively entertainment scene – as well as serving as a base for exploring a few local attractions: the mangroves at **Pedregal** or the wildlife reserve at **Playa Barqueta**.

West of David, the Interamericana speeds along 47km of flattish terrain to the frontier with Costa Rica. Just before the border post, the road veers off left down the narrow **Península Burica**, weaving through plantations and passing the former banana boom town of **Puerto Armuelles**, before an undulating road eventually peters out close to the southern tip, where the handful of travellers that make it that far can stroll along deserted beaches and watch the waves.

David

The only one of three Spanish settlements founded in the area in 1602 to survive repeated attacks from indigenous groups, **DAVID** developed slowly as a remote outpost of the Spanish Empire, only beginning to thrive when Chiriquí's population swelled in the nineteenth century. Today, despite being a busy commercial city of around one hundred thousand – the third largest in Panama – and the focus of Chiriquí's strong regional identity, it retains a sedate provincial atmosphere.

Oppressively hot and either humid or dusty, its unexceptional modern architecture spread out on a well-planned grid that derives from colonial days, David has few attractions per se, but its very ordinariness holds a certain appeal for a few days. It's also a good place to stock up before a trip to the Highlands or break a journey between Panama City and Costa Rica or Bocas del Toro.

David's annual highlight is its **international agricultural fair**, Feria Internacional de San José de David (Ⓦwww.feriadedavid.com), whose ten days of festivities coincide with the patron saint day for San José on March 19. Although principally a trade show, there's plenty to entertain the public, with rodeo and lasso competitions, music and dancing, not to mention the annual *cabalgata*, a colourful horseback parade through the city streets.

Arrival and information

As a major transport hub, strategically located between San José, Costa Rica and Panama City, David is easily accessed. **Flights** (see p.216) from Panama City, Bocas del Toro and San José, Costa Rica arrive at the **Aeropuerto Enrique, Malek**, about 5km out of town, a $4 taxi ride away. Both Air Panama and Aeroperlas have offices in town and at the airport, where it is easy to rent a car (see listings, p.215).

Boquete (37km)   Interamericana

DAVID

Bus Terminal

AVENIDA OBALDIA

PASEO ESTUDIANTE

CALLE H NORTE
CALLE G NORTE
CALLE F NORTE
CALLE E NORTE
CALLE D NORTE
Costa Rica
Consulate

CALLE C NORTE
CALLE B NORTE
CALLE A NORTE

Iglesia de la
Sagrada Familia

Parque
Cervantes

Museo de
Historia y Arte
José de Obaldia

Laundry
Culturama

Catedral San
José de David

Buses to
Pedregal

Cinema

Museo y
Antiguedades
La Casona

CALLE CENTRAL (DR ERNESTO PEREZ BALLADERES)
CALLE A SUR
CALLE B SUR

Hospital Chiriquí

CALLE C SUR

Super Strike
de David

Immigration

Mercado
San Mateo

CALLE D SUR
CALLE E SUR

Supermarket

Supermarket

CALLE F SUR (MIGUEL A BRENES)

Crown
Casino

0   200 m

Playa Barqueta

⑥(200m), Chiriquí Mall (3km), Costa Rica (47km) & Volcán (56km)   (25km)   Airport (5km) & Pedregal (10km)

NIGHTLIFE
Opium   10
Pirates   5

RESTAURANTS & CAFÉS
Asa 2 a la Leña   9
Bernard's   1
Casa Vegetariana   6
Jakalita   2
Multi-Café No.2   4
Restaurante Bar El Fogón 3
Restaurante Renegado   8
Restaurante La Típica   7

ACCOMMODATION
Bambu Hostel   G
Chambres en Ville   E C
Hotel Castilla   C
Hotel Gran Nacional   D
Hotel Iberia   B
Hotel Toledo   A F
Purple House Hostel   F

Long-distance luxury **buses** from Panama City (see p.98) and San José, Costa Rica (see box, p.216), as well as minibuses from the surrounding villages, pile into the bustling, well-organized **bus terminal** on Paseo Estudiante. The terminal has good facilities, including a self-service restaurant, toilets, a left-luggage office (daily 6am–8pm) and internet café. From there it's a fifteen-minute walk into the town centre, where numerous banks, pharmacies, hotels and the post office are located in and around the main square, with another area of commercial development – including the 24-hour Super 99 and Romero **supermarkets** with pharmacies and ATMs, plus restaurants – along Calle F Sur. **Taxis** are plentiful and should not cost more than $2–3 for a ride in town.

The city offers **consular services** for both Panama and Costa Rica. The Costa Rican consulate (Mon–Fri 8am–3pm; ☎774 1923) is opposite the Policlínica on Calle C Norte near Avenida 1 Este. If you need a Panamanian visa extension, go to Immigration (Mon–Fri 7.30am–2.30pm; ☎775 4515) on Calle C Sur. For the latest information on the region's several national parks, contact the **ANAM** office (☎775 3163). The **tourist office** on Calle Central between avenidas 5 Este and 6 Este is friendly and courteous but thin on information.

Accommodation

A broad range of good-value **accommodation** exists in David, most near the city centre and all with hot water and a/c unless indicated.

Bambu Hostel C Virgincita, San Mateo district ☎730 2961, ⓦwww.bambuhostel.com. Further out than most places, though within reach of amenities on C "F" Sur; for the mellow-minded or party-fond folk. Offers fan-ventilated dorm bunks and private rooms with a/c as well as all the usual hostel amenities, plus a small pool with *rancho* bar in the garden for cooling off. Also runs tours. Dorm $8. ❸

Chambres en Ville Av 5 Este between C "A" Sur & C "B" Sur ☎775 7428, ⓦwww.chambresenville.info. Friendly family hostel with seven large, fan-ventilated rooms (a/c extra) with good storage space. Shared kitchen, laundry room, terrace with hammocks and small pool as well as free transportation to and from the bus station or airport make this place excellent value. French, English and Spanish spoken. Bed $10. ❷

Hotel Castilla C "A" Norte between Av Cincuentenario & Av 3 Este, ☎774 5236, ⓦwww.hotelcastillapanama.com. The pick of the hotels in terms of good-value comfort, and centrally located. The tiled rooms are slightly chintzy but bright and clean, and you might fancy splashing out the extra $15 for a balcony view of the main park. The decent, if dark, onsite restaurant draws in the local business community for the special lunch menu ($4.75, Mon–Sat), though prices otherwise are mid-range. ❸

Hotel Gran Nacional C Central & Av 1 Este, ☎775 2221. As the name and marble lobby floor suggest,

the grandest hotel in town, conveniently located a couple of blocks from the main square. Rooms are tastefully furnished with flat-screen cable TV and other mod cons. There's also a bar, pool, casino, cinema and three restaurants. ❻

Hotel Iberia C "B" Norte between Av 1 Oeste & Av 2 Oeste ☎777 2002. ⓔhoteliberia@cwpanama.net. Popular with business folk for its immaculately clean, functional rooms with cable TV and free wi-fi, friendly staff and on-site restaurant offering tasty fare. ❹

Hotel Toledo Av 1 Este between C "D" Norte & C "E" Norte ☎774 6732. Conveniently situated for the bus terminal, this clean, comfortable hotel offers good value for money with firm beds, cable TV and friendly service. On-site bar-restaurant closed on Sundays. ❸

The Purple House Hostel C "C" Sur at Av 6 Oeste ☎774 4059, ⓦwww.purplehousehostel.com. A David institution, this small, efficient, rule-bound, purple-clad hostel is 15min walk from the city centre, though close to many amenities. There are two small dorms and a couple of private rooms with fans (a/c extra) and comfortable mattresses, plus a patio garden. Amenities include a kitchen, free coffee and wi-fi, and there's excellent tourist information. Transfer to Boca Chica can be arranged for around $30. ❷

The City

David's heart is vibrant **Parque Cervantes**, where snow-cone sellers, shoe-shiners and hawkers peddling sugar cane and fresh fruit juice all vie for business, overlooked by the nondescript Iglesia de la Sagrada Familia. The park's curved stone seating maximizes the leafy shade, making it a prime spot for watching urban life unfold. Its design, with its large geometric fountain at the centre, exemplifies the city's striving for modernity, whereas a stroll three blocks southeast down Calle "A" Norte takes you back to the city's colonial past in **Barrio Bolívar**, where you can take a tranquil stroll through the district's sprinkling of russet tiles, balconies and intricate wrought iron. The sorry state of the historic colonial mansion on the corner with Avenida 8 Este that houses the **Museo de Historia y Arte José de Obaldía** – currently closed awaiting restoration – is symptomatic of numerous governments' indifference towards cultural heritage, though a rescue package has now been promised. The building was home to successive generations of the distinguished Obaldía family – José Vicente was the president of New Granada (combined Colombia and Panama) and his son José Domingo became the second president of Panama. Adjacent, the city's oldest building is in better repair; another delightful tiled, adobe structure, dating back to 1794, it is home to the **Fundación C Gallegos y Culturama** (ⓦwww.semanarioculturama.com), an NGO and cultural centre that puts on alternative theatre, films and events, sometimes in English.

Just east of here, a crumbling bell tower stands over the messily restored nineteenth-century **Catedral San José de David**. See what you make of the recently renovated colonial Romanesque facade and the interior's gaudy murals. Heading north back up Calle Central, just round the corner from the Fundación

Gallegos, make sure you pop into the **Museo y Antiguedades la Casona** (Mon–Sat 9am–noon, 3–6pm; free) an antique shop-cum-private museum. The seven small rooms are stuffed full of curiosities including original bottles from the city's first pharmacy, intriguing early photos of the region and stacks of period furniture interspersed with colonial religious art.

Eating and drinking

There are plenty of good-value **restaurants** and **bars** in David, several of which double as nightspots at the weekends.

Asa 2 a la Leña C "F" Sur between Av 4 Oeste & Av 5 Oeste. Pleasant, airy joint serving a range of tasty grilled and roasted meat and seafood mains ($5–8) with fried yuca, *patacones* and salad. Daily 7am–midnight.

Bernard's Av 1 Oeste between C "F" Norte & "G" Norte ☏ 6751 5028. This excellent recent venture offers a menu as colourful as its owner – from delicious spice-infused Indian and Thai creations to lasagne, burgers and even fish and chips, most for under $9. Tues–Sun from 5pm. There's a branch at the airport too, serving legendary all-day breakfasts.

Casa Vegetariana C Central at Av 2 Este. Easy-to-miss casual hole-in-the-wall café with a handful of small tables to sit at and enjoy your pick-and-mix veggie dishes washed down with a refreshing fruit juice. Mon–Sat 6.30am–4pm.

Jakalita C "E" Norte at Av Central. Very popular take-away venue famous for its goat's milk yoghurt and fresh-fruit ice creams, now branching out into Chilean empanadas. Daily 7am–11pm (from 4pm on Sat).

Multi-Café No. 2 C "A" Norte between Av 2 Este & Av 3 Este, next to *La Castilla*. Modern self-service restaurant with a/c and parking that attracts a busy weekend crowd. Vast array of local and international staples on offer, rarely totalling more than $4, and made-to-order omelettes for breakfast. Mon–Sat 7am–8pm, Sun 7am–3pm.

Restaurante Bar El Fogón Av 2 Oeste between C "C" Norte & C "D" Norte ☏ 775 7091. Recently expanded spacious and airy restaurant, painted in warm colours with a friendly atmosphere. Deservedly popular with Davideños, serving various grilled meat, poultry and seafood mains (from $5) – try the *pescado parmesano* – plus burgers and sandwiches ($3–4.50). Daily noon–midnight.

Restaurante Renegado Interamericana, opposite Autocentro ☏ 774 5977. A cosy setting in which to savour excellent, moderately priced Peruvian and Catalan specialities, such as paella with black rice and *ceviche* ($20 for two), reflecting the two owners' origins. Wash it down with first-rate sangría. Mon–Sat noon–10pm, Sun noon–4pm.

Restaurante La Típica Av 3 Este & C "F" Sur. Busy, no-nonsense Chinese–Panamanian cafeteria serving decent food around the clock at reasonable prices. A reliable budget choice. Open 24hr.

Nightlife and entertainment

Discotecas open and shut with predictable regularity. Calle "F" Sur is currently the happening part of town with *Opium* (next to the Crown Casino) the hottest club among 20-somethings and *Pirates* at the Fiesta Casino (across from the *Gran Nacional*) a slightly older alternative. Round the corner, the hotel's six-screen **cinema** shows the latest Hollywood releases. The Superstrike **bowling alley** is on Avenida 5 Oeste, and there are plenty of **pool halls** (one on Calle "F" Sur opposite Super 99) and casinos.

Listings

Airline offices Aeroperlas (☏ 775 7779) is on Av Ernesto Peréz Balladeres between C 3 & Av 2; Air Panama (☏ 775 0812) is on C 2 in Plaza Oteima; Copa Airlines (☏ 775 6110) is on Av Central at C "C" Norte.

Car rental Alamo (☏ 721 0101), Avis (☏ 774 7075), Budget (☏ 775 5597), Dollar (☏ 721 1103), Hertz (☏ 775 8471), Hilary (☏ 775 5459), National (☏ 21 0974) and Thrifty (☏ 721 2477) are all at the airport.

Hospitals Hospital Chiriquí, on C "B" Sur between Av 3 Oeste & Av 4 Oeste, and Hospital Mae Lewis, on the Interamericana, are the two largest private hospitals, both open 24hr with English-speaking doctors.

Post office A block northeast of the park on C "C" Norte (Mon–Fri 7am–6pm, Sat 7am–5pm).

Two companies offer twice-daily departures from David to San José. **Tracopa** (☎775 0585, ✆www.tracopacr.com) buses leave from the main bus terminal (8.30am, noon; 8–9hr; $15 one way), where they have an office. **Ticabus** (☎777 2511) transport leaves from outside their office on the Interamericana (5am, 5pm; 10hr; $15 one way). Tickets are available in advance and should definitely be booked for peak holiday periods.

It is often quicker, though, to take one of the frequent **minibuses** ($1.75) from the bus terminal to the border at **Paso Canoas**, walk across, with the usual bureaucracy surrounding getting exit and entry stamps, and hop on one of the regular buses to San José. Tracopa also has an office at the border (daily 7am–4pm Costa Rica time, which is 1hr behind Panama) between the two immigration offices, adjacent to the Banco de Costa Rica, with two daily departures, at 8am and noon, to San José. If you miss one, take a shuttle to Ciudad Neily, the first sizeable population over the border 18km away, where there are even more connections with the capital.

Moving on from David

Aeroperlas and Air Panama operate several daily **flights** to Panama City ($105 one way), with fewer at the weekend. Aeroperlas flies to Bocas del Toro (Mon, Wed, Fri; $58.30) while Air Panama flies to San José (Mon, Wed, Fri, 10.30am; $176.75 one way, plus $15 departure tax). Two **bus** companies also operate daily connections to the Costa Rican capital (see box above). From the main bus terminal there are frequent departures to Panama City (every 50min–1hr, 5am–8.30pm; 6–7hr; $12.60, $15 for the express buses at 11.45pm & 3am), dropping off in Santiago en route (3hr; $7), and Boquete (every 30min, 6.30am–9pm; 1hr; $1.45). Buses to Río Sereno (every 45min–1hr, 5am–5pm; 2hr 30min; $4.25) and Cerro Punta (every 15min, 5am–8pm; 1hr 50min; $2.90) also pass through Volcán (1hr 20min; $2.50). Other destinations include Caldera (10 buses, 6am–7pm; 1hr; $2), and Puerto Armuelles (every 15min, 5.30am–11.45pm; 1hr 30min; $1.75) via the Costa Rican border at Paso Canoas.

Around David

Several pleasant **day trips** are within striking distance of the city, all reachable on public transport. At weekends many Davideños pile into their cars and head to the nearest beach, a grainy stretch of sand hosting a couple of places to eat 25km southwest at **Playa Barqueta**, a meandering forty-minute bus ride away (8am, 11.20am, returning 2.30pm & 5pm; $2 or bus to Guarumal and taxi to the beach $4). A large portion of the beach lies within the boundaries of the low-key **Refugio de Vida Silvestre de Playa Barqueta Agricola** (8am–4pm; $5; park warden ☎6602 5770) whose 14km stretch of sand, scrub and mangrove protects nesting sites for hawksbill, olive ridley, leatherback, loggerhead and green sea **turtles**. Arrange visits to check out the night-time nesting (May–Nov is best) with the park warden or visit the ANAM office outside David (see p.213). The reserve entrance lies east of *Las Olas Resort*, where the bus stops.

A far nicer place to cool off from the sweltering heat is **Balneário Barranca** (daily from 11am), a natural swimming pool with a *rancho* bar-restaurant and hammocks on a meander of Río Chiricagua, 20km west of David. While a festive family atmosphere prevails at weekends you can have the tarzan swing all to yourself midweek. Take any bus heading west to the border, Volcán or Concepción, getting off on the Interamericana just before the Boquerón turn-off and walking 100m up a track to the right.

▲ Exploring the mangroves near Pedregal

Ten kilometres south of the city, past the airport, the road fizzles out at **Pedregal**, David's small port and marina, a convenient place to contract a **boat** (Ronald ☎6642 7576 or Marciana "Pollo" ☎6446 9656; around $160/boat for 2hr) to explore the morass of mangroves and islands in the Golfo de Chiriquí, or to splurge on lunch at 🍴 *Stella's* (☎721 1951; Mon–Sat 11am–11pm, Sun 11am–9pm), a delightful waterside restaurant serving up mouth-watering mains such as curried jumbo shrimps in coconut cream or a rack of ribs. Buses leave from Avenida 2 Este between Calle Central and Calle "A" Norte (daily every 10–15 min, 6am–11pm; 15 min; 30c).

Peninsula Burica

Aside from a handful of die-hard surfers and fishing enthusiasts, few tourists venture down to the distant tip of the **Peninsula Burica**, resembling an upside-down skittle straddling the Costa Rican border. Here, 50km southwest of David, the remoteness is tangible and the sunsets spectacular. The gateway to the peninsula is **Puerto Armuelles**, for over seventy years Panama's thriving Pacific hub of the infamous United Fruit Company (now Chiquita Brands) until it pulled the plug in 2003 (see p.248). The rotting pier and abandoned wooden houses serve as poignant reminders of the town's former importance.

Though there is a comfortable fishing lodge halfway down the coast (Ⓦwww .aquaadventurespanama.com), most visitors choose to **stay** at *Mono Feliz* (☎6595 0388, Ⓔmono_feliz@hotmail.com, though contact is sporadic; camping $5, cabin ❸), a monkey sanctuary located at the tip of the headland overrun by troops of white-faced capuchins, howlers, Geoffroy's tamarins and endangered squirrel monkeys, which is either a major attraction or a deterrent depending on your views of encouraging contact with humans. With three basic free-standing cabins, shared kitchen (or home cuisine if you don't fancy cooking) a freshwater pool, horse riding and expanses of deserted sand and sea, this is the ultimate chill-out spot, though getting there can be a challenge, especially in the rainy season. Timing for the daily *chiva* (90min–2hr journey; $3) that makes the 30km trip down the peninsula from the waterside transport depot in **Puerto Armuelles**, depends on the tides since much of the "road" is on the beach, only accessible at low tide – make sure you arrive before noon. Get off just after the village of El Medio, and hike 45 minutes along the beach.

Paso Canoas and the Costa Rican border

It's a speedy forty minutes by **minibus** from David (every 15min, 4am–10.30pm; $1.75) along the Interamericana to Panama's main border crossing with Costa Rica at **Paso Canoas** (others are at Río Sereno, west of Volcán and Guabito over the *cordillera* in Bocas Province), open 24 hours. The busy frontier town exudes an edgy tackiness, with stalls, money changers and taxi drivers all competing for business. A couple of **cafés** right in front of the border offer filling fry-ups. To the left, on the corner, minibuses (every 15min, dawn–late) from David pick up passengers bound for Puerto Armuelles. A few metres down the road are a couple of banks, both with **ATMs**. Neither changes money, but if you're heading for Costa Rica and require colones, note that a Banco de Costa Rica with ATM sits between the Panamanian and Costa Rican immigration buildings.

If you're entering Panama and want onward transport, walk 100m down the Interamericana, where the hole-in-the-wall office of Padafront (daily 6am–10.45pm; ☎727 7230), on the left, sells tickets for six daytime departures for Panama City (6.15am–6.35pm; 8hr; $15) plus two express overnight services (9.30pm, 10.45pm; 7hr; $17). Next door, the similar-sounding Panafron (☎727 7054) operates five daytime and one overnight express bus (10.40pm) to the capital for the same prices. Alternatively, small minibuses scoot off down the highway to David (every 10–15min 4am–9pm; 40min; $1.75), from where onward transport is easy (see p.216); after the last shuttle, you'll need a taxi ($20–25). Don't forget that whether entering Panama or Costa Rica you'll need to show proof of onward travel and financial solvency.

Boca Chica and the Parque Nacional Marino Golfo de Chiriquí

The real appeal of the Lowlands lies along its little-explored coast, from the expansive beach at **Las Lajas** to the seemingly endless stretches of mangroves and numerous islands dotted round the **Golfo de Chiriquí**, surrounded by waters and coral reefs that nurture a veritable cornucopia of marine life. The tiny fishing village of **Boca Chica** and the nearby island of **Boca Brava** provide good bases for exploring the western area of the gulf, where you can go kayaking or arrange boats for snorkelling, scuba diving or sport fishing trips.

Parque Nacional Marino Golfo de Chiriquí

The laid-back fishing village of **Boca Chica**, 30km southeast of David as the vulture flies, provides the gateway to one of the province's most prized natural treasures, the **Parque Nacional Marino Golfo de Chiriquí** ($10 park fee). It's nirvana for **scuba diving**, **snorkelling** and **sport fishing** enthusiasts, though the very best spots actually lie round Islas Secas – which also host the country's most exclusive retreat (ⓦwww.islassecas.com) – and Islas Ladrones, just outside the reserve boundaries. When the wind drops in the rainy season, sandflies can be a nuisance, so bring repellent.

Arrival and information

The recently paved road has made it easy to **drive** to Boca Chica in a normal saloon, taking the turn-off to Horconcitos, 36km east of David on the Interamericana, and then the middle road at the three-way fork in the village, coming to a halt at the jetty in Boca Chica 14km later. The infrequent **buses** from David to Horconcitos,

5km south of the Interamericana ($1.50), are often cramped; you'll get a more comfortable ride in a bus bound for Tolé or San Félix, which can drop you off at the junction, where there's usually a taxi waiting to take you to Boca Chica ($15) during daylight hours. Alternatively, you might get a miracle sighting of the tatty Boca Chica minibus, which passes at around 12.30, and 4.30pm, if at all. If leaving a car overnight in the village ask around for Elvis ($1/night). Most of the accommodation lies offshore, on one of the islands; some offer free transfers (see below).

With **no bank** or ATM in Boca Chica – which is, after all, a fishing village – you need to take out enough cash in David, unless staying at *Cala Mia*, which accepts credit card payments. The going rate for a **boat** to *Cala Mia* on Isla Boca Brava or to the *Pacific Bay Resort*, on the mainland Peninsula Bejuco but only accessible by boat, is $30; you can get ferried across to *Hotel Boca Brava* for $3. For the return trip, a boat leaves for Boca Chica at 9am and 1pm to connect with the bus that heads up the Interamericana at 9.15am and 1.30pmish. In the not entirely unexpected event of a no-show, negotiate a ride.

There's a lively local **bar** just up from the jetty, which also serves simple **meals**, where you can enquire about a boat if you want to organize your own. Jay (☎6691 8450) or Chino (☎6444 6493) charge $65 for a half-day trip.

Accommodation

From luxury private island to laid-back backpackers' pad, there's a good spread of **accommodation**, mostly accessible by boat although these secluded spots generally mean you're limited to your lodging's restaurant.

Cala Mia Isla Boca Brava ☎851 0059, ⓦwww .boutiquehotelcalamia.com. No noisy a/c units or TVs spoil the tranquillity of this sophisticated yet rustic solar-powered eco-retreat. The eleven breezy bungalows have gorgeous private *ranchos* looking out to sea, and the lovely bar-restaurant deck serves gourmet Mediterranean cuisine – the three-course dinners ($32) draw on organic garden produce. Excursions start at $80 and there's a small spa. Breakfast and use of kayaks included. ❾

Hotel Boca Brava Isla Boca Brava ☎851 0017, ⓦwww.hotelbocabrava.com. Happily referred to as "Frank's Place" by backpackers, this long-standing favourite offers an affordable rub with nature. No advance bookings, but if you end up in a hammock or soggy mattress (bring a mozzy net) in the dorm one night, you'll be first in line for one of the sixteen private rooms (if you want one) the next. The vibey cliff-top bar-restaurant serves excellent food and lethal cocktails, and can be a spot to party on holiday weekends. There are trips to Isla Bolaños ($25), Islas Secas ($40) and the like

at very reasonable rates; alternatively flush out the howler monkeys on the trails or chill on the beach. $5 camping; $10 mattress/hammock. ❸

Isla Paridita ☎6464 2510 ⓦwww .expeditionpanama.com. Tranquil eco-getaway on a gorgeous private island with beaches, rainforest trails and freshwater lagoons, offering four simple open-sided bamboo and thatch *cabañas* (fans, solar energy) and communal gourmet dining. Rates include all meals, kayaks, snorkel gear and transfer from Boca Chica, and scuba diving and sport fishing can be arranged. ❾

Pacific Bay Resort Punta Bejuco ☎6695 1651, ⓦwww.pacificbayresort.net. There's an unequalled panorama of the bay from the hill-top bar-dining area, though you'll earn your food (which is of variable quality) hiking there from the four well-spaced, solar-powered, wood-furnished duplex cabins. Set in an extensive forested headland with three beaches, and coves to explore by kayak, it's wonderfully relaxing. Meals included; horse riding and moderately priced excursions are also on offer. ❼

The Park

Created in 1994 to protect almost 150 square kilometres of terrestrial and marine wildlife, the park comprises 25 islands and 19 coral reefs, teeming with hundreds of fish in a rainbow of colours. **Isla Parita**, by far the largest land mass, together with the much smaller **Isla Paridita**, are the only two inhabited islands on account of their fresh water sources; the rest are generally small, low-lying sedimentary

Diving and kayaking

Snorkelling outings in the park can easily be arranged through the hotels. For **scuba diving**, contact Carlos Spragge at Boca Brava Divers (T775 3185, Wwww .scubadiving-panama.com), who offers a one-day all-inclusive dive excursion ($150, minimum 4 people; visibility is best Dec–April). The area's islands, inlets, caves and channels have also helped establish it as a nascent **sea-kayaking** destination. Boquete Outdoor Adventures (see p.236) organizes overnight and multi-day trips, though most accommodation listed has kayaks if you just want to splash about.

outcrops that enjoy a tropical savannah climate, with beaches backed by coconut palms and manchineel trees, whose only visitors to disturb the hermit crabs and iguanas are nesting hawksbill and leatherback turtles.

The coastline to the west of Boca Chica is thick with **mangroves**, which means you'll have to venture to the more distant islands to find white sand or crystalline waters. Across the narrow water channel in front of the jetty is **Boca Brava**, an island hosting two contrasting lodgings, while on the mainland a couple of upmarket fishing lodges and a small guesthouse do little to disturb the tranquillity of the place. Snorkelling trips head out to the white-sand cove of **Isla Bolaños**, though even better snorkelling and diving is to be had round the more remote (and pricier) **Islas Secas**, **Islas Ladrones** and **Isla Montuoso**, where the marine life is breathtaking, from seahorses and starfish to giant manta and eagle rays, pods of dolphins, turtles, sharks and vast schools of fish swirling round volcanic pinnacles, with humpback whales arriving to calve from June.

Playa Las Lajas and around

The impressive broad belt of flat tan-coloured sand of **Playa Las Lajas** is by far the most popular weekend beach destination for urbanites from David (81km) and even Santiago (124km) in need of sand, sea and surf. However, since the beach, backed by wafting palms, stretches for kilometres both ways, there's plenty of space to escape the crowds. The benign waves are more suited to body surfing and playing around in than serious surfing; boards can be rented at *La Spiaza* and *El Mundo* (see opposite). Many people just roll up to breathe in the sea air, tuck into some seafood and chill at the **beachside bar-restaurants**. Developments have started to take root, with a couple of new low-key European-run establishments, while large-scale projects lurk on the horizon.

If you are interested in **Ngöbe** or **Buglé** culture, you should take time to visit the major communities of San Félix and Tolé north of the Interamericana; the latter, which lies east close to the border with Veraguas, is noted for its handicrafts (see *Arts and crafts* colour section), many sold at stalls along the Interamericana close to the turn-off.

Practicalities

The easiest way to reach the beach is to jump aboard a **bus** bound for Tolé or San Félix, which leaves David terminal every 20–30 minutes, and get off an hour later at the unmissable busy intersection, El Cruce de San Félix or "El Cruce". A major refuelling point for drivers and vehicles on a long-haul journey, it has a petrol station across the road, where you're most likely to find a **taxi** driver to take you to the beach ($7 one way); get a contact number for your return trip. If driving, take the turn-off 68km east of David. Bring sufficient cash with you since there is **no ATM**. Arriving at the beach you come to a T-junction; directions to the listings below are given from there.

Accommodation and eating

Las Lajas Beach Resort Right at the T-junction ☎6790 1972, ⊛www.laslajasbeachresort.com. Set back from the beach, a dozen expansive, tiled, minimally furnished rooms (one with wheelchair access) look onto the lawn through wall-to-floor windows. The two upstairs suites have spectacular sea views from the balcony and there's a large pool and bar-restaurant serving moderately priced American-style food. ❽

El Mundo Bar y Restaurante Left at the T-junction ☎6560 5478, ⊛www.el-mundo-bar .com. Try a little *wurst* and *wienerschnitzel* (burgers, snacks and sandwiches too) in a funky beerkeller-cum-beach bar under a *rancho* slap on the sand. Plenty of beer, cocktails and liquors make this the place to hang out and soak up the sunsets, or even check your emails. *Cabañas* are planned.

🏄 **Panamax** Left at the T-junction ☎6574 4986. The wooden A-frames are in need of attention and not even redeemed by a sea view, but the vibey beach-bar restaurant is a great spot to sway in a hammock, quench your thirst or stoke up on a burger or some solid Panamanian seafood dishes (mains $6–8) to a non-stop reggae beat. ❹

La Spiaza At the T-junction ☎6620 6431, ⊛www .laspiazapanama.com. Mellow Italian-owned backpackers venue 2min from the sand, with rustic two-storey wooden cabins, dorm beds, space to camp (in your own or one of their tents) and a small hammock-strung patio where you can enjoy real Italian espresso and pizza from a genuine wood-fired pizza oven. Bed $7. ❸

The Peninsula de Soná and Isla Coiba

Dwarfed by the Azuero Peninsula to the west, the hilly **Peninsula de Soná** has recently started to open up to small-scale tourism projects. Small cattle farms cover the interior and fishing villages dot the rocky coastline, which protrudes into the Golfo de Chiriquí. Panama's surfing capital, mellow **Santa Catalina**, continues to expand as more people use the fishing village as the launching pad for excursions to the primary rainforests and coral reefs of **Isla Coiba**, which offers some of the world's finest scuba diving, snorkelling and sport fishing.

Santa Catalina

At the southern end of the peninsula, the sleepy fishing village of **SANTA CATALINA** reels in visitors for its internationally renowned **surf** spots and is a jumping-off point for Isla Coiba. As a result, the village is rapidly developing into a pleasantly bohemian tourist centre, with mostly foreign-owned small-scale operations scattered along the main road into the village, or spilling off the potholed sandy track that leads to the main beach, **Playa El Estero**. Much of the surrounding coastline has been bought up by an American conglomerate, though the defiant sign on the beach, "La Isla Santa Catalina no se vende", emphasizes that the residents won't let their natural heritage go without a fight.

Arrival and information

Santa Catalina's location, 68km south of the Interamericana, and poor connections help ensure the place is only crowded for holiday weekends and surfing competitions. There are only three **minibuses** a day from Soná (5am, noon & 4pm; returning 7am, 8am and 2pm; $3.85, plus extra for a surfboard), an unendearing glorified crossroads, which offer six daily connections with Panama City (5hr; $8). **Taxis**, found hanging round Soná bus terminal, charge a hefty fixed rate ($30).

Once in Santa Catalina, you'll be on foot unless you've your own transport, but nowhere is further than a twenty-minute hike from the bus stop. Note also that there is **no bank** or ATM, and very few places take credit cards, so bring sufficient cash. The Soná ATM often runs out of money on busy weekends. **Self-caterers** – which includes anyone heading for Coiba – should stock up in Santiago or Soná since Santa Catalina is limited to a mini-super (with the emphasis on the "mini"),

5

an intermittently stocked fruit and vegetable shop and an excellent bakery. The **village website** (Ⓦ www.santacatalinabeach.com) has plenty of useful information, including a map and directions for driving.

Accommodation

Most **accommodation** in Santa Catalina is simple, catering for surfers and outdoor types, but more comfortable options are on the increase. There are three lovely **house rental** options: *Casa Verde* (Ⓦ www.lacasaverdepanama.com) and *Casa Maya* (Ⓦ www.santacatalinacasamaya.com) both sleep around six and are close to *Jamming*, off the beach road ($400 a week), while the cosy two-bedroom *Casa Kenia* (Ⓦ www.casakenia.com) in the village is less ($250 a week), with package rate deals which include tours to Coiba.

Places to stay are located either on the main road, which ends at Playa Santa Catalina, or are signposted from the 1.5km beach road that leads off left, where the bus stops. There are still no land lines apart from the two public phones (Ⓣ 998 9488 or 998 8600) and only sporadic internet and mobile phone connections, so you may have to wait several days for a response when booking.

Blue Zone Signed off the beach road towards the bluff Ⓦ www.bluezonepanama.com. Laid-back place set among trees, with five simply but nicely decorated rooms (one triple, four doubles) sharing bathroom, kitchen, BBQ and laundry facilities, with a couple of hammocks slung up in a *bohío* right on the clifftop. Can arrange horse riding and good deals with Fluid Adventures. ❸

La Buena Vida Main road Ⓣ 6635 1895, Ⓦ www.labuenavida.biz. Laden with original mosaic and wrought-iron work, these charming mid-range villas (with a/c, hot-water private bathrooms and patios) were designed by the artistic owners, who continue the theme on the terrace café. ❺

Cabañas Rolos Main road, by the beach Ⓣ 998 8600 (public phone) or 6598 9926, Ⓦ www.rolocabins.net. This locally owned place a stone's throw from the beach is the top choice for backpacking surfers. Its brightly painted, clean dorm rooms house 2–4 people, with comfy beds, fan and shared bathrooms. Use of kitchen, pleasant dining and social area is included, and the board rental is the cheapest in town. Double rooms with private bathroom will set you back $40. ❶

Hibiscus Garden 10min drive from Santa Catalina on the Soná road, at Lagartero, Ⓣ 6615 6095, Ⓦ www.hibiscusgarden.com.

Spacious rooms painted brilliant white with tasteful dark-wood furnishings (private hot-water bathroom & a/c) and patio space in a serene beach- and riverside setting. The terrace restaurant offers a tasty European menu (mains $5–10), or you can self-cater in a shared kitchen, and there's no shortage of activities, on site or in Santa Catalina (shuttle service provided): table tennis, horse riding, yoga, sailing, boat trips, diving. Children under 14 free. ❹

Oasis Surf Camp Playa El Estero, contact David Bortolletti (in David) Ⓣ 6588 7077, Ⓦ www.oasissurfcamp.com. Great beach location among the palms offering no-nonsense fan-ventilated double cabins alongside a good-value house for six ($70) and camping ($5/person) – though there's no potable water. Italian dinners in the restaurant *rancho* are a highlight (usually open to non-residents). Watch out for the river – you'll need to wade across at high tide. a/c $10 extra. ❹

Sol y Mar Main road, Ⓣ 202 9214 or 6920 2631, Ⓦ www.solymarpanama.com. Stacked up the hillside, on the right as you ease into the village, these comfortable cabins offer home comforts; the newest have a/c, fridge, sitting room with satellite TV, internet and a terrace, shaded by tropical fruit trees, offering distant sea views. Cheaper, more basic cabins with shared bathroom and kitchen access lie behind. ❺

Activities

While the Santa Catalina website mantra of "surf, dive, fish and chill" just about sums up what the village is about, it doesn't do justice to an array of activities that also includes kayaking, yoga, massage and horse riding. For specialized trips you're best off going with a tour (see box opposite), but for general **snorkelling**, **surfing**, **fishing** or jaunts to **Coiba** you'll pay less by negotiating directly with the fishermen hanging out on the beach by their *pangas* (small flat-bottomed metal

Several **tour operators** now run trips to Coiba from Panama City, or, in the case of sport fishing, from Boca Chica, but better deals are to be had in Santa Catalina – offices are spread along the main road into the village.

Eco-Tours to Coiba ⓦwww.casakenia.com. Bilingual (English–Spanish) Javier Elizondo has a good knowledge of flora and fauna and specializes in safety-conscious day- and multi-day eco-tours to Coiba and surrounding islets, ranging from $82 for one day to $235 for three (assuming six people), including park fees, meals, snacks and lodgings. He also guides for Fluid Adventures and will take his boat to surfing spots.

Fluid Adventures ⓣ832 2368, ⓦwww.fluidadventurespanama.com. Versatile, acclaimed Canadian outfit offering everything from yoga sessions and surfing lessons, through snorkelling round Isla Santa Catalina ($40), to a six-day (five-night) kayaking adventure in Coiba that offers wonderful access to wildlife (approx $1200).

Santa Catalina Boat Tours ⓦwww.santacatalinaboattours.com. If you are not looking to catch a monster marlin for a monster fee (see ⓦwww.coibaadventure.com for that), Richard Brady is your man. He also offers boats to surf spots, surfing and snorkelling combos and a one- or two-day tour to Coiba (one day $300; two day $450), with accommodation, park fees, food etc on top.

Scuba Coiba Next to *Rolos* ⓣ6575 0122, ⓦwww.scubacoiba.com. Top billing for diving goes to pioneering Austrian Herbie Sunk. Rates are $55 for two-tank trips close to Santa Catalina, $120 for Coibà National Park. Multi-day trips with three-tank dives to Coiba are also available. Rates include full board and lodging at the ANAM station, transportation and park fees. Gear rental is $15/day on top. Canadian-run **Coiba Dive Center** (ⓣ6565 7200, ⓦwww.scubadivecenter.com) offers similar deals.

boats). Expect to pay $150–200 for a boat (usually carrying up to six) for a full-day of snorkelling, surfing or fishing, excluding food and drinks; budget more for Parque Nacional de Coiba ($300/boat) since it involves extra fuel, time and park fees ($20), which aren't usually included (see p.224), and possibly more again for extra fuel to visit the old prison. Although the marine life is truly astounding in the reserve, you won't be disappointed round **Isla Cébaco**, noted for its sparkling clear waters and good coral, since you're still guaranteed to be sharing the sea with colourful schools of snappers, jacks, tunas, butterfly, angel and puffer fish alongside moray eels and white-tip reef sharks.

Surfers should head for the Santa Catalina Surf Break, which boasts an international reputation, with waves often topping 5–6m in the season (Feb–April). *Oasis*, *Blue Zone*, *Sol y Mar*, *Hibiscus Garden* and *Fluid Adventures* all offer beach-based lessons for beginners at varying rates ($20/hr to $30/4hr, including board rental); *Rolos* and *Paradise Surf Camp* also rent out boards (usually $15/day).

Eating, drinking and nightlife

Most of the surf camps have some on-site catering facilities but a sprinkling of **restaurants** cater to a range of culinary tastes.

La Buena Vida Main road. Delightful mosaic-filled terrace that's great for a leisurely breakfast – eggs, pancakes, fruit and granola ($3.50–5) – or a light lunch of salads, tacos and sandwiches ($5–7.50). Daily 7am–2pm.

The Dive Main road, near the beach. Lively, tourist-oriented bar-restaurant down by *Rolo's*,

serving up Mexican tacos, burritos and veggie options washed down with *mojitos* and margaritas. Daily 2–10pm.

Donde Vianca On the beach road. A former national surf champion serves simple, freshly prepared and moderately priced seafood in a delightfully relaxed atmosphere.

Arrive early and be prepared for a wait. Daily 11am–9pm.

Jamming Signed off the beach road, this genuine pizzeria is the hub of the tourist-based nightlife, serving crispy clay-oven-cooked pizzas (from $6) plus pasta. Dining is either under thatch or in the garden, accompanied by a steady dose of reggae. Tues–Sun from 6.30pm; closed Oct.

Los Pibes Off the beach road. Pleasant Argentinian-run open-air bar-restaurant (with TV) dishing up empanadas, home-made burgers, fish and other meats char-grilled to perfection, complemented by fresh salads. Mains $6–7. Daily 6.30–9.30pm, usually closed Wed.

Tropical Beach Main road by the beach. Local restaurant at local prices serving filling Panamanian favourites – fish and chicken with beans, rice and salad (around $2.50 for lunch), and a fry-up breakfast for under $2. Can fix up boat trips too. Daily 7am–7pm.

Parque Nacional de Coiba

Some say "Panama" means "abundance of fish", and nowhere is this more apparent than in the crystalline waters of the **Parque Nacional de Coiba**. The 2700 square kilometres of reserve encompass Panama's largest island, **Isla Coiba**, plus eight smaller islands and forty islets, but the vast majority consists of ocean brimming with spectacular sea life, including the second largest coral reef along the Eastern Pacific. As part of the nutrient-rich Central Pacific Marine Corridor, the park is on the migration route of humpbacks (Jun–Sept), orcas, pilot and sperm whales. Diving conditions are good year round, but for land-based activities, it's better to visit the island in the **dry season** since the trails are less boggy and there's a better chance of spotting mammals.

The island still possesses large tracts of **virgin forest**, most of it still unexplored, home to 36 mammal and 147 bird species. Of the estimated 2000 different types of plant, only around 850 have so far been formally classified. The surrounding **oceans** contain 760 species of fish, ranging from delicate sea horses to vast manta rays, with 33 species of shark – including tiger, hammerhead and whale sharks, though most are harmless reef varieties.

For years, the island's gruesome history as a penal colony (see p.226) helped protect its forests and waters, but the colony's animals (cattle, buffalo and dogs) are now roaming free, threatening the **ecological balance**. Incursions by large fishing vessels (limited artesanal fishing is permitted), illegal timber extraction and resort development could also damage the reserve, and ongoing negotiations between the government, environmental pressure groups and interested businesses will have a critical impact on Coiba's future.

Arrival and information

Every visitor has to buy a **park permit** ($20), theoretically in advance at the Santiago ANAM office (T 998 4271) – in practice it can be acquired on arrival at the ANAM ranger station on Coiba. **Getting to** the island is fairly straightforward. Fishermen on the beaches at Santa Catalina should do the return trip for $250–350 but it'll cost more if you want them to take you round the island to some of the sights; each journey can take anything from ninety minutes to several hours, depending on the weather conditions and the boat. Make sure you establish your itinerary and pick-up times beforehand, and check that any boat has a decent-sized engine, and preferably a roof to stop you frying.

Once on the island you can engage a ranger to accompany you on trips ($10), but to truly appreciate this vast, pristine wilderness and its prolific wildlife, it pays to spend several days on Coiba with a boat and guide willing to take you out at first light, which is why it's worth splashing out the extra for a hassle-free multi-day deal with a **tour operator** (see box, p.223). For this reason, too, the day-trips from Santa Catalina can be both costly and a little disappointing since the lengthy journey there plus the unavoidable *tramites* (bureaucracy) at the ranger station

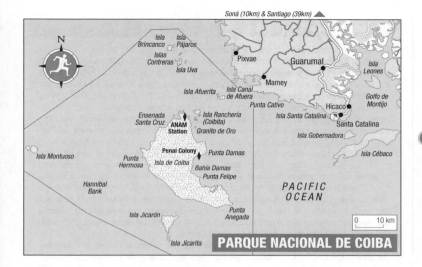

PACIFIC OCEAN

0   10 km

PARQUE NACIONAL DE COIBA

mean that by the time you actually venture into the rainforest any animal or bird with sense will be hiding from the heat and humidity. As there are no limits on visitor numbers, holiday periods should be avoided at all costs.

Accommodation

Coiba's **accommodation** is, in some ways, a great leveller – whether you're on an exclusive all-in deal or you've hitched a ride with the park wardens, everyone has to stay in the same basic huts.

ANAM cabins ANAM ranger station. Forty-odd beds spread dormitory-style around five double cabins with screening and shared bathrooms. You will need to book ahead through the Santiago office (☎ 998 4271) in the dry season. If you're travelling independently, bring your own bedding and supplies from Santa Catalina, including some gas; the rangers let you share their kitchen (but not the fridge), but the gas occasionally runs out. The cabins have a/c and electricity 6–10pm, though power cuts are frequent. Other useful items to bring include mosquito coils and net, a torch, candles and plenty of insect repellent and bite cream. Limited camping spaces are available ($10 for a two-person tent). ❷

The Island

You can spend a pleasant day just hanging out round the camp. There's some moderate snorkelling in the sandy cove and a couple of easy short **walks** affording pleasant views and some tranquil birdwatching. Iguanas and agoutis are frequent dawn visitors to the lawn-cum-part-time football pitch fronting the main beach, and spider monkeys are often sighted swinging through the surrounding vegetation. A strenuous but fascinating four-hour hiking route from the ANAM station through primeval rainforest, crossing crocodile-infested rivers to the west coast at Santa Cruz, was recently completed.

Access to the flora and fauna on the rest of the island, however, is extremely limited without a **boat**. Most of the tourist spots are inconveniently spaced out along the lengthy eastern coastline, hence the cost of trips. The first stop is usually the 1km **Sendero de los Monos**, though you'll need to be here early to encounter the elusive white-faced capuchins or the island's unique variety of howler monkey.

The penal colony on Coiba

For almost eighty years Coiba was synonymous with fear and brutality, as horror stories of forced labour and torture, political assassinations and gang warfare leaked from the island. Designated as a **penal colony** in 1919, it was intended to be an open prison, staffed by civilians and aimed at reforming serious offenders – hence the inclusion at the main camp of a school, rehabilitation centre and church. But with up to three thousand prisoners on the island at one stage, scattered round sixteen different camps, most offenders were unable to access these resources, and the planned civilian custodians never materialized. Instead, prisoners worked twelve-hour shifts on farmland and forest on only one meal a day, suffering violence from gangs and guards, malnutrition, poor sanitation and scant medical care. A peek inside the decaying **high-security block** is sobering. Here ten to twenty people used to share a humid, windowless cell no more than 3m across, with nine bare concrete "beds" and a hole for a toilet, incarcerated for 24 hours a day, with no exercise, no visitors, and little chance of release. Unsurprisingly, **escape attempts** were frequent but usually resulted in failure as those who managed to get through the island's dense undergrowth, avoiding the crocodiles and snakes, generally came to grief in the shark-infested waters and strong sea currents.

Far from the public gaze, the island also gained notoriety during the **military dictatorships** of Omar Torrijos and Manuel Noriega as a prime location for "losing" political opponents, some of whose tortured bodies were unearthed in around 180 graves discovered during President Moscoso's Truth Commission investigations. The penitentiary finally closed in 2004; the only former convict still remaining on the island is "Mali-Mali", now the park's most famous ranger and much sought-after tourist guide.

Just across the water from the trail lies one the most popular snorkelling spots, **Granito de Oro** ("the little grain of gold"), a speck of soft sand surrounded by translucent water, plentiful coral and prolific fish. However, smaller cruise ships periodically stop off here and smother the sand with deckchairs and assorted aquatic paraphernalia, causing the fish to scarper. The park rangers can advise you on timing (usually Tues & Thurs, Dec–April).

Heading further south, you come to the main camp of the former **penal colony** (see box above), whose the crumbling, eerie buildings are slowly being reclaimed by nature; through the iron bars you can glimpse half-opened filing cabinets and decaying documents waiting to be sorted. Continuing south across **Bahía Damas**, the aquamarine reef-filled shallows of the eastern coast provide many of the prime diving and snorkelling sites. Panama's last remaining nesting site of the spectacular scarlet macaw is at the south of the island, near **Barco Quebrado**, though these magnificent birds are more easily heard than seen in the forest canopy. Some tours take a plunge in the invigorating thermal springs at **Punta Felipe** or venture into tangled mangroves at **Boca Brava**, or at **Punta Hermosa**, on the more unexplored west coast.

The Chiriquí Highlands

North of David rise the slopes of the eastern limits of the Cordillera de Talamanca, home to Volcán Barú (3475m), the country's highest point. These are the **Chiriquí Highlands**, or Tierras Altas, a region of forested peaks, fertile valleys and mountain villages. The cool, temperate climate and stark scenery give the highlands a distinctly Alpine feel, an impression reinforced by the influence of the many European migrants who have settled here since the nineteenth century. Sadly, their agricultural success poses a threat to the survival of the region's spectacular **cloud forests**, which have been cleared at a devastating rate over the past thirty years, while Chiriquí's picturesque rivers have attracted major hydro-electric projects, which are beginning to cause serious environmental damage. More positively, large tracts of forest are now protected by **Parque Nacional Volcán Barú** and **Parque Internacional La Amistad**, whose flanks are home to wildlife including jaguars, pumas, tapirs and resplendent quetzals, and whose trails offer some of the best hiking in Panama.

Two roads wind up into the highlands on either side of Volcán Barú. The first climbs due north to **Boquete**, an idyllic coffee-growing town cradled in a pictur-esque valley, which has become popular among foreign retirees and tourists and is the easiest place from which to climb **Volcán Barú**. The second runs north from the town of La Concepción, 25km west of David, winding 32km through countless dairy farms to the smaller settlement of **Volcán**, before threading its way through a steep-sided valley to **Cerro Punta**, the highest village in Panama and the best base for visiting the cloud forests and Amistad.

Boquete

Set in a scenic valley on the banks of the Río Caldera, 37km north of David and 1000m above sea level, **BOQUETE** has a population of around twenty thousand. The largest town in the Chiriquí Highlands, it's also the centre of Panama's gourmet coffee production and a popular weekend resort, with some of the country's best hiking, birdwatching and adventure sports as well as a refreshing climate.

Technically, the town is separated into Alto Boquete, on the lip of the escarp-ment leading into the valley, and Bajo Boquete, considered by most to be Boquete proper. Dubbed the *Valle de las Flores y la Primavera Eterna* (Valley of Flowers and Eternal Spring), the slopes surrounding the town are dotted with shady coffee plantations, lush flower gardens and orange groves, and rise to rugged peaks. The thick cloud that envelops them frequently descends on the town as a veil-like fine mist known as *bajareque*, producing spectacular rainbows when the sun emerges. Only when the sky clears, most often in the early morning, can you see the imperious peak of Volcán Barú, which dominates the town to the northwest.

Some history

Though the **Guaymí** were the first inhabitants of this remote valley, seeking refuge from the conquistadors, the valley was not formally settled until 1911, when **European and North Americans migrants** joined the existing population. Drawn to Panama during the canal construction eras, these pioneering settlers started up the various coffee estates and hotels as Boquete continued to develop, especially when, in 1916, the now defunct national railway improved connections with David and other lowland centres.

In recent years, the retirement and **real-estate boom**, driven by the govern-ment's attempts to increase foreign investment, has forced major changes on the tranquil mountain community. Though unemployment has been vastly reduced, the cost of living has shot up, and it's difficult for locals to get jobs if they don't speak English. Fifty percent of the vegetation protecting the Río Caldera's catchment area has been lost in the frenzy to cash in on the real-estate boom. Many Guaymí are only resident nowadays for the duration of the coffee harvest (some time Oct–March, depending on the estate), when families migrate from across the province for the tiring work of picking the "cherries", the earnings from which have to support many for the rest of the year.

Boqueteños themselves remain ambivalent about the effects of the boom. Yet for all the unforeseen ill-effects of growth – particularly in the last decade – Boquete has retained its charm.

Arrival and information

The only way to reach Boquete by **bus** is from David bus terminal (every 20min, 4.50am–9pm, returning at similar intervals 5.45am–9.45pm; 50min; $1.45),

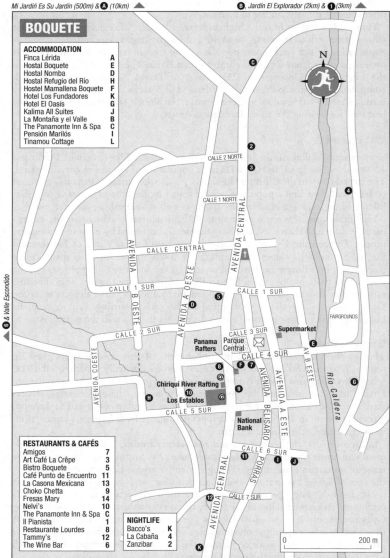

Mi Jardín Es Su Jardín (500m) & Ⓐ (10km) ▲   Ⓑ, Jardín El Explorador (2km) & ❶ (3km) ▲

◀ ❻ & Valle Escondido

BOQUETE

ACCOMMODATION
Finca Lérida	A
Hostal Boquete	E
Hostal Nomba	D
Hostal Refugio del Río	H
Hostel Mamallena Boquete	F
Hotel Los Fundadores	K
Hotel El Oasis	G
Kalima All Suites	J
La Montaña y el Valle	B
The Panamonte Inn & Spa	C
Pensión Marilós	I
Tinamou Cottage	L

N

CALLE 2 NORTE

CALLE 1 NORTE

AVENIDA CENTRAL

AVENIDA B OESTE

CALLE CENTRAL

AVENIDA A OESTE

CALLE 1 SUR

CALLE 1 SUR

CALLE 2 SUR

AVENIDA COESTE

FAIRGROUNDS

Panama Rafters

Parque Central

CALLE 3 SUR

Supermarket

CALLE 4 SUR

AV B ESTE

AVENIDA A ESTE

Chiriquí River Rafting

Los Establos

CALLE 5 SUR

Río Caldera

AVENIDA BELISARIO PORRAS

National Bank

CALLE 6 SUR

RESTAURANTS & CAFÉS
Amigos	7
Art Café La Crêpe	3
Bistro Boquete	5
Café Punto de Encuentro	11
La Casona Mexicana	13
Choko Chetta	9
Fresas Mary	14
Nelvi's	10
The Panamonte Inn & Spa	C
Il Pianista	1
Restaurante Lourdes	8
Tammy's	12
The Wine Bar	6

AVENIDA CENTRAL

CALLE 7 SUR

NIGHTLIFE
Bacco's	K
La Cabaña	4
Zanzibar	2

0   200 m

⓭ (100m), ⓘ (600m), ⓮ (3km), Ⓛ (5km), Volcancito (5km), ▼ Caldera (20km) & David (37km)

which arrive and depart from the main square, Parque Central. From David **airport**, faster and more luxurious transport is offered by the Boquete Shuttle Service (☎720 338, ⓦwww.boqueteshuttle.com; $10–12.50), which connects with flights to and from Panama City, Bocas and Costa Rica (see p.216 for details). In Boquete minibuses head up to the surrounding hillside hamlets from various streets close to the park.

Getting around is easy accomplished on foot, while a $2 taxi will get you to most places on the fringes. The majority of services lie within a stone's throw of the bus stop. The **post office** is on the main square, while several **banks** with ATMs lie on the main drag, and near the fairground bridge, along with a couple of pharmacies and a laundry. The **tourist office** (Mon–Fri 8am–4pm, Sat & Sun 7am–3pm; ☎720 4060) and adjacent café is inconveniently, if splendidly, located on the bluff overlooking the town at Alto Boquete, on the road to David. Although few speak English, the staff members are reasonably helpful but you can get better advice from the hotels or tour operators. Though there is an ANAM office in Alto Boquete, all enquiries about the national parks should be made through the office in David (☎775 3163).

Romero's (open 24/7) off the square is the best stocked **supermarket**, while Deli Barú (daily 8am–8pm) on the high street offers imported treats. Boquete's fertile surroundings also ensure that the **market** (6.30am–6pm), just off the main square, supplies plentiful fresh produce.

Accommodation

Unsurprisingly, there's a decent range of predominantly foreign-owned **accommodation**, all with hot water, in a burgeoning mid-range market. Since most places only have a handful of rooms, everywhere fills up during holiday and festival periods – when prices are hiked – so book ahead.

Finca Lérida Alto Quiel, 10km up the valley ☎720 2285, ⓦwww.fincalerida.com. This is all about location: plum in the middle of a historic coffee estate, with cloud-forested slopes and birding trails above. The eleven spacious terraced rooms of the lodge have vast windows and private patios affording stellar views down the valley on clear days. In the evenings, snuggle up in the cosy common room. Pricier rooms with old-world charm are available in the original family home. Breakfast included. ❼

Hostal Boquete Av "B" Este ☎720 2573, ⓦwww.hostalboquete.com. Great central riverside location (noisy during the festival). Four of the nine compact rooms (one of which is a four-bed dorm) have balconies overlooking the fast-flowing waters at the back for an extra $10, but there's a great communal deck and hammock space out there too. Dorm $12. ❸

Hostal Nomba Av "A" Oeste between C 1 & 2 Sur ☎6401 6278, ⓦwww.nombapanama.com. Small, spartan but popular backpacking hostel with friendly staff, offering dorms and rooms, plus a group cabin with eight bunks and fully-equipped kitchen (from $75). Mirador Adventures (ⓦwww.miradoradventures.com) are based here and can sort out various excursions and rent out

camping gear, bikes ($20/day) and the like. Communal facilities, too. Dorms $10. ❹

Hostal Refugio del Río Av "B" Oeste ☎720 2088, ⓦwww.refugiodelrio.com. Lovely, spacious private house converted into a veritable Rolls-Royce of a hostel, containing two private rooms and two comfortable dorms, each with their own bathroom. Set in a tropical garden beside a babbling brook, there's also a flash kitchen, TV in the lounge, free wi-fi and a gazebo with a barbecue pit. Dorms $10. ❸

Hostel Mamallena Boquete South side of Parque Central ☎720 1260, ⓦwww.mamallenaboquete.com. Set right on the square in a lovely renovated wooden property, this friendly, efficient place offers small four-bunk dorms and private rooms with a large kitchen, TV lounge and garden and all hostel amenities. Can get noisy from *Amigos* next door. Dorm $11. ❸

Hotel Los Fundadores Av Central ☎720 1298. You can't miss the whacky Walt Disney castle facade as you arrive in town. This family-run enterprise makes up in friendliness what it lacks in sophistication, though rooms are clean and functional. The hotel's star feature is a stream that runs through its midst. ❺

Hotel El Oasis Av Buenos Aires ☏720 1586, ⓦwww.oasisboquete.com. A moderately priced, friendly, locally owned hotel located the other side of the river near the fairgrounds with a couple of communal hammock-hung balconies. Rooms vary – avoid the bunker by reception – but some have lovely views and all are clean and comfortable. Good complimentary breakfast on the patio, and great on-site bar-restaurant too. ❺

Kalima All Suites Av "A" Este ☏720 2884, ⓦwww.panamatropicalvacations.com. Six, large, clean, sparsely furnished self-catering suites offer good value, especially for longer stays, only two blocks from the centre of town. Some open onto the garden. ❺

🏃 La Montaña y el Valle Just along the road from El Explorador ☏720 221, ⓦwww.coffeeestateinn.com. A deluxe retreat in lush gardens consisting only of three bungalows, each with kitchen, lounge, dining room and terrace affording spectacular vistas across to Volcán Barú, this intimate B&B (also known as the *Coffee Estate Inn*) enjoys an unparalleled reputation – advance booking is a must. Light suppers and gourmet candlelit dinners are also on offer and you get a coffee tour thrown in with your stay. ❽

The Panamonte Inn & Spa Av 11 de Abril off the top end of Av Central ☏720 1327, ⓦwww .panamonte.com. This historic hotel, founded in 1914, which has hosted the likes of Roosevelt and Ingrid Bergman, offers refined elegance in flower-filled surroundings; when the chill nights close in, huddle next to the cosy log fires while you sip your wine. Excellent fine-dining restaurant. ❾

Pensión Marilós Av "A" Este at C 6 Sur ☏720 1380, ⓔmarilos66@hotmail.com. Homely place, with bags of character, knick-knacks and a talking parrot whizzing round the dining area. The good-value clean rooms (the ones at the rear are particularly light) have comfy beds and shared hot-water bathroom. ❹

Tinamou Cottage Finca Habbus de Kwie, Jaramillo de Abajo ☏720 3852, ⓦwww .coffeeadventures.net. Choice retreat for birdwatching enthusiasts, with three snug self-catering cottages tucked away in a small Dutch-owned hillside coffee estate a 10min drive from Boquete. Reduced rates for internet booking and long stays. You'll need 4WD access or arrange to be picked up in town. Meals can be ordered. ❻

The Town

Whether it's swinging across a valley in a harness, sampling gourmet coffee or chilling with a beer by the river, there's plenty to occupy visitors to Boquete for several days. But while many head straight for the outdoor activities and tours described on p.232, the town itself, spread out along the west bank of the Río Caldera and set against an impressive mountainous backdrop, has a handful of low-key attractions on its fringes. Life revolves around the small, leafy central square and the main street, dotted with several souvenir shops, of which Tucan Tile stands out, selling innovative, locally inspired hand-painted tiles.

A couple of quirky gardens are also worth a visit. The nearest, Jardín Santa Marta, lies 200m beyond *Café Ruiz*, whose welcoming words above the entrance, **"Mi Jardín Es Su Jardín"** ("My Garden is Your Garden"; 9am–6pm; free) have stuck as its more common name. Delightful formal gardens brimming with bougainvillea and carpeted with geraniums and hydrangeas are interspersed with water features, gazebos and bizarre giant painted cows and flamingos. The place is packed with families at weekends. In the opposite direction, the similarly eccentric **Jardín El Explorador** (Tues–Sun 9.30am–6pm; $3) lies a forty-minute climb northeast of Boquete's centre – cross the new bridge after the *Panamonte*, follow the road north and then right up a major incline to Jaramillo Arriba. Its steep gardens are decorated with tin men and scarecrows, with plants protruding from wellington boots and old TV sets, plus scattered homilies in Spanish. On a clear day the views of the Caldera Valley and Volcán Barú from the rose garden are fabulous, as are the strawberry juices at their café.

In contrast, **Paradise Gardens** (Tues–Sun 10am–4pm; $5 minimum donation), just south of Boquete in Bajo Volcancito, is an ANAM-certified animal rescue centre set in flower-filled grounds. Tour groups flock here, with the butterfly house a highlight, though a visit might make you question the amount of human contact that is appropriate for animals that will be eventually released into the

▲ Ngöbe and Buglé women arriving in Boquete

wild, as well as the pros and cons of employing unqualified volunteers. To get there, take the Volcancito bus outside the supermarket (every 45min; $0.75).

Boquete's main festival, **Feria de Flores y Café** (Ⓦ www.feriadeboquete .com), takes place mid-way through the coffee harvest in January, its ten-day riot of craft stalls, flowers, stage shows and throbbing late-night music centred on the fairgrounds bordering the eastern banks of the Río Caldera. $20,000 is spent annually on ensuring a vibrant floral carpet – which you can still admire once the fair has ended. The fairgrounds burst into colour again for the annual **Feria de las Orquídeas** in April, while the **Boquete Jazz Festival** (Ⓦ www .boquetejazzfestival.com) reels in visitors in March.

Eating and drinking

Aside from a few local **restaurants** serving up Panamanian staples, the eating scene is pricey though varied, and predominantly foreign-owned. Things change quickly, and places open, close or move every few months. Many take credit cards.

Amigos South side of Parque Central. The shady garden is a popular gringo gathering spot for hearty breakfasts ($4–5), snacks or more substantial burgers, chicken, salads or meat dishes (from $5) – though you can have the *almuerzo del día* for under $3. With live music during the week, there's a fair bit of drinking here, too. Free wi-fi. Daily 7.30am–midnight.

Art Café la Crêpe Av Central at C 2 Norte ☏6769 6090. More Paris than Panama, the café is as colourful as the adjoining art gallery, bright wooden furniture, patterned tablecloths and poster art giving it an authentic French feel. Deliciously light but filling savoury crêpes will set you back $6–7, while the sweet ones are around $5. Other French favourites such as *boeuf bourguignon* are also on the menu. The daily fixed price three-course meal option offers the best value at $12. Tues–Sun 9am–9pm.

Bistro Boquete Av Central at C 1 Sur. A long-standing favourite unashamedly aimed at tourists that consistently serves good, if pricey North-American-style food. Linger over a deli-sandwich or crisp salad at lunchtime ($6–9), or tuck into a succulent steak or rack of ribs for dinner ($12–16), with plenty of veggie options. Leave room for the delicious calorie-laden desserts. Daily 6am–11pm.

Café Punto de Encuentro C 6 Sur off Av Central. This pleasant terrace overlooking a garden is a popular spot for brunch, attracting Panamanians and foreigners alike, who can feast on a varied menu of omelettes, French toast, tortillas, pancakes or waffles ($2–4). Service can be slow when it's busy. Daily 7am–noon.

231

La Casona Mexicana Av Central south of C 7 Sur. Very popular with Panamanian tourists, dishing up huge platefuls of burritos, *chimichangas*, *enchiladas* and tacos for $4–7.50. The quality can be a bit hit and miss but the rustic ambiance is warm. Daily noon–9.30pm.

Choko Chetta Av Central, next to *Pizzeria La Volcánica*. "Chetta" is short for *brochette* – kebab – and kebabs dripping in chocolate are the house speciality – with a choice of marshmallows, chunks of brownie and, best of all, strawberries on your stick ($2–3). The sheltered roadside tables are great for basking in the afternoon sun. Tues–Sun 2–10pm.

Fresas Mary On the Volcancito road just down from Paradise Gardens. Great little kiosk serving delicious *liquados* and *batidos* and fabulous bowls of strawberries with *natilla*, a particularly mouthwatering local cream concoction. Daily 10am–7pm, sometimes closed Mon.

Nelvi's Local eatery at the back of Plaza Los Establos with terrace and indoor seating which arguably serves the tastiest Panamanian dishes in town. Breakfasts or a full lunch for under $3. Daily 7.30am–3.30pm.

The Panamonte Inn & Spa Av 11 de Abril ☎720 1327, ⊛www.panamonte.com. Hands-down the most sumptuous dining in Boquete, laid on by celebrity chef Charlie Collins. Inventive gourmet dishes can either be savoured seated at candlelit damask-covered tables in the formal dining room or more casually in the fireside lounge or out on the terrace. A three-course meal for two without drinks is around $50, or try a gourmet brunch weekend special (7–11am; $6–8). Lunch daily noon–2.30pm, dinner from 6pm.

Il Pianista Palo Alto road ☎720 2728. Intimate split-level stone restaurant a $2 taxi ride northeast of town next to a bubbling stream, illuminated at night. The Italian chef produces Boquete's best pizzas ($6 medium), various *bruschetti* and *antipasti* and excellent home-made pasta ($8.50–14). Tues–Sun noon–10pm.

Restaurante Lourdes Av Central at C 4 Sur. Grandstand views of the main square from the terrace provide the main attraction, though the *comida típica* is decent enough – a small cafeteria selection plus à la carte. A full lunch with rice, beans and salad costs $2.50–3.50, with mains otherwise $4.50–5. Daily 7am–8.30pm.

Tammy's Just off Av Central on the way into town. Nice location by a stream with indoor and outdoor seating. Slow roasted firewood-smoked chicken is the house speciality (get a whole bird for under $7), with an otherwise eclectic menu of burgers, hot dogs and a handful of very tasty Middle Eastern dishes. Free wi-fi. Mon–Thurs 11.30am–8pm, Fri–Sun 11.30am–10.30pm.

The Wine Bar 400m west of the town centre along the road to Valle Escondido at *Hotel Valle del Río*. The trademark plastic vines replicate those in Panama City's *Wine Bar*, and the food and wine are similarly pricey but high quality, to be enjoyed at delightful riverside balcony tables – though the numerous TV screens may not be to everyone's liking. Daily 7.30am–11pm.

Nightlife

Unless it's festival-time (see p.231) the streets are often deserted after 9pm, even at weekends. There are a few options, though, or you could also head into *Amigos* (see p.231) for pool, darts, films (Wed) and NFL games.

Bacco's *Hotel los Fundadores* A friendly and occasionally lively basement venue to dance and chat (the volume's not too high) playing a mix of Latin and Anglophone music. Thurs–Sun from 7pm.

La Cabaña Left after the bridge up past the fairground. For a louder blast of a variety of sounds and blinking plasma screens, try this joint's dark recesses. Wed–Sat from 6pm.

Zanzibar Av Central. Bars come and go, but this unlikely African-themed watering hole has established itself, attracting trendy young locals and travellers. Dim lighting, comfy zebra-striped cushions and mellow music provide the backdrop for sampling the vast array of excellent cocktails ($4). The place occasionally gets going on weekends when there is sometimes live jazz. Daily from 6pm.

Activities around Boquete

Generated by the region's wonderful topography and climate, Boquete's signature activities revolve round **coffee tours**, **birdwatching**, **hiking** and **whitewater rafting**, although the main rafting river is actually some way west by the Costa Rican border.

Learning Spanish

As a place to hang out and **learn Spanish,** Boquete is a more relaxing venue than Panama City. Both Spanish by the River (Alto Boquete ☎720 3456, ⑩www .spanishatlocations.com) and Habla Ya Panama (Plaza los Establos ☎720 1294, ⑩www.hablayapanama.com) come recommended, though the latter has an extensive extracurricular programme and enjoys a more central location.

Coffee tours and fairs

Boquete is to **gourmet coffee** what Bordeaux is to fine wine, and even those not particularly enamoured of the drink should not leave the region without at least going on a basic tour to learn about the fascinating intricacies of this labour-intensive industry. Visits offered in English or Spanish (and Dutch in the case of Café Kotowa) range from a 45-minute introduction to a three-hour interactive marathon, involving a lesson on how to hone your cupping (tasting) skills and a tour of the estate and roasting facilities.

Café Kotowa Palo Alto ☎720 3852, ⑩www .kotowacoffee.com. The entertaining full-length tour here of this scenic hacienda is highly recommended. The visit takes in the original century-old wooden coffee mill brought over from Scotland. Mon–Sat 2–4.30pm; 2hr 30min; $28.50 including hotel transfer.

Café Ruiz Av Central 500m north of town ☎720 1000, ⑩www.caferuiz.com. Panama's largest producer of gourmet coffee offer a nuts-and-bolts tour (Mon–Fri 8am; 45min; $9) led by multilingual Ngöbe or Buglé cuppers at the roasting facility covering the production process from plucking the cherries to packaging, distinguishing the different varieties and learning how to judge quality. It ends at their very pleasant coffee shop (Mon–Sat 7am–6pm, Sun 10am–6pm). More extensive tours focus on the tasting process (Mon–Fri 7.15am; 90min; $25), while the full works (Mon–Sat 9am–1pm; 3hr; $30) includes a visit to the plantation. The two longer tours include hotel transfer.

Finca Lérida Alto Quiel ☎720 2285, ⑩www .fincalerida.com. Spectacular setting for a comprehensive estate tour (Tues, Thurs 1.30pm, Sat 9am; 3hr 30min; 4 days' notice necessary; $68.25), which includes watching the action in the original 1922 processing plant. Take the Alto Quiel bus ($1) or a taxi ($6) – transfers are not included.

Geisha coffee

In most of the world, the word **geisha** evokes elaborately made-up Japanese entertainers. Mention the word in Boquete and you'll be naming a deluxe beverage that took the speciality coffee world by storm in 2003, prompting ecstatic experts to exhaust their thesauruses. As with wine, the world of coffee-tasting or **cupping** is full of hype, jargon and poetry. Geisha has variously been characterized as spicy, honeyish, chocolatey and citrusy, with one critic likening the experience to "diving head first into a swimming pool of mixed fruits". The fuss started when the small Hacienda Esmeralda began sampling individual cups of beans from different parts of the farm – usually combined in blends – and discovered an extraordinary Abyssinian variety that had been growing neglected for some years. Setting three online coffee auction records, from $21 per pound in 2004 to a ludicrous $130 per pound in 2007 – an online purchase of a pack of beans will currently set you back $50 – as well as being declared the world's best coffee from 2005 to 2007 and in 2010 by the prestigious Specialty Coffee Association of America, the estate's Esmeralda Especial is very much in demand. Since almost all the farm's slender annual hundred-bag crop is exported you have a better chance of locating it at Fortnum & Mason than anywhere in Panama. Now everybody in Boquete wants to plant geisha, though, since bushes take five years to grow, only time will tell whether the success of Esmeralda Especial can be replicated elsewhere in the area.

Hiking and birdwatching

The jade-coloured cloud forests sitting in the mist high above Boquete, many of which lie within the boundaries of the **Parque Nacional Volcán Barú**, which stretches west towards the town of Volcán, are prime birdwatching territory – and the favoured habitat of the metallic green resplendent quetzal, the Holy Grail of Boquete birding. The male in particular, with its ruby breastplate and lengthy trailing iridescent tail, which it only dons for the breeding season, is a dazzling sight. These otherwise elusive birds are at their most visible from the end of December to April, just after first light, when breeding pairs can sometimes be seen on the path.

The area's **trails** range from a gentle undulating stroll round Finca Lérida to a marathon assault on Volcán Barú, which promises one of the country's finest panoramas. You can undertake the shorter trails (see box below) on your own, but only experienced hikers with emergency equipment should attempt the longer routes – including the popular, scenic Sendero de los Quetzales – without a **guide** – see p.236.

Sendero de los Quetzales

A far more beautiful, rugged hike than the slog up the brooding volcano it skirts, the **Sendero de los Quetzales** ($5 park fee) offers the additional thrill of a possible glimpse of a male quetzal in full regalia (Dec–April). Though formerly easily doable on your own, severe floods and landslides have made the route difficult to navigate in places, and hiring a guide will substantially enhance your chances of spotting a quetzal as well as allowing you to learn more about other flora and fauna. The trail can be hiked in both directions, though conventional wisdom has it that it's easier to start from the Cerro Punta side (over 2400m) because of the drop in altitude between there and eastern trailhead at Alto Chiquero (over 1800m). A moderately fit person soaking up the scenery and making occasional stops to spot the odd shy bird in the undergrowth should count on 5–6 hours to complete the trail.

Though the distance between the two ranger stations is only around 10km, both trailheads are several kilometres from public transport. At the eastern end, the Alto Chiquero **park office**, accessible by 2x4, is a steep, almost completely tarred 11km up from Boquete, reachable by taxi ($12), or by bus as far as the T-junction followed by a 3km hike. Accessing the western side from Volcán, you can hire a

---

The shorter trails

The shorter walks listed below can generally be managed without a guide.

Finca Lérida This eco-lodge (see p.229) offers good-value hikes through the 10km of trails on its estate, with a chance of seeing quetzals as well as highland hummingbirds such as the white-throated mountain gem, sulphur-winged parakeets, silver-throated tanagers and the impressive black guan. The tour includes lunch ($26.25; two days' advance notice necessary), or you can pay $10 for a sketch map and head off up through the coffee fields and cloud forest on your own. The finca's café-restaurant (daily 7am–8pm) is a good place for a pit stop en route.

Sendero Il Pianista Steep route, starting near *Il Pianista* restaurant, taking you up to the continental divide (buses bound for Alto Lino or Arco Iris can drop you off on the way back down), offering great views on a clear day.

Sendero Pipa de Agua This modest trail follows a water pipeline up a dead-end valley from a T-junction, 8km from Boquete, on the way to the start of the quetzal trail. Beware of a scam by the occasional unscrupulous taxi driver who, in order to save petrol, leaves hikers there claiming it's the start of the quetzal trail.

4WD taxi ($20–25) or get dropped off any Cerro Punta-bound bus and walk the rough 5km road to the El Respingo park office.

Anyone wanting to catch the early bird should consider bedding down in the **bunkhouse** at either of the ranger stations (advise the ANAM office in David ☎775 3163; ➋) though you'll need to take warm bedding and food, and be prepared for cold water showers. You can also **camp** there ($5), though a far nicer location is Mirador la Roca, a picnic spot complete with tables, though no other facilities, about halfway along the trail. Tours generally include transfer to and from each trailhead, whereas an option for backpackers who want to hike the trail one way and not have to return, yet don't want to be encumbered with their rucksack, is to send it with Transportes Ferguson (Boquete ☎720 1454, Volcán ☎771 4566; both Mon–Fri 8am–4pm, Sat 8am–noon; $5–6 for each pack plus $2 for delivery to accommodation), which has an office on Avenida Central in Boquete and one behind the Shell garage in Volcán.

Climbing Volcán Barú

The unremarkable haul up **Volcán Barú** (3474m), Panama's highest point, is rewarded at the summit, which on good day boasts a truly breathtaking panorama of the Pacific and Caribbean, both dotted with a myriad of islands. The dry season is the best time to attempt the ascent but even then clouds and rain can close in quickly. To maximize your chance of a clear view, you should attempt some, or all, of the climb at night – for which you'll need a guide (see p.236) – to arrive at dawn. Leaving at 11pm to midnight, the 13.5km ascent from the **park office** ($5 entry, $5 camping permit) takes 4–6 hours, arriving in time to enjoy a sunrise picnic before descending. No rock-climbing skills are necessary, just the grit to plod up a boulder-strewn track and a little rock-scrambling. Once on top, you'll need to turn a blind eye to the radio masts and graffiti-covered rocks on one side.

If you prefer a daytime hike, but still want to enjoy sunrise on the summit, you can **camp** on the volcano's upper slopes, although there are no formal camping facilities, including no water, and nowhere particularly pleasant to pitch a tent. *Hostal Nomba* (see p.229) rents out camping equipment. As well as warm, water-proof clothing, plenty of water and the usual hiking essentials, you'll need a 4WD taxi to take you to the trailhead ($12) and should arrange a pick-up unless you walk down to the main road and flag down a taxi or bus.

Climbing Volcán Barú from the western side is more physically demanding, and takes longer, but is more rewarding as you are taken up a path, rather than a road, and across more varied terrain. See p.239.

Whitewater rafting

Hugging the coast of Costa Rica, the tumbling waters of the **Chiriquí Viejo** constitute one of the world's great **whitewater rafting** rivers. Rising in the folds of Cerro Picacho, Amistad's highest peak, it gushes its way through ravines and forested slopes in a series of spectacular falls and torrents before eventually sliding into the Golfo de Chiriquí, 128km later. There are, however, other equally scenic and enjoyable rivers to paddle within closer striking distance of Boquete, such as the **Chiriquí**, **Dolega**, **Gariché** and **Majagua**, with category II and III rapids. The rafting season predictably dovetails with the rains, generally June to November, though the Chiriquí Viejo, by far the most popular run, is navigable all year.

Although the rafting outfits are all located in Boquete, the entry point for the Chiriquí Viejo is a good three hour's drive away (whatever the tour operators may claim) by the time you've picked up all passengers and crawled up the spectacularly sinuous road to the drop-off point. It's therefore actually better to

Inevitably in a tourist-boom area, everyone wants a piece of the cake, and some "guides" and operators lack the skills for the job. If in doubt, seek advice from someone at your accommodation. Finca Lérida and Habla Ya Language School (see p.229 & p.233) also have good guides and the latter accepts non-students on its tours.

Boquete Mountain Safari Plaza Los Establos ☏6627 8829. The main recommendation for this outfit is the scenic horseriding excursion to Caldera. $40 includes transfer and 2hr 30min riding across the scenic undulating terrain round Caldera. Other excursions are offered involving dudes in shades speeding around in a yellow safari jeep.

Boquete Outdoor Adventures Plaza Los Establos ☏720 2284, ⓦwww.boquete outdooradventures.com. A range of highly acclaimed whitewater kayaking and rafting trips as well as multi-day sea-kayaking adventures in the Golfo de Chiriquí, including a five-day excursion to Coiba. Family adventure holidays are also a speciality. Prices are from around $500 for three days.

Boquete Tree Trek Office in Plaza Los Establos, the zipline in Palo Alto ☏720 1635, ⓦwww.aventurist.com. The impressive canopy tour ($60, including transfer from town) allows you to soar across valleys along steel cables, fastened into a harness high above Boquete (1600m) in a 3km series of adrenaline surges that scarcely give you time to admire the breathtaking scenery. After a 90min thrill you can chill at their pleasant terrace café-bar – you can even stay overnight in spacious cabins here. Departures are at 8am and 10am Mon–Sat and 10am on Sun. A recently expanded repertoire now offers guided downhill mountain-bike tours or hikes on trails within the reserve with a naturalist guide. Both excursions depart from Boquete daily at 7am and 1pm.

Chiriquí River Rafting Av Central next to Plaza Los Establos ☏720 1505, ⓦwww .panama-rafting.com. Run by Héctor Sánchez, Panama's pioneering rafter, and

arrange a pick-up from lodgings in David, or, if you're staying in Volcán, on the Interamericana at the turn-off in Concepción, which the tour operators regularly do, thus saving yourself a couple of hours' travel time. On arrival, everyone dons life-jacket and helmet before slithering down a steep, often muddy descent into a ravine. The safety talk and paddling instructions are fresh in your mind as you hit the first serious rapids almost immediately. In the upper stretches the rapids range from category II to V, while on the lower section categories II and III predominate with more time to take in the stunning scenery and watch egrets, herons, cormorants and kingfishers fly past. A decent picnic lunch is provided after two hours of hard paddling to fortify you for the remaining two-hour descent, which ends at the Intermericana bridge close to Paso Canoas.

The three rafting companies in Boquete (see box above) are a professional bunch, but the sport is not without risk. Bring sun block, trainers and a change of clothes (you will get wet and possibly thrown out of the raft); don't be afraid to ask for clarification on safety issues, and know your limits – the major rapids on the Chiriquí Viejo can be truly hair raising.

Other activities

Aerial thrills coupled with spectacular views draw people to a lofty valley in Palo Alto, home to Boquete Tree Trek's **canopy tour** (see box above), Panama's premier Tarzan experience. A more relaxing way to appreciate the surroundings is to go on a **horse riding** tour. Franklin Rovetto (☏776 2047; $35, including Boquete transfer) leads a two-hour excursion across the open countryside in the foothills of the cordillera round Caldera, 26km southeast family, offering full-day all-inclusive rides down the Chiriquí Viejo ($105) and half-day rafting trips to a range of rivers ($85–95). Has now extended business to offer five-day multi-activity tours ($1200), fishing charters in the Golfo de Chiriquí and stays on his farm.

Coffee Adventures Jaramillo Abajo ☎720 3852, ⓦwww.coffeeadventures.net. A Dutch couple who, in addition to running coffee tours (see p.233), offer pricey but very professional hiking and birding excursions in English, Spanish or Dutch ($45–50/ half day, $100–125/day, not including lunch).

Feliciano González ☎6624 9940, ⓔfelicianogonzalez255@hotmail.com. González has taken people up and down Volcán Barú so often over the last twenty years he almost lives up there. Enthusiastic, popular and with constantly improving English and a little French, he charges modest rates that vary depending on numbers ($25–60 for two) and offers a very special four-day trip over the cordillera and down to the coast in Bocas, camping and staying in indigenous villages. If he is booked up, try Cristian (☎6685 9813).

Panama Rafters Av Central at C 4 Sur ☎720 2712, ⓦwww.panamarafters.com. Well-established outfit, offering cheaper full-day runs down the Chiriquí Viejo ($95) and half-day trips for $80. Multi-day camping and whitewater trips are also on offer, as well as mountain-bike rental.

Pete's Mountain Tours ☎6647 7564, ⓔpetesmnt.tours@yahoo.com. Bilingual guide offering informative walking tours through the forests. Look for his truck round *Amigos*.

Santiago Chago ☎6626 2200. "Chago" is a reliable birding guide ($120 for two, $150 for three or more), whose rates include transport.

of Boquete. Boquete Mountain Safari (see box above) also organizes horse riding there.

Mountain biking is another possibility, either on your own (*Hostal Nomba* and Panama Rafters rent out bikes – see p.229 and box above) or on a 25km downhill guided run organized by Boquete Tree Trek (see box above). If you want to explore the area expending less energy, hire a **scooter** ($7.50/hr, $25/day) from Panascoot, run by the owner of *Hostal Boquete*. **ATV** tours, predominantly tailored for thrills, roar around noisily (☎6678 5666, ⓦwww.boqueteatvtours. com), with rates starting at $45. **Rock-climbing** and **abseiling** (rappelling) are relatively new to Panama – try local outfit Vertical Adventure Boquete (☎6764 7918, ⓔboqueteclimbing@yahoo.com; $40/2hr). Run by experienced, certified bilingual guide César Meléndez, the most well-known destination is the Gunko de Boquete, a fascinating lump of basalt that was spewed out of Volcán Barú when it last erupted, only a ten-minute drive from town.

After exhausting yourself with any of the above, consider recuperating with some serious pampering at one of the town's **spas**. A range of massage and reflexology treatments are available at the *Isla Verde* ($40–45/hr) while the deluxe Haven Spa is located at the *Panamonte Inn*, offering massages, facials, pedicures, manicures and the like (approx $90/hr). Those in search of more natural reinvigoration might head for the **thermal pools** (*pozos termales*; $2) just outside **Caldera** (buses from Boquete 9am, 2.30pm, 5pm; 1hr; $2 plus a 45min hike; taxis $15 one way) – although, despite the scenic location, the pools themselves are nothing special, set among the cow pats on a farm. There's also a lovely boutique lodge and gourmet restaurant in the vicinity (☎772 8040, ⓦwww.ranchodecaldera.com).

Volcán

Spreadeagled on the lower western slopes of Volcán Barú, at an altitude of 1700m, the twelve-thousand-strong town of **VOLCÁN** (formally known as El Hato de Volcán) is little more than a glorified road junction en route to the more appealing fertile valleys of Cerro Punta and the cloud forests of the Parque International La Amistad, or the little used Costa Rica border crossing at Río Sereno. That said, it does offer the most impressive views of Volcán Barú, and as the retirement and real estate boom gradually seeps west of Boquete, tourism is beginning to take root, offering a handful of diverting excursions, not least of which is to scale the adjacent **volcano**. A couple of enjoyable days can easily be spent exploring the area, though if you're short of time push on to Cerro Punta and Guadalupe. Even if you don't overnight here, a clutch of good restaurants and relaxed ambiance make Volcán a convenient pit stop and anyone set on self-catering up in the mountains should stock up on supplies (leaving the fruit and vegetables to Cerro Punta) and visit a bank.

Arrival and information

Buses from David pass through Volcán (5am–8pm; 1hr 20min; $2.50) every 15 minutes bound for Cerro Punto and Guadalupe, and every 45 minutes en route to the frontier at Río Sereno. Most places of interest are spaced out along or just off the main road, including petrol stations, two **banks** with ATMs, a couple of **supermarkets** (a 24hr Romero's with pharmacy and the meat specialist Berard's), a bakery, a laundry, tour operators and hotels. *Hotel Don Tavo* runs a small internet café. A few hundred metres into the town at the police station, the road forks: right (past the post office) takes you up to the highlands surrounding Cerro Punta and La Parque Internacional Amistad, while straight ahead lies the route to Costa Rica. There is no tourist office in Volcán; your best bet is to quiz the tour operators, mindful of their agenda. Taxis hover near the main junction, charging $1 for a short hop round town.

Accommodation

Volcán's **accommodation** scene is not stellar, but still offers the greatest variety of anywhere on the western flank of the volcano.

Cabañas Reis On the left just before Volcán ☎771 4025, ⊛www.cabanasreis.com. Twelve brightly painted new cement cabins (some with car porches), aimed squarely at the domestic market and accommodating two to twelve guests. Excellent value as they're clean and comfortable with decent bathrooms, cable TV, wi-fi and a helpful owner. ❺

Cerro Brujo 1km northeast of the town centre, turn right off Av Central before the fork ☎6669 9196. Twee cottage divided in two cosy living spaces opening onto a patio with hammock and chairs, set in lovely wooded grounds with a stream – great for birdwatching – with a gourmet restaurant next door. ❹

Hostal Llano Lindo Av 2A, 1km up the Cerro Punto road off to the left ☎6514 0094, ⊛www .hostalllanolindo.com. Basic seven-room hostel in a friendly family atmosphere with shared kitchen-dining-TV room. Multi-day package deals also available and local tours at $75/person. Breakfast included. ❷

Hotel Don Tavo Av Central, on the right ☎771 5144, ⊛www.hoteldontavo.com. Reliable, moderately priced central hotel comprising sixteen clean en-suite rooms, each holding two to five people, set around a courtyard garden. Service can vary. On-site restaurant (daily 7am–11pm) and 24hr internet café. ❹

Hotel Dos Rios Av Central, on the left, exiting towards Río Sereno ☎771 4271, ⊛www.dosrios .com.pa. The most upmarket and overpriced option in Volcán, its fabulous tree-filled grounds bisected by a bubbling stream. The ample, wood-furnished rooms are fairly worn – grab a brighter end room, or at the very least one upstairs, else the creaking floorboards will niggle. Breakfast included. Avoid the dreary restaurant. ❻

Las Plumas Paso Ancho, 2km north of Volcán ☎771 5541, ⊛www.las-plumas.com. Excellent value for groups or families, comprising four fully equipped (laundry, satellite TV, internet, phone) two- or three-bedroom modern self-catering

bungalows set in manicured wooded grounds. Good long-term rates ($250/week) with three-night minimum stay $66.

Activities

Hiking and **birdwatching** are very much the order of the day, in particular exploring the forested slopes of the volcano within the protected boundaries of the **Parque Nacional Volcán Barú**, which lies between Volcán and Boquete. The **Sendero de los Quetzales** (see p.234) is by far the most popular destination both for hikers and birding enthusiasts, offering a wonderful twisting trail through verdant forest round the northern flanks of the volcano. Accessing the **summit** of Volcán Barú itself from this western side (see p.235) is a much more daunting though potentially satisfying prospect, clambering across overgrown lava flows and navigating round precipitous tors, where you should look out for the spectacular black and white hawk eagle soaring above.

The town has several **tour operators** that offer guiding services and rent out camping kit. The well-established Highland Adventures (℡ 771 4413, Ⓔ ecoaizpurua@hotmail.com) run by Gonzalo Aizpurúa has an unmissable garden shed-office on the Cerro Punta road with uncertain hours. Rates are per person based on two people and include guiding service and transport, with a maximum of five per guide. Excursions include overnight treks to the summit of Volcán Barú ($75/person), or a day-long slog ($55), which only the super-fit should attempt. Guides can also be provided for the Sendero de los Quetzales or to explore other trails in the national park or in Amistad. Less energetic excursions take in the **Pozos Termales de Tisingal**, a collection of thermal pools, or the breathtaking 80m cascade of the **Salto de Tigre**, both in a lovely setting off the Río Sereno road. Specialist birding excursions can also be arranged ($70 for several locations), although you might want to contact Gonzalo's brother Nariño Aizpurúa, a keen ornithologist (℡ 771 5049, Ⓔ westernwindadventure@yahoo.com), who has his own company. Both brothers speak some English.

A newer outfit, Green Mountain Adventures (℡ 6457 6080, Ⓦ www.gmavolcan .tripod.com), has an office on the right towards the far end of Avenida Central adjoining *Kfé Essenzia* with bilingual local guides and offers rock climbing and mountain biking as well as hiking tours.

Eating and drinking

Volcán boasts some excellent **dining** options, reflecting a range of culinary traditions.

Café Gladys y Gladys Av Central, entering town on the left. Set back from the road, this hole-in-the-wall restaurant, with blue-checked tablecloths, dishes up the usual fried favourites for under $3, with an even cheaper *almuerzo del día*. Daily 6am–6pm.
Cerro Brujo Gourmet Restaurant 500m up a dirt road signed off to the right from Av Central before the fork ℡ 6669 9196. The delightful, Mediterranean-style stone and tile interior here is decked out with artwork and overlooks a garden. An eclectic changing menu of gourmet dishes (mains $13–16) such as dorado fillet coated in sesame seeds and mushrooms does not disappoint. Musical or artistic evenings are often hosted here. Reservations only: lunch noon–3pm, dinner from 6pm.

Kfé Essenzia Av Central on the right, heading out of town. Pleasant, touristy café attached to Green Mountain Adventures serving local Janson's Estate coffee plus great *batidos*, hot chocolate and sandwiches. Daily 9.30am–5pm.
Ristorante Il Forno Signed off to the left from midway down Av Central ℡ 771 5731. Warm wooden furnishings provide an intimate environment to enjoy some excellent genuine Italian cuisine. Gas-fired oven-baked pizzas ($7–9) and pasta ($6) are supplemented by meat options – pork chops in apricot sauce, or veal in Masala (from $10). Thurs–Sun noon–9pm.
Restaurante Mary Av Central on the left. Popular local restaurant on a breezy upstairs terrace (with

inside seating in a/c) serving moderately priced chicken, pork and seafood dishes ($4–6), though try the local trout ($8) alongside tasty soups and fresh juices. Daily 6am–6pm.

🏃 **Restaurante Polineth** Cerro Punto road on the left ☎6594 8313. Freshly ground spices and loving preparation (this isn't the place to come if you're in a hurry) means mouth-watering delights (mains $6–8). Evening dining in the conservatory-style building requires a sweater. Bring your own booze. Chef-owner Paul is an authority on carnivorous plants and will gladly show you his collection. Daily noon–9pm.

Around Volcán

A few kilometres west of Volcán lie several modest attractions – a couple of **lakes**, a **coffee estate** and an **archeological site** – which will appeal to enthusiasts or may be worth swinging by if you've a free couple of hours and your own transport. South of the town, the **waterfall** of Cañon Macho de Monte is a spectacular sight in season.

The Lagunas de Volcán

The **Lagunas de Volcán** (1300m) are Panama's highest wetlands and an important sojourn for migrating birds, and will appeal to birders, who will be keen to spot northern jacanas, masked ducks and, in the forested fringes, the rare rose-throated becard. The casual visitor is more likely to bemoan the lack of decent paths around these two shallow lakes. To reach the lakes take a **taxi** ($4, $7 for the return plus wait time); if you're driving, turn left off Avenida Central, by the sign to El Oasis Place, bearing right at the mini-super and following the tarred road until you hit the disused airstrip; continue across and keep on the rutted or muddy track for another 4km (4WD needed in the wet season and high-clearance vehicle at other times). Turning right at the airstrip takes you to the **coffee estate** of Finca La Torcaza (☎771 4087, 🌐www.estatecafe.com), which you can explore on horseback.

Sitio Barriles

Five kilometres west of Volcán ($5 by taxi), the private *finca* of the Landau family harbours one of Panama's most important archeological sites, **Sitio Barriles** (9.30am–4.30pm; $1–3), named after the barrel-shaped stones unearthed in 1947 that provided the first modern-day evidence of what is presumed to be the country's oldest pre-Columbian culture, which was prominent around 500 AD. The most interesting artefacts have been carted away to Panama City's anthropology museum (see p.84). Nevertheless, the farm possesses a couple of **petroglyphs** with the *pièce de résistance* a silky smooth slab of basalt, which when doused with water reveals yet more squiggles. There's also an unconvincing recreation of an archeological dig chamber and a small display of ceramics. For $1 you can wander about the orchard with a full tour ($3) in Spanish or English.

Cañon Macho de Monte

A worthwhile detour for those with their own transport, east of the Concepcíon–Volcán road, is **Cañon Macho de Monte**, a dramatic waterfall (less so in the dry season) that tumbles into a gorge. Travelling almost 13km south of Volcán, turn left at the mini-super in the hamlet of Cuesta de Piedra, continuing 2.5km along the road, and crossing two bridges until you come to the hydro-electric project. Park up on the left; across the road, a path leads down across stone slabs to the precipice above the fall. Returning to the main road, a few minutes drive further south, the **Mirador Alan-Her** (daily 6.30am–7.30pm) lives up to its promised view, and is one of the best places in Chiriquí to pick up sweet delicacies, from local mozzarella and ricotta to *bienmesabe* – a slow-cooked dessert of rice, milk and

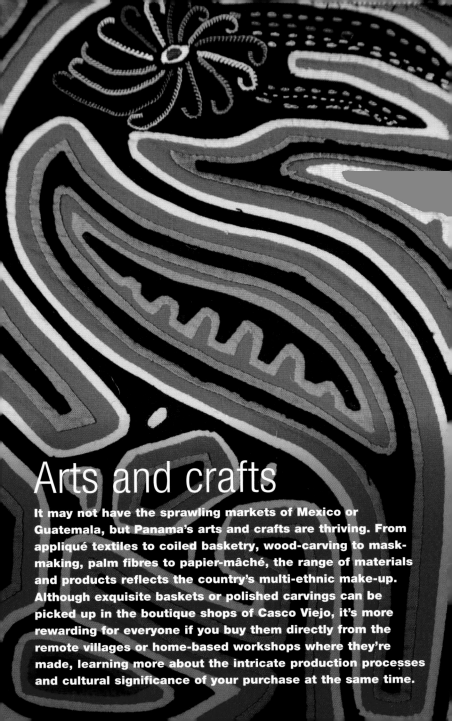

Arts and crafts

It may not have the sprawling markets of Mexico or Guatemala, but Panama's arts and crafts are thriving. From appliqué textiles to coiled basketry, wood-carving to mask-making, palm fibres to papier-mâché, the range of materials and products reflects the country's multi-ethnic make-up. Although exquisite baskets or polished carvings can be picked up in the boutique shops of Casco Viejo, it's more rewarding for everyone if you buy them directly from the remote villages or home-based workshops where they're made, learning more about the intricate production processes and cultural significance of your purchase at the same time.

Kuna woman embroidering a *mola* ▲

Stitching a *pollera*, Chitré ▼

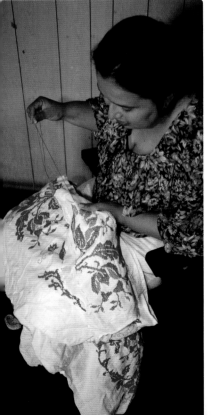

Textiles

You can't walk far in Panama City without tripping over **molas** — literally, as they're spread out on pavements and draped over park benches. Comprising layers of brightly coloured cloth, with shapes cut out and overturned edges painstakingly stitched, Panama's most abundant and distinctive textile is made by and for Kuna women. Originally worn as decorative panels on their blouses, they are nowadays transformed into everything from cushion covers to Christmas stockings. Though the traditional geometric designs are still popular, you are just as likely to come across helicopters or even Batman.

Far more elaborate and costly is the multi-layered **pollera**, Panama's national dress. With probable origins in Afro-colonial slave dress, the floral or patchwork versions of the **pollera congo** unsurprisingly form an integral part of congo celebrations in the communities around Colón (see pp.138-139).

The plain, everyday **pollera montuna**, comprising full skirt and simple white blouse, was later adopted and adapted by the Panamanian social elite, culminating in the *pollera de gala*, a wedding-cake-like confection embellished with intricate stitching, appliqué and embroidery. Taking up to two years for even the most skilled seamstresses to make, working out of their homes in the villages around Las Tablas, they are either passed down as family heirlooms or made to order at a cost of several thousand dollars.

Masks

Most in evidence in the extravagant celebrations of Corpus Christi and the pre-Lenten congo festivals of the Caribbean coast, **devil masks** are made predominantly from papier-mâché coated onto a greased clay or earthen mold; their horns, wooden teeth and eyes – usually ping-pong balls or marbles – are added later. The most famous (male) mask-makers hail from La Villa de los Santos and Chitré (see p.187), their workshops stuffed full of terrifying salivating dragon or gargoyle-like monsters in kaleidoscopic colours.

An entirely different tradition of mask-making is passed down through generations of women in the Wounaan and Emberá communities, using the same palm fibres as for basketry but with more colourful dyes (which have generally spent longer in the pot). Rainforest animals important in folklore, such as tapirs, jaguars, macaws, toucans and monkeys, inspire fanciful elaborate masks and head-pieces, some taking a couple of years to make.

▲ Painting a devil mask, Chitré

▼ *Sombreros*, La Pintada

Hat-making

Though Panama's hat-making industry shows due deference to the "true" Panama hats that originate from Ecuador, it produces a fine array of its own **sombreros**, made from sisal, junco or the oft-dubbed "Panama hat palm" (*carludovica palmata*), as much for working in the fields as for special occasions.

Best known is the **sombrero pintado** (or *pintao*) – the "painted hat" from Coclé, whose name derives from the decorative black rings in the weave. The most sophisticated examples, known as *finos* on account of the finer, denser weaving, can only be made early in the morning or late at night, to avoid quality being compromised by the sweat that builds up on the weaver's hands.

Ngöbe and Buglé artisans produce some of the finest-quality straw hats, though most *sombreros* found in craft markets and shops derive from the mestizo cottage industries in Herrera and Coclé provinces (see p.167 & p.190).

Emberá baskets ▲

Roadside stall selling Ngöbe and Buglé necklaces ▼

Baskets, bags and necklaces

The Wounaan and Emberá women of eastern Panama are renowned for their **baskets** (*hösig di* in Wouneu), the finest examples of which are so tightly woven they can even hold water. Fibres from the nahuala palm are split into strands of varying thickness, with chunga palm filaments used to sew the coils together. Traditional designs are sold alongside more modern depictions of flora and fauna. In contrast, the Ngöbe **kri** (*chácara* in Spanish), a versatile string **bag** woven from fibres of pita, cabuya or cortezo plants, still adheres to geometric designs, evoking folklore, historical events and natural surroundings.

Less traditional is the colourful beaded **necklace** or **nguñunkua** (*chaquira* in Spanish); once fashioned out of dyed pebbles, shells and bone and worn by Ngöbe and Buglé warriors, the modern-day equivalent is donned by both sexes and remains a marker of cultural identity.

Woodcarving

Wounaan and Emberá men are as renowned at **woodcarving** as their women are at basketry. Initially embellishing household utensils and the spirit sticks of the shaman, they now also carve free-standing animals from **cocobolo**, an attractive reddish-brown tropical hardwood, as well as intricately painted animals etched from **tagua nuts** (vegetable ivory). Less refined but equally colourful, and found in abundance at the market in El Valle, are the brightly painted Ngöbe **trays** (*bateas*), ornamental versions of the plain ones used to toss grain and rice.

panela – and their other Chiricano speciality, *sopa borracha* ("drunken soup"), sponge cake soaked in cinnamon-flavoured rum.

Río Sereno and the Costa Rican border

From Volcán, a well-paved road snakes its way 45km to the small border town of **Río Sereno**. Unless you're bound for Costa Rica, the only reason to make this glorious drive is to visit **Finca Hartmann**, a birding hotspot and charming coffee estate a thirty-kilometre spectacular drive from Volcán. Heading out through open pastures scattered with dairy cattle, the journey intensifies as the road swoops round tight bends across cascading rivers and through coffee and banana plantations.

Finca Hartmann

A family-run, eco-friendly coffee estate whose biodiversity acts as a magnet to birdwatchers and biologists, **Finca Hartmann** (☏6450 1853, Ⓦwww.finca hartmann.com) has recorded over 280 species, and is considered the best place in Panama to see the dazzling turquoise cotinga and fiery-billed aracari, as well as 62 different mammals. Birds are more easily spotted round the main farm at Palo Verde, where the coffee roasting and other operations take place, but the real treat lies 3km up the mountain in Ojo de Agua, where two rustic cabins are tucked away in the forest. The smaller one-bedroom *cabaña* (Ⓞ) is cosier and has a kitchenette whereas the larger six-bedroom cabin with full kitchen and fireplace is more of a bunkhouse ($140 for four, plus $10/extra person). Both have hot-water showers (though neither has electricity – gas lamps and candles are used) and are regularly visited by howler and white-faced capuchin monkeys. A sturdy 4WD is necessary for access, or you can arrange transfers. The **coffee tour** in Spanish or English (best during the harvesting season, Oct–March; 1hr; $15) also allows you to stroll the five trails on the estate, one of which leads up to Amistad national park. Trail access alone is also $15. The *finca* is signposted right at the entry to Santa Clara, just after the petrol station, up a 1km dirt track (high-clearance 2x4, or better, required) to the farm.

Río Sereno

Twenty kilometres west of Volcán lies the somnolent frontier town of Río Sereno and the least-used border crossing with Costa Rica. To the right of the T-junction marking the entrance to the small town, **buses** leave for David via Volcán (every 45min–1hr, 5am–5pm; 2hr 20min; $4.25; to Volcán same times; 70min; $1.95). Turn left and pass the central park, where there's a **bank** (though no currency exchange) with an ATM. Should you get stranded here for the night, the town's lone accommodation, *Posada Los Andes* (☏722 8112; ❷), which will provide you with a rudimentary room, is tucked away at the far side of the plaza. Four hundred metres from the bus stop, look for the radio mast and flag of the police station to locate Panamanian **immigration** next door (daily 8am–5pm), with the Costa Rican office not far beyond. Note the one-hour time difference, the tendency towards extended lunch breaks and infrequent transport to San Vito, the nearest town in Costa Rica. Border crossing experiences here range from the ultra laid-back to the downright pernickety.

The road to Cerro Punta

Shortly after leaving Volcán, the road starts to twist and turn, threading its way up a mist-filled ravine, through which the Río Chiriquí Viejo gushes, flanked by almost vertical pine-clad slopes dotted with alpine chalets, some established by early European settlers. Roadside stalls overflow with locally produced vegetables; stop off and gorge on a heaped bowl of strawberries or blackberries and *natilla* (a local creamy custardy melange) or pick up a pot of home-made jam.

Six kilometres north of Volcán, squeezed into a picturesque ravine, the village of **Bambito** contains a few upmarket but overpriced accommodation options and a trout farm, but you're best pushing on a couple of kilometres to the ⚘ *Hostal Cielito Sur* (☎771 2038, ⓦ www.cielitosur.com; $95), tucked away in the community of **Nueva Suiza**. This outstanding B&B is run by genial hosts, who provide a perfect blend of knowledgeable warm hospitality and privacy. Set amid beautiful grounds, four vast, immaculate rooms, some with kitchens, are decorated with traditional Panamanian artwork and share a homely living room. Rates include a substantial breakfast with plenty of home-made goodies.

Cerro Punta and Guadalupe

From Nueva Suiza the road continues to climb as the landscape opens out to expose a patchwork of agricultural holdings and pastureland arriving 4km later in **CERRO PUNTA**. Set almost 2000m above sea level in a fertile basin-shaped valley – the scarcely recognizable crater of an extinct volcano – surrounded by densely forested, rugged mountains, it is the highest village in Panama. In the ninety or so years since it was formally settled, partly by Europeans, agriculture has expanded so rapidly that the area now supplies over sixty percent of all the vegetables consumed in Panama, with fields forming a tapestry of produce from lettuce, onions and carrots to commercial flowers and strawberries. This agricultural boom has come at the expense of the surrounding forests, but the village, frequently swathed in cloud, and surrounding fields are still undeniably beautiful, filled with abundant flowers and buzzing with hummingbirds. The spectacular scenery, together with the cool, crisp mountain air (temperatures drop to well below 10°C at night), makes Cerro Punta a superlative base for **hiking**, and the pristine cloud forests of La Amistad (see opposite) and Volcán Barú (see p.234) national parks are both within easy reach.

Three kilometres further on, you arrive at **Guadalupe**, an enchanting flower-filled hamlet of around four hundred inhabitants, dominated by the rustic *Los Quetzales Lodge & Spa*. From there, the road (and bus) sweeps round to the left in a wide loop, passing the turn-off to Las Nubes and Amistad to the right, then the church, before a steep climb back to the junction with the main road at the police station, where taxi drivers often hang out.

Besides hiking and admiring the scenery, there are a couple of niche-interest attractions. **Finca Dracula** (daily 8am–5pm; $5, $10 for guided tour), far from being the country retreat of a Transylvanian bloodsucker, is home to one of Latin America's premier orchid collections, boasting 2200 species, and is about five minutes' walk beyond *Los Quetzales*. It best justifes its hefty entrance fee in March and April, when more flowers are in bloom. Those interested in horses might consider **Haras Cerro Punta** (☎227 3371, ⓦ www.harascerropunta.com), which offer tours in Spanish round a stud farm that breeds racing stallions with greater lung capacity due to the altitude. The foaling season (Jan–May) is probably the most rewarding time to visit.

Practicalities

Buses from David (every 15min, 5am–8pm; 1hr 50min; $2.90) via Volcán pull up on the one main street before heading up to Guadalupe. After 6.45pm at night, you'll need a taxi to get down to Volcán ($10); they tend to hang around the police station or the Shell garage.

There are only a couple of **places to stay** round here. *Hotel Cerro Punta* (☎771 2020; ❸), on the left-hand side of the main road, is a friendly spot with clean, comfortable rooms and a reasonable **restaurant** serving local fare. There are also a couple of *fondas* in the village where you can get inexpensive *comida típica* and excellent *batidos* made with local strawberries and blackberries. ☕ *Los Quetzales Lodge and Spa* (☎771 2182, ⊛www.losquetzales.com; dorm $18, double ④) up in Guadalupe has a range of accommodation options, from dormitories to vast two-storey wooden cabins ($160) that offer splendid wildlife-spotting opportunities in the cloud forest of Parque Nacional Volcán Barú, all with blankets to ward off the chill nights and hot water to wash off the hiking mud. The usual room package includes breakfast and a free half-day guided hike into the forest. Upstairs, the central lodge building has a wonderful large comfy lounge with a log fire, various board games, table-tennis table and a bar while the moderately priced restaurant serves predominantly locally sourced organic produce, including various vegetarian items, and the menu ranges from tasty home-made soups to boeuf bourguignon.

The lodge, owned by prominent Panamanian conservationist Carlos Alfaro, can organize tours with horses and knowledgeable guides into the parks, taking in the well-known Los Quetzales trail. The adventurous might consider an eight-day venture to Changuinola, camping and staying with indigenous communities en route, although it's only really feasible towards the end of the dry season. Aching limbs from hiking can be soothed with a massage at the spa.

Parque Internacional La Amistad

Covering four thousand square kilometres of precipitous forested mountains straddling Panama and Costa Rica, **Parque Internacional La Amistad** (International Friendship Park), often abbreviated to PILA or Amistad, forms a crucial link in the "biological corridor" of protected areas running the length of Central America. Given its varied topography, Amistad is the most ecologically diverse park in the region, including more than four hundred different bird species (see p.272), making it the most important protected area in Panama after the Darién. Although almost all of the Panamanian section lies in Bocas del Toro, it is far more accessible from the Pacific side of the country. There are three short **trails** with *miradores* offering excellent views of some of the highest mountains in Panama (at least before the cloud descends) and a 50m waterfall. A longer, steeper and less distinct trail (8km round trip) leads through virgin cloud forest to the summit of Cerro Picacho (2986m), but you'll need to get one of the park wardens to guide you.

To **get to the park** ($5 entry) from Cerro Punta, walk or take a taxi ($5) the 5km to **Las Nubes**, on the northern fringes of the crater. There's a permanently staffed **park office** and one of the larger, better-equipped **refuges** with kitchen facilities ($15/night) but only cold water – bring your own food and, ideally, a sleeping bag, as it gets cold at night. A local women's cooperative runs a **restaurant** five minutes before the park entrance, and is well worth patronizing.

Along the La Fortuna road

Highway 4, the serpentine road that traverses the continental divide to the Caribbean coast, is Panama's most spectacular drive, with **breathtaking views** on a clear day; conversely, if you find yourself peering through thick fog to see the edge of the asphalt, it can be one of the scariest journeys you ever make. During the October and November rains, landslides are frequent, sometimes blocking the route for days. Midway across the cordillera, before descending into Bocas del Toro province, you cross the dam wall of **Lago Fortuna**, Panama's main source of hydro-electric power. Look out for the Oleoducto Trans-Panama (Trans-Panama Oil Pipeline) on the left shortly after the dam.

At 1200m **Finca La Suiza** (℡ 6615 3774, Ⓦ www.panama.net.tc; $50 – meals or packed lunch to order; 3 nights min; closed mid-Sept to mid-Oct), 40km north of the junction with the Interamericana on the right-hand side, is both a comfortable three-room **guesthouse** and a **private reserve** with a substantial network of immaculately maintained trails open to the public. An entry fee ($8) will get you a map and access to the trails (3–7hr circuits) and for a serious all-day climb to Cerro Hornito (2100m) you can hire a guide ($72/group). Day-visitors should arrive between 7 and 10am.

Contrasting accommodation lies slightly further up the mountain, at the **Lost and Found Ecolodge** (℡ 6581 9223, Ⓦ www.lostandfoundlodge.com; dorm $12, camping $8; ❸), a lodge-cum-hostel with shared kitchen or food provided that's worth visiting for the views alone. At over 1200m, the establishment is surrounded by cloud forest with numerous trails to explore and offers local and regional excursions ($40–75 day-trip, $125–175 an overnight venture) and opportunities for volunteering.

To get to either, take the David–Changuinola **bus**; the *finca* entrance is on the road after approximately 40km, whereas for the lodge alight at the 42km marker, at the hamlet of Valle de la Mina, where a sign directs you up a lengthy flight of steps to the right – the point at which you may regret having a heavily laden backpack. Fares vary for both lodgings, generally $2.50–3 from David (1hr journey) or $5–8 from Almirate or Changuinola (3–4hr journey), though with few pick-ups en route drivers can be reluctant to take people not travelling the distance. If you arrive with your own vehicle, the lodge can arrange for it to be looked after locally for a couple of dollars; note also that the small community of **Gualaca** has the last petrol station before the Caribbean coast. The lodge sits on the edge of **La Reserva Forestal La Fortuna**, established in 1976 to protect the reservoir's catchment basin comprising primary and secondary cloud forest, inhabited by thirty percent of all Panama's reptile species and the best place in Panama to spot the rare bare-necked umbrella bird.

6

Bocas del Toro

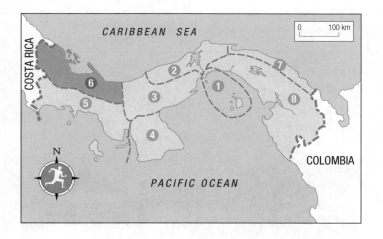

CHAPTER 6 # Highlights

* **Cocktails in Bocas** The finishing touch to a hard day at the beach is an iced cocktail at one of Bocas Town's many waterside bars. See p.259

* **Isla Bastimentos** Explore the Caribbean community of Old Bank, Ngöbe villages and windswept surfing beaches while looking out for the famous red frogs. See p.262

* **Cayo Crawl** Snorkel among gorgeous soft corals before tucking into a seafood platter at a restaurant over the water. See p.265

* **Humedales de San San Pond Sak** This wetland manatee refuge also provides nesting sites for marine turtles and hosts an array of birdlife. See p.271

* **Stay in a Naso village** A unique opportunity to learn about Panama's only monarchy and explore the surrounding rainforest. See p.272

▲ The waterfront in Bocas Town

Bocas del Toro

solated on the Costa Rican border between the Caribbean and the forested slopes of the Cordillera de Talamanca, **Bocas del Toro** ("Mouths of the Bull") is one of the most beautiful areas in Panama. It's also one of the most remote – the mainland portion of the province is connected to the rest of Panama by a single spectacular road that carves its way over the continental divide, often blocked by landslides during the heaviest rains, while the island chain offshore requires a ferry ride to reach.

For most people, Bocas – confusingly, the abbreviation for the province, archipelago, provincial capital and even sometimes Isla Colón – means the **tropical islands**, which attract more visitors than anywhere else outside Panama City, offering opportunities for relaxing on pristine **beaches** and snorkelling and diving among unspoilt **coral reefs** in a maze of tangled **mangroves** and undisturbed **rainforest**. The archipelago's unique history has made it the most ethnically diverse region in Panama outside the capital, its Afro-Caribbean, Panamanian-Chinese, *mestizo* and indigenous Ngöbe residents recently joined by North American retirees and US and European hotel owners. English is the dominant language, though Spanish is still widespread. However cosmopolitan Bocas has become, it is the languid pace of the dominant **Afro-Caribbean culture** and its distinctive vernacular wooden architecture that most clearly defines the place.

Yet the archipelago only constitutes a small percentage of the province, much of which is taken up by the Comarca Ngöbe-Buglé in the east and the inaccessible but spectacular Talamanca mountain range to the southwest, whose lofty peaks form the backbone of the vast **Parque Internacional La Amistad**, which boasts an awe-inspiring array of wildlife. The lowlands of the mainland, often dismissed as an endless stream of banana plantations, also offer a couple of notable attractions. Panama's banana capital and the province's main commercial centre, **Changuinola**, provides access to the magical **Humedales de San San Pond Sak**, the country's main refuge for the manatee and an important beach for nesting marine turtles. Inland, on the banks of the picturesque Río Teribe, a stay with the **Naso**, one of the less well-known indigenous peoples, provides a unique opportunity for inter-cultural exchange in a stunning natural setting.

Some history

Archaeological evidence suggests that **indigenous peoples** inhabited the islands and mainland of present-day Bocas del Toro two thousand years ago, long before an ailing Christopher Columbus limped into the bay on his final voyage in 1502 in search of a route to Asia. Later, during the colonial era, the calm waters of the archipelago provided shelter for European pirates and, by the early nineteenth century, the islands were already becoming the ethnic melting pot that characterizes them today, attracting British and US trading **merchants**, who came with their West African slave workforce, founding the town of Bocas del Toro in 1826. Following construction of the **Panama Railroad** and the French canal effort, West Indian migrants continued to drift into the area.

For the last two centuries, the ebb and flow of the **banana trade** has most clearly defined the province. The small plantations that started up in the 1880s were soon swallowed into the US trans-national United Fruit Company (UFC – now Chiquita Brands International). By 1895 bananas from Bocas accounted for more than half of Panama's export earnings, and Bocas Town boasted five foreign consulates and three English-language newspapers. Around 6500 were employed by UFC in its heyday, and the company was responsible for building the now-defunct mainland railroad system and constructing canals, hospitals, telegraph networks and entire towns. But following repeated devastation by disease early in the twentieth century, the banana harvests failed, causing the archipelago's economy to languish. When the banana trade started up again in the 1950s and 1960s, Kuna and Guaymí workers were also integrated into the workforce, many suffering serious ill-health from noxious pesticides. Now, the business is confined to the plantations round Changuinola, the headquarters of Bocas Fruit Company, the current incarnation of "the company", which with almost four thousand employees is still the most important employer in the province though since the trade in "*oro verde*" (green gold) is flagging, workers now earn pitifully low wages.

In recent years, **tourism** and **real estate** speculation have soared, generating employment and income for some residents while leaving others behind to struggle with the inevitable rise in the cost of living, increased pressure on services and the threat of being thrown off their land. Foreign investors have been allowed to purchase huge portions of the archipelago for luxury resorts and holiday homes, despite local opposition. Given the complex eco-systems involved and the lack of infrastructure on the islands due to years of government neglect, much concern exists over the sustainability of such developments.

Archipiélago de Bocas del Toro

Most tourists make a beeline for the **Archipiélago de Bocas del Toro**, scarcely setting foot on the mainland except to catch a bus or ferry. Despite the existence of several hundred atolls, islets and cays scattered across the bite-shaped gulf that shelters much of the archipelago, most tourist activity is centred on the handful of larger islands, covered in rainforest and fringed with mangroves, populated by small Ngöbe communities or, in the cases of Islas Colón and Bastimentos, largely Afro-Antillean settlements.

The majority of visitors stay in the laid-back provincial capital **Bocas del Toro**, which spills off a peninsula at the southeast tip of **Isla Colón**, the archipelago's largest and most developed island. During the day, launches brimming with tourists scatter outwards, heading for the reefs, beaches, mangroves and forests of the neighbouring islands of **Bastimentos**, **Solarte** and **Carenero** or the distant cays of **Zapatillas**. Other popular destinations include the **Laguna de Bocatorito**, often dubbed Dolphin Bay for the frequent sightings of dolphins, and the sea-bird colonies of **Swan Cay** off the north coast of Isla Colón. In late afternoon, the sandy streets of Bocas fill as the **waterfront bars** come to life. Dining options are plentiful and varied, reflecting the cosmopolitan population, and at weekends the energetic can usually find somewhere to dance till dawn.

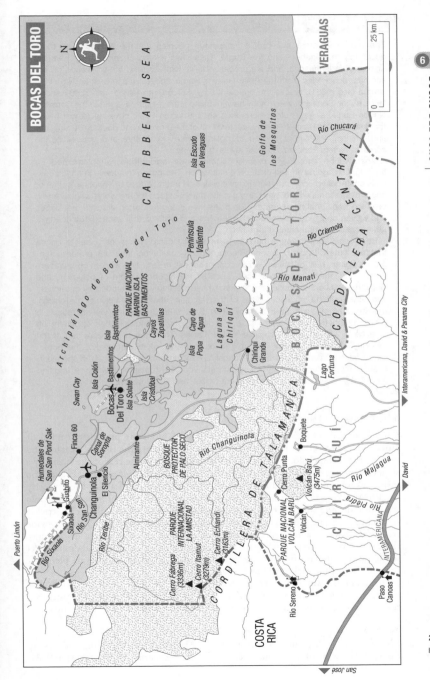

The Ngöbe and Buglé

The province's most high-profile indigenous peoples are the **Ngöbe** – or more accurately the Ngäbe – and the **Buglé**. These two related peoples speak mutually unintelligible languages, and are probably the oldest surviving ethnic groups on the isthmus, descended from the great Guaymí warrior tribes, whose best-known chief, Urracá (see p.331), graces the one-cent coin. Forced into remote and mountainous lands by the Spanish, where many have remained, the majority live within the Comarca Ngöbe-Buglé, a semi-autonomous area established in 1997, covering almost seven thousand square kilometres in the eastern half of the province and pockets of Veraguas and Chiriquí. With poor access to potable water, healthcare and education, the *comarca* suffers Panama's highest levels of poverty.

Most Ngöbe and Buglé practise **subsistence agriculture**, supplemented by hunting, fishing and limited cash crop cultivation. Struggling to survive in an increasingly cash-based economy, some make seasonal migrations to the banana, coffee or sugar plantations, where they carry out the harshest jobs for the worst wages. A few produce traditional handicrafts – the distinctive colourful cotton dresses, necklaces and woven bags – to sell to tourists (see *Arts and crafts* colour section); others have abandoned the rural areas altogether.

Traditionally, both groups have lived in small kinship groupings – half a dozen thatched huts with dirt or wooden floors, though coastal communities prefer rectangular lodgings built on stilts – which control access to land and work in cooperation. These, and other cultural practices, such as the Ngöbe custom of polygamy (the Buglé have always espoused monogamy), have inevitably been eroded by missionary and other outside influences. One of the traditions that clings on in some places, despite attempts to outlaw it, is the **krün** (*balsería* in Spanish), a violent "sport" in which members of two teams take it in turn to try and knock their opponent off balance by hurling a wooden pole at their calves. The contest is a core part of the four-day **chichería**, which inevitably involves plenty of its namesake, the potent maize-based *chicha fuerte* brew, alongside dancing and music. Much of the significance of these festivities has been lost but if you can stomach the violence, and find a host, there is still plenty to learn about Ngöbe and Buglé culture.

Bocas Town

On a headland off the southeastern tip of Isla Colón, the provincial capital of **Bocas del Toro** is the easiest base from which to explore the islands, beaches and reefs of the archipelago. **BOCAS TOWN**, connected to the rest of the island by a slender isthmus, explodes with tourists in high season (Dec–April); whenever you visit, rickety wooden buildings painted in faded pastels and a laid-back, mostly English-speaking population welcome you to the island's casual melee. The town went into decline after the banana trade collapsed (see p.248), until a steady trickle of backpackers and American retirees in the 1990s, followed by a country-wide real estate boom, catapulted the town into another era. Just over a decade ago, there were only three hotels in Bocas; now there are over sixty lodgings. Yet while Bocas Town is a fine spot for hedonistic young travellers, there are plenty of options for anyone seeking a more mellow vibe.

The main festival is the **Feria del Mar**, held on Playa del Istmito in late September, whose endless rows of exhibition stands, craft stalls, mountainous fry-ups and late-night partying on the sands draw visitors in their thousands.

Arrival

All **flights** arrive at, and depart from, Bocas Airport, a small building and airstrip three blocks west of the main street, Calle 3. Aeroperlas (℡757 9341) and Air

Panama (☎757 9841) both offer multiple daily flights from and to Panama City ($105 one way), which get booked up over long weekends and holiday periods. Aeroperlas also offers morning connections three times a week with David, via Changuinola (Mon, Wed & Fri; $55 one way), while the Costa Rican domestic airline Nature Air (☎757 9341, ⓦwww.natureair.com) has direct flights between Bocas and San José (Mon, Wed, Fri, Sat & Sun; 50min; $180 one way, including carbon offsetting) and several other locations in Costa Rica. All flights allow 14kg checked baggage plus hand luggage, and charge supplements for surfboards.

In terms of **buses**, the Bocas Shuttle (Bocas ☎757 7048, Puerto Viejo ☎2750 0626, ⓦwww.bocasshuttle.com) offers a hassle-free door-to-door service between Puerto Viejo, Costa Rica and Bocas (departure from Puerto Viejo at 2pm, and departure from Bocas at 9am; 4hr 30min; $28). Otherwise, if you are arriving from the Costa Rican border at Guabito, take the bus to Changuinola (every 25min, 5.30am–7pm; 30min; 70c) or taxi (*colectivo* $1.25/person, private $6), and transfer to a bus bound for Almirante (see p.268). See p.269 for details on bus connections with Panama City and David.

Two companies run **water-taxis** across the bay between Almirante and Bocas (every 30min, 6am–6.30pm; 30min; $4, $5 at night, see p.268 for details); Taxi 25 has a dock by the *Barco Hundido* in Bocas, while Bocas Marine Tours operates from the main jetty. The unreliable and slow **car ferry** from Almirante also takes foot passengers (Mon–Sat 8am; 2hr; $1.50) but should be given a wide berth. It docks at the southern end of the main street.

Information

The **tourist office** (Mon–Fri 8am–4pm; ☎757 9642) has toilet facilities, an upstairs exhibit on the history and ecology of the archipelago and may be able to provide a map. ⓦwww.bocas.com is a good resource for hotel and tour operator information and the free monthly *Bocas Breeze* (ⓦwww.bocasbreeze.com) advertises local events. **ANAM**, located a couple of doors down from the tourist office on Calle 1 (Mon–Fri 8am–4pm; ☎757 9244), hands out permits to camp within Parque Nacional Marino Isla Bastimentos and can organize a visit to see turtles laying their eggs (May–Sept; $10) though see p.266 for details about volunteering for the turtle conservation programme. The *Alianza de Turismo Sostenible de Bocas del Toro* (Tues–Sat 11am–7pm) on C 3, opposite the *Starfish Café*, has information on tour operators, community-based tourism and hoteliers who are committed to sustainable environmental practices.

Safety in Bocas

The collapse of the banana trade and the social inequalities exacerbated by the mushrooming tourism and real estate industries have led to an increase in **petty crime**. Valuables can go missing from even the most apparently empty beach, especially on Islas Colón and Bastimentos, despite police patrols. Robbery on the path across to Wizard Beach from Old Bank even in daylight is on the increase, with the occasional report of guys threatening with knives. If you hike this path, seek local advice and ensure that you are in a group. However tempting, camping on any of the beaches on the main islands outside an official campsite is very unwise.

Another safety issue concerns **boats**. Serious, even fatal collisions have occurred in the bay, usually at night, generally involving an unlicensed or inebriated boatman and/or a lack of lights on the vessel. Don't get into a boat until you've assessed the level of risk. And finally, take note of **riptides**, which are prevalent in the archipelago. Ask locals about currents and tides before swimming, especially on Bastimentos.

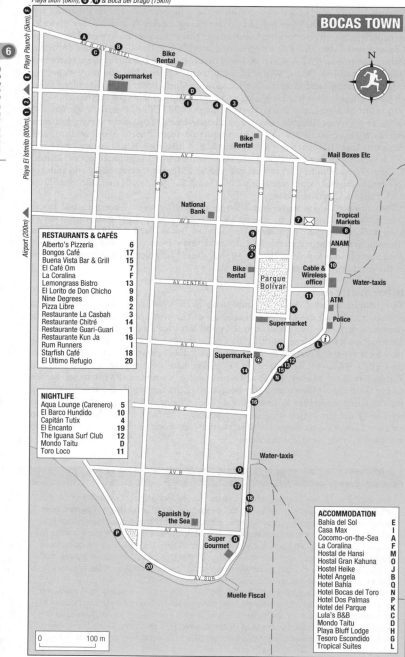

Playa Bluff (8km), G , H & Boca del Drago (15km)

BOCAS TOWN

N

Bike Rental

Supermarket

AV H (AV NORTE)

A
C
B

E , Playa Paunch (5km)

Playa El Istmito (800m), 1 2

AV G

D
I
4
3

Bike Rental

Airport (200m)

Mail Boxes Etc

Isla Carenero & 5

AV F

Bike Rental

6

National Bank

Tropical Markets

AV E

7
8
ANAM

9
@
J

Cable & Wireless office

10

Water-taxis

ATM

Police

Bike Rental

Parque Bolívar

AV CENTRAL

11
Toro Loco

K

Supermarket

M
L
i

AV D

Supermarket
@

14
15
13
12
N

16

AV C

Water-taxis

AV B

O

17
18
19

Spanish by the Sea

AV A

Super Gourmet
Q

P

20

AV SUR

Muelle Fiscal

Isla Bastimentos

252

0   100 m

Boca del Drago, Changuinola & Almirante

RESTAURANTS & CAFÉS

Alberto's Pizzeria	6
Bongos Café	17
Buena Vista Bar & Grill	15
El Café Om	7
La Coralina	F
Lemongrass Bistro	13
El Lorito de Don Chicho	9
Nine Degrees	8
Pizza Libre	2
Restaurante La Casbah	3
Restaurante Chitré	14
Restaurante Guari-Guari	1
Restaurante Kun Ja	16
Rum Runners	I
Starfish Café	18
El Último Refugio	20

NIGHTLIFE

Aqua Lounge (Carenero)	5
El Barco Hundido	10
Capitán Tutix	4
El Encanto	19
The Iguana Surf Club	12
Mondo Taitu	D
Toro Loco	11

ACCOMMODATION

Bahía del Sol	E
Casa Max	I
Cocomo-on-the-Sea	A
La Coralina	F
Hostal de Hansi	M
Hostal Gran Kahuna	O
Hostel Heike	J
Hotel Angela	B
Hotel Bahía	Q
Hotel Bocas del Toro	N
Hotel Dos Palmas	P
Hotel del Parque	K
Lula's B&B	C
Mondo Taitu	D
Playa Bluff Lodge	H
Tesoro Escondido	G
Tropical Suites	L

The town's one **bank** is on Calle 4 and has a 24-hour **ATM**, with a second **ATM** on Calle 1 by the police station. A couple of blocks north, along Avenida E, is the **post office**, which will keep post for a month. Most shops are along the main drag, Calle 3, including a couple of **pharmacies** and several basic **supermarkets** with Super Gourmet (C 3 at Av "A") and Tropical Markets (C 1 by Av "E") stocking more luxury food items.

Getting around

Though everything in town is within easy walking distance, **taxis** are readily available (50c/person). Transporte Boca del Drago (☎774 9065) operates the island's only **bus** service to and from Boca del Drago, 15km away at the north-western tip of the island. It leaves from Parque Bolívar at (every 2hr, 6am–6pm; $2) departing from outside *Restaurante Yarisnori* at similar intervals for the return trip. The island's other dirt road heads up the east coast, petering out at the northern end of Playa Bluff. A taxi to Boca del Drago usually costs around $25 whereas a water-taxi can be around $6; a 4WD to nearer Playa Bluff, where taxis are reluctant to go, will set you back $30.

For most of the time transport involves **boats**. Water-taxis regularly ferry people back and forth from Bocas to Isla Carenero ($1.50 to the near shore) and Old Bank on Bastimentos ($3) at fixed rates from around dawn to dusk. Taxis leave once they've gathered a few passengers, every ten to fifteen minutes or so, and the rates go up at night. The main water-taxi dock for Carenero is by the Barco Hundido on Calle 1, though you can also find boats leaving from the main water-taxi dock, where the boats to Old Bank hang out. For other destinations you can join an organized tour (see p.256), or get a group together to hire a boat to head for a particular destination. If you head for a remote spot, make sure you make arrangements for a return pick-up, preferably reserving most of the payment until the return trip. Otherwise, loiter on the end of one of the numerous jetties and wave at passing boats until someone swings by to pick you up.

Accommodation

There's a good range of **accommodation** in Bocas, and more hostels here than anywhere else in the country outside Panama City, reflecting the island's status as a firm fixture on the backpacker trail. Even so, rooms are scarce during high season and on holiday weekends. Advance booking is therefore a good idea though backpacker lodgings don't accept reservations, so try to arrive before 11am. A sprinkling of foreign-owned lodges and guesthouses are now opening up in more remote corners of Isla Colón, getting you closer to nature but more reliant on their amenities, since public transport between Bocas Town and the rest of the island is largely limited to taxis. Water shortages, power cuts and floods can affect these isolated islands, however much you're paying.

Camping out on the beach is not recommended for safety reasons. Instead, try *Camping Playa Bluff* (ⓔcgrisini@hotmail.com; $3/person), an informal campsite with a cheap on-site restaurant, though it doesn't operate during the turtle nesting season. Alternatively, enquire at the tourist office.

Hostels

Hostal Gran Kahuna C 3 at Av "B"
☎757 9038, ⓦwww.grankahunabocas.com. A fantastic lounge area, full of comfy chairs, hammocks, internet and table football, accompanied by mellow reggae. No a/c, but the traditional, large-windowed dorm rooms allow ocean breezes (and bugs – no screens) to drift through. Good surfing packages. Dorms $10.

Hostal de Hansi C 2 at Av "D"
☎757 9932. Immaculately clean and tidy, catering to couples and single travellers on a budget who want to avoid the dorm party scene. Fan-ventilated singles (private or shared bathroom)

and en-suite doubles have use of a communal kitchen. Singles $12. ❸

Hostel Heike C 3 between Av Central and Av "E" ☎ 757 9708, ⓦ www.hostelheike.com. The town's largest hostel offers packed dorms with fans (one with a/c) that share spotless, hot-water bathrooms. The communal kitchen, balcony overlooking the main street, free wi-fi and internet and purified water on tap make it a popular hangout. Rates include a DIY pancake breakfast. Dorms $10. ❸

Mondo Taitu Av "G" between C 4 & C 5 ☎ 757 9425, ⓦ www.mondotaitu.com. Legendary funky hostel whose daily happy hour and several themed party nights ensure the tiny cocktail bar is piled high with bodies. Not the place to stay if you want some sleep, but it is great for hooking up with other travellers. All rooms and dormitory accommodation share hot-water bathrooms, plus there's a communal kitchen, unlimited filtered water and free pancake breakfast. Dorms $10. ❸

Hotels and B&Bs

Casa Max Av "G" between C 4 & C 5 ☎ 757 9120, ⓦ www.casamax.netfirms.com. A friendly, reliable choice for budget travellers not wanting a dorm, with cheerful, fan-ventilated rooms – some with balconies, though noise from nearby can spill over here. The wi-fi patio, which also hosts the bar-restaurant *Rum Runners*, is a pleasant spot to hang out. ❹

Cocomo-on-the-Sea Av "H" at C 6 ☎ 757 9259, ⓦ www.cocomoonthesea.com. Very popular, comfortable four-room B&B in a lovely painted wooden Bocatorian house, where you'll be well cared for. Two rooms face the ocean but all have access to a waterside veranda plus free use of kayaks. Advance credit card booking a must. Substantial breakfast included. ❻

Hotel Angela Av "H" between C 5 & C 6 ☎ 757 9813, ⓦ www.hotelangela.com. Popular, friendly hotel offering good value in twelve clean and functional en-suite rooms with a/c and orthopaedic mattresses. The complimentary breakfast is a treat to be enjoyed on the waterside bar-restaurant terrace, which at other times dishes up succulent Caribbean seafood. ❻

Hotel Bahia C 3 at Av "A" ☎ 757 9626, ⓦ www.hotelbahia.biz. You're definitely paying more for this 1905 hotel's history than its facilities (though rooms have a/c, cable TV and wi-fi) and the impressive former headquarters of the United Fruit Company is steeped in it. Hang out on the fabulous first-floor wooden veranda and splash out the extra $10 for the larger, brighter rooms upstairs. Breakfast included. ❻

Hotel Bocas del Toro C 1 between Av "C" & Av "D" Excellent, well-managed hotel in the centre of town. Attractive polished wood abounds and the eleven rooms are elegantly furnished (also with a/c, cable TV, wi-fi), some with stunning ocean-view balconies. The restaurant deck overlooks the water at the back. The hotel also organizes tours, rents out kayaks and offers massage. ❽

Hotel Dos Palmas Av Sur at C 5 ☎ 757 9906. On the quieter southern tip of town in a residential area, offering the best budget over-the-water deal, with a handful of faded but tidy rooms (a/c, cable TV and hot water) plus a terrace with hammocks and chairs from which to watch the sun set. ❹

Hotel del Parque C 2 ☎ 757 9008. This warm, family-run place has a balcony overlooking the main square and a quieter hammock-hung one at the back. Cool, homely rooms include cable TV, wi-fi, good hot-water showers and a/c (or fan) and use of the kitchen. ❺

Lula's B&B Av "H" at C 6 ☎ 757 9057, ⓦ www.lulabb.com. Excellent-value B&B offering half a dozen spotless rooms with private bathroom, a/c or fan, hot water and wi-fi with a spacious communal balcony and a book exchange. ❺

Tropical Suites C 1 at Av "D" ☎ 757 9081, ⓦ www.tropical-suites.com. Sparkling new apart-hotel with sixteeen well-equipped suites and helpful staff. Particularly good value for families, they comprise a kitchen, one large double bed and pull-out double sofa bed, with a jacuzzi bath. Amenities include a laundry room, a good terrace restaurant and a marina complete with water slide to shoot into the sea from. Reasonable weekly and excellent monthly rates, when it's worth paying the extra for the sea view. ❽

Out of town

Bahía del Sol Saigon Bay ⓦ www.bocasbahiadel sol.com. Situated in a local community, a 15min walk from town, overlooking the water towards the mainland, this fabulous guesthouse offers a range of rooms and prices from affordable rustic comfort (in the adjoining *Casa Rosada*) to rustic luxury. The most sought-after suite boasts an ocean veranda with open-air jacuzzi and shower. Wonderful sunsets, scrumptious breakfasts (included in the rate) and gracious hosts make this place a treat. ❺–❼

La Coralina Playa Paunch ☎ 6788 8992, ⓦ www.lacoralina.com. Splendidly restored Spanish colonial-style house set on a breezy forested bluff surveying the surf. It offers a range of accommodation, from small fan-ventilated rooms with shared bathrooms ($66) to expansive suites with a/c, cable TV and private patios – all designed with a high level of artistry. The attractive *rancho* bar-restaurant is a great place to hang out, while there's also horse riding, bike rental and a spa due to open in 2010. **❼ Playa Bluff Lodge** Playa Bluff ☎6798 8507, ⓦwww.playablufflodge.com. Set back in forest midway along the beach road, this highly recommended lodge has four spacious rooms in cream and beige with private or shared bathroom, all with terraces, in verdant surroundings a stone's throw from the beach. **❻**

 Tesoro Escondido Playa Bluff ☎6749 7435, ⓦwww.bocastesoroescondido.com.

Delightful eco-friendly resort that generates its own wind and solar power as well as harvesting rainwater. A handful of rustic rooms, a couple of cottages and a small apartment (sleeping 2–4) are set amid lush tropical forest up on the cliff or down near the beach with plenty of terrace and porch space. Rooms and cabins are simply yet funkily furnished with artwork from recycled items; mosquito nets are provided. You can self-cater in the communal kitchens or enjoy home cooking at reasonable rates. Good weekly discounts. **❹**

The Town

Bocas is laid out on a simple grid system with most activity centred on Calle 3, the broad sandy main street that runs north–south, spilling into Calle 1, which bulges out into the bay, where the decks of attractive wooden hotels, bars and restaurants stretch over the water on stilts. Halfway up the main drag, lined with supermarkets, souvenir shops, hotels and hostels, sits the newly revamped **Parque Bolívar**, the social heart of the town, shaded by coconut palms and fig trees, with a bust of the Liberator the town's sole monument. There's no sightseeing to be done in town; experiencing Bocas is more about hanging out in the waterfront bars and restaurants, soaking up the mellow vibe, getting out on the water during the day and partying at night.

Activities

Bocas has traditionally been all about surfing, diving and snorkelling, but as tourism has expanded so has the range of **activities** on offer, with forest walks, kayaking and wildlife-viewing organized by several lodgings and tour operators, as well as yoga and massage.

Surfing

Though Bocas can't match Santa Catalina for **surfing** consistency, it offers some excellent rides when conditions are right, with the best waves encountered between December and March. Several places offer packages: *Hostal Gran Kahuna*, *Red Frog Bungalows* on Bastimentos and *Hotel Lula's B&B*, whose owners have recently taken over the *Bocas Surf School* (see p.257). *Bocas Surf School* and *La Buga* both offer surf lessons ($50–60 half day, $90–100), as do *Gran Kahuna* and the *Buccaneer Resort* (ⓦwww.bocasbuccaneer.com) on Isla Carenero. Numerous places rent out boards in various states of repair (see listings, p.259). Several surf breaks lie on the east coast of Isla Colón, with other hot spots off Isla Carenero and along the northern coast of Isla Bastimentos; between the two islands, the giant waves of Silverbacks are only for expert practitioners.

Diving and snorkelling

Diving and **snorkelling** are the most established diversions around Bocas Town, which is no surprise as the area offers the healthiest coral on the Caribbean coast, covered in sponges and anemones, fed on by an array of colourful reef fish and frequented by turtles and nurse sharks, while moray eels, lobsters and crabs hide in the crevices.

The snorkelling highlights include the distant Cayos Zapatillas in the national marine park, though currents are strong, and, off the southern tip of Bastimentos, the magical soft coral gardens of Cayo Crawl. Closer to base, the shallows by Hospital Point off Isla Solarte are favoured by both snorkellers and divers, who can explore the impressive wall and rocky outcrop sheltering schools of fish. Dive sites further out are only accessible when the sea is calm, with Tiger Rock offering

Tours

Generally, you get what you pay for in a **tour**, in that the more established, pricier ones tend to use better and safer boats, take fewer people and show greater customer service and respect for the environment. To avoid misunderstandings, ask plenty of questions, establishing what is included, where you will be taken and what extra costs are involved. Of course, it's often cheaper for a group to negotiate a deal with one of the boatmen hanging out around the dock. But bear in mind, for example, that operators who speed around Laguna Bocatorito to encourage the dolphins are putting the animals at risk of injury, and that cut-price trips to the Sendero Peresoso and the Cueva Nivida may also cut out local Ngöbe guides – who desperately need the income.

Several of the **operators** listed opposite offer a variety of excursions combining snorkelling with other activities, which make up several standard day-trip itineraries. They cater predominantly to budget travellers and cost $20–25 per person (for a minimum of four to six people), depending on the destination and boat quality. Most leave at around 9.30am, returning about 4–4.30pm and stopping off for a seafood meal (not included) at a local restaurant along the way. Be aware that bad weather can result in a change of itinerary or cancellation and that the seas further out can get very rough.

The itineraries

There are three popular itineraries offered by most operators. The first takes you to **Laguna Bocatorito** (Dolphin Bay), where you have a good chance of seeing the rather shy **bottle-nosed dolphins** that live there year-round. This can be a hit-and-miss experience, to be boycotted in high season when the place is overrun with boats, many engaging in potentially harmful practices (see above). The next stop is the gorgeous rainbow-coloured soft coral of **Cayo Crawl**, where lunch is at one of the three over-the water restaurants ($6–10), before returning to spot Bastimentos's star amphibians at **Red Frog Beach** ($3 entry) on the way back, sometimes with an additional spot of snorkelling nearer home.

Another similar but pricier option takes you on from Cayo Crawl to the national marine park and **Cayos Zapatillas** ($10 entry fee on top) for further snorkelling and beach lounging, stopping off at one of the other top snorkelling spots, such as **Hospital Point**, on the way back. Alternatively, boats head round Isla Colón to the easy shallows of **Boca del Drago**, with lunch at a restaurant on the beach, and to marvel at the wonderful starfish of **Playa Estrella** as well as heading out to see the sea birds at **Swan Cay** before donning the snorkel mask once more at **Punta Manglar** on the way back. Endless possibilities exist for boat excursions further afield as well: up one of the rivers into the rainforests of the mainland to visit isolated **indigenous communities** or east around the Peninsula Valiente to the remote **Isla de Escudo de Veraguas**, which aficionados consider one of the best diving spots in the whole Caribbean – *La Buga* offers overnight camping dive trips, though the seas are too rough to reach it most of the year.

experienced divers the chance to explore pinnacles teeming with schools of larger fish and Polo Beach boasting caverns and swim-throughs. The main problem with snorkelling and diving in Bocas is drastically reduced visibility caused by run-off from the mainland following heavy rains, which are frequent, even in the dry season. Strong winds and rough seas limit accessibility to more remote dive sites too.

Cultural eco-tourism

Several **Ngöbe communities** in the archipelago have initiated cultural **eco-tourism** projects to supplement their subsistence livelihood: Bahía Honda and Quebrada

Bocas tour operators

There are loads of **tour operators** in town – below is just a small selection of the best.

ANCON Expeditions At *Bocas Inn* Av "H" at C 3 ⓉT757 9600, ⓌWwww.ancon expeditions.com. Excursions into the marine park and the forests on the mainland. More expensive than other operators but very organized, with good boats and experienced naturalist guides.

Bocas Surf School Phone *Lula's* on ⓉT757 9057, ⓌWwww.bocassurfschool.com. Offers professional private lessons with qualified instructors ($60 half day, $90 full day, including board) at all levels.

Bocas Water Sports C 3 at Av "A" ⓉT757 9541, ⓌWwww.bocaswatersports.com. Professional and well-established US-run outfit with bilingual Panamanian staff offering diving (two tanks $60–70), including PADI open-water certification ($225) and a taster course, plus snorkelling outings as well as kayak rental (single $3/hr, $18/day; double $5/hr, $35/day) and water skiing.

Boteros Bocatoreños C 3 ⓉT757 9760. An association of local boatmen formed to try and compete against some of the slicker foreign tour operators, offering the usual tour favourites, often at slightly lower prices, and with bags of local tales to tell.

La Buga Dive Av Sur next to *El Ultimo Refugio* ⓉT6781 0755, ⓌWwww.labugapanama .com. Originally a dive centre (Open Water $265), now branching out into surfing and fishing trips.

Catamaran Sailing Adventures Av Sur, opposite the park, ⓉT6637 9064, ⓌWwww .bocassailing.com. Offers day trips to see dolphins en route to Cayo Crawl ($44 including picnic lunch) or heads for Boca del Drago, with private charter possible for overnight self-catering trips at very reasonable rates ($300 for four) and sailing lessons.

Jampan Tours C 1 just south of the tourist office ⓉT757 9619. You can't miss the bright Jamaican colours of their office or boats, which run water-taxi services (including to Almirante) and the standard day tours ($20–25), plus one to the mainland Ngöbe community of Silico Creek (see p.268).

J&J and Transparente Tours C 3 next to the water-taxi dock ⓉT757 9915, ⒺEtransparentetours@hotmail.com. Run by experienced locals, this long-established company offers the regular trips ($20–25) plus sport fishing, and rents out snorkel gear.

Starfleet Scuba C 1 near Av "D" ⓉT757 9630, ⓌWwww.starfleetscuba.com. British-run company with a friendly, professional team focusing on diving (two-tank $60), including full PADI open-water diving courses (about $235) and taster courses ($75), but also offering massage and spa treatments. English, Spanish and German spoken.

Yellow Jack's Old Bank, Bastimentos ⓉT6912 0695, ⓌWwww.yellow-jack.com. Fun, friendly dive hostel catering to backpackers so offering good rates (one-tank $30, two-tank $55) with supplements for more distant sites. Also offers Open Water certification ($250) and taster courses for beginners ($60).

---

de Sal (Salt Creek) on Bastimentos, Sandubidi on Isla Popa and Silico Creek on the mainland are all trying to attract visitors. While several day tours now include communities in some of their itineraries, you learn and experience much more by staying overnight (see p.256, p.267 & p.268) for details). In addition to the obvious interest of being able to interact with the Ngöbe and learn about their culture, the communities often offer traditional dishes, crafts for sale and guided walks into the rainforest, during which you can learn about medicinal plants. These walks are generally the nearest you get to hiking in the archipelago since although the islands are carpeted in rainforest, the potential for serious walking is yet to be realized.

Other activities

One luxurious way to enjoy the area is to take a relaxing **sailing cruise** on Catamaran Sailing Adventures' 42ft craft, either to Laguna Bocarito and Cayo Crawl, or to Boca del Drago ($40; see p.257). If you want to do your own thing on the water, **sea kayaks** are available for hire at Bocas Water Sports (see p.257), though you'll need to keep a sharp eye out for motor boats in the bay; or you can ask any local boatman to take you out for a spot of line **fishing**.

A good day out on land is to rent a **mountain bike**, which range from the dirty and worn to the downright dilapidated (see opposite), and in high season should be booked a day in advance. Then either head 7km up the potholed east coast road (impassable after heavy rains) to Playa Bluff, where you can also arrange **horse riding** at Bluff Beach Stables (☎6803 4966; $30 for 3hr). Alternatively, make the more demanding 15km bike ride over to Boca del Drago, taking snorkel gear and plenty of water with you.

In keeping with the boho vibe of Bocas, there's no shortage of people to **massage** your aching surfing limbs or restore your good karma. Just check the hostel notice boards and other posters round town. **Yoga** too is popular. The unmissable lilac *Bocas Yoga Centre* (top end of C 4, near *La Casbah* ☎6658 1355, 🌐www.bocasyoga .com; $5 per session, with discounts for multi-class passes), which only opened its doors in 2009, has already garnered rave reviews.

Restaurants and cafés

Bocas has an excellent range of **restaurants**, with vegetarians enjoying a decent selection. Lobster, conch and other local seasonal specialities taste particularly delicious in local coconut milk and Caribbean spice preparations. Some of the restaurants here, as in Panama City, add on a ten percent service charge as well as the five percent tax, while opening hours can be erratic, especially in low season, and service seriously soporific. Tap water here is not safe to drink.

Alberto's Pizzeria C 5 between Av "E" & Av "F" ☎756 9066. Though the entrance appears more car workshop than restaurant, this relaxing spot away from the party scene serves good pizza and pasta dishes ($6–12) as well as real cappuccino or espresso. Mon–Sat 5–11pm.

Bongos Café C 3 at Av "C". Raised wooden deck with plastic chairs and table on the main drag which is great for people-watching. Busy at lunchtimes with clientele tucking into the *menu del día* ($4.25) to the salsa beat. Fresh fruit juices and extensive happy hours; the food is variable. Tues–Sun 7.30am–11pm.

Buena Vista Bar & Grill C 1 at Av "D". This seafront spot draws visiting Americans with US sports on cable TV and burgers, sandwiches and salads (from $6), with larger meals in the evening. Closed Tues.

El Café Om Av "E" at C 2. The Canadian–Indian owner draws from traditional family recipes, dishing out excellent curries (mains $7–10), including a spread of vegetarian dishes, as well as juices and lassis, on a pleasant upstairs balcony. The eggs vindaloo *roti* wrap will set your day off with a blast, or choose from bagels and bowls of fruit, granola and yoghurt. Open for breakfast and dinner, closed Wed.

La Coralina Playa Paunch. This breezy hilltop *rancho* offers fantastic views best enjoyed over a leisurely (though pricey once you've factored in twenty percent in charges), appetizing lunch. Popular with surfers from nearby Playa Bluff, who come to play pool. Daily 8am–9pm.

Lemongrass Bistro C 1 between Av "C" & Av "D" ☎757 9630. More boutique than bistro, but you can't argue with the food. The creative and varied menu of predominantly Thai cuisine, served in a delightfully airy upstairs balcony, changes daily. Mains $11–14. 6–10pm, closed Thurs.

El Lorito de Don Chicho C 3 at Av "E", across from Parque Bolívar. *Lorito* serves tasty, inexpensive, self-service Panamanian food – locals seldom eat anywhere else. Breakfast and lunch for under $3 and $5, respectively. Daily 6am–9pm.

Nine Degrees Tropical Markets C 1 ☎757 9400. Elegant restaurant on a polished plant-filled wooden deck. With ceiling fans, comfy sofas and white tablecloths, it has a sophisticated but relaxed ambiance. Great for soaking up the views while enjoying a leisurely lunch ($6–10). For dinner try the Caribbean lentil soup or lobster chicken crêpes (mains $12–17). Wheelchair accessible. Lunch noon–3pm, dinner 6–10pm.

Pizza Libre *Mar e Iguana* hotel by the fairgrounds
☎6852 3600. Gourmet pizzas to eat in the garden
rancho, to take away or even have delivered,
including several vegetarian options, with the Madre
Teresa – pear, walnut and goat's cheese – a hot
favourite. Tues–Sun noon–10pm.
Restaurante La Casbah Av "H" at C 4. An
intimate, vibey restaurant offering freshly prepared
and tasty Mediterranean cuisine (mains $8–13).
Closed Sun & Mon lunch.

Restaurante Chitré C 3 between Av "C" &
"D". Probably the best hot sauce and fried
chicken in town: tuck into traditional staples for
under $3. Mon–Sat 6am–9pm, Sun 10am–9pm.
Restaurante Guari-Guari 2km from town centre
along the isthmus, near the petrol station ☎6627
1825. Gourmet prix fixe six-course meal ($19) and
some of the most innovative dishes in Panama,
exquisitely prepared by a Spanish chef. Served in

intimate open-air surroundings, this is the place
for a special night out. Reservations essential.
6–10pm, closed Wed.
Restaurante Kun Ja C 3 at Av "C". This Chinese
restaurant, with indoor and waterfront seating, is
one of the friendliest budget spots in town. It serves
large portions of tasty meat and seafood dishes
with either fried rice, chow mein or chop suey ($4).
Takeout is available. Noon–11pm, closed Tues.
Starfish Café C 3 between Av "A" & Av "B". A great
hole-in-the-wall spot for breakfast, specializing in
gourmet coffees, organic chocolate drinks and fancy
teas as well as bagels, deli-sandwiches and snacks
($5–7). The Saturday brunch extravaganza ($6.95)
includes a cocktail. Mon–Sat 8am–9pm.
El Ultimo Refugio Av Sur between C 4 & C 5.
West-facing waterfront venue affording the best
sunset views in Bocas and an interesting, daily
changing menu (mains $8–11). Tues–Sat from 5pm.

Nightlife

Several restaurants double as drinking venues in the evening, and there are a few
good **bars** where you can relax with a chilled Balboa or cocktail. On weekends,
many locals head to the seafront Calle 3 to dance to pounding reggae. For more
seafront partying, you can head across to Isla Carenero's *Aqua Lodge* (see p.262).

El Barco Hundido C 1, beside Cable & Wireless.
Fondly known as the "Wreck Deck" both for the
illuminated shipwreck by the dancefloor and the
late-night state of its clientele, this legendary
hangout has DJs most nights, playing everything
from salsa through reggae to rock. In high season
the "Barco Loco" heads out for the sunset booze
cruise round 5pm ($5). Opens at 7pm, gets lively
after 10pm, closed Wed.
Capitán Tutix Av "G" at C 4. Chilean-owned mildly
pirate-themed dancefloor and watering hole also
serving food – more to absorb the alcohol from the
expensive cocktails than satisfy the taste buds. DJs
play Fri–Sun & Tues, with live music from bolero
to rock on other nights. Very much the place to be.
Open from 5pm–late.
El Encanto C 3 between Av "A" & Av "B". Hard to
tell what music is being played here, so deafening

is the volume in this dilapidated local men's
drinking bar, where you could easily fall through
the floorboards before you reach the counter.

La Iguana Surf Club C 1 at Av "D". A
mellow hangout with tree-trunk furniture,
funky music, fairy lights and great cocktails to
linger over either in the palm-fringed patio or on
the waterside deck. Daily 6.30pm–midnight.
Mondo Taitu Av "G". Tiny bar attached to the
groovy hostel bursting at the seams with exuberant
backpackers, who come for the daily happy hour and
lethal cocktail hour, plus wild, themed party nights.
Toro Loco Av Central between Parque Bolívar & C
1 US-style sports bar (formerly *Baumfalks*) serving
gringo comfort food – fries, burgers and wings – for
under $6 and ice-cold beer, enlivened by drinks
promos, darts, poker nights, occasional live music
and free wi-fi. Daily noon–midnight (2am weekends).

Listings

Bike rental Bicycles can be rented from Bocas Bikes,
Av "G" at C 3, Ixa's Bicycle World on Av "H" at C 5 and
Bicicletas Lau, C 3 at Parque Bolívar (all $2/hr or $10/
day), which also has mopeds ($15/hr, $90/day).
Hospital Av "G" & C 10 ☎757 9201. The island's
only hospital has 24hr emergency services.
Language school The relaxed Spanish by the
Sea, Av "A" at C 4 (🌐www.spanishatlocations
.com) offers affordable lessons for extended

vacationers (from $80 for 2hr Mon–Fri) and oppor-
tunities for volunteering.
Laundry Don Pardo up by *Restaurante La Casbah*
charges $3.75 a load.
Surfboard rental Surfboards generally rent for
$15–20/day, but prices vary with size, quality
and availability; try *Flow Boardshop*, Av "E",
Hostal Heike/Mondo Taitu, C 3 at Av "G" and *Gran
Kahuna*, C 3.

Though **ISLA COLÓN** is covered in lush primary and secondary rainforest, most tourist activity happens along the coastline, on the wild and relatively deserted **beaches** of the east coast or the more sheltered shallows of Boca del Drago, on the north western point close to the mainland. The nearest stretch of sand and general town beach is tatty **Playa del Istmito**, on the eastern side of the causeway that links Bocas with the rest of the island, which is a decent place for a beer, especially during September's Fería del Mar festivities (see p.250).

On the western side, the impoverished neighbourhood of Saigon is becoming a more popular residential area for expats and its bay is the planned site for a new luxury marina. Heading round the top end of horseshoe-shaped Bahía Sandfly, which abounds with its pesky namesakes, and skirting the very un-Bocas *Tortuga Playa Resort*, the road divides at "la Ye", where the funky horse-saddle seats at *Alma Bar* provide a good pit stop; left takes you over the hilly terrain to Boca del Drago, 12km away, while right hugs the coastline, another bumpy or boggy 5km past **surfing** hotspots **Playa Paunch** (or Punch) and **Dumpers**, until the start of the glorious 4km swathe of sand that is **Playa Bluff**. An important nesting site for leatherback and green **turtles**, it can be visited at night during the nesting season (May–Sept) by arrangement with ANAM (see p.251). None of these beaches is suitable for swimming, with powerful waves and strong currents, but the thundering breakers on Bluff beach are a sight to behold and the golden sands provide a lengthy, scenic promenade.

Colonia Santeña

Halfway across the island on the bumpy, tarred Boca del Drago road lies the small settlement of **Colonia Santeña**. The main reason to stop off here is to visit a sacred cave, often referred to simply as **La Gruta** (grotto; $1), a place of pilgrimage

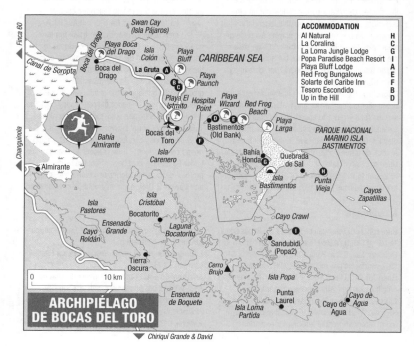

ACCOMMODATION	
Al Natural	H
La Coralina	C
La Loma Jungle Lodge	G
Popa Paradise Beach Resort	I
Playa Bluff Lodge	A
Red Frog Bungalows	E
Solarte del Caribe Inn	F
Tesoro Escondido	B
Up in the Hill	D

ARCHIPIÉLAGO
DE BOCAS DEL TORO

on July 16 for the Festival de la Virgen del Carmen. Push the fronds of greenery aside and, depending on the time of year and the amount of rain, you'll be wading in a delightful freshwater creek or a stream of guano. The shrine to the virgin is near the entrance; flash a torch around and you'll see hundreds of bats clinging to the rock. The place is signposted off the main road to the right by an even larger Coca-Cola sign and is a short walk. To reach there, take the Boca del Drago bus ($1) or taxi ($15 return, including wait time).

Boca del Drago

Follow the road to the northern end of the island, turning left at the T-junction as it peters out in the Ngöbe community of **Boca del Drago**, which hosts a small field station for the Institute of Tropical Ecology (see p.266 for details on volunteering for its turtle conservation programme). Supposedly the first place in Panama that Christopher Columbus set foot, Boca del Drago is a great place to spend a relaxing day. The beach, though slight, consists of lovely white palm-fringed sand but the real appeal are the sheltered translucent waters, perfect for safe bathing and a little snorkelling while you wait for your seafood order at *Yarisnori* (8am–6pm, closed Tues; ☎6613 1934), the mellow sandy-floored open-air restaurant plum on the beach. The simple but tasty mains average a touristy $9. Further along the shoreline, **Playa Estrella**'s shallows are dotted with an amazing number of orange cushioned starfish, which should not be touched. While Boca del Drago is an excellent destination for the hardy cyclist, most visitors avoid the hill-climbs by taking a taxi ($30), or the occasional bus (every 2hr, 6am–6pm; 30min; $2) from Bocas.

The area's other main attraction is a bird sanctuary, a fifteen-minute boat ride off the north coast and included in several tours, though it's accessible only when conditions are benign. **Swan Cay**, known locally as *Isla Pájaros* (Bird Island), is an impressive 50m stack topped with cascading vegetation. Sea birds wheel above, with star billing going to the elegant white **red-billed tropicbird**, which shares this nesting spot with a colony of brown boobies.

Isla Carenero

A short water-taxi ride from Bocas Town, **Isla Carenero** presents a 2km sliver of low-lying land surrounded by shallow waters and a thin necklace of beach that periodically dissolves into mud, tangled roots and, round the northeastern end, jagged rocks, where one of the archipelago's best surf breaks pounds the reef. Most of the four hundred occupants are squeezed onto the southwestern tip, in makeshift wooden housing on littered and boggy ground. The main reason to base yourself on Carenero, rather than in busier Old Bank or Bocas, is to stay over water you can swim in or right on the beach. That needs to be weighed against the island's vicious sandflies and the fact that there's not much to do or see; most visitors hop across for a day-trip ($1 **water-taxi** ride from the dock beside *El Barco Hundido*) for a drink, a bite to eat or just a change of scene.

Popular tourist and expat **watering holes** built over the water on the eastern side with great Caribbean views include *Bibi's on the Beach* at the *Buccaneer Resort* (daily 7.30am–9pm) and the *Pickled Parrot* (daily 11am–9pm; karaoke on Wed), which both serve up fresh seafood and refreshing cocktails. For a more authentic, Panamanian flavour, offering mid-priced seafood mains ($9–13), head for *Restaurante Doña Mara* (daily 11am–9pm).

Two places to **stay**, along the southeastern edge, stand out. ⚓ *Casa Acuario* (☎757 9565, ⓦ www.casaacuario.com; ⑥), a delightful wooden structure built over the water, has five spacious rooms (fan, a/c and cable TV) with vast windows. The best ones at the front have their own hammock and deckchairs and there's a wraparound deck and communal kitchen-dining area, ideal for lolling about on. At the other end of the scale, the *Aqua Lounge Hostel* (℡757 9975, Ⓦwww.bocasaqualounge .info; dorm $10, hammock $5) is a friendly over-the-water party venue with its own swimming pool carved out of the deck, swings and a diving board. Two cramped dorms house eleven bunks each, or you can bag a hammock, though you'll need a mosquito net. Don't expect any sleep on party nights (Wed & Sat), or any water left for a shower the next day.

Isla Bastimentos

The sprawling and beautiful 52 square kilometres of **ISLA BASTIMENTOS** boasts the mellow, Afro-Antillean fishing community of **Old Bank**, lush inland **forest** inhabited by strawberry poison-dart frogs and marble-sand **surfing beaches**. Most visitors are day-trippers: some come independently to tuck into tasty Creole seafood in Old Bank or to hike across the island to the surfing beaches; others visit with organized tours, which generally cut across the western arm of the island to the much vaunted Red Frog Beach. If you want to escape the unashamedly tourist-oriented scene in Bocas, Bastimentos is a good place to hang out and the place where you're most likely to hear Guari-Guari, English patois embellished with Spanish and Ngäbere.

The island's two Ngöbe communities of **Bahía Honda**, in the crook of the bay of the same name on the island's south side, and **Quebrada Sal** (Salt Creek), over towards the eastern end by Punta Vieja, both welcome visitors. Despite protests, developers have plans to mar this unspoilt natural habitat with enormous resorts, the first of which, over by Red Frog Beach, is well on the way to completion.

Old Bank (Bastimentos Town)

Old Bank, the island's main settlement of around nine hundred, sits on the westernmost point, a mere ten-minute ($3) ride by **water-taxi** over from Bocas. An undulating, cracked concrete path acts as its main thoroughfare, snaking its way

▲ Houses on stilts are a common sight on Isla Bastimentos

between tightly packed houses built out over the water on stilts, past reggaeton beats, discarded bikes and old men slamming down dominoes and up to a steep, green hillside dotted with some precariously built wooden homes. A jungle **path**, occasionally impassable after heavy rains, leads to several glorious beaches twenty minutes away on the other side of the island (see p.265). Be sure to bring cash, as there's **no bank** or ATM on the island.

Accommodation

The handful of **lodgings** in Old Bank are budget-oriented and attract those wanting to experience the "real" Bocas, who need to be prepared to be lulled to sleep by ear-splitting music on occasions. The all-inclusive lodges elsewhere on the island (also listed below) offer a more back-to-nature experience.

Old Bank

Beverly's Hill Guesthouse ☎757 9923. Good budget option fabulously located on the hillside behind the main path, offering rooms in *cabañas* with basic wooden furnishings, fans and mosquito nets, set in a garden of fruit trees. ❸

Caribbean View Hotel ☎757 9442, ⊛www .bocas.com/caribbean-view.htm. Impressive two-storey structure stretching over the water containing eleven neat, compact rooms (with fan or a/c, TV and hot-water bathrooms), some with private balconies. A friendly, locally run establishment, it has a pleasant restaurant-lounge deck serving predominantly Creole seafood dishes (mains $9–14). Takes cards. ❹

🏃 **Hostal Bastimentos** ☎757 9053. A friendly maze of a backpackers' hostel spread over the hillside behind town, offering everything from dorms to posh bedrooms with a/c and hot water plus great views. Has two communal kitchens, hammock space and a mellow vibe. Dorms $6. Doubles ❸

Pensión Tío Tom ☎757 9831. Long-standing thatched-roof inn built over water in the thick of things (so can be noisy), with five simple bamboo-partitioned rooms and great breakfasts cooked by the German owners, who also offer informed and enthusiastic tours of the islands' natural wonders. ❸

Rafael's House ☎6446 0787, ⊛www.panamas paradise.com. Beautifully renovated two-bedroom Caribbean house with fully fitted kitchen and balconies front and back, one overlooking the meanderings along the main street, the other the sea. $135 for the whole house. ❻

The rest of the island

🏃 **Al Natural** Punta Vieja ☎757 9004, ⊛www.alnaturalresort.com. Beautiful, isolated spot with half a dozen single or double-decker palm-thatched huts that open onto the sea. Decorated with hewn driftwood, and using solar-powered fans and showers (which don't always deliver), the simple bungalows have comfy beds with netting that keeps out the bugs while letting in the sounds of the forest. Delicious meals are served in the bar-restaurant area, with games and reading room plus an observation deck on the upper storeys. Rates include transfer from Bocas, meals (including wine and beer), use of kayaks and snorkel gear with moderately priced excursions extra. The superior bungalows are well worth the extra $50. ❾

🏃 **La Loma Jungle Lodge** Bahía Honda ☎6619 5364, ⊛www.thejunglelodge .com. On a hilltop surrounded by lush rainforest and butterflies, only reachable by boat, this working cocoa and butterfly farm offers three very private airy Ngöbe-style *ranchos* at incredibly modest prices. Rates include transfer, meals, a tour of the farm, trip to Red Frog Beach and use of *cayucos*, with plenty of sailing, surfing, hiking and excursions on offer for an extra fee. Gourmet cuisine, much derived from their organic garden, makes this very popular so book ahead. Some of the accommodation costs go to support the Bahía Honda community development fund. ❼

Red Frog Bungalows Red Frog Beach ☎6717 2304, ⊛www.redfrogbungalows.com. Bali meets Bastimentos in this upmarket, surfer-friendly eco-lodge – carbon-offsetting, solar power, rainwater harvesting, composting toilets etc – made from sustainably farmed Javanese teak, sat a coconut's throw from Red Frog Beach. Accommodation is in two-storey Balinese-style bungalows (for up to four) or luxury safari tents (for up to three) on platforms under thatch. There's a great bar-restaurant for guests with pool and ping pong, plus a hot tub outside. Rates include airport transfer, accommodation and all meals. Surfing packages offered, though there's a range of other excursions, plus kayak and snorkel rental. ❾

Strawberry poison dart frogs

Probably the island's most famous residents, the dazzling **strawberry poison dart frogs** (*oophaga pumilio*), no larger than a thumbnail, are actually widespread along the Caribbean lowlands from Nicaragua to western Panama. But nowhere is their colouration and size – "morphs" as they are termed – as varied as in Bastimentos.

The most commonly sighted is the smart "blue-jeans" morph, whose brilliant scarlet torso fades into cobalt blue or purple legs, though on Bastimentos these seductive amphibians span red, orange, gold, green or even white, and are often speckled with black. The "poison dart" title given to the family derived from the likes of the Colombian golden poison frog (*phyllobates terriblis*) that secretes a particularly lethal toxin – sufficient to kill up to twenty people – and which has traditionally been used by the Chocó (ancestors of the present-day Emberá) to coat darts and arrows for hunting.

While the dazzling colouration aimed at alerting would-be predators to the poison beneath their skin is what most attracts tourists to these fluorescent creatures, their behaviour is equally striking. Extremely territorial, male dart frogs can be seen locked in combat among the leaf-litter like miniature wrestlers, comically teetering on their hind legs trying to pin their opponent down in submission with the front legs. Mating occurs at any time of year and after the small clutch of eggs has been laid and fertilized, the male periodically pees on them to keep them moist. Once hatched, the female gives each tadpole a piggy-back ride, one by one, up to the canopy, depositing them in separate water-filled bromeliads. Over the next few weeks, she returns frequently to deposit unfertilized eggs in the water for the tadpoles to feed on as they mature.

Restaurants and nightlife

Most eating options in Bastimentos are low-key, with local flavourings at locally affordable prices. You're likely to find traditional Caribbean dishes such as *rondón*, a fish and vegetable stew in coconut milk, or *pescado* "Escobich", a spicy marinaded fish dish. On **Blue Mondays** (every Mon), vast speakers at the *cantina* crank up the volume, cheap beer flows and you may be lucky enough to catch the island's most famous musicians, the Bastimentos Beach Boys.

Café One Love Up the hill on the way to the beach. Let the reggae beat pull you in to this rasta haven for a beer or soda. So laid-back it is almost horizontal, as are some of its clientele after a heavy night's drinking.

Island Time ☎ 6844 7704, ⓦ www.island timethairestaurant.com. Mouth-watering authentic Thai cuisine for under $6 an invigorating 15min hike up the hill from Old Bank, past the church. There are only a handful of tables, so booking is advisable. Dec–March Mon–Sat noon–8pm.

Restaurante Ali Katy Main path. Run by the famous local Archibald family, and popular for its hot pepper sauce and chicken with ice-cold beers. Dishes $3–10. Generally only open high season.

The Rooster Up by the path near *Tío Tom's*, offering some good, moderately priced vegetarian options, most for around $5. Try the stir-fry or falafel. Tues–Sun 8am–10pm.

Roots A Bastimentos institution that serves up cracking fresh seafood and coconut rice dishes ($4–10). Just follow the music and you can't miss it. Noon–9.30pm, closed Tues.

Up in the Hill ☎ 6607 8962, ⓦ www.upinthehill .com. Well worth the 20min hike, this organic snack and craft shop offers fresh lemonade, delectable brownies and numerous other goodies ($3–5). From town, follow the path near the police station and continue through the jungle, keeping watch for markers.

The rest of the island

Renowned for riptides that claim lives every year, the sea that pounds the northern **beaches** of Bastimentos is often too dangerous to swim in, but the beaches are lovely to walk along, offering curved broad belts of creamy sand backed by palms and thick vegetation. Heading overland from Old Bank, you pass **Playa Wizard** (Playa Primera) and, further east, **Red Frog Beach** (Playa Segunda). While you won't find its namesake waving to you from a beach towel, just peer around the leaf litter off the back of the beach and you're sure to spot one before too long. If you arrive along the trail most tours take, enterprising local kids will charge $1 to find you one or photograph one they've picked up earlier. Don't touch the frogs (see box opposite), whatever the kids may urge, both for the obvious reasons of animal welfare, but also since the poison can get into the bloodstream if you have a cut or abrasion, though it won't kill you.

The 25 or so thatched homes of the dispersed Ngöbe community of **Bahía Honda** are hidden among a dense tangle of mangroves at the eastern end of the bay of the same name, with a few across the water on Isla Solarte. In addition to a chapel and school, they have a restaurant, the heart of the community tourism project (☎6726 0968 – ask for Rutilio Milton, ⓦwww.timorogo.org) – whose star attraction is a guided excursion up the **Sendero del Peresoso** (Trail of the Sloth) to the Cueva Nivida. You'll be paddled up a nearby creek, where you can often see the trail's namesake furled round a branch and crabs and caimans in the shallows, before heading off on foot through forest that was once a cocoa plantation, to wade through a series of caves thick with stalagmites and coated with several species of Bastimentos bats. If you ring a day in advance, you can stop off at the community restaurant on the way back and sample some traditional cuisine, such as *morongodo,* a green plantain pancake.

Heading several kilometres almost due south through a myriad of mangrove islets, you round the southern tip of Bastimentos and arrive at tiny **Cayo Crawl**, where three thatched **restaurants** do a roaring trade in seafood lunches (mains $6–10) for day-trippers in the season, though the original *Restaurante Cayo Crawl* gets top billing. After rounding the point, you come to the gorgeous soft coral fields of the same name. Some 4km further along Bastimentos's south east coast, close to Punta Vieja, the larger Ngöbe community of **Quebrada Sal** (☎6592 5162; $22/person plus $5 community fee, $1 guide) sees fewer visitors, generally from the lodges around that end of the island, but now offers basic accommodation in the village – with electricity, which the village itself lacks, and private bathroom. The surrounding wetlands and nearby Playa Larga can be explored via several trails during the stay, which also provides a chance to learn about medicinal plants and other aspects of Ngöbe culture.

Practicalities

The sea is rarely calm enough to land at either Wizard or Red Frog Beach. Sometimes, experienced boatmen can make it through the reef at the more sheltered Playa Polo, from where it's a short hike back to Red Frog beach. Alternatively you can hop over to Old Bank (water-taxi $3 from Bocas) and take the steep beach trail over the hill (15–20min), a real challenge if it's muddy and you're carrying a surfboard (but see box, p.251). The easiest route lies southeast of Old Bank, accessible by boat, along a flatter well-tramped trail (5–10min) across to Red Frog Beach ($3 entry). If you're planning a whole day at the beach, take enough water with you since apart from a funky **beach bar** complete with swings at the back of Red Frog Beach (which may not have water, or much food), you're on your own.

Water-taxi fares one way and per person to the various places from Bocas Town are as follows: Red Frog Beach via walk from Magic Bay ($5), Wizard and Polo Beaches ($10), Bahía Honda ($5), Cayo Crawl ($15) and Quebrada Sal ($20), though costs will depend on fuel prices at the time; you may want to negotiate a return excursion fare including wait time. If you want to visit one of the Ngöbe communities and are struggling to make your own arrangements, contact the sustainable tourism office on Calle 3 in Bocas (see p.251).

Parque Nacional Marino Isla Bastimentos and Cayos Zapatillas

One of the major attractions of the archipelago is the **Parque Nacional Marino Bastimentos**. The 130 square kilometres of boomerang-shaped reserve sweep across a central swathe of the island and include a chunk of the northern coastline, dominated by the 6km Playa Larga, an important nesting site for hawksbill, leatherback and green turtles (March–Sept). There's a park office here, where you may be charged a $10 park entrance fee, and a basic refuge where you can camp for another $10; you'll need to stay overnight if you want to see the turtles lay their eggs, which requires permission from ANAM in Bocas; if you arrive between March and July, ANAM is likely to refer you to the Endangered Wildlife Trust (see below) since the refuge will be occupied by conservation volunteers, though you could overnight in slightly more comfort at Quebrada Sal (see p.265).

Marine turtle conservation

One of the most poignant scenes in the natural world is the laborious nesting process of the female **turtle** as she drags herself up the beach beyond the high tide mark, excavating a hole with her flippers, before depositing fifty to two hundred eggs, their sex later determined by the temperature of the sand. After around sixty days, usually under cover of darkness, the hatchlings break out from their shells en masse and scuttle down to the sea, unless they become disoriented by lights or emerge in daylight and are picked off by sea birds. Each egg has less than a one in a thousand chance of reaching maturity.

Of the five species of turtle found in the country, three are known to nest along the beaches of Bocas del Toro. Historically the **hawksbill** (*eretmochelys caretta*) and **green turtle** (*chelonian mydas*) reproduced prolifically on the province's sands but over the last fifty years, as eggs were overharvested and adults killed for their meat and shells, the populations were decimated – though significant numbers of hawksbill still nest on Islas Zapatillas (May–Sept). The 29km expanse of Playa Chiriquí, which lines the Golfo de los Mosquitos, east of the Peninsula Valiente, is the most important rookery in all Central America for gigantic **leatherbacks** (*dermochelys coricea*). Measuring around 1.5m on average and weighing half a ton, these leviathans dig seven thousand nests annually (March–June). Whether and where **loggerheads** (*caretta caretta*) deposit their eggs remains a mystery, though they are often seen swimming off the islands.

For the last few years, ANAM has been working together with various national and international bodies monitoring and tagging turtles and patrolling beaches. The main beaches involved are Playa Larga and Cayos Zapatillas, Playa Chiriquí in the Comarca Ngöbe-Buglé and Playa Soropta in the Humedales de San San Pond Sak. You can volunteer through the Institute for Tropical Ecology (@ www.itec-edu.org /conservation.html), based in Boca del Drago, for the season. Alternatively, if you have less time available, you can also volunteer on the spot in Bocas (March–July); visit the Endangered Wildlife Trust next to ANAM (☎757 9962, @turtlevolpanama @yahoo.com). A three-day minimum period is required for volunteering, though a week is preferred.

Increasingly turtle-watching is being offered by hotels and tour operators, and by ANAM in Bocas (see p.251). This can be a captivating experience, though bear in mind that female turtles can easily be spooked into not depositing their eggs. For this reason it's best to go with an experienced turtle guide and a very small group. Avoid bright clothes and try to go when there is a good moon, so as not to be tempted to use a torch (unless infrared), leave your camera behind and maintain a respectful distance from the turtle.

Southeast of Isla Bastimentos, but still within the park boundary, are the **Cayos Zapatillas** (Little Shoes), so named because they resemble a pair of footprints in the sea. The two dreamy, coral-fringed islands, encircled by powdery white sand, offer snorkelling off the beach, where you'll find more and larger fish than in Cayo Crawl. The main reef is exposed to the ocean, often with strong currents and choppy water. An ANAM officer will usually find you to collect the entry fee. On the prettier northern island, camping is also possible with permission from ANAM in Bocas Town, where you can watch the stars and share the sand with nesting turtles.

Practicalities

The easiest way to visit the marine park is with one of the area's **tour operators** (see box, p.256) on one of their day trips or by contracting a **boat** (see box, p.256). If the latter, arrange for an early start to miss the tour boats at Laguna Bocatorito and Cayo Crawl. For an overnight **stay** in the forest and the chance of acquainting yourself with some of the park's thirteen species of bat and improving your chances of spotting white-faced capuchins, night monkeys, red-lored Amazons or blue-headed parrots, consider staying at Quebrada Sal.

Other islands

Other islands in the archipelago are far less frequently visited and far less populated, though some of the scattered Ngöbe communities are now opening up to visitors through community-based tourism projects.

Sheltered in the leeward crook of Isla Bastimentos, thin, hilly **Isla Solarte** is surrounded by tranquil waters. Its most famous feature, Hospital Point, at its northwestern tip, was the location of a hospital built by the United Fruit Company in 1900 during the banana boom to quarantine malaria and yellow-fever sufferers, though it also served as the region's main hospital until 1920. The point is now one the most popular dive and snorkel spots, at the end of many day-trip itineraries, with a healthy reef of cauliflower and brain coral and an impressive wall full of tropical fish, shelving off a pencil-thin strip of beach.

Solarte, also known as Cayo Nancy, a corruption of "nance", the cherry-sized yellow fruit much in evidence on the island, is home to a Ngöbe village of around 250, which has a school and even a football field. Most of the villagers live from fishing and subsistence agriculture though a handful work for the island's sole hotel, the *Solarte del Caribe Inn* (℡ 757 9032, ⓦ www.solarteinn.com; ⑥), an attractive cedar guesthouse perched on the hilltop, offering a handful of fan-ventilated rooms and spectacular sea views across to the mainland. Free transport is provided to Bocas for dining though evening catering can be provided.

Just off the southern tip of Isla Bastimentos lies the archipelago's second largest land mass, **Isla Popa**, home to five Ngöbe fishing communities and the only island where you can spot toucans. The northern village of Sandubidi (Popa 2) has a community-based tourism project (ⓦ www.meri-ngobe.org), which includes a restaurant serving simple dishes of fried fish, *patacones* or fried yuca with coconut rice to visitors, who can also take a guided walk along a trail with a local guide. A breezy hilltop wood-and-thatch *cabaña* with a bathroom has also been constructed for overnight guests. The acclaimed luxury *Popa Paradise Beach Resort* (℡ 6550 2505, ⓦ www.popaparadisebeachresort.com; ⑧) lies nearby on the northeastern tip, spread over substantial grounds, which include several thin sandy beaches leading off into coral-filled shallows and acres of rainforest. In addition to eight *casitas* and three luxury suites, there are five more economical lodge rooms, though restaurant and excursion costs remain pricey.

Mainland Bocas

Mainland Bocas covers the vast majority of the province, yet its imperious jagged peaks clad in virgin forest, boggy wetlands and powerful rivers are ignored by most visitors. True, the three mainland towns of **Chiriquí Grande**, **Almirante** and **Changuinola** have little to offer the visitor, but the **Humedales de San San Pond Sak**, home to countless aquatic birds and the endangered manatee, and the spectacular wilderness **Parque Internacional La Amistad** are definitely worth the effort to reach. The two main obstacles to exploring the region – accessibility and lack of infrastructure – have helped preserve the province's natural heritage and the indigenous Bri-Bri, Naso and Bokota populations' livelihoods are now under threat from various hydro-electric projects (see box, p.273).

From the village of Chiriquí, 14km east of David on the Interamericana, a spectacular road passes over the Fortuna hydroelectric dam, cresting the continental divide that marks the entry into Bocas del Toro before descending to the small town of Chiriquí Grande, the Atlantic terminus of the Trans-Panama Oil Pipeline, visible on the left shortly after crossing the dam. The road then hugs the crinkled coastline for 60km to the port of Almirante, before continuing to the main provincial town, Changuinola, a mere 17km from the Costa Rican border.

In contrast, virtually no visitors venture east of Chiriquí Grande, into the increasingly deforested **Comarca Ngöbe-Buglé**, where rivers cut through the Caribbean slopes of the Cordillera Central, flowing into the Golfo de los Mosquitos, backed by the 29km Playa Chiriquí, home to a major turtle conservation programme (see p.266).

Almirante

The ramshackle town of **Almirante**, its rusting tin-roofed wooden houses propped up on stilts over the Caribbean, is the departure point for **water-taxis** to the Bocas del Toro archipelago. Like Bocas, the port is a product of the banana boom, and suffered a similar decline. Unlike Bocas, there is no tourism-fuelled renaissance on the horizon. Basic services are lacking; unemployment and its associated ills are a major concern; and most visitors pass through as quickly as possible.

In contrast, between Chiriquí Grande and Almirante, at Kilometre 24, on the border of the Comarca Ngöbe-Buglé, lies the Ngöbe community of **Silico Creek** (☎6449 3503, ⓦwww.urari.org), a dynamic village that has successfully retained traditional values while adapting to the modern economy. Though day-visits are common, you can also stay in the community's two thatched *cabañas*, giving you more time to browse the Ngöbe crafts and learn about their organic permaculture projects in coffee, plantains, banana, yuca and, most successfully, cocoa, which for the past few years has been exported to Switzerland.

Practicalities

Buses heading to destinations beyond Almirante will drop you at the intersection ("*La Y*"), on the main road, from where it's a ten-minute walk or short hop in a taxi (50c–$1) to the dock. Buses stopping at Almirante go into the town itself to the small bus terminal; ask to be let off just before at the water-taxi stop "*parada de las lanchas*". Two companies run **water-taxis** to Bocas Town with little to choose between them. Bocas Marine Tours (☎758 4085, ⓦwww.bocasmarinetours.com) and Expreso Taxi 25 (☎758 3498) both charge $4 ($5 at night) and have boats leaving every 30 minutes from around 6am until 6.30pm. Find out when the next departure is from both companies before committing and watch out for touts, who will offer to carry your luggage and book your ticket for a fee, and may try to dissuade you from checking out the competition by claiming the office is closed. If you're coming by car, you can leave it in a secure compound at nearby Leiza's ($3 per day). Anyone wanting to take a bike or motorcycle across will need to head for the car ferry dock and get the Palanga (℡ 261 0350), which makes one very slow crossing a day (Mon–Sat 8am; $1.50).

Minibuses career between Almirante and Changuinola (every 20–25min, 6am–10pm; 30min; $1.25), where you can get connections for the border. There are also regular larger buses passing Almirante en route to David from Changuinola (every 25min, 3.15am–7pm; every 55min on Wed; 4hr 30min; $7) and twice-daily to Panama City (8.30am, 7.30pm; 10hr; $23), stopping to pick up passengers at the intersection with the main road, by the roadside restaurant. If you want to be sure of a seat, get on in Changuinola.

If you're unfortunate enough to miss the last water-taxi, the fairly modern *Hotel Alhambra* (℡ 758 3001; ❸) is the best **accommodation**, offering clean, functional en-suite rooms with air conditioning, cable TV and hot and cold water. The small on-site restaurant saves you venturing out at night – unwise, especially if you're travelling alone – though *Bocas Marinas* by the ferry terminal is a good place to eat seafood during the day. The **bank** diagonally opposite the hotel has a 24hour ATM.

Changuinola

From Almirante the road dips and twists its way through endless banana plantations, past wooden Ngöbe houses on stilts, offering occasional tantalizing glimpses of the mangroves and islands of the archipelago. After 29km it arrives at the hot, dusty town of **CHANGUINOLA**. Panama's most important banana centre lies 17km from the Costa Rican border; in between, lie flat, drained wetlands, a patchwork of planta-tions and pastureland. A bustling, unattractive town of around fifty thousand, Changuinola possesses little of interest to the visitor but provides a launch pad for trips to the Humedales de San San Pond Sak or Parque International La Amistad, and is the best place to stay if you've missed the last water-taxi to Bocas or are too late to make the Costa Rican border.

Arrival and information

The town has two **bus terminals**. Terminal Urracá, on the northern end of the congested main street, Avenida 17 de Abril, serves the long-distance buses to and from Panama City and David. TRANCEIBOSA (℡ 758 8455)

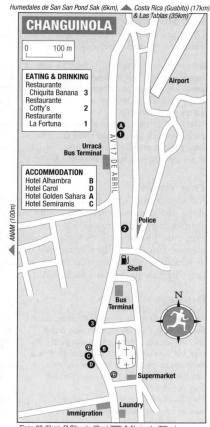

Humedales de San San Pond Sak (6km), Costa Rica (Guabito) (17km) & Las Tablas (35km)

CHANGUINOLA

0   100 m

EATING & DRINKING
Restaurante
  Chiquita Banana   3
Restaurante
  Cotty's   2
Restaurante
  La Fortuna   1

Airport

AV 17 DE ABRIL

Urracá
Bus Terminal

ACCOMMODATION
Hotel Alhambra   B
Hotel Carol   D
Hotel Golden Sahara   A
Hotel Semiramis   C

ANAM (100m)

Police

Shell

Bus
Terminal

N

@ B
@ C
@ D

@   Supermarket

Laundry

Immigration

Finca 60 (5km), El Silencio (8km) & Almirante (29km)

has two daily departures for Panama City, leaving at 7.30am and 6pm ($24; 11hr). They fill up fast, so buy tickets as early as possible. Buses to and from David are much more frequent (every 25min, 3.15am–7pm; every 55min on Wed; 5hr; $8).

Everything else arrives and departs from the busier SINCOTAVECOP bus terminal, set back from the road near the petrol station. This includes the daily bus to San José, operated by Transporte Bocatoreño, which leaves at 10am (6hr; $10); pay on the bus. **Diablos rojos** for the village of Las Tablas swing by the border at Guabito (every 20min, 5.30am–7pm; 30min; 80c), or you can grab a **colectivo** ($1.25/person) or **private taxi** ($6); **minibuses** depart for El Silencio on the Río Teribe at a similar frequency (every 20min, 6.30–8pm; 25min; $1), as do minibuses heading in the opposite direction to Almirante (every 20–25min, 6am–10pm; 30min; $1.25). The **airport** lies northeast of the town centre – both Aeroperlas and Air Panama operate daily flights to and from Panama City (1hr; $105).

A major commercial centre, Changuinola is well served with **banks** and **ATMs**, dotted along the main drag, as well as countless grocery stores and supermarkets, the best being the 24hr Romero, a block east of the Global Bank, which also has a pharmacy. The **immigration office** (Mon–Fri 7.30am–noon, 1–3pm) is also on Avenida 17 de Abril, while the **ANAM office** (℡ 758 6822) is a couple of blocks west of the centre.

Accommodation

There are several functional **hotels** on the main street, mainly serving business travellers. All suffer periodic lapses in water and electricity supply.

Hotel Alhambra ℡ 758 9819. Probably the best value in town but check out several rooms since quality varies, though all are clean with a/c and cable TV. Those at the back overlook a graveyard and are much quieter. ❸

Hotel Carol ℡ 758 8731. Rooms range from cheap, cheerless, fan-ventilated rooms to slightly better pricier ones with a/c and hot water. The nearby *cantina* can be noisy at weekends. ❸

Hotel Golden Sahara ℡ 758 7478. Has 28 reasonably modern rooms (a/c, cable TV, hot water), though some lack windows. ❹

Hotel Semiramis ℡ 758 6006. Probably the most upmarket place to stay in town. The a/c rooms are clean with foam mattresses on the beds, cable TV and the bathrooms have decent hot-water showers. ❹

The Town

An unendearing town with little to detain the visitor, most of the action occurs along the congested Avenida 17 de Abril, whose crowded central pavements overflowing with cheap goods soon give way to broken, potholed ground. The road runs north–south but cut through east to the parallel street and you can glimpse rusting carriages in railway sidings and disused tracks, the last vestiges of what was once an impressive rail network built by the United Fruit Company extending along the coast back to Almirante and well into Costa Rica.

Restaurants

Restaurante Chiquita Banana Off-putting prison-like bars mask a friendly enclosed patio where you can tuck into tasty breakfasts with fresh fruit juice, the usual chicken and fish mains ($5–6) and even cheaper risottos. A chintzy room with a/c, tablecloths and a pricier menu lies at the back. Daily 7am–11pm.

Restaurante Cotty's Mounds of cheap noodles and rice dishes with indeterminate accompaniments in this small cafeteria. Daily 7am–11pm.

🏃 **Restaurante La Fortuna** Very popular a/c Chinese next to the *Golden Sahara* offering friendly, efficient service, including takeaways. The wide-ranging menu has several veggie options and set menus starting at $16 for two. Choose a sizzling hotplate dish with first-rate chips. Daily 11.30am–10.30pm.

Humedales de San San Pond Sak

One of the premier natural attractions of mainland Bocas is the **Humedales de San San Pond Sak** (with numerous variant spellings), which encompass over 160 square kilometres of coastal wetlands stretching from the Costa Rican border, past Changuinola, to the Bahía de Almirante. Only a small section of the reserve is accessible to visitors ($5 entry) but its mix of seasonally flooded swampy forests, dense mangroves and peat bogs makes for a magical boat trip, especially at first light when the prolific birdlife – 160 species at the current tally – is at its most active.

As you glide along the river, keep an eye out for sungrebes, green ibis, least bitterns, muscovy and masked ducks as well as the more commonly sighted egrets, herons and kingfishers. Caimans and river otters lurk in the waters. A dawn visit will also heighten your chances of spotting the wetlands' most celebrated inhabitant, the shy, endangered **manatee** (see box below); though there are now an estimated 150–200 in the area, they remain fairly elusive except when banana leaves are provided at the viewing platforms when tour boats enter the reserve. The river eventually fills out into a coastal lagoon before emptying into the sea, its progress blocked by a sand bank, on which the poorly maintained **ANAM refuge** is located. Behind the hut lies a long stretch of beach, where hawksbill, leatherback and green turtles nest.

Practicalities

If you want to **visit** the reserve, try to make arrangements at least a day in advance with AAMVECONA (Kierstin Félix de Léon ☎6666 0892, Ruiz ☎6494 5001, Ⓦwww.aamvecona.com), who manage activities in the wetlands; failing that, check with ANAM in Changuinola. Boat tours (3hr; $45) leave from outside the AAMVECONA office by the road bridge on the Río San San, which you can reach by taking the Guabito–Las Tablas **bus** (see opposite), getting off at the Puente Río San San, 6km north of town.

You can also spend the night in the reserve, and in the season, go out on a turtle watch ($15). AAMVECONA offers rudimentary **lodgings** in a new bunkhouse, where you can self-cater or arrange for meals ($5) to be prepared. Though

The West Indian manatee

Occasionally called a "sea cow", the **West Indian manatee** (*trichechus manatus*) resembles a cross between a sea lion, a hippo and an elephant, its barrel-like greyish-brown body propelled by two flippers and a spatula tail, its large snout equipped with a prehensile upper lip that helps it feed. Adults average 3m in length though can reach 4.5m, including tail, and weigh in at 200–600 kilos; to sustain such a size, they have to spend 6–8 hours a day munching floating or submerged greenery. When not feeding, they often rest, floating like large logs on or below the surface, frequently surfacing to breathe. Moving easily between freshwater and marine environments, the shy yet playful mammals are surprisingly agile, and can exceed 25km/h for short bursts. In Panama, the vast majority of these aquatic behemoths inhabit the wetlands of Bocas del Toro, though in 1964 a small number were relocated to Lago Gatún by the Americans in a failed attempt to tackle the rampant spread of water hyacinth in the canal. Though lacking natural predators, manatees are threatened by **human activity**, experiencing collisions with motor boats and getting tangled up in fishing nets or canal locks, while suffering from loss or pollution of habitat. What's more, since they only give birth to a single calf every three to five years, it takes a long time to boost numbers.

spending a couple of nights here greatly enhances your chances of spotting the elusive manatees, as well as other wildlife you'll need to bring all your water, food and supplies – including the usual paraphernalia to keep the unspeakably vicious sandflies at bay. Some lodgings and tour operators in Bocas run their own day excursions to the wetlands.

Parque Internacional La Amistad

Divided equally between Panama and Costa Rica, the remote **Parque Internacional La Amistad** (International Friendship Park), often abbreviated to PILA or Amistad, covers a vast 4000 square kilometres of the rugged Talamanca massif, with a topography and biodiversity unmatched in Central America. Precipitous volcanic tors clad in prolific cloud forest, containing the greatest density of quetzals in the world, plunge into deep ravines, providing Panama's most dramatic mountain scenery.

From the treeless *páramo* of Cerro Fábrega (3,336m), the park's highest peak, to the Caribbean rainforests only 40m above sea level, the park encompasses an incredible range of **flora** and **fauna**, including many endemics and endangered species. All five of Panama's resident cat species prowl the forests while the soaring canopy contains impressive specimens of ceiba, almendro and cedar, home to endangered harpy and crested eagles and great green macaws. A crucial link in the "biological corridor" of protected areas running the length of Central America, it is now under threat from agricultural incursions, illicit timber extraction and poaching, but most of all from the ill-considered hydro-electric projects under way. As well as imperilling the area's unique biodiversity, the projects are threatening numerous indigenous communities.

Given the park's remoteness and the ruggedness of the terrain, any **visit to Amistad** proper is a major undertaking, to be made with a good guide, suitable hiking and camping gear, a readiness for rain (over 5m tip down annually in places), and therefore mud, plus a spirit of adventure. Most visitors content themselves with a trip (see opposite) organized through one of the Naso communities dotted along the banks of the Río Teribe, in the buffer zone of the **Reserva Forestal de Palo Seco**, a haven for colourful butterflies, dazzling birdlife, and a host of other wildlife.

The Naso villages

The **Naso**, boasting Central America's last remaining monarch, are one of the country's least numerous indigenous groups. As well as inhabiting the park, they also live on the San San and Yorkin rivers and around Changuinola, where, seeking further schooling and employment, many have abandoned their traditional lifestyles. Those that have remained generally inhabit wooden houses built on stilts covered in thatch or occasionally zinc, practising animal husbandry and subsistence agriculture supplemented by fishing and hunting. Though western clothing predominates, you will still see some women wearing more customary floral prints with short puffed sleeves and the men in plain shirts with black trousers. Though the spiritual heart of the Naso lies in their ancestral lands high up the headlands of the Teribe, the present-day capital is **Sieyik**, the largest Naso community, its five hundred inhabitants dispersed over a pleasant hillside overlooking the river, around ninety minutes upriver from Changuinola. In the grassy clearing at the centre of the village stand a medical centre, primary school and the **royal palace**, a forlorn cement-block covered in graffiti that has remained empty since its former incumbent was deposed (see box opposite).

The Naso Kingdom

When the Spanish arrived in the region, the **Naso** (or Teribe) were both numerous and widespread, but centuries of conflict with the conquistadors and other tribes decimated their numbers, which declined further in the early twentieth century due to tuberculosis. Of the remaining 3500 Naso, around a third have been assimilated into the dominant Latin culture, living and working in Changuinola, while the rest mostly inhabit settlements along the Río San San and Río Teribe. Teribe is believed to be a corruption of "Tjër Di", meaning water of Tjër, the grandmotherly guardian spirit of the Naso, one of the more tangible traces of a sorely eroded culture. Since the Naso language is not taught at school, only an estimated twenty percent still know how to speak it, with Spanish often the preferred language even in the villages, though the Naso legends and colourful characters that populate them are still widely recited.

The more immediate threat to the Naso lies in the form of a hydro-electric dam project upstream on the Río Bonyik, a tributary of the Teribe, which has ripped the kingdom apart. In 2004, the reigning monarch **Tito Santana**, seemingly won over by promises of a primary school, clinic and jobs, approved the project without proper consultation, for which he was deposed and chased into exile. His uncle, **Valentín Santana**, has subsequently been recognized as the new monarch by most, but significantly not all, Naso and has garnered the support of national and international environmentalists and human rights groups – though crucially not the Panamanian government – in a battle to stop the dam and safeguard their lands and livelihood. The beleaguered Naso are also fighting on another front as two communities on the Río San San were flattened in April 2009 by bulldozers – backed up by police with riot shields and tear gas – belonging to a cattle-ranching firm that had bought the land they were living on. After a failed protest camp in Panama City, the bulldozers returned in November 2009 to destroy the homes that had been subsequently rebuilt. The Naso have repeatedly demanded their own *comarca*, which they hope will afford greater protection to their ancestral lands.

Community tours

Two communities are involved in **eco-tourism**, both charging similar rates for trips exploring the surrounding rainforest. You'll learn about medicinal plants, Naso history and culture, and visit the capital, Seiyik. The Naso are warm and welcoming and the spectacular river trips set against the brooding backdrop of the Talamanca range alone make a visit worthwhile, though to do the place and the people justice you should plan at least a two-night stay. Lodgings are basic and meals consist of traditional dishes made from local organic produce, with main expense the huge amount of fuel needed to power a dugout against a strong current. A national **park fee** ($5) is generally collected for ANAM even though most excursions stay within the buffer zone.

OCEN Bonyik, 10km up the Río Teribe ⌖6569 3869, ⓦwww.ocen.bocas.com, ⓔecoturismo_naso @yahoo.es. Raúl Quintero arranges visits to the welcoming community of Bonyik, across the river from WEKSO, the former site of General Manuel Noriega's Pana-Jungla training camp and one-time eco-tourist station. Guests are lodged in a rudimentary cinder-block building and a more appealing balconied wooden house. You will need to bring mosquito nets and torches. Guided hikes range from a 4hr stroll to a 12hr marathon that reaches into Amistad proper; bring snacks and make sure you have a water bottle (with purification tablets advisable). Costs are à la carte (accommodation $15; three meals $13; return boat from El Silencio to Bonjik, or Bonyik to Seiyik $70; hikes $25–30). All organization will need to be done in Spanish. To reach the Naso jetty (*embarcadero*) on the Río Teribe, get the regular minibus to El Silencio (every 20min, 6.30am–8pm; 25min; $1) from the main bus station in Changuinola.

Soposo Rainforest Adventures Soposo ⓦwww.soposo.com. The better advertised and more patronized project is run by a US–Naso couple, which makes for easier organization if you're not comfortable making arrangements in Spanish. Well organized and professional, they offer pleasant wooden cabins with porches, lit by solar lanterns, and have set rates for trips ranging from one to six days ($100–595) inclusive of lodging, meals, transport from Changuinola and a range of excursions.

Guabito and the Costa Rica border

From Changuinola, the road runs 17km to the border with Costa Rica at **Guabito–Sixaola**, where, on the Panamanian side, there is little more than a handful of shops. It's a short walk from **immigration** (daily 8am–6pm, closed 1hr for lunch) across the old railway bridge to Costa Rica (an hour behind Panama time), where you can change currency in the town of Sixaola. There you can catch a through-bus to San José (6am, 8am, 10am, 3pm; 6hr; $10) or to Puerto Viejo in southeastern Costa Rica (hourly; 90min; $3). To reach the border from Changuinola, take a *colectivo* or private taxi ($1.25; $6) hanging around the bus terminal, or, if you're in no hurry, the lumbering bus marked for Las Tablas (every 20min, 5.30am–7pm; 30min; 70c). If you're arriving from Costa Rica, head down the flight of steps to hang around for the bus, which may well have "Las Tablas" on the windscreen whichever direction it's headed, so be sure to check with the driver; or cross back under the bridge to find a taxi. The rate to Almirante is $10.

Kuna Yala

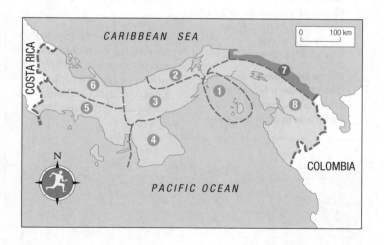

CHAPTER 7 # Highlights

* **Kuna villages** Experience a compelling mix of tradition and modernity in crowded communities such as Cartí Sugdup or Ailigandi, making sure you get to see the meeting house, *chicha* house and *mola*-making first-hand. See p.290 & p.300

* **Blissful islands** Camp out in a thatched *cabaña*, laze in a hammock or float in the turquoise shallows of the palm-topped white-sand islands of western Kuna Yala – choose from Islas Aguja, Perros or Wailidup. See p.291, p.289 and p.290

* **Cayos Holandéses and Coco Bandero** Marvel at a marine wonderland of corals and tropical fish, the archipelago's best snorkelling. See p.292

* **Río Azúcar** Head upriver by dugout along one of the archipelago's loveliest rivers, cutting through plantations and forests brimming with birdlife. See p.297

* **Isla Tigre** Stay in the fascinating home of the Kuna dance, one of the few remaining communities that still practises community-based traditions. See p.297

* **Armila** A very different Kuna village on the forested mainland at the far eastern end of the *comarca*, from which you can head into the jungle by dugout and watch leatherback turtles nesting. See p.302

▲ An *ulu* (dugout) passes Cartí Sugdup

Kuna Yala

Kuna woman in traditional attire – hair bound in a scarlet headscarf, colourful blouse tucked into a sarong-like patterned skirt, her forearms and calves bound with intricate beadwork and her nose pierced with a golden ring – is a sight that has launched a thousand travel brochures. Yet the Kuna's relationship with tourism remains ambivalent, and their suspicion of outsiders (*uagmala*) and determination to ensure that tourism is conducted on their terms has been borne of bitter experience. This can make a trip to Kuna Yala a challenging experience, though the benefits more than outweigh any frustrations or inconveniences. A visit is an opportunity to engage with an evolving, unique indigenous culture, to experience village life first-hand, to loll on heavenly white-sand islands and to explore the little-visited, wildlife-packed mainland.

The Kuna – or the Dule or Tule, as they call themselves – are Panama's most high-profile indigenous people. They inhabit a vast semi-autonomous region (or **comarca**) along the eastern Caribbean coast, which stretches some 375km from the Gólfo de San Blas to Puerto Obaldía and comprises almost four hundred islands and a swathe of land whose limits extend to the peaks of the Serranías de San Blas and the Darién. Around 33,000 Kuna live within the Comarca de Kuna Yala, with a further 33,000 predominantly spread among two smaller inland *comarcas* in eastern Panama and in the capital. For the most part the population is packed onto a chain of 36 low-lying coral outcrops close to the shore, with eleven communities established on the coast and two further inland. Though the crowded island-villages rarely possess a beach, the waters of the western archipelago, in particular, are sprinkled with near-deserted **cays** covered in coconut palms, surrounded by dazzling **beaches** that shelve into turquoise waters, whose coral reefs provide great opportunities for **snorkelling** (diving is prohibited across the *comarca*). Trips to the luxuriantly rainforested mainland are equally magical, whether gliding upriver in a dugout, visiting a Kuna burial ground, or seeking out the spectacular birdlife. These attributes make Kuna Yala a wonderfully idyllic location for a holiday, but to appreciate its unique nature, engaging with **Kuna culture** in all its variations, complexities and contradictions is essential.

Names in Kuna Yala

All island communities have a Kuna name, which has several variant spellings, and a Spanish name. In each case, we have tried to use the more common name, be it Spanish or Kuna, and given the alternative name in brackets when introducing the place.

There are basically two types of islands, though all are small and flat. The palm-topped **deserted islands** so cherished by brochures are predominantly distinguished by their accommodation, ranging from simple cane *cabañas* to comfortable rustic lodges, all owned by particular families or communities from the more densely populated **village-islands**. Choc-full of cane and thatch buildings interspersed to varying degrees with cement structures – schools, medical centres and the occasional shop – these overcrowded coral outcrops generally lack beaches. To the casual visitor, they are very much alike: jetties hold tethered dugouts and traditional over-the-water toilets, with litter often floating among the pilings, while sandy streets gravitate towards the centre, where meeting and *chicha* houses (see p.285) and the basketball court and public phone boxes (see p.296) stand out. Only by spending several nights in different places will you begin to appreciate the subtle differences between communities.

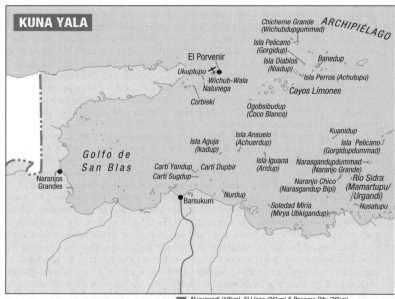

Visiting Kuna Yala

It's easy to feel bewildered at the mere thought of visiting Kuna Yala – **getting there** is no easy matter, involving a pre-dawn start whether travelling by air or by land. **Getting around** is not much better, relying for the most part on sporadic transport in a motorized dugout. You've over 365 islands to choose from – one for every day of the year, as some Kuna will remind you – most with two names (one in Dulegaya or Kuna, one Spanish) and a handful with the same name. However, the fact that only 36 support villages, and many are conveniently arranged in identifiable clusters, simplifies planning. During one visit it is unlikely that you will have time to visit more than a couple of these clusters, and most visitors are satisfied to explore just one. Note that in addition to the tourist tax levied by the Onmaked Summakaled (Kuna General Congress) at your point of entry into the *comarca*, you will generally have to pay a community tax ($3–10 on the island villages, $1–3 on near-deserted beach islands), even if only

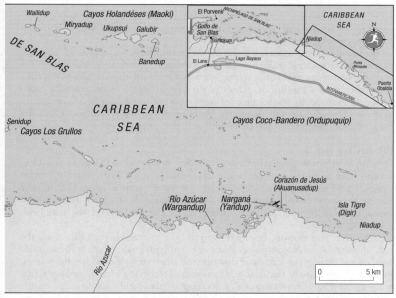

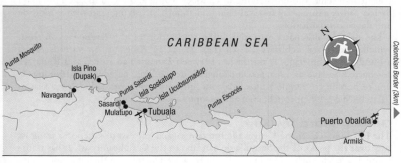

What to take

Flights into the *comarca* have an 11kg checked luggage allowance, but in any case, you should limit yourself to what can easily be lifted in and out of a dugout. A mosquito net may be a good idea, together with lashings of repellent, sun cream, a basic first-aid kit and a torch and/or candles since there is limited or no electricity on some islands. A travel hammock can prove useful if you're intending to venture to communities with no hotels, though your host family should be able to provide one, and a thick book will fill time while waiting for transport to show up. Some kind of waterproof protection, such as a plastic bin liner, is desirable to protect your gear from the water which inevitably breaks over the bows. It's not advisable to drink tap water in Kuna Yala, except in the coastal community of Playón Grande (Ukupa), which boasts the *comarca*'s first decent water treatment system; most hotels will provide purified water for guests at meals. Bottled water is on sale in most islands, but is very expensive and its disposal an environmental headache; using a water filter or purifying tablets (see p.43) is preferable.

stopping there for half an hour – these costs are often not included in the packages (see p.282).

The islands in the **western area** of the archipelago are the most popular, possessing the greatest sprinkling of tiny Robinson Crusoe style islands and the best snorkelling, as well as the widest spread of accommodation. Moreover, they – together with a handful of islands in the central region – are generally more geared up for tourism. Visitor numbers in this part of the archipelago have shot up in the last few years, mainly due to the vastly improved 40km El-Llano–Cartí dirt road – the only significant terrestrial link with the *comarca*.

When to go

In terms of **when to go**, both the dry (late Dec–April) and wet (May to mid-Dec) seasons have their advantages. In the **dry season**, you'll suffer from the trade winds (Dec–Feb/March), which whip up the waters, impairing snorkelling and leaving the outer islands inaccessible. That makes much of March and April an appealing time to visit, although water levels can be low on the mainland, restricting river trips.

In the early **wet season**, from May to July, the unbearable humidity from the lack of breeze is balanced by a sea that can be millpond still – perfect for snorkelling, except during the afternoon downpours, when run-off muddies the waters. June to October spells the season for *chocosanos*, terrifying electric tempests that whip up monstrous waves capable of flooding an island and dashing a ship onto a reef in an instant, though arriving in October would allow you to catch the Feria de Isla Tigre, a three-day **festival** held mid-month, involving craft displays, music and dance competitions.

The other major party to catch is the celebration of the **Kuna Revolution**, which takes place February 23–25 (Feb 19–21 in Ailigandi) in various forms around the archipelago as skirmishes between Panamanian forces and Kuna are re-enacted on land and sea, accompanied by storytelling, parades and drinking. If you're hoping to sample Kuna Yala's succulent **lobster**, avoid the closed season (March–May), when conch, crab and octopus are also off limits.

Getting there by land

The **El Llano–Cartí road** leaves the Interamericana just east of Chepo, snaking its way over the peaks of the Serranía de San Blas to the Caribbean coast. It has transformed access to the region, but still requires a 4WD, and even then it is not always navigable year round. A mere three-hour trip in the dry season can treble following downpours in the rainy season, which create treacherous conditions surmountable only by sturdy high-clearance 4WDs, generally travelling in convoy. The small number of enterprises that transport backpackers, and dry goods from Panama City to sell to the Kuna, manage to make the trip most of the year. **Hostels** can arrange a pick-up ($25 one way from the hostel to a waiting motorized dugout at the mouth of Río Cartí, which will take you to your island), which will be at around 5am; drivers often stop off at a hypermarket on the Interamericana in the outer suburbs of Panama City, allowing passengers to stock up on supplies, but check in advance. To make your own arrangements, contact Junior (☎6019 4151) or Alfonso Navarro (☎6004 6410). On a clear day the road can afford fabulous views, with glimpses of toucans and deer as you slither round the bends.

At the entrance to the *comarca* at Nusugandi, all non-Kuna, including Panamanians – a source of some friction – have to pay a **tourist tax** ($6 for foreigners, $2 for nationals), which is not included in the transport cost. On arrival at the hamlet of Barsukum, on the banks of the Río Cartí ($2 fee), visitors pile into a collection of waiting motorized dugouts ready to transport them to various islands, a cost included in some deals. If travelling independently without pre-booking any package, it's worth asking the waiting boatmen about vacancies – popular backpacker islands often book up – or ask to get dropped off in Cartí Sugdup ($1), a transport hub for neighbouring islands, where you can check out what other transport is leaving that day.

Note that the Burbayar Lodge, located at the *comarca* entrance in Nusugandi, conducts guided **hikes** (6–8hr) down through the rainforest to Cartí while an overnight hike there starting just north of Chepo is also a possibility (see p.309 for details of both).

Getting there by plane

For much of the year, and for islands in the central and eastern regions of the *comarca* year-round, small twin-prop **planes** provide the main form of transport. All flights depart from Albrook Airport at 6am – except for the plane for Puerto Obaldía, which leaves at 8.30am, though times are prone to change, as are the destinations served by the two domestic airlines, so check beforehand. At the time of writing, Aeroperlas (☎378 6000, ⓦwww.aeroperlas.com) offered daily flights to Mamitupu and Playón Chico. Air Panama (☎316 9000, ⓦwww.flyairpanama .com) flies to Corazón de Jesús, El Porvenir and Playón Chico (Mon, Wed, Fri & Sun), Achutupu, Mulatupu and Ogobsukum (Tues, Thur & Sat) and Puerto Obaldía (Tues, Thurs and Sun).

Departures are often delayed and planes hop from one destination to another so make sure you're at the right place before you disembark. All flights return to Panama City the moment they've dropped off their last passengers, generally

---

Kuna glossary

The most essential word to grasp in Dulegaya (Kuna language) is the versatile "*nuedi*", meaning "hello", "yes" and "it's good/OK" or "welcome". Other key terms include:

saila – chief; *nele* – traditional healer or shaman; *ulu* – dugout canoe; *Onmaked Summakaled* – Kuna General Congress; *onmaked nega* – meeting house; *inna nega* – chicha house; *neg uan* – burial ground; *Iboergun* – Kuna prophet and religion; *Bab Dummad* and *Nan Dummad* – Great Father and Mother, the creators; *Baba Nega* – heavenly spirit world; *boni* – evil spirits; *nuchu* – carved wooden totem to ward off evil spirits; *uaga* (*uagmala*) – outsider(s); *absoguedi* – chanter.

around 7am. **Prices** range from $58 to $79 (including taxes) one way. Most of the Lilliputian airstrips are located on the mainland a few hundred metres from the islands themselves. When organizing return flights from the *comarca*, you can ring and book with a credit card, making the payment on arrival at Albrook. It is exceedingly difficult to book flights between islands.

Getting there by boat

Travelling to Kuna Yala by **boat** is more difficult. The two entry points by sea are via El Porvenir in the west, and Puerto Obaldía in the southeastern corner, where you'll almost inevitably be arriving from Colombia – see p.22 for information on customs and immigration. No scheduled ferries exist anywhere in the region: occasional transport leaves Miramar in Colón Province (see p.146), arriving in El Porvenir, and from the Colombian end of the *comarca*, you can sometimes catch a ride on a boat heading up the coast from Puerto Obaldía (see p.301). From either direction, be prepared to hang around until a sufficient number of people are interested and sea conditions are favourable before the boat will set out. Backpackers travelling to and from Colombia by boat from Puerto Lindo usually spend a couple of days in Kuna Yala en route (see box, p.22). Do not try to arrange passage from Coco-Solo port in Colón; though once the main, albeit extremely dangerous, sea route east, it should now be discarded in favour of the other safer options, though none are without some risk.

Accommodation

Given the complexities of travelling independently around the archipelago, which generally also necessitates reasonable Spanish, the easiest way to visit the region is to go on a **package tour**; in fact most hotels only offer package deals, charging per person – our codes, unless otherwise stated, cover the cost for a double, or two people – and including all meals. The majority are aimed at budget travellers, as there's very little mid-range (and no luxury) accommodation. Panama City hostels can help organize a multi-day trip, or you can make arrangements yourself; one way is to ask the Kuna selling handicrafts along Vía Veneto, in Casco Viejo or in Mi Pueblito, many of whom have links with a village in the *comarca*; alternatively contact one of the places listed in the chapter. See box opposite, for information on tour companies.

Most packages in the western region include transport from the end of the Cartí road, or the nearby airstrip, three basic meals, rustic accommodation and a daily excursion, usually to a near-deserted (there's usually someone living there to look after the place) palm-fringed island, or a cultural visit to an inhabited island or mainland cemetery (see box, p.293). Check in advance exactly what's included. On the sandy atolls, all of which are privately owned, accommodation is usually provided in simple white cane *cabañas*, with either a thin mattress or a hammock and perhaps somewhere to keep your belongings out of the sand. The often-basic **toilets** are shared and **electricity** is not a given; washing may be under overhead **showers**, or may involve a barrel of water and a jug or calabash (gourd).

Camping is occasionally permitted on the near-uninhabited islands, but not in the villages, and you will need to bring all utensils and food (from Panama City), or arrange to pay for meals there, prepared by the caretaker family. Travellers looking for a little more **comfort** will find that several lodges in the central area fit the bill, offering fan-ventilated cabins with private bathrooms (flush toilets, hand-basins and showers), often with private balconies over the water, fancier cuisine and English-speaking guides. Only the *Coral Lodge*, which lies just outside the confines of the *comarca* (see p.287), can be described as luxurious.

At the budget end, **package rates** are generally $25–50 per person per night, with $70–100 or more for more comfortable options, but these depend heavily on

Tour companies visiting Kuna Yala

In theory only Kuna-owned companies are entitled to operate within the *comarca* though several others do, including backpacker boats to and from Colombia (see box, p.22). Given the time needed to get to the islands, the three-day tours offered by some outfits are rarely worth the expense and are not listed below – short trips are better organized directly with the lodging involved. Itineraries may change depending on sea conditions.

Ecocircuitos ⓣ314 0068, ⓦwww.ecocircuitos.com. Nine-day sea-kayaking trip with naturalist guides that starts at Isla Tigre and involves camping on near-deserted islands. $2685/person (assuming two people) including return flights from Panama City.

Expediciones Tropicales (Xtrop) ⓣ317 1279, ⓦwww.xtrop.com. Excellent sea-kayak tours working with trained Kuna guides and communities, offering a six-day package in the vicinity of Isla Tigre, camping on deserted tropical islands with plenty of snorkelling. $1600/person including return flights from Panama City.

Mola Tour ⓦwww.molatour.com. US-run operation based within Kuna communities with in-depth focus on Kuna culture and *mola*-making.

Panama Exotic Adventures ⓣ223 9283, ⓦwww.panamaexoticadventures.com. French-run adventure company offers a package based on Naranjo Chico, with rates including lodging and a daily activity – usually snorkelling, a cultural tour or fishing trip. $65/night.

San Blas Sailing ⓣ314 1800, ⓦwww.sanblassailing.com. Pricey but idyllic way to see the archipelago, offering 4–21-day sailing tours (in French, Spanish and English), generally in western Kuna Yala, including kayak or dinghy forays onto the mainland. Prices depend on the boat capacity and season – in high season it's cheaper to share ($175/day per person rather than $210/day for a private yacht). Flights not included.

fuel prices. If there's interest among other travellers and weather conditions are favourable, you can often pay extra for a boat to travel out to one of the outlying cays (see p.292), which offer the best snorkelling in the archipelago.

Getting around

Transportation within the *comarca* is almost exclusively by boat. This can mean being paddled in the customary **dugout** (*ulu* in Kuna, *cayuco* in Spanish) for short distances or **sailing** in a highly effective canoe with a cotton-sheet sail attached to a rough-hewn mast and boom. More often than not, though, travelling around the archipelago entails chugging along in a (sometimes leaking) **motorized dugout**. If staying at one of the more expensive establishments on a package deal, you are likely to travel in a fibre-glass **panga**, possibly with a roof to shade you from the sun. Otherwise, be prepared for hours of exposure to the elements and water leaking over the bow of the boat. Since there are no fixed schedules, enquire at the village's main jetty about possible boats and be prepared to hang about for some time, even until the next day. This is especially true the further east you travel, where transport is much sparser.

It is fairly easy, though expensive, to **hire a boat** (with some Spanish) privately. If you're on an island with a hotel, and want to visit a beach, you may be able to negotiate a ride with one of their tours. Colombian **trading vessels** also ply the coast but are not always willing to take passengers, and even if they do you should be cautious (see p.301). The small prop **planes** from Panama City often hop along the coast, but it's hard to book a ticket between locations since seats are nearly always full with passengers travelling to or from the capital.

Some history

Kuna oral history traces their origins to the Sierra Nevada de Santa Marta of present-day Colombia. Fleeing from tribes such as the Emberá, they took refuge in the mountainous areas of the **Darién**, including Mount Tacarcuna – the highest peak in eastern Panama (1875m), lying just outside the *comarca* – which became a sacred place in folklore. Violent conflict ensued against the Spanish, with the Kuna often forming unlikely alliances with English and French pirates, and gradually being forced towards the Caribbean. Though Kuna had visited the coast for many years, colonization of the **islands** they inhabit today did not start until the mid-nineteenth century as they sought greater access to passing traders and escape from disease-carrying insects on the mainland.

Geographical isolation ensured the Kuna were pretty much left to their own devices until Panamanian independence in 1903, when the new state refused to recognize the Comarca Tulenega, which has been established by Colombia in 1870. It covered Kuna territories straddling the two countries and had guaranteed a certain measure of independence. Tension between the Kuna Congress and Panamanian authorities escalated as the latter granted concessions to outsiders to plunder resources in Kuna territory and persistently attempted to suppress Kuna culture – banning women's traditional attire or force-feeding communities with missionaries and colonial schooling. Matters came to a head in 1925, when a gathering of Kuna leaders on Ailigandi resolved to declare independence and rose up in what is proudly commemorated as the **Revolución Dule** (Kuna Revolution). Around forty people lost their lives, and only the intervention of the US – concerned for the safety of the canal – prevented further government reprisals.

A settlement was finally reached in 1938, when the Kuna agreed to recognize Panamanian sovereignty in exchange for a clearly defined *comarca* and a high degree of political autonomy. Onmaked Summakaled (Kuna General Congress), the supreme Kuna authority, comprises three openly elected Sailadummagan (regional chiefs), who also participate in the Panamanian national assembly, along with an appointed Kuna administrator, or *intendente*, and the principal *sailas* (chiefs) elected within the 49 communities in the *comarca*. Arguably a further Kuna triumph occurred in 1999 when Enrique Garrido became the first Kuna to be elected leader of Panama's national assembly.

Kuna puberty rituals

Whereas adolescent boys pass into adulthood unheralded, a **young girl** undergoes two important ceremonies. The first, *innamutiki*, at her first menstruation, prompts several days of confinement in a small ceremonial enclosure cloaked in banana leaves (*surba*) within the house, where she is purified in herbal baths and finally painted from top to toe in the indigo *jagua* dye before being allowed to join the festivities outside. The second celebration, *innasuit*, involving the whole village, entails the young woman being officially named and receiving a ceremonial haircut, a protracted affair signifying that she is now available for marriage. Food is shared, pipes are passed and *chicha* abounds, though the presence of cigarettes and *seco* in some communities reflects the changing times.

Ironically the young woman at the heart of the festivities misses out on most of the fun, remaining in seclusion until the actual hair-cutting. In an increasing fog of rituals, chants, cocoa-bean incense, tobacco and alcohol, the celebrations, aimed partly at affirming the coexistence of the material and spiritual worlds, continue for several days, until the *chicha* has run out, by which time several people have usually passed out.

Tourism in Kuna Yala

Tourism has a shaky history in Kuna Yala and even now is viewed with suspicion by some Kuna, though after witnessing some visitors treating the place as a human zoo or a *mola* supermarket it is easy to see why. In the 1970s the Panamanian government tried to foist a multimillion-dollar six-hundred-room hotel on the Kuna, which left them so distrustful of outsiders that they booted out the two American hoteliers already operating in the *comarca* and banned non-Kuna ownership of hotels. More recently, the previous Panamanian government pursued the idea of a huge floating hotel anchored offshore, another plan that was roundly rejected by the Kuna. The Kuna General Congress prefers to promote sustainable, low-impact cultural tourism that benefits the whole community.

Even putting aside the anomaly of allowing **cruise ships** into the archipelago – they are especially visible in the west between December and April – this laudable vision is hard to put into practice. Since most visitors flock to the more accessible western region, with its abundant islands and coral-filled shallows, the distribution of tourist income is skewed from the outset. Yet these cays lack the toilet facilities to accommodate the numbers they receive and the boat traffic does little for the already deteriorating coral and aquatic life. Although the Kuna General Congress has ruled that all tourist projects require its prior approval, some communities have set up unofficial hotels, or have negotiated unsanctioned deals with outsiders, which can result in fines.

The traditional Kuna way of life

Historically the Kuna have lived collectively and worked cooperatively. Though some hunting was practised, fishing and subsistence agriculture – yuca, plantain, rice, maize, sugarcane, cocoa, occasional fruit trees and the harvesting of coconuts – were the mainstay of the economy for many years. In the late 1960s, coconuts accounted for seventy percent of the *comarca*'s revenue, bartered for dry goods, fuel, clothing and cooking oil with the brightly painted Colombian trading vessels you still see tethered to the main jetty at communities across the region. Over three million are still harvested annually.

Kuna society is traditionally both matrilocal (when a man marries he moves into his in-laws' compound and works for them) and matrilineal (as property is inherited down the female line). But these practices are slipping, and while women's views are respected, men play a larger role, as chiefs, healers and interpreters, in community meetings. Men undertake most of the agricultural labour, and the entire Kuna Congress is male.

Families traditionally live in compounds of cane and thatch dwellings, the living quarters crammed with hammocks and the rafters laden with clothing, buckets and utensils. Villages without aqueducts bring fresh water by canoe from the mainland. Seafood accompanied with plantain, rice and coconut are staples and *tule masi* – a fish stew containing boiled green plantains, coconut and an assortment of vegetables – is effectively the Kuna national dish.

At the heart of community life stands *onmaked nega* (the meeting house), where villagers, including children, congregate most evenings. The *saila* – usually recognizable by his hat – is the leader in all village matters though some communities now have several *sailas* to fulfil particular functions. A mixture of songs, chants, stories and talk filter through the walls as Kuna history, mythology and religion are as much a part of the reunions as information-giving, public debate and conflict resolution. Another key community building is the *inna nega*, where the *chicha brava* (*inna* in Kuna), the potent mind-numbing sugar-cane-based homebrew, is left to ferment in large clay urns for major celebrations such as a young girl's puberty, ritual (see box opposite).

Changes to Kuna society

As in any society, Kuna life is evolving. Numerous communities now have aqueducts bringing fresh water from the mainland, electricity is available on most inhabited islands, cement block buildings are increasingly common, shops stock canned food, sweets and biscuits, whose wrappers often litter the streets, mobile phones are mushrooming and the iconic Kuna traditional dress is declining among women. Christian churches have taken root on some islands, on the understanding that they respect traditional religion. Despite the Kuna authorities' success in insisting on bilingual education, schooling is primarily about preparing young people for a modern industrialized society. In this respect, many Kuna hope that tourism, if managed carefully, may help ensure that changes in lifestyle can coexist with more established mores (see p.285).

Already, tourism has played a pivotal role in the Kuna's reluctant but inevitable metamorphosis from a collective barter economy – the word for "money" does not exist in Kuna – to a more individualistic cash economy. The resulting economic inequalities have put a strain on communities that are already struggling to deal with major social upheavals due to increasing contact with outsiders (*uagmala*) and returning urbanized Kuna who are no longer prepared to live as their ancestors. Environmental damage by outsiders and the Kuna themselves constitutes a further challenge, often exacerbated by tourism. Issues include overfishing, particularly of lobster, reef degradation, the deforestation of the mainland and waste disposal.

Etiquette when visiting Kuna Yala

In Kuna Yala, particularly in the more remote areas, it is important to remember that you are a guest of the Kuna, irrespective of how much you have paid for the privilege, and should abide by their laws. It is customary to ask **permission** from the local *saila* when you visit a particular community or wish to stay on an island, as indeed the Kuna themselves do. Though this courtesy is often waived in the less traditional islands that see many visitors, else the *saila* would never get any other work done, you should still enquire on arrival since rules vary among communities. **Photography** is another contentious area: on some islands it is forbidden, on others it is governed by strict regulations. Never photograph anyone without asking. Traditional beliefs still held by some of the older generation maintain that a photograph takes away a part of the soul, which is why you should resist the temptation to surreptitiously snap away. Generally $1 is charged to take a single photograph, more for group shots whereas video cameras, if permitted, can cost around $15. Women selling *molas* – the distinctive brightly coloured embroidered cloth panels (see *Arts and crafts* colour section) - will usually allow you to photograph them if you purchase an item but do not presume that the cost includes the photo charge.

While lazing in a hammock on one of the coconut islands, beachwear is fine, but you should **dress** more modestly in villages – no bikini tops or bare chests; villagers may not say anything, but it doesn't mean you haven't caused offence. The Kuna are particularly sensitive about the *onmaked nega* (meeting house) and the cemeteries on the mainland – never enter or photograph these without permission. **Alcohol** too is a thorny issue. Traditionally large clay pots of *chicha* are prepared for the whole village for ceremonies; once the jars are exhausted, the drinking spree is over. Nowadays, communities vary in their regulations on alcohol: in some places drinking is unregulated, but people are fined if found drunk; some allow *seco* and beer to supplement the *chicha* at celebrations but not at other times; some have licensing hours; and others ban alcohol completely, though may allow its sale to tourists. Always enquire first, and drink discreetly if alcohol is available to tourists but not to villagers.

Western Kuna Yala

Most visitors to Kuna Yala visit the **western end** of the *comarca*. It's more accessible by land, sea and air, with more idyllic islets enclosed in white-sand beaches and better snorkelling and more accommodation, though most on the basic end of the scale. For independent travellers, there is also more inter-island transport available and more shops to purchase supplies, though choice it limited and prices high. The downside of greater exposure to tourism, especially in communities that have put up with more than their fair share of insensitive visitors, is that some Kuna are understandably jaded with outsiders.

El Porvenir and around

The diminutive, scarcely inhabited island of **El Porvenir** belies its status as administrative capital of Kuna Yala and gateway to the western isles at the northwestern extremity of the *comarca*. A sliver of bare land, it barely manages to squeeze on an airstrip. Nearby are busy **Wichub–Wala** and **Nalunega**, the latter offering some decent accommodation, and the smaller tourist destinations of **Ukuptupu**, **Ogobsibudup** and the appealing **Cayos Limónes**.

El Porvenir (Gaigirgordup)

With a handful of buildings, including a police post, hotel and museum, plus a couple of pay phones and a clump of palm trees, **El Porvenir** is merely a transit point for most arrivals though the water off the island's thin strip of sand is cleaner than the more heavily populated neighbouring islands.

It's worth pausing to call in at the **Museo de la Nación Kuna** (open daily – you may need to ask around to get someone to open up; $2; ☎ 314 1293), unless you're travelling on to Cartí Sugdup, where a privately owned museum covers similar ground. The exhibition hall displays photos of festivals and numerous ceremonial artefacts such as a necklace of pelican bones worn by the *absoguedi*'s (chanter's) assistant and a headdress decorated with macaw feathers. There's also a model Kuna kitchen and a notable collection of basketry and bamboo flutes. Notices are in English, Spanish and Kuna. The nearby **Cooperativa de Molas de Porvenir** (open daily) has a small selection of crafts for sale.

Practicalities

Air Panama flights arrive from and depart for Panama City four times a week (Mon, Wed, Fri & Sun; $58 one way). The island's only **accommodation**, the long-established *Hotel El Porvenir* (☎ 221 1397 for Sra Vélez in Panama City, who speaks English or ☎ 6760 5571 for Sr Vélez in El Porvenir, ⓦ www.hotelporvenir .com; ❸, ❻ for full board plus excursions to nearby islands), is pleasantly situated in grassy grounds with its own veranda bar-restaurant and eighteen simple dark concrete rooms with tin roof and private cold-water bathrooms.

The *Coral Star Lodge* (reservations ☎ 232 0200, lodge ☎ 832 0795, ⓦ www .corallodge.com; accepts credit cards, ❾) lies just outside the *comarca*, on an isolated beach surrounded by rainforest and mangrove near the mainland community of Santa Isabel. This luxury adventure eco-resort on the doorstep of Kuna Yala (60min boat ride from El Porvenir, or 30min transfer from Miramar in Colón Province; see p.146) provides the only possible base from which to explore some of the *comarca* from a high level of comfort – though given the wilderness location, you shouldn't be surprised to see the odd crab crawling up to have a closer look at your cocktail. Six deluxe thatched bungalows connected by a boardwalk stretch out over the water, stylishly furnished and each equipped with air conditioning, jacuzzi and private sundeck with stunning ocean vistas. Rates include meals and a daily tour, which can include hiking, birdwatching, kayaking and snorkelling, with additional charges for diving (including PADI courses), fishing, horse riding and trips to Kuna Yala, as well as for all transfers.

Wichub-Wala

Wichub-Wala is a bustling yet relaxed island that's often visited by cruise ships, hence the proliferation of arts and crafts. Beyond some decaying cement structures, including a former swimming pool, now full of large tropical fish, stands the overpriced but popular *Kuna Niskua Lodge* (☎225 5200, ⓦwww .kuna-niskua.com; ❼), a two-storey concrete, cane and thatch building plum in the middle of the village, with a pleasant first-floor hammock-strewn veranda and communal dining area from which to observe village life. Of the ten rooms (eight with private and two with shared bathroom), the upper ones are much nicer; some beds have orthopaedic mattresses and there is solar-powered electricity at night. Rates include meals and a trip to Nalunega, a Kuna cemetery, or to one of the nearby uninhabited islands to swim and snorkel. The budget *Hostal Nadi* (☎293 8709, ⓦwww.hostalnadi.com; ❻ including meals, tour and airport transfer from El Porvenir – you'll have to pay the $4 return transfer if coming from Cartí) has four small dorm rooms (eighteen beds) containing bunks and single beds, mattresses of varying degrees of comfort, three shared bathrooms and a waterside *rancho* dining area. The downside is its proximity to the noisy generator of the island health centre.

Ukuptupu

Formerly home to a Smithsonian marine research station, until the institute was ejected from the *comarca* in 1998, the *Cabañas Ukuptupu* (☎293 8709 or 6746 5088, ⓦwww.ukuptupu.com; ❼ including meals, daily tour and transfer) now occupy the tiny semi-submerged private coral outcrop of **Ukuptupu**. The friendly owner, Juan Garcia, who speaks good English, and his family are its only inhabitants. A maze of wooden boardwalks leads between fifteen spacious but simple wooden doubles, each looking out onto the sea, with hammocks strung up in front of the rooms. Good food is served under a communal central *rancho* and traditional showers (bucket of water and soap) and toilets (a mix of traditional and flush) are shared. There's nowhere to stretch your legs, but the island provides a mellow hide-away and Wichub-Wala and Nalunega are a stone's throw away.

Nalunega

Just south lies **Nalunega**, "the house of the macaw" in Kuna, since these brightly coloured birds were resident on the island when it was first colonized. A more appealing village than Wichub-Wala, with a population of around five hundred, it has broader streets dotted with shady trees populated with parrots, while traditional cane and thatch buildings rub shoulders with occasional aluminium-topped cement structures. At the centre lie a primary school, the meeting hall and the basketball court, off which is signposted the island's **museum** (daily 7am–6pm; $2). This unusual collection is worthwhile if you have reasonable Spanish since the curator, Teodoro Torres, offers a fascinating narrative of Kuna culture illustrated through his wood carvings and paintings from recycled materials, such as boat sails that have washed up on the beach.

The oldest **hotel** in the *comarca*, offering the best value in the area, ☀ *Hotel San Blas* (☎6749 9667, ⓔhotelsanblas@hotmail.com; ❻ including three meals and tour), where several staff speak some English, enjoys a great location, overlooking a small beach – though since it's squeezed between a couple of traditional communal toilets over the water, swimming is not advised. Six simple rooms, with gaps between the walls and the ceiling – prioritizing ventilation over privacy – lead off the wraparound balcony, which affords lovely views of the sun setting over the thatched rooftops as you listen to the sounds of the healer (*nele*) singing in the home of someone who is ill. A few more traditional sandy-floor cane *cabañas* stand on the beach, with some cheaper well-ventilated cement rooms round the back (❹ including two meals, with tours extra), opening out onto a cooking area. The hotel's rather gloomy restaurant serves some of the best food you're likely to taste in the archipelago – lobster, crab and a host of delicious accompaniments.

Ogobsibudup (Coco Blanco)

Another coral-sand drop in the ocean southeast of El Porvenir, **Ogobsibudup** (☎265 6335 or 6700 9427 for Sra Beatriz Sanchez, ✉coco_blanco@hotmail.es; ❽ including meals, daily tours and transfer) offers six superior sandy-floored cane and thatch *cabañas* (sleeping 2–4) with comfy beds and private bathrooms, tapped in to the island's septic system. Though possessing more decorative trimmings than most and fabulously positioned on the tiny beach, the *cabañas* are tightly packed. The food is nicely prepared and the small sandy beach slides into reef-protected shallow waters, with better swimming off Nidirbidup a few hundred metres away, where you can also **camp** ($35/person), being ferried over for meals on Ogobsibudup, which makes the place ridiculously crowded in peak season.

Cayos Limónes

Offering perfect tranquillity (provided you don't coincide with a cruise ship stopover), the gorgeous islands that comprise **Cayos Limónes** are clustered east and northeast of El Porvenir. Once dedicated to harvesting coconuts, they now function primarily as prime day-trip destinations, but it's worth stopping overnight, allowing you to soak up the stillness by a campfire and admire the sparkling night sky. **Isla Perros** (or Achutupu, not to be confused with a far more populated namesake further east) is the most visited, offering the best snorkelling round an accessible reef and sunken cargo boat in the narrow channel separating it from adjacent **Isla Diablos**, a favourite camping spot for backpackers from Cartí Yandup (see p.291). Further out lies another rewarding snorkelling spot, the idyllic, pinprick-size **Isla Pelicano** (Gorgidup) – one of several with the name – surrounded by a necklace of soft white sand and carpeted with trimmed grass among the all-too-sparse palm trees, which sometimes struggle to provide sufficient shade for all the visitors on high season weekends. The fact that there is currently no toilet on the island is another reason to avoid peak periods. Hammocks can be hired for the day and camping is possible if you bring your own tent ($5/person), and food can be prepared by the one caretaking family (Deliano Davies ☎6840 9850).

Some trips offer an entertaining detour via a speck of sand housing a single battered palm tree, reminiscent of Popeye or Tintin cartoons, commonly referred to by tourists as "**one-tree island**". Heading towards the outer perimeter of the archipelago, the large palm-covered island of **Chicheme Grande** (Wichudup Dumad), home to a handful of families, is predominantly another day-trip location though sailing vessels on the Puerto Lindo–Cartagena route often stop off here for the night. Waves thunder over the protective outlying reef, which prevents rubbish from washing up on the gorgeous beach, and the island's relative size coupled with its isolation engender a more away-from-it-all feel, though it's not really a place for snorkelling. Umberto Burgos (☎6880 4054) offers basic hammock accommodation (❷) in a thatched hut and meals; you'll pay $3 per person if you bring a tent. There are currently no toilet or shower facilities.

Tucked away behind a mangrove-fringed islet, **Isla Wailidup** is arguably the nicest place to stay in the area, comprising a windward stretch of alabaster sand and an open grassy patch surrounded by willowy palms. ⚓ *Cabañas Wailidup* (☎259 9136, Ⓦwww.kuna-niskua.com; ❼ including meals and trips, camping $10) on the island of the same name, which has the rare luxury of a fresh water supply. Run by the owner of the *Niskua Lodge* (see p.288), three superior *cabañas* are built on stilts right on the beach with sea-facing balconies, solar-powered electricity and private bathrooms, complemented by a bar-restaurant favoured by yachties.

Cartí and around

The dirt road connecting Panama City funnels backpackers and day-trippers into the coastal hamlet of Barsukum close to the largely disused Cartí airstrip. Only a coconut's throw away, the **Cartí** group of islands, together with the nearby uninhabited palm-covered retreats of Aguja, Ansuelo and Iguana, inevitably experience the greatest number of tourists in the archipelago. Close to the mainland, populated Cartí Sugdup forms the stadium-sized hub of this island group and is one of the *comarca*'s busiest communities, with motorized dugouts constantly coming and going. It is also a favourite pit stop for cruise ship passengers. The best recommendation is to stay on one of the smaller islands – Cartí Yandup if you want to sample Kuna village life, or Isla Aguja for the desert-island experience – and drop by Cartí Sugdup during the day to visit the excellent museum, or in the evening if some community event is on.

Cartí Sugdup (Suitupu)

With around two thousand inhabitants, **Cartí Sugdup** is one of the most densely populated communities in the *comarca*, comprising a few large functional cement buildings, such as a secondary school, medical centre, library and post office, standing amid a maze of cane and thatch. The numerous stalls selling soft drinks and snacks and the archipelago's only **pizzeria** testify to the island's popularity with tourists. The large number of people and proliferation of consumer goods has resulted in rubbish collecting in the streets and at the water's edge, and the place should be avoided at all costs when a cruise ship has dropped anchor as Kuna women selling *molas* appear from every doorway and the population almost doubles.

The main reason to visit the island is to learn more about Kuna culture at the **Museo de Cultura y Arte Kuna** (daily 8am–4pm; ☎6691 3904; $2.50). Stuffed full of artefacts and pictures from floor to ceiling, covering many aspects of Kuna culture – *mola* making, funerary rites, traditional medicine, religious beliefs – with some bilingual signage in Spanish and English, the place really comes alive through the informative explanations of the curator, José Davies, who is happier conducting tours in Spanish but can manage some English.

Practicalities

Davies also offers **accommodation** in the form of a home-stay programme (❸ for meals and a hammock and an extra $10 for a tour). Being a transit point for other parts of the *comarca*, the village also has a very basic, noisy community dormitory, *Dormitorio Gardí Sugdupo* (☎6751 1026; ❷ for a hammock or mattress, ❹ for a room), though since there's a lot of coming and going you should not leave valuables lying about. It sits above the *Cafetería Don Leonidas Kantule Valdéz*, which sounds grander than it is, serving simple main dishes for around $4. Alternative lodgings are available the other side of the island at *Cartí Homestay* (☎6734 3454, Ⓦwww.cartihomestay .info; ❻ for lodgings, meals and a daily excursion). Run by Eulogio Pérez, who speaks English, the place is actually more of a hostel, consisting of a communal downstairs kitchen-dining area and a few upstairs dorm rooms, somewhat cramped but with comfy mattresses and large windows overlooking the village. Most visitors, however, choose to overnight on one of the smaller neighbouring islands.

Cartí Yandup

A few hundred metres across the water, the pretty village – by the cramped standards of Kuna Yala – of **Cartí Yandup** has around four hundred inhabitants in a collection of traditional cane-built household compounds, interspersed with flowers and shrubs, with *molas* hanging out for sale. A favourite with backpackers, *Cabañas Cartí Yandup* (☎250 6059 or 6537 0416, ⓦwww.cabanascarti.es.tl; ⑤), run by the effervescent Nixia, provides a friendly environment offering a handful of rooms in and around the family compound. Traditional toilet and shower facilities over the water are shared with the family. It's easy to arrange for some time in the village and a night or two in a hammock on Isla Diablos (see p.289), thus experiencing both sides of Kuna Yala living.

Just off the main street, the two-storey *Cabañas Cartí* (☎6740 7535, ⓔkunatours1@hotmail.com; ⑦) is run by Nixia's brother Aaron, an engaging and enthusiastic guide, who speaks good English. Rooms are upstairs and barely large enough to contain their double mattress, though the pleasant communal balcony allows you to scan the rooftops and the open sea. Aside from a few shops selling basic supplies, there is a recently opened **museo botanico** ($2) run by Kenny González, the former president of the healers of Kuna Yala, although you'll struggle to get much from the experience without a Kuna interpreter.

Islas Aguja, Ansuelo and Iguana

The trio of **Islas Aguja**, **Ansuelo** and **Iguana** provide accessible day-trips from the Cartí villages and, when the El Llano-Cartí road is dry, from Panama City. All are very similar postage-stamp-sized islands, great for lying in a hammock under the coconut palms, surrounded by gorgeous turquoise waters to swim in with some pleasant though not outstanding snorkelling – ideal for unwinding for a few days.

Isla Aguja (Ikadup)

Of the three, tiny **Isla Aguja** stands out. An archetypal Caribbean picture postcard, with a wide band of sparkling white sand and translucent turquoise waters encircling a carpet of coconut palms, it is one of the nicest places in Panama to laze in a hammock, provided you time your visit to miss the dry season day-trip rush, when up to two hundred city dwellers armed with giant cool boxes cover every speck of sand until the mid-afternoon exodus when they are ferried back to their vehicles parked up on mainland Cartí.

Kept immaculately tidy despite this influx, the island offers better facilities than most without spoiling the ambiance. José Fernandez offers **accommodation** in ⚓ *Cabañas Ikadup* (☎6724 7260, ⓦwww.renatonannini.blogspot.com; ⑤ including meals), four simple cane structures, each divided into two rooms with beds or hammocks, plus wind- and solar-powered electricity, showers and flush toilets. Hammocks and deckchairs can be rented for the day ($1), and the well-prepared, simple meals are served in a pleasant *rancho* – all of which justifies the slightly higher $3 visitor's fee. There are also tents for rent ($20/person) and space to pitch your own tent ($7/person). **Transport** is extra, and pricey – $20 return from the mainland, and $20–40 per person for a tour.

Isla Ansuelo (Achuerdup)

Closer to the mainland, **Isla Ansuelo** is another tiny tropical islet, though with a slightly thinner strip of beach than Isla Aguja, greater ground foliage and banana trees interspersed among the coconut palms. It's owned by a large family of 33, whose members take it in turns to run the business. **Accommodation** here comprises a few tents with mattresses ($5/person) or hammocks ($3/person). A campfire is lit at night and you can have whatever's on the menu for the day ($2.50 per meal) or bring your own food and cooking equipment. There's no electricity or toilet, though traditional over-the-water conveniences are planned, which will sadly cut down the very pleasurable swimming options; water from the island well is used for washing.

Isla Iguana (Aridup)

With its slender necklace of sand, shallow waters and ground foliage, there's little to choose between **Isla Iguana** and neighbouring Isla Ansuelo. But *Cabañas Aridup* (☎6807 2764; ❻ with tours and meals; boat transfer to the mainland $10 each way), though pricier, more resemble lodgings on Isla Aguja with three well-maintained cane huts containing three neat beds in each, and a volleyball net and ball is at your disposal should you tire of beachside torpor. Fully inclusive package deals are also available from Panama City ($190).

Very close to the coast, four families occupy the tiny outcrop of **Nurdup**, welcoming visitors to their simple inexpensive ⚐ *Cabañas Nurdup* (Elixto Tejada ☎6698 3491; ❹ plus $3 each way boat transfer), usually travelling to Isla Perros for the day excursion. Provided your Spanish is up to the task, this intimate environment is ideal for deepening your understanding of Kuna culture.

Cayos Holandéses and around

Three groups of predominantly **uninhabited cays** forming an equilateral triangle provide the archipelago's most spectacular underwater scenery. At the top of the triangle, marking the outer limit of the *comarca* 30km from shore, **Cayos Holandéses (Maoki)** are the most remote, yet most visited of the three. Effectively out of bounds during the fierce winds and high waves of December to the end of February, at other times this chain of around twenty islands, some fairly large (by the standards of Kuna Yala) and densely forested, act as a magnet for yachts drawn to the sheltered anchorage and shallow, translucent waters. The protection is afforded by the outlying **Wreck Reef**, which has ensnared Spanish galleons and the odd drug-smuggling vessel, parts of which still protrude through the pounding surf. The resulting bays form clear natural swimming pools displaying a stunning array of sponges and soft and hard corals – fire, elkhorn, brain, fan – that attract rays, reef sharks, moray eels, starfish and a plethora of polychromatic fish.

For budget travellers staying on the inner isles near Cartí or Río Sidra, an **excursion** to Cayos Holandéses usually requires a $20 supplement – well worth the additional expense – for the extra fuel needed and will involve several hours in a boat, where you need to be prepared to get wet since even in the calmer months the wind can suddenly whip up. Make sure you're climbing aboard a robust and fairly substantial *cayuco* or, better still, a fibreglass *panga*.

At the southwestern and southeastern tips of the triangle, respectively, lie **Cayos Los Grullos** and **Cayos Coco–Bandero (Ordupuquip)**, two clusters of around a dozen or so cays, with thin powdery beaches peppered with driftwood encircling densely forested isles and coral-filled shallows. Popular with cruising yachts, they attract Kuna dugouts selling *molas* and fresh produce to the visitors.

Río Sidra and around

Fifteen kilometres east of Cartí, just off the mainland, **Río Sidra**, consisting of the twin communities of **Urgandi** and **Mamartupu**, provides a key portal into the archipelago. Since the airport closed in 2008, this major population centre and the surrounding palm-studded sandy islands are usually accessed by **boat** from the Cartí road, from where it's a 45-minute boat ride ($15 return but included in some packages), or by **plane** to El Porvenir (see p.287) and a similar-length boat ride. Offering some of the cheapest packages in the archipelago, the palm-shaded sandy islands of **Senidup** and **Isla Pelicano** are favourites with backpackers, who often arrive in groups arranged by the Panama City hostels. Río Sidra is also the main gateway to the dozen or so cays renowned for the sublime snorkelling of their coral-filled shallows that make up **Cayos Los Grullos** (see opposite), and is within reach of the slender island of **Kuanidup**, and the slightly larger, well-forested and rather glorious **Naranjo Chico**, where there are several lots of *cabañas*. Other scenic excursions in the area include the lovely sandy island of **Pigirtupu** and starfish haven of **Isla Salar**, while the mainland attractions include a boat trip up the **Río Masargandi**, calling in at the cemetery at its mouth, and a trek through luxuriant rainforest to the once-sacred waterfall of Saiba ($10 per group), where you can cool off in the delightful freshwater pool at its base.

Río Sidra

Originally two separate islands, the communities of **Urgandi** and **Mamartupu** combined to make **Río Sidra** – a community of close on two thousand – by reclaiming the land in between. Each retains its own identity, maintaining separate *sailas*, meeting houses and churches, though they share a school and basketball court, plus the two nearby public pay phones. Facing the town from the main jetty, Urgandi lies to the right, Mamartupu to the left and the main drag, a broad sandy boulevard with a number of grocery stores, bisects both, running the length of the island.

If you arrive on the island having skipped breakfast, the home-baked fresh bread and accompanying shot of coffee from the friendly *Restaurante Petita*, by the main jetty, will soon revive you. A decent main meal with dessert and coffee for a mere $3.50 does the trick at any other time of day. Señor Umberto, the owner, who speaks English and whose son-in-law is the administrator of *Cabañas Kuanidup* (see p.295), also has a few rudimentary wooden **rooms** for rent, with uncomfortable plank beds (❺ for full board), which would do if you got stuck there, though nearby Nusatupu (see p.294) has better accommodation. The proximity to the mainland of both islands means sandflies are a major nuisance in winter (May–Dec).

Kuna cemeteries

One of the most fascinating tours offered by Kuna communities is to their traditional Kuna **burial ground** (*neg uan*) on the mainland. From afar the cemetery resembles a miniature village, a mass of thatched rooftops, which turn out to be shelters protecting the graves from the rain. Beneath each one is an elongated mound of earth, representing the pregnant belly of Napguana (Mother Nature) as she gives birth to the deceased in the heavenly spirit world (Baba Nega), as well as everyday utensils, clothing and food, which are left to accompany the deceased on their journey and serve as gifts for relatives who have already passed away.

Before burial the deceased is bathed in aromatic herbs and dressed in their best clothes, their cheeks painted with the natural reddish dye of *achiote*, a colour believed to ward off the evil spirits (*boni*). After villagers have paid their respects, the body is laid to rest in a deep grave in a hammock oriented towards the rising sun in the east, symbolic of the beginning of new life, which is also sometimes alluded to by laying cotton threads – representing the umbilical cord – across the corpse. A dugout tethered nearby is left to carry the deceased to their ancestors.

Nusatupu

A smaller community of around four hundred just across the water from Río Sidra, the unfortunately named **Nusatupu** (Isla Ratón or "Rat Island") does not harbour any more of these rodents than anywhere else; it does, however, boast an adequate **hotel** offering some interesting excursions. *Hotel Kuna Yala* (☏ 315 7520, public phone, ask for Manuel Alfaro; ❼ including meals and daily tour) is a two-storey cement structure with a canteen producing tasty meals on the ground floor and a handful of breezy rooms upstairs, each with two windows ensuring views of both the congested village and the sea. Rooms are basic with beds of varying quality and minimal, if any, other furniture and a shared flush toilet and shower. Make sure you get up onto the rooftop, which affords a splendid panorama of the surrounding village and neighbouring Río Sidra. Diminutive nearby **Isla Maquina** (Mormarketupo), whose four hundred plus inhabitants are unused to visitors, is known for its fine *molas*.

Isla Pelicano (Gorgidup) and Senidup (Isla Chiquita)

The postage-stamp-sized islands of **Isla Pelicano** and **Senidup**, crowned with coconut palms and fringed with strips of soft sand, are perennial favourites with backpackers at the budget end of budget since they offer the cheapest packages in the *comarca* and stays are easily organized through Panama City hostels. As a result there can often be something of a holiday-camp atmosphere on them.

Rather scruffy *Cabañas Robinson* (Río Sidra public phone ☏ 299 9007 or 6721 9885; ❹, plus $15 return transfer from Cartí), owned by the engaging and charismatic Arnulfo Robinson, who speaks English, has relocated on a couple of occasions but at the time of writing was based on Isla Pelicano around a 30-minute boat ride north of Río Sidra.

Though slightly larger and better tended, nearby **Senidup** is now rather cluttered with *cabañas* belonging to two owners. Half the island is run by Sr Franklyn, who operates *Cabañas Dubasenika* (Río Sidra public phone ☏ 299 9058 or 6540 5478; ❹, return transfer from Cartí $15 return), currently the cheapest deal in the archipelago, comprising nine traditional cane and thatch huts (for 2–4 people) with basic washing facilities using a bucket. For a few dollars more, *Cabañas Senidup* (☏ 6712 9816 or 6042 1507; ❹, plus $15 for return transfer from Cartí), run by a family cooperative from Soledad Miria, offers eight simple *cabañas*, plus an occasionally functioning shower and a shady volleyball court. Both operations have solar-powered electricity in communal dining areas, which provide the focus of evening social life. Possible **excursions** take in the village of Soledad Miria (Mirya Ubkigandup), which is noted for fine *molas*, or the glorious white-sand beaches of Naranjo Chico or Pidertupu.

Naranjo Chico (Narasgandup Bipi)

Belying its diminutive tag, **Naranjo Chico** is the second-largest island in the area after Naranjo Grande. It is particularly lovely for its distinctive hourglass shape, gorgeous swathe of white-powder sand, off which you can snorkel, and vegetation of coconut palms, shrubs and delightful hibiscus flowers.

Cabañas Narasgandup (☏ 299 9007 or 256 6239, ✉ narasgandup@yahoo.com; ❼ including transfers to the mainland) at one time provided the only **lodgings** here and still has its own beach set apart from the competition at the back on which a row of six traditional *cabañas* (for 2–5 people) look out to sea. Though rustic, they are nicely done with bamboo tables and towels provided. The dining room is superbly located on a coral landfill promontory off the beach.

Several families have now jumped on the tourism bandwagon, erecting cane and thatch dwellings, and slinging up hammocks – some cordoning off their patch.

Still, with most *cabañas* set back off the sand, nestled in the undergrowth, the nicest stretch of beach remains unspoilt. Contact Sr Miro (℡6769 2758; ❹, plus $15 transfer from Cartí and extra for tours). Exotic Adventures (see p.283) also organises multi-day packages here.

Kuanidup

Approaching the wafting coconut palms of **Kuanidup**, 10km north of Río Sidra, a row of seven smart cane and thatch **cabañas** at the edge of the sparkling white sand seemingly stand to attention. The lodgings of *Cabañas Kuanidup* (contact Sra Petita, ℡6742 7656, ⓦwww.kuanidup.8k.com; ❽ including transfer) are neat and well kept with shared toilet and shower facilities and electricity in the cabins; across the central grassy area there's a bar and a couple of open-sided restaurant areas. Though idyllically located, within striking distance of the Cayos Holandéses, the tear-drop island offers relatively little shade and the beach is small.

Central Kuna Yala

The main appeal of the **central isles** lie in **Isla Tigre**, which sustains many traditional Kuna practices, and **Río Azúcar**, one of the most beautiful rivers in the *comarca* – both accessible by **plane** via the twin-island hub of **Corazón de Jesús** and **Narganá**. Forty kilometres further east, sprawling **Playón Chico** presents an interesting combination of modernity and tradition but is generally only visited by guests at two of the *comarca*'s more comfortable lodgings, which lie close by and make sound bases for exploring the area. The region possesses a handful of delightful sand-fringed coconut isles on which to idle, but its beaches don't match the breathtaking beauty of many in the western end of the archipelago, though the mainland excursions into primeval rainforest more than compensate.

Narganá, Corazón de Jesús and the central isles

Narganá and **Corazón de Jesús**, linked by a pedestrian footbridge, are the least traditional communities in the *comarca* and hence rarely a tourist destination in themselves but act as the access point to **Isla Tigre**, 10km to the east and one of the more intriguing traditional communities in the *comarca*, and to the lovely **Río Azúcar** – the river, that is, 8km west, rather than the village of the same name. Lying 50km east of El Porvenir, they are accessed by daily **flights** by Air Panama (see p.296).

Narganá (Yandup) and Corazón de Jesús (Akuanusadup)

A quick glance round either Narganá or Corazón de Jesús and it's easy to forget you're in Kuna Yala. The paved squares are dotted with benches, lampposts flank wide sandy streets, evening sound systems blast out reggaeton and traditionally clad women are conspicuously absent. Some Kuna see the twin islands as a warning of the fate of the *comarca* if the spread of *uaga burba* – the spirit of outsiders – proceeds unchecked. On the plus side, however, the location of the two islands is enchanting, nestled in a bay, fringed with mangroves fronting forest-clad hills. Moreover, if you've been travelling around the *comarca*, you might find Narganá's western-style hotel with a/c a welcome relief, while two good restaurants offer a more varied menu than the fried fish and plantain you're likely to be fed at many of the more basic island lodgings.

Corazón de Jesús, in keeping with its name, has a statue of Christ in its central plaza, which is illuminated at night. Other than that, the island's main features are its airstrip, a handful of government buildings and a church; there's a small cemetery at the northern tip. Most of the action occurs down at the wharf and at its opposite number across the dividing channel of water in Narganá: boats load up with supplies and drop off passengers, and yachts bob at anchor.

Across the bridge, the gleaming golden statue of Carlos Inaediguine Robinson, educator and major player in the 1925 Kuna Revolution, stands as if in defiance at the centre of **Narganá's** main plaza, where spacious sandy streets lead off in grid formation, in stark contrast to most Kuna communities' cramped, labyrinthine layouts. Cement houses, occasionally surrounded by a hedge or garden, alternate with traditional cane and thatch dwellings sometimes sprouting satellite dishes. Given that the first missionaries to the *comarca* settled in Narganá, it's no wonder the place has four churches.

Practicalities

Air Panama **flights** from Panama City at arrive at Corazón de Jesús (6am on Mon, Wed, Fri & Sun; $62 one way). The island has two mini-supers and the *comarca*'s only **bank** (Mon–Fri 8am–2pm, Sat 9am–noon) which, with no ATM and no facilities to change travellers' cheques or advance cash against a credit card, is not much help to foreign tourists.

Most visitors **stay** in the *Hotel Noris* (public phones ☎ 299 9090 or 299 9001, ask for Paco; ❹) in Narganá, which has seven pleasant basic rooms (with a/c or fan, private or shared bathroom), though minimize the amount of toilet paper you use since it all ends up in a rotting mass at the back of the small garden. Laid-back owner Paco also runs a fuel depot by his home at the back of the primary school, so is a good source of information if you're looking for passage on a boat. A couple of blocks further down the road, *Hostal Anayuri* (☎ 231 0943; ❷) has half a dozen simple partitioned rooms, where ventilation takes precedence over privacy, and clean shared bathrooms in a small waterside garden. The town now has an occasionally functioning **internet café**, which operates out of school hours behind an unmarked grey door at the front of the school building.

Eating options are limited but good. *Restaurante Nali's Café* (daily 6.30am–10.30pm) enjoys the nicer location, behind the primary school in Narganá, overlooking the

---

Public phones

As mobile technology becomes more widely available across the *comarca*, the social importance of **public telephones** is likely to diminish. In the meantime, the blue and aluminium units provide a focal point for people to congregate and chat in the evening. Nowhere is this more pronounced than in Narganá, where the three phone boxes enclosed in a wire fence are tightly regulated by community employees. A waiting bench seems excessive, until you catch on to the system, which dictates that one of the three booths has to remain free for incoming calls but that the moment a call comes in – and someone is sent racing across the village to fetch the person being called – then the next available free phone becomes the one for incoming calls. In this way, the waiting line only makes any headway when two phones become available at once, hence the need for the bench. Once you've witnessed the log jam first-hand you understand why community numbers are always engaged – they can be out of order too, meaning getting through to someone needs great persistence. In Narganá, and in various other communities, you are charged to use the phone – presumably to pay for the services of the phone managers; sometimes it is a set fee, sometimes a percentage of what you have used on the phone card that they give you.

channel between the two islands. Simple but well-prepared mains ($5) of fish or chicken with sauces and vegetable or salad accompaniments are served while breakfast too is surprisingly varied for the *comarca*. Across the bridge off the square in Corazón de Jesús, the slightly cheaper and more popular *Fonda Mas Kuleguet* serves up tasty fish dishes for under $4. The obvious nightlife occurs in the bar and pool hall by the plaza in Corazón de Jesús with the alternative social scene centring on the public phone boxes in Narganá's plaza (see box opposite).

Río Azúcar (Wargandup)

Five kilometres west of Narganá, the distinctive faded blue tower of the Catholic church and a large water tower herald your arrival at the crowded, vibrant village of **Río Azúcar**, where Westernization has left its mark. Yos Aranda (public phones ☏ 299 9069 or 299 9013), one of the community's many *sailas*, is in charge of tourism and can sort out a family homestay, but, more appealingly can organize a day-trip or overnight stay (extremely basic hammock accommodation) up the beautiful Río Azúcar (Guebdidiwar), where you can awake to the sound of howler monkeys in the morning and the birdlife is truly spectacular. This trip is highly recommended, especially when the water level is high enough for you to penetrate further upriver by dugout.

Isla Tigre (Digir)

A thirty-minute ride east by motorized *cayuco* from Narganá takes you to the populous yet spacious, elongated **Isla Tigre**, which has the rare luxury of a couple of slender beaches. It is a community which is managing better than most to sustain Kuna mores while opening up to tourism, partly due to partitioning off the village, including a rare football pitch, from the grassy community-run tourist areas, which include **accommodation** in the form of seven simple beachside *cabañas* (❷), toilet and shower facilities and an excellent open-sided ⫚ **bar-restaurant** ($5 per meal), which offers some of the *comarca*'s best cuisine, embellishing delicious sea-food dishes with Chinese-influenced sauces, and rotates chef and staff every three months. It's also a great place to chat to some of the (male) members of the community. Book by ringing the public phones (☏ 333 2005 or 333 2006),

In the tourist-designated area, you can loll in a hammock or sit on the sliver of **beach** in your swimwear provided you cover up to go into the village. If you notice anyone pointlessly clearing ground or cutting grass round you, the chances are they're carrying out community punishment for some misdemeanour. Possible **excursions** for modest fees include to the mainland cemetery, a three-hour hike to waterfalls or snorkelling round one of the nearby islands, where coconuts are harvested.

Many aspects of **traditional living** are still practised: the conch is sounded to call men to plant or harvest the crops and families rotate to harvest coconuts. Yet wander into the village one night and you could well catch the community TV showing a cartoon or action flick. The Kuna dance – involving men playing panpipes and women shaking maracas – originated here and during the mid-October **Feria de Isla Tigre** dance troupes from across the *comarca* compete for prizes. You can catch them practising Saturday and Sunday evenings.

Playón Chico (Ukupseni)

Between Isla Tigre and the next main settlement, 40km away, the coastline becomes more rugged, the horizon devoid of islands, but as you approach the next main administrative hub, **Playón Chico**, home to around three thousand, the flat, palm-crowned, sandy islands begin again and two cemeteries atop hills on the mainland announce your arrival. Few people stay in the community but it forms the customary village outing for the two relatively luxurious lodgings situated on tiny private islands a five-minute boat-ride from the community. Other attractive excursions include hikes into pristine rainforest taking in the cascading waterfall of Saibar Maid, birdwatching up Río Grande and some lazy sun-lounging, moderate snorkelling and fishing off nearby coconut isles.

The Island

A large flat coral-filled pancake packed with cane and thatch dwellings, interspersed with functional concrete buildings, sprawling **Playón Chico** is wrestling to balance traditional customs with modern developments but a vibrant and welcoming place for all that. There's a police station at the wharf (where you need to sign in), which opens out onto the main square-cum-basketball-court, and a stage painted in the Kuna colours of red and yellow. A concrete pedestrian bridge, which young lads fish from, leads to the mainland where a football pitch, airstrip and several government buildings, including a secondary school, are located. In the early morning, men armed with machetes stride up the path leading to the cultivated lands (*nainumar*). Westernizing influence is evident in the numerous churches scattered round the island and in the weekend film night held at the community hall by the basketball court – for $0.25 you can enjoy a Hollywood action flick, though you may find *Die Hard* competing against *Ice Age II* to serenade you to sleep whether you like it or not, since electricity on the island means competing TV sets penetrate the paper-thin cane walls. Note that the community tax is a hefty $10. The airstrip receives daily **flights** from Panama City by Aeroperlas and four times a week by Air Panama (Mon, Wed, Fri & Sun; all flights 6am; all flights $64 one way).

Accommodation

There is limited **accommodation** on Playón Chico, with most tourists ferried out to the relatively swish lodgings of *Sapibenega* and *Cabañas Isla Yandup*, which lie a five-minute boat ride from Playón Chico.

Cabañas Isla Yandup ☎394 1408, ⓦwww.yandupisland.com. Five lovely octagonal *cabañas* with private balcony and bathroom sit over the water, while three slightly cheaper rooms offering sea views are set further back. The tiny island, with a small beach and nearby reef, has a breezy waterside *rancho*-restaurant with full bar, which serves excellent seafood-based cuisine, and service is friendly and attentive. Costs include two daily excursions with an English-speaking guide. Credit cards accepted. ⑧

Hostal Golebir Public phone ☎299 9168 or 299 9169; ask for "Domy". Two cement-floor rooms (one double and one triple), each with private bathroom, with tasty meals served in a convivial family environment. Trips can include an island beach outing, where you can swim or fish, and a tramp through the mainland rainforest, taking in the village cemetery. Bed only ⑤, with meals and excursions ⑦.

Sapibenega "The Kuna Lodge" ☎215 1406 in Panama City, ⓦwww.sapibenega.com. The most luxurious accommodation in the *comarca*, though overpriced, consisting of a handful of spacious bamboo twin cabins (for 2–4 people) decorated with Kuna art, built over the water and set round a grassy interior covering the entire coral outcrop of Iskardup. Each room has a private balcony, hammock and tiled bathroom. Credit card payments can be made for the basic package, which includes standard excursions, but extras such as snorkel rental, additional excursions and alcohol need to be paid for in cash. A well-stocked bar-lounge area complements the top-notch over-the-water restaurant-gazebo. ⑧

San Ignacio de Tupile (Dad Nakue Dupbir)

Ten kilometres southeast of Playón Chico, midway along the *comarca*, lies the well-organized community of **San Ignacio de Tupile** (Dad Nakue Dupbir, which translates as "where the sun rises"). As you step out of a boat at the community pier, you are greeted by a statue of the Virgin Mary – an indication of the island's fairly widespread evangelization – who is often surrounded by an assortment of goods awaiting shipment from the adjacent warehouse of one of the *comarca*'s main distributors. Soft drinks, dry foodstuffs, fuel and vegetables such as onions, potatoes and garlic, all pass through, and shops here are consequently better stocked than on many islands so it's a good place to stock up if you're travelling through the *comarca*. Though tourists rarely visit, the vibe among the 1500 inhabitants is relaxed and welcoming, particularly if your visit coincides with the patron saint festivities (July 28–31), when you can join in the celebrations marked by rowing races and various competitions.

Beyond the statue stands the primary school, where a wide main boulevard peels off left. The streets are kept spic-and-span as community regulations mean families are held responsible for disposing of rubbish on the mainland. Rules are equally strict about getting a permit to leave the island, aimed at curbing what elders see to be the moral decline among some of the younger members of the community. Squeezed between two public phone boxes, the strangely whitened face of General Inatikuña, the community's first *saila* when the settlement relocated from the mainland to the island in 1903, stares out across the street.

Practicalities

The community's only **restaurant** is up the stairs to the right by the wharf, and serves a decent plate of fried fish with rice and plantain. The only **accommodation**, *Obued Nega* (public phones ☏333 2001/2/3/4; ❷ bed only), is tucked away at the far end of the island behind the vast church, where the evening tranquillity – the name means "place of relaxation" – is compromised by the insistent throbbing of the island generator. Basic cement and wooden rooms have reasonable mattresses with private or shared bathroom; the better upstairs rooms have a balcony and hammocks from which to survey the sea and the village. Down below, a green turtle and barracuda kept in a small natural aquarium eye you up as you tuck into a meal in the waterside *rancho*. The price of a bed is fine but the all-inclusive package (❽) is on the high side. Tours are led to the unremarkable nearby beach on Ilestup ("Isle of the Englishman", after a gent who lived there in the 1700s) and to Río Yuandup Gandi, where large alligators laze on sandbanks and a rainbow of birds flit in and out the foliage. The nearest airport is a forty-minute boat ride away at Playón Chico.

The eastern isles

What might loosely be described as the **eastern isles** stretches over the whole of the eastern half of the *comarca*, which, outside the sprinkling of lodges near Achutupu and Mamitupu, sees precious few outsiders beyond the odd yacht and Colombian trading vessel. Here, lacking the protection of an offshore reef, the seas are rough and transport between communities sparse.

From Ailigandi to Mamitupu

Another 10km southeast along the coast, and around 100km from the Colombian border, the island communities of **Ailigandi**, **Achutupu** – not to be confused with the tiny palm-covered spot in the western *comarca* – and **Mamitupu** mark the last main area with some tourist infrastructure. They are generally accessed by plane at Achutupu, though Mamitupu also has an airstrip a few hundred metres southeast. Like the lodges round Playón Chico, they are aimed at the upper end of the market, though as with all accommodation in Kuna Yala the lodgings are rustic. The islanders generally see fewer visitors here and so are less tourist-weary than some of the communities further west.

Ailigandi

Westernmost of these islands, overlooking coastal mangroves (*ailan* means mangrove), **Ailigandi** has its spot firmly cemented in Kuna history as the first place of organized resistance in the Kuna Revolution of 1925, symbolized in the Kuna swastika flag (representing an octopus) fluttering proudly above the rooftops. A pivotal figure in the rebellion was Chief Olokindibipilelel (Simral Colman), whose statue – incongruously clad in suit and bowler hat – claims a central position on the densely populated island of around 1200, next to the obligatory basketball court. A warren of pathways weaves through tightly packed thatched dwellings, in the midst of which is squeezed the tiny **Museo Olonigli** (donations welcome). As with other museums in the *comarca*, it is a single room stuffed with artefacts whose significance only become clear through the explanations (in Spanish) of the owner-curator. Willing to open up at any time, Roy Cortéz Olonigli elaborates on traditional culture drawing on his own wood carvings, which depict Kuna symbols and rituals.

The only **accommodation** is on the private island lodge of Dadibe (Ⓦwww .dadibelodge.com; ❾ including meals, excursions and airport transfer from Achutupu or Mamitupu) – named after a Kuna prophet who was transformed into the sun – whose three brightly painted wooden waterside cabins are visible as you approach Ailigandi by boat from the west. The tiny island is a place to curl up in a hammock with a book and open yourself to cultural and jungle excursions rather than lounge on a beach or snorkel.

Achutupu

Five kilometres east of Ailigandi, the unusual crescent-shaped island of **Achutupu** has a deceptively spacious feel, dotted with banana trees and coconut palms. There's a strip of sand that might optimistically be called a beach, though swimming is inadvisable due to the usual pollution. The village has a primary school, health centre and restaurant by the pier, alongside a basketball court.

Two higher-end **accommodation** options, both with the same owner, lie off Achutupu; one, *Uaguinega Eco-resort* (Ⓣ263 7780, Ⓦwww.uaguinega.com; ❾), meaning "house of the dolphin", is literally a stone's throw across the water on tiny Isla Uagutupo. This easy-going place has eleven simple wood and cane *cabañas* facing the water and three superior "junior suites". Palm trees are sprinkled over a grassy area with a central *bohío* and a pleasant and breezy restaurant, where you can tuck into delicious seafood while gazing out to sea. The hotel is also the first place in the archipelago to offer satellite internet access.

The new and supposedly more exclusive *Akwadup Lodge* (Ⓣ263 7780, Ⓦwww .sanblaslodge.com; ❾), a five-minute boat ride to the west of Achutupu, offers greater seclusion in wooden bungalows, but is probably not worth the extra $70 per night you'll pay to stay here.

The **airstrip**, which was laid through community labour and is a source of local pride, lies 200m across the water on the mainland and has three Air Panama flights a week from Panama City (Tues, Thur & Sat, 6am; $68 one way).

Mamitupu

Mamitupu has ten *sailas* governing a traditional village of about 1200; photography is forbidden here though it is permitted on excursions to the mainland. *Cabañas Waika Mamitupu* (public phones Ⓣ333 2032 or 333 2033; ❽, ❶ bed or hammock only) on the island of the same name, are an affordable option for travellers on a more modest budget. In **Mamitupu**, contact the extremely hospitable Pablo Nuñez, who speaks English and a little French, or organize your visit through *Hotel Costa Azul* in Panama City (see p.67) – ask for Agostín. Set apart from the main village in a palm-shaded grassy end of the island stand five simple sandy-floor cane huts, with decent mattresses protected by mosquito nets, a good-size table, private washing area (for bucket and water ablutions) and solar-powered electricity, which is more than the village has. Flush toilets (using a septic tank) are shared, as is the pleasant *rancho* dining area. Photography is not permitted in the village. Only a few hundred metres east of Achutupu, Mamitupu airstrip receives daily flights by Aeroperlas (6am; $68 one way).

Along the coast to Puerto Obaldía

Beyond Mamitupu, completing the remaining 75km to Puerto Obaldía, you pass the densely matted thatch rooftops of the *comarca*'s most populous communities: the four-thousand strong twin settlements of **Ogobsukum** and **Ustupu**, served by the airport of Ogobsukum (see p.281). Noted for their gold craftwork, they rarely see tourists. Beyond them lies the swampy Bahía de Masargandi. Rounding the aptly named Punta Mosquito, the next landmark of interest is the pine-clad **Isla Pino** (Dupak), which unlike any other island in the *comarca* has a large hill; though only just over a square kilometre in size, it boasts a couple forest trails and a picturesque waterside thatched village. Hugging the coastline further southeast you pass a host of other islands clustered round the mainland airport of Mulatupo (see p.281).

Despite the communities' accessibility by air, the lack of tourist facilities and scarcity of picture-postcard islands to bask on mean that travellers rarely venture this far east, so are treated as curiosities when they do; communities are more traditional, and you will need to check in with the police and ask permission of the *saila* to visit or stay on an island (make sure you are appropriately clad – see p.286), where it is usually possible to negotiate with a family for a hammock or bed and engage the services of someone to explore some of the rivers and rainforest on the mainland. Many of the mammals have been hunted into obscurity, but smaller reptiles, insects, amphibians and an array of birdlife are much in evidence. The seas along this stretch of coastline are particularly rough here and should only be navigated in a decent boat – not the shallow leaking dugout favoured by many.

Puerto Obaldiá

Puerto Obaldía, the last major "town" before the Colombian border, is an unendearing encampment where police in combat gear guard against drug runners, Colombian guerrillas and smugglers. Though technically within the *comarca*, the community has a mixed population of Kuna, Colombian refugees and non-Kuna Panamanians. Before or after crossing the **border**, you'll need to visit immigration, for an entry or exit stamp (see p.22 on crossing the border) and the police post, where you will need to register. If you're entering Panama your belongings are likely to be thoroughly searched and you may be asked for proof of onward travel out of the country and evidence of the means to support yourself financially. You could end up with a more intimate knowledge of the town than you would like unless you've booked an air ticket to Panama City in advance since seats are often oversubscribed. Air Panama (☎316 9000, ⓦwww.flyairpanam .com) operates three morning flights a week (Tues, Thurs & Sun at 9.40am; 1hr; $78), though times are liable to change. Flights can be booked over the phone using a credit card as security or online.

Heading west up the *comarca* by **boat** is tricky; departures are sporadic at best and generally involve hitching a ride (for a fee) on one of the Colombian trading vessels which ply the coast all the way to the western extremity in El Porvenir, but you need to be prepared for a lot of discomfort – cramped hammock space (you may need to provide your own), limited diet and scarce shelter from rain on a journey that may take days longer than originally envisaged – added to the possibility that the boat may be carrying drugs or contraband. Sailings also depend on sea conditions; it is highly inadvisable during the storm season (Dec–Feb). Ask around, however, since occasionally faster motor boats take a few hours to head up the coast to one of the larger communities.

Visitors travelling on to **Colombia** from Puerto Obaldía will need to take the likely roller-coaster ride on the launch (1hr, generally around $15, life jackets provided (see p.21) to Capurganá, a pleasant resort town, from where a further ferry to Turbo and bus on to Medellín are possible.

Most visitors who need **accommodation** in Puerto Obaldía stay in the rudimentary *Pensión Condé* (no reservations; **❶**), which offers cell-like rooms with private or shared bathroom. The owner also runs a restaurant, where the *comida corriente* will cost you less than $3, and can help change any lingering Colombian pesos.

Armila

If you fancy staying in the area, you might consider visiting the small Kuna village community of **Armila**. With lodgings that are relatively dispersed the abundant greenery, in contrast to the overcrowding of most Kuna villages, the hamlet is idyllically located at the base of a forest-cloaked hill where two rivers empty into the sea and over 4km of cream-coloured windswept beach extends along the coast. This is one of the world's most important nesting sites for **leatherback turtles**, consisting of several thousand nests protected by the community – around thirty to forty females lay their eggs nightly between February and August – and turtle-watching is one of several tourist activities; others include jungle walks and river trips by dugout.

Although only a twenty-minute boat ride up the coast from Puerto Obaldía, landing on the beach (there is no jetty) is frequently impossible due to rough waves (especially Dec–Feb and sometimes July–Aug), or water spilling out of the river mouths following torrential rain. An alternative route involves a two-hour hike close to the shoreline (though this should only be attempted with a guide and after consulting the police on the security situation, since FARC incursions have been known). Accommodation is provided in *Cabañas Ibedi*; contact Ignacio Crespo, known as "Nacho" (☎ 212 318 or 6563 0554, ✉ ibedilodge@hotmail.com), who can usually be found in person at Mi Pueblito in Pananama City. On offer is a three-day, two-night package for $120, including basic lodging in a large cabin, which houses fourteen and offers food and activities, but no electricity. Alternatively, enquire at *Cabañas Aridup* on Aridup (Isla Iguana – see p.292), in the western end of the *comarca*, whose owner, Luis Espitia (☎ 6807 2764), also has a cabin in Armila.

The Darién and eastern Panama

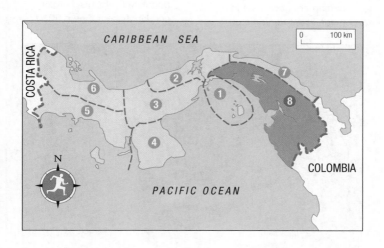

CHAPTER 8

Highlights

* **Lago Bayano** Take a boat ride in search of caiman lurking in the lake's muddy fringes, and venture into the bat-infested Cuevas de Majé. See p.309

* **Rancho Frío** On the banks of a picturesque river, this ANAM refuge provides the best access to the natural wonders of Parque Nacional Darién. See p.316

* **Cana** One of the world's birding hot spots, set in a magnificent rainforested

valley teeming with wildlife, right in the heart of the Darién. See p.318

* **Staying with the Emberá** Spend a few nights in Mogué or, better still, La Marea, a choice village where you can learn about Emberá culture and the surrounding rainforest. See pp.319–320

* **Río Sambú** A gloriously sinuous river, lined with mangroves and rainforest, and populated with ibis, herons and kingfishers. See p.322

▲ Body painting at the Emberá village of Mogué

8

The Darién and eastern Panama

M ention of **the Darién** conjures up a host of images, some alluring, others less so; some true, others vastly exaggerated. What is not in dispute is the region's status as one of the last true tropical wildernesses – though even this is under threat – encompassing swathes of mountainous forest containing an astounding array of wildlife, most notably in the **Parque Nacional Darién**, which provides unparalleled opportunities for serious hiking and birdwatching.

The largest of Panama's nine provinces, the Darién abuts Colombia and covers a sparsely populated rugged expanse that sprawls across almost twelve thousand square kilometres, reaching its highest point at Cerro Tacarcuna (1874m) by the border, but including numerous peaks over a thousand metres. The province also boasts Panama's longest river, **Río Tuira**, which empties into the Golfo de San Miguel, a vast mangrove-lined body of water that opens out into the Pacific Ocean. Yet travellers are increasingly drawn to the Darién as much by its people as by its compelling scenery. The main indigenous groups, the closely related **Emberá** and **Wounaan**, are gradually opening up their communities to tourists; in the **Comarca Emberá–Wounaan** or in communities outside such as **Boca Lara**, **La Marea** and **Mogué**, you can stay overnight in a village and learn the intricacies of basketry or wood-carving, for which they are world-renowned, or hike through steaming rainforest to spot harpy eagles – the area boasts the greatest concentration of these raptors in the world. **Kuna** communities are also present, mainly in eastern Panama province, historically considered part of the Darién. Their two small *comarcas* stretch along the shores of **Lago Bayano**, a vast reservoir 100km east of Panama City, which enjoys a picturesque setting in an increasingly deforested landscape, and has an impressive network of caves.

Some history

The Darién bore witness to some of the bloodiest confrontations between the invading conquistadors, greedy for gold and power, and the indigenous groups desperate to defend their territories, most notably at **Santa María la Antigua del Darién**, the first successful Spanish settlement on the mainland since the time of Columbus (over the border in present-day Colombia). Balboa took Santa María in 1510, and later intercepted an attempt to reclaim the city, led by Cacique **Cémaco**, a pivotal figure in the indigenous resistance; he captured all the alliance's chiefs, bar

Cémaco, and had them hanged as an example. It is perhaps only fitting that Balboa, who first espied the Pacific from the Darién, also met his end here – beheaded by Pedrerías Dávila in the coastal town of Acla (in present-day Kuna Yala) – while Santa María was eventually abandoned by the Spanish in favour of Panama City, and was razed to the ground by indigenous forces in 1524.

The indigenous peoples most in evidence today are the **Emberá** and **Wounaan**. Both groups may have migrated from the Chocó regions of Colombia (which is why they are often referred to collectively as Chocós). **Kuna** presence is still recalled in some of the place names, notably the snaking Río Tuira, and though most Kuna moved to the Caribbean coast, pockets remain in the more recently formed *comarcas* of Madugandi and Wargandi, and in isolated communities in Panama and Darién provinces. The other substantial population, dominant in the regional capital of Las Palmas and in settlements lining the Golfo de San Miguel, are the **Afro–Darienites**, descendants on the whole of the *cimarrones* – escaped slaves brought over by the Spanish, who fled and waged warfare from their own strongholds (*palenques*) in the rainforest, forming strategic alliances with pirates and indigenous tribes. Some of their communities are now mixed with Emberá and Wounaan, and in some parts with **Afro–Colombian refugees**, escaping the civil conflict across the border. The completion of the Interamericana to Yaviza in 1979 opened the floodgates to **colonos** (the name often given to migrating cattle ranchers and farmers predominantly from the Azuero Peninsula), who have now cleared vast tracts of land along the highway for pasture and constitute around fifty percent of the total population of Darién province.

Though the joint Comarca Emberá–Wounaan was established in 1983, covering around 25 percent of Darién province, there have been increasingly violent clashes with *mestizo* settlers encroaching on their lands, while overlap with the national park, whose regulations restrict traditional hunting and agricultural practices, fuel frictions between indigenous communities and government.

The Emberá and Wounaan

Two separate but related ethnic groups speaking mutually unintelligible languages, the majority of Panama's **Emberá** (warriors famed for their poisonous blow-darts) and **Wounaan** (more noted for their artistry) inhabit wood-and-thatch huts along the Darién's numerous rivers – though the increasing presence of zinc roofs and cement buildings is indicative of encroaching modernization. As former semi-nomadic hunter-gatherers, it is only relatively recently that their communities started to live in fixed villages, a government-encouraged project primarily to facilitate schooling and access to modern healthcare; before, family homes, though still sprinkled along the rivers as they are today, formed temporary bases from which to hunt and practise limited slash-and-burn agriculture before moving on, allowing the forest to recover.

The groups' wooden **houses** are built on stilts, to protect them from wild animals and unwelcome intruders, as well as rising floodwaters. Semi-open sides allow cooling breezes to enter while preserving a degree of privacy. The platform, accessed by a tree trunk, with notches carved out as steps, constitutes a living space with a fire pit for cooking; crucially, the heat prevents the thatched roof from rotting during the rainy season. Traditionally, the largest building in the community is the *casa comunal*, a splendid circular construction with a soaring conical ceiling, where meetings are held, guests are received and ceremonies take place. Missionaries have been chipping away at traditional **beliefs** since the time of the conquistadors, and while shamanism persists, villagers are more likely today to head for the government medical centre than put their trust in traditional medicine.

For details on **staying the night** in an Emberá or Wounaan village, see box on p.319.

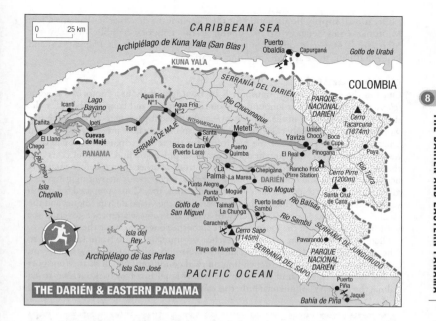

THE DARIÉN & EASTERN PANAMA

Visiting the Darién

Most tourists visit the Darién **on a tour** but it is entirely possible, and becoming more common, to visit **independently** – though you need to be flexible and have sufficient time, Spanish and, more often than not, funds. The Darién can be tough, often lacking flush toilets, electricity, running water or even sometimes a bed. On the other hand, you do not have to undergo Indiana Jones-type endurance feats to get around a lot of the region, though you should always engage a **guide** if you're heading into the rainforest, and inform the ubiquitous frontier police of your plans.

Getting there

Aeroperlas (☎315 7500, ⓦwww.aeroperlas.com) and Air Panama (☎316 9000, ⓦwww.flyairpanama.com) operate mid-morning **flights** from Albrook Airport to Jaqué via Bahía Piña (Aeroperlas Tues & Thurs, Air Panama Mon & Fri; 10.30am; approx 1hr 15min; $70 one way), with return flights to the capital almost immediately. Air Panama serves the region's other airstrips, Garachiné and Sambú, in two hops (Tues & Thurs; 10.30am, returning 11.25am from Sambú, 11.45am from Garachiné; $69/$66); La Palma flights depend on demand – departing only with five or more passengers (Tues & Sat 10.30am, returning 11.30am; 50min; $62) – so ring the office to check.

Now that the road to Yaviza has almost completely been tarred, a journey by **bus** is thankfully not the bone-breaking experience it once was – direct services from Albrook bus terminal leave before dawn (7 daily, 3.15–7.30am; 7hr; $14), or you can take a later bus to Metetí (hourly until 4.30pm; 5hr; $9) and transfer to a local minibus to Yaviza or, for the Golfo de San Miguel, grab a seat on the shuttle to nearby Puerto Quimba, from where you can catch one of the regular water-taxis to La Palma.

Occasional **supply boats** bound for the Darién leave the wharf at Panama City; Multimar Food Services (Ⓣ262 6848), at the temporary public dock by the Mercado de Mariscos, offers limited places on their boats to La Palma ($15) and Jaqué ($20) but these are slow and uncomfortable.

Getting around

Once in the Darién proper, transport is by **boat**, generally in a motorized dugout (*piragua*), and entails a fair amount of enquiring at jetties and hanging about for the tide to rise – especially in the dry season – and sufficient passengers to make the trip worthwhile. It's infinitely cheaper, however, than hiring a boat privately, where you will have to cover the cost of the fuel (often for the return trip, even if you're only travelling one way), the captain and probably a poleman; find out fuel costs and the likely amount required for your journey from another source before you start negotiating prices, and note that if hiring someone's services for an overnight stay in a village, you'll need to pay for *their* lodging and meals, too. Come prepared for rough sun-baked roller-coaster rides in the open waters of the Golfo de San Miguel and the Pacific – bring a hat, sunscreen, plenty of water and some waterproof covering for your luggage – though the journey will be smoother once you enter the rivers.

There are a couple of isolated stretches of unmade **road** from La Palma to Chepigana and from Garachiné to Taimatí via Sambú and Puerto Indio, where you can occasionally hitch a ride depending on road conditions. Much of the transport to and from villages round the Golfo de San Miguel involves backtracking to La Palma, the Darién's commercial hub; this can sometimes be avoided by hiring a local

Tours to the Darién

Though customized itineraries can also be arranged (with a minimum number of participants), these **all-inclusive tours** generally leave Panama City on fixed dates, the majority from December to the end of April, and include transport to and around the Darién as advertised, accommodation, meals and bilingual guiding services in Spanish and English. If you're on a tight budget but lack the confidence or Spanish to make arrangements, you could contact Rafael Calvo (Ⓣ672 0799, Ⓔcrjourneys@gmail.com), who can organize personalized ethno-cultural itineraries in the Darién (and Kuna Yala).

Advantage Tours Ⓣ232 6944 or 6676 2466, Ⓦwww.advantagepanama.com. Focused on birdwatching, and offering multi-day excursions to the scenically situated biological field station in Chucantí, a three-hour hike (or shorter horse ride) south of the Interamericana, and the Emberá village of La Marea. Five-day tours cost around $630, with a minimum of four people, or $900 if there are just two of you.

ANCON Expeditions Ⓣ269 9415, Ⓦwww.anconexpeditions.com. The Rolls-Royce of tour operators, with top-notch bilingual naturalist guides, offering five-day tours to its comfortable lodges in the Cana Valley ($1590) and Punta Patiño Reserve ($740), with prices to match (see p.318 and p.322). The two-week Darién Explorer Trek takes you from Cana to Punta Patiño via Mogué, though you'll rarely need to carry your pack (around $3000).

Panama Exotic Adventures Ⓣ223 9283, Ⓦwww.panamaexoticadventures.com. French-run organization with the greatest variety of trips to the Darién (and Kuna Yala) often involving more camping and hiking. Three- to five-day tours to the Golfo de San Miguel include a lodge stay at the Reserva de Filo de Tallo near Metetí, the Wounaan community of Boca Lara and camping on an island near La Palma. A four-day Sambú area expedition involves plenty of hiking in the rainforest and visits to Emberá villages of Villa Queresia and Pavarandó; with four more days, you can trek over the Serranía del Sapo to Playa de Muerto for around $1030.

guide (and a horse if you don't want to carry your pack) to **hike** cross-country, which is also a great way to see more of the rainforest. In the wet season, **rubber boots** are the footwear of choice for coping with the incredibly boggy paths.

Panama province

Aside from the Altos de Cerro Azul, **Panama province** east of the canal is known more for the continuing urban spread out towards Chepo and rampant deforestation than for any sightseeing charms. **Lago Bayano**, some 90km east of Panama City and voted one of the country's top ten attractions in a nationwide tourist-board poll, is worth at least a day's sojourn, while the indigenous communities just off the Panamericana at **Ipetí** provide the other main reason to stop en route to the Darién proper, though the relatively barren location lacks the rainforest charm of other villages in Darién province.

Chepo

It's hard to imagine the agro-commercial town of **Chepo**, which looks set to be swallowed up in Panama City's greedy expansion eastwards, as the gateway to the Darién Gap only forty-odd years ago, where the Pan-American Highway ended and rainforest began, so devastating has been the pace of deforestation. Though the town itself holds little to detain you, nearby **Puerto Coquira** on the Río Bayano is the jumping-off point for boats (from $40 return) to the delightful island of **Isla Chepillo**, 4km from the mangrove-filled river mouth. A popular weekend day-trip from Panama City, the tiny island supports a pretty fishing village plus a beach pounded by good **surfing** waves, a **surf camp** (℡519 2407, ⓦwww .chepillosurfcamp.0catch.com/1.html) and basic accommodation available at *Eco-Cabañas Cimmarón* (℡6620 7116), or you can pitch a tent on the beach for free.

Around 20km beyond Chepo, a dirt road to the left heads up across the *cordillera* to Kuna Yala, passing *Burbayar Lodge* (℡390 6674 or 6654 09520, ⓦwww .burbayar.com; $115pp) on top of a ridge, just before the entrance to the *comarca*. The slightly cooler climate is just one of the many plus points of this delightful rustic eco-lodge that attracts serious birders, with a list of over three hundred species, as well as casual nature lovers. All-inclusive rates include lodging, meals and two guided walks a day, as well as pick-up in Panama City (book in advance). Popular day-trips from the lodge include Lago Bayano, and an exhausting trek down to the coast in Kuna Yala (6–8 hr). It's also possible to make a two-day hike across the cordillera to the coast, passing the night in a hammock or tent en route, starting a short *chiva* ride northeast from Chepo in the village of San José (contact Fernicio Alfaro or his son, Yahir, on ℡296 8660 or 6529 5230).

Lago Bayano

Though now earmarked for "development", **LAGO BAYANO** remains a pictur-esque location, perfect for boat rides and picnics, and with a fascinating cave network at its southeastern tip. Its apparent charm and tranquillity, however, belie the anger of indigenous communities – displaced when the reservoir was formed in 1976 and still awaiting full compensation from the government – and the acres of forest that were submerged when the Río Chepo (or Río Bayano) was dammed to supply Panama City with more hydro-power; dead tree trunks protruding eerily from the water act as poignant reminders. The economic mainstay of the sixteen lakeside communities – including those of the Kuna **Comarca de Madugandi**, as well as Emberá, Wounaan and Ladino settlements – is the commercial fishing of tilapia.

El "Rey Negro Bayano"

While his origins and death remain enveloped in a fog of conjecture, it is unequivocal that El **"Rey Negro Bayano"** (also known as Ballano or Vaino) was the most successful leader of the *cimarrones* and the undisputed king, referred to as such even by the Spanish. Commanding the loyalty of between 400 and 1200 followers, he constructed an impenetrable hilltop fortress from where he repeatedly attacked Spanish forces and plundered mule trains on the Camino Real. Despite conducting three major campaigns against him (1553–56), the Governor of Panama failed to quell the resistance, prompting the Viceroy of Peru to charge a certain Captain Pedro de Ursúa with the specific task of crushing the *cimarrones* rebellion. Realizing it would be impossible to take Bayano's mountain stronghold by force, Ursúa pretended to offer him a peaceful settlement, in which the land would be divided equally between the Spanish and Bayano and his followers. At the celebratory feast that ensued, Ursúa ordered poison to be mixed with the wine to stun Bayano and his men. The plan worked: feeling the worse for wear from the potent cocktail, they were easily taken, thus ending six years of triumphant revolt against the Spanish Crown.

Named after Bayano, a charismatic leader of a major settlement of *cimarrones* (see box above), the 350-square-kilometre reservoir is a popular day-trip destination from Panama City; at weekends, families spill out of vehicles at the impressive Puente Bayano, which fords the lake's narrowest point, and pile into motor **launches** for island picnics, fishing trips or tours of the lake, on the lookout for caimans, crocodiles and otters slithering around the muddy banks. The most fascinating destination is the **Cuevas de Majé** ($2 entry), which lie at the southeastern end of the reservoir and comprise a 1km-long system of limestone caverns, replete with colonies of bats clinging to calcitic formations. Towards the end of the dry season, it's possible to wade (up to your chest) your way through the entire system, emerging in a steep-sided verdant gully, dripping with mosses and ferns. At other times, the raised water level means you'll need to go part way in a boat before stepping into the water, and may not be able to make it through on foot. In either case, you'll need a headlamp, footwear with a good grip and a minimum amount of clothing that you're happy to get soaked. The impressive **rock walls** that enclose the entrance to the nearby Río Tigre should also not be missed.

Comarca de Madugandi

The indigenous community of **Akua Kuna** (or Loma de Piedra) at the western end of the bridge marks the entry to the Kuna **Comarca de Madugandi** ($2 entry), established in 1996, which includes eighty percent of the reservoir's surface area and extends from the forested northern shores of the lake up the mountainous backdrop of the Serranía de San Blas. Well over three thousand Kuna inhabit the *comarca*, dispersed among fourteen communities, some of which, such as **Icantí** and **Pintupu** (contact Ramón Bayarismo ☎ 6448 6672 or enquire at Akua Kuna) are beginning to open up to tourists. The easiest **overnight** option is to book a camp bed at the basic Kuna community hostel ($10) by the bridge (with an equally basic *fonda* over the road), a single large room with a TV/DVD player the centre-piece, where some Hollywood action film is likely to be drawing a crowd.

Practicalities

Frequent **buses** depart from Albrook bus terminal for Puente Bayano (daily every 40min, 4am–4.40pm; 2hr 15min; $2.40), which hosts the first of several **police checkpoints**, where passports will be painstakingly checked.

It's worth reserving your launch in advance (especially at weekends) as organizing a boat and guide on the spot (from $60 per boat) may take time: for **lake tours**, contact Noy Ortega (☎6815 1969, prefers 24hr notice), who also runs the small bar by the bridge, or Mateo Cortéz (☎297 0157). Increasingly, tour companies are also offering excursions here from the capital (around $135), which also include a visit and lunch at the community of Unión Emberá on the Río Majé, but it's far cheaper and not too difficult to organize a visit yourself.

Ipetí

Kuna and Emberá communities exist either side of the highway at **IPETÍ**. South of the road by the bus stop, a dirt road leads a kilometre down to what was formerly a single community, relocated after their lands were flooded by Lago Bayano, which has split in two, situated on the very picturesque banks of the Río Ipetí. The first and larger settlement announces itself as **Ipetí-Emberá** and is well set up for tourists, with a couple of handicraft shops and two coordinators (Secairo Dojirama ☎6014 6161 and Olga Dojirama ☎6012 6743) to facilitate your stay in the large *casa comunal* ($5) and organize meals ($2 each) and activities: horse riding, birdwatching or excursions upriver when there's sufficient water ($10). The smaller splinter community of **Bahu Pono** is even more delightful, in a cleaner, quieter (lacking the noisy generators – and electricity), shadier spot, with a miniature *casa comunal* but otherwise offering similar activities at comparable rates (contact Diana Dumasa ☎6062 2955). Both make an ideal weekend excursion from Panama City (under 3hr from the capital), but with more time it's worth pushing on much deeper into the Darién proper, especially in the dry season, when the river here is too low to paddle and the countryside too denuded to enjoy.

Along the Interamericana to Yaviza

Agua Fría No. 1, a place easily missed were it not for the police checkpoint, marks the entry into Darién province. From here, traffic tends to speed along the remaining 110km of virtually straight tarmac, past pastureland, the odd settlement and occasional teak plantation to the end of the road at Yaviza, measuring time by the number of huge articulated lorries that lumber past, vast trunks of valuable hardwoods bound for North America and Europe chained to their trailers. Twenty kilometres further along the highway, a dirt road right leads to the Wounaan community of **Boca Lara**, which sees a fair number of visitors, and is renowned for its crafts. From **Metetí**, an important staging post and access point to the low-key **Reserva Forestal Filo de Tallo**, there's little to detain you until the bus rolls into **Yaviza**, a further 50km along the asphalt, spelling the end of the Interamericana.

Boca Lara

Fifty kilometres east of Ipetí, and 3km south of the highway, lies the fairly substantial village of **Santa Fé**, one of the Darién's major agricultural centres with a population of about eleven hundred, served by half-hourly buses from Metetí. Though of no particular interest to tourists, its location on the banks of the Río Sabaná allows you to travel (at high tide) the 5km downriver to the Wounaan village of **BOCA LARA** (or Puerto Lara), otherwise only accessible by 4WD car or taxi, and even then not in the wettest months. One of the few communities to receive plenty of technical support and funding, Boca Lara has a functioning fishing association, an organized tourist industry and produces high-quality crafts.

Though both Emberá and Wounaan are renowned for their basketry and woodcarving, it is the Wounaan who historically have been artists and have the greater reputation; many pieces from Boca Lara are sent straight to Panama City for sale, but some can still be perused in the village, where workshops in *artesanía* are also held.

Accommodation is in a plain open-sided wooden lodge ($15), with several partitioned rooms with mattresses (and one pricier, relatively de luxe room with private bathroom ❸). Simple but tasty meals ($2.50) are served on the deck out front; overlooking the main street, which slopes down to the dock, it is the perfect spot for watching village life unfold, though not so well located for the marathon Friday-night church service nearby. Boat trips to various destinations, guided hikes (within a small patch of forest of modest appeal), fishing and traditional dances can all be arranged by contacting Neldo Pisario (☎299 660 or 6848 3070), president of the tourism committee.

The most enjoyable way to **move on** from here is to head for Puerto Quimba by boat ($80 for the boat unless you can get a cheaper *colectivo* ride), past exposed mangrove roots and mud flats at low tide and the occasional burnt patch of hillside. Otherwise, you have to hitch a ride out to the Interamericana.

Metetí and around

A police security checkpoint that looks set for a siege heralds your impending arrival in **METETÍ**, a long, strung-out settlement that is an increasingly important commercial and administrative hub. It's hardly an endearing place, but if you're travelling around much in the Darién, you're likely to pass through more than once, since it offers good links with both Yaviza – from where it a shortish hop to El Real, the main gateway to the national park – and Puerto Quimba, which provides a water-taxi link to La Palma, capital of the Darién and access point for many of the surrounding Emberá and Wounaan communities.

The village's de facto centre lies across the bridge at the turn-off to Puerto Quimba, where there's a taxi rank, a handful of warehouse-like shops and, for people heading to the national park, the Darién's regional **ANAM** office (Mon–Fri 8am–4pm; ☎299 6965).

Practicalities

A few hundred metres up the Puerto Quimba road from the junction, **buses** depart regularly for Yaviza (1hr; $5), picking up passengers at the Interamericana, though seats can be scarce by then. Transport for Panama City leaves hourly from 3am to 5pm (5–6hr; $9), or you can flag down one of the buses coming from Yaviza. Buses also head off from the terminal to Puerto Quimba (hourly; 20min; $2.50) to meet the **water-taxi** to and from La Palma (hourly 5am–6pm; 40min; $3); the "port" consists of little more than a ramp, a jetty with a few tethered boats and the inevitable police checkpoint. There are also a couple of small *fondas*, one by the water's edge, where you can sip a beer or tuck into *pollo asado* while waiting for transport to show up.

Metetí has one of two **banks** in the Darién (the other is in La Palma) though it is inconveniently located a couple of kilometres before the town centre on the Interamericana; its **ATM** is only accessible during banking hours. Turning right up the road to Puerto Quimba, there are a couple of **pharmacies**, a very small **internet café** and a **health centre**.

Choices for **sleeping** are extremely limited, with the *Hotel Felicidad* (☎299 6544; $12) on the left-hand side of the Interamericana heading into town from the west, earning unequivocal top billing – a solid budget bet, it is a motel comprising thirty clean, compact rooms with private bathroom ($5 extra for fan or a/c) and secure parking, though like most places in Metetí, it suffers from water shortages.

Eating is slightly better: over the road next to the petrol station, 200m down the hill from the hotel, the cosy patio of *Restaurante Paso a Paso* (daily 6am–10pm) is a pleasant enough spot to tuck into a tasty breakfast fry-up for a couple of dollars. Another reasonable alternative, though with considerably less charm, is the *Restaurante Chiman* (daily 6.30am until late), down by the junction; the Chinese–Panamanian proprietors also own the adjacent **supermarket**, which occasionally surprises by stocking fresh fruit, and is a good place to load up with supplies if you're venturing further into the Darién. A few hundred metres up the Puerto Quimba road on the right, *Restaurante Brisas Darienitas* (Mon–Sat 6.30am–8.30pm) has a brighter feel and serves a wider variety of dishes, enhanced by a discerning use of spices, though the bill still won't top $4.

Reserva Forestal Filo de Tallo
Though lacking the wilderness appeal of the Darién, the **Reserva Forestal Filo de Tallo** nevertheless constitutes a refreshing oasis of woodland in an increasingly deforested landscape; along with the contiguous Reserva Forestal El Canglón, it aims to protect the water sources for 26 communities stretching 60km from Santa Fé, northwest of Metetí, to the optimistically named Nuevo Progreso, 20km before Yaviza. The two-room refuge, located off the road to Yaviza, with **bunks** ($15) and a space to **camp** ($10), is infinitely preferable to staying in the environs of Metetí or Yaviza, but it's expensive given that it has no facilities whatsoever, there's no public transport and you'll need to hire a guide. What's more, any stay requires organizing in advance with **ANAM** in Metetí (see opposite). Currently, there's only one short 2km interpretive trail, though longer hikes with a guide are possible. Exotic Adventures (see p.308) has a lodge on the edge of the reserve.

Yaviza
The gently rolling final 50km of the Interamericana to **YAVIZA** – now tarred except for a few kilometres – is mercifully more tree-lined than the stretch between Chepo and Metetí, though pastureland still prevails until the highway comes to an abrupt halt at the banks of the Río Chucunaque, where a flotilla of motorized *piraguas* remains moored by the wharf. Marking the official start of the infamous **Darién Gap** (*Tapón del Darién* – Darién cork or plug), the highway hiatus between Central and South America, Yaviza simultaneously exudes a lethargic end-of-the-road torpor and an edgy frontier-town feel – the mixed population of around three thousand (Afro-Darienite, Emberá, Wounaan and *mestizo*) eyes outsiders warily, while pairs of gun-toting police officers routinely patrol the town, togged up in full camouflage combat gear.

The town's only interest to visitors is as a stepping stone to El Real, the gateway to Parque Nacional Darién, or to the Distrito Cémaco, the northern segment of the Comarca Emberá–Wounaan, though you may want to make a quick detour to the edge of town upriver to view the last stand of the **Fuerte San Jerónimo de Yaviza**, as its one remaining wall slides unchecked into the murky water. One of several Spanish fortifications constructed in the Darién in the mid-eighteenth century, it protected the gold mines at Cana from marauding pirates. Thanks to the insouciance of INAC, the government department charged with caring for the country's patrimony, most of these historical sites have been fully reclaimed by the forest or are in terminal decline.

During the day, most of the action occurs by the **waterside**, where buses pull in: supplies are loaded onto boats headed for communities upriver, while mounds of plantain and yuca bound for the city are heaved onto trucks, and the surrounding makeshift *fondas* and restaurants do a thriving trade.

Buses from Panama City (6 daily, 3.15–7.30am; 6–7hr; $14) grind to a halt at the jetty, where **minibuses** from Metetí (1hr; $5) also pull in; on arrival, the heavily fortified **police station**, tellingly referred to as the *cuartel* (barracks), should be your first port of call – your intended travel plans will require police approval and will depend on the security situation. The handful of **buses** that head to Panama City are often dilapidated *diablo rojos*; it might be better to catch the regular shuttle to Metetí and hope for comfier transport to the capital from there. **Piraguas** regularly make the 45-minute journey to El Real, unless delayed by a major downpour; *colectivo* rates are generally $5 per person.

If you're unfortunate enough to have to **spend the night** in Yaviza, the *Hotel Yadarien* (T 299 4334: $20), just up the paved footpath that leads off from the dock, is the best option: it has twenty rooms, containing beds in varying states of repair, with air conditioning and private bathrooms, and a small first-floor balcony affording a prime view of happenings in the street below. The various comings and goings during the evening are unlikely to make for a peaceful sojourn, though it's infinitely quieter than the older, hardcore *Hotel 3 Americas* (no phone; ●), which offers dilapidated fan-ventilated rooms in the centre of town by the basket-ball court, with an on-site music-thumping bar and restaurant.

At night, you'd be wise to hunker down in your hotel room after **eating**: a reasonable option is the *Restaurante Oderay*, a few doors down from the *Hotel Yadarien*, which dishes up a decent plate of fried chicken or fish (and has a good toilet), but note that after 7.30pm, you'll be unlikely to unearth anywhere serving food. The country's priciest **internet café** is a block up from the dock at *Casa Lefy* (daily 6am–7pm; $2.50/hr).

Parque Nacional Darién

Outranking all of Panama's national parks in both size and reputation, the **PARQUE NACIONAL DARIÉN** is nevertheless one of the least visited protected areas in the country – reaching the refuge at Rancho Frío requires considerable organization, while the alternative, more comfortable option at Cana requires a great deal of cash – yet the awe-inspiring greenery, laced with rivers and waterfalls, all rich in wildlife, are well worth the time and money, providing a truly magical experience. Created in 1972 and, at 5790 square kilometres, the most expansive protected area in Central America, it hugs the Colombian border, a forested carpet rising from the mangroves, coastal lagoons and deserted beaches of the Pacific, rippling over the volcanic ranges of the Serranía del Sapo and Cordillera de Jungurudó northeast to the park's highest point of Cerro Tacarcuna (1845m) on the continental divide of the Serranía del Darién, and stopping just short of the Caribbean coast. Numerous important rivers scythe their way through the green mantle, including the Tuira, Sambú and Balsas.

The **biodiversity** is staggering even as it is shrinking. Over 450 bird species have been recorded, including an array of vibrantly coloured macaws and parrots and strange-named rarities such as the beautiful treerunner, scale-crested pygmy tyrant and Chuck-will's-widow. Mammal species top 168, with numerous endemics and endangered animals lurking in the lush vegetation; the park offers the best chance, albeit slender, of glimpsing any of the big-five cats, or a Baird's tapir – though spotting their footprints in the early morning mud is more likely – and even the occasional spectacled bear has been sighted. Yet the arboreal richness of the Darién demands just as much attention, with tracts of primary and secondary growth and a towering canopy of barrigón, spiny cedar and graceful platypodium. A visit in

▲ Harpy eagle, Parque Nacional Darién

March or April is rewarded with the golden crown of the guayacán, heralding the start of the rains, and the russet bloom of the silvery cuipo trees looking down on the already lofty forest canopy, favourite nesting site of the world's largest concentration of **harpy eagles** (see box, p.320). Most of this can only truly be appreciated from the air, or from breaks in the tree line when ascending the region's peaks. On the forest floor, the scene is very different: dark and dank, and dominated by gnarled tree trunks entwined with vines or studded with vicious spines, vast buttress roots, dangling lianas, ferns and rotting leaf litter.

Declared a UNESCO World Heritage Site in 1981 and a Biosphere Reserve in 1983, the **protection** offered the park in practice is worth little more than the paper it's written on, as illegal hunting, logging, extraction of rare plants and animals, and slash-and-burn agriculture continue unchecked. Ironically, the long list of undesirables that have taken refuge in the rainforest – FARC guerrillas, right-wing paramilitaries, drug traffickers, smugglers and bandits – have acted as unwitting conservationists by frightening off most settlers and major developments, though the fighting over the border in Colombia has also resulted in an influx of refugees, who themselves are clearing land to cultivate.

Now that hiking the Darién Gap has been consigned to history, **visiting the national park** these days means going on a guided tour (see p.308) or staying at one of the permanent camps: ANAM's run-down refuge Rancho Frío (often dubbed Pirre Station), to the west of Cerro Pirre (1200m) and reached via the town of El Real, and, on the eastern side of the Pirre ridge, Cana, site of a colonial-era gold mine, and accessible only on an expensive all-inclusive tour (see p.308 & p.318).

El Real and around

The deceptively fast-flowing waters of Río Chucunaque snake down 6km from Yaviza through variegated walls of water chestnuts, banana plantations, expansive trees and pastureland to the low-key grassy bank "jetty" of **EL REAL** on Río

Scotland's doomed Darién venture

In one of Panama's lesser-known historical footnotes in the late 1600s, the Scots gambled their country's future on a **trading colony in the Darién** in the hopes of transforming **Scotland** into an imperial power to rival England. The undertaking was the brainchild of **William Paterson**, one of the founders of the Bank of England, who, having failed to convince the English government of the plan's viability, managed to rouse the nationalist pride of the Scots, forming the Company of Scotland in May 1695 and persuading rich and poor alike to pour their often meagre savings into the scheme. In the excitement that accompanied preparations, the fact that Paterson had never set foot in Panama and was wholly ignorant of conditions there passed unnoticed. Soon, a sizeable chunk of the kingdom's wealth resided with the company.

A fleet of five ships and 1200 Scots, including Paterson and his family, set sail from Leith in July 1698, their hulls laden with the most unlikely collection of personal possessions and trading goods, including 4000 wigs, 25,000 pairs of shoes and 1500 Bibles. Within days, many of the ships' supplies – including meat, butter and cheese – had spoiled and rations were cut, quickly demoralizing the crews. After four months at sea, the fleet finally anchored in Caledonia Bay, and for five months the settlers worked hard to build **New Edinburgh** (in modern-day mainland Kuna Yala), despite disease, low rations, drunken infighting – 5000 gallons of brandy had been transported along with copious amounts of claret and rum – and the tropical environment constantly conspiring against them. To make matters worse, the English king, who was keen not to upset the Spanish, had forbidden any of the Caribbean colonies to assist, despite the fact that the Scots were also his subjects. Only **the Kuna** were prepared to help – the Scots seemed infinitely preferable to the

Tuira. From the jetty, it's a sweltering fifteen-minute walk into the town proper – another one-time fortified colonial settlement, now a pleasant if somnolent collection of houses constructed from various combinations of wood, zinc and concrete and a couple of churches, interwoven with a network of cement pathways. The vibe is far more relaxed than in Yaviza, though the **accommodation** is on a par, namely the dilapidated wooden two-storey *Hotel el Nazareño* (☎299 6548; $10), which looks on the verge of collapse, has intermittently functioning plumbing and a DIY shower. Round the corner near the church, the friendly ⚔*Restaurante Doña Lola* serves very tasty **food** in a relaxed environment; if you're just after a drink, head for the aptly named *Caña Blanca*, a traditional thatch-and-cane *cantina*, which is just the place for quenching a post-expedition thirst.

As with Yaviza, El Real is only likely to serve as a jumping-off point to somewhere else, either a boat trip down the sweeping meanders of the Río Tuira, or, more likely, a hike into the ANAM refuge at Rancho Frío. For the latter, a permit, which ANAM prefers you to purchase in Metetí, and guide ($15–20 per day) are both needed, requiring a visit to the **ANAM park office** (Mon–Fri 8am–4pm; no phone) as well as the obligatory registration with the police.

Rancho Frío

The only ANAM refuge still in operation within the park, ⚔**Rancho Frío** ($10 entry, $10 per bunk, $5 for camping), sometimes called Pirre Station, is scenically situated on the shady banks of the Río Perescenico, with several **trails** leading off from the camp, including the serious overnight trek to the cloud forest of **Cerro Pirre** (1200m), which requires lugging tent, sleeping bag and provisions up the mountain; it can be chilly at night, so pack something warm.

Spanish – though they were as uninterested as everyone else in trading with any of the colonists' bizarre wares. When the promised supply ships failed to materialize, and the onset of the rainy season brought another wave of disease, morale slumped further. After ten months, and news that a Spanish fleet was on its way, the colony's council called it a day and decided to weigh anchor. Only one ship made it back to Scotland, carrying a quarter of the original population, including Paterson, though his family had died in Panama.

When rumour of the colony's abandonment reached the ears of the company directors, it was roundly dismissed; refusing to believe that the men they had sent forth "could be guilty of so much groundless cowardice, folly and treachery", the directors sanctioned a second fleet of four ships and 1300 would-be settlers, no better equipped than the first. Arriving to find a deserted colony, the second expedition soon encountered the same problems that had ruined the first and, worse, their renewed presence further riled the Spanish along the coast in Portobelo. Small **battles** soon broke out between the Scots, aided by the Kuna, and the Spanish, and despite one unlikely victorious raid on a Spanish stockade, six months after arriving in April 1700, the Scots finally surrendered to the Spanish force. Thanks to the respect bestowed on them by the Spanish governor, they were all allowed to leave, though none of the ships made it home and only a handful of folk survived.

The venture crippled Scotland financially, leaving the many subscribers to the company penniless, and the country at the mercy of rival England, which in 1707 eventually agreed to compensate all investors as part of the deal for Scotland conceding to the creation of the United Kingdom of Great Britain.

The **Sendero de las Antennas** provides a stiff all-day alternative that culminates in a hilltop police post, affording sweeping views of La Palma and the Golfo de San Miguel, with the Pacific as backdrop. Less strenuous walks can be had closer to camp, but still require a guide – the most popular is the two-hour circular **Sendero Rancho Frío**, which takes in a waterfall and natural *piscina*. During the wet months, the rivers and waterfalls are truly spectacular, though the refuge and mountain trails are often swathed in mist and the quantity of mud to wade through can scarcely be imagined, making even the shortest hike a major physical achievement. In the dry season, paths are easier to hike, views more frequently glimpsed and your chances of spotting mammal life – driven to the river to drink – is greatly enhanced.

The refuge itself suffers from neglect, with two dirty dormitories, collapsing bunk beds and torn mosquito netting, which makes a mosquito net, coils, candles, repellent and anything else to keep the ferocious insects at bay essential. The kitchen has a gas stove, but the place lacks electricity, and water supply is inter-mittent. Ensure you have a good torch to pick out scorpions or snakes at night, since the toilets are separate from the main block. All **provisions** need to be brought with you, including enough for the park warden and/or guide; be sure to pack bottled water or, better still, purifying tablets. Yaviza is a better place to stock up with supplies than El Real, having lower prices and slightly more tinned food to choose from.

In the dry season, the easiest **access from El Real** is to arrange transport by (4WD) vehicle as far as the village of Pirre Uno, 12km upriver, from where it is a gentle ninety-minute walk to the refuge. In the rainy season, you can sometimes get further upriver to Pijebaisal (around $40 for the *piragua*, plus the cost of three gallons of diesel each way), an hour's hike away.

Cana

On the eastern side of the Pirre ridge, nestled in the folds of Cerro Pirre, lies the forested valley of ⅄ Cana. Now a biological field station and considered one of the world's top-ten birding sites, it is hard to picture this stunning place as the bustling mining community of over twenty thousand that it was in the seventeenth century. Santa Cruz de Cana, to employ its little-used full title, was originally the site of the most lucrative gold mine of the New World, reliant on a vast slave workforce. Abandoned in the early eighteenth century after repeated attacks by pirates and indigenous resistance forces, it was revivified briefly in the nineteenth century when a railroad was built down to Boca de Cupe, where the bullion was transferred to boats. Deserted again in 1912, the forest soon clawed back the land, though you can still glimpse a few sleepers amid the vegetation, and a forlorn railway engine incongruously peeks out from under the foliage at the end of one of the trails.

Cana is everything that Rancho Frío is not: comfortable and expensive, since it can only be visited through **ANCON Expeditions** (see p.308), and its remoteness – a two-day hike to the nearest village – means flying into the valley on a charter plane. The well-kept lodge-cum-field-station offers eight simple double rooms with ample shared facilities, a spacious veranda and separate dining terrace. It's easy to spot **wildlife** in the immediate vicinity, and a dawn or dusk stroll down the grassy airstrip can be rewarded with sightings of deer and agoutis, while herds of white-lipped peccaries occasionally grunt and snaffle in the undergrowth. With a decent pair of binoculars, though, you can observe a wealth of dazzling birdlife without shifting from your hammock: copious hummingbirds gorging on nectar, toucans and parrots squawking from the surrounding cecropia trees, and raptors wheeling overhead.

Since the lodge is located at an elevation of 500m, it is a shorter three-hour ascent into the cloud forest of **Cerro Pirre** – though the trail does not connect with the Rancho Frío route – where most packages spend a night in the more rudimentary tented camp (with latrine and a bucket of river water for ablutions) in search of the elusive golden-headed quetzal and other highland species.

Around the Golfo de San Miguel

Stacked up on a hilly peninsula, the ramshackle collection of wooden buildings that constitute the lively provincial capital of **La Palma** jut out into the widening expanse of the Río Tuira as it empties into the **Golfo de San Miguel**, a large bite-shaped body of water penetrating into Panama's southeastern Pacific coastline. Just across the water from La Palma, Isla El Encanto (or Boca Chica) hosts the scarcely visible crumbling remains of the overgrown **Fuerte de San Carlos de Boca Chica**; though little more than a watchtower, it was a crucial link in a chain of defences that safeguarded the gold mines at Cana. Sprinkled along the coastline amid the mangroves are several predominantly Afro-Darienite communities such as **Garachiné** – comprising a collection of fairly dilapidated buildings and negligible services. The rivers that flow into the Golfo de San Miguel are the means of access to the **Comarca Emberá–Wounaan** and to the villages of **La Marea**, **Mogué**, **La Chunga** and, of course, **Sambú** itself.

La Palma and around

Resembling no other town in Panama, **LA PALMA**, a predominantly Afro-Darienite settlement of around six thousand, is the regional administrative and

Staying the night (or preferably several nights) in an **Emberá or Wounaan village** is a great way to interact with villagers, and learn about their day-to-day activities – fishing, basketry, cooking or making a dugout – as well as venturing into the rainforest. Communities used to tour parties tend to have slightly better **facilities** (showers, flush toilets and maybe even mattresses and mosquito nets), whereas others may provide little more than a wooden floor for you to sleep on, possibly with a family, a fire to cook your own food, and a bucket of water for washing.

The location of many settlements on tidal rivers only accessible at high tide often entails a lot of hanging around by jetties waiting for the water level to rise – generally, you need to be flexible yet more organized, taking **food supplies** with you where possible, since many communities expect you to provide the food to cook and village shops are thinly stocked. Whereas **bottled water** – or the means of purifying it – is both necessary and scarce, beer is more widely available, though check on the village etiquette before indulging and be discreet in your drinking except when the whole village is having a party.

Most visitors head for villages round the **Golfo de San Miguel** or in the **Distrito Sambú** section of the **Comarca Emberá–Wounaan**, where you first need to report to the *comarca* office in Puerto Indio (see p.323). Mobile-phone signals are fickle, so a better bet is to ring the village public phone (numbers are listed in the phone directory), though they are often out of order, and ask to speak to the tourist coordinator (*coordinador de turismo*), who is also the person to ask for on arrival. They can tell you the prices and whether money needs to be paid to them (to be disbursed later to the relevant people) or directly to anyone who provides a service. Families usually take turns in hosting visitors to ensure that wealth is distributed across the community, but it is essential to sort out what's to be paid to whom from the outset to prevent misunderstanding. **Costs** are itemized separately – village community fee, accommodation, meals, guided hikes or fishing trips, *jagua* dye body painting and dance performances – so assuming one excursion and three meals a day, you should budget around $30–40 per day, plus **transport** ($10–20/person if you manage to catch a *colectivo piragua*, $60–150 if you hire a boat privately).

Sales of **handicrafts**, for which the Wounaan and Emberá are renowned, are also an important aspect of village visits, displayed in a small shop or by the artisans themselves, and at set prices that are inevitably lower than in Panama City. If you don't intend to buy anything, alert the tourist coordinator to avoid embarrassment; otherwise, try to spread your purchases round several artisans.

commercial hub, where motorized dugouts from the coastal and riverine communities jostle for position at the narrow and non-too salubrious main jetty. The town's one sultry street is choc-full of small hole-in-the-wall restaurants, bars and hotels, and shops selling welcome piles of fresh produce and other goods that are regularly shipped in from Panama City. Most visitors gravitate to La Palma to connect with transport to Emberá communities such as **La Marea** and **Mogué**, or those further afield up the Río Sambu, and you'd be well advised to stock up with supplies while here – the (pricier) village stores are unlikely to provide much beyond tinned fish, rice and biscuits. If you don't have the means to purify water, make sure you pick up a flagon or two of the bottled variety.

Practicalities

Water-taxis to La Palma run from Puerto Quimba (hourly, 5am–6pm; 40min; $3), a short bus ride from Metetí. Aside from decent fresh supplies, La Palma boasts a **bank** with an ATM (Mon–Fri 8am–3pm, Sat 8am–noon), located at the far end of town, towards the airstrip, as well as a **post office**. At the opposite end of the main drag, by Cable & Wireless, a tiny but invitingly air-conditioned **internet café** (daily 8am–9pm) makes a good place to escape the heat. Though you are unlikely to want to **spend the night** in La Palma, the family-run ⚘ *Hotel Blaquirú Bagará* (☏299 6224; ❷–❸) is the place to head for, with a dozen neat wood-panelled rooms, most with fan and shared bathroom, a couple with a/c, private bathroom and balcony. If you're on a shoestring and fancy being in the thick of the noisy action, then *Hospedaje Pablo Benita* (☏299 6490; ❶) and the slightly nicer *Hotel Tuira* (☏299 6316; ❷) are both more centrally located on the main street, with communal balconies overlooking the estuary. For **food**, you could do worse than head across the street to *Restaurante Nayelis* (daily 5am–9pm), which serves inexpensive Panamanian and Dominican dishes. As for entertainment, cockfighting bouts feature high on the list, as elsewhere in the region, accompanied by plenty of betting and boozing.

La Marea

Forty minutes' boat ride southeast from La Palma up the sinuous tree-lined Río La Marea, the welcoming community of **LA MAREA** provides a perfect introduction to the Emberá way of life. The *"marea"* (tide) is crucial to village logistics since the place is only reachable at high tide, and even then, at the backend of the dry season, the *piragua* scrapes along the riverbed. Traditional open-sided wooden-and-thatch dwellings are dotted across a sloping expanse of neatly trimmed grass ending at the riverbank, where a small *rancho* is used for dance performances and craft displays; opposite this, a tiny shop sells beer and a few tinned essentials. An infectious tranquillity pervades the settlement, which is devoid of any generator hum and illuminated by starlight and kerosene lamps at night, and unlike some

---

Saving the harpy eagle

Instantly recognizable for its splendid slate-grey back, brilliant white chest and distinctive crest, the **harpy eagle** (*águila harpía*) is the largest eagle in the Neotropics and one of the most powerful worldwide, with talons the size of a grizzly bear's claws. The larger female can weigh up to 9kg and measure over 1m long, yet despite a vast wingspan of over 2m, it can reach speeds of up to 80kph while accelerating through trees to stab its prey.

Formerly widespread across the lowland primary forests of the Darién and Bocas del Toro, the harpy eagle has suffered years of decline due to loss of habitat and hunting. However, recent concerted **conservation efforts** are beginning to pay dividends. An increasingly successful breed-and-release programme run by the Peregrine Fund (ⓦwww.peregrinefund.org) has caused numbers to swell to over two hundred pairs, resulting in Panama now having the greatest concentration of harpy eagles in Mesoamerica. It will be a long recovery process, though, as harpy eagles are lethargic breeders, laying two eggs once every three years; worse still, once the first egg has hatched, the second is discarded as the pair focus on nurturing the single chick in the nest for another six months, and taking care of it for a further two years.

Working with local communities and conducting educational campaigns in schools, the conservation project has succeeded in heightening public awareness and interest in the harpy eagle. Fittingly, it was legally recognized as the **national bird** in 2002, and since 2006 must by law top the national coat of arms. Additionally, the raptor now even enjoys its own **national day**, on April 10. All this publicity, it is hoped, will help ensure the harpy eagle's continued survival.

For more on the efforts to save the harpy eagle, see Fondo Peregrino-Panamá (ⓦwww.fondoperegrino.org) and Patronato Amigos del Águila Harpía (ⓦwww.aguilaharpia.org).

communities, many of the 160 villagers choose to go about their business clad in traditional attire, except when heading into town. The surrounding forest abounds in **wildlife**, worth exploring with a guide ($8) following a trail leading to a waterfall or a lake, or embarking on a substantial three-hour hike, or a shorter horse ride, to a **harpy eagle nest**, where a willingness to stake the place out for several hours can often be rewarded by a truly special sighting. Otherwise, the days can happily slip by interacting with villagers, getting your body painted in jagua dye and cooling off in the river.

A traditional house is set aside for visitor **accommodation** ($5), with space to hang your hammock or spread a sleeping bag, and a family allocated either to cook food (which they prefer you to provide) or lend you their fire pit and some pans to prepare your own meals. Since the village receives small tour groups, comfortable accommodation (with private rooms, beds and mattresses) will soon be possible when groups aren't there.

To **reach the community**, contact the chief, Gabriel Mengisana (℡6736 4368) – who can also organize visits to the less-frequented community of Aldea, another hour upriver and accessible via the La Palma–Chepigana road in the dry season – or pop into the office of Radio Voz Sin Fronteras in Metetí; alternatively, in La Palma, contact Jerairo Grajales (℡299 6232, @jgrajales@dgi.gob.pa), who works in the Ministerio de Economía y Finanza office and is from the village.

Mogué

There's a Heart of Darkness feel about entering the **Río Mogué**, enclosed by forbidding walls of mangroves, flecked with perching white ibis, which eventually clear at a scenic mooring, ten minutes' walk from the village of **MOGUÉ**. The name derives from Mogadé, a mythical Emberá creature that lived in the mountains and ate people – though Panama City would seem to have devoured more of the dwindling village population as they leave in search of employment. Besides a little tourism, agriculture – plantain, yuca and a variety of other fruits and vegetables – constitutes the economic mainstay of the community, though a minority still fish or hunt iguanas, agoutis and other small animals with traditional arrows or a gun.

Mogué's facilities are well organized, with a relatively luxurious yet rustic shower and toilet block and **accommodation** on a mattress, or in a hammock ($10) in a lofty cathedral-like *casa communal*, whose breezy raised platform affords a prime spot to eavesdrop on village life. Food is served at a table there ($10 per day for the cook's services per group, plus $2.50 per meal, though you should preferably provide the food), where on Saturdays or Sundays the leaders preside over the weekly village gathering. Though there's no electricity, there are a couple of private generators, causing loud music to occasionally blast across the rooftops and enabling some families to congregate round a television at one of several village *tiendas*, located at the far end of the basketball court.

Since Mogué is predominantly surrounded by cleared land and fields of plantains, it takes fifteen minutes to reach the more luxuriant rainforest, and a further ninety minutes along a well-trodden trail to an active **harpy eagle nest**, though there are numerous less-frequented paths to explore with a guide ($10, plus $10 per group for the guide) populated with toucans, sloths and monkeys. Horse riding and fishing trips ($10) are also on the menu and Mogué is definitely a place to acquire some fine-quality basketry, especially masks.

Once again, **transport** to the village makes the journey expensive unless you're travelling in a group ($50 one way from La Palma). If you ring (public phone ℡333 2519, Emilio Chami ℡6962 0166) to arrange a boat pick-up in La Palma, ask for the cooler box to be brought along, which you can fill with fish, chicken or shrimps from the market for meals.

Established in the early 1990s, **RESERVA PUNTA PATIÑO** is Panama's first and, at 300 square kilometres, largest private reserve, occupying the entire headland at the tip of the choppy Golfo de San Miguel, just beyond the lively Afro-Darienite fishing village of **Punta Alegre**.

While the landscape is nowhere near as dramatic as the jungle-carpeted peaks of the interior, the regenerating hinterland forest – once devastated by cattle ranching, timber extraction and coconut plantations – is filling up with native hardwoods, though it's an hour's hike to primary forest. Aeroperlas sponsors a **carbon-offsetting reforestation project** within the reserve, which also covers a stretch of charcoal beach, an important expanse of mangroves and mud and salt flats that attract an abundance of resident and migratory sea birds.

Managed by the environmental organization ANCON, the reserve is not without its critics, not least the Emberá, who feel the land should be theirs. Moreover, the area can only be visited by splashing out around $740 per person for an all-inclusive four-day **tour** (full board, with bilingual naturalist guide and charter flight) through ANCON Expeditions (see p.308), which includes an excursion to Mogué. You do get what you pay for, though: comfortable lodgings comprising ten *cabañas* with single beds, air conditioning, private cold-water bathrooms and balconies. The lodge, perched on a bluff overlooking the bay, has a wraparound, hammock-strewn balcony – the perfect spot to soak up glorious sunsets, aerial displays by diving pelicans, and occasional sightings of bottle-nosed dolphins and humpback whales. On land, mammals to look out for include the weasel-like tayra, grey foxes and the extraordinary-looking capybara, the world's largest rodent, which resembles a giant guinea pig and weighs in at 55kg. Needless to say, the location necessitates lashings of insect repellent to ward off the prolific uninvited guests.

Garachiné

Set against the imposing backdrop of Cerro Sapo (Toad Hill), the small neglected fishing community of **GARACHINÉ** surprisingly boasts an airstrip and a road (leading to Sambú before looping back to the coastal Wounaan community of Taimatí, further north along the bay), making it another entry point into the Darién rainforest – though time your visit for low tide and you'll be wading knee-deep across slate-coloured alluvial mud flats to the shore. If you're hungry for a plate of rice and fried chicken or fish, *Fonda Carlos Alberto* on the main street should hit the spot, washed down by a beer from the rather grim local *cantina*. A couple of doors down, the two-storey wooden *Hospedaje San Antonio* (public phone, opposite the hotel ☎299 6428, or Efraim de Olmedo ☎6042 8504; ❷) offers the only **accommodation** and is a good place to enquire about transport to Sambú or further afield. Alternatively, contact Solarte Barqueño Carpio (☎6655 0984, Ⓦwww.traveldarienpanama.com), who offers various multi-day packages ($550 for three nights all-inclusive from Panama City) to Taimatí, a thirty-minute boat ride away, or across the mountains to Playa de Muerto on the Pacific coast, six hours' hike – or a two-hour boat ride – away (see p.325). Whichever itinerary you choose, it will need to be approved by the police first.

Río Sambú and the Comarca Emberá-Wounaan

Portal to the twelve communities of the **Distrito Sambú** of the **Comarca Emberá-Wounaan**, 12km up the serpentine **Río Sambú**, the twin settlements of **Sambú** and **Puerto Indio** are generally only reached by river at high tide. As the Río Sambú's waters swell during the rainy season, so *piraguas* can penetrate as far upstream as the tiny village of Pavarandó; more easily accessible downriver is the fairly dispersed community of **La Chunga**, which lies a few minutes' paddle up a quiet tributary.

Sambú and Puerto Indio

Outside the small thatched waiting room at the airstrip, a hyperbolic wooden sign announces the "Sendero del Paraíso Sambú!". While **SAMBÚ** and its counterpart **PUERTO INDIO**, connected by a narrow footbridge across the river, are pleasant enough places to hang out, they serve more as a gateway to what might more aptly merit the description: swathes of primeval forest and a serpentine waterway leading to Emberá and Wounaan communities further upriver.

The contrast in mood and architecture between the two villages is striking: in bustling Sambú, cement pathways wind between tightly packed houses of various architectural styles, accommodating a mixed population of Emberá, Wounaan, *mestizos* and Afro-Darienites; across the river, quieter Puerto Indio, at the western limit of the Distrito Sambú, of which it is the capital, comprises an indigenous population living in traditional wooden housing raised on stilts.

Arrival

The least expensive way to reach both communities is by **plane** from Panama City via Garachiné (see p.307), though arriving by **boat**, sweeping round the river's tortuous bends, causing flocks of white ibis to fly off in unison, is far more atmospheric; most commercial traffic ($15 from La Palma, $20 from Puerto Quimba) occurs on Monday and Fridays, though you may be wedged in between containers of fuel and bottle-filled crates. There are also regular connections (Mon, Wed & Fri, timings depending on tides) from La Palma ($13) and Puerto Quimba ($15) to Garachiné, from where, between January and April, you can usually **hitch a ride** along the dirt road; this will set you back $4–5 per person for a *colectivo*, $40 in total if a special trip is necessary. Fortnightly sailings to Panama City (10–12hr; $15) can provide a rough passage and are not for those with a queasy stomach.

Before you get too settled, don't forget the obligatory detour via the **police checkpoint**, tucked away at the edge of the runway in Sambú; since Puerto Indio is the administrative capital of the southwestern area of the *comarca*, you need to check in at the Oficina del Congreso there and pay the **entry fee** ($10) before venturing any further into the territory.

Accommodation

Almost all visitors **stay** in Sambú; a couple of lodgings overlook the airstrip, with a couple more options in town.

Mi Sueño By the airstrip, public phone ☎333 2512. Eleven small, wooden-fan-ventilated rooms with shared bathroom, and a large communal balcony affording a pleasant view of the surrounding hillside. Downstairs is an occasional restaurant. ②

Sambu Hause Village centre, ☎268 6905, ⓦwww .sambuhausedarienpanama.com. A US-Darienite couple offers the Darien's most affordable stay with home comforts – a cosy, painted wooden house consisting of three fan rooms with single beds and shared bathroom (⑥), and a slightly pricier a/c en-suite double; all have shutters and mosquito netting. There's a shared, fully equipped kitchen and a nicely furnished living-dining room, plus spacious shady terrace and BBQ area; B&B rates can also be arranged. Local guides are engaged for river trips and village visits. The only snag is the recently opened *cantina* opposite, which is heavy on the ears at weekends. ⑧, including all meals

Villa Fiesta By the airstrip, public phone ☎333 2512 or 6687 2271. Three bright, good-value rooms (a/c & fan) with excellent beds, private bathroom and fridge; meals can also be arranged. Former Emberá *cacique* Ricardo Cabrera, the genial owner and proprietor of the downstairs shop, is fluent in English and a mine of local knowledge. ③

Tours

In **Puerto Indio**, the tourism committee, based in the Oficina del Congreso, offers a range of day **excursions to the Distrito Sambú** (for which you'll need to provide your own food and water), including a guided walk round the village taking in a nearby lake, a half-day excursion to a waterfall involving a 45-minute boat ride and a modest rainforest walk, and lengthier ventures to the communities of La Chunga ($78 for groups of up to 6 people), Villa Quiresia ($84) or remote Pavarandó ($114). In all cases, overnight stays can easily be arranged, either in the *casa comunal* or in someone's house. Arquinio Dogirama (@emberaguia@yahoo.es) and Domicilio Cardena, president of the tourism committee at La Chunga (public phone ☏333 2516), are **guides** authorized by the *comarca*'s tourism committee ($15 per group), though each village has its own guide.

In **Sambú**, *Werara Pum*, an organization of local **guides**, offers similar tours, though they are not allowed to guide within the *comarca* boundaries ($10 for a walk, around $100 for a 6hr boat-trip); contact Juan Murillo Moreno, known as "Juancito", who lives a few doors down from *Sambu Hause*, or Arnulfo at the shop on the right-hand side before the bridge. Ricardo Cabrera, of *Villa Fiesta*, offers pricier **tours** than others in the town, but then you pay for his experience and English language proficiency: $115 (including transport, food and guide) for the four-hour Sendero Bayamón to the community of Villa Quiresia, with the option of an overnight stay.

Eating and drinking

A couple of **restaurants** offer tasty inexpensive *platos típicos*: Benedicta's *Aqui me Quedo* (daily 6–7am or 8pm), in a sturdy cane building behind the shop near the airstrip, prepares excellent breakfasts in particular, while *Restaurante Maranata* (Mon–Sat 6am–8pm, Sun until 6pm), before the bridge on the right, serves up a decent plateful of fish or chicken for under $3. Several *cantinas* in Sambú constitute the **nightlife**.

La Chunga

Closer to the mouth of the Río Sambú, a small tributary navigable only at high tide leads to the hamlet of **LA CHUNGA**, named after the ubiquitous palm used for basketry. At other times, you land at a pontoon on the main river, from where it's a twenty-minute walk along an impressive raised wooden boardwalk through mosquito-infested swamp to the village.

A pleasant avenue of cedar trees marks the entrance, opening out onto an overgrown basketball court surrounded by a handful of traditional homes; although possessing four hundred inhabitants, the place seems smaller, with homes dispersed and hidden amid the lush vegetation. **Basketry** is still widely practised by the women, though potential buyers are scarce these days – when former *cacique* Ricardo Cabrera was based in La Chunga, his contacts and US-honed English ensured a steady flow of cruise-ship groups, but following his relocation to Sambú, the village is struggling to attract tourists and the *cabañas* have fallen into disrepair (though new ones are planned). Despite this, overnight guests are made comfortable, accommodated on mattresses, with mosquito nets and even sheets and pillows, in someone's home ($5 per night, payable to the community), while a cook is appointed to prepare basic meals ($10), worth perking up with a few tinned extras.

For $20 per group, a village guide will take you **birdwatching** upriver, or you can make a six-hour round trip to a **harpy eagle nest**. Make sure you check out the village **stocks** (*sepo*); miscreants who commit an offence and are unable to pay the fine are placed there for a couple of hours, an experience made particularly painful by being made to sit on a pile of cooked rice, which attracts vicious ants that tuck in to the penitent's buttocks.

The southeastern Pacific Coast

The Darién's **Pacific coast** is as remote and unexplored as the jungle-filled interior: to the northwest of the Golfo de San Miguel, the coastline is dominated by mangroves, but to the southeast it comprises miles of deserted beaches interspersed with rocky outcrops, cliffs and expanses of pristine forest, with the contiguous brooding Serranías del Sapo and Jungurudó a dramatic backdrop. Three places of interest stand out along this stretch of land: the Emberá village of **Playa de Muerto**, the sport fishing magnet of **Bahía Piña** and **Jaqué**, the last sizeable community before the Colombian border, with kilometres of unpredictable ocean in between.

Playa de Muerto

A stiff six-hour hike or bruising two-hour boat ride from Garachiné, the isolated Emberá community of **PLAYA DE MUERTO** receives more visitors than you would imagine given its isolation and therefore the time, effort and cost involved in getting there. The rewards, however, are considerable: a small welcoming village of a couple of hundred inhabitants, fronted by a swathe of silvery sand sprinkled with coconut palms and backed by vast tracts of virgin forest. The settlement gained its rather gruesome name – "Beach of the Dead" – from the corpses that would wash up on shore following sea battles between bullion-bearing Spanish galleons and pirate ships. Nowadays, only the occasional turtle lands on the sand – with numbers dwindling, since the villagers take their eggs – along with the odd tourist boat. You couldn't ask for a more tranquil spot with more hospitable hosts.

Accommodation is provided in two thatched bamboo *cabañas* by the beach ($7) with hammock or mattress, as well as shower and toilet; additional hammock-swinging space is afforded in an open *rancho*. The more active can head off into the rainforest on a guided hike ($20 per group), with a two-hour **trail** from a nearby beach to a waterfall a popular trip. Fish, shrimps and even lobster dishes are on the menu at a small inexpensive **restaurant** in the village, and a fridge ensures ice-cold beer and soft drinks.

For **transport** here, ring the village public phone (☎299 6428) or enquire at the *Hospedaje San Antonio* in Garachiné ($130–150 per boat, plus $10 per day each for the pilot and assistant, and their meals), or contact Solarte Barqueño Carpio (☎6655 0984, ⓦwww.traveldarienpanama.com) in Panama City. You'll need to show your passport for the frontier police in Garachiné and on arrival in the village. An alternative route to the village takes a mountainous six-hour cross-country route, cutting through primary forest, for which you would need a guide (see p.308).

Bahía Piña

The sheltered **BAHÍA PIÑA** is synonymous with sport fishing: it's rated the number one saltwater fishing destination in the world, boasts 250 world records at the last count and attracts enthusiasts from across the globe. The natural aquarium is mainly due to the **Zane Grey Reef** just offshore, a huge underwater mountain that ensures vast quantities of black and blue marlin, Pacific saltfish, dorado, amberjack, yellowfin tuna and the like, whose continued abundance is guaranteed by the commercial-fishing exclusion zone that the government enforces rigorously. The place to indulge this pastime is the *Tropic Star Lodge* (toll-free in the US ☎1 800 682 3424, ⓦwww.tropicstar.com; $6000 for a seven-night all-inclusive package), an exclusive fishing resort with landscaped grounds set in the rainforest above a beach, built by a Texas oil tycoon in the 1960s. Facilities have been subsequently upgraded to ensure plenty of home comforts (minus phones and cable TV), and there are over a hundred employees to make sure the 36 guests are properly pampered. For those who don't actually want to fish, there's plenty to enjoy: kayaking up the Río Piña, which runs through the property; hiking in the surrounding rainforest; or sipping a cocktail while birdwatching from your veranda. There are substantial reductions for non-fishing and low-season rates. Most of the workforce for the lodge comes from the nearby impoverished agricultural and fishing community of **Puerto Piña**; though locked in an almost feudal relationship, with little development occurring in the village without the lodge's nod of approval, the two sides continue to wrangle over land rights.

Jaqué

A few kilometres further down the coast, and 45km from the Colombian border, lies the far more populated village of **JAQUÉ**. A mixed community of about 2500 Emberá, Wounaan, Afro-Darienites and Afro-Colombian refugees, it sprawls across the flat and mainly deforested plain at the wide mouth of the Río Jaqué, at the western end of a four-kilometre belt of tan-coloured sand. Another community struggling to make a living from agriculture and fishing, made harder by its isolation from markets, Jaqué also boasts several NGO-sponsored development projects including an agricultural college, a women's craft cooperative, a school recycling and composting initiative, and a leatherback turtle conservation programme.

The rudimentary *Anamal Lodge* (℡7383 233 5976 or 6032; ❶), a rickety two-storey structure with large windows, offers adequate **accommodation** with shared bathrooms and fans and can organize guided excursions. Despite the denuded plains, primary forest is only just over an hour's hike away, covering the folds of the Serranía de Jugurundó. A more popular excursion, however, is 45 minutes upriver in a motorized dugout to the Wounaan village of **Biroquera**; also visited by groups from the *Tropic Star Lodge*, they are accustomed to entertaining tourists and selling their exquisite crafts. Three other Emberá villages lie further upriver, which are usually beyond the safe limits that the frontier police will allow.

Reaching Jaqué requires either **flying** from Panama City to the settlement's new airstrip (see p.307) or risking the rough seas in one of the regular supply **boats** from Panama City (see p.308).

Contexts

Contexts

History

Though the Republic of Panama is only over a century old, humans have lived on the isthmus for thousands of years. Its location as a slender bridge between two vast land masses has proven as crucial to its development as its eventual link between two expanses of ocean.

Pre-Columbian society

Panama's scarce archeological remains give little clue to the societies that inhabited the region, in part because many early excavations were poorly executed and finds were damaged or looted. Lacking the huge structures and sophisticated carvings that epitomize the Mayan, Aztec and Toltec civilizations of Mesoamerica, the trading societies of Central America have always taken an historical back seat. Yet central Panama boasts the earliest traces of **pottery-making** in the Americas with ceramics from Monagrillo, in the northern Azuero Peninsula, carbon dated to 2500–1200 BC. A nearby fishing village in Sarigua is considered to be the isthmus' **oldest settlement**, from around 11,000 BC.

The most sophisticated societies inhabited central Panama, with the richest archeological finds in the **necropolis** of Sitio Conté, outside Penonomé. Excavations by American academics in the 1930s opened up around a hundred **tombs** to reveal thousands of intricate **gold pieces of jewellery** alongside sophisticated **polychrome ceramics** and other artefacts dating back to the first century, most of which were shipped off to the States.

Just down the road at El Caño, near Natá, lies a **ceremonial site** believed to have become a cemetery dating from 500 to 1200 AD, though its original function and significance is left to conjecture, not helped by the fact that a US adventurer decapitated the heads of over a hundred basalt **standing stones**. In the Western Highlands, outside Volcán, another important site indicates the existence of what has been termed the **Barriles culture**, at its apogee around 500 to 800 AD, whose curious **stone statues** of a figure wearing a conical hat carrying another on its shoulders are on display at the anthropological museum in Panama City. A large **ceremonial grinding stone**, or *metate*, adorned with human heads – also in the museum – has led to speculation about human sacrifice. Sprinkled round Sitio Barriles and elsewhere in western and central Panama on moss-covered boulders are numerous **petroglyphs**; the largest example is La Piedra Pintada outside El Valle.

Arrival of the Spanish

The first European credited with setting foot on the isthmus was the Spanish aristocratic notary **Rodrigo Galván de Bastidas**, who in 1501 made a low-key arrival, trading his way peacefully up the Caribbean coast as far as present-day Colón. In contrast, **Christopher Columbus** (Cristóbal Colón), who arrived a year later on his fourth and final voyage to the "New World", headed for the western and central Caribbean coast, keen to lay his hands on the legendary gold. He attempted to establish the first European settlement on the isthmus, prompting violent conflicts with indigenous populations. Though relations between Columbus and the local chief or *cacique*, **Quibián**, known as "El Señor de la Tierra", were initially friendly, the mood changed once it was clear the Spanish intended to stay. When Columbus left his garrison at Santa María de Belén (in present-day Veraguas) to seek reinforcements, Quibián rallied local leaders to destroy the settlement but was captured by Columbus's brother Bartolomé, who had been left in charge. While being transported as a prisoner downriver to Belén, the chief dived out of the dugout and was presumed drowned. He survived, however, and went on to lead the assault against the invaders, eventually forcing them to flee.

The respite was short-lived. In 1505 the King of Spain, Ferdinand II, intent on expanding and consolidating his empire, dispatched two men to take charge of what had been named *"Tierre Firme"* (extending from present-day Venezuela to Panama): **Alonso de Ojeda** was to govern the land between Cabo de la Vela in present-day Colombia through to the Golfo de Urabá, known as Nueva Andalusia, while **Diego de Nicuesa** was to oversee the west from the gulf to Gracias a Dios on what is now the border between Honduras and Nicaragua (and was known as Castilla de Oro, after its supposed riches). Both campaigns ended in disaster; indeed, of Nicuesa's eight hundred men only a hundred survived.

Though estimates of the indigenous population at the time of the Spanish conquest vary from two hundred thousand to two million, what is not in dispute is the speed at which the local communities were decimated, as much by **disease** brought by the conquistadors as through **massacre** and **enslavement**. The remainder retreated to inhospitable remote mountain areas, where they either lay low or continued their resistance against the invaders. The Spanish instituted a feudal-style system of **encomiendas**, theoretically entrusting "free" indigenous peoples to the stewardship of colonizers for their well-being and instruction in the Catholic faith in return for labour; in practice, workers were more often treated like slaves. Though the system was eventually abolished in 1720, it did not spell the end of intense hardships for many of the rural population.

Balboa and the Mar del Sur

There's little in **Vasco Núñez de Balboa**'s inauspicious early life to suggest he would rise to prominence. After setting foot on the isthmus as a member of Bastidas's expedition, he settled on Hispaniola, where, failing as a pig-farmer, he fled his creditors by stowing away on a boat bound for the mainland. Upon discovery, he was saved from being thrown off the ship thanks to his knowledge of the isthmus. As the incipient Spanish settlements struggled to survive, including the new regional centre **San Sebastián de Urabá** founded by Ojeda, Balboa recommended relocating across the gulf. **Santa María de la Antigua del Darién** (located just on the other side of the current Panama–Colombia border) was thus established on a site that had been seized from followers of Cacique **Cémaco**, a pivotal figure in the indigenous resistance. It was the first successful Spanish settlement on the isthmus, eventually becoming the capital of **Castilla de Oro** until the seat transferred to Panama City in 1524.

In the meantime Balboa continued his acquisition of power by subjugating, negotiating and making peace with local tribes; popular with his men and brutal with the local population, he was, nevertheless, judged to be fair in comparison with his cruel, murderous successors. Hearing from the locals about another sea to the south and land dripping in gold and pearls, Balboa found a route through the forests of Darién to become the first European to look out onto the **Pacific Ocean** on September 25, 1513. Several days later, in true imperialist fashion, Balboa waded into the water in full body armour, sword in one hand, statue of the virgin

Mary in the other, and claimed possession of the "Mar del Sur" in the name of the King of Spain. Yet he received scant reward for his "discovery" – in 1519 his jealous superior **Pedro Arias de Ávila**, known as Pedrarias the Cruel or *Furor Domini* (Wrath of God), the first governor of Castilla de Oro, had him beheaded despite having given him one of his daughters in marriage.

Panama City and the Camino Real

In the face of appalling losses from disease, Pedrarias moved his base from the Caribbean side to the slightly more salubrious Pacific coast, where he **founded Panama City** (the ruins at Panamá La Vieja) in 1519. The new settlement became the jumping-off point for further Spanish inroads north and south along the coast, and, after the conquest of Peru in 1533, began to flourish as the transit point for the fabulous riches of the **Incas** on their way to fill the coffers of the Spanish Crown. From Panama City, cargo was transported across the isthmus on mules along the paved **Camino Real** to the ports of Nombre de Dios and later Portobelo, on the Caribbean coast. A second route, the **Camino de Cruces**, was used to transport heavier cargo to the highest navigable point on the Río Chagres, where it was transferred to dugout canoes that carried it downriver to the coast.

The flow of wealth attracted the attention of Spain's enemies, and the Caribbean coast was under constant threat from European **pirates**, the first of whom, the Englishman **Francis Drake**, successfully raided Nombre de Dios. He received support from the **cimarrones**, communities of escaped African slaves that lived in the jungle and often collaborated with pirates in ambushing mule trains and attacking their former masters. In the most daring assault, in 1671, Welshman **Henry Morgan** and his men sailed up the Río Chagres, having destroyed the fortress at San Lorenzo at the river mouth en route, and crossed the isthmus to ransack Panama City. Though Morgan is generally blamed for the fire that then engulfed the place, it was more likely due to the detonation of the city's gunpowder supplies ordered by the defeated Spanish governor.

The city was rebuilt in 1673 on today's Casco Viejo behind defences so formidable that it was never taken again, but the raiding of the Caribbean coast continued, until finally in 1746 Spain rerouted the treasure fleet around Cape Horn. With the route across the isthmus all but abandoned, Panama slipped into decline.

Independence from Spain

Independence movements in South America, headed by **Simón Bolívar** and **José de San Martín**, were gathering pace by the turn of the nineteenth century. Though the isthmus initially remained fairly detached from the process, it was not devoid of nationalist sentiment. On November 10, 1821, the tiny town of La Villa de Los Santos unilaterally declared that it would no longer be governed by Spain, in what was known as the *Primer Grito de Independencia* (First Cry for Independence); the rest of the country soon followed suit, declaring **independence** on November 30. It retained the name of Panama, as a department of what historians have subsequently termed "Gran Colombia"; with the secession of Ecuador and Venezuela it quickly became Nueva Granada. Almost immediately conflicts emerged between the merchants of Panama City, eager to trade freely with the world, and the distant, protectionist governments in Bogotá, leading to numerous, if half-hearted, attempts at separation. As the century wore on, US influence asserted itself, most notably in the 1846 **Mallarino–Bidlack Treaty**, which granted the US government rights to build a railroad across the isthmus and, significantly, accorded them power to intervene militarily to suppress any secessionist uprisings against the New Granadan government – a theoretically mutually beneficial accord that was to seriously backfire on Bogotá.

The **discovery of gold** in California in 1849 sparked an explosion in traffic across the isthmus. Travel from the US east coast to California via Panama – by boat, overland on foot, and then by boat again – was far less arduous than the trek across North America, and thousands of "Forty-niners" passed through on their way to the goldfields. In 1850 a US company began the construction of a **railway** across Panama. Carving a route through the inhospitable swamps and rainforests proved immensely difficult – thousands of the mostly Chinese and West Indian migrant workers died in the process – but when the railway was completed in 1855, the Panama Railroad Company proved an instant financial success, earning $7 million in profit in the first six years, despite having cost $8 million to construct. The railway also marked the beginning of a new era in foreign control:

The Watermelon War

The completion of the railroad left many Panamanian labourers, including the new immigrant workforce, unemployed and resentful of their well-paid US counterparts, some of whom showed scant respect for their hosts or local customs. On April 15, 1856, tensions spilled over. An intoxicated (white) American named Jack Oliver, who had been killing time in the bars waiting for the boat, grabbed a slice of **watermelon** from a local (black) stall holder and refused to pay. When the trader drew a knife, Oliver's mate tossed a dime at him, further enraging the merchant, and as he advanced on Oliver, the latter drew a gun. An attempt to disarm the American resulted in a bystander getting shot, prompting a full-scale anti-US **riot**. Many Americans holed up in the railway depot and gunfire was exchanged with the crowd, which was attempting to batter down the door. Rather than control the situation, the **police** joined in the affray, which continued until a trainload of the vigilante **Isthmus Guard** arrived to disperse the mob. While the number of casualties in the so-called "Watermelon War" – 17 dead and 29 wounded, predominantly American – was not disputed, blame for the violence was. Amid claims and counter-claims of racism, the US government dispatched two warships to Panama and occupied the railway station – though only for three days – but their demand for total control of the railroad was refused.

within a year, the first **US military intervention** in Panama had taken place (see box opposite).

The French canal venture

In 1869 the opening of the first transcontinental railway in the US reduced traffic through Panama, but the completion of the **Suez Canal** that same year made the longstanding dream of a canal across the isthmus a realistic possibility. Well aware of the strategic advantages such a waterway would offer, Britain, France and the US all sent expeditions to seek a suitable route. The French took the initiative, buying a concession to **build a canal**, as well as purchasing the Panama Railroad, from the New Granadan government. In 1881, led by ex-diplomat **Ferdinand de Lesseps**, the driving force responsible for the Suez Canal, the Compagnie Universelle du Canal Interocéanique began excavations.

Despite de Lesseps' vision and determination, the "venture of the century" proved to be a disaster, not least because of his technical ignorance and arrogance. In the face of impassable terrain – forests, swamps and the shifting shales of the continental divide – the proposed sea-level canal proved unfeasible, while yellow fever, malaria and a host of other unpleasant diseases ravaged the workforce. In 1889 the Compagnie collapsed; \$287 million had evaporated as a result of financial mismanagement and corruption, implicating the highest levels of French society in what an official described as "the greatest fraud of modern times". Hundreds of thousands of ordinary French investors lost everything.

The War of the Thousand Days

At the end of the nineteenth century the simmering feud between the Conservative and Liberal parties erupted into a bloody three-year **civil war** referred to as the **War of the Thousand Days** (*Guerra de los Mil Días*). Though there were distinct ideological differences – ruling elite **Conservatives** supported a strong central government, limited voting rights and close bonds between church and state whereas the merchant class and educated **Liberals** wanted more decentralized, federal government, universal voting rights and a greater division between church and state – there were also many factions within each party. The violence was triggered by alleged election fraud by the landed Conservatives in their bid to remain in power, but by the time the bloody conflict had ended in 1902, claiming around a hundred thousand lives, it was hard to pinpoint what much of the fighting had actually been about. It's also not conclusive whether key Liberal protagonists were motivated more by the desire for separation or greater democracy and social justice; regardless, most Liberals were subsequently elevated to the status of nationalist heroes.

In Panama the initial Liberal revolt was led by **Belisario Porras**, the popular exiled lawyer, who later won three periods of office as president of Panama. With the support of the presidents of Nicaragua and Ecuador, Porras entered western Panama on March 31, 1900, with an invasion force commanded by Colombian **Emiliano Herrera**, at the insistence of President Zelaya of Nicaragua. Their antagonism was a major factor in the ultimate Liberal failure. Moving towards Panama City, they gathered numerous supporters, but slow progress allowed reinforcements to arrive from Colombia. On arrival outside the capital, Herrera

Pedro Prestán and the Fire of Colón

Another ugly episode between Liberals and Conservatives and a further example of US intervention resulted in the public hanging of **Pedro Prestán**, a Liberal revolutionary who took advantage of the absence of Colombian troops in Colón – they had headed over to Panama City to quell an attempted coup by Liberal Rafael Aizpuru – to seize control of the city. After looting businesses to raise money, he and his band of rebels purchased arms from the US, which arrived on a steamship that anchored in the bay. When the steamship agent refused to unload the arms, Prestán took the agent, US consul and several other Americans **hostage**, threatening to kill them if the US naval vessel stationed nearby landed troops and if the arms were not handed over. Though the weapons were promised and the hostages released, the Americans reneged on the deal. Fleeing to Monkey Hill outside the city, Prestán and his poorly armed combatants fought with the Colombian troops now back from Panama City. The rebels were routed and the **city caught fire**; built entirely of wood, it was totally engulfed in flames, killing eighteen and leaving thousands homeless. Prestán, who had fled by boat to his native Cartagena, became the scapegoat. Many of his men were rounded up and **executed** while Prestán himself was captured, tried and convicted by a partisan jury, and left to hang above the railway tracks in Colón.

rejected Porras's attack plan and led a botched single-pronged assault on the city that resulted in a thousand dead. Though the Conservatives reasserted their authority, small bands of Liberal sympathizers ran riot in the interior, especially in the central rural areas under the leadership of **Victoriano Lorenzo**, a local official of mixed race from Coclé and a champion of the indigenous population.

In 1901, a second Nicaraguan-backed Liberal force managed to take Colón and effectively immobilize the railway, forcing the Colombian government to ask the US to broker an armistice. The Liberals, fearing intervention by the US government, agreed to the peace conditions but Lorenzo refused to accept the terms. In a sordid collusion between both Conservative and Liberal social elites, Lorenzo was tricked into capture. In disregard of the amnesty detailed in the accord, he was summarily tried and executed by firing squad on May 15, 1903, in the Plaza de Armas (today's Plaza de Francia) of Panama City. Six months later Panama separated from Colombia.

Separation from Colombia

Despite the French canal debacle, the dream of an interoceanic waterway remained as strong as ever. The US government took up the challenge; President **Theodore Roosevelt**, in particular, felt that the construction of a canal across Central America was an essential step to becoming a major sea power. At first the favoured route was through Nicaragua, but the persuasive lobbying of Philippe **Bunau-Varilla**, former acting director and major shareholder in the French company, swung the Senate vote in Panama's favour. His masterstroke was to buy ninety Nicaraguan stamps that showed an erupting volcano – a major argument against the Nicaragua route – and send one to each senator just three days before the vote. In 1903 a **treaty** allowing the US to build the canal was negotiated with the Colombian government, whose senate refused to ratify it, understandably wary that the US would not respect their sovereignty. Outraged that "the Bogotá lot of jackrabbits should be allowed to bar one of the future highways of civilization", Roosevelt gave unofficial backing to Panamanian secessionists.

In the event, the **separation** was a swift almost bloodless affair with only one casualty. The small Colombian garrison in Panama City was bribed to switch sides and a second force that had landed at Colón agreed to return to Colombia without a fight after its officers had been tricked into captivity by the rebels. On November 3, 1903, the **Republic of Panama** was declared and immediately recognized by the US, whose gunship standing offshore prevented Colombian reinforcements from landing to crush the rebellion.

The Canal

A new **canal treaty** was quickly negotiated and signed on Panama's behalf by the slippery Bunau-Varilla, who had managed to get himself appointed a special envoy, theoretically only with negotiating powers. The Hay-Bunau-Varilla Treaty gave the US "all the rights, power and authority...which [it] would possess and exercise as if it were the sovereign", in perpetuity over an area of territory – the **Canal Zone** – extending five miles (8km) either side of the canal. In return, the new Panamanian government received a one-off payment of $10 million and a further $250,000 a year. (Of particular interest to Bunau-Varilla was the $40 million the French canal company received for all its equipment and infrastructure.) Even American Secretary of State John Hay admitted the treaty conditions were "vastly advantageous to the US and we must confess...not so advantageous to Panama". Panama's newly formed national assembly found the terms outrageous, but when told by Bunau-Varilla that US support would be withdrawn were they to reject it – a claim he invented on the spot – they ratified the treaty, and work on the canal began.

It took ten years, 50,000 workers from 97 countries and some $352 million to complete the task, an unprecedented triumph of organization, perseverance, engineering and, just as crucially, sanitation, during which time chief medical officer Colonel **William Gorgas** established a programme that **eliminated yellow fever** from the isthmus and brought malaria under control. As a result the **death toll**, though still some 5600 workers predominantly of West Indian descent, was substantially lower than it would otherwise have been. Meanwhile the two men in charge, **John Stevens**, a brilliant railway engineer, and his successor **George Goethals**, a former army engineer, managed to solve the problems that had stymied the French. The idea of a sea-level canal was quickly abandoned in favour of constructing a **series of locks** to raise ships up to a huge artificial lake formed by damming the mighty Río Chagres. Stevens was responsible for maximizing the potential of the railway, devising an ingenious pulley system that enabled them to excavate over 170 million cubic metres of earth and rock, three times the amount removed at Suez. The thirteen-kilometre **Gaillard Cut**, which ran through the continental divide, required a mind-boggling 27,000 tonnes of dynamite. The end result, overseen by Goethals, was the largest concrete structure, earth dam and artificial lake that the world had ever seen, accomplished with pioneering technology that set new standards for engineering. On August 15, 1914, the SS *Ancón* became the first ship to officially transit the canal, which was completed six months ahead of schedule.

An enormous **migrant workforce**, at times outnumbering the combined populations of Panama City and Colón, was imported to work on the canal's construction, and many of these workers – Indians, Europeans, Chinese and above all West Indians – stayed on after its completion, indelibly transforming the racial and cultural make-up of Panama. Work was carried out under an apartheid labour system, where white Americans were paid in gold and the rest – the vast majority of whom were black – in silver. Employees were "**gold roll**" or "**silver roll**", a categorization that permeated every aspect of life. The gold roll employees and their families enjoyed higher wages, superior accommodation, better nutrition, health care and schooling; even toilets and drinking fountains were set aside for the exclusive use of one group or the other. As well, the mortality rate among black workers was four times higher than of whites.

The New Republic

Though their economy boomed during the canal's construction, it was soon apparent to Panamanians that they had exchanged control by Bogotá for dominance by the US. The government, largely controlled by a ruling **oligarchy** known as the "twenty families", was independent in name only; the US controlled everything – trade, communications, water and security. Moreover, the de facto sovereignty and legal jurisdiction that the US enjoyed within the Canal Zone made it a strip of US territory in which Panamanians were denied the commercial and employment opportunities enjoyed by the US "**Zonians**", a situation that lasted well beyond the completion of the canal. The US agreement to guarantee Panamanian independence came at the price of intervention whenever the US considered it necessary to "maintain order", a right they exercised on several occasions.

Once such action followed the Dule or **Kuna Revolution** in 1925, an eventual result of the Panamanian government refusing to recognize the relative autonomy granted by the Colombian authorities in 1870 through the Comarca Tulenega. Pressure mounted when outside groups were given concessions to plunder Kuna resources and persistent attempts made to suppress Kuna culture. Following an **armed revolt** led by Sailas (chiefs) Nele Kantule and Olokindibipilele (Simral Colman), which resulted in around twenty fatalities on each side, the Kuna declared independence. Forestalling government retaliation, the US stepped in and mediated a **peace agreement** that granted the Kuna the semi-autonomous status they still retain.

The Republic of Panama's first president, the respected Conservative **Manuel Amador Guerrero**, was actually from Colombia, though he had been heavily involved in the separatist movement, and more important, was well known to the Americans as the former medical officer for the Panama Railroad. But the first Panamanian president of real impact was **Belisario Porras**, elected to office in 1912 for the first of three terms (1912–16, 1918–20, 1920–24). A trained lawyer and prominent Liberal leader from the War of a Thousand Days, he is largely credited for establishing the basic infrastructure necessary for a newly independent state – roads, bridges, hospitals, schools, libraries, a legal system, communication networks, even the cherished national lottery.

The rise of nationalism

Despite a **new treaty** limiting the US right of intervention in 1936, resentment of American control became the dominant theme of Panamanian politics and the basis of an emerging sense of national identity. **Arnulfo Arias Madrid**, a fascist and Nazi-sympathizer – earning him the nickname "Führer Criollo" – exploited this while going on to become one of the country's most popular leaders. Of middle-class farming stock from Coclé, he was the first Panamanian graduate of Harvard Medical School but abandoned medicine in favour of politics on his return to Panama. He founded Acción Communal, the political precursor to the Partido Nacional Revolucionario and present-day **Partido Panameñista** (PP), which espoused his nationalistic and initially racist doctrine of **Panameñismo**. After assisting his older brother Harmodio Arias Madrid to the presidency in 1932, he won office himself in 1940, for the first of three periods (1940–41, 1949–51 and 1968).

During his first term he set about disenfranchising Afro-Antillean and Chinese Panamanians and pursuing **racist** immigration policies. On the positive side he instigated the social security system, improved many workers' rights (a policy strand abandoned in his later term), modernized banking and gave the vote to women. Crucially, he was adamant about pushing for a better deal with a US government intent on expanding its military defences outside the Canal Zone. But the US-backed Panamanian *Policía Nacional* (National Police) and its successor, the *Guardia Nacional* (National Guard), made sure that no president who challenged the status quo lasted long in office and Arias was ousted by military coup each time, the last after only two weeks.

Nevertheless, **anti-US riots** erupted periodically over the next thirty years. The ten-thousand-strong protest in 1947 against the US attempt to extend the lease on World War II-era bases outside the Canal Zone helped persuade the deputies not to ratify the proposal. By 1948, the US military had withdrawn from outside the Zone. The most infamous disturbances, however, were the so-called **flag riots** of 1964. The flying of flags was a trivial but symbolic battleground for Panamanian–US antagonism. To ease tensions, the US government agreed to the Panamanian flag being flown beside the Stars and Stripes in selected places in the Zone. When in Balboa High School the US flag was flown on its own for two days in succession, two hundred Panamanian students arrived at the school to raise a Panamanian flag. A skirmish broke out during which the Panamanian flag was torn, prompting full-scale mob violence. The twenty Panamanians who died in the fracas were later elevated to the status of **national martyrs**, commemorated annually on January 9, *Día de los Mártires* (Martyrs' Day). A diplomatic protest about US aggression ensued, going all the way to the UN and resulting in President Lyndon Johnson's promise of a new canal treaty.

Omar Torrijos and the new canal treaty

After a brief power struggle following the coup to oust Arnulfo Arias in 1968, Lieutenant Colonel **Omar Torrijos** of the National Guard established himself as leader of the new military government. Fracturing the political dominance of the white merchant oligarchy (known disparagingly as the *rabiblancos*, or "white tails") in his pursuit of a pragmatic middle way between socialism and capitalism, he was a charismatic, populist leader. Over twelve years he introduced a wide range of reforms – a new constitution and labour code, nationalization of the electricity and communications sectors, expanded public health and education services – while simultaneously maintaining good relations with the business sector, establishing the **Colón Free Zone** and initiating the banking secrecy laws necessary for Panama's emergence as an international financial centre. On the debit side, he was extremely intolerant of political opposition and his critics were often imprisoned or simply "disappeared"; several **mass graves** from the period were unearthed during a Truth Commission instigated by President Moscoso, though there was no evidence of Torrijos' direct involvement in the atrocities.

Central to Torrijos' popular appeal was his insistence on gaining Panamanian control over the canal. After lethargic negotiations with the Nixon and Ford administrations, Torrijos signed a new canal treaty with US President Jimmy Carter on September 7, 1977. Under its terms the US agreed to a gradual withdrawal, passing complete control of the canal to Panama on December 31, 1999; in the meantime it was to be administered by the **Panama Canal Commission**, composed of five US and four Panamanian citizens. Even so, the US retained the right to intervene militarily if the canal's neutrality was threatened. Under pressure from Washington to democratize, Torrijos formed a political party, the **Partido Revolucionario Democrático** (PRD), and began moving Panama towards free democratic elections. In 1981, however, he died in a plane crash in the mountains of Coclé Province. Many Panamanians believe that there was some involvement by the **CIA** or by Colonel **Manuel Noriega**, Torrijos's former military intelligence chief.

Manuel Noriega and the US invasion

After a period of political uncertainty, Noriega took over as head of the National Guard, which he restructured as a personal power base and renamed the *Fuerzas de Defensa de Panamá* (**Panama Defence Forces** or PDF), becoming the de facto military ruler in 1983. Although the 1984 elections gave Panama its first directly elected leader in nearly two decades, Nicolás Ardito Barletta, the real power lay in the hands of Noriega, backed by the US government.

A career soldier, Panama's new military strongman had been on the US Army's payroll as early as the 1950s and the CIA's from the late 1960s. After training at the notorious School of the Americas, he was made chief of intelligence for the National Guard in 1970. In the early 1980s, Noriega assisted the US by supporting its interests elsewhere in Central America, especially Nicaragua. Whereas Torrijos had supported the leftist Sandinistas in Nicaragua's civil war, Noriega allegedly became an important figure in covert US military support for the Contras, helping to funnel money and weapons to the guerrilla force – a charge he denies. Noriega was also busy building his relations with the Colombian cocaine cartels in Medellín. Although this extracurricular activity was ignored by the US for years, in 1986 the **Iran-Contra Affair** – in which the US government sold weapons illicitly to Iran and used the proceeds to fund the Contras – brought an unwelcome glare of publicity on the cosy arrangement between Noriega and the CIA. Deciding it was politically expedient to drive Noriega from power, the US government began economic sanctions in 1987, followed by Noriega's indictment on drug charges in the US in February 1988.

On December 20, 1989, US President George H.W. Bush launched the ironically named "**Operation Just Cause**", and 27,000 US troops invaded Panama. They quickly overcame the minimal organized resistance offered by the PDF. Bombers, helicopter gunships and even untested stealth aircraft were used against an enemy with no air defences, and hundreds of explosions were recorded in the first twelve hours. The poor Panama City barrio of El Chorrillo was heavily bombed and burned to the ground, leaving some 15,000 homeless; indeed, a Human Rights Watch report noted that civilian deaths were over four times higher than military casualties among the PDF. Noriega himself evaded capture and took refuge in the papal nunciature, before being forced to surrender on January 5 after a round-the-clock diet of ear-splitting heavy metal and rock music blasted from the car park. He was taken to the US, **convicted of drug trafficking** and sentenced to forty years in a Miami jail before being extradited to France to face trial on money-laundering charges.

Estimates of the number of Panamanians killed during the invasion vary from several hundred to as many as ten thousand. That the invasion was **illegal**, however, was clear: it was condemned as a violation of international law by the United Nations and the Organisation of American States, both of which demanded the immediate withdrawal of US forces. Despite most Panamanians being relieved to see the back of Noriega, they were outraged at the excessive use of force and America's blatant disregard for Panamanian sovereignty.

Post-invasion, the US installed **Guillermo Endara**, winner of the 1989 elections annulled by Noriega, as president. He replaced the PDF with the Panamanian Public Forces, branches of which carry out limited military duties when necessary. In 1994 PRD-leader **Ernesto Pérez Balladares** defeated Endara, who had little national support. After taking office, Pérez Balladares implemented neoliberal economic policies, like the privatization of state-owned companies and reduction of public expenditure, aimed at meeting payments on the vast external debt that was the legacy of the Torrijos years.

Twenty-first-century politics

In an interesting twist, the presidential elections of 1999 were contested between Martín Torrijos, son of the former military ruler, and the widow of Arnulfo Arias (the man Torrijos ousted in 1968), **Mireya Moscoso**, who became Panama's first female leader. On December 31 she presided over the seamless **handover of the canal**, which is now efficiently managed by the independent Autoridad del Canal de Panamá. The US withdrawal was a mixed blessing for Panama's economy: many jobs disappeared with the closure of the bases, but the valuable real estate and infrastructure Panama inherited created investment opportunities. Still, a number of the former US buildings lie abandoned, and relations with the US remain complex.

Moscoso's term in office got off to a rocky start when, before the first budget vote, she gave Cartier watches and jewellery as "Christmas presents" to the 72 members of the legislative assembly. It set the tenor for the presidency, which was scarred with accusations of corruption and incompetence. Her term ended in similarly controversial fashion as she tried to push through construction of a tarred road linking Boquete and Cerro Punta through the national park of Volcán Barú, rather than upgrading an existing route south of the mountain in a far less environmentally sensitive area. Opposition to the outrageous plan successfully united numerous national and international environmental groups and became a major election issue in 2004, when **Martín Torrijos**, of the PRD, was elected with 47 percent of the vote.

Though Torrijos junior was elected on a platform of "zero corruption" it did not take long before scandals started to emerge; nor was his administration's record on the environment particularly memorable, approving countless hydroelectric projects in Chiriquí and Bocas del Toro Provinces with scant environmental assessment studies and little negotiation with the indigenous

Panama's indigenous population

While Panama's national economy enjoys one of the highest growth rates in Latin America, the distribution of wealth remains highly skewed, the poorest twenty percent living below the poverty line, receiving less than 1.5 percent of the earnings. This includes most of Panama's 286,000 indigenous citizens, who comprise around ten percent of the total population according to the outdated 2000 census. Some have been assimilated to varying degrees into urban life; most, though, inhabit the rural regions, with around half living in the various *comarcas* – semi-autonomous areas demarcated by the state over the last sixty years – many without access to clean water, health care, electricity, decent schooling or paid employment.

Panama has eight indigenous groups, the most numerous by far being the **Ngöbe** (170,000), who share a vast *comarca* in western Panama, spanning Bocas del Toro, Chiriquí and Veraguas, with the less numerous **Buglé** (18,000). The groups are culturally similar but speak mutually unintelligible languages. The first comarca established was **Kuna Yala** in 1953, the result of a revolution by the **Tule** (or Kuna) people (62,000) in 1925, which stretches out along the coastal strip of eastern Panama to the Colombian border, incorporating over four hundred tiny islands. Much later, the smaller inland comarcas of Wargandi and Madugandi were added. The **Emberá** (23,000) and **Wounaan** (7000) inhabit the forests of the Darién, though some have now migrated to the Chagres river basin nearer Panama City. Around 35 percent remain in the two *comarcas*; many others are scattered among around forty riverside communities across the province. At the other end of the isthmus in Bocas del Toro Province, the **Naso**, also known as the Teribe, number just over three thousand and live around Changuinola and along the rivers heading up into the mountains. A few kilometres north, on the banks of the Río Sixaola, live the **Bri-Bri** (2500). The oft-forgotten **Bokota** number less than a thousand and are often mistakenly considered Buglé since they speak Buglere; they live around the Bocas–Veraguas provincial boundary in the Comarca Ngöbe-Buglé.

populations most affected. One of his major challenges was to reform the Social Security Fund, which was on the verge of financial collapse, but unpopular proposals to increase workers' contributions and raise the retirement age provoked angry street protests, forcing the government to back down and pass a watered-down bill. He did, however, help to tighten measures against drug-trafficking and money-laundering. And in his biggest gamble, he green-lighted a $5.3 billion project to **widen the canal**, to be completed in 2014. The **canal expansion programme** aims to fit most post-Panamax vessels (ships that don't currently fit in the canal) through a larger set of locks and improve the canal's efficiency by widening the Gaillard Cut.

Future prospects

The elections in May 2009 broke the political stranglehold that the PRD and PP had enjoyed for the previous seventy years as conservative multimillionaire supermarket magnate **Ricardo Martinelli** swept to power. Head of the new

Suffering the highest levels of poverty, some Ngöbe and Buglé migrate for seasonal jobs on banana, coffee and sugar plantations to earn cash to sustain them the rest of the year. Kuna, Emberá and Wounaan women, in particular, earn an income from their fine craftwork – though villages in remote areas more or less compete with each other for the small percentage of visitors that venture past Panama City and the canal.

Although the *comarcas* cover a fifth of Panama's land, these territories as well as those of indigenous communities residing outside their boundaries are under constant threat. Some lands lie within national parks and reserves, which has enabled government, generally through ANAM, to apply restrictions on traditional lifestyles in the name of conservation, while simultaneously allowing mining or hydro-electric projects to go ahead often with minimal or no consultation with indigenous authorities and no compensation to those forced to move. Government and big business are not the only threats: poor cattle farmers, colonos, desperate for fresh grazing land, have been encroaching on indigenous lands for years, particularly in eastern Panama.

By far the most organized politically are the Kuna, who have had the greatest success in defending their rights against the state and possess three representatives at government level. The other main indigenous groups have tended to follow the Kuna model, electing a General Congress consisting of a cacique and community representatives. Leaders from the various indigenous parties have begun working together to tackle attempts to marginalize them or incorporate them into models of development they do not espouse. In 2008, a petition listing indigenous peoples' grievances against the state was presented to the American Commission on Human Rights. The resulting landmark victory for the Ngöbe living along the Río Changiunola, who secured an injunction to halt the dam threatening their village, gives reason for some optimism.

Cambio Democrático (Democratic Change) party, he claimed sixty percent of the vote campaigning against corruption, violent crime, unemployment and poverty.

To demonstrate his intentions, Martinelli immediately stormed into the Amador Causeway to close down illegal landfill operations and deliver ultimatums to businesses for payment of overdue rent. Other high-profile policy initiatives included: raising the minimum wage by at least fifty dollars per month; ensuring free books and uniforms for school children; setting up a system of free internet access countrywide; and establishing a task force for a new underground system designed to solve Panama City's gridlocked traffic problems. In a surprising move, the new president also agreed to the US installing two anti-narcotics naval bases in Panamanian waters – a move his predecessor had roundly rejected. Not everyone has cause for optimism: a businessman and real estate vendor has been put in charge of ANAM; mining and hydro-electric projects continue apace; and the violent forced removal of the Naso from their villages in Bocas del Toro in November 2009 suggest little has changed for some sectors of society (see p.273). The battle lines for this presidency are only just being drawn.

Wildlife

One of Panama's major attractions is its varied and abundant **wildlife**. For its diminutive size – slightly larger than the Republic of Ireland, smaller than the US state of South Carolina – Panama's **biodiversity** and level of **endemism** is astounding. Located at the barely touching fingertips of two continents, the country hosts fauna from both land masses: deer and coyotes more readily associated with temperate North America as well as jaguars and capybaras from the tropical South. But the animal life is dependent on equally varied flora, ensured in part by Panama's **topographical range**, from the low-lying swamps of the Humedales de San San Pond Sak to the grassy *páramo* on Cerro Fábrega. An estimated ten thousand vascular plant species, including more than a thousand different types of tree, grow on the isthmus, predominantly in the country's luxuriant **tropical rainforests**, which cover an estimated 45 percent of the land. Panama's tropical forests also include five species of **mangrove**, constituting the so-called "rainforests by the sea". Covering vast swathes of coastline and tidal estuaries, they provide vital nutrients and shelter for a host of fish and invertebrates and protect the **coastal coral reefs** from the effects of terrestrial erosion.

Flora

Panama's **tropical wet forests**, or **rainforests**, which by definition receive an annual rainfall of more than two metres and can receive up to three times that amount on some of the Caribbean slopes, are what most excite nature-lovers. **Primary** rainforests – original, undisturbed growth – are highly prized for their greater biodiversity, comprising seventy percent of the country's forested area. In these complex ecosystems most animal and plant activity occurs in the forest "roof" or **canopy** and the **sub-canopy**, where dangling vines and lianas provide vital transport links. Poking out of the canopy, which filters out over ninety percent of the sunlight, are a sprinkling of robust **emergent trees**, generally around 60–70m tall, able to withstand being buffeted by storms and scorched by sunlight. Most easily recognized, and visible from a great distance, is the ringed silvery grey trunk of the **cuipo** (*cavanillesia platanifolia*), which exhibits a bare umbrella-like crown during the dry season; particularly abundant in the Darién, it is a favourite nesting site of the harpy eagle. Equally distinctive from above is the lofty **guayacán** (*tabebuia guayacan*), whose brilliant golden crown stands out against the dense green canopy carpet, blooming a month in advance of the first rains. Not atypically, both species drop their leaves in the dry season to reduce water loss through evaporation. From the forest floor, the vast buttress roots of the **ceiba** (silk-cotton or kapok tree; *ceiba petandra*), or thinner versions on the **Panama tree** (*sterculia apetela*), are more striking; so, too, the vicious protective spines on the **spiny cedar** (*pachira quinata*), or the swollen midsection of the aptly named **barrigón** (*pseudobombax septenatum*) – "*barriga*" meaning "pot belly" in Spanish – which can double its waist size to store water and whose pretty pompom flowers open for evening pollination.

Dominated by vines, ferns, saplings and shrubs typically 10–25m tall, the forest **understorey** and **forest floor** below are relatively sparsely populated in the cathedral-like primary forest, in contrast to the dense and tangled vegetation of **secondary** forest. It's in these lower layers that you'll come across the pinkish hues of **heliconias**, such as the vividly named **"lobster's claw"** (*heliconia rostrata*), edged with yellow, and the more solid **"beefsteak"** (*heliconia mariae*), a "medium-rare" dark pink, or the pouting scarlet bracts of the Warholian **"hotlips"** (*psychotria poeppigiana*), which lure butterflies and hummingbirds to the almost invisible central flowers.

Topping the higher mountainous ridges, especially in western Panama, and almost permanently enveloped in mist, are dense patches of eerie fern-filled **cloudforest**, characterized by shorter, stockier trees covered in **lichen** and dripping with **mosses**. Boughs here are more heavily laden with **epiphytes**, including many of Panama's thousand-plus species of delicate **orchid** and **bromeliads**, whose leaves trap moisture, providing water for numerous tree-dwelling organisms. Back down on the coast, some 1700 square kilometres of mostly **red, white** and **black** mangroves constitute a vital buffer zone, serving both terrestrial and marine ecologies.

Fauna

Though most visitors yearn to catch sight of a jaguar or tapir, you'll likely have to settle for smaller mammals and the less elusive members of the avian and amphibian populations, which can be just as fascinating.

Birds

Panama lays claim to 976 recorded species of **bird**, more than Canada and North America combined, and greater than any Central American state. Cana, in the heart of the Darién, consistently features in the world's best birding spots while the 17km Pipeline Road in the former Canal Zone boasts a species list of over four hundred. Even Panama City harbours egrets to elaenias, parakeets to pelicans: avian-rich locations within the greater city boundaries include the Metropolitan and other parks, Panama Viejo, the Amador Causeway and round Cerro Ancón and Balboa.

Acting as a continental funnel, Panama sees many **migrants**, with numbers peaking in September and October and returning in more dispersed fashion from March to May. During this period, over a million shore birds carpet the Pacific coastal mud flats, though it is the **raptor migration** that captures the imagination: hundreds of thousands of **turkey vultures**, interspersed with **Swainson's** and **broad-winged hawks**, ride the thermals, wheeling their way along the isthmus (late Oct–Nov), a spectacular sight best appreciated from the summit of Cerro Ancón or one of Gamboa's several canopy lookouts.

While twitchers may get excited locating a dull-coloured rare endemic in the undergrowth, average nature-lovers will be more impressed by the visually dazzling birds. The cloud forests of Chiriquí afford an unparalleled opportunity to spot the iridescent emerald-and-crimson **resplendent quetzal** – especially visible and striking during spring courtship displays – while the Darién jungle maintains a similar reputation for the **harpy eagle**, Panama's gigantic national bird and arguably the world's most powerful raptor, with its distinctive tousled crest and ferocious giant talons (see p.320). Other glamour birds include the country's multi-coloured, raucous **parrots** (loros), including five species of endangered **macaw** (*guacamaya*); sadly depleted through the pet trade, loss of habitat and hunting – their flashy tail feathers make a customary adornment for some traditional costumes and dances – they have been forced into more remote areas, with the **scarlet macaw** making its last stand on the island of Coiba. Panama's seven varieties of **toucan** (*tucán*), including toucanets and aracaris, are another psychedelic feature of the landscape; their oversized rainbow-coloured bills help pluck hard-to-reach berries and regulate body temperature. Abundant in the canal area and round Cerro Ancón, they are most easily spotted croaking in the canopy early morning or late afternoon. Panama's 55 types of **hummingbird** (*colibrí*) are spellbinding as they hover round flowers and feeders as if suspended in air, or whizz past your ear at some 50km/h. Lustrous **tanagers**, smart **trogans** and the distinctive racquet-tailed **motmots** will also turn heads.

Some birds are more notable for their behaviour: **jacanas**, whose vast, spindly feet enable them to stride across floating vegetation, are nicknamed "lilly-trotters"; minute fluffy **manakins** conduct manic acrobatic courtship displays in their communal mating arenas known as *leks*; and the prehistoric-looking **potoo** is a nocturnal insectivore that camouflages itself on the end of a tree stump during the day, invisible to would-be predators. Spend enough time in the western highlands, especially in the breeding season (March–Sept), and you're likely to hear the distinctly unbell-like metallic "boing" of the strange-looking **three-wattled bellbird** complete with what look like strands of liquorice hanging from its beak; audible from almost a kilometre away, it is considered one of the loudest bird songs on earth. Mention should also be made of the ubiquitous **oropéndola** (gold pendulum); these large, generally russet-toned birds with outsize pointed beaks and golden tails, are renowned for their colonies of skillfully woven hanging nests, which dangle from tall trees like Christmas decorations.

Terrestrial mammals

Spotting any of Panama's 230-plus mammal species – half of which are small **bats** – requires luck and persistence and is nigh on impossible when it comes to Panama's "big-five" wild cats, which in descending size order are the **jaguar**, **puma**, **jaguarundi**, **ocelot** and **margay**. Nocturnal and shy at the best of times, from years of human predation, they are most numerous in the country's two remaining wilderness areas at either end of the isthmus: the Darién and Amistad.

Spotting tracks in the morning mud is the closest you're likely to get to a jaguar in the wild. Referred to as a "*tigre*" (tiger) by indigenous populations and revered as a symbol of power and strength, the jaguar is the world's third largest feline after the lion and tiger, weighing in at around 60–90kg, and with leopard-like markings. It's more probable you'll encounter its dinner, be it **deer** (*venado*), the raccoon-like **coati** (*gato solo*), or large rodents such as the **agouti** (*ñeque*) or the nocturnal **paca** (*conejo pintado*, literally "painted rabbit" on account of its white spots). Panama also harbours the world's largest rodent, the **capybara**, which can tip the scales at 65kg; resembling a giant guinea pig, it wallows in the shallows round Gamboa and grazes at Punta Patiño, in the Darién. A more ambitious feature of the jaguar's diet is the **peccary**, a kind of wild boar. Two barely distinguishable species forage through the rainforest undergrowth in Panama: the more frequently seen **collared** peccary (*saíno*), which lives in small herds, and the elusive, aggressive **white-lipped** peccary (*puerco de monte*), which can travel in battalions of several hundred and be dangerous when threatened.

One of the largest, most extraordinary-looking mammals in the Neotropics is **Baird's tapir** (*macho de monte*). Another endangered nocturnal creature, it resembles an overgrown pig with a sawn-off elephant's trunk stuck on its face, which is actually a stubby prehensile nose and upper lip used to grip branches and eat off the leaves and fruit. Though the adults are dull brown, baby tapirs have spotted and striped coats for camouflage. More commonly espied are **sloths** (*perezosos*) and **anteaters** (*hormigueros*), both of which arrived on the planet shortly after the demise of dinosaurs. Panama's **two-toed** and **three-toed** sloths spend much of their time literally hanging around treetops, either curled round a branch camouflaged as an ants' nest, or gripping with their long curved claws, doing everything in slow motion to conserve energy. Inexplicably, they make a near-suicidal descent to ground level once a week to defecate. In contrast, the **northern tamandua**, a type of anteater, moves nimbly along the branches, hoovering up ants and termites. Not an uncommon sight in the Metropolitan Park, even though mainly nocturnal, they are widespread across the country, whereas the wholly terrestrial **giant anteater** is verging on extinction nationally, as is the **spectacled bear**, named after the cream-coloured markings around its eyes.

Monkeys are an almost guaranteed sighting in Panama, which hosts all seven Central American species. A distinctive feature of the tropical landscape, the large, shaggy **mantled howler monkey** (*aullador negro*) is more likely to be heard before being seen; the ape's stentorian cries travel for kilometres, with large troops announcing dawn and dusk and even the onset of heavy rain. The other two more widespread species are the cherub-like **Geoffroy's tamarin** (*mono tití*), found in central and eastern Panama, and the larger, highly intelligent **white-throated capuchin** (*mono cariblanco*). Named for their physical resemblance to brown-robed Capuchin friars, though also somewhat misleadingly dubbed "white-headed" or "white-faced", the monkey's pink anthropomorphic face makes it a popular pet. Catching sight of a troop of **black-headed spider monkeys** (*mono araña negro*) – one of several types of endangered Panamanian spider monkey – elegantly gliding through the canopies of eastern Panama is a magical experience. At the other end of the isthmus, the **owl** or **night monkeys** (*mono de noche*), with their saucer-like eyes, are restricted to the Caribbean lowlands of Bocas, while over on the Pacific side, the delicate **squirrel monkey** (*mono ardilla*) is occasionally sighted in the Burica Peninsula in southwestern Chiriquí.

Reptiles

Mention the fact that you intend to hike in the jungle, and someone is bound to alert you to the dangers of **snakes**, though a relatively small percentage are venomous and snake bites are rare – most serpents are as wary of humans as humans are of them. The most feared, accounting for almost all fatal snakebites in Panama, is the **fer-de-lance** pit viper, which inhabits a variety of lowland habitats. Commonly dubbed "*equis*" ("X") for the markings on its well-camouflaged brown, cream and black skin, it often exceeds 2m. The female gives birth to fifty to eighty live young, which incredibly are already 30cm, not to mention venomous, when born. Initially arboreal, feeding on frogs and lizards, they become terrestrial with age. The world's largest pit viper, the dangerous **bushmaster**, can reach three metres, but fortunately is only encountered in remote forests and like most pit vipers is nocturnal. In contrast, Panama's various species of **coral snake**, both venomous and benign, all possess striking black, red and yellow banded markings; since it's difficult to differentiate among them, it's best to assume danger. Positively mellow in comparison – though packing a powerful bite if provoked – the giant **boa constrictor** is Panama's only endangered snake, hunted for its prized skin.

Similarly endangered is the **green iguana**, which ranges from lime-green to dusty brown in colour and is pursued for its eggs and tasty meat, earning it the nickname "*gallina de palo*". Despite its dragon-like appearance, it is a docile forest-living herbivore that likes to be near water; the large flaps of skin under its chin (dewflaps) are used to regulate body temperature and for courtship and territorial displays. The tetchier, charcoal-grey **spiny-tailed** or **black iguana** is most commonly found on the Azuero Peninsula. The world's fastest lizard, it escapes predators by hitting speeds of up to 35kp/h; the miniature version, a 30cm **basilisk**, takes flight across water on its hind legs and partially webbed feet, earning it the nickname "**Jesus Christ**" **lizard**.

In Panama's mangrove-filled estuaries and mud-lined waterways, including around Lago Gatún and Lago Bayano, **crocs** and **caimans** lurk. The endangered, aggressive **American crocodile** has actually increased its numbers here, as has the smaller, more docile **spectacled caiman**.

Amphibians

Of all amphibians, **frogs** are the most compelling. The country's emblematic and revered **golden frog** (see p.160) is, sadly, under grave threat due in part to the **chytrid fungus**, which has been decimating amphibians worldwide; this has prompted an Amphibian Ark rescue mission (ⓦwww.amphibianrescue.org) to seek out healthy specimens to breed in captivity (see El Valle, p.159, and the Summit Botanical Gardens and Zoo, p.119). The brilliantly coloured miniature **poison-dart frogs**, with markings as varied as wallpaper, are relatively easy to see, especially in Bocas del Toro (see p.264), as they hop around the leaf litter under trees by day. But the rainforests harbour other equally extraordinary specimens, less visible since they're primarily nocturnal: the tiny lime green **glass frog**, whose inexplicably transparent belly affords you the dubious pleasure of observing its viscera and digestive processes; the **flying frog** with giant webbed feet that help parachute it through the air; and the **milk frog** – so named after the toxic mucous it secretes when threatened – which possesses two giant vocal sacs either side of the head that also function as buoyancy aids in water.

Insects and arachnids

Although **insects** don't generally set the pulse racing, **butterflies** are the exception. With sixteen thousand species, Panama hosts approximately ten percent of the world's Lepidoptera, from the enormous **owl butterfly**, so-called after the large "eyes" on its mottled brown wings, to the tiny delicate **glasswing**, whose translucent wings suggest the restrained beauty of a stained-glass window. Most magnificent of all, however, is the iridescent **blue morpho**, whose drunken zigzagged flight in the forest makes it particularly difficult to photograph.

Ants can be found in abundance; tiny Isla Barro Colorado alone has 225 species. Most distinctive are the packed highways of industrious **leafcutter** ants bearing enormous segments of leaf to their vast underground complex, where they are pulped to cultivate a "fungus garden", which in turn feeds the ants. Also easy to spot is the enormous black **bullet ant**; the size of a large grape and prevalent in low-lying forests, it holds the dubious distinction of causing the world's most painful insect sting.

Panama also possesses over a thousand species of **spider**, a fair proportion of which are poisonous though rarely lethal to humans. One such is the innocuous-sounding **wandering spider** – until you realize its scientific name derives from the Greek for "murderous" (*phoneutes*) – which is a hairy arachnid that stalks the forest floor at night rather than ambushing prey in a web or lair. It is often mistaken for the stockier, hairier and relatively harmless **black tarantula**; also a night-time predator, it can be seen poking out of its lair, in a hollowed out log or semi-submerged under leaf litter, during the day. Worth avoiding is the female **black widow spider**; recognizable by the glossy black abdomen and red hourglass mark on the underbelly, she has a potent venom with which to inject her prey. The **golden silk orb-weaving spider** makes the largest web; a magical sight on a sunlit morning in the rainforest, it really does glisten like gold thread.

Marine life

With coastlines on two oceans, Panama's **marine biodiversity** is impressive, especially where warm ocean currents and upwellings of cool nutrient-rich waters converge along the Pacific's Golfo de Chiriquí. **Humpback whales** (July–Oct) calve in this area and can also be sighted off the Pearl Islands and the tip of the Azuero Peninsula. Cavorting in the waves, with males engaging in acrobatic courtship rituals, these fifteen-metre giants are exciting to behold though **whale-watching** in Panama is in its infancy. Earlier in the year (Feb–July), you may be lucky enough to catch sight of the gargantuan but placid **whale shark**, the world's largest fish, as it moves submarine-like through the waters round Coiba. **Hammerhead** and **tiger** sharks are occasionally spotted though **white-tipped reef** sharks are more common. The distinctive black and white **killer whales**, or **orcas** – actually the world's largest dolphin – prey on younger and weaker marine mammals, but aren't as widespread as **bottle-nosed** dolphins. From October to December schools of diamond-shaped **golden rays** glide like floating autumn leaves, occasionally leaping two metres into the air, as well as more solitary **manta** rays; boasting a colossal six-metre wingspan, one weighs as much as a small car.

In general the Pacific coast boasts a greater number of large fish – **blue** and **black marlin**, **amberjack**, **wahoo**, **dorado** and **tuna**, to name a few – while the **coral reefs** on the Caribbean side, particularly around the archipelago of Bocas del Toro and parts of Kuna Yala, are populated with a greater variety of soft and hard corals. These feed and shelter aquatic life from sinuous **moray eels** and spiky **sea urchins** to delicate **sea horses** and a rainbow of dazzling fish. Iridescent **parrot fish** (30–50cm) are among the most distinctive, named less for their technicolour coats than for their serrated parrot-like "beaks" that gnaw algae and coral polyps off the reef. The ground coral is digested and excreted as sand – up to an estimated 90kg per fish annually – a major factor in the formation of Panama's glorious **white-sand beaches**. The Caribbean's other mammalian draw is the **manatee**, or sea cow, an amiable elephantine herbivore with a paddle-like rudder and flabby fleshy snout, found in the San-San Pond Sak Wetlands of Bocas del Toro.

Five species of **marine turtle** lay their eggs on both Atlantic and Pacific shores, roughly between March and October/November (timings depend on species and location; see p.266). In the Caribbean, Bocas del Toro is the easiest place to visit **hawksbill**, **leatherback** and, to a lesser extent, **green** turtle nesting sites while **loggerheads** frequent the shallows. On the Pacific side, Isla de Cañas, off the Azuero Peninsula, is renowned for the mass **olive ridley** nesting (May–Nov), though the other species also deposit their eggs there in smaller numbers.

Environmental issues

As elsewhere in the tropics, the rainforests of Panama are disappearing at an alarming rate, threatening the country's wildlife and, ultimately, human survival. While 45 percent of the country is still covered in forest, and **deforestation** rates have slowed substantially since the millennium, the country is losing around one percent of its species-rich primary growth a year. A third of the land lies in **national parks** and reserves, but many of these are "paper parks" since the perennially underfunded ANAM – the government's environmental department – is short of money and, in some cases, political will to enforce the regulations.

Deforestation

Drive along the newly tarred road in eastern Panama and you'll frequently pass enormous trailers carrying vast trunks of mahogany, cedar or purpleheart destined for European and North American markets. The timber industry inevitably is a major contributor to **deforestation** but in recent years has been more stringently controlled even if illegal logging, and more insidiously, selective thinning continues.

By far the main driver of deforestation is **colonization**, clearing the land for cattle ranching and subsistence agriculture. Having already denuded the entire Azuero Peninsula and most of the Pacific slopes of central and western Panama, *colonos*, or "colonists", have been moving into eastern Panama in recent years along the Darién highway and Caribbean coast. Despite the richness of tropical forests, the layer of nutritious topsoil is particularly thin so that once cleared it soon becomes worthless, forcing farmers to move on to fell new areas. Some indigenous communities are also contributing to deforestation thanks to population increases and forced changes in lifestyle. In some cash-strapped communities they are even leasing land to farmers for cattle grazing or colluding with illegal timber extraction. Panama's coastal mangrove forests – considered to be the most extensive, healthiest and most diverse in all Central America – are critically threatened, from agricultural expansion and coastal development on the mainland and water pollution, overfishing and sedimentation on the islands and marine areas.

Small-scale initiatives have begun across the country aiming to improve **environmental awareness**, ranging from assistance for micro-enterprises such as plant nurseries, production of organic fertilizers and agroforestry projects to tree-planting and recycling, often backed by NGOs and international environmental organizations. One such programme is supported through Fundación Nacional Parque Chagres, the result of a "debt-for-nature" swap whereby $10 million of debt to the US government is eradicated as long as Panamanian government banks spend $700,000 annually over fourteen years on green-oriented projects and education. Of course it's no coincidence that this is taking place in the Chagres river basin, which is vital to the functioning of the Panama Canal, the lifeblood of Panama's economy and not insignificant to the US.

As well, **reforestation programmes** in Panama have become more common in the last few years. Initially they were all teak plantations, which arguably further degrade the soil, do nothing to sustain biodiversity and being a monoculture are more susceptible to disease; however, there has been a positive recent move towards more sustainable mixed plantations of native species.

Mining and hydroelectric projects

Another area of environmental concern is the **mining industry**. In the 1990s a lot of prospecting was done but plans ceased as mineral exploitation became unprofitable; however, prices are rising and the threat looms once more. In 2008 a sobering revelation was made by a new Panamanian environmental watchdog, CIAM (Centro de Incidencia Ambiental), namely that the amount of land involved in mining concessions that have either already been granted or are awaiting consideration totals three times the country's surface area. The Petaquilla open-cast gold mine has restarted operations despite still owing $2 million in fines and damages for environmental negligence and trampling on local people's rights. Cerro Colorado, potentially one of the world's largest copper mines, smack in the middle of the Comarca Ngöbe-Buglé, looks to be next on the list for production as indigenous groups and environmental lobbyists begin to gather forces.

Protests are also likely to continue against the many **micro-hydroelectric projects** underway or planned for western Panama, one of which has already resulted in intervention by the Interamerican Human Rights Commission. Environmentalists are particularly concerned about projects that lie within the Amistad National Park or its buffer zone of Palo Seco.

Tourism and environmental impact

In the midst of this ecological gloom stands the difficult balance between promoting tourism, which has been on the rise, and limiting the environmental and social impact – something the government doesn't always seem to take into account.

Indigenous communities above all are being encouraged to engage in **cultural eco-tourism**, inviting visitors to learn about their traditional ways of life and selling their handicrafts. With little financial support from the government, some groups have benefited from assistance from NGOs or local Peace Corps workers. Emberá communities along the Chagres, in particular, have gained valuable income from cruise ship tours and day-trip groups from travel agencies in Panama City because of their proximity to the capital. But the long-term effect when large groups swamp small villages in high season, eroding the land of the village and tramping en masse down the same rainforest trail, is more difficult to gauge. Moreover, the impact on the marine environment of the cruise-ship industry – the area of tourism in which the government has invested most heavily – is a further unknown.

By and large, visitor numbers are small in most indigenous communities that engage with tourism, the exception being in the western end of Kuna Yala. This is partly due to the completion of a dirt road across the cordillera from the Panamerican Highway, which has allowed faster, cheaper access. Day-tripping Panamanians and beach-loving backpackers make up the bulk of the visitors: for small, overpopulated islands with inadequate sanitation and often ad-hoc waste disposal, there's untold pressure on the natural resources.

The beautiful islands of Bocas del Toro, the most visited area outside the capital, suffer from similar problems: whereas once a handful of bohemian backpackers hung out in Bocas Town's three hotels, sixty lodgings now attempt to accommodate the town's seven thousand annual visitors. The main water and electricity systems struggle to cope with the numbers and without proper sewage and water treatment works, the current situation is unsustainable. On the positive side, turtle watching is taking off here, which as an income-generating project might eventually help protect their nesting sites.

However, in Bocas, as elsewhere in Panama, there is no attempt at regulation, be it the number of boats dolphin watching or snorkellers accessing the most popular reef. Even in the cruise ship industry, where the government has actively invested in infrastructure, environmental regulation is hard to enforce, and there are tales of vessels dumping untreated or inadequately treated waste and toxic chemicals out at sea.

Other business ventures suffer from lack of strict oversight, too. One prominent example is the vast luxury resort being constructed on Isla Viveros in the Pearl Islands, complete with private international airport. Already fined a paltry $50,000 – in comparison with the $300 million investment – for starting to build without even a pretence of an environmental impact assessment, the developers were then assessed a similar penalty for bulldozing through eight archeological sites. Adding to the double-edged nature of such developments, many big-ticket projects have an international consortium at the helm, so much of the profit leaves the country while indelibly altering the natural and social landscape.

Books

Bookshops are far from plentiful in Panama, with most located in Panama City (see listings p.96), generally stocking a small, pricey selection in English. The colossus of contemporary Panamanian literature is Enrique Jaramillo Levi – internationally acclaimed short-story writer, poet, essayist, editor and critic, who, despite such accolades, has had relatively few works translated into English.

The Canal

William Friar *Portrait of the Panama Canal: From Construction to Twenty-first Century.* Very readable account by a former Zonian and *New York Times* journalist. This paperback coffee-table offering contains a few wonderful historical photos as well as some more mundane contemporary glossies of the canal and Panama.

Julie Greene *The Canal Builders: Making America's Empire at the Panama Canal.* The builders of the title are the work force, the men and women who in dreadful conditions and facing all sorts of discrimination worked to achieve the realization of America's grandiose dream of empire. You also meet the big players whose ambition ignored the human cost.

Ulrich Keller *The Building of the Canal in Historic Photographs.* A clear case of pictures speaking louder than words, as 164 detailed black-and-white photos evoke the lives of both rich and poor engaged in the monumental struggle to build the canal.

David McCullough *The Path Between the Seas: The Creation of the Panama Canal, 1870–1914.* Though a detailed scholarly work of nigh on seven hundred pages, it is the plot-twisting narrative and larger-than-life characters that sweep the reader along, together with a consistent emphasis on understanding the underlying causes of events.

Matthew Parker *Hell's Gorge: The Battle to Build the Panama Canal* (also published as *Panama Fever*). A gripping account of the struggle with jungle, disease, engineering impossibilities and disastrous ignorance, which is a meticulously researched yet wide-ranging narrative that focuses on the oft-neglected labour force that lived and died digging the Big Ditch.

Other history and politics

Kevin Buckley *Panama.* Written by a former *Newsweek* correspondent, this book provides what many consider to be the most reliable account of events leading up to the US invasion of Panama in 1989. Buckley vividly brings the complex web of corruption and political intrigue to life.

Peter Earle *The Sack of Panama: Captain Morgan and the Battle for the Caribbean.* A swashbuckling account of the real-life pirates of the Caribbean and the efforts of the Spaniards to defeat them, focusing on the Welsh privateer Henry Morgan and his exploits along the Caribbean coast, and culminating in the sack of Panama in 1671.

John Esquemeling *The Pirates of Panama: True Account of the Famous Adventures and Daring Deeds of Sir Henry Morgan and other Notorious Freebooters.* Based on a lively firsthand account originally written in Dutch, the first English edition was published in 1684. The author was barber surgeon to

Henry Morgan and accompanied him on his notorious expedition against Panama City.

Aims McGuinness *Path of Empire: Panama and the Californian Gold Rush.* A look at the key role played by the isthmus during the Gold Rush in the mid-1800s as the fastest link between New York and San Francisco, the consequences of building the Panama Railroad and the first of many military interventions by the US.

Andrew Parkin *Flames of Panama: The True Story of a Forgotten Hero, Pedro Prestán.* A dramatized true story of a man of mixed race from Cartagena who rose to eminence in Colón as a lawyer and became a Member of the Assembly only to be hanged as a leader of the rebel forces, falsely accused of burning Colón to the ground in 1885. A poignant tale, but it would have worked better as a factual account.

John Lindsay Poland *Emperors in the Jungle: The Hidden History of the US in Panama.* A human rights campaigner and investigative journalist explores the role of the US military in Pamana and the dubious uses to which it put the land it acquired.

John Prebble *The Darien Disaster.* Highly detailed and often turgid exploration of the doomed attempted by the Scots to colonize the Darién. The minutiae, such as the numbers of cases of rum loaded onto the ships, obscure the depth of the tragedy that bankrupted Scotland.

John Week and Phil Gunson *Panama: Made in the USA.* Written in 1991, this much-praised analysis of the 1989 American invasion of Panama and its historical background deals with the legal implications and political consequences, while shining a light on the part Noriega played leading up to the attack.

Art and culture

James Howe *Chiefs, Scribes and Ethnographers: Kuna Culture from Inside and Out.* Written by a professor of anthropology who has spent considerable time among the Kuna over a 35-year period, this recent book deals with the accounts which the Kuna chiefs themselves have given of their life and culture. Like his previous *A People Who Would not Kneel: Panama, the United States and the San Blas Kuna* and *The Kuna Gathering: Contemporary Village Politics in Panama*, a serious but rewarding read.

Salvador Mary Lyn (ed.) *The Art of Being Kuna: Layers of Meaning among the Kuna of Panama.* Glossy coffee-table book full of fascinating photos and scholarly insights on the interweaving of Kuna art, culture and environment.

Michael Perrin *Magnificent Molas.* Lavishly illustrated, this book explores the *molas* or fabric "paintings" of the

Kuna women, tracing the links between the patterns used and traditions and rituals in the lives of the women.

Anton Rajer *Paris in Panama/Paris en Panama: Robert Lewis and the History of His Restored Art Works in the National Theatre of Panama.* Intriguing bilingual book tracing the history and restoration of Panamanian-born Roberto Lewis's (1874–1949) masterpieces painted in Paris but installed in the National Theatre of Panama (see p.72).

Joel Sherzer *Stories, Myths, Chants and Songs of the Kuna Indians.* The author, a linguistic anthropologist, lived among the Kuna people photographing and recording their oral tradition of songs and ritual performances. He reveals their close association with plants and animals and their belief in myths and magic.

Jorge Ventocilla, Heraclio Herrera and Valerio Nuñez *Plants and Animals*

in the Life of the Kuna. Written by two Kuna biologists and a Panamanian colleague, this book is aimed at the Kuna reader as well as outsiders, providing fascinating insights into the Kuna perspective on ecology and cosmology as they relate to environmental issues.

Fiction

Iain Banks *Canal Dreams*. More nightmare than dream in which an unloveable famous Japanese cellist is trapped on a ship in the Panama Canal that is captured by guerrillas. The violence she and her lover suffer at their hands leads her to an equally violent revenge.

Jane Bowles *Two Serious Ladies*. An avant-garde classic of 1943, this story follows two ladies seeking freedom from the confines of social convention. On holiday in Panama, one falls in love with a young prostitute and leaves her husband to live in the brothel in Colón. Offering a glimpse of the city's red-light district, it also includes a scene in the historic *Washington Hotel*.

Douglas Galbraith *The Rising Sun*. A detailed, somewhat rambling historical novel about the Scottish expedition to the Darién, fuelled by human greed but leading to unbelievable hardship and the eventual bankruptcy of Scotland. It is difficult to warm to the main character who tells the story, but the horror comes across.

James Stanley Gilbert *Panama Patchwork Poems*. A fascinating collection, published between 1901 and 1937, by a one-time employee of the Panama Railroad Company. Though "Poet Laureate of the Isthmus" may be a tad exaggerated, his accessible verse provides a powerful evocation of pre-canal hardships for settlers in Colón.

John Le Carré *The Tailor of Panama*. With an explicit nod to Graham Greene's *Our Man in Havana*, this satirical spy thriller is a classic. Set just before the US handover of the Canal, a young unscrupulous British agent embarks on an elaborate fiction of intrigue. While both American and British intelligence services are lampooned as much as Panamanian high society, the novel, nevertheless, caused some upset in Panama on its publication.

Enrique Jaramillo Levi *The Shadow: Thirteen Stories in Opposition*. Short stories by Panama's pre-eminent (post)modern writer, though some tales are scarcely more than vignettes. You'll either be seduced by the originality of his imagination and fluid prose or left baffled and irritated as meaning slips through your grasp. More accessible is his edited collection of short stories by Costa Rican and Panamanian women, *When New Flowers Bloomed*, tackling a range of subjects from gender relations to political events.

William Penn *The Panama Conspiracy*. A thriller which manages improbably to link all the US enemies, from Fidel Castro through Red China to Osama Bin Laden, in a complex plot culminating in a plan to blockade the Panama Canal.

Eric Zencey *Panama*. All but the first chapter is actually set in Paris with a deftly drawn cast of real and imagined characters woven into a historically intriguing murder mystery that centres on the financial scandal surrounding the Panama Canal debacle.

Biography and memoirs

Darrin Du Ford *Is There a Hole in my Boat? Tales of Travel in Panama Without a Car*. The author sets out to explore Panama using public transport or hitching a lift, by dugout or on foot, aiming to get closer to the life and culture of the people than the average tourist; he never seems to turn down a new experience.

Christian Giudice *Hands of Stone: The Life and Legend of Roberto Durán*. Meticulously researched biography of Panama's most famous boxer and one of the sport's all-time greats, drawing on plenty of fascinating, original interview material. A warts-and-all rags to riches tale that tracks his rise to fame from the slums of Panama City, giving a view of his contradictory character inside and outside the ring.

Graham Greene *Getting to Know the General: The Story of an Involvement*. Greene provides a personal slant on Omar Torrijos, the country's most charismatic leader, whom the author befriended during his time in troubled late 1970s and early 1980s Panama.

Malcolm Henderson *Don't Kill the Cow Too Quick: An Englishman's Adventures Homesteading in Panama*. Entertaining and informative,

especially for expats thinking of following a dream, this book follows a couple's retirement in Bocas in the late 1990s, where they eventually established an organic farm.

Leo Mahon *Fire under my Feet: A Memoir of God's Power in Panama*. The moving story of a compassionate Roman Catholic priest sent in 1963 to a poverty-stricken town in Panama to found a church.

Martin Mitchinson *The Darien Gap: Travels in the Rainforest of Panama*. An entertaining account of eighteen months spent in the trackless jungle trying to retrace the route to the Pacific made by the first European, Balboa, in 1513. It's a successful blend of personal experience, history and local lore.

Manuel Noriega and Peter Eisner *America's Prisoner: The Memoirs of Manuel Noriega*. The other side of the story of a leader who was vilified, arrested and put on trial by America. This is a controversial book but worth reading for its revelations about the American attitude to Panama and Latin America.

Wildlife

George Angehr, Dodge Engleman and Lorna Engleman *A Bird-finding Guide to Panama*. You need to read the title carefully – this excellent, detailed guide tells you where to find the birds and how to get there by car, but is not a bird identification manual.

Juan Carlos Q. Navarro *Panama National Parks* (Ediciones Balboa). Bilingual Spanish/English guide to Panama's national parks accompanied by gorgeous glossy photos that will make you want to pack your rucksack and head for the hills immediately. The information is also on the ANAM website.

🏃 **Rainforest Publications** *Panama Field Guides* (numerous titles). This company has produced an excellent series of illustrated laminated

concertina-style pocket field guide pamphlets on Panama's flora and fauna, giving scientific, Spanish and English names. Available in Panama or online (www.rainforestpublications.com).

Robert Ridgely and John Gwynne *A Guide to the Birds of Panama*. This weighty tome is *the* birding bible for Panama although it's in desperate need of updating.

🏃 **Jorge Ventocilla and Dana Gardner** *A Guide to the Common Birds of Panama City* (Smithsonian Tropical Research Institute & Panama Audubon Society). Excellent, beautifully illustrated pocket book aimed at the average nature-lover – perfect for anyone basing their stay in the capital and wanting to identify the city's surprisingly abundant birdlife.

Language

Spanish

Spanish is the national and official language of Panama and the first language of more than two million of the population. A recorded thirteen other first languages are spoken across the country, including English, which is used by many black Afro-Antilleans (see p.49) – though outside Panama City and the touristy areas of Bocas del Toro and Boquete, it's not widely spoken. Learning at least the basics of Spanish will make your travels considerably easier and reap countless rewards in terms of reception and understanding of people and places; even the most faltering of attempts to speak it tends to be greatly appreciated.

Pronunciation and word stress

In Spanish, each word is **pronounced** as written according to the following guide:

A somewhere between the "A" sound of "back" and that of "father"
E as in "get"
I as in "police"
O as in "hot"
U as in "rule"
C is soft before E and I, otherwise hard; *cerca* is pronounced "SERka".
G works the same way – a guttural "H" sound (like the "ch" in "loch") before E or I, a hard G elsewhere; *gigante* is pronounced "HiGANte".
H is always silent.
J is the same sound as a guttural "G"; *jamón* is pronounced "ham ON".
LL sounds like an English Y; *tortilla* is pronounced "torTIya".

N is as in English, unless there is a "~" over it, when it becomes like the N in "onion"; *mañana* is pronounced "maNYAna".
QU is pronounced like an English "K" as in "kick".
R is rolled, **RR** doubly so.
V sounds like a cross between B and V, *vino* almost becoming "beano".
X is a soft "SH", so that *Xela* becomes "SHEla"; between vowels it has an "H" sound – *México* is pronounced "ME-hi-ko".
Z is the same as a soft C; *cerveza* is pronounced "serVEsa".

Getting the **word stress** right makes a big difference: *PAgo* means "I pay", *paGÓ* she/he paid. The rule is simple: if a word ends in a vowel, "s" or "n", the stress is on the syllable before last. If it ends in any other consonant, the stress is on the last syllable. Exceptions are marked with an accent on the vowel of the stressed syllable.

Latin American Spanish lacks the lisp common in Spain, where *cerveza* is often pronounced "therVEtha". One feature of the speech of many Panamanians which makes understanding more difficult is the aspiration of the "S" sound at the end of a syllable or word, such that the word *cascada* is pronounced more like "cahcada". Also, words containing a "ch" such as *muchacho* may sound more like "mushasho". Generally the Spanish of indigenous Panamanians is easiest to understand.

Formal and informal address

For English speakers one of the most difficult things to get to grips with is the distinction between formal and informal address. Generally speaking, the third-person **usted** indicates respect and is used in business, for people you don't know and for those older than you. Second-person **tú** is for children, friends and contemporaries in less formal settings. (Remember also that in Latin America the second-person **plural** – *vosotros* – is never used, so "you" plural will always be *ustedes*.)

Verbal courtesy is an integral part of speech in Spanish and one that – once you're accustomed to the pace and flow of life in Panama, especially out of the city – should become instinctive. Saying *Buenos días/Buenas tardes/Buenas noches*, or the abbreviated *buenos* or *buenas*, and waiting for the appropriate response is usual when asking for something at a shop or ticket office, for example, as is adding *señor* or *señora* (in this instance similar to the US "sir" or "ma'am").

On meeting, or being introduced to someone, people are likely to say *con mucho gusto*, "it's a pleasure", and you should do the same. On departure you will more often than not be told ¡*Que le vaya bien!* – literally meaning "May all go well with you", it often translates better as "Take care" or "Travel safely".

Words and phrases

Basic words

a lot	mucho	more	más
afternoon	tarde	morning	mañana
and	y	night	noche
bad	mal(o)/a	no	no
big	gran(de)	now	ahora
boy	chico	open	abierto/a
closed	cerrado/a	or	o
cold	frío/a	please	por favor
day	día	she	ella
entrance	entrada	sir/mister	señor
exit	salida	small	pequeño/a
girl	chica	thank you	gracias
good	bien/buen(o)/a	that	eso/a
he	él	their	suyo/de ellos
her	ella	there	allí
here	aquí	they	ellos
his	suyo	this	este/a
hot	calor/caliente	today	hoy
how much	cuánto	tomorrow	mañana
if	si	what	qué
later	más tarde/después	when	cuando/cuándo
less	menos	where	dónde
ma'am/missus	señora	with	con
man	señor/hombre	without	sin
maybe	talvez	yes	sí
miss	señorita	yesterday	ayer

Basic phrases

Hello	¡Hola!	What's your name?	¿Cómo se llama usted?
Goodbye	Adiós	My name is...	Me llamo...
See you later	Hasta luego	Where are you from?	De dónde es usted?
Good morning	Buenos días	I'm from...	Soy de...
Good afternoon	Buenas tardes	How old are you?	¿Cuántos años tiene? (usted)
Good evening/night	Buenas noches		
Sorry	Lo siento/Discúlpeme	I am...years old	Tengo...años.
Excuse me	Con permiso/perdón	I don't know	No sé
How are you?	¿Cómo está (usted)?/ ¿Qué tal?	Do you know...?	¿Sabe...?
		I want/I'd like	Quiero/Quisiera
Nice to meet you	Mucho gusto	What's that?	¿Qué es eso?
Not at all/ You're welcome	De nada/para servirle	How much is it?	¿Cuánto es/cuesta?
		What is this called in Spanish?	¿Cómo se llama este en español/ castellano?
I (don't) understand	(No) Entiendo		
Do you speak English?	¿Habla (usted) inglés?	There is (is there)?	Hay (?)
I (don't) speak Spanish	(No) Hablo español/ castellano	Do you have...?	¿Tiene...?
		What time is it?	¿Qué hora es?
What (did you say)?	¿Mande?/¿Cómo?	May I take a photograph?	¿Puedo sacar una foto?
Could you... please?	¿Podría... por favor?		
...repeat that	...repetirlo	It's hot/cold	Hace calor/frío

Basic needs, services and places

ATM	cajero automático	market	mercado
bank	banco	money	dinero/plata
bathroom/toilet	baño/sanitario	museum	museo
beach	playa	pharmacy	farmacia
border crossing	frontera	post office	el correo
church	iglesia	restaurant	restaurante
internet café	cibercafé	supermarket	supermercado
laundry	lavandería/lavamático	telephone	teléfono
map	mapa	tourist office	oficina de turismo

Numbers (*números*), months (*meses*) and days (*días*)

1	un/uno/una	10	diez
2	dos	20	veinte
3	tres	21	veintiuno
4	cuatro	22	veintidos
5	cinco	30	treinta
6	seis	40	cuarenta
7	siete	50	cincuenta
8	ocho	60	sesenta
9	nueve	70	setenta

80	ochenta	July	julio
90	noventa	August	agosto
100	cien	September	septiembre
1000	mil	October	octubre
		November	noviembre
first	primero/a	December	diciembre
second	segundo/a		
third	tercero/a	Monday	lunes
		Tuesday	martes
January	enero	Wednesday	miércoles
February	febrero	Thursday	jueves
March	marzo	Friday	viernes
April	abril	Saturday	sábado
May	mayo	Sunday	domingo
June	junio		

Getting around

Transportation

bus	autobús
minibus	buseta/colectivo
bus station	terminal de autobuses
bus stop	parada de autobús
boat	barco/lancha/panga
dugout canoe	cayuco/piragua
dock/pier	muelle
airplane	avión
airport	aeropuerto
car	carro/auto(móvil)
engine	motor
4WD/4X4	doble tracción/ cuatro por cuatro
taxi	taxi
lorry/truck	camión
pick-up	camioneta

bicycle	bicicleta
motorcycle	moto
petrol/diesel/gas	gasolina
ticket	billete pasaje
ticket office	taquilla ventanilla
I'd like a ticket to...	(Necesito) un billete (pasaje) para...
...one way	...sólo ida
...return/round trip	...ida y vuelta
I would like to rent a...	Me gustaría alquilar un/una...
Where does... to... leave from?	¿De dónde sale ...para...?
What time does the ...leave for...?	¿A qué hora sale ...para...?
What time does the ...arrive in...?	¿A qué hora llega... en...?

Directions

Where is...?	¿Dónde está...?
How do I get to...?	¿Por dónde se va a...?
I'm lost	Estoy perdido/a
Is it far?	¿Está lejos?
left/right	izquierda/derecha
straight ahead	derecho/recto
north	norte

south	sur
east	este
west	oeste
street	calle
avenue	avenida
block	cuadra
corner	esquina
(main) road	carretera

Accommodation

Is there (a)…nearby?	¿Hay…aquí cerca?	…one person	…una persona
…hotel	…un hotel	…two people	…dos personas
…cheap, small hotel	…una pensíon/ un hospedaje	…for one night	…una noche
…hostel	…un hostal	…one week	…una semana
Do you have…?	¿Tiene…?	Does it have…	¿Tiene…?
…a room	…un cuarto	…a shared bath	…baño compartido
…with two beds	…con dos camas	…a private bath	…baño privado
…a double bed	…con cama matrimonial	…hot water	…agua caliente
		…air conditioning	…aire-acondicionado
…a dorm room	…cuarto colectivo/ dormitorio	…a mosquito net	…mosquitero
		May I see a room?	¿Puedo ver un cuarto?
…a cabin	…una cabaña	May I see another room?	¿Puedo ver otro cuarto?
It's for	Es para	Yes, it's fine.	Sí, está bien.

Food and drink

Basic dining vocabulary

almuerzo	lunch
cafetería	self-service restaurant
carta (la)	menu
cena	dinner
comedor	basic restaurant
comida corriente	cheap set menu, usually lunch
comida típica	traditional cuisine
cuenta	bill
desayuno	breakfast
fonda	inexpensive, informal local restaurant
mesa	table
plato fuerte	main course
plato vegetariano	vegetarian dish
silla	chair
vaso	glass
Soy vegetariano/a	I'm a vegetarian
Tengo hambre/sed	I'm hungry/thirsty

Basic food vocabulary

aceite	oil
ajo	garlic
arroz	rice
azúcar	sugar
chile	chilli
galletas	biscuits/crackers
hielo	ice
huevos	eggs
mantequilla	butter
mermelada	jam
miel	honey
natilla	sour cream
pan (integral)	bread (wholemeal)
pimienta	pepper
queso	cheese
sal	salt
salsa de tomate	tomato sauce

Frutas (fruit)

aceitunas	olives
chirimoya	custard apple
coco	coconut
fresa	strawberry
guanábana	soursop
guayaba	guava
guineo	banana
limón	lemon
manzana	apple
maracuyá	passionfruit
marañon	cashew
melón	melon
mora (zarzamora)	blackberry
naranja	orange

papaya	papaya
piña	pineapple
plátano	plantain
sandía	watermelon
uva	grapes

Legumbres/verduras (vegetables)

aguacate	avocado
cebolla	onion
champiñón (hongo)	mushroom
ensalada	salad
espinaca	spinach
frijoles	beans
gallo pinto	mixed rice and beans
lechuga	lettuce
lentejas	lentils
maíz	sweet corn/maize
menestra	bean/lentil stew
papa	potato
papas fritas	chips/French fries
tomate	tomato
zanahoria	carrot

Carne (meat), aves (poultry) and menudo (offal)

bistec/lomo	steak
carne	beef
cerdo	pork
chuleta	pork chop
jamón	ham
mondongo	tripe and chorizo stew
patas	trotters
pollo	chicken
res	beef
ropa vieja	shredded spicy beef and rice

Mariscos (seafood) and pescado (fish)

almejas	clams
anchoa	anchovy
atún	tuna
calamares	squid
camarón	shrimp
cangrejo	crab
ceviche	raw seafood marinated in lime juice with onions

concha	conch
corvina	sea bass
langosta	lobster/crayfish
langostina	king prawn
mejillónes	mussels
mero	grouper
pargo rojo	red snapper
pulpo	octopus
trucha	trout

Bocados or bocaditos (snacks)

carimañola	mashed boiled yucca stuffed with beef
churro	ribbed, tubular doughnut-cum-waffle
empanada	cheese/meat-filled pastry
emparedado	sandwich
hamburguesa	hamburger
hojaldre	deep fried doughy pancake
patacones	fried green plantains
salchichas	sausages
tortilla	thick fried maize patty
tortilla de huevos	omelette
tostada	toast

Bebidas (drinks)

agua mineral	mineral water
...con gas	...sparkling
...sin gas	...still
agua potable	drinking water
aromática	herbal tea
batido	fresh fruit milk shake
café	coffee
cerveza	beer
chicha	maize drink
chicha fuerte	fermented maize drink
jugo	juice
leche	milk
licuado	fresh fruit shake
pipa	fresh coconut juice
raspados	flavoured ice shavings
refresco/soda	(cold) soft drink
ron	rum
té	tea/coffee
vino blanco/tinto	white/red wine

Cooking terms	
a la parrilla	barbecued
a la plancha	grilled
apanado	breaded
asado	roast
encocado	in coconut sauce
frito	fried
picante	spicy hot
puré	mashed
revuelto	scrambled

Glossary and acronyms

ACP Autoridad del Canal de Panamá (Panama Canal Authority)

Afro-Antillano Panamanian of African heritage from the West Indies

Afro-Colonial Panamanian of African heritage from the Spanish colonial era

ANAM Autoridad Nacional del Ambiente (Department for the Environment)

ANCON Asociación Nacional para la Conservación de la Naturaleza – Panama's most prominent environmental NGO

artesanías traditional handicrafts

ATP Autoridad de Turismo Panamá, formerly IPAT (Instituto Panameño de Turismo)

barrio neighbourhood; suburb

bohío see *rancho*

bomba pump at a petrol station, often shorthand for the petrol station itself

cacique chief (originally a colonial term, now used for elected leaders/figureheads of indigenous *comarcas*)

campesino peasant farmer

cantina local, hard-drinking bar, usually men-only

chiva rural bus, which may be a converted pick-up

colectivo shared taxi/minibus, usually following fixed route (can also be applied to a boat – *lancha colectiva*)

colono generally a mestizo farming settler who originated from the Azuero Peninsula and central areas and moved to colonize other parts of the country

comarca semi-autonomous area demarcated for the major indigenous peoples

cordillera mountain range

diablo rojo colourful painted buses of Panama City

feria fair (market); also a town fête

finca ranch, farm or plantation

gringo/gringa any light-skinned foreigner, particularly a North American

guardaparque park warden

huaca pre-Columbian gold treasure buried with the dead in a tomb

INAC Instituto Nacional de Arte y Cultura (government department in charge of museums and preservation of cultural heritage)

indígeno/a an indigenous person (also used adjectivally)

ladino a vague term – applied to people it means Spanish-influenced as opposed to indigenous, and at its most specific defines someone of mixed Spanish and indigenous blood

mestizo person of mixed indigenous and Spanish blood, though like the term *ladino* it has more cultural than racial significance

metate pre-Columbian stone table used for grinding corn

mochilero backpacker

montuno traditional male costume consisting of a loose cotton shirt and knee-length trousers

(fiestas) patronales patron saint festivals enjoyed by every town or village

pollera embroidered dress with full skirt considered to be the national costume of Panama

quincha adobe

rancho open-sided (wooden) structure with palm-thatched roof (see bohío)

sancocho thick meat or chicken soup with root vegetables

STRI Smithsonian Tropical Research Institute

Small print and
Index

A Rough Guide to Rough Guides

Published in 1982, the first Rough Guide – to Greece – was a student scheme that became a publishing phenomenon. Mark Ellingham, a recent graduate in English from Bristol University, had been travelling in Greece the previous summer and couldn't find the right guidebook. With a small group of friends he wrote his own guide, combining a highly contemporary, journalistic style with a thoroughly practical approach to travellers' needs.

The immediate success of the book spawned a series that rapidly covered dozens of destinations. And, in addition to impecunious backpackers, Rough Guides soon acquired a much broader and older readership that relished the guides' wit and inquisitiveness as much as their enthusiastic, critical approach and value-for-money ethos.

These days, Rough Guides include recommendations from shoestring to luxury and cover more than 200 destinations around the globe, including almost every country in the Americas and Europe, more than half of Africa and most of Asia and Australasia. Our ever-growing team of authors and photographers is spread all over the world, particularly in Europe, the US and Australia.

In the early 1990s, Rough Guides branched out of travel, with the publication of Rough Guides to World Music, Classical Music and the Internet. All three have become benchmark titles in their fields, spearheading the publication of a wide range of books under the Rough Guide name.

Including the travel series, Rough Guides now number more than 350 titles, covering: phrasebooks, waterproof maps, music guides from Opera to Heavy Metal, reference works as diverse as Conspiracy Theories and Shakespeare, and popular culture books from iPods to Poker. Rough Guides also produce a series of more than 120 World Music CDs in partnership with World Music Network.

Visit www.roughguides.com to see our latest publications.

Rough Guide credits

Text editor: James Smart, Keith Drew, Andrew Rosenberg, AnneLise Sorensen
Layout: Pradeep Thapliyal
Cartography: Alakananda Roy, Jasbir Sandhu
Picture editor: Sarah Cummins
Production: Rebecca Short
Proofreader: Susannah Wight
Cover design: Nicole Newman, Dan May, Chloë Roberts
Photographer: James Brunker
Editorial: **London** Andy Turner, Edward Aves, Alice Park, Lucy White, Jo Kirby, Natasha Foges, Róisín Cameron, James Rice, Lara Kavanagh, Emma Beatson, Emma Gibbs, Kathryn Lane, Monica Woods, Mani Ramaswamy, Harry Wilson, Lucy Cowie, Alison Roberts, Eleanor Aldridge, Ian Blenkinsop, Joe Staines, Matthew Milton, Tracy Hopkins, Ruth Tidball; **Delhi** Madhavi Singh, Lubna Shaheen, Jalpreen Kaur Chhatwal
Design & Pictures: **London** Scott Stickland, Dan May, Diana Jarvis, Mark Thomas, Nicole Newman, Emily Taylor; **Delhi** Umesh Aggarwal, Ajay Verma, Jessica Subramanian, Ankur Guha,

Sachin Tanwar, Anita Singh, Nikhil Agarwal, Sachin Gupta
Production: Liz Cherry, Louise Daly, Erika Pepe
Cartography: **London** Ed Wright, Katie Lloyd-Jones; **Delhi** Rajesh Chhibber, Ashutosh Bharti, Rajesh Mishra, Animesh Pathak, Karobi Gogoi, Swati Handoo, Deshpal Dabas, Lokamata Sahu
Online: **London** Faye Hellon, Jeanette Angell, Fergus Day, Justine Bright, Clare Bryson, Aine Fearon, Adrian Low, Ezgi Celebi; **Delhi** Amit Verma, Rahul Kumar, Narender Kumar, Ravi Yadav, Debojit Borah, Rakesh Kumar, Ganesh Sharma, Shisir Basumatari
Marketing & Publicity: **London** Liz Statham, Jess Carter, Vivienne Watton, Anna Paynton, Rachel Sprackett, Laura Vipond; **New York** Katy Ball; **Delhi** Aman Arora
Digital Travel Publisher: Peter Buckley
Reference Director: Andrew Lockett
Operations Assistant: Becky Doyle
Operations Manager: Helen Atkinson
Publishing Director (Travel): Clare Currie
Commercial Manager: Gino Magnotta
Managing Director: John Duhigg

Publishing information

This first edition published Novembter 2010 by
Rough Guides Ltd,
80 Strand, London WC2R 0RL
11, Community Centre, Panchsheel Park, New Delhi 110017, India
Distributed by the Penguin Group
Penguin Books Ltd,
80 Strand, London WC2R 0RL
Penguin Group (USA)
375 Hudson Street, NY 10014, USA
Penguin Group (Australia)
250 Camberwell Road, Camberwell, Victoria 3124, Australia
Penguin Group (NZ)
67 Apollo Drive, Mairangi Bay, Auckland 1310, New Zealand
This paperback edition published in Canada in 2010. Rough Guides is represented in Canada by Tourmaline Editions Inc., 662 King Street West, Suite 304, Toronto, Ontario, M5V 1M7

Cover concept by Peter Dyer.

Typeset in Bembo and Helvetica to an original design by Henry Iles.

1   3   5   7   9   8   6   4   2

MIX
Paper from responsible sources
FSC
www.fsc.org   FSC™ C018179

Help us update

We've gone to a lot of effort to ensure that the first edition of **The Rough Guide to Panama** is accurate and up-to-date. However, things change – places get "discovered", opening hours are notoriously fickle, restaurants and rooms raise prices or lower standards. If you feel we've got it wrong or left something out, we'd like to know, and if you can remember the address, the price, the hours, the phone number, so much the better.

Please send your comments with the subject line "**Rough Guide Panama Update**" to ®mail @roughguides.com. We'll credit all contributions and send a copy of the next edition (or any other Rough Guide if you prefer) for the very best emails.
Find more travel information, connect with fellow travellers and book your trip on www .roughguides.com

Acknowledgements

The author is grateful to numerous people living in Panama who offered assistance, hospitality and understanding on countless occasions, willingly sharing their knowledge and experiences – such as those working for Áreas Protegidas in ANAM – but in particular to Raffa Calvo for his insight, support and friendship throughout.

Thanks to James Smart for unflagging support, a keen editorial eye and a balanced carrot-and-stick approach to deadlines (also to Andrew, Keith and AnneLise for pitching in); Dave Huxtable for panel-beating the section on Spanish pronunciation at short notice; and Rob for sound advice that often went unheeded.

Specific acknowledgements are also due to Jason for pre-trip input; Neil and Maria for culinary recommendations in Panama City; Enrique, Luchín, Nixia and Aaron for assistance researching Kuna Yala, Javier for Coiba insights; and James Brunker for assistance above and beyond his photography brief. Thanks to Raffa for raids along the Caribbean coast plus a cruise round the Azuero; to Helen for birdwatching in the rain, cruising the canal and coffee-cupping in Boquete; to Isabel and Raffa for muddy adventures by dugout in the Darién; and to Adrian, for tireless chauffeuring and explorations in Chiriquí and Bocas, and for keeping me fed and sane when writing up.

Photo credits

All photos © Rough Guides except the following:

Index

Map entries are in colour.

Map symbols

maps are listed in the full index using coloured text

- - - -	International boundary		⧫	Place of interest
·· —	Province boundary		⬦	Museum
· — —	Chapter division boundary		ⵟ	Gardens
▬▬	Interamericana		ⵟ	Cemetery
══	Major road		★	Transport stop
──	Minor road		@	Internet access
——	Unpaved road		ⓘ	Information centre
- - - -	Path		⊠	Post office
▬·▬·	Railway		⊞	Hospital
— —	Ferry route		◗	Fuel station
——	River		Ⓔ	Embassy
───	Wall		◉	Accommodation
▲	Mountain peak		▪	Restaurant
⌂	Cave		⬭	Stadium
⤋	Viewpoint		▬	Building
⚑	Ruin		⊞	Church
ⵙ	Lighthouse		▭	Market
✈	Airport		▦	Park
✗	Airstrip		⬓	Marshland/swamp
ⓟ	Beach		▦	Beach
⌘	Ranger station		⊞	Cemetery
⚑	Border crossing			

So now we've told you about the things not to miss, the best places to stay, the top restaurants, the liveliest bars and the most spectacular sights, it only seems fair to tell you about the best travel insurance around